North Carolina's Outer Banks and Crystal Coast

A Great Destination

Renee Wright

D0125576

THE COUNTRYMAN PRESS · WOODSTOCK, VT.

The Countryman Press   Woodstock, Vermont

SECOND EDITION

For my Mom, Betty Lou, better known to her many "kids"
across the country as RV Momma, who gave me the great gift of travel.
Without her, this book could never have been written.

And for Allan Maurer, the editor who helped me find my voice.

Interior photographs by the author unless otherwise specified
Maps by Erin Greb Cartography, © The Countryman Press
Book design by Bodenweber Design
Composition by Eugenie S. Delaney

Explorer's Guide North Carolina's Outer Banks and Crystal Coast: A Great Destination
978-1-58157-168-4

Published by The Countryman Press, P.O. Box 748, Woodstock, VT 05091
Distributed by W. W. Norton & Company, Inc., 500 Fifth Avenue, New York, NY 10110
Printed in the United States of America

10 9 8 7 6 5 4 3 2 1

EXPLORE WITH US!

OUR GUIDE COVERS an area stretching from the Virginia border south to the great Marine base of Camp Lejeune, outside Jacksonville, North Carolina. Between the two, you'll find as much water as land, and often a ferry offers a more direct route than a road. We'll island hop from north to south, with a chapter for each of the main destinations on the North Carolina Banks. Scattered throughout, we'll take closer looks at some common denominators, such as Banker horses, lighthouses, and lifesaving stations that stretch all along the coast. You'll also find a special section on the Inner Banks, perfect for day trips and rich in history. Special chapters on the history of the region, suggested itineraries, and a "What's Where on the Outer Banks and Crystal Coast" section help you design your perfect vacation.

All cities and towns mentioned in this guide are in North Carolina, unless otherwise noted. Wherever possible, we've included a website address for more information. We've also included places you can get connected with free Wi-Fi access. We provide lots of specific information for most of the attractions on the Outer Banks, and the information was checked as close to publication as possible. However, the Banks change from month to month and season to season. Please use the phone numbers provided to check for current information before you set out on a long trip to a particular place.

The Outer Banks no longer close down in the winter, as was once the norm. Seasonal closures now are quite random. Most everyone takes a month or two off during the winter; they just don't take the *same* month off. Even locals sometimes find themselves sitting in front of a favorite restaurant looking at a CLOSED sign. Telephone first to avoid disappointment.

LODGING While summer rates on accommodations still are the highest of the year, various special events or holiday weeks can bump up prices when you might not expect it. Most places go full tilt from Memorial Day to Labor Day, but we'll steer you to places where you won't notice the crowds.

These rate categories are per room, per night, based on double occupancy, or per unit for cottages or other rentals. They do not include room taxes or any special service fees that may apply. In Dare County, taxes add an additional 5 percent; in Currituck County, 6 percent; in Hyde County (Ocracoke), 3 percent; in Carteret County, 5 percent; and in Onslow County (Swansboro), 3 percent.

$	up to $80
$$	$80 to $150
$$$	$150 to $200
$$$$	$200 and up

RESTAURANTS These categories represent the average cost of an entrée, not including higher-priced specials, that super-size steak, or rack of lamb. They also do not include appetizers, desserts, beverages, taxes, or gratuities. Most restaurants on the Outer Banks will add a gratuity to bills for large groups.

$	under $10
$$	$10 to $20
$$$	$20 to $25
$$$$	$25 and up

GREEN SPACE This special section in each chapter covers the beaches that make the Banks so special, and other natural attractions, such as trails.

KEY TO SYMBOLS:

❄ Open during off-season

❧ Special-value spots that give you more than you expect

♂ Child-friendly spots that have special children's menus, or activities that appeal to families

🐾 Pet-friendly lodgings, restaurants, and shops

♿ Wheelchair-accessible establishments or attractions

☂ Rainy-day activity

♂ Venue that hosts weddings and civil unions

♟ Bar or nightspot

▼ Attractive to a gay clientele

((ᵩ)) Wi-Fi access available

↦ Ecofriendly establishments with green policies, or that feature local seafood and produce

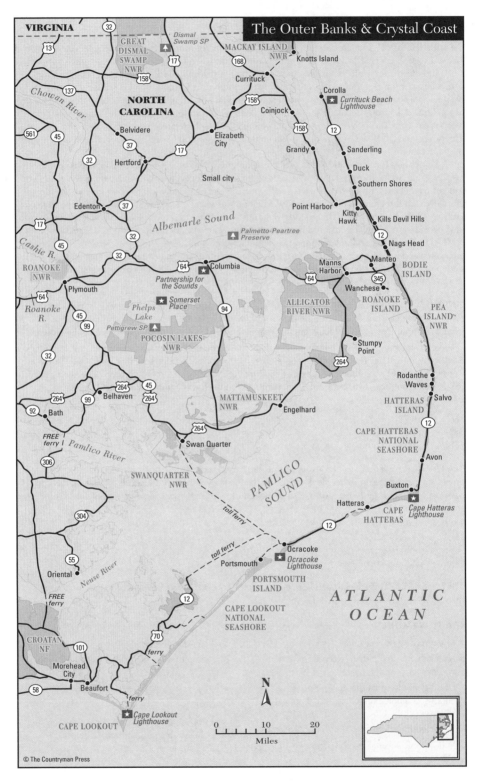

VIRGINIA

32

13

GREAT
DISMAL
SWAMP
NWR

Dismal
Swamp SP

17

158

Chowan River

137

NORTH
CAROLINA

561

45

Belvidere

37

Hertford

32

Small city

MACKAY ISLAND
NWR

168

Currituck

Knotts Island

158

Coinjock

158

12

Corolla

Currituck Beach
Lighthouse

Grandy

Sanderling

Duck

Southern Shores

Edenton

37

Point Harbor

Kitty
Hawk

Kills Devil Hills

17

32

Albemarle Sound

Palmetto-Peartree
Preserve

12

Nags Head

Cashie R.

45

32

ROANOKE
NWR

64

Columbia

64

Partnership for
the Sounds

Manns
Harbor

Manteo

345

BODIE
ISLAND

Plymouth

Somerset
Place

94

Wanchese

ROANOKE
ISLAND

PEA
ISLAND
NWR

Roanoke
R.

45

99

Phelps
Lake

Pettigrew SP

ALLIGATOR
RIVER NWR

32

POCOSIN LAKES
NWR

Stumpy
Point

264

Rodanthe
Waves

264

45

Belhaven

264

MATTAMUSKEET
NWR

HATTERAS
ISLAND

Salvo

92

Bath

99

264

Engelhard

CAPE HATTERAS
NATIONAL
SEASHORE

12

FREE
ferry

Pamlico River

264

Avon

306

Swan Quarter

PAMLICO
SOUND

Buxton

SWANQUARTER
NWR

toll ferry

Hatteras

CAPE
HATTERAS

Cape Hatteras
Lighthouse

304

12

toll ferry

Ocracoke

55

Portsmouth

Ocracoke
Lighthouse

Oriental

Neuse River

PORTSMOUTH
ISLAND

ATLANTIC
OCEAN

FREE
ferry

12

CROATAN
NF

101

70

CAPE LOOKOUT
NATIONAL
SEASHORE

ferry

Morehead
City

58

Beaufort

ferry

N

Cape Lookout
Lighthouse

CAPE LOOKOUT

0   10   20

Miles

© The Countryman Press

6

CONTENTS

INTRODUCTION

POISED BETWEEN SKY AND WATER, North Carolina's Outer Banks stand as a thin bulwark protecting the rest of the continent behind. A spearhead facing into the wind, a narrow wall marking the separation of land and sea, the Banks exist as they have for centuries, yet are never the same, season to season. Hurricanes and storms created the Outer Banks, mounding up sand scraped from the ocean floor. But Mother Nature is never satisfied. The face of the Banks changes constantly as nature resculpts this work of art. Behind the dunes shelter the rich brackish waters of the Sounds, where North Carolina's great rivers mingle their fresh waters with the incoming tides. The Sounds—Pamlico, Roanoke, and Bogue—are home to a teaming richness of sea life, including many varieties of shellfish and some of the best sportfishing to be found on the globe.

In this land of sky, sand, and water, it takes a special kind of people to thrive. Despite the flood of visitors that now visit the Banks, the families who have lived here for generations remain, practicing their traditions, preserving their heritage. They welcome, as they always have, the castaways that wash up on their shores, fall in love with the place, and stay. In this book, we introduce you to some of these people and help you seek out the authentic experiences the Outer Banks have to offer. Whether you're looking for a classic beach vacation, the thrill of extreme sports, immersion in a unique ecosystem, or a walk through history, the coast of North Carolina can be the destination of your dreams.

SUGGESTED ITINERARIES

IF TIME IS SHORT on your trip to the Banks (and when is any vacation too long?), we offer these suggested itineraries tuned to different interests.

If You Have a Week . . .

This trip goes down the Outer Banks, over the ferries to the South Banks, then loops back north on US 17. You can, of course, reverse the order, or just go one way. The trip can be comfortably done in a week.

Start with a trip to **Corolla,** on the northern end of the Outer Banks, where you can visit the elegant **Whalehead Club,** climb the **Currituck Beach Lighthouse,** and take an off-road adventure to see the wild horses of **Carova.** Traveling south on US 158, visit the **Wright Memorial** in **Kill Devil Hills,** and climb the dunes at **Jockey's Ridge State Park** in **Nags Head** to see the sunset. Cross the causeway to **Manteo,** where the **Roanoke Island Festival Park** brings you up to speed on the region's early history. On the way back across the causeway, stop for some fresh local seafood at the **Lone Cedar Restaurant,** owned by Marc Basnight, longtime president pro tem of the North Carolina Senate. Crossing to Hatteras Island, seek out the **Chicamacomico Life-Saving Station** in **Rodanthe,** and climb the famous **Cape Hatteras Light** for a bird's-eye view of Diamond Shoals. After a stop in **Hatteras Village** to tour the **Graveyard of the Atlantic Museum,** take the free ferry to **Ocracoke Island.** While there, visit the country's number-one beach, stop for a meal or beverage at famous **Howard's Pub,** and watch the sun set over **Silver Lake.** Take the ferry to Cedar Island and visit the historic town of Beaufort, where you'll find the main campus of the **North Carolina Maritime Museum.** Take in a meal at the famous **Sanitary Seafood** in Morehead City, before heading back north. You can take US 70 out to US 17 in New Bern, North Carolina's colonial capital, or turn off in Havelock to take the Cherry Branch–Minnesott Beach ferry and the Aurora–Bayview ferry to Bath, another colonial town, with a stop in Aurora to see some excellent fossils. (See "The Inner Banks: North Carolina's Secret Shore" for highlights on this leg of your trip.)

OBX for Kids Tour

Thanks to their summer beach patrols, the **best beaches for families** with young children are the Central Beaches of Kitty Hawk, Kill Devil Hills, and Nags Head, and on the Crystal Coast, Emerald Isle. Both areas also have many other kid-friendly activities, such as **minigolf, bumper boats,** and **go-karts. Skate parks** can be found at Corolla, Kill Devil Hills, Buxton, Manteo, and on the Currituck mainland. The Beach Road running along the Central Beaches still has several old-fashioned ice cream and burger hangouts, such as the **Snowbird** and **Dune Burger.** The **state aquariums** in Manteo and Pine Knoll Shores offer great rainy-day options, and the **Roanoke Island Festival Park** is fun rain or shine. The region's many headboats provide an easy and inexpensive introduction to **fishing** for all ages, as well as an exciting day on the water.

BEST ON THE BEACH

HERE ARE A FEW SUGGESTIONS for the best places to satisfy special interests on the Outer Banks and Crystal Coast.

BEST BIKING Roanoke Island has extensive dedicated bike paths leading to interesting destinations. Downtown Manteo is perfect for biking, and Wanchese makes a great biking day trip.

BEST KITEBOARDING AND WINDSURFING Hatteras Island is the East Coast hot spot for wind sports. The Tri-Villages have several dedicated kiteboarding resorts. Avon is a world-class destination for windsurfing.

BEST FISHING The fishing piers on the Outer Banks and Crystal Coast are legendary. Try for a giant red drum at the **Avon Pier** on Hatteras Island.

BEST FISHING CHARTERS Oregon Inlet and **Hatteras Village** on the Outer Banks are home to legendary charter fishing fleets.

BEST SURF FISHING The Core Banks in the **Cape Lookout National Seashore** offer a uniquely untamed opportunity to fish the break.

BEST BEACH Ocracoke! Dr. Beach gave the big nod to the lifeguarded beach here, but we love the miles of undisturbed sand with not a man-made structure in sight just as well.

BEST FAMILY BEACH Emerald Isle on Bogue Banks goes the extra mile with lifeguards, children's entertainment, tons of off-road bike paths, and plenty of family activities.

BEST BOAT TRIP The free **North Carolina State Ferry** between Hatteras Village and Ocracoke.

BEST FOODIE DESTINATION Beaufort, on the Crystal Coast, has the highest concentration of interesting restaurants, all within walking distance of the waterfront. On the upper banks, head for **Duck,** with many nationally recognized eateries.

BEST PLACE FOR HISTORY AND ART BUFFS Manteo, site of the Lost Colony, has the best history chops on the coast, plus an artist colony inspired by its fishing village charm. On the Crystal Coast, **Beaufort** is a close runner-up in both categories.

BEST SHOPPING Duck Village connects its many shopping villages, full of mostly locally owned shops, with boardwalks and paved paths. Throw in the awesome sunsets over the sound, and you have shopping nirvana.

BEST BIRDING The **Pea Island National Wildlife Refuge** has 365 birds on its list, with some species in residence all year.

BEST SURFING Hatteras Island near the Cape Hatteras Lighthouse is the traditional spot for surfers who love both solitude and a challenge. If you're looking for a crowd to applaud your hotdogging, head for Jennette's Pier in **Nags Head,** home of most of the region's surfing competitions.

BEST PLACE TO LEARN TO SURF The surf in **Corolla,** with shallow entry and a sandbar just off shore, is considered a great spot for beginners to catch a wave.

BEST BOAT EXCURSION Catch a ferry from **Harkers Island** to Cape Lookout for views of wild horses, dolphins, and sea turtles, all backed by the iconic diamond-patterned lighthouse.

BEST KAYAKING Swansboro on the Crystal Coast has enough saltwater and blackwater paddle trails to fill many vacations.

BEST OCEANFRONT RV CAMPING The **Tri-Villages** on Hatteras Island are the last great stronghold of oceanfront RV camping, once so common on the Banks. If you don't mind roughing it (no hookups), plan a vacation moving from one **Cape Hatteras National Seashore** campground to the next on Ocracoke and Hatteras Island.

BEST PRIMITIVE CAMPING The South Banks and Crystal Coast offer lots of places to camp away from civilization. Take a boat out to **Cape Lookout National Seashore,** set up camp along the trails in the **Croatan National Forest,** or get away from it all at the primitive sites on Bear Island at **Hammocks Beach State Park.**

WHAT'S WHERE ON THE OUTER BANKS AND CRYSTAL COAST

AIRPORTS AND AIRLINES Although no scheduled commercial flights touch down at the small airports that dot the Outer Banks, the heritage of flight is strong here. Kill Devil Hill, where the Wright Memorial now stands, is a place of pilgrimage for many pilots. They come to fly over the memorial, and to land and take off at the **First Flight Airport** (252-441-7430 or 252-473-2111; www.nps.gov/wrbr) next to the national monument, flying in the contrail of the Wright brothers themselves. Most visitors arriving by air land at one of the large commercial airports located near the Banks, where numerous rental cars are available. The major airports located closest to the Outer Banks include: **Newport News/Williamsburg International Airport (PHF)** (757-877-0221; www.flyphf .com) and **Norfolk International Airport (ORF)** (757-857-3351; www.norfolkairport .com), both about 90 miles from Kitty Hawk; and **Raleigh-Durham International Airport (RDU)** (919-840-2123; www.rdu.com), about 200 miles from Nags Head. **Wilmington International Airport (ILM)** (910-341-4125; www.flyilm.com) is the closest major airport to Beaufort and the Crystal Coast. The **Albert J. Ellis Airport (OAJ)** (910-324-1100; www .onslowcountync.gov/OAJ), in Onslow County, and **Craven Regional Airport (EWN)** (252-638-8591; www.newbernairport.com), in New Bern, offer service by smaller regional carriers.

Pilots can request free copies of the current North Carolina Aeronautical Chart or North Carolina Airport Guide from the North Carolina Department of Transportation's Aviation Division website (www.ncdot.org), or by calling 919-840-0112.

AIR CHARTERS Barrier Island Aviation (252-473-4247; www.barrierislandaviation.com) and **Outer Banks Air Charters** (252-256-2322; www.outerbanksaircharters.com) offer air tours and charters from Dare County Airport in Manteo.

FlightGest (919-840-4443; www.flightgest.com) offers charter service from several airports in the Mid-Atlantic region.

AQUARIUMS North Carolina state aquariums (www.ncaquariums.com) can be found in Manteo on Roanoke Island and Pine Knoll Shores on the Crystal Coast.

AREA CODES Area code 252 is used from the Virginia border south to Onslow County. In Swansboro, the gateway to Onslow, the area code changes to 910.

ART GALLERIES Manteo, Hatteras Island, Ocracoke, and Beaufort all have active colonies of artists and many galleries.

ATTIRE Whatever the season, dress is relentlessly casual on the coast, and the need for a suit jacket is very rare. Most people get comfortable in shorts and sandals in summer and bundle up when winter comes. A windbreaker is a must all year, and rain gear can come in handy. Closed toed, rubber soled shoes are safest on boats. Hats, sunglasses, and plenty of sunscreen and bug repellent make vacations trouble free, but they can be bought at numerous spots if you forget them.

BARBECUE In North Carolina, *barbecue* is a noun, and no vacation would be complete without a big order of take-out from one of the local joints. Be sure to order plenty, since ribs and chopped pork are favorite leftovers for many families. North Carolina barbecue is traditionally pork, hickory smoked, and served chopped with bits of fat moistening the mix. In eastern North Carolina the sauce, served on the side, consists of vinegar with various additions, usually including flecks of red pepper. Farther west, the barbecue parlors in Lexington, North Carolina, the self-proclaimed Barbecue Capital, use a sauce with both vinegar and tomato flavors. Western Carolina barbecue sauce is thicker and tomato based, with a ketchup consistency. South Carolina–style barbecue sauce is based on mustard. Most barbecue restaurants offer versions of all these, so try them all to find your favorite. Another Carolina tradition is putting coleslaw, either traditional or red "barbecue" slaw, on the bun with the chopped (or pulled) pork.

BEACH REGULATIONS North Carolina law says that all the sand below the high-tide line is public property. However, you must enter the beach from a public access, not across private property. Driving on the beach is a treasured local tradition, and one that has come under increasing pressure due to concern for beach nesting birds and sea turtles. When driving on beaches, especially in the national seashores, it is vital to observe closings established to protect certain areas. Driving on the beaches of the national seashores is especially changeable, with many environmental groups seeking to ban driving completely and locals fighting to maintain

TAKE SPECIAL PRECAUTIONS WHEN DRIVING IN SAND.

their traditional rights. Check with the local park visitors centers to find out areas that are currently available for vehicle and pedestrian access. Currently, the NPS requires those who want to drive on the Cape Hatteras beaches to purchase permits after watching a training video. No permits are currently required to drive on the Core Banks in Cape Lookout National Seashore, but you must ferry your vehicle to the island.

Many, although not all, of the communities along the North Carolina coast allow driving on the beach within their townships at certain times of the year. Usually this is October to March, but there are many variations. Many towns now ask drivers to buy a permit to drive on the beach. Check the town websites to find out the local laws. When driving on the beach, proceed with extreme caution and follow regular road rules: passing on the right, keeping to the left, wearing seat belts, et cetera. Speed limits are usually 15 miles per hour.

To avoid getting stuck in the sand, lower the air pressure in your tires to about 20 pounds and stick to the hard packed sand below the high-tide line. Enter only at beach access ramps, and stay off the dunes if you want to stay out of trouble.

BEACH EQUIPMENT AND LINEN RENTALS
You can rent just about anything from the companies that serve the area, and most deliver and pick up for free, with a minimum order. Linens and towels, beach chairs and umbrellas, baby

equipment, bikes, kayaks, boogie boards, and surfboards are standard items, but you can also rent sports equipment, metal detectors, binoculars, basketballs, volleyball and horseshoe sets, beach wheelchairs, coolers, charcoal grills, and roll-away beds. Businesses to try include **Just for the Beach Rentals** (www.justforthebeach .com); **Ocean Atlantic Rentals** (www.ocean atlanticrentals.com); **Moneysworth Beach Home Equipment Rentals** (www.mworth .com); on Ocracoke, **Beach Outfitters** (www .ocracokeislandrealty.com); and on the Crystal Coast, **Beach Butler Rentals** (www.beach butlerrentals.com) and **Emerald Isle Beach Gear & Linens** (www.emeraldislebeachgear .com). It's a good idea to make arrangements in advance, especially during the summer season.

BEACHES Dozens of public access points can be found in Corolla, along NC 12 (the Beach Road) and Old Oregon Inlet Road along the Central Beaches, and in both the villages and national seashore on Hatteras Island, as well as along NC 58 on Bogue Banks on the Crystal Coast. Look for signs that identify public access. Regional beach accesses have bathhouses with restrooms where you can shower and change. Contact the **Outer Banks Visitor Center** (252-473-2138 or 1-877-629-4386; www.outer banks.org) and the **Crystal Coast Visitor Center** (252-726-8148 or 1-877-206-0929; www .crystalcoastnc.org) for the latest information on lifeguards, handicapped access, and beach facilities.

BEACH MUSIC AND THE SHAG Shag is the state social dance of North Carolina, and shaggers crowd the dance floors in many beach communities. The R&B tunes that inspire the sweet moves of the shag are heard everywhere on the coast. Here's a list of **beach music classics** that have stood the test of time:
"Sixty Minute Man," Billy Ward and the Dominoes
"Carolina Girls," General Johnson and the Chairmen of the Board
"Be Young, Be Foolish, Be Happy," The Tams
"Ms. Grace," Tymes
"I Love Beach Music," The Embers
"Stay," Maurice Williams & the Zodiacs
"My Girl," Temptations
"Under the Boardwalk," The Drifters
"One Mint Julep," The Clovers
"With This Ring," The Platters

BICYCLING Eastern North Carolina is one of the most popular bicycling destinations in the country. In addition to many local bike paths, the area is included in several longer North

Carolina Department of Transportation bike trails that lead across the state. **Bike Route 2, Mountains to Sea,** leads from the Great Smoky Mountains to Manteo. **Bike Route 7** runs from Wilson to Cedar Island and the Ocracoke Ferry. The **Wright Brothers Bike Route** runs the length of the Outer Banks, 45 miles from Corolla to Hatteras Village, then over the ferry to Ocracoke. Most of the distance requires on-road riding. A popular 100-mile round-trip can be made by traveling from Manteo, down Hatteras Island, over the ferry to Ocracoke, then taking the ferry to Swan Quarter, connecting with US 264, and returning to Manteo. It can be done in one day if you start early in the morning.

Numerous companies offer bicycle rentals, and most will deliver weekly rentals right to your cottage. Every size and style of bicycle is available, as well as child seats, various tagalongs, and tricycles for children and adults.

You can order free maps of statewide and regional bicycling routes from the North Carolina Department of Transportation website, www.ncdot.org. North Carolina law requires that all bike riders and passengers 16 and under wear helmets.

BIRD-WATCHING With over 400 species documented on the Outer Banks, the area is one of the prime destinations for bird-watching on the East Coast. The annual **Wings Over Water** festival in November introduces many birding hot spots to newcomers through guided expeditions.

Among the many exceptional birding locations on the Banks are the **Pea Island National Wildlife Refuge,** which offers free

BIRDS HAVE THE RIGHT-OF-WAY ALONG MOST BEACHES.

birding walks all year, and the **Pine Island Audubon Sanctuary,** just north of Duck. Stop by the nearby Sanderling Resort to see its outstanding collection of bird art. If you are visiting in summer, be sure to see the huge flock of purple martins returning to roost at the **Umstead Memorial Bridge** in Manteo at sunset. In the winter, plan a visit to **Lake Mattamuskeet** to be amazed by the flocks of swans and other waterfowl that visit there. One of the largest colonies of the endangered red-cockaded woodpeckers can be seen at **Palmetto-Peartree Preserve** on the mainland.

At any time of year, a kayak trip through **Kitty Hawk Woods** rewards paddlers with serene views of wading and other birds. The maritime thickets of Jockey's Ridge State Park are visited by large numbers of migrating songbirds in late summer and fall, and migrating raptors can be seen along the **Soundside Trail.** The nature trails around **Bodie Island Lighthouse** yield views of wading birds and wintering waterfowl, while **Coquina Beach** across the road is visited by loons in winter, and other shorebirds during the spring and fall migrations. The world's largest population of black-capped petrels summers just off this coast. **Nags Head Woods** is the nesting spot of over 50 bird species. A list is available in the visitors center. **Kitty Hawk Woods** is equally well populated, and guides are being developed for this area. The **Wings Over Water Festival** (www.wings overwater.org) held every November offers many escorted birding tours to the region's numerous birding attractions. Download detailed maps of birding sites from the **North Carolina Birding Trail** (www.ncbirdingtrail .org).

BOATING Although most visitors arrive by car, an increasing number of travelers tour North Carolina's shores by boat. A steady stream of power yachts and sailing vessels makes its way along the Atlantic Intracoastal Waterway (ICW), the great, 3,000-mile-long water highway that stretches from Boston, Massachusetts, to Key West, Florida. The ICW has one of its longest stretches in North Carolina, making its way down black-water rivers and salt estuaries. The towns of Elizabeth City, Belhaven, Oriental, Beaufort, Morehead City, and Swansboro are major stops for mariners passing through, as well as for in-state boaters. An alternate route runs down the back side of the Banks, with stops at Manteo harbor, Hatteras Village, and Ocracoke. Visit the website of the **Atlantic Intracoastal Waterway Association** (www.atlanticintracoastal.org) for information and updates.

Many marinas lie along the ICW. We include listings in each section of facilities that welcome transient boaters. You can request a free copy of the official *North Carolina Coastal Boating Guide* by calling 1-877-368-4968 or by visiting www.ncwaterways.com.

BUS SERVICE Greyhound (214-849-8100 or 1-800-231-2222; www.greyhound.com) offers scheduled bus service along US 17. Jacksonville (910-346-9832), New Bern, Washington (252-946-3021), and Elizabeth City (252-335-5183) are the closest terminals to the Outer Banks and Crystal Coast. No tickets are sold at the New Bern station, but you can order tickets by mail through the main Greyhound contact numbers.

CAMPING RV campgrounds are now few and far between on the Outer Banks, except for the National Park Service campgrounds in Cape Hatteras National Seashore, which have very basic amenities. The exception is the Tri-Villages, where many RV campgrounds both on the oceanfront and on the sound welcome campers.

Bogue Banks, especially the communities of Emerald Isle and Salter Path, used to have a number of campgrounds. Today, most have disappeared under the wave of development washing across the island. However, a number of RV resorts on the mainland front on Bogue Sound. The Down East region also has several smaller campgrounds, most with boat ramps.

CANOEING AND KAYAKING The coastal region of North Carolina offers a wealth of paddling opportunities for canoes and kayaks. You can browse hundreds of trails on the **North Carolina Paddle Trails Association** website (www.ncpaddletrails.info). The website of the **OBX Paddlers Club** (www.obxpaddlers.org) lists suggested launch sites from Corolla to Ocracoke, including many spots on the mainland.

The **North Carolina Coastal Plain Paddle Trails** range from easy paddles on Lake Mattamuskeet to challenging trips across the open waters of the sounds. You can download maps at www.ncsu.edu/paddletrails, or order a copy by calling 919-778-9499, or by contacting the North Carolina Division of Parks and Recreation (345-B Park Entrance Road, Seven Springs, NC 28578).

One of the state's longest paddle trails, the 128-mile **Roanoke River Trail,** is also one of the best developed. It begins near Roanoke Rapids and follows the river to its mouth in Albemarle Sound, near Plymouth. Along the way, it passes through the **Roanoke River National Wildlife Refuge,** home of black bears, river otters, bobcats, and bald eagles.

Camping platforms and boat ramps have been built the length of the river by the Roanoke River Partners. You can find more information, including links to outfitters offering rentals and guided tours, on the website of the **Roanoke River Partners** (www.roanokeriverpartners .org).

CHOWDER One local specialty, which you'll find under varying names up and down this coast, is Hatteras clam chowder. It's a whole different take on the genre, having a clear broth with neither cream nor tomatoes. The clam's own juices are used, along with potatoes and onions sautéed in bacon drippings; it is seasoned with cracked pepper and salted to taste. Locals often add a splash of Texas Pete, a hot sauce that—despite its name—is made in North Carolina.

HATTERAS-STYLE CLAM CHOWDER, A UNIQUE DISH FOUND ON THE OUTER BANKS.

CLIMATE The coast of North Carolina generally enjoys a temperate climate, with very few days on which the temperature goes below freezing. In the Nags Head area, January is the coldest month, with average temperatures ranging from 36 to 51 degrees. July is the hottest month, with lows averaging 72 degrees and highs, 86 degrees. The water is warmest in August, when it reaches 80 degrees. However, a steady wind averaging over 10 mph blows all year, cooling even the warmest days and making cold weather very raw. August is generally the wettest month, when thunderstorms frequently develop in the afternoon.

The Crystal Coast faces south and is generally a little warmer in the summer, when average July temperatures reach 89 degrees.

Some of the best—and worst—weather is experienced in the spring and fall. Hurricane season begins before summer, on June 1. Late summer and fall are prime hurricane season, and storms can approach very quickly. Even

HAND-CARVED DECOYS ONCE WERE
ESSENTIAL TO THE RETAIL WILDFOWL TRADE.

outside of the official hurricane season, north-easters and other big storms can have devastating effects on the coast. The Ash Wednesday Storm of 1962 and the Thanksgiving Storm of 2006 live on in local lore.

DECOYS Decoy carving is a well established tradition on the Outer Banks, a cottage industry closely associated with waterfowl hunting. The region has several museums exhibiting antique decoys, as well as waterfowl created by contemporary carvers. The **Outer Banks Center for Wildlife Education** in Corolla contains the important Neil Conoley collection, with examples from all the most famed Currituck Sound school of carvers, and offers classes in carving.

Watch for decoys created by the famous carvers of the past, including Ned Burgess of Currituck Sound, Lee Dudley of Knotts Island, and Mitchell Fulcher from Down East. You can browse antique and modern decoys, as well as much other wildlife art, for sale at the **Bird Store** in Kill Devil Hills and the **Wooden Feather** in Duck. Look especially for hollow canvas-covered decoys, a local style carried on today by Wanchese carver Nick Sapone. Farther south, on Harkers Island, the **Core Sound Waterfowl Museum and Heritage Center** contains numerous examples of decoys donated by local families who have carved waterfowl for generations. Many of today's carvers gather at the H. Curt Salter Building, headquarters of the **Core Sound Decoy Carvers Guild,** just down the road from the museum. You'll often find carvers at work at these two locations, and auctions are held several times a year.

Other decoy collections are housed at the **North Carolina Maritime Center** in Beaufort and the **History Place** in Morehead City.

DRIVING TOURS Several special-interest tours will guide you through the Outer Banks, the Crystal Coast, and beyond. Select the itinerary that best suits your interests. **Charles Kuralt Trail** (www.northeast-nc.com/kuralt). Signboards identify 11 national wildlife refuges and a national fish hatchery in eastern North Carolina and along the Virginia border that were favorites of the North Carolina broadcaster and author. **Historic Albemarle Tour** (www.historicalbemarletour.org). Founded in 1975, this rambling journey follows brown signs to over 25 sites, most of historical significance, along with natural history and ecotourism highlights. The entire guide can be printed from the website for easy reference. **HomeGrown-HandMade Art Roads & Farm Trails** (www.homegrownhandmade.com). This website guides you to treasures scattered along the state's back roads, with listings of art studios, pick-your-own farms and farmer's markets, hiking trails, and unique events. **North Carolina Civil War Trails** (www.civilwartraveler.com). Markers tell of little-known battles fought on Roanoke, Ocracoke, and Hatteras islands.

You can also view sample tour itineraries on the Outer Banks and elsewhere in Northeast North Carolina at www.visitncne.com and www.outbanks.org.

EMERGENCIES Dial **911** for any emergency situation on land or sea anywhere on the Outer Banks. Major hospitals with emergency rooms are the **Outer Banks Hospital** (252-449-4500 or 1-877-359-9179; www.theouterbankshospital.com) in Nags Head and **Carteret General Hospital** (252-808-6000; www.ccgh.org) in Morehead City. For boating and water emergencies, contact the **U.S. Coast Guard 24-Hour Search and Rescue** at 252-247-4570.

EVENTS Many events are listed in the individual chapters in this book; however, some events involve the entire region and are a great time to visit the Banks.

January: **Outer Banks Wedding Weekend and Expo** (www.outerbanksweddingassoc.org). Tour area event venues and get plenty of free swag at the expo.

March: **Taste of the Beach** (www.obxtaste ofthebeach.com), a four-day festival for foodies with dozens of events.

April: **Outer Banks Bike Week** (www.outer banksbikeweek.com). **Flying Pirate Half Marathon and First Flight 5k** (www.obx marathon.org). 🌿 🐦 **Land of Beginnings Festival** (www.thelostcolony.org). Weeklong festival includes a fun run, Children's Faire, storytelling, lectures, Living Legend Luncheon, and final gala.

May: Spring **OBX Restaurant Week** (www
.outerbanksrestaurantweek.com).

September: **Bike Fest** (www.outerbankshd
.com). **Outer Bank Triathlon** (www.obx
marathon.org). 🦆 **Outer Banks Coastal Land
Trust Festival** (www.coastallandtrust.org).
Weekend of ecoactivities, including hikes, kayak
ecotours, and social mixers, benefiting the
Land Trust.

October: **North Carolina Big Sweep**
(http://outerbanks.surfrider.org). The Outer
Banks Brewing Station hosts an after-event,
TrashFest, for participants. **Outer Banks
Home Builders Parade of Homes** (www
.obhomebuilders.org). Tour dozens of homes
situated from Corolla to Hatteras. **Fall
OBX Restaurant Week** (www.outerbanks
restaurantweek.com). **Toast to the Coast
Restaurant Week** (www.toasttothecoast.org).
Special menus and culinary tours on the Crystal
Coast.

November: **Outer Banks Marathon** (www.obx
marathon.org), Kitty Hawk to Manteo. An expo,
art show, and social events are included in this
Veterans Day weekend of races. This marathon
is a Boston Marathon qualifier. 🦆 **Wings Over
Water** (www.wingsoverwater.org). Weeklong
birding festival includes over 100 birding tours,
plus special photography workshops, an art
show, and social events.

November–December: **Outer Banks Christmas Weekends** (www.obxmasweekends.com).
Special events and deals throughout the holiday
season.

December: **Festival of Trees** (www.obhotline
.org). **Crystal Coast Countdown** (www.crystal
coastcountdown.com). A multiday event with
bonfires, live music, tours, hikes, sand sculpture
contest, and more from Beaufort to Emerald
Isle leads up to the Pirate Plunge and Crabpot
Drop with fireworks on New Year's Eve.

FERRIES Although most of North Carolina's
outer islands are now linked by bridge and
causeway to the mainland, quite a few still
require a journey by boat. Call 1-800-BY
FERRY or visit www.ncferry.org for current
schedules and routes. No reservations are taken
for free ferries.

   The state of North Carolina maintains a
fleet of ferries that runs year-round on routes
throughout the eastern part of the state. These
link Ocracoke Island with Hatteras Island to the
north, Cedar Island to the south, and Swan
Quarter on the Hyde County mainland to the
west. They also cross rivers and sounds, linking
the sometimes isolated communities of the

Inner Banks, in addition to creating interesting
options for visitors. Any size vehicle can be
accommodated on the ferries, and pedestrians
and bikers are welcome. Pets must be on a leash
or remain in the vehicle. The ferries have restrooms, but no food service beyond vending
machines, so a box lunch is recommended for
longer voyages. The state ferries run on regular
schedules all year and in most weather, although
they may be canceled because of high seas or
strong winds. Call the terminal in advance to
check on current conditions. Current ferry
routes in the Outer Banks region include:

   Bayview–Aurora across the Pamlico River
near Bath. Crossing time: 30 minutes. Fare:
Free. **Cherry Branch–Minnesott Beach**
across the Neuse River below New Bern.
Crossing time: 20 minutes. Fare: Free.
Currituck–Knotts Island across Currituck
Sound. Crossing time: 45 minutes. Fare: Free.
Hatteras–Ocracoke. Crossing time: 40 minutes. Fare: Free. **Ocracoke–Cedar Island.**
Crossing time: 2.25 hours. Fare: $15 for vehicles
less than 20 feet; $1 for pedestrians; $3 for
bicycle and rider; $10 for motorcycles; $15–45
for motor homes, with the price increasing with
the length of the vehicle. Reservations recommended, especially during the summer season.
Ocracoke–Swan Quarter. Crossing time:
2.5 hours. Fare: Same as Cedar Island Ferry.
Reservations recommended.

   Please note that the tolls on North Carolina's
ferries are a matter of heated debate, with the
state government in favor of raising the tolls and
eliminating free ferry service altogether. Local
residents are understandably upset by these
plans, particularly Ocracoke folks who have no
other way to reach their homes. At press time,

A NORTH CAROLINA STATE FERRY

the issue is still undecided, although a proposed compromise will keep the Hatteras to Ocracoke ferry free, as well as the Knotts Island ferry, but raise tolls to as much as $27 on the Cedar Island and Swan Quarter ferries, plus impose $5 tolls on each passenger or pedestrian, and $15 on motorcycles. Vehicles or combination over 45 feet could be charged as much as $65. Check the ferry website for the current status of these increases.

State Ferry Terminals

Aurora/Bayview, 252-964-4521

Cedar Island, 252-225-7411 or 1-800-293-3779 (reservations)

Cherry Branch/Minnesott, 252-447-1055 or 1-800-339-9156

Currituck/Knotts Island, 252-232-2683

Hatteras, 252-986-2353 or 1-800-368-8949

Ocracoke, 252-928-1665 or 1-800-293-3779 (reservations)

Swan Quarter, 252-926-6021

FIRES While the idea of a campfire on the beach during the evening is an appealing idea, many communities along the coast do not permit them or require that you apply in advance for a permit, usually at the local fire station. Check individual town websites, listed in the appropriate chapters, for current information and requirements.

Bonfires are generally permitted in the national seashores if built below the high-tide line. You need a free permit, downloadable from the NPS website, for fires in Cape Hatteras National Seashore. Plan to bring your own wood for your fire, as it is illegal to cut any dead trees or use ship timbers that may have washed up on the shore. A fire should be extinguished with water, not sand, so it will not continue to smolder.

FIREWORKS After a series of near catastrophic brush fires, all private use of fireworks, including firecrackers, torpedoes, sky rockets, and sparklers, have been banned in Dare County, which includes the area from Duck to Hatteras Inlet. Ocracoke and Corolla also ban the private use of fireworks. Fines can range as high as $1,000 and are strictly enforced. Fireworks are prohibited in all national parks and seashores. Regulations for fireworks on the Crystal Coast vary. Check with each township to discover current laws. In general, the state of North Carolina prohibits the possession of any pyrotechnics that launch or propel into the air, or that explode, making a sound, or "report."

Public fireworks displays, once the signature of Fourth of July on the shore, have been severely curtailed in recent years, due to a deadly accident on Ocracoke Island before the 2009 Independence Day festivities. For many years, Fourth of July fireworks from ocean piers were a treasured and spectacular Banks tradition, with fireworks displays off Nags Head Pier, Avalon Pier in Kill Devil Hills, Avon Pier, and on the Crystal Coast, off Oceana and Bogue Inlet piers. Fireworks returned to Avon Pier on July 4, 2012, and pyrotechnic enthusiasts hope soon to see the return of these annual shows.

FISHING Fishing is the heart and soul of the North Carolina coast, with generations of watermen heading out into the ocean to make their livings. Some of the largest commercial fishing wholesalers in the country were founded here, including the **Wanchese Fish Company** (www.wanchese.com), founded in 1936. Other fishing industries, such as the menhaden fishing fleet once based in Beaufort, have seen their business disappear. In the 1930s, fishing captains, looking for an alternate source of income, began taking amateur fishermen out, first after the big old drum in the inlet, then out to the nearby Gulf Stream for blue marlin and other game fish. This was the beginning of the huge and lucrative charter fishing industry, now a year-round activity, on the North Carolina coast. Other fishing enthusiasts prefer to remain on shore, fishing from piers or casting from the beach.

Here's a guide to the several different kinds of fishing experiences available: **Charter fishing:** Charter boats typically accommodate groups of up to six. Prices range well over $1,000 for a full day of offshore action, half that

YELLOWFIN TUNA AT OREGON INLET FISHING CENTER

for a nearshore or inshore half-day excursion. All charters include fishing gear, tackle, and bait, plus any license you might need, and—sometimes—ice and fish cleaning. **Makeup charters:** If your group is smaller than six people, ask about a makeup charter to keep down the cost of your day of fishing. The captain matches interests to fill his boat, with the price split between all participants. **Offshore charters:** The offshore fleet goes out to the Gulf Stream after the big game fish: sailfish, white and blue marlin, as well as other pelagic fish, such as wahoo and mahi, plus giant bluefin tuna in the winter months. These are larger boats, especially designed for safety and comfort on offshore trips. It takes about an hour and a half for most boats to reach the Gulf Stream.

Nearshore charters: Nearshore captains fish the inlets or along the edge of the Continental Shelf, or go after bottom fish at one of the many wrecks in the area, home to snapper, grouper, pompano, drum, cobia, sea bass, tile fish, trigger fish, and more. **Inshore charters:** The inshore fleet typically is made up of smaller boats that fish within sight of shore, either in the inlets, on Diamond Shoals, or in the sound, for bluefish, king and Spanish mackerel, cobia, flounder, false albacore ("fat Alberts"), striped bass (rockfish), gray and speckled trout, and red drum. Trips on the calm waters of Pamlico Sound are usually the favorite for family fishing trips, offered by many inshore captains. **Headboats:** On headboats or party boats, rates are charged per person (per "head") and are reasonable, usually $30–40 for adults, less for children under 10. Bathrooms and refreshments are available onboard, and gear, bait, and licenses are provided. It's a great introduction to fishing for all ages. Some headboats also schedule 24- or 48-hour marathon trips to the Gulf Stream, or night shark hunts, for avid anglers. **Pier fishing:** Fishing from piers is a great Carolina tradition—one under attack in recent years due to high values on oceanfront property and a series of savage storms that have knocked down piers year after year. Today, many piers along the coast hang tough, hoping to preserve this family activity for future generations. The state of North Carolina has gotten into the mix as well, building concrete, hurricane-proof piers as part of the North Carolina aquarium system. Jennette's Pier in Nags Head has proved a tremendous success, and a similar state pier is in the design stages on Bogue Banks at Emerald Isle. A new pier is also in the planning stages for Hatteras Village. At these commercial piers, you pay a set fee to fish, usually in the $10–15 range, with licenses provided. Fishing tackle and bait, plus refreshments, are generally available at the pier store. Many fishing piers are also located on the sounds. These are often free piers, but you must have a North Carolina fishing license. Pier fishing reaches its peak in the spring and fall. **Surf fishing:** Another treasured tradition, fishing from the beach is hugely popular within the Cape Hatteras and Cape Lookout national seashores. As practiced on the Outer Banks, this activity requires a four-wheel-drive vehicle to drive to the surf line, loaded with gear, beach furniture, refreshments, and other necessities. Due to concern for the survival of nesting shorebirds and sea turtles, and an increasing number of accidents on the beach, the National Park Service has enacted a number of recent, and very controversial, regulations for driving off-road at the Cape Hatteras National Seashore, including ORV permits and closed areas to protect nesting sites. Those who want to experience "old-style" surf fishing, without permit fees, can ferry their vehicles over to the Core Banks at Cape Lookout, for up to 14 days of fishing and camping on the beach. A North Carolina Coastal Recreational Fishing License is required for all fishing from the beach or at public piers. **Fly and light tackle charters:** An increasing number of anglers choose to fish with light tackle or with fly-fishing rods for a greater challenge. While this is a popular method inshore, especially for sight fishing of red drum, and angling for fat Alberts and the tarpon that come into the sounds in the late fall, some captains also offer light tackle trips after big game fish on the open ocean. **Kayak or SUP fishing:** In this environmentally conscious form of fishing, you paddle out in a specially equipped kayak or stand-up paddleboard (SUP) to fly-fish and enjoy the serenity of nature.

The following is a guide to when certain types of fish are biting:

Winter (November–March): Rockfish (striped bass, called stripers locally), a good eating fish, inshore; giant blue tuna, 100–500 pounds, offshore.

April–May: The hard-fighting bluefish.

June–October: Spanish mackerel, inshore, a great eating fish.

Summer: Cobia, nearshore; the bright and beautiful dolphin (mahimahi), offshore, possibly the best tasting fish ever. The fighting game fish arrive in the summer as well: blue marlin, sailfish, wahoo.

July: White marlin, the acrobats of the billfish world, and a favorite for light tackle fishing.

Late summer: Pompano and tarpon in the sounds.

September–October: Runs of spots, a favorite meat fish, rock the piers. A classic Carolina fishing experience, this can hook you on fishing for life.

Fall: King mackerel are hooked all year, but fall brings the big "smoker kings," perfect for the smoker. Fall is also the best time for old drum (channel bass), the inshore fish most prized for eating by locals.

October: Specks (speckled trout), one of the best-tasting fish, inshore; king mackerel, offshore.

All year: Flounder, most often gigged at night; hard-fighting false albacore (fat Alberts) a favorite fly-fishing target.

FISHING LICENSES A North Carolina Coastal Recreational Fishing License (www.ncwildlife .org) will cover any fishing you might do from the beach, public piers, or private boats in the region. Licenses are required for all individuals 16 years and older. A short-term license good for 10 days costs $5 for North Carolina residents and $10 for those from out of state. Annual licenses are $15 and $30, respectively. Residents age 65 and over can get a lifetime license for $15. Special $10 lifetime licenses are available for the handicapped and disabled veterans. Check the North Carolina Wildlife website for legal sizes, seasons, and bag limits.

No license is required in North Carolina for the harvesting of shellfish, including oysters, clams, shrimp, mussels, blue crabs, conchs, and whelks, for personal consumption. However, size limits and bag limits may apply.

GETTING THERE The scarcity of causeways and bridges limit automobile access to the Banks to just a few routes. Despite their popularity, the Banks are a bit off the beaten track, far from the major interstates, so allow extra time to reach them, especially if you have an appointment to make.

From the North

There are two main routes from Virginia and points north, and one delightful "back way."

Approaching from the Norfolk airport or I-64E, the fastest route to the Outer Banks is VA/NC 168, a toll road. It joins US 158 in Barco, North Carolina, running down to the Wright Memorial Bridge and Kitty Hawk. This route is about 90 miles from airport to bridge, but it may be slow in summer, especially on weekends when people are coming in for their weekly rentals. A new toll causeway across Currituck Sound in the Jarvisburg/Grandy vicinity, intended to cut down on the congestion, is scheduled to open in 2018.

A second route from Virginia follows US 17, which has four lanes from the North Carolina border running parallel with the historic Dismal Swamp Canal. At Elizabeth City, a charming harbor town, you pick up US 158 out to Barco and beyond.

To sneak into the region via the scenic "back way," take VA/NC 618 from Virginia Beach through the **Mackay Island National Wildlife Refuge** and Knotts Island, noted for its vineyards, then cross via a free ferry to join NC 168. Call ahead to make sure the ferry is running (252-232-2683), as low water sometimes keeps it at the dock.

From the West

To reach Roanoke Island and the Central Banks from the west, you have your choice of two major roads, US 64 and US 264, both of them now four-lane, limited-access highways for most of the distance. The roads start out together from Raleigh, then separate to sweep along either shore of the great Albemarle Peninsula, joining again in Manns Harbor, on the mainland opposite Roanoke Island.

US 64 is the most direct and fastest route, being four-lane as far as Columbia. The trip from Raleigh to Roanoke Island takes about four hours via this route, with a rest stop in Columbia, or about three hours from I-95.

US 70E, a good four-lane, is the most direct route from Raleigh to the Crystal Coast, crossing both I-40 and I-95 along the way. Drive time to Beaufort is about three hours.

From the South

US 17 runs from Wilmington north to the Virginia border, passing through many old Inner Banks towns. To reach the Crystal Coast and Beaufort, turn east on NC 24 in Jacksonville.

GOLF Limited space and high land values make golf courses rare on the Outer Banks. The ones that do exist are wildly busy during the summer season, with tee times scheduled up to a year in advance. The demand has fueled an explosion of golf courses on the mainland just over the Wright Memorial Bridge in Currituck County, North Carolina's newest golf hot spot.

Packages and specials at several of the region's golf courses can be booked through the Outer Banks Golf Association (1-800-916-6244; www.golfouterbanks.com).

GUIDED TOURS Hatteras Tours (252-475-4477; www.hatterastours.com). Native historian Danny Couch conducts tours of Hatteras Island and other destinations.

Our Tour Guide (www.ourtourguide.net). A series of self-guided audio tours of the Outer

Banks are available on CD or audiotape. You can order from the website or buy the tours at local outlets.

Sandy Beach Tours (252-441-9800; www.sandybeachtours.com). Groups can tour the sights in a 12-, 15-, or 35-passenger coach. This company also provides shuttle service to Norfolk International Airport and transportation for weddings and other parties.

HAPPY HOURS Many North Carolina restaurants and clubs offer happy hours, but these are always specials on food. State law requires drink specials to be offered all day, from open to close. On the Outer Banks, happy hours are often scheduled earlier than in other areas, usually 3–5 PM, to avoid conflict with the big dinner rush.

HISTORIC DISTRICTS Despite the destruction of storms, the Outer Banks retains several historic districts, including Old Corolla Village, the Nags Head Historic Cottage District, downtown Manteo, and Ocracoke Village.

Farther south, several recognized historic districts are located along the Crystal Coast, including Cape Lookout Village and Portsmouth Village, both on Core Banks and today deserted. Other historic districts still occupied are the Beaufort, Morehead City, and Swansboro downtowns, all on the National Register of Historic Places.

HUNTING AND SHOOTING Waterfowl hunting has been a tradition on the North Carolina coast for generations, dating back to Native American days. In the years following the Civil War, many Northern industrialists bought large tracks of marshland, converting them to hunt clubs where they would spend weeks every winter, hunting the numerous ducks, geese, and swans that winter on the Banks. Commercial hunters came as well, shooting huge numbers of waterfowl, until the institution of seasons, bag limits, and other controls as the result of the Migratory Bird Treaty of 1918 between the United States and Canada.

Currituck County makes a limited number of blinds available to hunters with waterfowl hunting permits from the state. Contact the Currituck County Game Commission (252-429-3472; www.currituckgamecommission.org) and the North Carolina Wildlife Resources Commission (1-888-248-6834; www.ncwildlife.org) to start the process. The National Park Service allows waterfowl hunting on Bodie Island by registration request only and limits hunting through a lottery to 20 requests a day. You can get a Reservation Request Form (RRF) by picking one up at NPS Outer Banks Group Head-

quarters at Fort Raleigh National Historic Site in Manteo; by sending a written request to: Bodie Island Hunt, Cape Hatteras National Seashore, 1401 National Park Road, Manteo, NC 27954; or by printing the form from the NPS website (www.nps.gov/caha) and mailing it to the Manteo address, with a self-addressed stamped envelope for your notification. Twenty permanent blinds on Bodie Island are assigned to successful lottery applicants. To hunt legally at Cape Hatteras National Seashore, you must have on your person a valid North Carolina hunting license with North Carolina waterfowl privilege (1-888-248-6834; www.ncwildlife.org) and a Federal Duck Stamp (www.fws.gov/duck stamps). Ocracoke Island and the Down East region of the South Banks have strong family-based hunting traditions. One unique style of hunting available only in the area is a hunt using a curtain box, a similar setup to the now illegal sink box blinds, which allow hunters to hide below the surface of the water. Hunting licenses are still required.

Deer, bear, turkey, and other game are hunted in many national forests and wildlife refuges near the Outer Banks and Crystal Coast, mostly on the mainland. Check the North Carolina Wildlife Resources website (www.ncwildlife.org) for opportunities and regulations.

HURRICANES Hurricane season stretches from June 1 to November 30 each year, with the most active period from late August through September. The various islands of the Outer Banks often take the brunt of storms in the Atlantic, with extensive flooding, including overwash, pounding surf, and devastating winds. In recent years, hurricanes have cut new inlets through the banks, washing out roads and stranding residents. The National Weather Center may issue a mandatory evacuation when a hurricane approaches the Banks, and all visitors must leave the area. There are no emergency shelters in Dare, Currituck, or Hyde counties. Evacuation routes are marked with blue signs. If damage is significant, you may not be able to return to the Banks for an extended period of time. Most vacation rental agencies and hotels do not offer refunds if you have to leave during a storm. Some will refund or credit your money if a mandatory evacuation is ordered; however, most do not offer any reimbursement. If you leave before a mandatory evacuation is ordered, you will definitely not receive a refund. This policy makes it a very good idea to have trip cancellation and interruption insurance in the event of hurricanes or other storms. Most rental agencies now offer this option with your rental agreement.

For more information on hurricane preparedness, contact the county emergency management services: Carteret County Emergency Management (252-728-8470), Currituck County Emergency Management (252-232-2115), Dare County Emergency Management (252-475-5655), or Hyde County Emergency Management (252-926-4372).

INFORMATION The areas discussed in this book stretch across five North Carolina counties. Corolla is part of **Currituck County** (252-232-2075; www.currituckgovernment.com). Contact the **Currituck Outer Banks Visitor Center** (252-453-9612 or 1-877-287-7478; www.visitcurrituck.com) or the **Currituck Chamber of Commerce** (252-453-9497; www.currituckchamber.org) for visitor information. Kitty Hawk, Kill Devil Hills, Nags Head, Manteo and Roanoke Island, and Bodie and Hatteras islands make up **Dare County** (252-475-5878; www.darenc.com). For information on any of these destinations, contact the **Outer Banks Visitors Bureau** (252-473-2138 or 1-877-629-4386; www.outerbanks.org) or the **Outer Banks Chamber of Commerce** (252-441-8144; www.outerbankschamber.com). Ocracoke Island is part of **Hyde County** (252-926-9171 or 1-888-493-3826; www.hydecounty .org). Contact the **Ocracoke Civic and Business Association** (252-928-6711; www.ocracoke village.com) or the **Hyde County Chamber of Commerce** (252-926-9171 or 1-888-493-3826; www.hydecountychamber.org) for visitor information. Beaufort, Morehead City, and the towns along Bogue Banks are part of **Carteret County** (252-728-8450; www.carteretcounty gov.org). For visitor information, contact the **Crystal Coast Tourism Authority** (252-726-8148 or 1-800-786-8148; www.crystalcoast nc.org) or the **Carteret County Chamber of Commerce** (252-726-6350 or 1-800-622-6278; www.nccoastchamber.com). Swansboro, Camp Lejeune, and Jacksonville are part of **Onslow County** (910-347-4717; www.onslowcounty nc.gov). For visitor assistance, contact the **Swansboro Area Chamber of Commerce** (910-326-1174; www.swansborochamber.org) or **Onslow County Tourism** (1-800-932-2144; www.onlyinonslow.com).

You'll find information on all these destinations on the main tourism site for the state of North Carolina: **Visit NC** (919-733-8372 or 1-800-VISIT NC; www.visitnc.com); in the British Isles: http://uk.visitnc.com; in Germany: http://de.visitnc.com..

KITEBOARDING AND WINDSURFING Steady winds and shallow, protected water stretching for miles create what many boarders consider a paradise for wind-and-water sports. Wind gypsies make their way to the shallow waters of Roanoke and Pamlico sounds to experience the finest conditions on the East Coast. For the more adventurous, the ocean waves are just a few steps away. Kiteboarding, sometimes called kitesurfing, has a steep learning curve and requires a great deal of upper-body strength. Equipment for kiteboarding is generally not available for rent, but those interested can take a lesson that includes equipment. Those who complete Professional Air Sports Association–certified training courses may qualify to rent equipment. Windsurfing is also sometimes called sailboarding. Equipment for this sport is available for rent from a number of different services on the Outer Banks.

Hatteras Island is a world-recognized destination for both sports. The Tri-Villages have several top kiteboarding resorts, while Avon is the East Coast center of windsurfing.

LIQUOR Bottles of liquor are only available in North Carolina at state ABC Stores. The **ABC website** (www.ncabc.com) has a complete listing of stores and their hours of operation. Generally, the ABC stores are open Monday through Saturday 10–9 and are closed on Sunday. While a few towns in mostly unincorporated areas along the coast still don't allow liquor by the drink, beer and wine are universally available at restaurants, groceries, and convenience stores until 2 AM and after noon on Sunday. Liquor cannot be sold at restaurants before noon on Sunday in most towns or after 2 AM statewide.

For a safe, chauffeured night on the town, contact **Outer Banks University Pub Crawl** (www.obxpubcrawl.com).

LODGING Weekly cottage and house rentals are still the norm during the summer season; however, overnight and weekend accommodations are now available year-round, although two- and three-night minimums are still the rule on holiday weekends at all but the most expensive hotels. During the off-season, many shorter rentals are available, and most prices drop dramatically. Pay close attention to cancellation policies wherever you rent, including hotels. Many require early notice of cancellations to refund deposits. Trip insurance is a good idea, especially if you are making a considerable outlay in advance. Another thing to take note of is the hurricane or storm policy followed by your accommodation. These vary widely, but very few offer refunds, even for mandatory evacuations. You may receive a rain check or other compensation, or nothing at all.

What you see out of your window may affect

the price of your room. Ocean-view and ocean-front rooms will cost more than pool-view or so-called dune-view rooms that may look out on the parking lot. Prices are also often higher on the upper floors of hotels for rooms with ocean views, even though you may have to walk up several flights of stairs to get there. If stairs are a problem, it's a good idea to ask specifically whether a property has an elevator.

MAPS Download current maps of North Carolina from the state Department of Transportation website (www.ncdot.org), or you can order a free state transportation map to be sent by mail, either from the website or by calling 1-877-DOT-4YOU or 1-800-VISIT NC.

MARINE MAMMALS Report dead or stranded whales, dolphins, porpoises, or seals as soon as possible to the National Marine Fisheries Service's **North Carolina Marine Mammal Stranding Network** at 919-728-8762.

MILEPOSTS A long the NC 12 from Corolla to Oregon Inlet, and along the US 158 Bypass from the Wright Memorial Bridge to the Nags Head–Manteo Causeway, milepost markers (marked MP) help visitors find shops, restaurants, hotels, and other destinations. Farther south, Bogue Banks uses a similar MM system along NC 58, although the practice is not as widespread.

NEWSPAPERS AND PERIODICALS *Carolina Coast Online* (252-726-7081; www.carolinacoastonline.com), 4206 Bridges Street, Morehead City. *Coaster Magazine* (252-247-7442; www.nccoast.com). Free publication with information on the Crystal Coast. *Coastland Times* (252-473-2105; www.thecoastlandtimes.net), 503 Budleigh Street, Manteo. Published continuously since 1935, three times a week, Tuesday, Thursday, and Sunday. *The Gam* (252-728-2435; www.thegam.com), Beaufort. Weekly publication distributed on Thursday in Carteret County and Swansboro. *Island Free Press* (www.islandfreepress.org), Buxton. Extensive online coverage of Hatteras and Ocracoke islands. *North Beach Sun* (252-449-4444; www.northbeachsun.com), Kitty Hawk. Print and online editions cover news, arts, and real estate on the Outer Banks. *Outer Banks Sentinel* (252-480-2234; www.obsentinel.com), Nags Head. Local newspaper publishes on Sunday and Wednesday. Online and mail subscriptions available. A blog, Outer Banks Entertainment (www.obxentertainment.com), covers local events. *This Week Magazine* (252-726-6016; www.thisweekmag.com), Morehead City. Free weekly covers entertainment and dining on the Crystal Coast. *The Virginian-Pilot*

(252-441-1620; www.pilotonline.com), 2224 Bypass, Nags Head. Daily paper from Hampton Roads, Virginia, has a section of news from the North Carolina coast. A free section called *The Coast*, with Outer Banks entertainment listings and news, is published weekly March–December, monthly January–February.

PETS Rules governing pets on the beach vary widely and by season. In general, pets must be leashed. Several communities don't allow pets on the beach at all during the summer season. Again, check each town's website for its current rules. Pets on 6-foot leashes or caged are permitted within the national seashores, except at designated swimming beaches. Guide dogs may remain with their owners at all times.

PIRATES Ocracoke, Beaufort, and the Inner Banks village of Bath are the towns most associated with Blackbeard and his fellow pirates. On Ocracoke, visit the **Teach's Hole Blackbeard Exhibit,** then take a sail on the schooner *Windfall II,* where Captain Temple will entertain you with tales of pirate lore and point out the spot where Blackbeard met his end. In Beaufort, you can see artifacts recovered from the presumed wreck of Blackbeard's ship, *Queen Anne's Revenge,* in the **North Carolina Maritime Museum,** and take a ghost tour to the pirate's former home, said to be haunted by the one of his unfortunate "wives." Websites where you can find out more about Blackbeard's activities in North Carolina are www.blackbeardthepirate

EACH BEACH HAS ITS OWN SET OF DOG REGULATIONS.

.com, www.blackbeardlives.com, and www.qaron line.org.

RADIO For a local take on the news, community events, and a mix of alternative music, check out **WVOD The Sound 99.1 FM** (www.991thesound.com), broadcasting from Wanchese, and **WOVV FM 90.1**, **Ocracoke Community Radio** (252-928-WOVV; www .wovv.org), the voice of Ocracoke Village.

RECOMMENDED READING The **Eastern North Carolina Digital Library** (www.digital .lib.ecu.edu) contains hundreds of works of fiction and nonfiction, much of it from the 1800s and early 1900s, as well as museum artifacts, maps, and other educational material available free online.

A short reading list:

Cleary, William J., and Tara P. Marden. *Shifting Shorelines: A Pictorial Atlas of North Carolina Inlets.* Raleigh, NC: NC Sea Grant, 1999.

Daniels, Jaret C. *Butterflies of the Carolinas Field Guide.* Cambridge, MN: Adventure Publications, 2003.

DeBlieu, Jan. *Hatteras Journal.* Winston-Salem, NC: John F. Blair, 1998. A naturalist writes evocatively about the barrier island ecology.

Fletcher, Inglis. *Men of Albemarle.* New York: Bantam Books, 1970. Prolific author Inglis Fletcher wrote a dozen meticulously researched historical novels covering 200 years of North Carolina history (1585–1789). Hard to find, but worth the hunt.

Fussell, John O. *A Birder's Guide to Coastal North Carolina.* Chapel Hill: University of North Carolina Press, 1994.

Houser, Lynn. Edited by Jeannie Norris. *Seashells of North Carolina.* Raleigh, NC: NC Sea Grant, 2000.

Kaufman, Wallace. *The Beaches Are Moving: The Drowning of America's Shoreline.* Durham, NC: Duke University Press, 1983.

Kraus, E. Jean Wilson, and Sarah Friday, eds. *Guide to Ocean Dune Plants Common to North Carolina.* Chapel Hill: University of North Carolina Press, 1988.

McNaughton, Marimar. *Outer Banks Architecture: An Anthology of Outposts, Lodges & Cottages.* Winston-Salem, NC: John F. Blair, 2000.

Meyer, Peter K. *Nature Guide to the Carolina Coast: Common Birds, Crabs, Shells, Fish, and Other Entities of the Coastal Environment.* Wilmington, NC: Avian-Cetacean Press, 1991.

Pilkey, Orrin H. *How to Read a North Carolina Beach: Bubble Holes, Barking Sands, and*

Rippled Runnels. Chapel Hill: University of North Carolina Press, 2004.

Simpson, Bland. *The Inner Islands: A Carolinian's Sound Country Chronicle.* Chapel Hill: University of North Carolina Press, 2006. A guide to the often forgotten islands of the North Carolina sounds, written by one of the state's top naturalists, a professor at UNC–Chapel Hill and a member of the Tony award–winning string band the Red Clay Ramblers.

Stick, David, ed. *An Outer Banks Reader.* Chapel Hill: University of North Carolina Press, 1998. Excerpts from nearly five centuries of writings about the region, selected by the Banks' top scholar.

Young, Claiborne S. *Cruising Guide to Coastal North Carolina.* Winston-Salem, NC: John F. Blair, 2005. An invaluable guide for boaters.

SCENIC BYWAYS The **Outer Banks National Scenic Byway** runs 111 miles from Whalebone Junction in Nags Head to Beaufort, crossing two inlets by ferry. Other North Carolina scenic byways cross Roanoke Island, circle the Albemarle Peninsula, and loop through many towns on the Inner Banks. Maps and descriptions of the various routes can be downloaded from the **North Carolina Department of Transportation** website (www.ncdot.org).

SCUBA DIVING AND SNORKELING The Graveyard of the Atlantic brings divers from around the world to see German U-boats, 18th-century pirate ships, and everything in between on the bottom of the ocean. The hundreds of wrecks just offshore make the North Carolina coast the world's top destination for wreck diving. Warm Gulf Stream waters make diving possible year-round. Water temperatures in the area reach the low 80s, with visibility to 100 feet during the prime season, May to October. Temperatures, however, plummet at deeper depths. In addition to accidental wrecks, numerous ships, fishing boats, World War II Liberty ships, airplanes, landing craft, and even railroad boxcars have been purposely sunk off the Outer Banks. Two Falcon jet fixed-wing aircraft lie on the bottom approximately 8 nautical miles off Oregon Inlet. The original purpose of this program was to improve bottom fishing, but the artificial reefs also make excellent dive sites, harboring a wide variety of sea life, including the sand tiger sharks for which the area is known. A complete list of artificial reefs can be found on the website of the **N.C. Environmental and Natural Resources** (www.ncdenr.gov). The website of the **Association of Underwater Explorers** (www.uwex.us)

has an extensive listing of wrecks in these waters. BFDC, a club that organizes dive trips, lists over 50 frequently visited wrecks off the North Carolina coast on its **North Carolina Wreck Diving** website (www.nc-wreckdiving .com).

The Outer Banks is the only place on the East Coast where historic wrecks can be reached from the beach. Because they require you to swim on the surface through the surf, beach dives, while shallower than boat dives, are more physically demanding. You need to be in good physical shape and a strong swimmer. Snorkeling in Pamlico Sound is far safer, and it's an interesting experience, with small fish, shrimp, and crabs to be seen. The waters around Pea Island National Wildlife Refuge on Hatteras are usually some of the clearest in the area. The **Cape Hatteras National Seashore** (252-995-4474; www.nps.gov/caha) offers sound snorkeling adventures during the summer months. **Ocean Atlantic** (252-995-5868; www.oceanatlanticrentals.com) rents fins, snorkels, and masks.

SEAFOOD The North Carolina commercial fishing fleet brings home a wide variety of seafood, including shrimp, oysters, clams, and blue crab, plus stripers, tuna, mahimahi, mackerel, and much more from the rich ocean waters. The **NC Seafood website** (www.nc-seafood.org) has information on the species found in the state, along with local seafood recipes. Two organizations help you find fresh local catch at fish markets, roadside stands, and restaurants. On the Outer Banks, check the website of **Outer Banks Catch** (www.outer bankscatch.com). On the Crystal Coast, consult **Carteret Catch** (www.carteretcatch.org). Look for the logos of these organizations when you shop or eat out, and always ask: "Is it local?"

SEASONS High season on the Outer Banks has traditionally been Memorial Day to Labor Day. However, shoulder seasons are sometimes carved out of this period, and real estate agents each seem to have their own formula to determine the price of rental properties. While the Banks continue to host the most family groups during the summer, other seasons are becoming more popular, and businesses are increasingly open all year.

SMOKING Since 2010, smoking has been banned inside all restaurants and bars, as well as lodging establishments that offer food and drink, in the state of North Carolina. Many restaurants and bars have added smoking patios and decks since then. Lodging establishments must offer nonsmoking rooms, with no more

A HISTORIC BOARD ON DISPLAY AT THE COROLLA SURF SHOP

than 20 percent of rooms designated for smoking. Cigar bars and private clubs are exempt from the smoking ban.

SURFING AND SHAPERS The Outer Banks have some of the best breaks on the East Coast, and reports of a storm in the Atlantic set hordes of surfers in motion as they race to catch the big waves. On Hatteras Island, the Cape Point area around the lighthouse is considered the Eastern Seaboard's greatest "wave magnet" creating the best surfing available on the Right Coast.

Corolla is the North Banks' surfing hotspot, with easy entry and a reliable sandbar. Stop by the **Corolla Surf Shop** to find out where the waves are breaking. On the Central Beaches, you'll find surfers surfing at Jennette's Pier and partying at **The Pit.** On Ocracoke, surfers meet up at **Howard's,** where they can watch the waves from the rooftop deck. The great surfing has attracted many professional surfboard makers as permanent residents. Called "shapers" in surf lingo, some of these board artists own local surf shops; others work freelance. Their designs push the boundaries of boarding ever outward. Many shapers are now branching out into stand-up paddleboards (SUPs). **Wave Riding Vehicles** (www.waveridingvehicles.com), the largest surfboard company on the Eastern

Seaboard, makes boards in its Currituck County factory just across the Wright Memorial Bridge and sells its designs in its Kitty Hawk store. Tim Nolte's shop (www.timnoltesurfboards.com) is also on the Currituck mainland. Other well-known local shapers include Murray Ross; Mike Rowe, shaper of **Hooked Surfboards** (www .hookedsurfboards.com); Pat McManus; Lynn Shell, at the **Outer Banks Boarding Company** (www.obbconline.com); Ted Kearns, creator of **TK Shapes** (www.tkshapes.com), now based in Hawai'i; Mike Beveridge; Scott Busbey, creator of **In the Eye** (www.surfintheeye .com); Mike Clark, of **Clark Shapes** (www.face book.com/clarkshapes252); Rascoe Hunt, of Gale Force Glass; the late Robert "Redman" Manville, master of the big gun boards; Eric Holmes, of Formula Surfboards; and Mickey McCarthy, of New Sun. Other locally made boards to look for include Ability, Avalon, Broken Barriers, Cherry, Future Foils, Hot and Nasty, Tropix, and Secret Spot. Surf shops in the area typically carry a selection of new and used boards, many by local shapers. Serious surfers can order a board custom crafted by a master just for them.

You can catch a surf report on the local radio stations or call any of the local surf shops for expert advice. Online, you can see reports direct from the beach twice a day at www.obx surfinfo.com.

TRAILS Part of the 900-mile **North Carolina Mountains-to-Sea Hiking Trail** (www.ncmst .org) traverses the length of the Crystal Coast and Outer Banks, crossing the Croatan National Forest via the Neusiok Trail in Carteret County, then leaping to Ocracoke and Hatteras islands on the state ferries, before ending at Jockey's Ridge State Park in Nags Head. The sections of trail on Ocracoke, Hatteras, and Bodie islands run along the beach. Camping is available at established campgrounds within the Croatan National Forest and Cape Hatteras National Seashore.

TRAINS Amtrak (1-800-872-7245; www .amtrak.com) offers daily rail service from Boston, New York, and Washington, DC, to Newport News, Virginia, with bus connections to Norfolk and Virginia Beach. The Palmetto, Silver Meteor, and Silver Star trains offer service from New York City; Washington, DC; Charleston, South Carolina; and Florida, with stops in Richmond, Virginia, where you can connect with the train to Newport News. The Carolinian, running daily between New York City and Charlotte, North Carolina, also stops at Richmond, Virginia, as well as Rocky Mount, North Carolina.

Amtrak's new Thruway bus service connects with the Palmetto in Wilson, North Carolina, bringing travelers to downtown Morehead City daily, with stops in Havelock, New Bern, and Greenville, North Carolina.

VACATION RENTALS Real estate companies offer a wide variety of different properties for weekly rental. Shorter stays are sometimes available, especially off-season. Cottages generally have 2–8 bedrooms; some have as many as 18, making them suitable for large family reunions. Most real estate companies rent only to families. With so many properties now available for rental in this area, many management companies are increasing their efforts to make renting from them hassle-free. Linens and towels are now included with many rentals, formerly a separate charge, and some companies even make up the beds for you in advance. Companies are also dropping some of the many fees that traditionally have been added on, so that the price you see in brochures or online is actually what you pay, without the hundreds of extra dollars in administrative fees, damage waivers, and fees to use a credit card. Increasingly, you can browse available properties online and make your reservations there as well. We make specific suggestions for rental companies in individual chapters. Here are some companies that represent a wide range of properties all along the coast. Some also offer longer, off-season rentals. ❀ **Atlantic Realty** (1-877-858-4795; www .atlanticrealty-nc.com). Over 200 properties from Corolla to South Nags Head. All renters enjoy the company's Family Fun amenities package. ❀ **Cola Vaughan Realty** (252-449-2652; www.obxcola.com), 324 W. Soundside, Nags Head. Pet-friendly cottages from Southern Shores to South Nags Head. ❀ **Elan Vacations** (1-866-760-3526; www.elanvacations.com), 8624 US 158, Powells Point. Early-arrival policy lets you pick up your keys at the check-in office on the mainland. Three-day off-season getaways can be booked in advance. **Joe Lamb Jr. & Associates** (1-800-552-6257; www.joelambjr .com), 5101 Bypass, MP 2, Kitty Hawk. Over 500 properties available, most in the Central Beaches. **Kitty Hawk Rentals** (252-441-7166 or 1-800-635-1559; www.beachrealtync.com). Amenity package with some rentals. Partial weeks and long-term rentals available. **Nags Head Realty** (252-441-4315 or 1-800-222-1531; www.nagsheadrealty.com), 2405 Bypass, MP 10.5, Nags Head. Over 200 rentals; some three-day packages. ❀ **Outer Banks Blue Realty** (1-888-623-2583; www.outerbanks blue.com). Unique "check in by mail" program eliminates that time-consuming visit to the real estate office to pick up keys. **ResortQuest**

Outer Banks Vacation Rentals (1-800-467-3529; www.resortquest.com). Large national company lists hundreds of rental properties, from condos to 12-bedroom estates, all along the Outer Banks. *ᴓ* **Seaside Vacations** (1-888-884-0267; www.outerbanksvacations.com). Full-service management company with offices in Kitty Hawk and Corolla handles rentals at over 300 properties from the off-road area in Carova to Nags Head. Last-minute specials and dedicated-event properties available. **Sun Realty** (252-453-8822 or 1-888-853-7770; www.sunrealtync.com). One of the largest rental companies on the Outer Banks. **Wright Property Management** (252-261-2186 or 1-800-276-7478; www.wpmobx.com), 3719 Bypass, MP 4.5, Kitty Hawk. Over 100 properties, most in Kitty Hawk, Kill Devil Hills, and South Nags Head. Three- and four-night rentals available off-season.

VEHICLE RENTALS B&R Car Rentals (252-473-2142), 404 US 64, Manteo. Rentals at the Manteo airport. **Island Cruisers** (252-987-2097; www.islandcruisersinc.com), 26248 NC 12, Rodanthe. Rents fun, street-legal VW buggies, four-wheel drives for heading out to the beach for surf fishing, vintage classics, and golf carts. **Outer Banks Beach Buggies** (252-715-1295; www.obxbeachbuggies.com). Rents street-legal golf carts. **Outer Banks Chrysler Dodge Jeep** (252-441-1146 or 1-855-459-6555; www.outerbanksjeep.com), 3000 Bypass, MP 5.5, Kill Devil Hills. Rents four-wheel-drive vehicles for beach driving. **Outer Banks Harley-Davidson** (252-338-8866; www.outerbankshd.com), 8739 US 158, Harbinger. Rents Harleys to tour the Banks.

WINERIES Martin Vineyards (www.martinvineyards.com), on Knotts Island; the **Vineyard on the Scuppernong** (www.vineyardsonthescuppernong.com), in Columbia; and **Bennett Vineyards** (www.bennettvineyard.com), near Aurora, are all within an easy drive of the Outer Banks.

YOUTH HOSTELS The ❄ ❦ **Adventure Bound Hostel** (252-255-1130 or 1-877-453-2545; www.adventureboundnc.com), in Kitty Hawk, offers dorm and private rooms all year.

HISTORY AND CULTURE
A Story of Wild Waters and Independent Souls

THE OUTER BANKS, an isolated string of islands thrust into the Atlantic Ocean, stretch for about 175 miles from the Virginia border to Beaufort Inlet. These fragile bits of land are made entirely of shifting sand, exposed to extremes of wind and water. To keep a foothold on this uncertain terrain takes a special breed of people. And though they've seen their homesteads washed over with sand, water, and most recently by developers, the Bankers remain—independent, full of stories, and just a bit salty.

The Barrier Islands: A Fragile Ribbon Made of Sand

The island chain now called the Outer Banks juts into the ocean like the bow of a great ship. Here the two great currents of the western Atlantic—the warm, cobalt-blue waters of the Gulf Stream flowing north, and the cold, murky green Labrador Current traveling south—meet and mingle. It is not a peaceful encounter. The maelstrom where the currents meet extends some 8 miles off the tip of Cape Hatteras. The dreaded Diamond Shoals are a place of fog, shifting sandbars, and sudden surf that have led many ships to their ruin and caused the area to be called the Graveyard of the Atlantic.

The Banks are in constant motion, changed by every storm. Made almost entirely of sand, the land here is forever rolling westward, driven by waves, wind, and rising sea level. During storms, waves wash across the barrier islands, carrying sand from the ocean beach into the sound waters, moving the islands a little westward, and creating new salt marsh. It is a process called "overwash" and is now considered a necessary part of the health of the island ecology. It is also the reason most cottages stand on tall legs above the sand. This process has been going on for thousands of years and repeats as sea levels rise and fall. Other bands of barrier islands in the past have formed and moved west until they collided with the mainland. Roanoke Island, now situated between the outer islands and the mainland, is one example.

Viewed from above, the temporary nature of the Outer Banks is revealed. The pounding ocean surf is just yards away from the quiet sound waters at some points. Often these are sites where old inlets have closed—or where new ones are in the process of opening.

The Windswept Dunes

Although it is the ocean that provides the material, it is the wind gives shape to the great dunes of sand that are the most notable feature of the Outer Banks. Jockey's Ridge, at nearly 100 feet, is the largest dune on the East Coast and the most southern in a line of dunes that once stretched north over the Virginia border. Like all dunes, Jockey's Ridge began life with a wind shadow—a tree usually, or even a building—that blocked the wind. Sand behind the obstruction does not blow away, and a dune begins to form. The prevailing winds of the area come from opposite directions. From March through August, roughly, the winds come from the southwest, off the mainland. The rest of the year, September to February, the winds whistle in off the open ocean, across the cold Atlantic. These opposite winds are ideal for the formation of dunes. The winter winds are stronger, causing the dunes to move slowly to the southwest, usually just inches a year. Jockey's Ridge has slowly swallowed a hamburger stand and a miniature golf course since it became a state park in 1975. You can see the final turrets of a castle on the minigolf course poking above the sand just across the street from Kitty Hawk Kites. **Jockey's Ridge State Park** presents good exhibits on the processes that form the dunes, as well as a spectacular view from the top of the ridge. Dunes also shelter the land at their base from the salt spray, and rich pockets of maritime forest develop in their lee. The nature trails at Jockey's Ridge lead through pockets of forest called "blowouts," where fox,

THE WASH WOODS ON THE BEACH AT CAROVA ARE REMNANTS OF ANCIENT FORESTS.

deer, and rabbits make their homes. North of Jockey's Ridge, **Nags Head Woods** is a mature maritime forest full of pines, bayberry, wax myrtle, cedar, and live oaks. On its north side stands Run Hill, the next in the line of dunes; it can be accessed from West Airfield Road off US 158. From the top of Run Hill, you can see the sand slowly swallowing the forest on the sound side of the dune, while to the north the next dune in line can be seen. This is **Kill Devil Hill,** the dune used by the Wright brothers for their experiments in flight. No longer technically a dune, since it has been planted entirely with grass to stabilize it for the monument on top, in the Wright brothers' day it was as nude as Jockey's Ridge. The line of dunes continues on toward Virginia, looming to the west as you drive along NC 12 through Duck and beyond. Past the end of the road in Corolla stands the second largest of the untamed dunes, variously called Penny's or Lewark's Hill. The old settlement of Seagull, long buried, is slowly emerging from beneath the ever-traveling sand.

Another undisturbed dune system can be found on Bear Island, part of **Hammocks Beach State Park** near Swansboro. On Hatteras Island, **Buxton Woods** is the final remaining remnant of the great forest of cedar and live oaks laced with grape vines that once covered this island. The trees were timbered off for use in shipbuilding by the mid-1800s, and grazing livestock kept vegetation from regrowing.

Huge dunes, called "whaleheads" by locals, developed on Hatteras during this time and swept across the island. Today they are gone, dissipated into the sound, leaving a relatively flat landscape behind. The low dunes along the oceanfront today are the work of a Civilian Conservation Corps project, which constructed sand fences and planted sea grass to rebuild the dune line in the 1930s.

Inlets and Sounds

While the great dunes are the most obvious work of wind and water, inlets that break up the island chain are the most troubling. A single storm can change the face of the Outer Banks, destroying roads and stranding residents. In fact, Ocracoke Inlet and Beaufort Inlet are the only breaks in the barrier island chain that remain the same from the time the earliest explorers drew maps of the region in the 1500s. A great hurricane in September of 1846 opened the Hatteras and Oregon inlets we know today.

The process that gives birth to new inlets originates not from the action of the ocean but from the combination of wind and the fresh water flowing into the sounds from the rivers of the region. Pamlico Sound, the largest lagoon-style body of water on the East Coast, receives vast amounts of water from the Roanoke/Chowan river systems, via Albemarle Sound in the north, as well as the Tar/Pamlico and Neuse rivers farther south. All of this water reaches the ocean through the inlets that pierce the barrier islands. During a hurricane, the water in Pamlico Sound is often driven far northwest during the early hours of the storm, then returns with devastating force as the winds shift to the southeast during the later stages of the hurricane. It is this huge storm surge coming from the landside that opens new inlets in the Outer Banks. Inlets may close naturally, or they may get some help. In September 2003, with the Centennial of Flight celebration fast approaching, Hurricane Isabel opened a new inlet just east of Hatteras Village, isolating the community and its ferry dock. The U.S. Army Corps of Engineers moved swiftly to pump sand into the breach, closing it within a month, and rebuilding NC 12. By contrast, inlets are generally allowed to open and close as nature dictates on uninhabited Core Banks, within the Cape Lookout National Seashore.

Because of the prevailing winds, inlets tend to migrate southwest, along with the rest of the barrier island chain. This process can be seen at work at Oregon Inlet. Since the 2.5-mile long Herbert C. Bonner Bridge opened over Oregon Inlet in 1965, Bodie Island, on the north side of the bridge, has extended nearly a mile south, while, on the opposite shore, Pea Island retreated until the southern end of the bridge was threatened and the Army Corps of Engineers was forced to build a rock seawall to protect the underpinnings of the bridge. This is seen as a temporary measure, however, and plans for a new bridge are in the works. Meanwhile, dredging continues year-round to keep Oregon Inlet open for the sport- and commercial fishing fleets that depend on this route to reach the open ocean.

The Inner Banks

The sounds to the west of the Outer Banks vary in width from just a few hundred yards to more than 50 miles. Beyond lay the shores, if you can call them that, of the Inner Banks. Here brackish and fresh waters mix together in broad tidal estuaries, marshes, and wetlands, creating one of the richest breeding grounds for sea life on the planet. These swamps provide some of the last refuges for endangered species, such as the red wolf and red-cockaded woodpecker, and are at the northern limit of the American alligator. Black bear, deer, raccoon, turkey, squirrel, rabbit, quail, mink, and otter make this their home, as do a large variety of poisonous snakes and biting insects. Winter is considered the best time to visit. That's when the region's most beautiful visitors arrive for their winter vacations. Some 100,000 tundra swans—plus many more geese, ducks, coots, and other migrating waterfowl—make the lakes of this region their cold-weather home.

The Carolina bays are unusual features found within this wilderness. These round or oval depressions have been variously attributed to giant prehistoric beavers, an ancient asteroid shower, or—most likely—a remnant of falling sea level at the height of the last ice age. Found scattered all along the southern Atlantic seaboard, these bays, also called pocosins, are most numerous in eastern North Carolina, where thousands have been identified. Rimmed with sand, pocosins often contain acidic lakes surrounded by thick layers of peat. Bay trees, vines, and briars survive best in this nutrient-poor soil, and cypress trees grow along the water's edge.

Some pocosin plants have developed unusual behaviors to supplement their diets. This ecosystem is the evolutionary cradle of carnivorous plants, including the Venus flytrap and the less well-known pitcher plant and sundew. In fact, the Croatan National Forest is home to the nation's largest collection of carnivorous plants.

"A Land of Plentie"

Sir Walter Raleigh's captains sailed into the waters of the Outer Banks in the late 1500s and brought back stories of great abundance to entice settlers to make the voyage into the unknown. They described a land "so full of grapes as the very beating and surge of the Sea overflowed them." These grapes were the native scuppernongs, of which the 400-year-old Mother Vine on Roanoke Island is the oldest surviving example. Scientists speculate that the native tribes in the area began the cultivation of grapes, even before the arrival of the English settlers. The Banks, then and now, are home to white-tailed deer and the occasional black bear that makes the swim from the mainland. Today's bears have been known to make use of the causeways to reach the Banks. The ecosystem found along these shores is unique. Buxton Woods, at the base of Cape Hatteras Lighthouse, supports a population of rare plants and the greatest diversity of mammals of any barrier island along the East Coast. The forests, marshes, and freshwater ponds of the Banks also play host to a vast variety of birds, from migrating songbirds to waterfowl, and are the year-round home of ospreys and other raptors, as well as many wading birds. Rare pelagic species are found offshore on the Gulf Stream. Some 400 species have been spotted in this region, making it one of the prime birding destinations along the East Coast. Several beach areas provide important nesting grounds for the endangered piping plover. Endangered sea turtles also come to the Banks to nest from May to August. Loggerhead and green are the species most commonly found, with Kemp's ridley, hawksbill, and leatherback turtles making occasional appearances. The Network for Endangered Sea Turtles (252-441-8622; www.nestonline.org) maintains a 24-hour hotline for turtle sightings.

Beachcombers will find plenty to spark their interest on these shores. Although the heavy surf pounds many shells to fragments, a stroll along the beach, especially in early spring at low tide, may yield a trove of shells, including quahog clams, scallops, pen shells, olives, moon snails, Atlantic giant cockles, and Scotch bonnets, the state shell of North Carolina. Shelling is generally best at the ends of the islands, along the inlet shores. Excellent collections of shells are on permanent display at the **North Carolina Maritime Museum** in Beaufort and the North Carolina Coastal Federation in Newport, both on the Crystal Coast. On the North Banks, the **Hampton Inn and Suites Corolla** displays a fine private collection in its lobby.

Native Tribes

By the time the English first arrived off the Outer Banks, the area had been occupied for thousands of years by tribes of Native Americans. The coast of North Carolina had villages belonging to all three major linguistic groups then inhabiting eastern North America. The most numerous were the Algonquian-speaking tribes occupying the northern Banks and the shores of Albemarle Sound. Although often

THE SCOTCH BONNET, STATE SHELL OF NORTH CAROLINA AND A RARE FIND.

warring among themselves, the Roanoke, Croatan, and the tribes of the Chowan river valley spoke languages related to those of the tribes of Virginia and the Chesapeake Bay. To the west, the Tuscarora tribes spoke an Iroquoian language, indicating their origin in the eastern Great Lakes region. The southern Banks and the area around today's New Bern were home to tribes speaking Siouan dialects. The Woccon occupying Ocracoke, and the Coree who lived in Carteret County and gave their name to the Core Banks, belonged to this group. Early maps created by English explorers show dozens of native villages occupying the Banks and the shores of adjacent sounds and rivers. Population at the time of first contact is estimated to have been in the neighborhood of 10,000 souls.

The coastal regions occupied by the native tribes offered a rich selection of foods. In addition to deer, waterfowl, and much other game, the Indians depended on the ample fish and shellfish, including crabs, oysters, clams, scallops, and mussels, found in the waters of the sounds.

Many of the tribes apparently occupied their coastal encampments for just part of the year, retiring to mainland villages to grow crops of various tubers and root vegetables, as well as corn, squash, pumpkins, gourds, beans, and sunflowers. They also gathered wild walnuts, hickory nuts, and chinquapins, wild grains, and fruits. Early explorers reported that the local tribes drank wine made from local grapes, as well as a tea made from the leaves of the yaupon tree, still found abundantly in the maritime forests. Tobacco was grown as a sacred herb.

Roanoke Island was a center of Native American activity in precolonial times. Its name indicates it was a manufacturing center for making the shell money used by the native tribes in trade. *Roanoke* was a type of wampum that consisted of round disks of shell cut from whelk and clamshells. White was the most common color, but black or purple beads were worth more. The name seems to come from the Algonquian word that means to rub, smooth, or polish—a reference to how the beads were made.

The Croatan Indians had their main village, called Croatoan, on what is now the island of Hatteras, near the village of Buxton. Recently, archaeologists conducted excavations, discovering many pottery shards and a few English artifacts amid enormous numbers of discarded oyster shells. Like most tribes, the Croatans also held land on the mainland more suitable for agriculture. Growing crops on the Banks themselves was difficult because of the high salt content of the soil. Hatteras is derived from an Algonquian word, *hatorask,* which has been translated as "place where nothing will grow."

European diseases decimated the tribes, a process completed by the Tuscarora War. This uprising began in 1711 as the tribes protested the taking of their lands, as well as the capture and enslavement of their people. Most tribes in the area joined the rebellion in a last-ditch effort to expel the English and preserve their traditional ways of life. The natives were utterly defeated in 1715, and the survivors were enslaved or driven inland. Most of the Tuscarora migrated north to join with their cousins in the Iroquois Confederacy. The surviving Coree settled near Lake Mattamuskeet, while many of the Croatan people disappeared into the deep swamps surrounding Alligator River. Other Croatans migrated to the shores of the Lumbee River close to the South Carolina border and joined with the remnants of other tribes to become the forefathers of today's Lumbee Indians.

First Contact and the Lost Colony

Spanish explorers visited coastal Carolina as early as 1520, and in 1524, Giovanni da Verrazano, a Florentine captain sailing under the French flag in search of the Northwest Passage, landed on the Bogue Banks in Pine Knoll Shores, and again near today's Kitty Hawk. He was the first to comment on the vast quantities of grapes growing along the shore, but he mistook Pamlico Sound for the Pacific Ocean.

In 1584, Sir Walter Raleigh received a patent from his queen "for the discovering and planting of new lands not possessed by any Christian Prince nor inhabited by Christian

People." Raleigh sent a reconnaissance voyage out that very summer. Captains Amadas and Barlowe brought back two young Indians, a Croatan named Manteo and a Roanoke brave named Wanchese, and gave such a glowing report about the new land that Queen Elizabeth allowed Raleigh to name his colony Virginia, in her honor. Subsequent voyages in 1585 and 1586 didn't go as smoothly. Sir Richard Grenville grounded his ship in Ocracoke Inlet, the sailors spread smallpox through the native villages, and the men left on Roanoke Island were soon in conflict with the local tribe. In 1587, John White, an artist who had accompanied one of the earlier voyages, arrived with a party of colonists at Roanoke Island. Among the colonists were the first English women to cross the ocean, including White's pregnant daughter, Eleanor. Abandoned on Roanoke Island by the captain of their transport vessel, White's group soon found themselves reliant on the goodwill of Manteo and his mother, head of the Croatan people. Using the superiority of British arms, White drove off the local Roanoke tribe and installed Manteo as duke of much of the Albemarle Peninsula, including the Alligator River region.

After the birth and christening of his granddaughter, Virginia Dare, White was persuaded to return to London for additional supplies, but he was unable to return to "Virginia" until 1590 because of the attack of the Spanish Armada on England. When he finally set foot once again on

THE HISTORY OF THE BRITISH COLONIES IN AMERICA BEGINS WITH QUEEN ELIZABETH AND SIR WALTER RALEIGH.

Roanoke Island, he found only the letters *CRO* and *CROTOAN* carved in the logs of the colonists' palisade. A hurricane drove his ship back across the Atlantic before he could visit Manteo's people.

Despite extensive investigations, nothing certain about the fate of the 117 colonists was ever heard, and the enduring mystery of the Lost Colony was born.

Raleigh's Lost Colony: The Sassafras Theory and more Clues to Its Fate

Despite the 400 years since the colonists of the short-lived "Citie of Ralegh" disappeared, the mystery continues to attract public interest as well as scientific research and speculation.

Certainly the colonists died, but when, where, and by what means remain matters of debate. Perhaps they perished through starvation, disease, or massacre, at the hands of either the Spanish or the native tribes. Perhaps some trusted to the sea and tried to sail home on their small pinnace. Perhaps some joined the Croatan tribe, the friendliest of the natives, thanks to the continuing goodwill of Manteo. Most likely several of these theories are correct and the colonists' fates took them down different roads.

In the 1930s, a series of stones emerged that seemed to be engraved with messages from Eleanor Dare to her father, John White, as she moved southwest with Indian friends. They passed several scientific tests in the beginning but today are generally considered bogus.

In 1701, the Indians then inhabiting Hatteras Island told naturalist John Lawson that they were descended from English ancestors, and Lawson noted that many of the group had light hair and gray eyes. The Jamestown colonists made several efforts to find traces of the Roanoke Island group less than 30 years after their disappearance. They discovered nothing conclusive, but there were an abundance of rumors about men who dressed in European clothes and lived in two-story houses or who could "talk in a book." One chief claimed to have sent several youths and a "younge maide" to beat copper at his mine up the Roanoke River, but they were never found. Powhatan, the father of Pocahontas, when consulted on the missing colonists' fate, claimed they had been massacred after taking refuge with a Chesapeake tribe.

The political situation back in England gives perspective to these findings. It was to the benefit of the newcomers and their sponsor King James I if the colonists could be proved to have perished. A surviving colony would further Sir Walter Raleigh's continued claim to Virginia. Certainly, John White, who had perhaps the most reason to seek his daughter and granddaughter, initially felt minimal concern for their fate. The carved letters he found at the abandoned stockade indicated clearly to him that the colonists had taken refuge with the friendly Croatan tribe and were not in immediate danger, since he found no carved cross—the agreed-upon sign of distress.

Research into the fate of the colony picked up speed around the 400th anniversary of its disappearance. In the early 1990s, an archaeological dig at the Fort Raleigh site found a metallurgical workshop used by the 1585 expedition, but no trace of the living area of the colonists. Researchers speculate that the site may have washed away and is now underwater. In 1998, excavations conducted on Hatteras Island at the site of a large Indian village, believed to be the Croatan capital, turned up an English signet ring with ties to the English colonists. Two separate research organizations continue to investigate the mystery. The **First Colony Foundation** (www.firstcolonyfoundation.org), a group of historians, archaeologists, and concerned citizens, are concentrating their efforts on finding the area occupied by the 1587 colonists at the north end of Roanoke Island. They have conducted underwater surveys in the nearby sound, as well as archaeological digs within the national historic park.

The Lost Colony Center for Science and Research (www.lost-colony.com), a group of interested amateur scientists and historians, is looking farther afield for evidence of the Lost Colony. Using satellite technology, remote sensing, oral histories, and primary sources, they are exploring the fate of the lost colonists on several fronts. Currently they are conducting DNA studies in America and Britain, attempting to find mitochondrial and Y-chromosome matches among several populations.

One of the center's most intriguing theories is based on John White's statement that the colonists planned to move 50 miles into the mainland after his departure. Using old maps and other records, Philip McMullan speculates that the colonists relocated to a Croatan village about 50 miles away on the Alligator River, where abundant stands of sassafras trees were located. Sassafras was the main cash crop in the early years of American colonization, before tobacco came to the fore. The roots of the sassafras were at the time believed to cure syphilis, a newly introduced disease then running rampant through Europe. While Raleigh's early voyages are well-known, few are aware of the later voyages he sponsored to bring home cargos of sassafras. In 1602, sassafras was selling for up to 2,000 British pounds per ton, and the profits from one voyage in that year permitted Raleigh to fit out two more ships in 1603. The location where Raleigh's captains found these cargos, ready for shipment, was a closely guarded secret and may well have been the Alligator River region.

Lords Proprietors and the Iron Men of Albemarle

By the 1650s, planters from Jamestown began to move down the Chowan River and into the Albemarle area, spreading gradually south. In 1662 Charles II granted the lands south of Virginia to eight of his cronies, called the Lords Proprietors, who named the region Carolina in his honor.

Over the next several decades, the new owners of Carolina took measures to tighten their control over the Albemarle colonists, decreasing the power of elected officials. A series of clashes between the Proprietory and anti-Proprietory parties culminated in Culpeper's Rebellion in 1677, the first uprising against British tyranny in the colonies. The planters who inhabited the banks of Albemarle Sound earned the name of "Iron Men," thanks to their stiff determination on self-rule.

Beaufort, named for Henry Somerset, Duke of Beaufort, one of the Lords Proprietors, was established in 1713 next to the deep-water inlet then called Topsail, making it the third-oldest town in the colony.

The Civil War on the Banks

The Confederates built numerous fortifications along the Banks in the early days of the Civil War. Gun batteries were built on Huggin's Island (now part of Hammocks Beach State Park), on Beacon Island in Ocracoke Inlet, at the southern end of Hatteras Island, and on

> **FAST FACTS:** Bath, New Bern, and Beaufort are the three oldest towns in North Carolina. The Edenton Tea Party, organized in 1774 by the ladies of Edenton, another early town, to protest the British tax on tea, is one of the earliest political actions on record organized by women.

Roanoke Island. In April 1861, the Confederates occupied Fort Macon, built in 1826 to defend the port of Beaufort. Union general Ben Butler attacked the forts on Hatteras Island at the end of August 1861, the first amphibious attack of the war. Confederate troops based on Roanoke Island attempted

BLACKBEARD AND THE AGE OF PIRATES

Although the name of Blackbeard looms large in North Carolina history, his actual career of piracy was relatively short. Like many eventual pirates, Edward Teach, aka Blackbeard, originally served aboard a privateer with letters of marque from Queen Anne of Britain. These permitted him to capture French and Spanish ships during the War of Spanish Succession, called Queen Anne's War in North America.

After the war ended in 1714, many of the privateers continued to attack foreign ships, only their actions were now considered piracy. In 1717, the royal government offered a one-time pardon to English privateers turned pirates, and most of the active pirates accepted. Teach, which may or may not have been Blackbeard's true name, first rose to prominence as the magistrate of the short-lived Pirate's Republic on the island of Nassau. In 1717, he and his associate Capt. Benjamin Hornigold captured the French slave ship *Le Concorde*. Teach equipped the ship with 20 guns and made it his flagship, renaming it the *Queen Anne's Revenge* (*QAR*). In May 1718, he committed his most daring feat—a blockade of Charleston harbor. Blackbeard's demand was unusual: He would release his hostages and leave the harbor in return for a box of medicine. Shortly after Charleston met his demands, Blackbeard sailed his fleet of four vessels north, loaded with treasure taken from Spanish ships of the line. The *QAR* ran aground in Beaufort Inlet. Historians speculate that Teach purposely beached the vessel to rid himself of most of his

PIRATES PROVIDE SOME OF THE REGION'S MOST COLORFUL HISTORY.

crew. Certainly the flagship could never navigate the shallow inshore waters of the Outer Banks. Divers found what is believed to be the wreck of the *QAR* in 1996 in waters off Fort Macon.

Teach off-loaded most of his treasure onto the *Adventure,* a smaller vessel, left the majority of the crew on a convenient sandbar, and sailed up Pamlico Sound to Bath, where he accepted the royal pardon from Governor Charles Eden and reportedly married a local girl. The area was a familiar one for Teach. Legend says he had houses in both Beaufort and Bath at various times. His domestic bliss was short-lived, however, and by the fall of 1718 he was once again under sail. By November, reports located him at Ocracoke Inlet, roasting pigs, drinking meal wine, the local liquor, and partying with other pirates. Here Lt. Robert Maynard, of the Royal Navy, caught up with Blackbeard, and in a pitched battle at a spot called Teach's Hole, cut off the pirate's head, ending the career—but not the fame—of North Carolina's most notorious pirate.

to retake Hatteras in September. The armies chased each other up and down the island for several days, causing the locals to dub the battle the "Chicamacomico Races."

Union forces took Roanoke Island on February 7, 1862, and that spring New Bern and Fort Macon fell. The Confederate "mosquito fleet" was defeated off Elizabeth City, and Plymouth and other towns in North Carolina's northeast soon were under Union control. The Confederates managed to defend the Dismal Swamp Canal and the Wilmington & Weldon Railroad, keeping the supply lines to Richmond open. The port of Wilmington, defended by Fort Fisher at the mouth of the Cape Fear River, remained open until the final months of the war.

During the war, the Confederates built many ironclads in the rivers of North Carolina and sent them downstream to do battle with Union gunboats. In April of 1864, the Confederates successfully recaptured the port of Plymouth with the support of the ironclad CSS *Albemarle*. This was the last major Confederate victory of the Civil War.

RECOMMENDED READING: Author Drew Pullen has written extensively about the Civil War along the North Carolina Banks. His **Portrait of the Past Series,** published by Aerial Perspective, includes *The Civil War on Hatteras Island* (2001), *The Civil War on Roanoke Island* (2002), and *The Civil War in New Bern & Fort Macon* (2008).

During the war, Roanoke Island hosted a unique social experiment, the **Freedmen's Colony** (www.roanokefreedmenscolony.com). Many slaves from nearby regions escaped and made their way behind Union lines. Declared "contraband" by the U.S. military, these men, women, and children settled in a New England–style village, which included a sawmill, church, and school. By war's end, the population reached an estimated 3,500. The village was dismantled after the war, but many inhabitants of Roanoke Island today trace their family history back to the Freedmen's Colony.

QUICK TIPS:
• Civil War Trail markers dot the eastern North Carolina landscape. You can find a list of sites at www.civilwartraveler.com. A working replica of the ironclad CSS *Albemarle* still patrols the river at Plymouth.

• The boathouse and kitchen of the Pea Island Station have been moved to Roanoke Island and now house a museum detailing the history of the African American surfmen.

DID YOU KNOW? Bodie (pronounced BAH-dee) Island was named for the many shipwreck victims washing up on its shores.

Great Storms, Lost Ships, and Heroic Rescues

No one knows how many ships have been lost off the North Carolina Banks. Estimates range from the hundreds to many thousands. All agree, however, that this shore richly deserves its reputation as the Graveyard of the Atlantic. From the famous ironclad, USS *Monitor,* lost off Cape Hatteras in 1862, to the latest fishing trawler that fails to return to port, the ocean continues to exact its toll.

Storms are the greatest danger, and hurricanes arriving from the tropics June through November cause widespread devastation. But residents of the Banks fear the northeasters that blow in just as much. Storms, such as the Ash Wednesday storm of 1962, the Halloween storm of 1991, and the Thanksgiving storm of 2006, live on in local lore.

As early as 1792, the U.S. Congress authorized the building of lighthouses along this coast to aide navigation. Wooden light towers were constructed at Bald Head Island on the Cape Fear River in 1795, and on Shell Castle Island in Ocracoke Inlet in 1798. The first Cape Hatteras Lighthouse was

SEVERAL CIVIL WAR BATTLES TOOK PLACE ON THE OUTER BANKS.

completed in 1803, and a light tower began operation at Cape Lookout three years later. The lighthouses were upgraded over the years, but ships continued to run ashore, with crew and passengers perishing just yards from safety. The local fishermen and farmers along the Banks frequently came to the aide of shipwreck victims. Many of them were descendants of mariners who survived earlier wrecks and stayed to make a life on this harsh shore.

In 1874 the U.S. Life-Saving Service (www.uslife-savingservice.org), a division of the U.S. Department of the Treasury, established seven stations along the Outer Banks. One of the earliest was the **Chicamacomico Station** (www.chicamacomico.net) in Rodanthe, where the original buildings have been beautifully restored. In addition to Chicamacomico, several other early lifesaving stations survive, although not in their original forms. The Kitty Hawk station today houses the Black Pelican Restaurant, the Caffey's Inlet station serves as a restaurant at the Sanderling Resort, and the Kill Devil Hills station was moved to Corolla to become a real estate office. The Little Kinnakeet station near Avon is being restored by the National Park Service.

LIFESAVING STATIONS ONCE LINED THE COAST, GIVING AID TO SAILORS IN DISTRESS.

Most of the surfmen manning these stations were locals seeking to supplement their incomes and carrying on a tradition of service to those in peril at sea. A series of devastating wrecks during 1877 and 1878 caused Congress to authorize an additional 11 stations along the North Carolina coast. Life-saving stations were eventually located about 4 miles apart along the entire Outer Banks. The surfmen patrolled every mile of beach on foot or horseback 24 hours a day. When a ship in distress was sighted, they launched lifeboats through the surf or used a small cannon to send a line from the beach to the wreck, allowing them to bring survivors to safety using the breeches buoy apparatus or a metal life car. Many of the Life-Saving Service's most daring rescues took place on the Outer Banks. Some of the most notable include the rescue of the crew of the schooner *E. S. Newman* in 1896 by the men of the Pea Island Life-Saving Station, the only station staffed by African Americans, and the rescue by the Chicamacomico station of the crew of the British tanker *Mirlo,* after it was torpedoed by a German U-boat in 1918. In 1899, Rasmus Midgett of the Gull Shoal Station single-handedly rescued the 10-man crew of the barkentine *Priscilla.*

The men of the Life-Saving Service had a motto: "You have to go out, but nothing says you have to come back." This same brave spirit and commitment continue today in the U.S. Coast Guard, a service established in 1915 by the merger of the Life-Saving Service and the Revenue Cutter Service. One of the Coast Guard's largest bases is located at Elizabeth City.

RECOMMENDED READING: Mobley, Joe A. *Ship Ashore! The U.S. Lifesavers of Coastal North Carolina.* Raleigh, NC: Division of Archives and History, North Carolina Department of Cultural Resources, 1994.

Noble, Dennis L. *That Others Might Live: The U.S. Life-Saving Service, 1878–1915.* Annapolis, MD: Naval Institute Press, 1994.

Taking to the Air

The first years of the 20th century were important ones on the Outer Banks. The work of the Wright brothers that led to the first airplane flight at Kill Devil Hills in 1903 is well-known and the subject of the **Wright Brothers National Memorial** (www.nps.gov/wrbr). Wilbur and Orville Wright began coming to Kitty Hawk in 1900 to conduct glider experiments. They returned to test improved gliders the next two years, and in the fall of 1903 arrived with a powered flyer equipped with a wooden propeller and an aluminum engine created in their bicycle shop. On December 17, they successfully left the ground, and the Age of Flight began.

About the same time and not far away, inventor Reginald Fessenden was developing another important invention—the wireless telegraph, which led directly to radio and today's wireless technology. Working for the U.S. Weather Bureau, Fessenden successfully sent a message from Hatteras Island to Weirs Point on Roanoke Island on April 26, 1902, a demonstration witnessed by several navy officers. The development of wireless technology proved a great advance in weather forecasting and an important new aide to keep ships safe at sea.

The German U-Boat Invasion

During World War II, a major battle raged off the Outer Banks, still largely unknown to the American people. From the time of Pearl Harbor and the American declaration of war, dozens of German U-boats were active along the Atlantic Coast. Some came so close they reported seeing the lights from U.S. cities. Afraid of causing panic, the U.S. government did not call for a blackout until August 1942. Sinking tankers and cargo boats along the coast was so easy that German commanders referred to it as "the great American turkey shoot." The U-boats sank nearly 400 Allied ships off the North Carolina coast during this period, with over 5,000 lives lost. The seas off Diamond Shoals earned yet another ominous name: Torpedo Junction.

The war in the shipping lanes was no secret to the residents of the Outer Banks, who witnessed great explosions and fires off the coast and found the bodies of burned and drowned seamen washed up on their beaches. The people of Ocracoke buried several British sailors when a submarine sank the HMS *Bedfordshire*. The British Cemetery there is the only official bit of British soil in the United States, outside of the embassy in Washington, DC. By mid-1942, the U.S. military began to counterattack against the German subs. Air submarine patrols took off from the Manteo airport, and naval stations were established on Ocracoke and at Morehead City. The top-secret **Loop Control Station** on Ocracoke intercepted transmissions from the German U-boats that helped locate them.

The U.S. Coast Guard and U.S. Navy finally got the better of the German fleet. Four U-boats are known to rest on the ocean bottom off the Banks and are now favorite destinations for divers.

RECOMMENDED READING: Hickam, Homer. *Torpedo Junction: U-Boat War Off America's East Coast, 1942.* Annapolis, MD: US Naval Institute Press, 1996.

Tourism—Past, Present, Future

The first seasonal visitors to the Outer Banks arrived in the early 1800s as planters in the Albemarle region looked for a healthier place for their families to spend the summer. Francis Nixon, a Perquimans County planter, is the first on record. He brought his family to the Banks village at the base of Jockey's Ridge in 1830 to escape an outbreak of malaria. Soon after, Nixon bought 200 acres stretching across the Banks from the sound to the ocean, and Nags Head, the first resort destination on the Outer Banks, was born.

WINGED HORSES OF THE OUTER BANKS

During the Centennial of Flight in 2003, 99 life-size fiberglass winged horses and foals, decorated by local artists, lined the streets of the Outer Banks. The sponsor of the project, the *Outer Banks Press,* selected the horses to represent both the iconic herds of wild mustangs that still roam the Banks and the development of flight. The resulting works of art, each unique, were tremendously popular with residents and visitors alike. Seventy of the winged horses, some a bit battered by wind and rain, can still be seen at locations around the region, from Corolla to Ocracoke. A full listing of the current locations of the Winged Horses can be found on the *Outer Banks Press* website, www.outerbankspress.com.

ONE OF THE WINGED HORSES OF THE OUTER BANKS

HISTORIC LIGHTHOUSES OF NORTH CAROLINA

Beginning in Corolla and stretching nearly to the South Carolina border, the North Carolina coast has seven historic lighthouses. Built between 1818 and 1958, the lighthouses each sported a distinctive color pattern to help ships distinguish between them during the day; at night each flashed an individual light signature. Most of the North Carolina beacons are still in operation. This list travels north to south.

Farthest north, the **Currituck Beach Light** (www.currituckbeachlight.com), a 162-foot redbrick tower completed in 1875, operates under the stewardship of the Outer Banks Preservationists. Climbing is permitted seasonally. **Bodie Island Light** (www.nps.gov/caha), 156 feet tall, is painted in horizontal black and white stripes. Completed in 1872, it is still in operation under the care of the National Park Service (NPS) and retains its first-order Fresnel lens. The lighthouse reopened for climbing in 2013 after an extensive renovation. **Cape Hatteras Light** (www.nps.gov/caha), at 198 feet, is the tallest and most famous lighthouse in America. Painted in a black and white spiral pattern, it was moved to a new location in 1999 and continues to flash its signal out to sea. The National Park Service opens the lighthouse to climbers during the summer season. **Ocracoke Light** (www.nps.gov/caha), a 65-foot white tower built in 1823, is the oldest continuously operating lighthouse in North Carolina, and the second-oldest in the United States. Still owned by the U.S. Coast Guard, the lighthouse is maintained by the National Park Service. Climbing is not permitted; however, the base is open for limited hours during the summer months. **Cape Lookout Light** (www.nps .gov/calo), completed in 1859, is painted in a pattern of black and white diamonds. At 163 feet, it was the first tall lighthouse to be built and served as a model for later construction. The lighthouse can be reached by boat from Harkers Island, where the Cape Lookout National

CURRITUCK BEACH LIGHT

BODIE ISLAND LIGHT

In 1838, the 200-room Nags Head Hotel, located on the shore of the sound, opened. Visitors arriving at its dock could look forward to a season of balls and formal dinners, as well as bowling, card games, and ocean bathing. A boardwalk connected the hotel with the ocean, and local Bankers made good incomes transporting visitors to the shore in their pony carts. Today that hotel lies buried beneath the dunes of Jockey's Ridge, which slowly swallowed the property in the 1870s. By then, the vacation village had shifted its focus to the ocean beach.

Around 1855, Elizabeth City physician Dr. W. G. Pool bought 50 acres of oceanfront property from the Midgetts, who were then, as they are now, a prominent Banker family. Pool paid a reported $30 and sold lots to his neighbors in Elizabeth City for $1 each. By 1885 there were 13 cottages lining the shore, the first of the "Unpainted Aristocracy" of Nags Head. Several of these historic cottages still survive, although most have been moved back from the ocean several times, as storms washed away the sand in front of them.

In the years following the Civil War, Northern businessmen discovered the superb waterfowl hunt-

CAPE HATTERAS LIGHT   OCRACOKE LIGHT   CAPE LOOKOUT LIGHT

Seashore headquarters are located. The lighthouse is still operational, and open for climbing May to September. The remaining two lighthouses marked the treacherous entrance to the Cape Fear River in southern North Carolina: **Bald Head Island Light** (www.oldbaldy.org), no longer in service, was built in 1818, making it the oldest lighthouse still standing in the state. The 109-foot octagonal structure is built of brick covered with concrete. Open for climbing during the summer months, Old Baldy, as it's called by its fans, can be reached by ferry from Southport, North Carolina. **Oak Island Light** (www.oakislandlighthouse.org), a poured concrete 158-foot structure striped gray, white, and black, was built in 1958 to replace several earlier beacons and was one of the last manually operated lighthouses in the world. Tours of the first and second levels are conducted by the Friends of Oak Island Lighthouse.

Several other aids to navigation were used in North Carolina waters. Lightships, the most famous of which was anchored off Cape Hatteras on the Diamond Shoals until torpedoed by German submarines, helped mark extremely shallow waters. In the sounds, screw-pile lighthouses helped guide ships. Replicas of the screw-pile cottage-style lights can be found in Manteo on Roanoke Island and in Plymouth on Albemarle Sound.

For more information, visit the website of the Outer Banks Lighthouse Society (www.outerbanks lighthousesociety.org).

ing available in the region. Much of the land around the sounds was bought by hunt clubs, where sportsmen were accommodated in varying degrees of luxury during their annual winter visits.

The 1920s brought a new group of tourists to the Outer Banks as the first waves of motorists arrived in their Model Ts, crossing the sounds on ferries or taking an adventurous route along the tide line from Virginia Beach.

The year 1928 saw two causeways built to make access to the Banks easier. In Morehead City, a toll bridge linked the end of the rail line to an ocean bathing pavilion on Bogue Banks, in today's Atlantic Beach. And in the same year, the Washington Baum Bridge linked Roanoke Island with Nags Head. The Baum project was a true leap of faith. At the time, the only way to reach Roanoke Island was by a lengthy journey on rough roads followed by a ferry ride from the mainland. On the Nags Head end, the bridge ended in sandy ruts leading north and south; no roads had yet been paved on the Banks. However, Baum, then chairman of the Dare County Board of Commissioners, was a big believer in the philosophy "if you build it, they will come."

National attention was focused on the Outer Banks in 1928. It was the 25th anniversary of the Wright brothers' first flight, and the National Aeronautic Association commemorated the event by placing a 10-ton boulder at the point of takeoff. The next year, work began on the 60-foot-tall Wright Memorial pylon, which was dedicated in 1932, the beginning of the **Wright Memorial National Historic Site** (www.nps.gov/wrbr).

W. O. Saunders, founder and editor of the Elizabeth City *Independent* newspaper, was another of the area's notable boosters. He advocated the development of the Wright Memorial and helped organize the group of Elizabeth City businessmen who built the Wright Memorial Bridge from the Currituck mainland to Kitty Hawk. The 3-mile bridge was completed in 1930, and in 1931, the state paved the Beach Road, now NC 12, between the Nags Head and Kitty Hawk bridges. Dubbed the **Virginia Dare Trail,** the new road made it possible for motorists to drive on pavement from the mainland all the way to the gates of the "Citie of Ralegh" on Roanoke Island. This re-creation of Raleigh's colony, originally built by local history buffs, became part of the national park system in 1941.

The Lost Colony outdoor drama, another Saunders idea, was first performed in 1937. Franklin D. Roosevelt attended a performance, and the drama, originally intended to be a one-season affair to celebrate the 250th anniversary of Virginia Dare's birth, continues to be produced today, more than 70 years later.

In 1933, Saunders and one of his columnists, Frank Stick, began promoting another project in the *Independent,* this one for a coastal park that would restore and protect the rapidly eroding beaches of the Outer Banks. The idea caught on, and funds for the restoration of the dunes along the bald beaches were allocated at the federal level.

The Civil Works Administration and its successor, the Civilian Conservation Corps, began work constructing sand fences and planting sea grasses to rebuild the dunes in late 1933. The project was a success, and by 1940 a barrier dune as much as 25 feet high ran from the Virginia state line all the way to Hatteras Inlet, and along about half of the Ocracoke Island beachfront. It proved impossible to build dunes as far as Cape Lookout because the Core Banks were still being used as pasturage for free-roaming horses and cattle. Meanwhile, the Cape Hatteras Seashore Commission sought donations of land for the proposed seashore park. In 1935, the owners of a hunt club on Hatteras donated 999 acres surrounding the Cape Hatteras Lighthouse to the project. Other donations followed, until the beginning of World War II put seashore protection on hold.

The postwar years brought a boom in tourism and a rise in property values that almost put an end to the project, but in 1952 an anonymous donation for the purchase of park lands made the **Cape Hatteras National Seashore** (www.nps.gov/caha) a reality nearly 20 years after it was first approved by the U.S. Congress.

The **Cape Lookout National Seashore** (www.nps.gov/calo) followed in 1966. Together, these national parks preserve a unique and ever-changing ecosystem that continues to attract visitors from around the world.

SHARKS NOW HAUNT THE WRECKS OF GERMAN U-BOATS IN THE GRAVEYARD OF THE ATLANTIC.

DID YOU KNOW? The popular OBX nickname for the Outer Banks was invented in 1994 by Jim Douglas, owner of Chilli Peppers restaurant in Kitty Hawk. He marketed oval OBX stickers, modeled on the country stickers found on European cars, and they quickly became—and remain—a popular souvenir of an Outer Banks vacation. Douglas trademarked the symbol, and it appears on many authorized products. Check the Birthday Suits website (www.birthday-suits.com) or visit one of its three locations for a full selection of OBX gear. However, in recent years, OBX achieved fame in legal circles, after a judge ruled that the phrase had become generic and entered the common language as a geographical description, voiding the trademark.

The North Beaches

1

COROLLA AND CAROVA

DUCK AND SANDERLING

SOUTHERN SHORES

**CURRITUCK COUNTY
AND ELIZABETH CITY**

THE NORTH BEACHES
Where the Road Ends

THE NORTH BEACHES of the Outer Banks are not islands, but they have been. The original northern boundary of North Carolina was set at Currituck Inlet back in 1663. When the inlet closed in 1828, the island became a peninsula, connected with the Virginia mainland.

In the mid-1900s, many of the inhabitants of the North Beaches commuted up the beach to jobs in Virginia. But in 1974, a fence at the border blocked the route. On the Virginia side lie False Cape State Park and the Back Bay National Wildlife Refuge, neither of which allow any vehicular access. The fence was built to protect this pristine area. The border fence has become a tourist attraction in its own right for visitors on the North Carolina side. Numerous proposals were made over the years to build a paved road connecting the Virginia and North Carolina coastlines. But these all came to nothing, and NC 12 today ends at a beach access ramp about 12 miles south of the Virginia line.

The human history of the North Beaches is largely the story of NC 12, originally just a sandy track behind the dunes. Most locals drove on the beach. But when the Wright Memorial Bridge joined the mainland with the Banks in 1930, attention inevitably turned to the stretch of Banks to the north, more than 30 miles of dunes and marshes dotted here and there with fishing villages and lifesaving stations. As NC 12 was paved farther north over the following four decades, tourism moved with it up the Banks.

Bridge to the Future

As the summer population in Corolla multiplied, so did the traffic trying to reach the area up narrow, two-lane NC 12. Calls came to expand the road to four lanes, a move much opposed in Duck, where it would mean the sacrifice of a considerable portion of the trees that line the road through town. An alternative solution to the problem was found: a new bridge and causeway across Currituck Sound. Stretching from US 158 to NC 12 in Corolla north of TimBuck II, the 7-mile-long Mid-Currituck Bridge will join mainland Currituck County with its beachfront area, diminish drive-through traffic farther south, and cut the drive time to Corolla. The bridge, scheduled to begin construction in 2014 with completion by 2018, will charge a toll.

GETTING AROUND *By Bicycle:* The North Beaches are great for biking, with dedicated multiuse paths stretching along NC 12 from Corolla all the way to the junction with US 158 in Southern Shores. Bike paths wind through historic Corolla Village and Currituck Heritage Park, then paved paths parallel both sides of NC 12 as it heads south, reverting occasionally to a wide shoulder. A paved path runs along the road from the Dare County line through Duck and Southern Shores to the US 158 intersection, then turns west along 158 to Kitty Hawk Elementary School. From there you can cross 158 to the Woods Road Multi-Purpose Path through Kitty Hawk Woods. Other paved and unpaved paths lace the neighborhoods in Southern Shores, Duck, Sanderling, and Corolla.

By Car: Only one road threads north–south along this narrow strip of land, NC 12, named Ocean Boulevard in Southern Shores, Duck Road in Duck, and Ocean Trail in Corolla. Cross streets are short and generally dead-end at the water on both east and west.

TOP 10 DON'T MISS: THE NORTH BEACHES

1. Go off-road to see the Banker horses.
2. Climb the Currituck Lighthouse.
3. Have a picnic at scenic Currituck Heritage Park after visiting the Whalehead Club.
4. Discover the history of waterfowl hunting at the Outer Banks Center for Wildlife Education.
5. Check out the skateboard action at Corolla Light Town Center.
6. Have sunset cocktails on a west-facing deck along the shores of Currituck Sound.
7. See the bird art at the Sanderling.
8. Stroll the waterfront boardwalk in Duck, checking out the shops along the way.
9. Plan a foodie tour of Duck, with a course at each of the famous restaurants.
10. Pamper yourself with a day at a local spa.

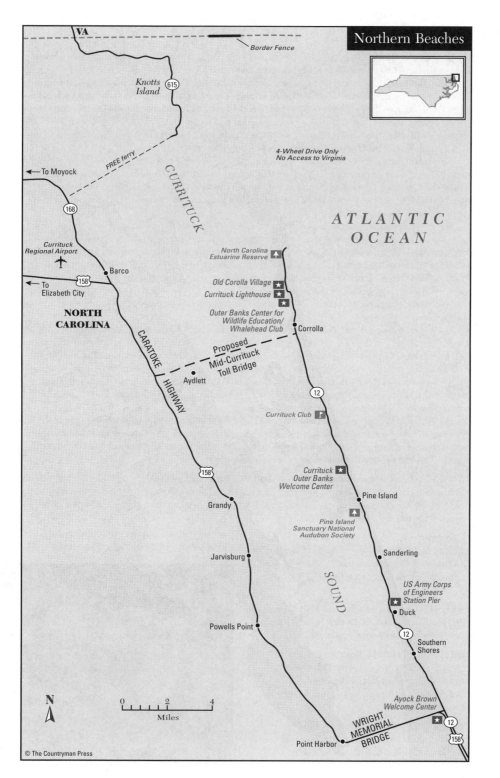

Northern Beaches

VA

Border Fence

Knotts
Island
615

4-Wheel Drive Only
No Access to Virginia

FREE ferry

CURRITUCK

← To Moyock

168

ATLANTIC
OCEAN

Currituck
Regional Airport

Barco

North Carolina
Estuarine Reserve

158

← To
Elizabeth City

Old Corolla Village
Currituck Lighthouse

NORTH
CAROLINA

CARATOKE

Outer Banks Center for
Wildlife Education/
Whalehead Club

Corrolla

Proposed
Mid-Currituck
Toll Bridge

Aydlett

HIGHWAY

12

Currituck Club

158

Currituck
Outer Banks
Welcome Center

Grandy

Pine Island

Pine Island
Sanctuary National
Audubon Society

Jarvisburg

Sanderling

SOUND

US Army Corps
of Engineers
Station Pier
Duck

Powells Point

12

Southern
Shores

N

0   2   4
Miles

Ayock Brown
Welcome Center

WRIGHT
MEMORIAL
BRIDGE

12

Point Harbor

158

© The Countryman Press

COROLLA AND CAROVA

NC 12 ENDS IN COROLLA, pronounced cuh-RAH-la by locals. Originally it was a small fishing village and home of the **Currituck Beach Lighthouse,** built in 1875.

Today, the lighthouse is part of a complex of attractions that make a popular day trip destination for visitors staying farther south on the Banks. Located on the sound side of NC 12, **Currituck Heritage Park** includes the lighthouse, the **Whalehead Club,** and the **Outer Banks Center for Wildlife Education,** all surrounding a boating lagoon and picnic area. On the north side of the lighthouse, the old village of Corolla houses a shopping district of charming shops with an off-the-beaten-track appeal. **The Wild Horse Museum** occupies the renovated schoolhouse.

The **Outer Banks Conservationists** (www.currituckbeachlight.com) led the drive to preserve the area's history. Starting in the late 1970s, the group raised more than $1.5 million in private dollars to restore the Currituck Beach Lighthouse and its keepers' quarters. The buildings had been standing open to the elements for over 40 years, and several had been hauled away by local residents, a time-honored Outer Banks tradition.

The restoration of these buildings dating to the late 1800s gives the area a unique group of what is today called "stick style" Queen Anne. Architectural features are notable in the keepers' house, now used as a museum store, and a storage building topped with sharp finials, now used for offices, as well as the 1878 Life-Saving Station on NC 12, today the office of Twiddy Realty. The design elements found in these buildings have provided inspiration for more recent architects and can be seen reflected in many new buildings in the area.

Another building of interest is the Whalehead Club, which houses exceptional examples of art nouveau decorative details.

A mile past the lighthouse, NC 12 comes to its end at a beach access ramp. Beyond a fence and livestock grate lie 12 miles of unpaved North Carolina, variously called the outback, the off-road area, and, most commonly, Carova, thanks to its position between the states of North Carolina and Virginia.

The land is a patchwork of public and private wildlife refuges, traveling sand dunes, and communities where owners and renters travel by four-wheel drive along sandy tracks or on the beach. Wild horses and 12-bedroom vacation cottages exist here side by side, along with a sprinkling of beachcomber shacks and year-round homes.

The best way to explore this area is with one of the local outfitters who knows how to get around, where to find the horses, and how to avoid getting stuck in the sand. ATVs are not permitted. Commercial businesses are also not allowed in the area north of the fence. All groceries and other supplies must be brought in by four-wheel-drive vehicle from Corolla.

GUIDANCE The **Currituck Outer Banks Visitor's Center** (252-453-9612 or 1-877-287-7488; www .visitcurrituck.com), at 500 Hunt Club Road, just off NC 12 in the Ocean Club Centre, provides a wealth of information on the area. Ocean Club Centre is the first shopping center you'll pass as you approach Corolla from the south.

Additional information on beach regulations and local attractions is offered by the **Currituck Chamber of Commerce** (252-453-9497; www .currituckchamber.org), P.O. Box 937, Moyock, NC 27958.

POST OFFICE The **Corolla U.S. Post Office** (252-453-2552) is at 1150 Ocean Trail/NC 12. The zip code throughout Corolla is 27927.

PUBLIC RESTROOMS Restrooms open to the public are located at the **Currituck Outer Banks Visitor's Center,** at the Currituck County Southern Beach Access, and at Currituck Heritage Park.

PUBLIC LIBRARY 🖉 📶 **Corolla Public Library** (252-453-0496; www.earlibrary.org /corolla), 1123 NC 12. Closed weekends. Public-use computers, Wi-Fi, and children's area available for visitors.

NO ONE KNOWS THE ORIGIN OF THE WILD PONIES THAT LIVE ON THE OUTER BANKS.

GETTING THERE *By Boat:* A few boaters come to Corolla by water from Back Bay in Virginia Beach or across Currituck Sound from Knotts Island or the Currituck mainland. However, the water here is very shallow, suitable only for flat-bottomed boats. There are no harbors or piers on the oceanfront.

By Car: The only road into Corolla is NC 12 coming from the south. There is no approach from the north. You cannot drive down the beach from Virginia. NC 12 is called Ocean Trail in Corolla.

GETTING AROUND If you plan to head north of the fence into the off-road area, you'll need a four-wheel-drive vehicle. You can use your own vehicle or rent one from several companies located in the area. However, if you plan on venturing off the beach into the interior to look for horses, your best bet is to join a guided tour. Getting stuck in the sand is a very real possibility on the sandy tracks that crisscross the area, and it can throw a serious wrench into your vacation schedule. Tour companies offer trips in both closed and open vehicles, to suit weather conditions. You can drive yourself or leave the driving to an experienced guide. Most companies operate year-round.

ONCE ALL ROADS ON THE OUTER BANKS WERE SANDY LANES, LIKE THIS ONE IN CAROVA.

✳ To See

A Village Garden (252-457-1190; www.twiddy.com/history). Behind the Parker House at 1129 Corolla Village Road, this delightful retreat features many native and heirloom species, including herb, vegetable, and butterfly gardens. Visitors are welcome.

🐚 **Currituck Beach Lighthouse and Keepers' Houses** (252-453-4939; www.currituckbeachlight .com), 1101 Corolla Village Road. The Outer Banks Conservationists have done a magnificent job restoring the lighthouse itself and the surrounding buildings. The 162-foot lighthouse was the last one built along this coast, illuminating the final "dark spot" starting in 1875, and retains its original first-order Fresnel lens. Climb the 214 steps to the top to enjoy an unsurpassed view of the Corolla area from Easter to Thanksgiving weekend (closed Thanksgiving Day) for a fee of $7 a person. Children under eight years old climb for free. The original keepers' cottage is now a museum gift shop. The buildings are arranged around a shady green lawn frequented by artists and photographers.

Currituck Heritage Park (252-453-9040; www.whaleheadclub.org), MP 11, NC 12. The 39-acre park is a small fraction of the original grounds of the Whalehead Club, but it seems pretty spacious amid today's development. A self-guided interpretive trail tells the history of the area. Launch your boat, kayak, or personal watercraft at the free boat ramp to access the sound. Or just admire the sunset from the arching bridge and gazebo. Many special events, from concerts and wine tastings to Halloween hayrides, are held here annually. Plenty of free parking.

Historic Corolla Village (252-457-1190; www.twiddy.com/history). Old Corolla, once a fishing village that was the largest town between the Virginia border and Kitty Hawk, has been renovated into a district of charming shops, largely through the efforts of the Twiddy family. Highlights include the **1900 Corolla School House** (1126 Schoolhouse Road); the **pre-1920 Parker House** (1129 Corolla Village Road), now housing the museum of the Wild Horse Fund; the **1895 Lewark-Gray House** (1130

QUICK TIP: History buffs with a taste for a bit of adventure can tour Corolla and Carova aboard Segways with **Outer Banks Tours** (252-453-0877; www.outerbanks tours.com).

CURRITUCK HERITAGE PARK PROVIDES THE PERFECT SETTING FOR CRABBING, PICNICS, AND SUNSET VIEWS.

Corolla Village Road), now home to Lovie's Kitchen Table; and the **1884 Corolla Post Office,** in the Austin Building on NC 12. Services are still conducted in the ♂ **1885 Corolla Chapel** (252-453-4224; www.corollachapel .com) at 1136 Corolla Village Road. Refreshments are available at Corolla Village Bar-B-Que next to the Parker House, and at Lovie's Kitchen Table.

U.S. Life-Saving Station/Twiddy & Company Realtors (252-457-1190; www .twiddy.com/history), 1142 NC 12. The 1878 Kill Devil Hills Life-Saving Station played an important part in the history of the Banks when surfmen from this station helped the Wright brothers complete their early flights. Preservationist Doug Twiddy moved the derelict building to Corolla and restored it. Visitors are welcome to view the Wright brothers and life-saving station memorabilia on display and pick up information on Corolla's historic district.

Wash Woods Coast Guard Station (252-457-1190; www.twiddy.com/history), North Swan Beach. This landmark in the off-road area served as a lifesaving and Coast Guard Station

THE HISTORIC SCHOOLHOUSE IN COROLLA VILLAGE

from 1917 and was restored by Twiddy & Company for use as a real estate office. Visitors are welcome to stop by to view the memorabilia and historic photos on display.

♂ ♂ **The Whalehead Club** (252-453-9040; www.whaleheadclub.org), Currituck Heritage Park. With copper roof shingles, cork floors, Tiffany light fixtures, duck-head doorknobs, and many art nouveau details, the Whalehead Club stands as a monument to a former age. This imposing 21,000-square-foot edifice began life in 1922 as the winter cottage of Northern industrialist Edward Knight and his bride, before becoming the most elegant hunt club on the southeast coast. After decades of other uses, ranging from a boys' school to a rocket-testing facility, the sumptuous structure has been

THE WHALEHEAD CLUB, ONCE THE MOST ELEGANT HUNT CLUB ON THE BANKS, NOW RESTORED TO ITS ART DECO SPLENDOR.

THE WILD HORSES OF CURRITUCK

restored to pristine condition. Ghost, children's, and other guided tours are offered daily, as well as a self-guided audio tour. All tours except the audio tour require reservations.

✎ **Outer Banks Center for Wildlife Education** (252-453-0221; www.ncwildlife.org). Spacious museum in Currituck Heritage Park explores the region's rich heritage of waterfowl hunting and fishing with exhibits that include a life-size duck blind, an 8,000-gallon aquarium stocked with native fish, and the 250-piece Neal Conoley collection of antique decoys, one of the finest in the country. A short film discusses Currituck Sound's role in the ecology of the region. The center provides a year-round schedule of classes suitable for ages two through adult, including decoy carving, crabbing, kayaking, fly tying, and nature photography. The classes are mostly free, but registration in advance is highly recommended. The center is open daily all year, including many holidays. Admission is free.

✎ **Wild Horse Museum** (252-453-8002; www.corollawildhorses.com), 1129 Corolla Village Road. The museum and headquarters of the **Corolla Wild Horse Fund,** dedicated to preserving and protecting the wild herd of some 100 horses, houses exhibits telling the history of the horses and the challenges they face. Some days, a "gentled" mustang is on hand to greet visitors. Children's activities are offered in summer for a small fee. Admission to the museum is free. The Wild Horse Fund also operates a seasonal **Wild Horse Museum Store** in the Corolla Light Town Center selling horse-themed gift items and offering information on the horses. Proceeds help keep the horses wild and free.

✳ To Do

BANKER HORSE TOURS No trip to the Outer Banks can be complete without a journey off-road to see the wild horses coexisting with villagers north of the fence in Corolla. To do this, you'll need a four-wheel-drive vehicle.

Numerous companies offer tours, but your best bet, and a must for horse lovers, is a trip with the **Corolla Wild Horse Fund** (252-453-8002; www.corollawildhorses.com). These tours, conducted by naturalists who oversee the welfare of the herds, often cost less than similar commercial tours, and they come with a year-long membership in the fund. Bonus: 100 percent of the tour price goes to help preserve the wild horses.

The following are other companies offering tours to the off-road area:

Beach Jeeps of Corolla (252-453-6141; www.beachjeepsofcorolla.com), Corolla Light Town Center. Drive your family on a guided tour up the beach "north of the fence." Vehicles with automatic transmission are available.

✎ **Corolla Outback Adventures** (252-453-4484; www.corollaoutback.com), 1150 NC 12. Enjoy a "ride-along" tour or drive a vintage Land Cruiser into the outback as part of a convoy of retro vehicles that visits several exclusive areas of the wild horse reserve. Tour guide Jay Bender's family has been leading off-road adventures since 1962, when the road ended south of Duck.

WILD HORSES: FREE SPIRITS OF THE BANKS

Manes flying in the wind, hooves leaving their imprint in sand, the herds of wild horses that make their home among the dunes are some of the most popular—and most endangered—tourist attractions of the Outer Banks. Once the herds roamed at will from Virginia to Shackleford Banks. Today they are confined to narrow stretches of land and a few islands, their numbers controlled by park rangers often more concerned with the survival of native grasses than that of the horses, which they consider an "exotic species."

These attitudes are at odds with the beliefs and wishes of most of the local inhabitants. Early settlers reported that the horses were there before them, and the old families of the Banks tell tales of taming the local horses. They pulled pony carts and plows, helped the surfmen of the Life-Saving Service rescue shipwrecked sailors, and raced around Jockey's Ridge.

On Ocracoke, locals held a pony penning on July 4th every year, rounding up the native ponies and selecting some to be sold off-island, thus stabilizing the size of the herd. The island's Boy Scout troop, established in 1956, was the first mounted troop in the country. Each boy caught, tamed, and trained his own horse.

When most of Ocracoke, including the area where the herds roamed free, became part of the Cape Hatteras National Seashore, the park rangers wanted to remove all the ponies to prevent overgrazing and to protect the ponies themselves from the traffic on NC 12. Local Ocracokers organized a protest and managed to keep some of the ponies on the island. About 25 to 30 ponies remain on Ocracoke, now confined to a 180-acre "pony pen."

Wild or feral horses are still found at several other locations on North Carolina's Banks. About 100 individuals live north of Corolla in the off-road area next to the Virginia state line. Once free-roaming, the Corolla herd is now confined to about 12,000 acres north of a fence and cattle guard near the end of NC 12. The horses were moved behind the fence after collisions with automobiles led to numerous fatalities. In one accident alone, six horses were killed. The **Corolla Wild Horse Fund** (www.corollawildhorses.com) operates an educational museum and store to support the herd.

Farther south, the horses of **Shackleford Banks** (www.shacklefordhorses.org) live much as their ancestors did, running free on a barrier island with no road or other traffic to threaten them. Nearby, an unrelated herd of feral horses, descended from a herd released here by a local farmer in the 1940s, occupies Carrot Island.

The origin of the Banker ponies and horses has been much debated, but scientific evidence is mounting to support the theory that they are descended from Spanish horses brought to these shores in great numbers by early explorers, as well as from ships wrecked along the coast. Horses are great swimmers and, according to records, were often driven overboard to lighten a ship stuck on a sandbar.

The Corolla, Ocracoke, and Shackleford horses all exhibit typical Spanish traits, including five rather than six lumbar vertebrae. In addition, a unique and rare blood variant found only in horses of Spanish descent is carried by the Shackleford herd. DNA tests are ongoing, but the Horse of the Americas organization recently officially recognized the Corolla and Shackleford herds as Heritage Herds of Colonial Spanish Horses. On a less positive note, the American Livestock Breed Conservancy in 2008 moved both herds from the threatened to the critical category, on the verge of extinction. The U.S. Congress recently passed legislation that will let the Corolla and Shackleford herds expand and interbreed to increase genetic diversity and hopefully assure the survival of these horses—descendants of the first Europeans to reach the Outer Banks.

WILD HORSES COEXIST WITH DEVELOPMENT IN CAROVA.

SEGWAYS MAKE A FUN WAY TO TOUR COROLLA.

Wild Horse Adventure Tours (252-489-2020; www.wildhorsetour.com), 610 Currituck Clubhouse Drive. Tours aboard air-conditioned four-wheel-drive SUVs, Range Rovers, or a variety of open-top vehicles, including a giant replica Hummer, guarantee you will see horses, or your money will be refunded. Check out the Wild Horse Art Gallery in the base shop.

BICYCLING The North Beaches are great for biking, with dedicated multiuse paths stretching along both sides NC 12, plus paved and unpaved paths lacing many Corolla neighborhoods. Paved paths and sandy lanes wind through historic Corolla Village and Currituck Heritage Park.

Several companies will deliver a wide-tired beach cruiser to your door. Tandem bikes, tricycles, child seats, and tagalongs are also available from most outfitters. Some also offer bikes with gears. Contact **Just for the Beach Rentals** (1-866-629-7368; www.justforthebeach.com) at the Ocean Club Centre or **Ocean Atlantic Rentals** (252-453-2440; www.oceanatlantic rentals.com) in Corolla Light Town Center. These companies also rent kayaks, surfboards, stand-up paddleboards, tennis racquets, and a variety of other things you might need for your vacation, from baby high chairs to outdoor grills. Both offer free delivery for orders over $95. Ocean Atlantic delivers to the off-road area.

FISHING Most of Currituck Sound is too shallow for oceangoing charter boats. However, fishing in the sound with light tackle is very good. This was once the sea bass capital of the world. On the beaches, surf fishing reigns. No public ocean piers are available along the north coast, but you can fish or crab in the sound from the pier and gazebo at Currituck Heritage Park. No fee is required, but you'll need a North Carolina Recreational Fishing License.

Corolla Bait and Tackle (252-453-9500; www.corollabaitandtackle.com), with two locations in Corolla Light Town Center and the Shoppes at Currituck Club, can set you up for offshore, inshore, backcountry, wreck, or big game safari fishing. They also offer surf fishing classes, rod and reel and crab pot rentals, plus a huge selection of tackle and bait. Drop by either store for free local fishing advice. Introductory crabbing and fishing trips aboard their pontoon boat are family favorites.

TW's Bait & Tackle and Fish Emporium (252-453-3339; www.twstackle.com), Monteray Plaza. Top of the line fishing equipment for sale or rent, plus plenty of free fishing advice.

FOR FAMILIES Biking, beachcombing, flying kites, and building sand castles are some of the most popular family activities on the North Beaches. Kids can learn crabbing or fishing at Currituck Heritage Park, and paint a horse (or ride one) at the ℰ **Corolla Wild Horse Museum** (252-453-8002).

The ℰ **Outer Banks Center for Wildlife Education** (252-453-0221; www.ncwildlife.org) in Currituck Heritage Park offers free classes geared for children as young as three throughout the year. Registration is required.

> **QUICK TIP:** Stay 50 feet away from any wild horse you encounter, or risk a ticket from local law enforcers. Never feed the horses anything. They have adapted to their sandy, salty environment, and any unfamiliar food, even things domestic horses love, such as carrots or corn, may kill them.
>
> **FAST FACT:** Currituck Sound is shallow and weedy, so flat-bottomed boats, such as kayaks, or very shallow draft vessels, such as pontoon boats, work best here. A free boat ramp is located at Currituck Heritage Park next to the Whalehead Club. Popular kayak excursions include a sunset paddle around the lagoon at the park or out into the salt marshes of the sound.

TimBuck II (www.timbuckii.com), known for its numerous shopping and dining options, is also a great destination for family activities. *Corolla Water Sports* (252-453-6900; www.corollawatersports.com), located at the docks along the sound behind TimBuck II, rents kayaks and WaveRunners, and offers kayak ecotours that paddle through the protected marsh waterway owned by the Currituck Hunt Club, one of the best paddling routes on the Banks. Parasailing is available for those looking for a thrill, and there's plenty of shady seating if you just want to watch. The complex also includes the **Golf Links** minigolf course, with several holes set on an island. Younger kids will enjoy a paddleboat cruise on the canals and a pond full of turtles, fish, and waterfowl.

WILD HORSES ROAM FREE IN CAROVA.

More fun at TimBuck II? *Corolla Raceway* (252-453-9100; www.corollagokarts.com) has a go-kart track, bumper boats, and video arcade. *Kitty Hawk Kites* (252-453-8845; www.kittyhawk.com), offers free kite-flying lessons.

Another minigolf opportunity, the *Grass Course,* is located at the **Corolla Light Resort** (252-453-4198).

Public playgrounds in Corolla are located at **TimBuck II Shopping Village** and **Corolla Light Town Center.**

GOLF *The Currituck Club* (252-453-9518; www.thecurrituckgolfclub.com), 620 Currituck Club Drive. Set amid dunes and marsh, this award-winning Rees Jones course is a links-style par 72, considered one of the top golf experiences in the state. Jones's design makes superb use of the land, formerly part of the legendary Currituck Hunt Club, yielding awesome views of the ocean, sound, and nearby lighthouse. *Bunkers Grille and Bar* serves lunch and after-golf libations. Call well in advance for tee times.

HUNTING The 35-mile-long Currituck Sound is shallow and grassy, ideal habitat for the migrating ducks, geese, and swans that visit in great numbers every winter. Currituck County makes a limited number of blinds available to hunters with waterfowl hunting permits from the state. Contact the Currituck County Game Commission (252-429-3472; www.currituckgamecommission.org) and the N.C. Wildlife Resources Commission (1-888-248-6834; www.ncwildlife.org) to start the process.

You can also arrange a hunt with a local guide service. One of the best known in the region is **Stuart's Hunting Lodge** (252-232-2309), run by Watson Stuart, world swan-calling champion.

SKATEBOARDING Island Revolution Skate Park (252-453-9484; www.islandrevolution.com), at Corolla Light Town Center, challenges boarders with dual bowls, grind pipes, and jumps. Rental boards and safety equipment are available.

SPAS Eden Day Spa and Salon (252-453-0712; www.edendayspasalon.com), Monteray Plaza. Get wrapped in rosemary mint or

QUICK TIPS:
• Send your kids to the free *S.E.A.L.S. for Kids Mini-Camp* (safety education and aquatic safety), offered by the lifeguards at Corolla Ocean Rescue, teaching kids ages 6–12 about ocean safety, first aid, and physical fitness. Parent/guardian seminars are offered at the same time. Call 252-619-2285 or visit www.corollaoceanrescue.com for details.

• Find out more about the region's hunting traditions in the books written by Travis Morris, including *Duck Hunting on Currituck Sound: Tales from a Native Gunner* (2006); *Currituck Memories and Adventures* (2007); *Ducks, Politics and Outlaw Gunners* (2008); and *Untold Stories of Old Currituck Duck Clubs* (2010). All are published by History Press (www.historypress.net) in Charleston, South Carolina, and are available at area bookstores.

Caribbean seaweed at this spa that specializes in Aveda products.

TENNIS Pine Island Racquet and Fitness Center (252-453-8525; www.thesanderling .com), NC 12, Pine Island. This full-service fitness and racquet sport center is open to the public, offering day and weekly memberships. Tennis facilities include two outdoor clay courts and three indoor cushioned courts.

WATER SPORTS ✍ Coastal Explorations (252-453-9872; www.coastalexplorations.com), 1118 Corolla Village Lane. This outdoor adventure company has a shop and boardwalk leading to the sound in Historic Corolla Village. Rent a kayak or paddleboard and launch from their dock to explore Currituck Sound, or sign up for a sail in their Hobie Cat, for a crabbing charter, or for a sunset cruise.

Corolla Surf Shop (252-453-9283; www.corollasurfshop.com), Monteray Plaza. With over a dozen years of experience, this outfit is the most knowledgeable on local surf conditions. New and used boards are for sale, including the shop's private-label boards made by top shapers. While you're there, check out the classic surfboards, including a 1930s hollow-wood board and experimental designs from the 1960s, on display.

Corolla Water Sports (252-453-6900; www.corollawatersports.com), Kitty Hawk Water Sports, Tim-Buck II. Truly a one-stop shop for fun, this complex behind TimBuck II rents WaveRunners, kayaks, paddleboats, and a flat-bottom party boat, or will take you parasailing. Guided kayak ecotours paddle north to the Whalehead Club or south through the protected marsh waterway owned by the Currituck Hunt Club, one of the best paddling routes on the Banks.

The Island Revolution Surf Company and Skatepark (252-453-9484; www.islandrevolution.com). Cool shop in Corolla Light Town Center schedules surfing lessons and rents surfboards and wet suits.

158 Surf and Skate (252-453-8158; www.158surfandskate.com), 794 Sunset Boulevard Rent a soft-top surfboard by the day or week, or sign up for surf or skateboard lessons.

Outer Banks Charter Fishing Adventures/Corolla Bait and Tackle (252-453-9500; www.corolla baitandtackle.com). Relaxing tours aboard the pontoon boat *Currituck Queen* include a sunset cruise and a trip around Monkey Island, once a famous hunt club. A wine tasting cruise takes you across Currituck Sound to a winery on Knotts Island.

✳ Green Space

With extensive marshes on Currituck Sound and unspoiled beaches on the Atlantic, plus the off-road playground beyond the end of the road, the North Beaches have some of the best ecotourism opportunities on the Banks.

Note that no ATVs are allowed in the off-road area, and four-wheel-drive drivers are requested to stay on the established sand roads through the communities. No access is available to the Virginia side of the state line through the locked gates.

You must keep 50 feet away from any wild ponies you come upon. Do not feed them any kind of food, even hay or apples. Ponies have died in recent years from well-meaning visitors feeding them food that their digestive systems are not adapted to handle.

BEACHES The beaches at the northern end of the Banks are wide, inviting, clean, and generally not crowded. An excursion onto the beach north of Corolla at the end of NC 12 is a fascinating journey, best taken with a local who knows how to navigate the maze of largely unmarked sand tracks. If you venture in with your own four-wheel-drive vehicle, stick to the beach, and you can't get lost—but keep an eye on the tides. There are no public facilities in the off-road area, and commercial development is forbidden. You can buy T-shirts, and perhaps get directions, at the fire station.

Here are some hints for driving on the beach that may keep you from getting stuck. Lower the pressure in your tires to 20 psi. Be sure you know the weather forecast and the tide tables. High surf can cut you off. Avoid getting too close to the water. If your tires do begin to spin, back up in your tracks for several car lengths, then move forward slowly. You may need to let out more air. Locals usually take along a shovel, wooden planks, and a towrope. Don't forget the sunscreen, hat, cell phone, and extra water.

If you do get stuck, don't call 911. This is not considered an emergency. Instead, use your cell phone to call the local tow service **A-1 Towing and Recovery** (252-453-4002). When you come off the beach, re-up your tires with air, and your cooler with beverages, at Winks grocery.

You can drive, walk, or bike onto the beach from Corolla's **North Beach Access** ramp where NC 12 ends, 24 hours a day, 365 days a year, and drive north on the beach all the way to the Virginia line. Beware of the many stumps that protrude from the sand, the remnants of an ancient forest, as well as other hazards, especially the wild horses that frequent the beach during hot weather. Many have been killed or maimed by speeding drivers.

You cannot drive south from the North Beach Access from May through September.

Elsewhere in Corolla, you can access the beach via East Corolla Village Road, the sand road across NC 12 from the lighthouse, also called the Lighthouse Ramp Road.

The **Currituck County Southern Beach Access** at 471 Ocean Trail (NC 12) has bathrooms, showers, and parking. There is a lengthy walk to the ocean.

Free public parking lots about a block from public beach walkways are available on Whalehead Drive at Sailfish, Bonito, Perch, Sturgeon, and Shad streets. The ban on parking on the shoulders of streets is vigorously enforced.

Another public beach access is located at the **Pine Island Audubon Sanctuary,** next to the Hampton Inn.

Bonfires, glass, personal watercraft, camping, and ATVs are all prohibited on Currituck County beaches. Pets must be on a leash.

TRAILS CAMA Sound Boardwalk, Currituck Heritage Park. Short boardwalk just west of the lighthouse leads through an abundance of native plants to a deck with great sunset views over the marsh.

♿ **Currituck Banks National Estuarine Preserve** (252-261-8891; www.nccoastalreserve.net). Just before the end of NC 12, a boardwalk and hiking trail lead from a parking lot through several barrier island habitats, including mature maritime forest and marsh to decks overlooking the sound. Interpretive signs explain the ecology of the area.

Currituck National Wildlife Refuge (252-429-3100; www.fws.gov/currituck). Several tracts in the off-road area are included in this national refuge, established to protect the fragile dune ecosystem and endangered species including piping plover, loggerhead sea turtle, and seabeach amaranth. Visitors must park on the beach and walk in to explore interior areas. No public facilities.

Pine Island Audubon Sanctuary (252-489-5303; www.ncaudubon.org). Occupying one of the last undeveloped parcels of land between Kitty Hawk and Corolla, this 6,000-acre sanctuary stretches from the ocean dunes to the marshes of the sound. A 2.5-mile, self-guided nature trail runs along the sound side of the sanctuary, beginning behind the Pine Island Racquet and Fitness Center. Two decks on the sound make great spots for birding. The old Pine Island Hunt Club is being renovated as an environmental educational center.

✳ Lodging

Corolla has very few hotels and inns, but it boasts some of the most luxurious rental homes on the Banks. During the last few decades, the entire ocean side of NC 12 became lined with tall beach houses, many with private pools, hot tubs, and elevators, well suited to large family get-togethers

INNS ✳ ♿ (ᵂⁱ) **Hampton Inn and Suites Outer Banks Corolla** (252-453-6565; www .hamptoninn.hilton.com), 333 Audubon Drive, Pine Island. Located north of the Sanderling, this low-rise hotel sits just behind the dune line, halfway between Corolla and Duck. The spacious 123 guest rooms and studio suites

all have balconies or patios, and most have a sleeper sofa. Complimentary breakfast is served daily in the lobby, where you can browse an extensive seashell collection. An indoor pool and hot tub are open all year, while outdoors a pool, kids' pool, and one of the few lazy rivers on the Banks are open seasonally. The hotel has its own game room, coin laundry, and fitness center, and guests also have access to the facilities at the Pine Island Racquet and Fitness Club. Summer $$$; off-season $$.

✳ 🐾 ♿ (ᵂⁱ) **The Inn at Corolla Light** (252-453-3340 or 1-800-215-0772; www.innatcorolla

.com), 1066 NC 12. The farthest north of all Outer Banks hotels, this inn sits within the Corolla Light community and shares its extensive amenities, including oceanfront and soundfront activity centers, and an inside sports center with pool, hot tub, and racquetball and tennis courts. The inn itself is charming, with friendly staff and a complimentary continental breakfast buffet served daily in the sunny dining room. Each of the 43 rooms and suites is unique, many with views of Currituck Sound, all with pillowtop beds, refrigerator, TV, and coffeemaker. All guests can enjoy the intimate hot tub and pool with views of the sound, or watch spectacular sunsets from the inn's gazebo, which sits at the end of a 400-foot pier. In the summer, kayaks, personal watercraft, sailboats, and other craft are available for rent. Bicycles are free for guests. Summer $$$$; off-season $.

RESORT ♂ **Corolla Light Resort** (252-453-2455; www.corollalightresort.com), 1197B Franklyn Street. The largest and most amenity-laden community on the North Beaches, this resort includes 400 homes on 250 acres that stretch from the ocean to the sound. Renters enjoy, among other amenities, an oceanfront recreation center with two pools; a sound-side swimming pool, pier, and gazebo; kayak rentals; minigolf; an ecology trail; fishing pond; an indoor sports center; a free summer trolley service; and weekly planned activities during the summer season. $$–$$$$.

VACATION COTTAGE RENTALS ☀ ⅃ ♂ **Corolla Classic Vacations** (252-453-9660 or 1-866-453-9660; www.corollaclassicvacations .com), 1196 NC 12. This property management company represents more than 200 properties in the Corolla area, many equipped with elevators, private pools, and hot tubs. Holiday rentals and partial week rentals available.

Karichele Realty (252-453-2377 or 1-800-453-2377; www.karichele.com), TimBuck II. Lists many properties, some pet friendly, in Swan Beach and Carova, where you may see wild ponies in your yard.

☀ ⅃ (ၐ) ↪ **Twiddy & Company Realtors** (252-457-1190; www.twiddy.com), 1127A Schoolhouse Lane. Twiddy specializes in the North Beaches and off-road area, listing over 700 properties, including more than 100 beyond the end of the road, some truly immense, with 16 to 18 bedrooms sleeping up to three dozen people.

☀ ⅃ **Village Realty** (252-453-9650 or 1-877-546-5362; www.villagerealtyobx.com), 501 Hunt Club Drive, Ocean Club Centre. Represents properties at Corolla Light and the exclusive Currituck Club. Last-minute specials available.

✳ Where to Eat

With the majority of lodgings in Corolla rental houses and cottages, take-out and gourmet markets play a huge role in the local dining scene, so you'll find lots of seafood, barbecue, and pizza take-out places here. Restaurants typically are accustomed to the large parties that stay at these beach castles, but it's always a good idea to call ahead for reservations.

DINING OUT ♂ **Agave Roja** (252-453-0446; www.agaveroja.com), Monteray Plaza. This upscale Mexican spot is wowing customers with authentic regional cuisine and a big selection of premium tequilas. Try a tequila tasting flight, a mojito, or sangria by the glass or pitcher. Seafood enchiladas, vegetarian entrées, gluten-free items, and lots of Mexican sweets highlight the interesting menu. $$.

✳ **Metropolis** (252-453-6167; www.metropolis obx.com), Ocean Club Centre. This intimate spot, serving dinner only, is everything other dining destinations in Corolla are not: no big servings at inexpensive prices, no children's menu, no split checks for big groups. At this destination of choice for foodies with deep pockets, plates are small, tapas-style; menus change with the season, featuring truffles, foie gras, and exotic mushrooms; and prices are high. Stop by for a late-night cocktail and a nibble of something interesting at the bar to have a look at the art on walls and plates. $$$$.

♂ ⅃ ♉ **Mike Dianna's Grill Room** (252-453-4336; www.grillroomobx.com), TimBuck II. Mesquite-grilled meats and seafood, plus some pasta entrées, are the specialties at this popular spot in TimBuck II that can accommodate large groups. USDA Prime beef, chicken, lamb, pork, and veal seared on the grill come with your choice of homemade sauces. A big wine list recognized by *Wine Spectator* complements the menu with vintages in every price range, including many bottles under $40. Try the mesquite-grilled banana split for dessert. You can eat inside in the white-tablecloth dining room, or outside on the casual deck, where you'll enjoy live music in season. Reservations recommended, especially for large groups. Dinner $$$.

♂ ⅃ ♉ ↪ **North Banks Restaurant & Raw Bar** (252-453-3344; www.northbanks.com), TimBuck II. Popular spot on the upper deck of TimBuck II's west building offers drink specials and a wide variety of steamed seafood. The small dining room does not accept reservations, so you may have to wait. Lunch $; dinner $$$$.

🍴 🍷 **Oceanfront Grille** (252-453-4748; www.oceanfrontgrille.com), 1197 Franklyn Street. The former private beach club at Corolla Light Resort is now open to the public, serving dinner along with magnificent ocean views from the second floor bar and deck. Seafood, steaks, and lamb chops dominate the menu, with a much-praised giant crabcake taking center stage. Located in the resort's pool complex, the grille is open for lunch for resort guests. Most seating is open-air. $$–$$$$.

🍴 ♿ **Route 12 Steak & Seafood Co.** (252-453-4644; www.rt12obx.com), TimBuck II. Chef Ron Davidson prepares a wide variety of popular dishes, from steak or tuna au poivre to pastas, duck, and shrimp, at this casual spot next to the Brew Thru. The pork ribs are locally famous. Reservations recommended. Lunch $$; dinner $$$.

EATING OUT 🍴 **Bad Bean Taqueria** (252-453-4380; www.badbeanobx.com), TimBuck II. The flavors of Baja California inspire the menu at this casual, inexpensive spot with a big-screen TV, fresh salsas, fish and shrimp tacos, vegetarian and gluten-free options, plus a large selection of Mexican beers and margaritas. $.

🍴 **First Light Breakfast & Burger** (252-453-4664; www.firstlightcorolla.com), TimBuck II. Full breakfast menu served until 2 PM in season, plus lunch, dinner, and a full bar. $.

Lighthouse Bagels & Deli (252-453-9998; www.lighthousebagels.com), Monteray Plaza. New Jersey natives bring authentic bagels and handmade doughnuts to the beach. $.

🍴 **Lovie's Kitchen Table** (252-453-0912; www.lovieskitchentable.com), 1130-E Corolla Village Road. Cute spot in a historic building in old Corolla Village serves breakfast and lunch on weekdays in summer. Try a signature sweet potato sticky bun and coffee or a salad made with locally caught tuna along with a North Carolina microbrew on the screen porch, or take a seat in the shady yard. Don't miss the chocolate room full of artisan truffles and other goodies. $.

🍴 **Smokey's Restaurant** (252-453-4050; www.smokeysrestaurant.com), 345 Audubon Drive, Pine Island. Located in the bright and shiny retro Pine Island Diner next to the Hampton Inn, this casual spot features seafood, marinated fried chicken, North Carolina–style pork barbecue, and ribs at lunch and dinner. Beer and wine available. $–$$.

How can you be sure that the seafood you order is locally caught? Look for the logo of Outer Banks Catch (www.outerbankscatch .com) at restaurants and markets up and down the Outer Banks. We've marked member organizations in our listing with 🍴.

❄ 🍴 🍷 **Tomato Patch Pizzeria** (252-453-4500; www.obxpizza.com), Monteray Plaza. Family-run spot has a menu that goes way beyond your typical pizza place, offering Italian and Greek classics, seafood, hot subs, gyros, po'boys, and vegetarian specials. The full-service **Dr. Unk's Bar** serves up a late-night menu. $–$$.

COFFEE AND SWEETS 🍴 **Big Bucks Homemade Ice Cream & Coffee Bar** (252-453-3188; www.bigbucksicecream.com), TimBuck II. More than 50 flavors of homemade ice cream, sorbets, sherbets, fruit smoothies, and an assortment of hot and iced coffee and fruit drinks, plus handmade chocolates and ice cream cakes to die for. Also in Nags Head, MP 4.5.

Northern Light Bakery (252-453-0201), Corolla Light Town Center. Doughnuts, cinnamon rolls, and other pastries baked fresh daily make a good breakfast with fresh roasted coffee drinks. Special order cakes in advance.

((•)) **Outer Banks Coffee Company** (252-453-0200; www.obxcoffee.com), Monteray Plaza. Beans are fresh roasted on-site, adding to the wake-up aroma as you walk through the door of this full-service coffee shop. Try a scoop of Edy's Ice Cream in your coffee for a mean espresso float.

PIZZA AND SANDWICHES Beach Road Pizza (252-453-0273; www.beachroadpizza .com), 1210 NC 12. Located a half mile north of the lighthouse, this spot serves pizzas, strombolis, calzones, salads, and subs, plus popular barrel rolls, crusty pinwheels of cheese-filled dough that are a hit with kids. Beach Road's real claim to fame, however, is that it delivers to the off-road beaches beyond the end of the paved road, although it will cost you extra.

Corolla Pizza and Deli (252-453-8592; www.corollapizza.com), 1152 NC 12, Austin Complex. Serving hand-tossed stone-oven pizza, including a cheese-free tomato pie, plus a variety of hot and cold subs, this local favorite is right next to Winks grocery and Corolla Scoops and Sweets ice cream shop. Free delivery in season.

Cosmo's Pizzeria (252-453-4666; www.cosmos pizzeria.com), Corolla Light Town Center. This popular spot with a great location offers fresh-made New York–style pizzas, whole or by the slice, salads, and subs. Cold beer on tap. Sister restaurant ✍ **Bambino's Little Italy** (252-453-4004) in the same shopping center has tables with lighthouse views and a popular and reasonably priced Italian American menu.

The Pizza Guy (252-453-9976; www.pizzaguy obx.com), Monteray Plaza. Free delivery of gourmet pizzas, oven-baked subs, and wings, to both Duck and Corolla.

TAKE-OUT ✍ **Bluewater Seafood Market** (252-453-9921; www.bluewaterseafoodmarket .com), Ocean Club Centre. Plan an eat-in evening with a designer steam pot or a mess of "dirty" crabs. Delivery available. $$$–$$$$.

Brew Thru Beverage Store (252-453-2878; www.brewthru.com), NC 12, TimBuck II. The ultimate in convenience: You don't even have to get out of your car to score a six-pack.

Corolla Village Barbecue (252-457-0076), 1129 Corolla Village Road. Serving Carolina pork barbecue, ribs, barbecue chicken, soft-serve ice cream, and homemade sides in the heart of Old Corolla Village, this local favorite offers take-out only, but you can eat at the picnic tables out front. $.

Dockside North Seafood Market (252-453-8112; www.docksidenorth.com), NC 12, Monteray Plaza. Full-service market will steam lobster, shrimp, king and snow crab to order, or you can get a Down East clambake, ready to go. Great for a crowd. $$$.

✍ **Fat Crabs Rib Company** (252-453-9931; www.fatcrabsobx.com), Corolla Light Town Center. A large selection of steamed seafood, including Maine lobster, is available à la carte or in steamer pot combos for dine-in or take-out. St. Louis–style ribs and North Carolina pork barbecue make up the flip side of the menu.

Seafood and barbecue sandwiches $; platters and steamer pots $$–$$$.

✍ **Sooey's BBQ and Rib Shack** (252-453-4423; www.sooeysbbq.com), Monteray Plaza. Family packs make it easy for your crowd to pig out. Second location (252-449-2271) at Scarborough Faire in Duck. $–$$.

❋ ✍ **Steamers Shellfish To Go** (252-453-3305; www.steamersshellfishtogo.com), Tim-Buck II. Take a steamer pot of seafood back to your cottage, or enjoy it on the deck overlooking Currituck Sound. There's also a long list of à la carte dishes, including several vegetarian options, and a lunch menu of seafood sandwiches, served before 4 PM. Lunch $$; dinner $$–$$$.

WINE, BEER, AND GROCERIES Bacchus Wine & Cheese (252-453-4333; www.bacchus wineandcheese.com), Monteray Plaza. This entertaining place stocks over 750 vintages from around the world and all the extras to go with them, from imported cheeses to steaks, pastas, and desserts, plus after-dinner cigars. Daily wine tastings are available in season, along with fat sandwiches and subs stuffed with Thuman's deli meats.

Corolla Wine, Cigar and Gourmet (252-453-6048; www.corollawinecigar.com), TimBuck II. Shop with a view specializes in North Carolina wines, premium cigars, gourmet food items, and wine-related gifts. Free wine tastings.

Seaside Farm Market (252-453-8285; www .seasidefarmobx.com), TimBuck II. Family-run open-air market at the entrance to TimBuck II offers locally grown produce from the Grandy family farm, baked pies and breads, and local seafood, plus beer and wine.

Winks of Corolla (252-453-8166), 1152 NC 12. Once the only spot in Corolla to get groceries, beer, wine, gas, and just about everything else, Winks anchors the shops in the historic Austin building, all local favorites.

❋ Entertainment

During the summer season, many local restaurants add music to their menus. In Corolla, bands play regularly at Mike Dianna's Grill Room, Uncle Ike's, and Sundogs Sports Bar.

CONCERTS Currituck Heritage Park (252-453-9040; www.whaleheadclub.org). The Whalehead Club sponsors a free summer concert series on the lawn Thursday evenings in July and August, and wine festivals with live music on Wednesday afternoons July through October ($20).

NIGHTCLUBS OBX Comedy Club (252-207-9950; www.comedyclubobx.com). Seasonal performances at the Currituck Club.

♈ **Sundogs Sports Bar and Grill** (252-453-4263; www.facebook.com/Sundogs2012), Monteray Plaza. Full-service bar, with a bar food menu, pool table, and late-night hours, is a favorite spot to watch sports on the big screen. Bands play several nights a week during the summer season. No cover.

♪ ♟ **Uncle Ike's Sandbar & Grill** (252-453-2385; www.facebook.com/UncleIkes), Corolla Light Town Center. Fun spot serves breakfast, lunch, and dinner but is best known for its nightly karaoke, live entertainment, and late-night dance scene. Outside covered deck is a great place for a fish taco. $–$$.

✳ Selective Shopping

In Corolla, dining, shopping, and entertainment venues are all concentrated into the shopping centers that sit along NC 12, often at the entrance of gated communities. The first, and still the most extensive, shopping destination is **TimBuck II Shopping Village** (www.timbuckii.com), a complex including over 60 shops and restaurants spread through several buildings, with ample parking. The complex backs up to Currituck Sound with a water-sports complex, go-kart track, paddleboat pond, and miniature golf course along the waterfront. Situated directly across the street from Currituck Heritage Park, and within walking distance of the Corolla Light Resort, the **Corolla Light Town Center** has a skate park hidden in its center amid pizza shops, bakeries, ice cream parlors, and surf shops. The statue of a rearing horse marks the location of the Wild Horse Fund store.

For a very special shopping experience, walk along the sandy streets of **Old Corolla Village,** poking your head into the various shops. Most of them are run by locals, born and bred, and they all have stories to tell.

ART GALLERIES Dolphin Watch Gallery (252-453-2592; www.dolphinwatchgallery.com), TimBuck II. Features a wide variety of arts and fine crafts, including gallery owner Mary Kaye Umberger's original works depicting wild horses and local landmarks.

Eclectic Treasures (252-453-0008; www.eclecticgallery.net), TimBuck II. Unique selection of fine art and crafts runs the gamut from blessing bowls to recycled glass art. Standouts are watercolors by former lighthouse keeper Lloyd Childers.

Ocean Treasures (252-453-2383; www.oceantreasures.net), TimBuck II. A 6-foot bronze dolphin welcomes you to the only gallery on the Banks representing Wyland, painter of whales, and Thomas Kinkade, Painter of Light. Both are represented by new releases and some sold-out items, as well as licensed gifts and collectibles.

Tarheel Trading Company (252-441-3132; www.tarheeltrading.com), TimBuck II. Handcrafted jewelry, gifts, and decorative art from over 200 American artists, including many from North Carolina.

BOOKSTORE The Island Bookstore (252-453-2292; www.islandbooksobx.com), 1130 Corolla Village Road, Historic Corolla Village. The Corolla location of this independent bookstore occupies a reproduction of the village's original general store. Signings and readings are frequent in season.

SPECIAL SHOPS ♪ Corolla Wild Horse Mustang Stores (www.corollawildhorses.com). The Wild Horse Fund maintains two stores that carry all sorts of horse merchandise, from books about horses to wild horse clothing, jewelry, and toys. The store in the museum at 1129 Corolla Village Road (252-453-8002) is open on weekdays, all year. The second location, in Corolla Light Town Center (252-453-9000), is open daily from Memorial Day through Labor Day. Visitors to the stores have an opportunity to meet and even ride a mustang (schedule varies). All proceeds go toward preserving and protecting the wild herds.

Currituck Beach Lighthouse Museum Shop (252-453-6778; www.currituckbeachlight.com), Little Lightkeeper's House, Currituck Beach Lighthouse. Sales of lighthouse and wild horse souvenirs benefit their respective charitable foundations. Look beyond the gifts to see the amazing architecture of this beautifully restored building.

♪ **DogNutz** (252-453-9955 or 1-866-364-6887; www.dognutz.com), TimBuck II. Make your dog the best-dressed barker on the beach in OBK9 gear. Store stocks gifts for cats and horses, as well.

♪ **Flying Smiles Kites** (252-453-8442; www.flyingsmileskites.com), Corolla Light Town Center. Store operated by competitive kite flyers hosts Fun Flies that are open to the public, and it stocks every kind of kite, from snowflakes to four-line stunt models. The experts here will patch up your kite if you crash.

♪ **Outer Banks Popcorn Shoppe** (252-453-4000; www.outerbankspopcornshoppe.com), TimBuck II. Family-owned shop creates popcorn in 20 flavors. Stop by for a free sample.

Spry Creek Dry Goods (252-453-0199; www.sprycreek.com), 1122 Corolla Village Road, Historic Corolla Village. From the outside, the unpresuming building may look like the auto repair shop it once was, but inside, Corolla native Karen Whitfield has gathered a colorful collection of local art, jewelry, and home accents, combining it with handmade crafts from around the world. Look for the line of locally made organic toiletries.

Whalehead Club Museum Shop (252-453-9040; www.whaleheadclub.org), Currituck Heritage Park. Unique jewelry, ornaments, birdhouses, and other art objects created from the house's original copper shingles join a nice collection of books, posters, and other gifts. Proceeds benefit historic preservation.

✳ Special Events

April: **Easter Egg-Stravaganza** (252-453-9040; www.whaleheadclub.org), Currituck Heritage Park. **Corolla Pedal-Foot-Paddle Triathlon** (www.whaleheadclub.org).

May: **Mustang Spring Jam** (www.mustangmusicfestival.com).

Late May: **Outer Banks Beach Music Festival** (www.outerbanksbeachmusicfestival.com). Memorial Day weekend event at Currituck Heritage Park brings out shaggers and lovers of old time R&B, as well as blues fans.

June: **"Under the Oaks" Arts Festival** (252-453-9040; www.whaleheadclub.org), Currituck Heritage Park.

June–September: **Whalehead Club Wine Festivals** (252-453-9040; www.whaleheadclub.org). Wednesday-afternoon events include live music, a souvenir glass, and tour of the Whalehead Club.

July Fourth: **Independence Day Festival of Fireworks,** Currituck Heritage Park.

July–August: **Summer Concert Series on the Lawn.** Free concerts at Currituck Heritage Park every Thursday evening.

July: **Wild Horse Days** (252-453-8002; www.corollawildhorses.com). Four-day annual fund-raiser at the Wild Horse Museum in Old Corolla Village.

August: **Corolla Surf Shop Longboard Invitational** (252-453-9283; www.corollasurfshop.com).

Mid-October: **Mustang Music Festival** (www.mustangmusicfestival.com).

October: **Haunted Corolla Village** (252-453-9040; www.whaleheadclub.org). Evening hayrides and treasure hunts at Currituck Heritage Park and Old Corolla Village.

November: **Black Friday Porch Sale** (252-453-9040; www.whaleheadclub.org). Holiday open house at the Whalehead Club features special sales.

December: **Currituck Heritage Park Tree Lighting Celebration** (252-453-9040; www.whaleheadclub.org), at Currituck Heritage Park, includes free tours of the Whalehead Club, caroling, and carriage rides.

DUCK AND SANDERLING

TODAY A SCENIC DESTINATION noted for exceptional shopping and gourmet dining, the small fishing village of Duck first appears on maps dating to the 1790s. The local folks, who traveled mostly by boat, developed the first crab-shedding business in the area, founding the commercial soft-shell crab industry. In the 1940s local residents and crabs alike were subjected to the sound of bombing practice on military land just north of the village. The bombing range is long gone. Its sole remnant is an impressive pier built by the U.S. Army Corps of Engineers, now used to conduct scientific studies of waves and currents.

Duck is Dare County's newest town, having incorporated in 2001. The new Town Waterfront Park lies along NC 12 on Currituck Sound. Public parking is available here, as well as at the numerous shopping villages that stretch along the road all the way through town. This stretch of coast is renowned for its sunsets, and many establishments look west over Currituck Sound. Most of the town's many rental condominiums and houses are tucked out of sight amid the maritime forest that makes Duck such a shady, pleasant place in the summer. The town has no public beach access but is still extremely popular as a destination for day trips.

Just north of Duck is one of the narrowest parts of the Banks, once the site of Caffey's Inlet. Today the **Sanderling Resort** occupies this prime property. The old lifesaving station has been restored as a restaurant.

Although officially part of Duck, Sanderling is often thought of as a separate community. The hotel's builder, Earl Slick, was the first to push the paved road north of Duck, and he put a gate across the road, protecting the exclusive neighborhoods he developed beyond it. The gate remained from 1975 until 1984, when the road became part of NC 12 and the state bulldozed the barrier. NC 12 is called Duck Road in Duck.

GUIDANCE Information on Duck can be found at the Dare County welcome centers. The closest is the **Aycock Brown Welcome Center** (1-877-629-4386; www.outerbanks.org), located at MP 1 in Kitty Hawk on US 158. Contact the **Town of Duck** (252-255-1234; www.townofduck.com), 1240 Duck Road, for information on town events and regulations.

POST OFFICE The U.S. Post Office in Duck is located at 1245 NC 12, inside the **Olde Duck Village Shoppe** (252-261-8555; www.oldeduckvillage.com). The zip code for Duck and Sanderling is 27949.

PUBLIC RESTROOMS The town maintains public restrooms in the Town Waterfront Park.

GETTING THERE Until the new toll bridge is completed across Currituck Sound (estimated to open in 2018), the only way to reach Duck is along NC 12. It is just two lanes from the junction with US 158 in Kitty Hawk, and traffic frequently backs up, especially on summer weekends, as guests check into and out of vacation cottages. Allow plenty of time to reach your destination, relax, and obey all traffic regulations. The slow speed zone through the Sanderling property often catches drivers by surprise.

GETTING AROUND *By Bicycle:* Duck is a small village, and many residents and visitors get around by bike. A shady paved bike path, the Duck Trail, runs under the trees through the heart of town. Several local restaurants, such as **Baldie's Burgers** (252-261-2660; 1215 Duck Road), next to Kitty Hawk Kites, cater to the two-wheel crowd with to-go windows and outdoor picnic tables.

On Foot: Many people who rent vacation cottages in Duck opt to walk to dining and shopping destinations, since most are localized in Duck Village. This can be a big time saver, especially when the traffic gets bad. The paved Duck Trail makes it easy and safe for bikes and pedestrians to navigate the village.

✳ To See

Duck Research Pier/Field Research Facility (252-261-3511; www.frf.usace.army.mil), 1261 NC 12. The equipment on this pier does important research into waves, currents, and other processes that create the Outer Banks. You can visit the facility on weekday mornings during the summer. Free tours begin promptly at 10 AM.

The Sanderling Resort (252-261-4111 or 1-800-701-4111; www.thesanderling.com), 1461 NC 12. The public rooms of this landmark resort display an outstanding collection of wildfowl art, including porcelain birds by Gunter Granget, the Boehm Studio, and Dorothy Doughty's Birds of North America Royal Worcester collection, as well as many impressive wood and metal bird sculptures by South Carolina artist Grainger McKoy. The main inn lobbies display 18 original Audubon prints in addition to a complete baby elephant folio.

✳ To Do

ART CLASSES ✿ ♈ **Duck Duck Art** (252-291-0092; www.facebook.com/DuckDuckArt), Duck Commons. Classes for children and adults in a variety of art forms, including watercolor, decoupage, tie-dye, acrylics, and pastels, are taught by local artists in the loft above Savvy Home Boutique. Special girls-night-out evening classes include wine and cheese.

BICYCLING A multiuse paved path, the **Duck Trail,** runs parallel with NC 12 from the Currituck/Dare County line through Duck to Southern Shores.

Duck Cycle (252-261-0356; www.duckcycle.com), 1211 NC 12. Shop in Duck Commons rents cruisers for adults and kids, plus jogging strollers, by the day or week.

Duck Village Outfitters (252-261-7222; www.duckvillageoutfitters.net), 1207 NC 12. Adult and children's beach cruisers, with or without gear, rent by the week. Training wheels available.

Ocean Atlantic Rentals (252-261-4346; www.oceanatlanticrentals.com), 1194 NC 12. Rents bikes and trikes, plus accessories such as bike lights.

FISHING **Bob's Bait and Tackle** (252-261-8589; www.bobsbaitandtackle.com), 1180 NC 12. A presence in the heart of Duck Village since 1982, Bob's has a big selection of equipment and bait, including live minnows, and will teach you how to catch crabs. Bob's also books inshore, offshore, and light tackle charters, specializing in makeup trips, with boats going out daily.

Sharky's Bait, Tackle and Charters (252-255-2248; www.sharkyscharters.com), 1245 NC 12, Barrier Island Station. Full-service bait and tackle shop across from the Sunset Grille offers rod and reel rentals, surf fishing clinics, fishing licenses, and arranges charter-fishing trips, plus fishing, sunset, and dolphin-watch cruises aboard the headboat *Miss Broad Creek*.

FOR FAMILIES The ✹ **Duck Town Waterfront Park** has a public playground. The town's two bookstores sponsor ✹ **Children's Story Time,** geared to ages three to seven, on the town green (252-255-1286; www.townofduck.com) during the summer.

KAYAK TOURS The sound-side waterfront, lined with boardwalks, restaurants, and shopping complexes, makes a popular and interesting paddle, especially as the sun sets into Currituck Sound. A public kayak/canoe launch in the Duck Town Park is free to use and will put you in the heart of the action.

Coastal Kayak (252-261-6262; www.outerbankskayaktours.com). Guided paddle trips explore the intricate marsh maze of the Pine Island Audubon Sanctuary.

Duck Village Outfitters (252-261-7222; www.duckvillageoutfitters.net), 1207 NC 12. Sign up here for kayak tours through Kitty Hawk Woods. The store rents single or double, surf or touring kayaks and canoes by the day or week. Delivery available. Or rent by the hour and take your craft directly across the street from the shop and put in at the Duck Town Park public launch.

Ocean Atlantic Rentals (252-261-4346; www.oceanatlanticrentals.com), 1194 NC 12. Rent a surf or touring kayak or stand-up paddleboard. Free delivery on weekly orders over $95. Or rent by the day at the shop along the sound and launch nearby for a peaceful paddle.

RUNNING **Outer Banks Running Company** (252-255-5444; www.outerbanksrunningcompany .com), Loblolly Pines. Stop in for information on upcoming running events and suggestions on where to stretch your legs, as well as a nice selection of top brand running shoes and apparel.

SPAS AND FITNESS **Aqua Essence Day Spa** (252-261-9709; www.spasouterbanks.com), 1174 NC 12. Waterfront spa upstairs from the Aqua Restaurant offers ayurveda treatments, organic facials, spa cuisine, and summertime yoga on the lawn.

Outer Banks Yoga (252-305-3791; www.outerbanksyoga.com), Duck Commons. Drop-in classes are offered in the loft above Savvy Home on weekday mornings during the summer.

The Sanderling Spa (252-261-4111 or 1-800-701-4111; www.thesanderling.com), Sanderling Resort. This elegant spa overlooking the tranquil waters of Currituck Sound is the perfect setting for the signature Serenity Ritual, in which two therapists work in tandem to give clients a hydro massage, facial, scalp treatment, sea salt glow, and sea mud wrap, then finish up with a Swedish hose massage and Vichy rain shower. The spa features products made from the native Russian olive tree and offers yoga and Pilates classes. Couple's suite available.

SURFING AND SKATEBOARDING **Duck Village Outfitters** (252-261-7222; www.duckvillageout fitters.net), 1207 NC 12. Centrally located shop rents surfboards, stand-up paddleboards, body boards, skim boards, fins, and wet suits, and will deliver to your rental property. Two-hour surf lessons include 24-hour board rental.

Kitty Hawk Surf Company (252-261-8770; www.khsurf.com), 1213 NC 12, Wee Winks Square. Rent surfboards, body boards, stand-up paddleboards, and kayaks from this location in the heart of Duck. Surfing lessons and three-day surf camps are available.

158 Surf and Skate (252-255-1581; www.158surfandskate.com), Waterfront Shops. The latest in streetwear and skatewear meets locally produced surfboards at this cool boutique operated by local shaper Mike Rowe. Skateboard and surf rentals and lessons, custom surfboards, and fast ding repair set 158 apart from the crowd.

Outer Banks Surf Shop (252-261-2907; www.obssurf.com), 1176 NC 12. Independent shop run by surfers offers equipment for surfers or skaters, as well as surf board and stand-up paddleboard rentals and lessons.

WATER SPORTS CENTERS From Duck Village to the Sanderling, the shore of Currituck Sound is lined with water-sports emporiums offering a wide variety of water-based fun. Sailing and kayaking are huge here, and parasailing is literally taking off. Kayaks, paddleboards, and personal watercraft, such as Jet Skis and WaveRunners, are widely available. On the other hand, the area is just beginning to explore the sports of windsurfing and kiteboarding. These centers are open seasonally, May to October, or as weather permits. Most have lawns where you can picnic. Bonus: All these docks and marinas face west, so you can expect some awesome sunsets as the day draws to a close.

Kitty Hawk Kites Watersports Center (252-261-4450; www.kittyhawk.com), 1214 NC 12. Wee Winks Square location offers on-site Jet Ski rentals, stand-up paddleboard rentals and lessons, parasailing, tubing, waterskiing, and wakeboarding. Kayaks, surfboards, boogie boards, and bicycle rentals are available.

Nor'Banks Sailing Center (252-261-2900; www.norbanks.com), 1314 NC 12. Full-service sailing center offers rentals and instruction, plus parasailing and WaveRunner tours. Kids' sailing camp and a weekly racing series are open to visitors. Nor'Banks rents a wide variety of catamarans, trimarans, and sailboats, as well as kayaks, stand-up paddleboards, WaveRunners, and motorboats. The calm waters of the sound are the perfect spot for tubing, waterskiing, wakeboarding, kneeboarding, and wakeskating afternoons.

North Duck Water Sports (252-261-4200; www.duckjetskirentals.com), 1446 NC 12, 2.5 miles north of Duck Village. Rent a pontoon boat or Jet Ski for a trip on the sound or go parasailing to see it all from above.

Soundside Water Sports (252-261-0855; www.soundsidewatersports.com), 1566 NC 12, Station Bay Marina. Rent WaveRunners at this casual spot across from the Sanderling, then stop out front at **Station Bay Seafood** (252-261-3267) for some fresh catch for dinner. Boat tours and sunset cruises available, or you can launch your own craft at the boat ramp here for a small fee.

Sunset Watersports (252-261-6866; www.sunsetgrillewatersports.com), 1264 NC 12. Rent sit-on-top kayaks, WaveRunners, skiffs, and pontoon boats to explore Currituck Sound, or sign up for a sunset cruise or parasail adventure at the dock behind the Sunset Grille, party place of the North Banks. Fishing, shrimping, and crabbing trips are also available. Follow up with a tropical cocktail at the tiki bar.

✳ Green Space

BEACHES Duck has an excellent 7-mile-long beach, uncrowded and watched over by lifeguards from May 1 to October 31, making it one of the most family-friendly beaches on the Atlantic Coast. However, the town has no beach access open to the public. Only residents, renters, and their guests may use the beach in Duck. Residents may drive on the beach between October 1 and April 30. Pets are allowed to run unleashed on the beach as long as they are with their owner. Fires are not allowed on the beach.

WALKS ✔ ✹ ⚑ **Duck Town Park and Soundside Boardwalk** (252-255-1286; www.townofduck .com), 1200 NC 12. Trails lead through a coastal willow swamp and maritime forest, and a boardwalk edges the Currituck Sound waterfront in downtown Duck. The Duck Boardwalk, famous for its sunsets, begins at Christopher Drive at the south end of Duck Village and ends at the Waterfront Shops north of the water tower, connecting several retail areas in between. A free launch ramp for kayaks and canoes, a fishing and crabbing platform, gazebo, picnic area, public restrooms, and playground, plus an amphitheater used for music, magic, and other programs, cluster in the Duck Town Park behind the Duck Town Hall. Four slips for transient boaters can be found at the northern end of the boardwalk. Drinking fountains, including a special one for dogs, are scattered throughout the park. A useful map with parking options can be found on the Town of Duck website. The park is open dawn to dusk. The boardwalk is open dawn–1 AM.

❦ ♿ **Duck Trail.** This paved multiuse path connects many of the businesses along NC 12/Duck Road. Along most of its 7-mile length, it runs along the east side of the road as a separate trail. However, through the village's commercial district, the trail runs along both sides of NC 12 and is not separated from traffic. Pedestrians, bicycles, and in-line skaters may use the trail; mopeds and other motorized vehicles, and Segways, may not. Pets must be on a leash.

Seahawk Overlook Sound Viewing Area, W. Seahawk Drive. A short hiking trail on the south side of Duck Village leads to an outstanding sound view.

✳ Lodging

RESORT ❦ ♿ ♂ ((ᵞ)) **The Sanderling Resort & Spa** (252-261-4111 or 1-800-701-4111; www.thesanderling.com), 1461 NC 12. The Sanderling serves up luxurious resort amenities with laid-back Outer Banks style 5 miles north of Duck Village. Two-story, cedar-shingled buildings keep a low profile on this stretch of land between sound and sea. The public rooms of the inn are virtual galleries of art featuring birds and wildfowl. The property recently enjoyed a $4 million refit that equipped guest rooms with king-size beds, 32-inch TVs, wireless Internet, and walk-in showers. Many rooms have private porches where guests can enjoy water views. The 88 guest rooms and suites, plus a conference center, the Lifesaving Station Restaurant, and several Jacuzzis, are located along the oceanfront, where a big deck and boardwalk provide access to the beach. Cocktails and sandwiches ($$) are available at the **Sand Bar** on the deck. Across the road, a full-service spa, indoor pool, and the elegant Left Bank restaurant overlook Currituck Sound. Guests also have access to the championship golf course at the Currituck Club and the indoor courts at the Pine Island Racquet Club. The eco-center conducts guided kayak trips and bird-watching hikes in the adjacent Audubon Nature Preserve. The resort also rents five oceanfront villas. A suite atop the conference center with balconies that face both the sunrise and sunset is a favorite with honeymooners. $$–$$$$.

VACATION COTTAGE AND CONDO RENTALS ✳ ❦ **Brindley Beach Vacations** (1-877-642-3224; www.brindleybeach.com), 1215 NC 12. Represents rental properties in more than two dozen communities in Duck, including many with pools, elevators, and hot tubs. All homes come with daily newspaper service, beach access, and limited early access beginning at noon. Some communities have indoor pools and tennis courts.

❦ ♿ ((ᵞ)) **Carolina Designs Realty** (252-261-3934 or 1-800-368-3825; www.carolinadesigns.com), 1197 NC 12. Specializes in some of the finest houses in the area.

((ᵞ)) **Ships Watch** (252-261-2231; www.shipswatch.com), 1251 NC 12. Rental homes in this centrally located community range from three to five bedrooms. Renters have access to a private beach access, sound-side pier, swimming pool and hot tub, tennis courts, and playground, plus numerous discounts at local establishments. Linens and Wi-Fi included.

✳ Where to Eat

Duck is the foodie capital of the Outer Banks, with numerous spots boasting *Wine Spectator* Awards of Excellence, restaurants practicing farm-to-fork creativity, a café selected as the best wine restaurant in the United States, and the AAA four-diamond Left Bank all within the town limits. There are plenty of spots to grab a casual meal as well, plus sound-side decks where you can kick back with a cocktail and watch the legendary sunsets.

Take note that the kitchen and waitstaff at even the best restaurants can get overwhelmed during the busy summer season. Make reservations if possible, or go to eat early. Prices and crowds are both generally smaller at lunchtime.

THE SANDERLING RESORT MAINTAINS A LAID-BACK PROFILE.

Duck Village

🌊 ♿ ✂ 🍸 ✈ **Aqua Restaurant** (252-261-9700; www.restaurantsouterbanks.com), 1174 NC 12. Big, beautiful house fronting on the sound serves food worthy of its setting: organic, local, and sustainable, although, with a spa upstairs, serving sizes are what you'd expect from "spa cuisine." Fish tacos and crab and corn chowder drizzled with truffle oil are local favorites. The best times here take place on the decks that surround the building, where a bar menu with happy hour prices 3–6 PM complements the amazing sunset over the water. On summer evenings, live music enhances the deck vibe most nights. Online reservations available. Lunch $$; bar menu $; dinner $$$$.

❊ 🌊 ♿ 🍸 ✈ **The Blue Point Bar & Grill** (252-261-8090; www.goodfoodgoodwine.com), 1240 NC 12, Waterfront Shops. Nationally recognized for its innovative cuisine, the Blue Point recently expanded to accommodate more of its avid fans but retains its diner charm, complete with checkerboard floors, red leather stools and booths, and the atmospheric screen porch overlooking Currituck Sound. While there are seasonal changes in the lineup, you'll want to try the much-praised Carolina She-Crab Soup laced with sherry. The crowds—and prices—max out at dinner, but you can eat lunch here for a much more moderate check. Locals are crazy about the meat loaf. Reservations are accepted only for dinner and are very much recommended. You can make them up to a month in advance and online. A new outdoor bar hosts live music (in season) as the sun sinks into the sound. Lunch $$; dinner $$$$.

♿ ✂ 🍸 **Elizabeth's Café & Winery** (252-261-6145; www.elizabethscafe.com), 1117 NC 12, Scarborough Faire. Named "Best Fine Dining Wine Restaurant in the United States" by *Santé* magazine in 2003, Elizabeth's is top of the line when it comes to wining and dining on the Banks. Owner Leonard Logan, an accepted expert in the world of wine, is on hand most evenings. Pairing wine with food is his area of expertise, and the nightly six-course prix fixe wine dinners are educational as well as delicious. An à la carte menu is also served, as well as a small plates menu at the bar and in the adjacent Wine and Art Gallery, where Chef Brad Price's original paintings are displayed. Menus change nightly; however, flame-seared barbecue shrimp served with mango chutney—a dish Logan developed himself—and a lobster, scallop, and Brie bisque are house specialties. Although definitely in the splurge category, Elizabeth's strives for a casual beach feel. Jazz

on the patio is a highlight of Duck's summer season. Dinner $$$$.

✂ 🍸 **Red Sky Café** (252-261-8646; www.red skycafe.com), 1197 NC 12, Duck Landing. Located across NC 12 from the Duck Town Park, the Red Sky has many fans despite its small size and sometimes lengthy waits. Chef Wes Stepp puts his wood-burning oven to good use, creating a wood-fired Trio each evening of fresh fish, shrimp, and crabcake. Wood-fired roasted duck and the Blue Moon, a filet mignon crusted with blue cheese, are popular favorites. The Chefs-on-Call service will bring your selected meal to you; no waiting for a table. Lunch $; dinner $$$$.

❊ 🍸 **Roadside Raw Bar & Grill** (252-261-5729; www.roadsideobx.com), 1193 NC 12. Occupying the oldest house in Duck, this tiny eatery earns raves for its seasonal menu featuring local fish and shellfish. Stained-glass-style windows made of recycled glass brighten the cottage's interior. Visit the upstairs bar for a bowl of the famous clam chowder and a tomato pie. Or have a seat on the pleasant patio, where you'll occasionally encounter live music. If you visit Duck in the off-season, check the schedule for Roadside's oyster roasts. Lunch $; dinner $$$$.

Sanderling

♿ 🍸 ✈ **The Left Bank** (252-261-8419; www.thesanderling.com), 1461 NC 12, Sanderling Resort. Modern, elegant decor highlighted by a bank of windows overlooking Currituck Sound sets off multicourse tasting menus and à la carte offerings created by the talented culinary team in the Left Bank's exhibition kitchen. The sophisticated menus emphasize sustainable, organic, artisanal, and local ingredients (a concept the restaurant refers to as S.O.A.L.), combining seasonal ingredients and locally sourced seafood with foie gras, lamb, truffles, and quail with spectacular results. Each course can be paired with a suitable wine by the sommelier, or you can order from the bar. *Santé* magazine named the Left Bank the "Culinary Hospitality Restaurant of the Year," and the wine list won approval from *Wine Spectator;* AAA awarded the restaurant four diamonds. The most magical time here occurs at sunset, when the blond onyx bar reflects the sun's glow. The dress code is "beachy casual": Men are asked to wear shirts with collars and "dress shorts" or slacks. Reservations are requested. Not recommended for children under 15. Bar menu $$; dinner $$$$.

✂ ♿ 🍸 ✈ **The Lifesaving Station** (252-449-6654; www.thesanderling.com), 1471 NC 12, Sanderling Resort. The Sanderling's casual

THE LIFESAVING STATION RESTAURANT AT THE SANDERLING RESORT

restaurant, the Lifesaving Station, occupies the renovated 1899 Caffey's Inlet Life-Saving Station boathouse. The paneled interior, beautifully restored, is studded with maritime memorabilia, historical objects, bird decoys, and culinary awards. Menus vary with the season but always feature local fish and shellfish. At breakfast, the Eggs Sanderling atop crabcakes and the sweet potato and country ham hash are both standouts. Upstairs you'll find the **Swan Bar,** a great place for a quiet drink and a bowl of the Sanderling's signature chowder, a creamy blend of shrimp, crab, and corn. Breakfast, Sunday brunch, and lunch $$; dinner $$$$.

The Paper Canoe (252-715-2220; www.paper canoeobx.com), 1564 NC 12. Renovated cottage on the shores of the sound just south of the Sanderling Resort is the latest venture of longtime OBX restaurateur Tom Karole, who also has the **Fin & Claw Sea Grill** in Corolla's Tim-Buck II. Locally sourced fish and seafood, handmade ravioli, and house-smoked pulled duck top the menu. During busy hours, grab a seat in the bar, with windows overlooking the sound, and enjoy a gourmet pizza cooked in the wood oven, accompanied by one of 10 craft beers on draft. Dinner only, $$–$$$$.

EATING OUT
Duck Village

🍴 ❖ **Coastal Cantina** (252-480-0024; www .coastalcantina.com), 1240 NC 12, Waterfront Shops. Tex-Mex on the boardwalk, with great views of the sunset, perfect for kicking back with a margarita. Try a duck taco for some local flavor. Live music in season. $.

❖ **Coastal Cravings** (252-480-0032; www .cravingsobx.com), 1209 NC 12. One of several restaurants operated by Coastal Provisions, the area's top gourmet grocery, Cravings occupies a former Burger King, complete with drive-through window, the only one in Duck. The restaurant serves breakfast, lunch, and dinner, including Coastal Provisions award-winning crabcakes, complemented by a nice by-the-glass wine list and draft microbrews. The take-out window, especially popular for a quick breakfast, opens at 7 AM. Breakfast and lunch $; dinner $$$.

🍴 **Duck Deli** (252-261-3354; www.duckdeli obx.com), 1223 NC 12. A landmark on the Duck Road for over 20 years, this casual spot serves breakfast and hickory smoked barbecue pork, chicken, and ribs to eat in or take out. The unique T-shirts are popular souvenirs. The deli does not serve any alcoholic beverages. $–$$.

❋ 🍴 ❖ **Fishbones Raw Bar & Restaurant** (252-261-6991; www.fishbonesrawbar.com), 1171 NC 12, Scarborough Lane Shoppes. A fun tiki bar with a thatched roof serves specialty cocktails in collectible glasses, as well as all the standard libations. The big menu of appetizers with Caribbean flair, such as Oysters Down East, topped with a lobster mushroom sauce and coconut shrimp, is served all day and night. The chowders here (clam, conch, and lobster corn) are award-winning. Lunch $; dinner $$–$$$.

🦞 🍴 ❖ **Sunset Grille & Raw Bar** (252-261-3901; www.fishbonessunsetgrille.com), 1270 NC 12. If you like Fishbones in Duck Village, you're going to love its big sister. It's hard to miss this edifice along the sound side of NC 12 north of Duck, and usually one look at the tiki bars and long dock stretching out to a gazebo is enough to make travelers hit the brakes. If you like a partying good time and spectacular sunsets, you'll come away singing this spot's praises.

THE SUNSET GRILLE, NORTH OF DUCK, CELEBRATES KEY WEST STYLE EVERY EVENING.

White tablecloth dining it's not, but take a seat at one of the outdoor tiki bars, order up an exotic cocktail in a neon glass, hum along to a Jimmy Buffet tune, and you'll soon catch the Key West vibe. Raw and steamed seafood is available all day, and sushi is served nightly on the upper level. The restaurant also offers an interesting and reasonably priced breakfast menu. Come early and plan to spend the day. You can rent Jet Skis and kayaks out back, or take a parasail ride. Breakfast and lunch $; dinner $$–$$$$.

Sanderling

🏖 ♿ (ᵖ) **Sanderling Sand Bar** (252-261-4111; www.thesanderling.com), 1461 NC 12. If the weather is good, grab a cocktail and sandwich with a view at the Sand Bar on the Sanderling's oceanfront deck. $$.

COFFEE AND SWEETS ♂ Duck Donuts (252-480-3304; www.duckdonuts.com), 1190 NC 12, Osprey Landing Center. Design your own doughnuts at this shop on the boardwalk. Fresh warm doughnuts are dipped in your choice of frosting and sprinkled with your favorite topping. Additional locations in Corolla, Kitty Hawk, and Kill Devil Hills.

Duck's Cottage Coffee and Books (252-261-5510; www.duckscottage.com), 1240 NC 12, Waterfront Shops. Run by java junkies, the historic, cedar-shingled cottage that once housed the Powder Ridge Gun Club now provides an early-morning stop for residents and visitors who come to browse the book selection, enjoy an espresso or herbal tea, or hang out on the porch with a Mucky Duck specialty drink.

♂ **Sunset Ice Cream and Cappuccino** (252-261-3553), 1240 NC 12, Waterfront Shops. Take-out window on the boardwalk is a family favorite for feeding the ducks. Cash only.

The Sweet Duck (252-715-1878), 1171 NC 12, Scarborough Lane. Homemade gelato, espresso, and hand-dipped Belgian chocolates from Argyles (www.argylesrestaurant.com), one of the top catering outfits on the Banks.

Tullio's Pastry Shop (252-261-7112; www.tulliospastry.com), 1187 NC 12, Loblolly Pines Shopping Plaza. Award-winning cakes, pies, doughnuts, cupcakes, breads, and rolls featured at some of the area's top restaurants are available at this retail outlet.

CRAFT BEERS AND WINES Elizabeth's Wine Bar and Gallery (252-261-6145; www.elizabethsofduck.com), 1117 NC 12, Scarborough Faire. Elizabeth's extensive wine selection is displayed in a unique, temperature- and humidity-controlled, walk-in wine cellar. Enjoy a glass on the patio or in the gallery decorated with original paintings by the café's chef.

(ᵖ) **Sweet T's Coffee, Beer & Wine** (252-480-2326; www.sweet-ts-duck.com), 1211 NC 12. Go the coffee and pastry route, or try a glass of wine or craft draft on the shady deck. Free wine and beer tastings happen weekly, along with live music in season.

PIZZA Duck Pizza Company (252-255-0099; www.duckpizza.com), 1171 NC 12, Scarborough Lane Shoppes. Gourmet pizzas come in three sizes, including the supersize 18-inch extra large. Beer available. Free delivery in Duck.

Pizzazz Pizza Company (252-261-8822; www .pizzazzpizza.net), Loblolly Pines. The original location of this local chain offers a lunch buffet. Eat inside, outside, or have your pizza or hot sub delivered (252-261-1111). Online ordering and free delivery from Corolla to Nags Head make this a local favorite.

((•)) **The Wave Pizza Café** (252-255-0375; www .thewavepizza.com), 1190 NC 12, Osprey Landing. Take advantage of the free delivery, or enjoy your hand-tossed pie on the waterfront deck with a cold beer.

TAKE-OUT AND GROCERIES Dockside N Duck Seafood Market (252-261-8687; www.docksidenduck.com), 1216 NC 12, Wee Winks Square. Family-owned spot makes a quick stop for Down East clambakes to steam on your stovetop, crabcakes, award-winning she-crab soup, live Maine lobsters,

and blue crabs, raw or steamed, along with homemade tomato pies and desserts. Out front, the **Green Acres Farm Market** sells sweet corn, vine-ripened tomatoes, watermelons, hot peppers, berries, and more, direct from the family farm in Currituck County in season.

Tommy's Gourmet Market and Wine Emporium (252-261-8990; www.tommys market.com), 1242 NC 12. Personal service and convenience are the hallmarks of this long-time Duck store that lets you order your groceries, or entire prepared meals, online or by phone. Drop by on Taste It Tuesdays for samples of Outer Banks products.

Wee Winks Market (252-261-2937), 1213 NC 12. The first store ever in Duck is still much beloved for its convenience and wide variety of necessities.

✳ Entertainment

The Duck Town Park hosts many special events in its new amphitheater, including concerts several times a week, magic shows, story time, and more. Most events are free. For a schedule and ticket details, visit www.townofduck.com or call the town's event hotline: 252-255-1286.

Several local spots schedule live music in season, including Coastal Cantina, the Blue Note, Aqua, Sweet T's, Elizabeth's Café, Coastal Cravings, and the Sunset Grille.

✳ Selective Shopping

Duck's main claim to fame has always been its compact collection of unique and eclectic shops, making it the prime shopping destination on the Outer Banks. Within a half mile or so along either side of NC 12, you'll find most of the shopping and dining options in Duck. The stores here are linked by paved walkways and boardwalks, making for excellent daylong browsing. Most of the boutiques, shops, and galleries are locally owned and operated, with a smattering of regional chains and high-end nationals.

Scarborough Faire Shopping Center (www.scarboroughfaireinducknc.com), at 1177 Duck Road, was one of the first shopping destinations in the village. Begun in 1983, it set the standard with sprawling live oaks, wooden walkways and porches, and plenty of spots to sit and relax. Next door at 1171 Duck Road is **Scarborough Lane Shoppes,** with ample parking beneath the building, and even more eclectic shops. **Loblolly Pines,** a bit farther north at 1187 Duck Road, is also on the east or ocean side of NC 12.

On the west or sound side of NC 12, several shopping destinations line the shores of Currituck Sound, offering pleasant decks and great views of the sunset. From south to north they are **Duck Soundside Shops,** 1180 Duck Road; **Osprey Landing** (www.ospreylandingshops.com), 1194 Duck Road; **Wee Winks Square,** 1216 Duck Road; and **The Waterfront Shops** (www.waterfrontshops duck.com), just north of the watertower at 1240 Duck Road. The Waterfront Shops occupy atmospheric buildings, some of them rescued from old hunt clubs, all joined by an expansive deck. This is a great place for lunch, and an even better one at sunset when nature puts on a show. A boardwalk connects the shops with Wee Winks and the Duck Town Park.

The **ABC Store** (252-261-6981; www.ncabc.com), Duck's only outlet for bottles of hard liquor, can be found in Wee Winks Square.

RECOMMENDED READING Mercier, Judith D. *Duck: An Outer Banks Village.* Winston-Salem, NC: John F. Blair, 2001.

Tate, Suzanne. *Bring Me Duck: Folktales and Anecdotes from Duck, N.C. (as told by Ruth Tate).* Nags Head, NC: Nags Head Art, 1986. Includes many photos and a glossary of local terms.

ART AND CRAFT GALLERIES Greenleaf Gallery (252-261-2009; www.outer-banks.com/green leaf), 1169 NC 12. Large gallery on the south side of Duck showcases paintings, ceramics, jewelry, woodcraft, and art glass primarily created by North Carolina and Virginia artists. Monthly openings in season.

Ocean Annie's Craft Gallery (252-261-3290; www.oceananniesobx.com), Scarborough Faire. A 30-year survivor of the Duck shopping scene, this gallery specializes in handmade pottery and jewelry from local and national artists, as well as gourmet coffees and locally made candles and soaps.

SeaDragon Gallery (252-261-4224; www.seadragongallery.com), Waterfront Shops. Arts and crafts selected by shop owner Paula Myott are handcrafted by artisans from across the United States, including many from the Outer Banks.

❋ **Solitary Swan** (252-261-7676), Scarborough Lane. Longtime Duck favorite stocks folk art, tin signs, decoys, samplers, and OBX photographs.

Tarheel Trading Company (252-441-6235; www.tarheeltrading.com), Scarborough Lane. Hand-crafted jewelry, gifts, and decorative art from over 300 American artists, including many from North Carolina.

The Wooden Feather Wildlife Gallery (252-261-2808; www.woodenfeather.com), Scarborough Lane. Decoys hand carved by local artists and wildlife art in wood and metal, plus artistic birdhouses, starfish, and sea urchins crowd this interesting gallery in Duck Village.

BOOKS AND MUSIC Duck's Cottage Coffee and Books (252-261-5510; www.duckscottage.com), Waterfront Shops. Handpicked selection of fiction and nonfiction fills this historic, cedar-shingled cottage. Summer signing series and monthly reading group, plus newspapers from up and down the East Coast and great coffee, make this a special spot.

The Island Bookstore (252-261-8981; www.islandbooksobx.com), Scarborough Faire. The original location of this local chain of independent bookstores features carefully selected books for every interest.

JEWELRY The Mystic Jewel (252-255-5515; www.themysticjewel.com), Scarborough Lane. Hand-crafted sterling silver jewelry set with semiprecious stones comes with information on the mystical powers of the gems. Second location (252-453-3797) in Corolla's TimBuck II.

Sara DeSpain Goldsmith (252-255-0671; www.saradespain.com), Osprey Landing. Seashell charms and OBX and duck beads are among the original designs created by this master jeweler.

SPECIAL SHOPS Christmas Mouse (252-261-5404; www.christmasmouse.com), Scarborough Lane. Specializes in nautical and beach-themed ornaments. Second location in Nags Head on the Bypass (MP 10.5).

The Culinary Duck and Rub-A-Dub Duck Bath & Body (252-261-0455; www.culinaryduck .com), Scarborough Faire. No vacation in Duck is complete without a rubber ducky to take home, and you'll find them here, along with gourmet foods and bath products.

Donna Designs Wearable Art (252-261-6868; www.donnadesignsobx.com), Waterfront Shops. Hand-painted clothing and jewelry are created by a local artist inspired by the beach.

Old Duck Village Shoppe @ Duck Post Office (252-261-8555; www.oldeduckvillage.com), 1245 NC 12, Barrier Island Station. The tiny Duck Post Office, founded in 1909, is inside this shop, featuring locally themed books and Duck souvenirs.

Outer Barks (252-261-6279; www.outerbarks.com), Scarborough Lane. Huge selection of gifts for dogs and dog lovers. Bring your pampered pooch to the Outer Barks Yappy Hour.

Plum Crazy (252-261-1125; www.ruplumcrazy.com), Duck Soundside Shops. Step through the looking glass at this local favorite, stocking one-of-a-kind jewelry, accessories, and functional art furniture, much of it by local artists, plus the hippest national brands.

✴ Special Events

March: **Outer Banks Wedding Show** (www.thesanderling.com), Sanderling Inn.

April: **Coastival Duck & Wine Festival** (www.duckandwine.com), Waterfront Shops. Food competition of dishes featuring duck and a wine-tasting festival benefits local children's charities.

SHOPPING LOCAL ON THE OUTER BANKS

As tourism surged, the Banks became an increasingly tempting market for national brands. That's why we send a shout-out to these local chains that have stood the test of time:

Birthday Suits/The OBX Store (www.birthday-suits.com). Frequent winner of the "Best of the Beach" award, this store has been selling swimwear for over half a century. The OBX Store sells some of the most sought-after souvenirs on the Banks. Currently there are three locations: in Duck (252-261-7297), at Scarborough Lane Shoppes; in Corolla (252-453-4862), at Monteray Plaza; and in Kill Devil Hills (252-441-5338), at 2000 Bypass, MP 10.

The Cottage Shop (www.cottageshop.com). Shops offer the latest in seaside decor for your vacation cottage or home, plus holiday decorations and gifts, including the popular "My Town" posters. A division of Kellogg Building Supply (www.kelloggsupplyco.com), founded on the Banks in 1946, Cottage Shops are located at the Kellogg store in Duck (252-261-8121) and in Nags Head (252-441-2522) at the Outer Banks Mall.

Gray's Department Store (www.grays-sportswear.com). The Outer Banks' homegrown department store chain carries the largest selection of Tommy Bahama and Fresh Produce on the Banks, and stocks a huge Vera Bradley collection, said to be the largest in the mid-Atlantic region. There are locations in Corolla at TimBuck II; in Duck at the Waterfront Shops and Scarborough Faire; and in Kitty Hawk at 3860 Bypass, MP 4.

❧ Nags Head Hammocks (www.nagsheadhammocks.com). Selling relaxation since 1974, the nation's largest retailer of hammocks still handcrafts all its products in North Carolina—a real "Made in America" story. Its stores are very welcoming, inviting you to relax on the many hammocks, swings, and rope chairs spread across the decks, lawns, and porches featured at each location, and to stay as long you like. Stores are located in Duck (252-261-1062), at 1212 NC 12, with a great deck on the sound; in Corolla (252-453-4611), at TimBuck II; in Kill Devil Hills (252-441-6115), at MP 9.5 Bypass; and in Point Harbor (252-491-5181), on the Currituck mainland on US 158. At the Kill Devil Hills location, you can see the company's full line on display and watch hammocks being made.

Soundfeet Shoes (www.soundfeet.com). The only full-service shoe stores on the Banks, Soundfeet carries all the top brands and styles, from sheepskin boots to sandals. Find stores in Duck (252-261-0490), at 1194 NC 12; and Nags Head (252-441-8954), at the Croatan Center, MP 14.

Try My Nuts (www.trymynuts.com). Local company, home of "the world's hottest nuts," hovers on the edge of fame for its Dirty White Trash snack mix. Three locations on the Banks, in Corolla at TimBuck II (252-453-4955); in Duck at Scarborough Lane Shoppes (252-261-0900); and in Kill Devil Hills (252-449-9022), at MP 8.5.

July: **Fourth of July Parade and Community Social** (www.townofduck.com), Duck Town Park. The 1-mile annual parade does not travel down NC 12, instead making its winding way along side streets.

October: **Duck Jazz Festival** (www.duckjazz.com), Duck Town Park. Free admission.

November: **Advice 5K Turkey Trot** (www.outerbanksrunningclub.org). Thanksgiving Day fun run.

SOUTHERN SHORES

IN 1947, NATURALIST FRANK STICK established the Kitty Hawk Land Company and began the first planned community on the Outer Banks, Southern Shores. Interested buyers were advised to cross the Wright Memorial Bridge and turn left at the ocean, directions that still hold true today. This left turn onto NC 12 leads through the heart of the original development, today an incorporated town in Dare County. The 4-square-mile community stretches from the oceanfront to the sound. Many of the largest homes are built along the sound side, and many year-round residents live here. Most vacation rentals are located closer to the ocean, along NC 12.

Scattered between the newer cottages are some survivors of the original homes built by Stick and his son David, who took over the company in 1955. Designed to withstand the local weather, these are generally flat-topped houses built of concrete made with local sand. Inside, they are paneled in native juniper (white cedar). David Stick took a great interest in Southern Shores, laying out many of the roads himself to take full advantage of the contour of the land. Today, the community is known for its natural beauty, with roads winding between tall pines, dogwoods, and live oaks draped with Spanish moss. Beautiful lagoons and canals intertwine along the sound.

> **DID YOU KNOW?** David Stick (1919–2009) was the foremost authority on Outer Banks history, authoring several books on the area, including *Graveyard of the Atlantic,* *The Ash Wednesday Storm,* and *The Outer Banks of North Carolina,* considered the definitive work on the region's history. His huge collection of books, maps, and papers are available to the public at the Outer Banks History Center in Manteo.

The local civic association owns and maintains the town's beach accesses and other community resources. No one can park a car inside the town limits except residents, property holders, and those renting cottages here, keeping the beaches free of crowds.

GUIDANCE Information on Southern Shores and Duck can be found at the Dare County welcome centers. The closest is the **Aycock Brown Welcome Center** (1-877-629-4386; www.outerbanks.org), located at MP 1 in Kitty Hawk on US 158.

For more on local ordinances, check in with the **Town of Southern Shores** (252-261-2394; www.southernshores.org), 5375 N. Virginia Dare Trail, Southern Shores.

POST OFFICE The nearest post offices are in Duck and Kitty Hawk. The zip code for all of Southern Shores is 27949.

GETTING THERE Southern Shores actually begins at the foot of the US 158 bridge from the mainland and runs down the north side of US 158 to its intersection with NC 12. All of the businesses in Southern Shores are located along this stretch of highway and at the junction of the two highways.

NC 12, called Ocean Boulevard at the south end of Southern Shores, then changing to Duck Road at the northern end, runs the entire length of the town from Kitty Hawk to Duck.

GETTING AROUND *By Bicycle:* While Southern Shores is a planned community, most of it is not gated. A system of bike trails, both paved and unpaved, runs throughout Southern Shores, connecting on the north with the Duck Path and to the south with US 158. These provide the best way to explore this unique beach community.

A map of multiuse bike paths can be found on the Southern Shores town website (www.southern shores.org) on the town parking areas map. A paved bike path runs along the southern side of US 158 from the Wright Memorial Bridge all the way to the junction with NC 12, then along NC 12 all the way to the Duck town border.

Parking is available in the Marketplace Shopping Center on the north side of US 158 and at Southern Shores Crossing Shopping Center at the corner where NC 12 turns off to the north.

MEDICAL EMERGENCY You can reach **Surf Rescue** directly at 252-599-2922.

✳ To See

OBX ARTspace (252-261-2787; www.obxartspace.com), 1 Ocean Boulevard, Southern Shores Crossing. Watch artists Bob Walker and Katy Caroline at work creating their locally themed paintings at this working art studio and gallery. The gallery also displays painted furniture, painted glassware, wooden bowls, pottery, and jewelry created by local artists, including Wendy Sisler of Family Jewels in Hatteras. Katy Caroline hosts popular Sip N Dip workshops where you can create your own work of art. Fridays are sale day.

✳ To Do

BOATING A boat launching area for Southern Shore residents and guests is located off Dogwood Trail on Currituck Sound.

FOR FAMILIES The privacy, low-traffic neighborhoods, uncrowded beaches, and residential quality of Southern Shores make it a favorite with families, especially those with young children. A community playground, basketball court, and soccer field can be found at ✐ **Sea Oats Park.** The ✐ **Soundside Wading Beach** off N. Dogwood Trail has a playground and picnic area. The water here is shallow and suitable for young children. Both facilities are under the management of the Southern Shores Civic Association.

GOLF Duck Woods Country Club (252-261-2609; www.duckwoodscc.com), 50 S. Dogwood Trail. Semiprivate course designed by Ellis Maples accepts public play on a limited basis. The course's traditional layout is sheltered by trees along the fairways, making this a good choice for windy days. Duck Woods is most easily accessed from US 158.

SPA Diva's Day Spa and Salon (252-255-1772; www.divasdayspa.com), 1 Ocean Boulevard, Southern Shores Crossing. Massages, facials and peels, waxing, plus full services for hair, feet, and nails, are offered at this award-winning spa. Couple's massages available.

✳ Green Space

BEACHES You must have a town parking tag to park in any of the parking lots at beach accesses in Southern Shores. No parking is permitted on the streets. You cannot drive on the beach here. Fires and fireworks are also prohibited. Dogs can go on the beach between 6 PM and 9 AM from May 15 to September 15, anytime the rest of the year. Pets must be leashed at all times. Lifeguards are stationed at the Hillcrest Drive, East Dogwood, and Chicahauk Trail beach accesses from May 1 to October 15.

✳ Lodging

Available vacation lodging in Southern Shores is composed entirely of cottages, most close to the ocean along NC 12. While many realty companies represent one or two properties in town, the original Southern Shores realty company founded in 1947 offers the greatest selection, including some of the original "flat-tops."

🐾 ♿ (ᵩ) **Southern Shores Realty** (252-261-2000 or 1-800-334-1000; www.southernshores .com), 5 Ocean Boulevard. This real estate company handles 400 rentals in Southern Shores, including some long-term rentals and partial-week stays.

✳ Where to Eat

DINING OUT ♈ **Coastal Provisions Wine Bar & Café** (252-480-0023; www.coastal provisionsmarket.com), 1 Ocean Boulevard, Southern Shores Crossing. Several evenings each week, dim lighting and romantic music transform the wine shop into a sweet spot to dine on antipasti, small plates, fresh seafood, prime steaks, and other goodies drawn from the shelves of this gourmet market. Over 20 wines are available by the glass, or select a bottle from the surrounding shelves and enjoy it at retail prices. Reservations suggested. $–$$$.

EATING OUT (ᵩ) **Bonnie's Bagels Deli Cafe** (252-255-2888; www.cateringobx.com), MP 2, US 158, The Marketplace. Bagels and breads are made from scratch daily here, then turned into sandwiches and subs for breakfast and lunch, topped with hand-blended cream cheese, Boar's Head meats, and house-made salads. Espresso bar and free Wi-Fi make this a good morning hangout. Breakfast and lunch $.

✐ ♈ **Coastal Provisions Oyster Bar and Deli** (252-480-0023; www.coastalprovisionsmarket .com), 1 Ocean Boulevard, Southern Shores Crossing. During the summer months, the patio at Coastal Provisions becomes an open-air eatery serving oysters on the half shell, Atlantic red crab, and a variety of steamed and fried seafood, plus the market's famous crabcakes and gourmet deli sandwiches. Live music some evenings. Year-round, you can pick up the same deli sandwiches, plus a wide variety of gourmet groceries, wines, and chef-prepared dishes, to go inside this full-service store. $–$$.

FAST FACT: Atlantic deep-sea red crab is a new sustainable seafood just getting started in the market. Caught with special traps in the deep, cold waters along the edge of the Continental Shelf, the crabs are fished commercially from New England to the waters off Cape Hatteras. The fishery has been certified as sustainable by the Marine Stewardship Council. These tasty crustaceans have sweet red meat, similar in texture to a Dungeness crab, and are challenging lobster as a favorite seafood at some restaurants.

PIZZA AND TAKE-OUT ❋ **The Pizza Stop** (252-261-7867; www.pizzastopobx.com), 5385 N. Virginia Dare Trail, Sandy Ridge Center. Hand-tossed New York–style thin-crust pizza is baked in a stone oven. Organic toppings are available. Hoagies on Amoroso rolls, salads, and pasta dishes made with organic marinara fill out the menu. Best of all, this pizzeria delivers for free from Duck to Kill Devil Hills—and will deliver beer with your order.

Shun Xing (252-261-0202), MP 1, US 158, The Marketplace. Classic Chinese dishes to eat in or take out.

❋ Selective Shopping

All of the retail in Southern Shores is concentrated along its southern edge. No free-standing retail exists in this community once you start up NC 12.

Southern Shores Crossing, where NC 12 splits with US 158, is the town's premiere shopping destination, with high-end restaurants, shops, and services. Most notable is **Coastal Provisions,** a foodie destination on this end of the Banks (see *Dining Out*).

The Marketplace, located on US 158 across from the Walmart, is anchored by a Food Lion grocery, plus a CVS pharmacy and a UPS store. Here you'll find a **Starbucks** (252-255-0790); **Rita's Ice** (252-441-4237; www.ritasice.com), with lots of wonderful cold treats; **Cosmo's Pizzeria** (252-261-8388; www.cosmospizzaobx.com), an off-shoot of the popular Corolla store; a Chinese take-out place; and **Bonnie's** bagel bakery (see *Eating Out*).

Sandy Ridge Center (5385 N. Virginia Dare Trail), located across from the Home Depot, is a smaller shopping area, home to a **Tropical Smoothie Café** (252-441-9996; www.tropicalsmoothie .com), with several healthy menu options, and the **Pizza Stop** (see *Eating Out*).

SPECIAL SHOPS Goodwill Community Foundation Store (252-255-5111; www.goodwillenc.org), 5381 N. Virginia Dare Trail. Located next to the Southern Shores Town Hall, this is a great place to pick up some gently used clothes, toys, and books to read on the beach.

CURRITUCK COUNTY AND ELIZABETH CITY

ON THE NORTHERN SIDE of the Wright Memorial Bridge, the mainland of Currituck County is the gateway to the Central Beaches. Here US 158 and NC 168, known as the Caratoke Highway, run along the west bank of Currituck Sound, providing the most direct route to the Banks from Norfolk and points north. Locals consider this area "north of the bridge" an extension of the Outer Banks, and, as property values on the Banks themselves have soared, some businesses have relocated there. It's a region of many farms, as well as shopping opportunities, often with prices less than you'll find on the beaches. Many of the area's golf courses are located here as well.

A ferry connects Currituck with Knotts Island, one of the most isolated parts of the Outer Banks, today a hot spot for wineries.

US 158 branches off from NC 168 and heads inland to historic Elizabeth City, one of the most charming and welcoming ports along the Atlantic Intracoastal Waterway (ICW), and a favorite destination for day trips and weekend getaways.

GUIDANCE Currituck County Welcome Center (252-435-2947 or 1-877-287-7488; www.visit currituck.com), 106 Caratoke Highway/NC 168, Moyock. Located on the Virginia border, this regional welcome center is on the most direct route from the Norfolk airport.

Dismal Swamp Welcome Center (252-771-8333 or 1-877-771-8333; www.dismalswampwelcome center.com). Located about 3 miles south of the Virginia border and 15 miles north of Elizabeth City, this North Carolina welcome center on both US 17/US 158 and the Dismal Swamp Canal offers exhibits on the history of the swamp and canal, information on regional destinations, moorings for boats traveling the ICW, friendly advice, and restrooms. A ♿ pedestrian bridge leads from the parking lot across the canal to the ♿ **Dismal Swamp State Park Welcome Center** (252-771-6593; www.ncparks.gov).

Elizabeth City Area Information Center (252-335-5330 or 1-866-324-8948; www.discover elizabethcity.com), 400 S. Water Street, Elizabeth City.

SWEET SPOTS TO SHOP ON THE BANKS

Forbes Candy & Gift Shop (1-800-626-5898; www.forbescandies.com). This company, founded back in 1930 in Virginia Beach and still based there, sells candies you may recognize from your childhood, including watermelon slices, fruit jellies, 15 flavors of saltwater taffy, fudge, peanut brittle, seafoam, and a variety of nostalgic penny candies. Four Forbes locations are on the Outer Banks: at MP 8, MP 9.5, and MP 15.5 on the Bypass in Kill Devil Hills and Nags Head; and in Waves Village in Rodanthe.

The Fudgery (www.fudgeryfudge.com). This national chain born on the Outer Banks over 30 years ago originated "fudge theater," where the audience sings for its fudge as the chocolate boils in a big copper kettle. Today in over a dozen states, the Fudgery has four locations on the Outer Banks: in Corolla, at the Shoppes at Currituck Club (252-453-8882) and TimBuck II (252-261-8882); in Duck, at Scarborough Faire (252-261-8283); and in Nags Head, at Jockey's Ridge Crossing (252-480-0163). On hot days, order the chiller fudge, with your choice of fudge blended into ice cream.

GETTING THERE People headed for vacations on the Outer Banks by either air or automobile all funnel through the mainland in northeast North Carolina. NC 168 (VA 168, the Chesapeake Expressway toll road, in Virginia) is the most direct route to the Outer Banks from the Norfolk and Newport News/Williamsburg airports, as well as from the I-95 corridor via I-64. The toll road ends at the North Carolina border, but NC 168 continues south, joining up with US 158 in Barco. It's about 42 miles from the Virginia border to the Wright Memorial Bridge and Kitty Hawk. This area will become increasingly prominent with the completion of the Mid-Currituck toll bridge connecting the mainland directly with the north beaches in the area of Corolla, due for completion in 2018.

An alternate (and free) route from Virginia follows US 17/158, running next to the historic Dismal Swamp Canal as far as Elizabeth City. There, US 158 heads east to its junction with NC 168, then south to the Wright Memorial Bridge, where it becomes the Bypass, focus of Outer Banks development.

Private pilots have a couple of choices among general aviation airports in the area:

Currituck Regional Airport (ONX) (252-453-8032 or 252-453-2876; www.co.currituck.nc.us), Maple. Public-use general aviation facility located off US 158 has a 5,500-foot concrete runway. Facilities include an Automated Weather Observing System, self-service fuel, free overnight tie-downs, and a new terminal. Hang gliding available.

Elizabeth City–Pasquotank Regional Airport (ECG) (252-335-5634; www.ecgairport .com), Elizabeth City. Full-service facility shares its 7,200-foot runway with the U.S. Coast Guard. Rental cars, 24-hour fuel service, pilot's lounge and flight planning room, courtesy car, and tie-downs available.

GETTING AROUND *By Boat:* Two routes are available for boaters arriving from the north down the Intracoastal Waterway. The **Dismal Swamp Canal,** originally chartered by George Washington, is the older and more scenic route. It is suitable for shallow draft vessels. The **Albemarle and Chesapeake Canal,** farther east, is the route used by most commercial and larger vessels. Both end near the friendly harbor of **Elizabeth City** (252-335-5330 or 1-866-324-8948; www.discoverelizabethcity.com), nicknamed the Harbor of Hospitality for its free docks and welcoming attitude. From here, boaters can continue to the ports of the Outer Banks.

ELIZABETH CITY IS RENOWNED AMONG BOATERS FOR ITS HOSPITALITY.

THE DISMAL SWAMP CANAL

One of the most scenic sections of the Intra-coastal Waterway, and certainly the most historic, is the Dismal Swamp Canal. Begun in 1793 by a group of investors that included George Washington, the canal connects Albemarle Sound with Chesapeake Bay. Along the way it traverses a great cypress swamp that stretches across the Virginia–North Carolina border. US 17 parallels the canal for much of its length.

The Great Dismal Swamp served as an escape route and refuge for enslaved indi-viduals during the years before the Civil War and today is recognized as part of the National Underground Railway Network to Freedom. The canal's strategic position caused Union forces to try to destroy the locks during the Civil War. The Battle of

THE DISMAL SWAMP CANAL IS PART OF THE INTRACOASTAL WATERWAY.

South Mills was fought nearby. In 2008, 14,000 acres within North Carolina became the **Dismal Swamp State Park.** The visitors center, a few miles south of the state border along US 17, gives visitors access to 16 miles of hiking and mountain-bike trails. The canal is also popular for kayaking and canoeing. At the annual **Paddle for the Border** held in early May, hundreds of craft make the run from South Mills, North Carolina, to Chesapeake, Virginia. For more informa-tion, contact the **Dismal Swamp Welcome Center** (252-771-8333 or 1-877-771-8333; www .dismalswampwelcomecenter.com).

By Car: Most people find an automobile essential for travel through this area. Numerous rental car companies serve the airports in the Hampton Roads area of Virginia.

✳ To See

✿ **Arts of the Albemarle Center** (252-338-6455; www.artsofthealbemarle.com), 516 E. Main Street, Elizabeth City. Housed in a historic building, once the city's premier department store, the center houses a gallery displaying works by over 200 artists and craftspeople, special exhibits of local and national artists, and the Maguire Theatre, an intimate 250-seat performance space.

Currituck County Public Library Art Exhibit (252-453-8345; www.co.currituck.nc.us), 4261 US 158, Barco. Exhibits organized by the Currituck County Arts Council hangs in the library's meet-ing room.

Grave Digger Dungeon (252-453-4121; www.gravedigger.com), 5650 US 158, Poplar Branch. Fans visiting the home of the legendary monster truck can have their pictures taken sitting in the Grave Digger and pick up logo merchandise. Check the website for scheduled autograph sessions and appearances by Dennis or Adam Anderson.

Historic Jarvisburg Colored School (252-453-8234; www.historicjarvisburgcoloredschool.com), 7300 US 158, Jarvisbug. The historic school that educated the African American community from 1868 to 1950 has been restored and is on the National Register of Historic Places. It will house a museum dedicated to local history.

✿ **Museum of the Albemarle** (252-335-1453; www.museumofthealbemarle.com), 501 S. Water Street, Elizabeth City. A wealth of artifacts and exhibits, including one of the area's oldest surviving wooden buildings, explore the history and culture of the 16-county northeast North Carolina region, from Native American times to the present. An early shad boat, the official state boat of North Car-olina, hangs in the museum lobby. Free.

A TRADITONAL SHAD BOAT HANGS IN THE LOBBY OF THE MUSEUM OF THE ALBEMARLE IN ELIZABETH CITY.

⚓ **Port Discover** (252-338-6117; www.port discover.org), 611 E. Main Street, Elizabeth City. Hands-on science center offers programs for all ages, from toddlers to adults. Exhibits help kids learn while having fun.

TCOM (252-330-5555; www.tcomlp.com), 190 TCOM Drive, Elizabeth City. TCOM builds airships (also known as blimps) at a huge facility just outside of Elizabeth City. Tours, offered on Wednesday afternoons, must be arranged in advance.

✳ To Do

BICYCLING Dismal Swamp Welcome Center (252-771-8333 or 1-877-771-8333; www .dismalswampwelcomecenter.com). You can borrow a bike (for free) to ride across the pedestrian bridge and explore the 18 miles of trails in the state park on the other side of the canal. The state park also rents mountain bikes at very low hourly rates.

GOLF Carolina Club (252-453-3588; www.the carolinaclub.com), 127 Carolina Club Drive, Grandy. A local favorite, just 15 minutes north of the bridge, is noted for its fine putting surfaces.

Goose Creek Golf and Country Club (252-453-4008; www.obxgolfgoosecreek.com), 6562 US 158, Grandy.

Holly Ridge Golf Course (252-491-2893; www.hollyridgeobx.com), 8818 US 158, Harbinger. This is the closest mainland course to Kitty Hawk, just 1.5 miles north of the bridge.

Kilmarlic Golf Club (252-491-5465; www.kilmarlicgolfclub.com), 215 West Side Lane, Powells Point. Three miles north of the bridge, this is the newest course in the area and a beauty.

The Pointe Golf Club (252-491-8388; www.thepointegolfclub.com), 308 Point Golf Club Drive, Powells Point. Located 3.5 miles north of the bridge. Designed by Russell Breeden, this was the first course in the country to use A1 bent grass greens.

HANG GLIDING ♿ Kitty Hawk Kites Tandem Gliding (1-877-359-8447; www.kittyhawk.com), Currituck County Airport. You are towed behind an ultralight plane to altitudes from 2,000 feet up to a mile high, then released to descend in lazy circles with no sound but the wind, as you get a unique perspective on the Banks. No experience is necessary for tandem gliding, and the activity is handicapped accessible.

KAYAKING One of the best paddles in the region is along the tea-colored waters of the historic Dismal Swamp Canal. You can put in next to the pedestrian bridge across the canal at the **Dismal Swamp Welcome Center** (252-771-8333; www.dismalswampwelcomecenter.com), about 15 miles north of Elizabeth City. The **Dismal Swamp State Park** (252-771-6593; www.ncparks.gov) rents canoes and kayaks for $5 an hour.

River City Outfitters (252-340-0900; www.perquimansriveroutfitters.com), Charles Creek Park, 719 Riverside Avenue, Elizabeth City.

On Knotts Island, **Stillwater Touring Company** (252-429-2089), 101 Shepherds Way, offers kayak instruction, rentals, and tours.

SKATEBOARDING Maple Skate Park (252-232-3007; www.visitcurrituck.com), Maple Airport Complex, 2826 US 158, Currituck. Designed by Grindline, a world leader in creating skate parks, this free county park on the mainland receives rave reviews for its 11-foot keyhole and pool coping. Helmets and elbow and knee pads required. The park also has a tot playground, a fitness trail, grills for picnics, and a paved walking trail that circles a fishing lake.

✴ Green Space

Dismal Swamp State Park (252-771-6593; www.ncparks.gov), 2294 US 17 North, South Mills. This section of the Great Dismal Swamp in North Carolina is crossed by 18 miles of logging roads and trails suitable for hiking or mountain biking. The area is a noted birding area, and the stands of Atlantic white cedar on the western edge of the park are home to a population of Hessel's Hairstreak, a rare butterfly species dependent on this tree. The park's visitors center houses exhibits on the history and ecology of the area. Several trails begin here, including the ♿ **Swamp Boardwalk** and the **Supple-Jack Trail,** where you may glimpse the remains of illegal stills half hidden in the woods. A replica still is located at the junction with Canal Road. Mountain bikes for riding the trails, and canoes and kayaks for paddling the Dismal Swamp Canal, are available for very low rates.

Mackay Island National Wildlife Refuge (252-429-3100; www.fws.gov/mackayisland), Marsh Causeway, NC 615, Knotts Island. Biking, hiking, paddling, fishing, crabbing, and bird-watching opportunities abound here. This is a stop on the Charles Kuralt Trail.

✴ Lodging

BED & BREAKFAST INN ♂ **Culpepper Inn** (252-335-9235; www.culpepperinn.com), 609 W. Main Street, Elizabeth City. Located in the heart of Elizabeth City's historic district, this welcoming inn is the perfect base for exploring the city. $$.

CAMPGROUND Sandy Point Resort Campground (252-429-3094; www.sandypointresort campground.com), 176 Sandy Point Drive, Knotts Island. Full RV hookups, rental cabins, and trailers available, plus a boat ramp and fishing supplies. Camping $; cabins $$.

✴ Where to Eat

EATING OUT Bay-Villa Marina and Pearl's Bay-Villa Restaurant (252-429-3559), 112 Bay-Villa Lane, Knotts Island. Full-service restaurant and lounge on the shores of Knotts Island Bay at the end of Brumley Road. $–$$.

♂ **Currituck BBQ Company** (252-453-6618; www.currituckbbq.com), 4467 US 158, Barco. Classic barbecue and Southern sides are cooked on-site. $–$$.

Knotts Island Market (252-429-3305), 395 Knotts Island Road, Knotts Island. Established in 1937, this store carries a little bit of everything and is the only gas station on the island. The deli serves quick meals all day. $.

Southland Trade Corporation (252-435-6247; www.southlandtrade.com), 141 NC 168, Moyock. Located close to the Virginia border, the restaurant here is a great place to stop for a first (or last) taste of NorthCarolina–style barbecue. You can fill your tank with gas and your backseat with gifts here as well. $.

♞ ↪ **The Weeping Radish Farm Brewery & Eco Farm** (252-491-5205; www.weeping radish.com), 6810 US 158, Grandy. Formerly located in Manteo, the Weeping Radish is North Carolina's oldest microbrewery, founded in 1986. Its new 24-acre location in Jarvisburg allowed the business to expand its operations into sustainable agriculture. The Farmer to Fork Natural Foods Market offers organic vegetables; as well as hormone- and antibiotic-free beef, pork, and chicken from local farms; smoked local fish; and nitrate-free homemade sausages, bacon, pastrami, and award-winning sweet potato liver pâté; plus fresh beer brewed in accordance with the strict Bavarian purity laws. Meals featuring these products, including sausage sampler platters and German dinner entrées, are served in the Weeping Radish Pub. Brewery tours are available. Lunch $; dinner $–$$.

FARMER'S MARKETS AND VEGETABLE STANDS A couple of produce stands are located on the Beaches, but most of the farming action is just over the Wright Memorial Bridge in Currituck County. There you'll find farm stands selling sweet white corn, vine-ripened tomatoes, strawberries, blueberries, blackberries, melons, tree-ripened peaches, and other fruits, plus some more exotic items such as herbs and honey. Farm stands line the Caratoke Highway (NC 168/US 158) from the Virginia line all the way to the Wright Memorial Bridge. All are open seasonally, so it's a good idea to call ahead for hours and availability.

> **QUICK TIP:** Stop by the Weeping Radish on your way to the Banks to pick up a Grill Box of all-natural sausages to cook on the grill at your vacation cottage. It makes a nice change from fish.

KNOTTS ISLAND: BETWEEN TWO STATES

One of the most isolated communities on the East Coast lies on an island caught between North Carolina and Virginia. Connected by a causeway to Virginia, Knotts Island is actually a part of North Carolina's Currituck County, although the only connection is by boat. A free state-run ferry takes 45 minutes to reach this island, surrounded by marsh in Currituck Sound. From the ferry dock, NC 615 travels a dozen miles north to the Virginia border and then on to Pungo, Virginia, just south of Virginia Beach. Several boat tours also visit the island from the Corolla area of the Outer Banks, just a few miles across the sound.

Once known as the home of duck-hunting preserves, Knotts Island today is a quiet, friendly community. Peaches are the biggest crop here, and the community hosts an annual peach festival in July. The actual name of the town on Knotts Island is Fruitville.

The ducks and snow geese still come by the thousands, finding a winter home in Mackay Island National Wildlife Refuge along the Virginia border. The land was once the estate of publishing magnate and philanthropist Joseph P. Knapp, founder of Ducks Unlimited, the organization that has done more than any other to preserve the great migrating flocks for future generations. Throughout the refuge, hiking trails and observation decks invite visitors to see the rich wildlife that made this part of the world famous. You can find out more about this unique community at its website, www.knottsislandon line.com.

MARSHES AT THE MACKAY ISLAND WILDLIFE REFUGE HARBOR NUMEROUS WATERFOWL.

Downtown Waterfront Market (252-338-0169; www.downtownwaterfrontmarket.com), Mariners Wharf, S. Water Street, Elizabeth City. Saturday-morning markets feature local foods, cooking and craft demonstrations, and live music, spring through fall.

Grandy Farm Market (252-453-2658), 6264 US 158, Grandy. Free samples and local peaches.

Morris Farm Market (252-453-2837), 3784 NC 168, Barco. This market, featuring melons, ciders, tomatoes, and homemade canned goods, has a great collection of tractors.

The Peach Basket (252-429-3317), 208 South End Road, Knotts Island. Peaches, plums, nectarines, pears, and apples, along with jams, jellies, peach pies, and cobblers, are available in season.

☞ Point Harbor U-Pick Strawberries (252-491-8266), 135 James Griggs Road, off US 158, Point Harbor. Season runs late April to mid-June.

☞ Roberts Ridge Farm Market (252-202-9665), 489 N. Indiantown Road, at US 158, Shawboro. Farmer's market specializing in sweet corn. Cornfield maze in the fall.

☞ Watkins Apiary (252-429-3134 or 757-563-2275), 121 Wade Cove Lane, Knotts Island. Honey fresh from the hive available in summer, and kiwis in winter. Tours available.

HEALTH FOODS ☞ Beach Organics (252-457-0200; www.beachorganicsinc.com), 6622 US 158, Grandy. Full-service health-food store carries vitamins and supplements, pet supplies, natural and organic meats, gluten-free products, and local produce. You can also order and pick

GRAPE VINES GROW WELL ON KNOTTS ISLAND.

up dishes prepared by **Chef Amy Huggins** (www.outerbanksepicurean.com), featuring whole foods, wild-caught seafood, organic produce, and no GMOs (genetically modified organisms).

SEAFOOD I Got Your Crabs (252-207-GOTM; www.igotyourcrabs.com), Border Station, 101 NC 168, Moyock. Stock up on crabs near the Virginia border. Open weekends, Memorial Day through October. Sister restaurant in Kitty Hawk.

Rose Produce & Seafood Market (252-453-2911), 6378 US 158, Grandy. Mr. Rose catches the shrimp, blue crabs, flounder, and scallops sold here.

WINE Martin Vineyards (252-429-3542 or 252-429-3564; www.martinvineyards.com), 213 Martin Farm Lane, Knotts Island. Tastings available of dry reds and whites, plus fruit wines. Pick your own apples, peaches, scuppernong grapes, and pumpkins in season.

Sanctuary Vineyards (252-491-2387; www.sanctuaryvineyards.com), 6957 US 158, Jarvisburg. Vineyards planted with Sangiovese, Norton, and French hybrids produces signature blends. Tasting room located in the Cotton Gin.

Trio Point Harbor (252-491-5311; www.obxtrio.com), 9138 US 158, Point Harbor. Formerly Native Vine, this is the sister store of the new Trio in Kitty Hawk, offering wine, beer, and gourmet food from around the world, plus daily free tastings of North Carolina wines and a huge selection of microbrews.

Art lovers should plan a visit to Elizabeth City to coincide with the **First Friday Art Walk** (www.ecdowntown.com or www.ecncart.com), when numerous downtown galleries and shops host open house events beginning at 5:30 PM. Special kids' Art Walk events take place at Port Discover.

✳ Entertainment

✦ **Dennis Anderson's Muddy Motorsports Park** (252-453-8586; www.dammpark.com), 5243 US 158, Aydlett. Mud Sports weekend competitions include monster trucks, teeny-man stunts, power wheel races, and carnival rides. Weekend camping available.

Weekly Acoustic Wine-Down (252-491-2387; www.sanctuaryvineyards.com). Free evening concerts on Thursday evenings at Sanctuary Vineyards and the Cotton Gin. Late May through September.

Selective Shopping

ANTIQUES US 158, the Caratoke Highway, has earned another name among lovers of all things old: **Antique Alley.** Numerous antiques stores and malls line the road north of the bridge, inviting shoppers to stop and browse.

Coinjock Antiques (252-453-0453), 4901 US 158, Coinjock.

✤ **Lammers Glass Gifts & Antiques** (252-491-2303; www.lammersglass.com), 7715 US 158, Powells Point. Area's largest selection of stained glass, plus antique advertising signs, a museum-quality collection of "petroliana" (antique gas station signs, pumps, and maps), blown glass balls, soy candles, and more.

BOOKS ✦ **Page After Page Bookstore** (252-335-7243; www.pageafterpagebook.com), 111 S. Water Street, Elizabeth City. Independent bookstore hosts many community events, including book signings and readings. Special kids' area has books and trains.

SPECIAL SHOPS Beach Bums (252-453-0502; www.beachbumsobx.com), 4402 US 158, Barco. Gallery carries many works by local artists, plus unique gifts and home decor.

Carolina Christmas Shoppe (252-435-0528; www.carolinachristmasshoppe.com), 384 NC 168, Moyock.

Cotton Gin (252-491-2387; www.cottongin.com), 6957 US 158, Jarvisburg. Expansive shop houses a wide range of country and coastal themed decor, clothing, and gifts, plus a historic cotton gin. Complimentary tastings of Sanctuary wines are offered on weekends. Additional locations in Corolla (252-453-4446), at TimBuck II; and in Nags Head (252-449-2387), at MP 14.5 Bypass.

Nolte Surfboards (252-491-2590; www.timnoltesurfboards.com), 8576 US 158, Powells Point. Top shaper Tim Nolte presents his own lines of surfboards and stand-up paddle boards.

✤ **Outer Banks Harley-Davidson** (252-338-8866; www.outerbankshd.com), 8739 US 158, Harbinger. You can rent a Harley here to tour the Banks or schedule a test ride. The showroom features the history of transportation circa 1903 with a Wright brothers replica flyer overhead and an exact duplicate of the original Harley-Davidson backyard garage.

✳ Special Events

April: **North Carolina Governor's Cup Mothboat Regatta** (www.mothboat.com), Elizabeth City harbor.

May: **Paddle for the Border** (www.dismalswampwelcomecenter.com), Dismal Swamp Canal. **The Burg: Currituck Food and Wine Festival** (www.sanctuaryvineyards.com), Cotton Gin, Jarvisburg. **NC Potato Festival** (www.ncpotatofestival.com), downtown Elizabeth City. The Miss Tater Tot contest, Lucky Duck Derby, potato peeling contest, music, dancing, craft fair, amusement rides, and food on the waterfront.

June–July: **Mariners Wharf Film Festival** (www.marinerswharffilmfestival.com). Free classic films are screened weekly outside in downtown Elizabeth City. Kidz Flix are scheduled once a month during the summer.

July: **Knotts Island Peach Festival** (www.knottsislandonline.com).

September: **Currituck Wildlife Festival** (www.visitcurrituck.com), Currituck High School. Local decoy carvers, wildlife artists, decoy collections, and local food celebrate the duck hunting traditions of the region. **Currituck Fall Food & Wine Festival** (www.sanctuaryvineyards.com), Cotton Gin, Jarvisburg. **Classic Mothboat National Championship** (www.mothboat.com), Elizabeth City harbor.

October: **Dismal Day and 5K Run** (www.ncparks.gov), Dismal Swamp State Park. ✎ 🐾 **Bark in Maple Park** (www.currituckanimallovers.org), Maple Park, next to the Currituck Airport. Dog costume contest and festival with live music benefits the local animal shelter. **Elizabeth City First In Flight Festival** (www.ecfirstinflight.com), Elizabeth City Regional Airport. Includes a candy drop commemorating the Berlin Airlift.

November: **The Big Curri-Shuck** (www.sanctuaryvineyards.com), Cotton Gin, Jarvisburg. All-you-can-eat steamed crabs and oysters, plus a wine sampling. **Downtown Holiday Celebration and Grand Illumination** (www.ecdowntown.com), downtown Elizabeth City.

December: **Christmas Parade & Tree Illumination** (www.visitcurrituck.com), Currituck Cooperative Extension Center, Barco. **Downtown Holiday Stroll and Jaycees Christmas Parade** (www.ecdowntown.com), downtown Elizabeth City.

The Central Beaches 2

KITTY HAWK

KILL DEVIL
HILLS AND
COLINGTON
ISLAND

NAGS HEAD
AND
WHALEBONE
JUNCTION

SOUTH BODIE
ISLAND AND
OREGON
INLET

THE CENTRAL BEACHES
Kitty Hawk to Oregon Inlet

ONE HUNDRED YEARS AGO, tall sand dunes, migrating with the wind, dominated the landscape. Today, this is the most accessible—and the most visited—region of North Carolina's Outer Banks. On this part of the coast, you will find the greatest variety of accommodations, the most restaurants, and the most active nightlife. These beaches have an intimate connection with the history of flight. Orville and Wilbur Wright first took to the air from a tall dune in Kill Devil Hills, a flight that changed the world. The persistent breezes that helped lift the Wright brothers into the air today make this one of the premiere destinations for air sports on the East Coast.

John Harris, an early proponent of the sport of hang gliding, established Kitty Hawk Kites in 1974. Today he heads the largest hang gliding school in the world and, with 11 locations, is one of the guiding forces on the Outer Banks. Over the years, Harris has branched out into many other sports that combine the area's unique blend of wind and water, helping to popularize surf kayaking, parasailing, and the latest extreme sport, kiteboarding. Kitty Hawk Kites sponsors numerous festivals, competitions, and workshops throughout the year. Its 35 instructors introduce 10,000 visitors annually to the thrills of hang gliding. Instruction takes place at Jockey's Ridge State Park atop the highest dune on the East Coast. After a lesson, you can spread your nylon wings to the breeze and, like Wilbur and Orville and a million birds before you, take to the sky.

The Central Beaches present two faces to the world. The most public face is the well-known beachfront, mile after mile of some of the finest sand and waves in the world. Here you'll find surfers, boogie boarders, sandcastle artists, beachcombers, and surf anglers having the time of their lives. The other, more hidden face of the Central Beaches overlooks Roanoke Sound. The marshes are full of wildlife, attracting both hunters and birdwatchers. The shallow water is perfect for Jet Skis and kayaks, while the steady winds make this an ideal location to learn to windsurf or kiteboard.

In between these two coasts, the Central Beaches hold a wealth of both history and natural wonders. The great dunes that brought the Wright brothers to this neighborhood now lift hang gliders on their own first flights. The deep maritime forests give nature lovers and birdwatchers many pleasant options.

As one of the East Coast's earliest summer getaways, the Outer Banks helped define the beach vacation. The traditions of the Central Beaches are ones of laid-back summers spent in hammocks on the cottage porch, beachcombing, and dancing in the sand on warm summer nights. With the burgeoning of the tourism industry, large hotels and condominiums have made inroads along the beachfront, but the coast here is far from being lined with high-rises, and steps have been taken to preserve reminders of the early days on the Banks. Dare County imposes a 35-foot maximum height on most new development. Numerous public beach accesses make it easy to find a quiet piece of beach, and small family-run cottage courts preserve the beach vacation of an earlier day.

TOP 10 DON'T MISS: CENTRAL BEACHES

1. Climb the tower at Jockey's Crossing for a look at both the Unpainted Aristocracy and the hang gliding action.
2. Drop a fishing line at Jennette's Pier.
3. Learn about the history of flight—from Kitty Hawk to the stars—at the Wright Brothers National Monument.
4. Climb the Jockey's Ridge dune at sunset, after exploring the secret forest at its base.
5. Bike the west shore along the road used by the Wright brothers.
6. Have breakfast at Sam and Omie's and listen to the fishing stories.
7. Score a snow cone or a soft-serve at a stand along the Beach Road.
8. Watch the fleet come in at Oregon Inlet.
9. Eat a classic Outer Banks meal at Basnight's (or Owens' or the Black Pelican).
10. Go airborne with a hang gliding lesson.

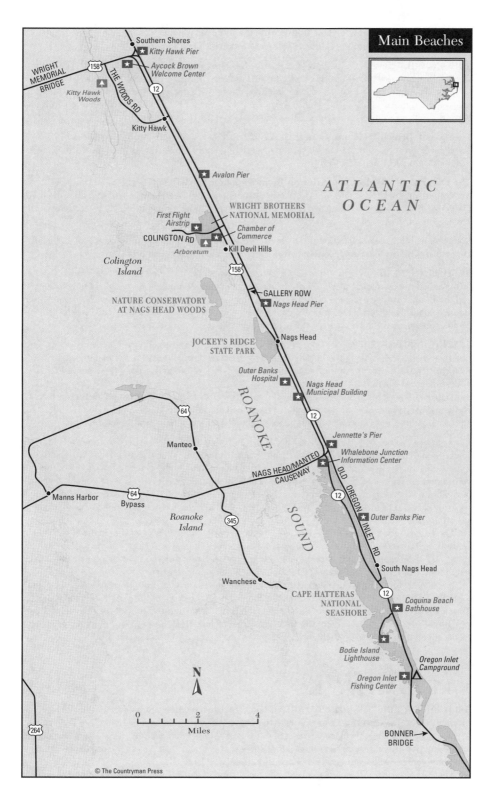

Main Beaches

ATLANTIC OCEAN

Southern Shores
Kitty Hawk Pier
158
Aycock Brown
Welcome Center
12
WRIGHT
MEMORIAL
BRIDGE
Kitty Hawk
Woods
Kitty Hawk

Avalon Pier

WRIGHT BROTHERS
NATIONAL MEMORIAL
First Flight
Airstrip
Chamber of
Commerce
COLINGTON RD
Arboretum
Kill Devil Hills

Colington
Island

158

NATURE CONSERVATORY
AT NAGS HEAD WOODS

GALLERY ROW
Nags Head Pier

JOCKEY'S RIDGE
STATE PARK

Nags Head

Outer Banks
Hospital
Nags Head
Municipal Building

ROANOKE

64

Manteo

12

Jennette's Pier

Whalebone Junction
Information Center

NAGS HEAD/MANTEO
CAUSEWAY

64
Manns Harbor
Bypass

SOUND

12

Roanoke
Island

345

OLD OREGON INLET RD

Outer Banks Pier

Wanchese

South Nags Head

CAPE HATTERAS
NATIONAL
SEASHORE

12

Coquina Beach
Bathhouse

Bodie Island
Lighthouse

Oregon Inlet
Campground

N

Oregon Inlet
Fishing Center

0   2   4
Miles

264

BONNER
BRIDGE

© The Countryman Press

A nightlife scene is growing here as well, with the action continuing well into the night at clubs and bars, a nice addition to the traditional all-night action on the fishing piers.

GUIDANCE Two causeways, the only land accesses from the mainland to the Outer Banks, join the Central Beaches with the rest of the world. In the north, the Wright Memorial Bridge leaps Albemarle Sound, connecting Kitty Hawk and Southern Shores with mainland Currituck County. About 20 miles south, the Nags Head–Manteo Causeway leads to Roanoke Island and the Albemarle Peninsula beyond. Each approach has an Outer Banks welcome center to greet visitors.

The Aycock Brown Welcome Center (1-877-629-4386; www.outerbanks.org), located at MP 1 in Kitty Hawk, provides information for vacationers arriving on the Outer Banks from the north via the Wright Memorial Bridge (US 158).

The Outer Banks Welcome Center on Roanoke Island (252-473-2138 or 1-877-OBX-4FUN; www.outerbanks.org) is located on Roanoke Island along the US 64/264 Bypass between the Virginia Dare Memorial Bridge and the Nags Head–Manteo Causeway, providing information for visitors arriving from the west.

Both centers offer accommodation reservations, restrooms, public phones, and a picnic area. The Outer Banks welcome centers close only two days a year, on Thanksgiving and Christmas.

GETTING THERE Traveling south from the Wright Memorial Bridge, you pass through three separate incorporated towns, all part of Dare County, plus a national seashore, before reaching Oregon Inlet and the Bonner Bridge to lonely Hatteras Island. The towns may appear alike, but each has its individual personality, history, laws, and attractions. All three, Kitty Hawk, Kill Devil Hills, and Nags Head, stretch across the Banks from the ocean beaches to the waters of the sound.

GETTING AROUND *By Bicycle:* Bike riding is a popular way to get around the Central Beaches. The best bike route of all is along the beach, where you can travel for miles without encountering any motorized traffic during the summer months. However, each of the towns along the Central Beaches has excellent bike paths.

Maps of bike routes and paths are available from the **Outer Banks Welcome Centers** in Kitty Hawk and on Roanoke Island. Contact the **Wheels of Dare Bicycle Club** (252-261-3068), 6072 Currituck Road, Kitty Hawk, or one of the local bike shops for advice and more information.

By Car: Between the two causeways at Kitty Hawk and Nags Head, two highways run north and south through the Central Beaches: NC 12 and US 158, otherwise known as the Beach Road and the Bypass. The Beach Road, NC 12 and also the Virginia Dare Trail, is the older and narrower of the two, and the most scenic. Sand frequently blows in little drifts across the two lanes, there are few traffic lights, and bicycles are as popular as cars for getting around. Take your time as you drive, and you'll spot raw bars and taverns lining the west side of the road, and beach cottages about to wash into the sea on the east.

The Bypass, just a block or two west, is quite the opposite: a large, fast-moving highway with two lanes in each direction. Although not many hotels are located here, the majority of the newer retail stores and restaurants line both sides, in a sometimes bewildering procession of shopping centers and strip malls. The Bypass is officially US 158 and also the Croatan Highway.

Fortunately for visitors, the milepost system is well established along both these roads, and looking for the MP signs will speed locating your destination. MP 0 is at the foot of the Wright Memorial Bridge. The milepost distances are not quite the same on the Beach Road and Bypass, but they are helpful anyway. Street addresses can also help with locations, so we include them here. Even-numbered establishments are on the west side of the highways; odd numbers are on the east or ocean side.

KITTY HAWK

ORIGINALLY A QUIET FISHING VILLAGE and port for arriving visitors, among them the Wright brothers, Kitty Hawk became the gateway to the Outer Banks with the completion of the Wright Memorial Bridge. The old village lies west of the Bypass, hidden in a deep maritime forest and marsh, with many year-round residences set back in the trees. The Beach Road lies very close to the ocean here, and many seaside cottages have been lost to the sea.

The area appears on the earliest maps as "Chickahauk," a native Indian name meaning "goose hunting grounds," which may have evolved into both Kitty Hawk and Currituck, the county across the bridge on the mainland. Certainly, the Native Americans considered the area essential to their welfare and once complained to the colonial government when incoming settlers kept them from hunting there.

Other historians speculate that the name Kitty Hawk came from the skeeter hawk, a local name for the dragonflies that gathered to feast on the mosquitoes so plentiful in earlier days. The name Kitty Hawk was well established by the 1790s.

QUICK TIP: The Kitty Hawk Fire Department (252-261-2666; www.kitty hawkfd.com), 859 W. Kitty Hawk Road, sells T-shirts and patches featuring the Wright brothers airplane that make great souvenirs.

At the base of the Wright Memorial Bridge, MP 0, Kitty Hawk is on the south side of the highway, and Southern Shores is on the north for about 2 miles to the junction with NC 12. One of the oldest developed parts of the coast lies around Winks Store at MP 2 on the Beach Road.

GUIDANCE Be sure to stop at the **Aycock Brown Welcome Center** (1-877-629-4386; www.outer banks.org), located at MP 1 on US 158, for maps, information, and much more. Have a look at the adjacent **Monument to a Century of Flight,** designed by local artist Glenn Eure and North Carolina sculptors Hanna and Jodi Jubran.

For information on beach rules and other local regulations, visit the **Town of Kitty Hawk** (252-261-3552; www.townofkittyhawk.org) website, or the Kitty Hawk town hall, at 101 Veterans Memorial Drive.

POST OFFICE The **Kitty Hawk Post Office** (252-261-2211) is located at 3841 Bypass on the east side at Kitty Hawk Road. The zip code for Kitty Hawk is 27949.

PUBLIC RESTROOMS Public facilities are found at the Aycock Brown Welcome Center, at MP 1 on US 158; Kitty Hawk Park, on West Kitty Hawk Road; Sandy Run Park, on the Woods Road; David Paul Pruitt, Jr. Park, near the junction of US 158 and the Woods Road; and at the public boat ramp on Bob Perry Road. On the Beach Road (NC 12), public facilities are located at the Kitty Hawk Bath House, at the junction of Kitty Hawk Road next to the Black Pelican Restaurant, and at the Byrd Street beach access.

THE BEACH ROAD IN KITTY HAWK AS IT APPEARED SEVERAL HURRICANES AGO.

GETTING THERE Most visitors coming from the north cross the Wright Memorial Bridge on US 158 and proceed down US 158, called the Bypass. Alternatively, you can follow NC 12, called the Beach Road, north to Duck and Corolla, or south to Nags Head, Manteo, and Hatteras Island.

GETTING AROUND Kitty Hawk Road, beginning at the ocean and running west almost to the sound, is the major road through Kitty Hawk. It crosses US 158 (the Bypass) at about MP 4. The Woods Road turns off US 158 across from Kitty Hawk Elementary School and runs through the heart of Kitty Hawk Woods, with several parks located along its route, then joins Kitty Hawk Road.

MEDICAL EMERGENCY Regional Medical Center (252-255-6000; www.albemarlehealth .org), 5200 Bypass, MP 1.5, a facility associated with Albemarle Hospital in Elizabeth City, offers outpatient surgery, diagnostic imaging and testing, and the services of doctors representing some 20 specialties.

☀ To See

☝ ↑ **Children @ Play Museum** (252-261-0290; www.childrenatplayobx.com), 3809 Bypass, MP 4.5. Open Tuesday–Saturday. Kids can visit the Teddy Bear Wellness Center and an Open Air Market, try their hand at fishing, explore a lighthouse and a tree fort, and more. Special birthday party packages available. Admission $5; infants 12 months and under free.

& **Monument to a Century of Flight** (1-877-629-4386; www.monumenttoacenturyofflight.org). Adjacent to the Aycock Brown Welcome Center at MP 1 in Kitty Hawk, this memorial commemorates the accomplishments that led from Kitty Hawk to outer space. Stainless-steel pylons and black granite panels chronicle the 100 most significant events of the first 100 years of flight. The poem "High Flight" is engraved on a marker at the entrance. Free.

& **Old Kitty Hawk Village.** Off Kitty Hawk Road on the west side of the Bypass, turn south onto Moore Shore Drive to drive through Old Kitty Hawk, where the Wright brothers stayed when they came to the Outer Banks. A memorial marks the spot where their boardinghouse stood. Another site associated with the Wright brothers is the old **Kitty Hawk Life-Saving Station,** now the Black Pelican Restaurant.

& ↑ **USS *Kitty Hawk* Exhibit** (252-261-3552; www.townofkittyhawk.org), 101 Veterans Memorial Park Drive. Kitty Hawk's town hall displays artifacts from the supercarrier USS *Kitty Hawk* CV-63, decommissioned in 2009. The Veteran's Memorial and Memorial Park are adjacent to the town hall.

☀ To Do

BICYCLING In Kitty Hawk, the & **Pruitt Multi-Use Trail,** a separate paved path, runs along Woods Road through the maritime forest. It connects at its northern end with the Southern Shores bike path along US 158, and at its southern end with a bikeway along the wide, paved shoulders of Kitty Hawk Road. Parking is available at Pruitt Park, near the junction of US 158 and the Woods Road, and at Kitty Hawk Park, on W. Kitty Hawk Road.

From Kitty Hawk Road, head south on Moore Shore Road to find the historic village of Kitty Hawk, where the Wright brothers first stayed when they came to the Banks. Moore Shore Road leads down to the & **Wright Brothers Multi-Use Path,** which follows a historic roadbed along the sound. This bikeway, a paved road not accessible to motorized traffic, leads to Windgrass Circle and Bay Drive in Kill Devil Hills with a beautiful ride along the sound for several miles.

Another bike route through Kitty Hawk is along a multiuse path running beside Twiford and W. Kitty Hawk roads to Kitty Hawk Landing.

Farther east, Lindberg Avenue, between the highways in east Kitty Hawk, is a popular north–south biking route paralleling NC 12. The Beach Road is narrow here and not recommended for children on bikes.

Kitty Hawk Cycle Company (252-261-2060; www.kittyhawkcyclecompany.com), MP 2.5, Beach Road at Eckner Street. Repairs, rentals, and sales of beach cruisers, road and mountain bikes. Group rides for road bikers offered most days.

Moneysworth Beach Home Equipment Rentals (252-261-6999 or 1-800-833-5233; www.mworth .com), 947 W. Kitty Hawk Road. Bike rentals conveniently located near the Kitty Hawk Woods bike paths.

BOATING A Dare County public boat ramp is located on Bob Perry Road in Kitty Hawk Woods, with a picnic area, public toilets, and parking available for about 30 vehicles. The 200-foot canal leading to Kitty Hawk Bay is approximately 5 feet deep. A floating dock is provided for launching kayaks and canoes.

Dock of the Bay Marina (252-255-5578; www.dockofthebay.info). Located just beyond the public boat launch on Bob Perry Road, this marina, with easy access to Albemarle Sound, has a fuel dock, plus a convenience store with all the essentials (beer, wine, ice, snacks) as well as fishing tackle and bait.

OBX Sail (1-877-FLY-THIS; www.obxsail.com). Enjoy a daytime or sunset sail of Roanoke Sound aboard the ketch *Pomaika'i.*

☝ **Promenade Watersports** (252-261-4400; www.outerbankswatersports.net), 105 Promenade Lane, MP 0, Bypass. Rent kayaks, stand-up paddleboards, pontoon boats, fishing skiffs, Jet Skis, catamarans, and sailboats at this complex, located on the sound at the foot of the Wright Memorial Bridge.

PIER FISHING IS A TREASURED NORTH CAROLINA TRADITION.

FISHING AND HUNTING ✍ ♂ **Kitty Hawk Pier** (252-261-1290; www.hiltongardeninn.com), MP 1, Beach Road. Restored and operated by the Hilton Garden Inn, the pier house is a popular spot for events. The pier is usually open for fishing 8 AM–10 PM for a modest fee. Contact the inn for access information.

Outer Banks Fishing School (252-255-2004; www.obxfishingschool.com). Private and group lessons in saltwater sportfishing are taught by top local experts. Sound-side kayak fishing trips are available all year, all equipment included.

Outer Banks Waterfowl and Fishing Guide Service (252-261-7842; www.outerbankswaterfowl .com). Kitty Hawk resident and decoy carver Capt. Vic Berg leads fishing trips in the sound and bird-watching excursions in his flat-bottom skiff, able to navigate in the shallowest water. During the hunting seasons (usually scattered from October to January), he and his experienced guides lead dog hunts after as many as 27 different species of wildfowl.

Soundside Charters (252-475-0090 or 252-261-2551; www.soundsidecharters.com), Dock of the Bay Marina, 4200 Bob Perry Road. Go fishing or crabbing or take a sunset cruise with Capt. Chad on the lovely waters of the sound, and keep what you catch for tonight's dinner.

TW's Bait and Tackle (252-261-7848; www.twstackle.com), MP 4, Bypass; second location (252-441-4807) at MP 10.5, Bypass, Nags Head. Custom rods are a specialty at these full-service shops, which also carry hunting accessories, fish decor, and camouflage outfits for all ages.

FOR FAMILIES ✍ **Kitty Hawk Park** (252-475-5920; www.darenc.com/parksrec), 900 W. Kitty Hawk Road. New Dare County park has a 5,000-square-foot skate park, and a dog park (registration required). There's also a playground, picnic area with grills, restrooms, and a half-mile walking trail.

✍ ♂ **The Promenade** (252-261-4900; www.outerbanksfamilyfun.com), MP 0, Bypass. This 30-acre entertainment complex located at the foot of the Wright Memorial Bridge is a convenient place to cool off if you arrive before your rental house is ready. Rent a watercraft, go parasailing, play a round of minigolf, stroll out on the 600-foot pier, or check out the arcade.

✍ **Pruitt Park,** Woods Road at US 158. Small town park has play equipment for young children, a picnic area, a portable restroom, and parking.

GOLF ✐ **The Promenade** (252-261-4900; www.outerbanksfamilyfun.com), MP 0, Bypass. Practice your short game on this chip and putt course along the sound or hit a basket of balls on the full-size driving range. Young golfers like the waterfall-themed minigolf course. Golf clubs are available to rent, and the courses are lit for evening play.

⛳ **Sea Scape Golf Links** (252-261-2158; www.seascapegolf.com), 300 Eckner Street, MP 2.5, Bypass. The windswept dunes and ocean views at this links-style, par 70 public course just a block from the ocean remind many golfers of Scotland. **The Sea Scape Bar & Grill** (252-261-2243) serves breakfast, lunch, and weekend brunch. The full bar hosts live music for Friday happy hour. Pro shop on-site rents clubs.

HEALTH AND FITNESS CLUBS ❋ **Barrier Island Fitness Center** (252-261-0100; www.bistation.com), Cypress Knee Trail, MP 1, Bypass. Day and weekly passes provide access to an indoor pool, hot tub, sauna, steam room, tanning beds, massage therapists, aerobic and free weight equipment, and tennis courts, along with on-site babysitting and a cyber-arcade.

❋ **Knuckleup Family Fitness Center** (252-489-8239; www.fitnessouterbanks.com), 3712 Bypass, MP 4.5. Work out with kickboxing or jiujitsu; join a beach boot camp; or sign up for on-the-water classes from the **Outer Banks Paddle Board School.** Single classes available, or sign up for a free-week pass.

❋ **Outer Banks Yoga and Pilates** (252-480-3214; www.outerbanksyoga.com), 5230 Beach Road, MP 1.5, Ocean Centre Shops. Single, three-class, and five-class passes available. Drop-ins welcome.

KAYAKING AND CANOEING The floating dock launch facility on Bob Perry Road gives access both to Kitty Hawk Bay and a paddle trail that runs through the Kitty Hawk Woods nature preserve. The trail follows a canal, variously called High Bridge Creek, Jean Guite Creek, or Ginguite Creek, once used by loggers and opens into the sound at both ends. Narrow and lined by tall trees on either side, it is protected from the often strong winds that sweep the Banks, besides being a haven for wading birds, turtles, and other wildlife. A covered bridge, the only one in eastern North Carolina, is one of the creek's highlights. This trip is highly recommended and perfect for children and novice paddlers.

> **QUICK TIP:** To see the Kitty Hawk covered bridge without launching a kayak, take Covered Bridge Road off the Woods Road.

After launching at the Bob Perry boat ramp, paddlers have the choice of heading north, deeper into the maritime forest, or south toward the marshy islands lining Kitty Hawk Bay. Experienced paddlers can cross the sometimes choppy open waters of the bay to Colington Island (about 7 miles one-way), or follow the creek all the way north to Currituck Sound, then around Martin's Point and back along the shore (about 18 miles round-trip).

A second put-in is located at the point where High Bridge Creek crosses under US 158, near the Wright Memorial Bridge, at the **Kitty Hawk Kayaks Paddling Center** (252-261-0145; www.khkss.com), where you can rent kayaks to explore on your own or sign up for a tour. The covered bridge is located less than a mile south of the paddling center; the public boat ramp is 2 miles south.

Several outfitting companies offer tours along High Bridge Creek, considered the finest paddle on the Banks. Most launch at the Bob Perry boat ramp and head south to the marshes of Kitty Hawk Bay.

The exception is the ⚓ **Kitty Hawk Kayak and Surf School** (see *Water Sports*), which specializes in tours of the northern end of High Bridge Creek, including the covered bridge. A portion of proceeds benefits the 1% for the Planet organization (www.onepercentfortheplanet.org). Sunrise and sunset ocean kayaking tours, full-moon paddles, and overnight kayak trips to platforms around Albemarle Sound, including some key birding areas, are also available.

Outfitters offering tours of the southern end of High Bridge Creek include: **Coastal Kayak** (252-261-6262; www.outerbankskayaktours.com) and **Duck Village Outfitters** (252-261-7222; www.duckvillageoutfitters.net). **Kitty Hawk Kites** (1-877-359-8447; www.kittyhawk.com) and **Deep Country Outfitters** (252-573-1114; www.deepcountryoutfitters.com), owned by a local family, offer paddles on Kitty Hawk Bay as well as tours of the creek and marsh.

Sandy Run Park, Woods Road. Kayak and canoe launch leads to quiet paddle trails along ponds and canals in the maritime forest.

DID YOU KNOW? SUP is the abbreviation for stand-up paddleboarding, one of the fastest growing sports in the country. SUPs can be used on either ocean surf or flat water, and they make excellent substitutes for either a kayak or a surfboard. Plus they give paddlers a great core workout.

&. **Windgrass Circle Sound Access,** W. Tateway Road at Bay Drive. A good spot to launch directly into Kitty Hawk Bay.

SPAS Lotus Day Spa & Boutique (252-261-0800; www.lotusdayspaobx.com), 3810 Bypass, MP 4.5, Buccaneer's Walk. Intimate day spa specializes in Dermalogica skin care products, therapeutic massage, microdermabrasion, and pedicures and manicures.

WATER SPORTS Kitty Hawk Kites (252-261-0145; www.kittyhawk.com), 6150 Bypass, MP 1. Try a Jetpak, the latest water sports thrill, which shoots you through the sky like a character out of the *Jetsons*. Lessons take place at Promenade Watersports on the sound. Minimum age is 16.

&. **Kitty Hawk Kayak and Surf School** (252-261-0145 or 1-866-702-5061; www.khkss.com), 6150 US 158, MP 1. Experienced instructors conduct surf, kayak, and SUP (stand-up paddleboarding) clinics, private lessons, and three-day camps. Rentals are available, and used equipment is for sale at the shop. Several packages combine surfing, kayaking, and even yoga, including a "Shredder" package that combines catching waves on boards, SUPs, and surf kayaks. Kids' Coastal Explorer camps are a great value.

&. **OBX Wakeboard and Waterski** (252-256-2018; www.obxwakeboardwaterski.com), 251 N. Dogwood Trail. Wakeboarding, waterskiing, tubing, wakesurfing, kneeboarding, and sunset cocktail cruises.

Wave Riding Vehicles (252-261-7952; www.waveridingvehicles.com), 4812 Bypass, MP 2.5. WRV, the largest surfboard manufacturer on the East Coast, is located across the bridge in Currituck County and employs many top shapers. Its retail shop in Kitty Hawk carries the full line of WRV surf-, body-, skim-, snow-, and skateboards, many hard-to-find brands, and cool swim and surf wear with the popular "wave of porpoises" logo, besides offering rentals and repairs.WRV has another store in Hawai'i. You can order your custom longboard here and pick it up there.

✳ Green Space

BEACHES Kitty Hawk Beaches. Many public beach access points line NC 12 (the Beach Road) in Kitty Hawk. Bathhouses with parking and restrooms where you can shower and change are located at Byrd Street and at the large **Kitty Hawk Bath House,** also known as the Old Station Bathhouse, just south of Kitty Hawk Road. Eight other access points on the Beach Road have parking.

Handicapped access is available at several beach accesses. Beach wheelchairs are available from the **Kitty Hawk Fire Department** (252-261-2666; www.kittyhawkfd.com).

Lifeguards are on duty at the Byrd Street, Eckner Street, and Kitty Hawk Bath House accesses from Memorial Day to September 30. Roving beach patrols also keep watch. Driving, glass, fires, and fireworks are all prohibited.

Dogs are permitted on Kitty Hawk beaches while under the control of their owners. From Memorial Day weekend to Labor Day weekend, dogs must be on a leash. Check the town website (www.townofkittyhawk.org) for current regulations.

NUMEROUS LIFEGUARDS MAKE THE CENTRAL BEACHES THE MOST FAMILY FRIENDLY ON THE OUTER BANKS.

&. **Kitty Hawk Bath House,** Kitty Hawk Road at the Beach Road. Public showers, restrooms, and parking. Free.

♿ **Windgrass Circle Sound Access,** W. Tateway Road at Bay Drive. This fully accessible town access to the quiet waters of Kitty Hawk Bay is located at the southern end of the ♿ **Wright Brothers Multi-Use Path** (Moore Shore Road).

TRAILS ☘ **Kitty Hawk Woods Coastal Reserve** (252-261-8891; www.nccoastal reserve.net), 983 W. Kitty Hawk Road. Nearly 2,000 acres of unspoiled maritime deciduous swamp, forest, and marsh occupy the center of the town of Kitty Hawk. The area contains ancient dunes and bald cypress swamp, and is home to a variety of wildlife and plants, including several rare and endangered species. Birds are numerous, especially wading birds, and bald eagles and ospreys nest here. The Woods Road (NC 1206) runs through the heart of the preserve and is paralleled by a paved multiuse path. Unpaved trails lace the park and can be accessed at the end of Eckner Street, Barlow and Amadas roads, Birch Lane, and Ridge Road, and at Pruitt Park on the Woods Road. Horseback riding and biking are allowed on designated trails. Hunting is permitted in season with the proper licenses.

♿ **Sandy Run Park,** 4000 block, Woods Road. A pleasant new nature trail with interpretive signs circles a pond, home to wading birds, many turtles, and an osprey nest. A picnic pavilion, crabbing dock, restrooms, and canoe/kayak launch, plus horseshoe pits, shuffleboard court, and basketball half court, make this a good destination for a family outing.

> **FAST FACT:** Cottonmouth and water moccasins, both poisonous snakes, are numerous in Kitty Hawk Woods. Take precautions, especially when hiking or paddling under low-hanging limbs.

✳ Lodging

BED & BREAKFAST INN ✳ ⚓ **Cypress Moon Bed and Breakfast** (252-261-5060 or 1-877-905-5060; www.cypressmooninn.com), 1206 Harbor Court, at MP 2 Bypass. Innkeepers Greg and Linda Hamby rent three guest rooms that open directly onto the sound. The elegantly appointed inn, furnished with antiques and Greg's professional photography, sits tucked into the maritime forest in Kitty Hawk Village. Rooms each have private bath, private dining area, and semiprivate porch looking out on the water, as well as satellite TV, stereo, and refrigerator. Hot breakfast is served daily, and vegetarian requests can be accommodated. Take one of the inn's complimentary kayaks for a tour of the shoreline. The inn is nonsmoking and does not accept guests under 18. You must climb stairs to reach the rooms. The Hambys also rent two fully equipped cottages nearby at the same nightly rate. $$–$$$.

CAMPGROUNDS AND HOSTEL ✳ ☘ ♿ **Adventure Bound Campground and Hostel** (252-255-1130 or 1-877-453-2545; www .adventureboundnc.com), 1004 W. Kitty Hawk Road, at MP 4.5, Bypass. Tent-only campground in Kitty Hawk Woods has 20 sites, hotwater showers, laundry, large lawn for games, and a campfire area. The year-round hostel next door offers dorm and private rooms, with shared kitchen and bath. Pets are allowed at the campground, but not at the hostel. $.

✳ ☘ **Kitty Hawk RV Park** (252-261-2636; www.kittyhawkrv.com), MP 4, Beach Road. The last survivor of the oceanside campgrounds on this stretch of beach rents RV sites with full hookups, including cable. Sites stretch from the Beach Road to the Bypass, with a private beach access. No tents or pop-ups. Longer leases available. $.

HOTEL ✳ ♿ ⚓ **Hilton Garden Inn Outer Banks** (252-261-1290; www.hilton gardeninnouterbanks.com), 5353 Beach Road, MP 1. Conveniently located at the northern end of Kitty Hawk where the Beach Road and the Bypass meet, this Hilton has an added amenity unique on this stretch of beach—its own private fishing pier. You can fish 24 hours a day on the former Kitty Hawk Pier as a hotel guest. This hotel, which opened in 2006, offers every amenity, with the Hilton emphasis on quality, including an indoor pool and whirlpool, fitness center, outdoor seasonal pool, 24-hour convenience shop, and a lobby restaurant serving breakfast, lunch, and dinner. Room service is available in the evenings. The 180 rooms and suites all have private balconies with views of the ocean, and the beach is right out the back door. Standard equipment in each room includes a hospitality center with refrigerator, microwave, and coffeemaker; large-screen cable TV; a large desk with ergonomic chair; and both wired and wireless Internet access. A free business center, open around the clock with remote printing and complimentary fax, make this a good place to stay when traveling on business. Guest laundry is available. Children under 18 stay free with parents. $$–$$$$.

MOTELS AND COTTAGE COURTS ❄ ((ψ)) **Saltaire Cottage Court** (252-261-3286; www.saltairecottages.com), MP 2.5, Beach Road. Recently renovated two-bedroom apartments and three-bedroom cottages are across the street from the ocean. All have screened porches. Nightly rentals available off-season. Linens and cable TV included, plus pool, beach access, deck, barbecue pit, and coin laundry. No smoking or pets in units. $$–$$$.

♿ **Sea Kove Motel** (252-261-4722; www.seakove.com), MP 3, Beach Road. Efficiencies and cottages on both sides of the Beach Road are operated by an old beach family. Outdoor pool and playground. No pets. Off-season $; high season $$.

✷ Where to Eat

DINING OUT ♿ ⚥ **Argyles Events & Catering** (252-261-7325; www.argylesrestaurant.com), 4716 Bypass, MP 2.5. Formerly one of Kitty Hawk's most sophisticated restaurants and piano bars, Argyles now concentrates on being one of the top catering and event destinations on the Banks. However, dinner is still served to the public on a limited basis, usually one night a week. Call for details. $$$.

❄ 🖍 🍸 ⟴ **Black Pelican Oceanfront Restaurant** (252-261-3171; www.blackpelican.com), 3848 Beach Road, MP 4. Located in the 1874 lifesaving station where the Wright brothers came to telegraph news of their successful flight to the world, the Black Pelican makes a great destination before, during, or after a day at the beach. The public beach access is just across the street, and you can even shower off at the adjacent town-operated bathhouse. The restaurant has three levels and a lofty deck with a bar and a view of the ocean. Late-night menu, daily specials, daily happy hour, and vegetarian dishes ensure something for everyone. Families will like the magic shows on summer Friday nights. Lunch $; dinner $$–$$$.

❄ ♿ 🍸 **Ocean Boulevard Bistro & Martini Bar** (252-261-2546; www.obbistro.com), 4700 Beach Road, MP 2. A casual spot just steps from the beach, this bistro serves artfully designed dishes that appeal to the upscale palate. *Southern Living* described it as "beachy and swanky all at once." The menu is divided into "Big Plates," which are serious entrées of lamb, fresh fish, duck, or beef, sold at equally serious prices, and "Small Plates," a nicely varied tapas menu that may range from gourmet macaroni and cheese to an antipasto plate with goat cheese, olives, and cured duck. Menus change with the season. Martinis are a specialty, and the wine list received the *Wine Spectator* Award of Excellence. Live jazz is featured on the OceanSide Patio in season, and late night on Friday all year. Reservations recommended. $$–$$$$.

EATING OUT ❄ 🍸 **Art's Place** (252-261-3233; www.facebook.com/artsplaceobx), 4624 Beach Road, MP 2.5. Tiny spot on the Beach Road (look for the cottage covered in cool aquatic murals) serves breakfast, great burgers, and live music all year to a loyal clientele. Join the locals for happy hour on the upper deck with ocean view. $.

🖍 ♿ 🍸 ((ψ)) **Barefoot Bernie's Tropical Grill & Bar** (252-261-1008; www.barefootbernies.com), 3730 Bypass, MP 4.5. The menu at Bernie's features tropical flavors drawn from Caribbean, Hawaiian, Jamaican, and other island cuisines, with a bit of Greek thrown in. Fish tacos, gyros, hot subs, and pizzas are on the menu all day. In addition to satisfying meals, this casual spot books live entertainment and is a gathering place for sports fans. Bernie's, official home of the Pittsburgh Steelers OBX fan club, has a dozen or so TVs, so you can

FOODIES ON THE BEACH

Taste of the Beach (www.obxtasteofthebeach.com), a four-day festival for foodies with dozens of events—including wine-pairing dinners, pig and oyster roasts, chowder cook-off, cooking classes, tapas crawl, brewing lessons, a tasting expo, and more—is held every March. The Outer Banks Restaurant Association also sponsors **Outer Banks Restaurant Weeks** (www.outerbanksrestaurantweek.com) in May and late October with bargain-priced three-course meals at many local eateries.

If your visit doesn't coincide with any of these events, contact **Outer Banks Restaurant Tours** (252-722-2229; www.outerbanksrestauranttours.com). The company offers walking and driving tours of eateries in Kitty Hawk, Duck, and Corolla, plus beer and wine tours and cooking classes, on a regular schedule from May to October.

watch your favorite game. Tabletop Sound Dog wireless receivers let you tune in to the audio, too. $–$$.

♂ ♀ (•) **Good Life Gourmet** (252-480-2855; www.goodlifegourmet.com), 3712 Bypass, MP 4.5. A real find, this place is a bakery and coffee shop in the morning, a deli with a big menu of salads and subs at lunchtime, and a bistro with occasional live music at night. Breakfasts served in a frying pan are a local favorite. Breads and sweets are baked on-site, the in-house wine shop carries unusual vintages and beers, the whole place has free Wi-Fi, and prices are some of the most reasonable on the Banks. Off-season, don't miss the popular Pasta Nites. $–$$.

❋ ♂ **Henry's Restaurant** (252-261-2025; www.henrysobx.com), 3396 Bypass, MP 5. Classic American food is served all day in a friendly, no-frills environment. A local favorite for breakfast, served until 1 PM. Breakfast and lunch $; dinner $$–$$$.

♀ **Outer Banks Taco Bar** (252-261-8226; www.obxtacobar.com), 3723 Bypass, MP 4.5, Ocean Plaza. Chef-designed tacos and enchiladas made with house-pressed corn tortillas come with a variety of fillings, including vegetarian options. $.

♂ ♀ ↷ **Rundown Café & Tsunami Surf Bar** (252-255-0026; www.rundowncafe.com), 5218 Beach Road, MP 1. Named for the traditional Jamaican fish-and-coconut soup that tops the menu, this cool spot right at the head of the Beach Road provides a gathering spot for locals and a favorite dinner stop for everyone who discovers its laid-back charm and eclectic menu. Known for its huge dinner salads and Oriental sesame noodle bowls, both available with a wide variety of toppings, the Rundown successfully combines the flavors of the Caribbean with Asian influences. Vegetarians will be pleased with the numerous offerings designed for them. The Hula Deck hosts frequent live music. Upstairs, a bar offers ocean views, cold brews, and a surfer vibe. $–$$.

BARBECUE ♂ ♿ **High Cotton Barbeque** (252-255-2275; www.highcottonbbq.com), 5230 Beach Road, MP 2. Authentic North Carolina–style pulled pork flavored with vinegar and hot pepper shares the menu with Texas beef brisket, St. Louis–style ribs, and chicken, smoked or fried. The big family packages are a real bargain. Dine in or take out. $–$$.

BEACH BARS ❋ ♿ ♀ (•) **Hurricane Mo's Beachside Bar and Grill** (252-255-0215), 120 E. Kitty Hawk Road, at MP 4, Bypass. Fun

tropical bar just steps from the beach has fun nightly happy hours featuring steamed shrimp, wings, and $1 tacos. Lunch and dinner $$.

♂ ♀ **Pete's Pourhouse** (252-715-2290; www.petespourhouse.com), 4020 Bypass, MP 3. Family-friendly sports bar has 20 flat-screen TVs, live music and karaoke, outside deck, and a full-service ice cream bar. Big menu is full of family favorites. $–$$.

BEACH FAST FOOD ❋ ♂ ♿ **Capt'n Frank's** (252-261-9923; www.captnfranks.com), 3800 Bypass, MP 4.5. Don't let the boat out front fool you. Hot dogs, topped with everything imaginable, are the main event here, plus North Carolina barbecue, wings, cheese fries, and steamed shrimp in season. An OBX favorite since 1975. $.

❦ **John's Drive-In** (252-261-6227; www.johnsdrivein.com), 3716 Beach Road, MP 4.5. A longtime favorite across the street from the beach, John's keeps busy, making its signature milk shakes with added fruit, burgers, and legendary fried dolphin (mahimahi) sandwiches. Take-out only; for fastest service, call ahead (but not from your cell phone; they don't accept calls from off-beach area codes) and pick up your order at the side service window. Closed Wednesday. $.

♂ **Spanky's Grille** (252-261-1917; www.spankysnc.com), 4105 Bypass, MP 3.5. Serving 79-cent hotdogs and $3 cheeseburgers, plus fish sandwiches, barbecue, and home-cooked meat loaf (a dinner special), this spot is one of the top rated eateries on the Banks. Only the two-pound Viking Burger tops the $10 mark—finish one and you enter the hall of fame. Sides come separately, however, and can add up quick. $.

Winks Market and Deli (252-441-9465), 4626 Beach Road, MP 2. This family-run grocery across from the ocean has stood the test of time by providing what beachgoers need for more than 50 years. Pick up a deli sandwiches or one of the daily specials for a quick lunch. $.

BREAKFAST ♂ **Stack 'Em High** (252-261-8221; www.stackemhigh.com), 3801 Bypass, MP 4.5. Family-owned and family-operated cafeteria-style breakfast restaurant offers made-to-order French toast, pancakes, omelets, and eggs, plus unusual items such as clam hash and red flannel hash from 7 AM to 1 PM daily. Kids love the specialty pancakes in flavors like banana split. Senior menu. $.

COFFEE AND ICE CREAM ❋ **Southern Bean** (252-261-5282), 3701 Bypass, MP 4.5, Dunes Shops. Locally owned coffee shop serves fresh-brewed coffee, along with vegetarian and seafood sandwiches and salads, pastries, fresh-squeezed fruit juices, and ice cream. $.

DELI Max's Bagels & Deli (252-255-311; www.maxsrealbagels.com), MP 3.5, Bypass. Freshly baked bagels stuffed with homemade cream cheese spreads and smoked salmon, plus a menu of deli sandwiches made with Thumann's products, are offered at this friendly, nonchain spot. Deli items available by the pound. $.

HEALTH FOOD Health-A-Rama Nutrition Center (252-261-9919), 3105 Bypass, MP 4.5, Seagate North Shopping Center. This health-food grocery stocks gluten-free products, organic produce, vitamins, and herbs.

PIZZA (ᵗᵖ) **Max's Pizza Company** (252-261-3113; www.maxspizza.net), 3733 Bypass, MP 4.5, Ocean Plaza. Hand-tossed pizzas, baked subs, paninis, calzones, and strombolis delivered free to Southern Shores, Kitty Hawk, and Kill Devil Hills. Beer and wine available for eat-in customers. $–$$.

Pizzazz Pizza Company (252-255-0050; www.pizzazzpizza.net), 4146 Bypass, MP 3.5. Locally owned and operated pizzeria, with other locations in Duck, Corolla, and Nags Head, has been making pizza lovers happy since 1986. You can order online and have your pie delivered free, or come down to the restaurant for the lunch and dinner buffets that include a 40-item salad bar. $–$$.

SEAFOOD Carawan Seafood (252-261-2120), 5424 Bypass, MP 1. Family-owned operation next to the Walmart specializes in local seafood, steamed crabs, and shrimp, plus beer, wine, organic produce, and other groceries.

✳ ↩ **I Got Your Crabs Seafood Market & Steam Bar** (252-449-2483; www.igotyour crabs.com), 3809 Bypass, MP 4.5. Local family pulls blue crabs out of Currituck Sound daily and brings them direct to market. Order them live to cook at home, or steamed to eat at this casual spot. Hard shell and soft shell available, along with crab dip, crab bisque, and lots of other seafood and veggies, steamed

and fried. Fried shrimp are sold by the piece. $–$$.

↩ **Jimmy's Seafood Buffet** (252-261-4973; www.jimmysobxbuffet.com), 4117 Bypass, MP 4. If you decide to forgo the pricey 100-plus item all-you-can-eat buffet, now including lobster, call ahead for a seafood bucket to steam at home or have the kitchen do it for you. Curbside pickup. Kids 4–12 pay their age, plus $2 for the buffet. $$–$$$$.

SWEETS The Belgian Chocolate Company (252-261-7325; www.thebelgianchocolateco .com), 4716 Bypass, MP 2.5. Division of Argyle's Catering specializes in truffles and bonbons made with natural ingredients.

Distinct Delights (252-715-0779; www.distinct delights.com), MP 4.5, Bypass, Buccaneer's Walk. Small-batch chocolates and caramels made by hand.

TAKE-OUT ↩ **Seaside Gourmet to Go** (252-255-5330; www.seasidegourmet.com), 3701 Bypass, MP 4.5, Dunes Shops. Formerly the Seaside Vegetarian, this take-out-only spot has expanded its offerings to include seafood but retains a dedication to local products and vegetarian dishes. Lunch $; dinner $$.

Vilai Thai Kitchen (252-441-8424), 5230 Beach Road, MP 2. Classic Thai dishes, including several vegetarian selections, available for take-out, delivery, or to eat in the tiny dining room. $–$$.

WINE, BEER, AND SPIRITS ABC Liquor Store (252-261-2477; www.ncabc.com), MP 1, Bypass. All liquor by the bottle is sold at these state-run stores, which are closed on Sunday.

🍴 ♈ (ᵗᵖ) **Trio** (252-261-0277; www.obxtrio.com), 3708 Bypass, MP 4.5, Harbor Bay Shops. Unique store stocking a huge selection of wine, beer, cheese, and gourmet food items from around the world lets you taste before you buy. Downstairs, sample 24 different wines by the taste or glass from the automat-style WineStations, or try one of the two dozen draft beers at the copper-top bar in the Tap Room. A menu of cheese and charcuterie plates, panini, and other small dishes makes a great lunch or light supper. Upstairs, the Carolina Tasting Room offers free samples of North Carolina wines and beers, along with free Wi-Fi. Live music plays most nights during the summer season. $.

The Wine Specialist (252-305-7911; www.the winespecialistobx.com), 3810 Bypass, MP 4.5, Buccaneer's Walk. Enjoy a glass of your favorite beverage while you browse the big selection of wine, beer, and gourmet cheese. Wine tastings are held weekly. Discounts for wedding parties. $.

✳ Entertainment

LIVE MUSIC Spots in Kitty Hawk offering live entertainment in season include the Black Pelican, Ocean Boulevard Bistro, Art's Place, Barefoot Bernie's, Pete's Pourhouse, the Rundown Café, OBX Taco Bar, the Sea Scape Bar & Grill in the Sea Scape Golf Course, and Trio.

✳ Selective Shopping

BOOKS **The Island Bookstore** (252-255-5590; www.islandbooksobx.com), 3712 Bypass, MP 4.5, Ocean Plaza. With sister stores in Corolla and Duck, the Island Bookstore is a powerhouse on the local literary scene, hosting book signings, author readings, book clubs, and many special events. Local subjects are a specialty, as well as large collections of children's titles, audiobooks, and magazines. *New York Times* best-sellers are discounted.

SHOPPING CENTERS Along US 158, shopping centers pass in sometimes bewildering profusion. Here we list the major shopping destinations and some of their outstanding features, starting at the north end of Kitty Hawk. Even-numbered addresses are on the west or sound side of the road. Odd numbers are on the east or ocean side. Here are some to watch for, arranged from north to south:

Shoreside Center, 5400 Bypass, MP 1. National chains including Walmart, Harris Teeter grocery, Radio Shack, and Dollar Tree are found at this large complex, as well as several locally owned shops and the new **Beach Boys Frozen Yogurt** (252-261-2697; www.facebook.com/BeachBoysFrozen Yogurt). RVs may overnight in the lot here.

Ocean Centre, 5230 Beach Road, MP 1. Strip of shops at the northern end of the Beach Road houses barbecue and ice cream shops, and the oh-so-tasty **Duck Donuts** (252-261-3312; www.duck donuts.com), plus an art supply store.

Kitty Hawk Plaza, 3836 Bypass, MP 4. Specialty stores include a sporting goods store, a party store, a **Sound Feet Shoes** outlet (www.soundfeet.com), and an excellent thrift store with lots of bargains (see *Special Shops*).

⚓ **Buccaneer's Walk,** 3810 Bypass, MP 4.5. Lots of specialty stores crowd this nautically themed center, including two antiques stores; shops specializing in chocolates, wine, homemade ice cream, and peanuts; plus ⚓ ☂ **Puzzles, Pranks & Games** (252-261-4323; www.facebook.com/PuzzlesPranks AndGames), with tons of fun options for rainy-day activities, including game demos.

Ocean Plaza, 3723 Bypass, MP 4.5. Home of the Island Bookstore (see *Books*), a bakery, a tobacco and beer store, and the **OBX Romance Store** (252-715-1605).

Harbor Bay Shops, 3708 Bypass, MP 4.5. Home of Diamonds 'n Dunes jewelry (see *Special Shops*) and the new Trio wine emporium (see *Wine, Beer, and Spirits*).

MADE ON THE OUTER BANKS

Local entrepreneurs are busy producing a variety of food and gift items that make great souvenirs of your vacation. Here are a few to look for at local produce markets, groceries, restaurants, and stores.

Good Karma Foods (252-261-3589; www.brynnsfoods.com). All-natural foods including granolas, Karma Krunch pancake mix, Beach Brittle, and the notorious EVILnuts.

Kill Devil Rum Ball Co. (570-220-6375; www.killdevilrumballs.com).

Outer Banks Bees Honey (252-441-8277). Made from hives in Wanchese.

Outer Banks Kettle Corn (252-202-2469; www.obxkettlecorn.com). Created by two teenage sisters from family recipes, this company's products are widely available at special events and festivals.

Outer Banks Rum Cakes (252-441-9090; www.outerbanksrumcakes.com).

Outer Banks Sea Salt (252-267-7884; www.obxseasalt.com). All-natural salt hand-harvested from Atlantic Ocean water using heritage techniques.

Dunes Shops MP 4.5, 3701 Bypass. Here you'll find the Seaside Gourmet to Go (see *Take-Out*) and the Southern Bean coffee shop (see *Coffee and Ice Cream*), both popular stops for vegetarians.

SPECIAL SHOPS CHKD Thrift Store (252-255-5437; www.chkd.org), 3838 Bypass, Kitty Hawk Plaza, MP 4.5. Thrift store benefits the Children's Hospital of the King's Daughters.

Diamonds 'n Dunes (252-255-0001; www.diamondsanddunes.com), 3708 Bypass, MP 4, Harbor Bay Shops. A showroom full of innovative and sophisticated jewelry designs capture the beauty of the ocean.

Islander Flags (252-261-6266; www.flagfinder.com), 6146 Bypass, MP 0. Blink as you come over the Wright Memorial Bridge and you'll miss this spot, selling flags, banners, and windsocks in colorful profusion.

✴ Special Events

August: **Sandbar 5K** (252-261-2004; www.outerbanksrelieffoundation.com), Beach Access at MP 4.5. Charity run/walk takes place on the sand in front of the historic Old Station public bathhouse.

KILL DEVIL HILLS AND COLINGTON ISLAND

REFERRED TO BY LOCALS AS KDH, Kill Devil Hills occupies the middle portion of the Central Beaches and was the first town in Dare County to incorporate, taking that step in 1953. The Wright Brothers Memorial was the area's first nonbeach attraction, and many hotels located close to it. More chain hotels and condominiums are found in this part of the beach than any other. The Wrights took flight from a dune called Kill Devil Hill by locals, some say because it was used as a hiding place for scavenged rum that would "kill the devil."

Avalon, centered on the Avalon fishing pier in KDH, was one of the first beachfront neighborhoods on the coast. Today, KDH is Dare County's largest municipality, with over 7,000 year-round residents and a distinctly family focus.

Located west of the Wright Memorial, Colington Island—about 2 miles long by 2 miles wide—is connected by bridges and a single road to Kill Devil Hills. Named for Sir John Colleton, one of Carolina's Lords Proprietors, Colington was the location of one of the earliest plantations on the Banks and eventually became the home of a thriving fishing village where crab-shedding (the process that creates soft-shell crabs) was—and remains—a major industry. Development was slow to come to Colington, but recently many upscale subdivisions have appeared among the more modest homes of families who have lived here for generations. The few restaurants and inns set among the old live oaks are worth seeking out for an Outer Banks experience different from both the beach and the Bypass.

GUIDANCE Outer Banks Chamber of Commerce (252-441-8144; www.outerbankschamber.com), 101 Town Hall Drive, Kill Devil Hills.

Kill Devil Hills Town Hall (252-480-4000; www.kdhnc.com), 102 Town Hall Drive, Kill Devil Hills.

POST OFFICE The **Kill Devil Hills U.S. Post Office** (252-441-5666) is at 302 Bypass, MP 8. The zip code in Kill Devil Hills is 27948.

PUBLIC RESTROOMS Ocean Bay Boulevard Bathhouse, at MP 8.5 on the Beach Road, along with several public parks off Colington Road, as well as **Kill Devils Hill Field** on the Bypass, MP 6, behind the KDH fire department, offer public facilities.

PUBLIC LIBRARY ((ᵖ)) **Dare County Library at Kill Devil Hills** (252-441-4331; www.earlibrary .org), 400 Mustian Street. This library, with a Wi-Fi hotspot and six computers available for public use, houses a local history collection. Closed on weekends in summer, and on Sunday year-round.

GETTING THERE *By Air:* Kill Devil Hill, where the Wright Memorial now stands, is a place of pilgrimage for many pilots. They come to fly over the memorial, and to land and take off at the First Flight Airport next to the national monument, flying in the contrail of the Wright brothers themselves.

First Flight Airport (FFA) (252-441-7430 or 252-473-2111; www.nps.gov/wrbr). Unattended airfield next to the Wright Brothers Memorial. Unlighted 3,000-foot runway. Amenities include a weather and flight planning pilot's facility, and free 24-hour tie-downs.

By Car: KDH runs roughly from MP 5 to MP 10 on both the US 158 Bypass and the Beach Road (NC 12), between the towns of Kitty Hawk and Nags Head.

GETTING AROUND The KDH town offices, as well as the Outer Banks Chamber of Commerce, a library, recreation facilities, the senior center, the Veteran's Memorial, and an arboretum, are located west of the Bypass off Colington Road, the first street south of the Wright Brothers Memorial. Turn east on this road instead, and you'll be on Ocean Bay Boulevard, headed for one of the largest ocean bathhouses in KDH.

> **QUICK TIP:** Thinking of retiring to the Outer Banks? Take a few minutes to stop by the **Thomas A. Baum Senior Center** (252-475-5635; www.darenc.com/adult/baum.asp), at 300 Mustian Street in Kill Devil Hills, to see all the activities and support services Dare County has to offer seniors. Visitors 55 and over are welcome to attend the center's many exercise classes.

❋ To See

GARDEN ❧ **Outer Banks Arboretum and Teaching Garden** (252-473-4290; http://dare.ces.ncsu .edu), 300 Mustian Street. Located next to the Thomas A. Baum Senior Center, this pleasant spot has gardens of dune, aquatic, butterfly, and native plants, including many pest- and salt-resistant species, labeled for identification. Free.

HISTORIC SITES ❧ ⬆ **First Flight Shrine** (252-441-7430; www.firstflight.org/shrine.cfm), MP 7.5, Bypass. Over 50 portraits of outstanding figures in the history of aviation hang in the Wright Brothers National Memorial Visitor Center. Reading their biographies is an education in itself. Free with admission to the national memorial.

♦ ❧ ⬆ **Wright Brothers National Memorial** (252-473-2111; www.nps.gov/wrbr), MP 7.5, Bypass. Open daily. Many improvements to the exhibits at this national shrine were made during the 2003 Centennial of Flight. The visitors center has a replica of the 1903 flyer, plus a bookstore, restrooms, and an aviation hall of fame. The Centennial Pavilion houses exhibits on the history of aviation, NASA space exhibits, and an interactive area showing what the Outer Banks were like when Wilbur and Orville arrived. Close by, the park service has reconstructed the Wrights' living quarters and hangar. The Flight Line of the first four successful powered flights is marked by a series of granite boulders. The 60-foot granite pylon, the memorial's most noticeable feature, stands atop Kill Devil Hill. On the far side, a life-size group of bronze statues, accurate down to the barefoot photographer snapping the most famous picture in history, captures the moment of the First Flight. During the summer months, park rangers give tours and talks throughout the park. Admission $5, good for seven consecutive days; ages 15 and under free.

THE WRIGHT BROTHERS MEMORIAL PROVIDES A FOCAL POINT FOR THE CENTRAL BEACHES, AND A STARTING POINT FOR THEIR MODERN HISTORY.

❋ To Do

BICYCLING A paved multiuse path begins at the East Ocean Bay Boulevard beach access on the Beach Road and runs west, crossing the Bypass and following Colington Road along the south side of the Wright Brothers Memorial, then cuts through the woods to connect with First Street, Canal Road, and Bay Drive along the sound. Many paved paths cut off from Colington Road, including paths along Bermuda

Bay Boulevard, Veterans Drive, and Mustian Street, connecting the facilities of the **Dare County Family Recreation Park** and the public schools found in the area. The Beach Road has widened paved shoulders for the use of bikes and pedestrians on its stretch through Kill Devil Hills.

The Bike Barn (252-441-3786), 1312 Wrightsville Boulevard. Rents hybrids and road bikes.

Just For the Beach Rentals (252-441-6048; www.justforthebeach.com), 1006 Beach Road, MP 9, and **Ocean Atlantic Rentals** (252-441-7823; www.oceanatlanticrentals.com), MP 10, Beach Road. Both these companies rent bikes, kayaks, surfboards, paddleboards, coolers, baby equipment, beach chairs, grills, linens, and every sort of equipment you need at the beach.

Outer Banks Bicycle (252-480-3399), 203 Beach Road, MP 8.5. Dedicated bike store offers rentals, sales, and repairs. BMX, scooters, hybrids, and tandems also available.

BOATING Kitty Hawk Bay and the canals and streams that surround Colington Island provide peaceful places to paddle or fish. On Colington Island, put your kayak in at the foot of the second bridge, where you'll find a parking area on the western side.

&. **North Carolina Wildlife Boat Ramp and Access** (www.ncwildlife.org), Dock Street at Bay Drive. Open 24 hours. Two paved boat ramps and 12 parking spaces, plus a canoe launch area, give access to Kitty Hawk Bay. Free.

CRAFTS ⚡ ↑ (((•))) **Garden of Beadin'** (252-449-5055; www.obxbeads.com), 2200 Bypass, Milepost 6 Plaza. Take a beading class, or just get a cup of coffee at the Front Porch Café next door and browse the many beads and semiprecious stones available. Children's beading projects and paint-your-own pottery next door make this a great rainy-day stop.

⚡ ↑ (((•))) **Glazin' Go Nuts Paint Your Own Pottery** (252-441-2134; www.obxpottery.com), 2200 Bypass, Milepost 6 Plaza. Create a unique souvenir of your vacation.

FISHING Avalon Pier (252-441-7494; www.avalonpier.com), 2111 Beach Road, MP 6.5. This 696-foot pier, built in 1958, is open 5 AM–2 AM during the summer, shorter hours in spring and fall. No shark fishing. Live pier cam on the website.

Colington Road Bridge. The second bridge on Colington Road is noted for its fine crabbing. A paved parking lot can be found just past the bridge, with a path leading down to the water.

Stop N Shop Gourmet Deli & Beach Shop (252-441-6105; www.stopnshopobx.com), MP 8.5, Beach Road. Longtime local convenience store is a surf-fishing hot spot offering advice and all the equipment you'll need to bring a string of speckled trout to shore. Deli sandwiches are some of the best on the beach and include vegetarian items.

FITNESS Aloha Yoga (252-441-5994; www.alohayogaobx.com), Ocean Bay Boulevard Beach Access, MP 8.5, Beach Road. Enjoy a peaceful yoga class on the sand with surfer and certified yoga instructor Susan Krause.

FOR FAMILIES ⚡ **Colington Speedway** (252-480-9144), 1064 Colington Road. Find these $5 go-karts off the beaten track on Colington Island.

⚡ **Lost Treasure Golf** (252-480-0142; www.losttreasuregolf.com), 1600 Bypass, MP 7. Wild West mining theme features a free train ride to the first hole.

⚡ &. ↑ **OBX Pet Gallery** (252-480-1799; www.obxpetgallery.com), 1210 Bypass, MP 9.5. The Outer Banks are short on zoos, but young animal lovers will enjoy a visit to this pet shop, with a Reptile Row full of snakes, lizards, and turtles, plus spiders, frogs, gerbils, and birds on display. One room is devoted to saltwater aquariums complete with live coral and Nemo look-alikes. Next door, the **Toy Gallery** (252-480-0209; www.obxtoygallery.com), under the same ownership, offers a huge selection of kids' books, games, and toys to try out, plus free daily activities, usually a story followed by a themed craft project. (Think princess tiara or pirate eye patch.)

⚡ **Paradise Golf & Arcade** (252-441-7626), 3300 Bypass, MP 5.5. Play all day for one price at two 18-hole, natural grass courses that appeal to both kids and adults.

PARKS ⚡ **Aviation Park,** Veterans Drive off Colington Road. Town park has a fitness trail, skate park, lighted roller-hockey rink, playground, and restrooms. The **Kill Devil Derby Brigade** (www.facebook.com/outerbanks.rollerderby or www.obxrd.wordpress.com) practices here.

🌊 ⛵ **Dare County Youth Center and Recreation Park** (252-475-5920; www.darenc.com/parksrec), 602 Mustian Street. A wealth of activities are available in this compact area just west of the Bypass off Colington Road. Inside are two full-court gyms for open play of basketball or volleyball, TV room, foosball, Ping-Pong, pool table, and computer room. Visitors can use the facilities for a small daily or weekly fee. Outside, lighted tennis courts, volleyball and basketball courts, game fields, horseshoe pits, picnic pavilion with grills, a playground, Alpine Tower, and climbing wall offer more activity options. Public restrooms available.

🌊 **Kill Devils Hill Field** (252-475-5920; www.darenc.com/parksrec),1634 Bypass, MP 6. Lighted tennis courts, athletic field, playground, picnic area, and restrooms, behind the KDH fire department.

SHORE SNORKELING AND DIVING The **Triangle Wrecks** (two ships, a freighter and a tanker, now in three pieces) lies about 150 yards offshore in 20 feet of water near Second Street beach access, MP 7.

For 14 summers, the **Outer Banks Daredevils** (www.facebook.com/outer.daredevils), made up of top-notch college athletes, played ball from late May to early August against rivals in the Coastal Plain League (www.coastalplain.com), the hottest and largest collegiate wood-bat summer baseball league in the nation. Daredevils merchandise became a favorite souvenir. Games were played at the First Flight Baseball Complex, 111 Veterans Drive, in Kill Devil Hills. Unfortunately, the team's owners suspended play in 2012, citing financial concerns, and put the team up for sale. But stay tuned. Some baseball lover is bound to buy the team and bring back one of the favorite ways to spend a long summer evening on the Banks.

SURFING In Kill Devil Hills, the area around Avalon Pier has some of most rideable waves. Surfing is not allowed within 75 feet of the pier.

The Pit Surf Shop (252-480-3128; www.pitsurf.com), 1209 Bypass, MP 9. A great hangout for surfers of all ages, this shop carries its own line of boards made by expert local shapers and is especially friendly to beginning surfers. Boards are available for sale or rent, and lessons and surf camps are offered for beginning and intermediate riders.

TENNIS Lighted courts for public play are located in KDH at MP 6 on the Bypass next to the Kill Devil Hills Fire Department, and at MP 8.5 on Mustian Street next to the Kill Devil Hills library and water plant.

✳ Green Space

BEACHES Kill Devil Hills is particularly rich in beach access points, with nearly two dozen along NC 12 (the Beach Road). Seventeen of them have paved parking, and most of these are handicapped accessible and have open-air showers. The ♿ **Ocean Bay Boulevard Bathhouse** (MP 8.5) has parking, restrooms, and inside showers. Beach wheelchairs are available from the **Kill Devil Hills Fire Department** (252-480-4060). Fires, fireworks, motor vehicles, and glass are not permitted on the beach in Kill Devil Hills. Dogs are not allowed on the beach from 9 AM to 6 PM between May 15 and September 15. They must be leashed at all other times. Lifeguards are on duty at many beach access points along this stretch of coast from Memorial Day to Labor Day.

SOUND ACCESS Several public access areas are located along Bay Drive on the sound side of Kill Devil Hills.

Hayman Boulevard Estuarine Access, Bay Drive at W. Hayman Boulevard. Crabbing pier, gazebo, picnic area, and parking.

N.C. Wildlife Boating Access (www.ncwildlife.org), Dock Street and Bay Drive. Boat-launching area, with picnic tables and free parking, is a popular spot to jump in the water.

Third Street Estuarine Access, Bay Drive at W. Third Street. Gazebo with a pleasant view of the sound. No parking.

TRAILS 🌊 🐾 ♿ **Nags Head Woods Ecological Preserve** (252-441-2525; www.nature.org), 701 W. Ocean Acres Drive, at MP 9.5, Bypass. Located mostly in Kill Devil Hills, this 1,000 acres of maritime forest, protected by the Nature Conservancy, includes pine and hardwoods, with some trees over 500 years old, and provides a nesting area for over 50 species of birds. The property features several ponds full of frogs and other amphibians, plus historical remains of farmsteads and cemeteries. Trails and dirt roads crisscross the preserve, passing through the forest and down to the shore of the sound. The new boardwalk trail is fully ADA accessible. Bikes, horses, and dogs on leashes are allowed on the gravel roads through the preserve, but not on the trails. However, you can take your dog down the Roanoke Trail to the beach on Roanoke Sound. Maps are available at the visitors center.

NAGS HEAD WOODS, A MARITIME FOREST PRESERVE

✳ Lodging
BED & BREAKFAST INNS
Colington Island

♿ (ꚛ) **Colington Creek Inn** (252-449-4124; www.colingtoncreekinn.com), 1293 Colington Road. Enjoy waterfront views from the two-story screened porch at this cedar-shingled bed & breakfast on Colington Island, or take a dip in the private pool. The inn's four bedrooms all have private baths, spacious beds, and private sunporches with excellent water views. Boat dockage is available along Colington Creek if you arrive by water. Innkeepers Bob and Mae Lunden sometimes take guests on an evening cruise aboard their private boat to enjoy the sunset. A full breakfast and evening hors d'oeuvres are served daily. The inn has an elevator for handicapped access; children and pets cannot be accommodated. Although the inn enjoys a secluded location off the main highway, public beach access is an easy drive away, without getting into traffic. $$$.

Kill Devil Hills

✳ ♂ (ꚛ) **Cypress House Inn** (252-441-6127 or 1-800-554-2764; www.cypresshouseinn.com), 500 Beach Road, MP 8. Known to locals as the Cherokee Inn, this 1940s hunting lodge has been designated a local historic landmark. The six guest rooms feature cypress tongue-and-groove paneled ceilings and walls, and modern amenities, including private baths, small refrigerators, ceiling fans, air-conditioning, and cable TV. Bicycles, beach chairs, and towels are complimentary. A public beach access is located directly across the street. Innkeepers Bill and Veda Peters place coffee, tea, and fresh-baked muffins outside each door in the morning for guests to enjoy on the inn's wrap-around porch or in front of the fireplace in nippy weather.

Room rates include a full breakfast served in the dining room and afternoon tea and cookies. $$–$$$.

CAMPING
Kill Devil Hills

✳ **Joe & Kay's Campground** (252-441-5468), 1193 Colington Road, west of the Bypass at MP 8.5. Dump station, restrooms with warm water, boat ramp. Full-hookup sites are rented by the year. Several grassy tent sites are available for overnight camping.

CONDO RENTALS
Kill Devil Hills

✳ (ꚛ) **Outer Banks Beach Club** (252-441-6321; www.spmresorts.com), 1110 Beach Road, MP 9. One of the largest condominium groups directly on the ocean rents completely equipped one-, two-, and three-bedroom units by the week year-round. Amenities include indoor and outdoor pools and hot tubs, tennis and shuffleboard, barbecue grills, and a large clubhouse with planned activities all year.

COTTAGE COURT
Kill Devil Hills

✳ (ꚛ) **Wright Cottage Court** (252-441-7331; www.obxlodging.com), 301 Beach Road, MP 8. Next door to the Days Inn Oceanfront, and enjoying pool privileges there, these two- to six-bedroom oceanfront cottages rent by the day or week, at rates that include free linen setup and cable TV, plus full kitchens and, in some, dishwashers and washer/dryers.

INNS AND HOTELS
Kill Devil Hills

✳ (ꚛ) **Atlantic Street Inn** (252-305-0246; www.atlanticstreetinn.com), 205 E. Atlantic

Street, MP 9.5. Six comfortable suites, all with refrigerator, microwave, cable TV, phone, coffeemaker, and a personally controlled heat and air, are available in this recently renovated beach house. Located close to all the action in KDH, the inn is also just down the street from the Atlantic Street Beach Access. Bright colors and local art decorate the suites, which are available by the day or week. Backyard grill, full kitchen, enclosed outdoor showers, and bikes are available for guest use. Two-night minimum stay required. $–$$.

✿ ♿ (๏) **Best Western Ocean Reef Suites** (252-441-1611; www.bestwesternnorthcarolina .com), 107 Beach Road, MP 8.5. The only all-suite hotel directly on the beach in the Outer Banks, this five-story Best Western received a three-diamond rating from AAA. Each suite accommodates up to six people and has a completely equipped kitchen. To get above it all, book the hotel's penthouse suite, where the rooftop deck with Jacuzzi offers an unimpeded view. Room rates include a full continental breakfast daily, free local calls, cable TV, and access to the hotel's hot tub, sauna, steam room, fitness center, and outdoor heated pool (open seasonally). The hotel also has a guest laundry room open 24 hours. Most rooms in the hotel are nonsmoking. Children under 13 stay free with paying adult. $–$$$$.

❄ ✿ ♿ (๏) **Days Inn Oceanfront—Wilbur and Orville Wright** (252-441-7211 or 1-800-325-2525; www.obxlodging.com), 101 Beach Road, MP 8.5. The longest continuously operating hotel on the beach, this 52-room property opened in 1948 and has a nostalgic "Old Nags Head" appeal. Built in the style of a mountain lodge, the hotel's inviting lobby features a big fireplace where guests gather for hot cider and popcorn in the cooler months. In summer, lemonade and cookies are the afternoon refreshments. A full hot breakfast with eggs, sausage, waffles, and more is included in the room rate. Double, queen, and king rooms, plus efficiencies with a full kitchen, as well as non-smoking and handicapped-accessible rooms, are available. Children under 13 stay free. The property has a large outdoor pool, open seasonally, and a boardwalk to the beach. Guests also can take advantage of free passes to the local YMCA. Oregon Inlet Fishing Center parties qualify for special discounted rates. $–$$$.

The same company operates a number of other properties nearby, including the **Days Inn Mariner** (252-441-2021), located on the oceanfront at MP 7, and the budget-conscious **Driftin' Sands Motor Court** (252-441-5115), across the street from the ocean at MP 6.5.

❄ ♿ (๏) **Shutters on the Banks** (252-441-5581 or 1-800-848-3728; www.shuttersonthebanks .com), 405 Beach Road, MP 8.5. Recently refurbished with new bedding, furniture, and carpet, the family-owned and family-operated Shutters offers four floors of rooms with two double beds and efficiencies with full kitchens on the oceanfront. Amenities include a new indoor heated pool, whirlpool, family game room, and exercise room, in addition to an outdoor heated pool, gazebo, and walkway to the beach. Rooms on the second through fourth floors have private balconies. Rates include a deluxe continental breakfast. $–$$$$.

MOTOR LODGE
Kill Devil Hills

✿ ❦ **Outer Banks Motor Lodge** (252-441-7404 or 1-877-625-6343; www.obxmotorlodge .com), 1509 Beach Road, MP 8.5. Located directly on the ocean, this is one of the Banks' original motels, established in 1961, and belongs to the Miller family, which operates several restaurants in the area. Now completely refurbished, the two-story lodge offers both oceanfront and poolside double rooms and efficiencies. A seasonal outdoor pool, plus picnic area and playground, fish cleaning station, and coin-operated laundry, are on the grounds. Free Wi-Fi in Coffee Corner. Children under 13 stay free. Open seasonally, April to November. $–$$.

RESORTS
Kill Devil Hills

❄ ❦ ♿ ♂ (๏) **Ramada Plaza Resort and Conference Center** (252-441-2151 or 1-800-635-1824; www.ramadaplazanagshead.com), 1701 Beach Road, MP 9.5. This five-story hotel offers a host of amenities in a convenient, oceanfront location. Rooms have a king or two queen beds, private balconies, cable TV, Wi-Fi access, microwaves, refrigerators, coffeemakers, hair dryers, and irons. A free guest laundry, fitness center, and business center are located off the spacious lobby, where complimentary coffee and newspapers are available each morning. The large indoor pool and Jacuzzi are open all year. Outdoors, guests enjoy lots of deck space, a seasonal gazebo bar, and a boardwalk to the beach. Free passes to the nearby YMCA and to the Kitty Hawk Pier are available by request. Most rooms are nonsmoking. . The Ramada's restaurant and bar, ♈ **Peppercorns,** offers nightly specials, frequent entertainment, and full cocktail service with an ocean view. The breakfast served here, both buffet and à la carte, is a real bargain. Room service available. The outdoor **Dragon Fly Deck Bar** serves lunch during the summer months. The resort is also home to the **OBX Comedy Club** (252-207-9950; www.comedyclubobx.com). $$–$$$$.

♂ (ʲ) **Sea Ranch Resort** (252-441-7126 or 1-800-334-4737; www.searanchresort.com), 1731 Beach Road, MP 7. Completely renovated in 2004, the Sea Ranch is located on the oceanfront. A glass-enclosed pool fronts on an oceanfront deck. The new fitness center offers seasonal exercise classes. An on-site restaurant, the ♂ ♈ ↪ **Beachside Bistro** (252-255-1063), serves three meals daily in an airy dining room with ocean view, or on the outdoor deck, which hosts weekly deck parties during the summer. Room service available. Waterfowl hunting packages are available. $$–$$$$.

✳ Where to Eat

DINING OUT

Colington Island

♂ ♿ ↪ **Colington Café** (252-480-1123; www.colingtoncafe.com), 1049 Colington Road. Located in a lovely Victorian house well away from the crowds on the Bypass, this local favorite is not such a secret since *Southern Living* named it the "Best Restaurant for the Best Price" on the Outer Banks. Inspired by owner Carlen Pearl's French background, the cuisine here features the freshest seafood and other local ingredients in classic preparations. The she-crab bisque and crabcakes are legendary, and the homemade desserts, especially the white chocolate crème brûlée, inspire raves. The atmosphere is romantic, with several small rooms downstairs. However, larger family groups can be accommodated in the upstairs room. Reservations are highly recommended, especially during the busy summer season. The Colington closes during the winter but often reopens for holidays. Dinner daily, $$–$$$$.

Kill Devil Hills

♂ ♈ **Bad Bean Baja Grill & Cantina** (252-261-1300; www.badbeanobx.com), 3105 Bypass, MP 5, Seagate North Shopping Center. Stop by to see what Tex-Mex can be when designed by a professional chef. Created by owner Rob Robinson, formerly a chef at the Left Bank (a fine dining landmark), the reasonably priced menu features award-winning treatments of classic dishes, such as duck comfit tostones, shrimp ceviche, and soft-shell crab tacos, and includes many vegetarian items, all prepared from local ingredients. The salsas are legendary. Sister restaurant, the **Bad Bean Taqueria** (252-453-4380), is in Corolla. Lunch $; dinner $–$$.

Flying Fish Café (252-441-6894; www.flyingfishcafeobx.com), 2003 Bypass, MP 9.5. One of the highest-rated restaurants on the Banks, Flying Fish has a nice wine list, racks of lamb, and a wonderful dessert called the Chocolate Hurricane. Reservations suggested. Dinner only, $$$$.

✳ **JK's Restaurant** (252-441-9555; www.jksrestaurant.com), 1106 Bypass, MP 9; second location in Corolla (252-453-9555) in Monteray Plaza. Established in 1984, this fine-dining spot has stood the test of time. Hand-cut house-aged steaks, rack of lamb, grass-fed veal chops, and local seafood are cooked over mesquite coals on the wood-fired grill. Sides are priced separately. A popular special occasion spot for locals, this is definitely a splurge. If you are visiting OBX in the off-season, drop by JK's to sample its daily specials at considerable savings. Dinner only, $$$–$$$$.

♂ ♈ ↪ **Kill Devil Grill** (252-449-8181; www.thekilldevilgrill.com), 2008 Beach Road, MP 9.5. Located in an authentic 1939 railroad dining car listed on the National Register for Historic Places, this Beach Road favorite offers meals that far surpass typical diner fare. Talented chefs create daily seafood and blue-plate specials (think meat loaf), great crab-cakes, white pizza topped with goat cheese and fresh basil, wood-roasted chicken, steaks, and chops. Everything is prepared from scratch here, so specials often sell out. Popular dishes include the chicken wings, the Kahuna burger, and for dessert, award-winning Key lime pie. Closed Sunday and Monday. Lunch and dinner $–$$$.

EATING OUT

Colington Island

♿ ♈ **Dockside Grill** (252-441-0444), 1469 Colington Road. An inexpensive menu, plus fresh, fresh seafood make this a real find several miles out winding Colington Road, or you can arrive by boat at the dock off Colington Creek. Soft-shell crabs, shucked just across the road, are menu highlights in season, as are various shrimp dishes. North Carolina–style barbecue and ribs fill out the menu, along with popular daily specials on a chalkboard out front. Eat inside or take a table on the screened porch, where you can listen to the cicadas sing. A big fan keeps the porch cool in summer, and in winter it's heated. The outside is rimmed with strands of tiny white lights, casting an atmospheric glow. The regulars here are locals who come to play pool and listen to live music. Lunch and dinner $–$$.

Kill Devil Hills

❋ ✇ ⵈ (ⵈ) **Awful Arthur's Oyster Bar** (252-441-5955; www.awfularthursobx.com), 2106 Beach Road, MP 6. Serving steamed oysters the authentic North Carolina way for two decades, Arthur's has a casual, kicked-back atmosphere much beloved by locals and the regulars who return here each year. Between peeling the famous spiced shrimp (*Esquire* named them one of "67 Things Worth a Detour" in the United States), slurping oysters, and cracking crab legs, things may get a little messy, but that's part of the fun. During summer, the crowds can get thick as the sun heads west. If you want to sit at a table, you may have a long wait. At this point, adopt the local strategy: Head upstairs to the lounge, order some steamed shrimp and a cold beverage, and enjoy the view of the ocean and Avalon Pier, just across the Beach Road. Locals usually opt for a stool at the copper-topped bar. Or order from the take-out window and stake out a picnic table outside. *Coastal Living Magazine* named this one of the top 10 oyster bars in the nation, but the menu also offers fried seafood, burgers, barbecue, and steaks. Open every day of the year (another reason the locals love it) for lunch and dinner. You can pick up logo'd souvenirs and gifts, or maybe a hermit crab, at the **Awful Arthur's Beach Shop** (252-449-2220), next door to the restaurant. It even rents surfboards. $–$$.

✇ **Bob's Grill** (252-441-0707; www.bobsgrill obx.com), 1219 Bypass, MP 9. Breakfast is served all day at this restaurant, where the motto is "Eat and Get the Hell Out!" (a great idea to maximize vacation time). Big servings of homestyle food arrive fast, but the line can be long midmorning. Check out the great deals on lunch specials. Full bar; gift shop with logo'd gear. Breakfast and lunch $; dinner $$.

❋ ⵈ **Chilli Peppers Coastal Grill** (252-441-8081; www.chilli-peppers.com), 3001 Bypass, MP 5.5. Live entertainment, along with a late-night menu, steamer bar, daily enchilada specials, and some of the spiciest food on the beach, keep regulars coming back. Something is going on here almost every night, from live music to surfer videos. In the off-season, check out the Thursday tapas nights. The bar features a big selection of premium tequilas and margaritas. Weekend brunch here was voted "Best of the Beach." Brunch and lunch $; dinner $$.

✇ ⵈ **Food Dudes Kitchen** (252-441-7994), 1216 Beach Road, MP 9, Seashore Shops. Two popular OBX chefs team up to offer gourmet food to take out or eat in the casual dining room. Organic produce and locally sourced seafood are whipped up into a variety of wraps, sandwiches, and blackboard specials. This is an excellent choice for Sunday brunch (featuring sweet potato biscuits) as well. Thursday is taco night. Beer and wine available, along with great bottled hot sauce. Brunch and lunch $; dinner entrées $$.

❋ ✇ ⵈ (ⵈ) **Jolly Roger Restaurant & Bar** (252-441-6530; www.jollyrogerobx.com), 1836 Beach Road, MP 6.5. A pirate greets you at the Jolly Roger, offering a huge menu of pastas and Italian specialties served nightly. Locals know this is also a great spot for breakfast, served 6 AM–2 PM.. Pier-style eggs and Belgian waffles topped with ice cream are specialties, and, for the true pirate, homemade bread pudding with a hearty bourbon sauce. The decor is pure pirate kitsch, but the service is famous for its warmth. The bar, with karaoke nightly, plus Wii and other video games, stays open late. A gift shop sells pirate gear. Breakfast and lunch $; dinner $$.

❋ ✇ ⵈ ⵈ **Mako Mike's** (252-480-1919; www.makomikes.com), 1630 Bypass, MP 7. Promising "killer food" at reasonable prices, Mako Mike's serves all the family favorites, from pizza cooked in a wood oven and a variety of pasta dishes to standard beef, chicken, and pork entrées. Prime rib is a specialty. The long list of seafood features Outer Banks Catch local seafood, including blackened mako shark. Wildly painted decor, and huge sharks hanging from the ceilings, create an underwater atmosphere popular with children. Early-bird specials make it a favorite with seniors. Head for the Sunken Bar to escape the crowds. Owned by Mike Kelly, this is the sister restaurant of **Kelly's,** farther down the Bypass. Reservations available. Lunch $; dinner, $$.

❦ ✇ ⵈ (ⵈ) ⵈ **Outer Banks Brewing Station** (252-449-2739; www.obbrewing.com), 600 Bypass, MP 8.5. Fresh award-winning beer, frequent specials, and live entertainment keep the crowds coming to one of the Outer Banks' most popular establishments. Much of the food served is locally sourced, and the desserts and breads are baked in-house. The kids' menu is special, too, featuring a filet mignon and home-brewed root beer, and there's a pirate-themed playground with picnic tables out back. Stop by the bar (shaped like an old lifesaving boat) for a sampler of some of the most creative beers anywhere and to check out the week's entertainment lineup. This is a hot spot for live regional and national bands. The building itself is inspired by one of the old lifesaving stations that once dotted the Banks and is powered by a wind turbine, making it the first wind-powered brewpub in the United States. Bottles and growlers are available to go. Weekend brunch, lunch, and bar $; dinner $$–$$$.

BARBECUE ♪ **Pigman's Bar-B-Que** (252-441-6803; www.pigman.com), 1606 Bypass, MP 9.5, Kill Devil Hills. Besides the usual pork and beef barbecue, this place offers heart-healthy 'cue made from tuna or turkey, plus country ham rolls, smoked chicken and ribs, homestyle sides, and sweet potato fries, washed down with iced tea or a beer. Eat in or take out. $.

BEACH BARS ⅄ **Dare Devil's Pizzeria** (252-441-6330; www.daredevilspizzeria.com), 1112 Beach Road, MP 9, Kill Devil Hills. A landmark along the Beach Road since 1987, this cool spot shows surf videos while you wait for your pizza or stromboli. Or chow down on some wings or nachos at the full-service bar. $–$$.

♪ ⅄ **Goombay's Grille and Raw Bar** (252-441-6001; www.goombays.com), 1608 Beach Road, MP 7, Kill Devil Hills. Cool vibes, Caribbean-inspired food, big beer selection, daily happy hour, and live music some nights make this a favorite hangout. A late-night menu features raw and steamed shellfish until 2 AM. Lunch $; dinner $$.

⅄ **Mama Kwan's OBX Grill & Tiki Bar** (252-441-7889; www.mamakwans.com), 1701 Bypass, MP 9.5, Kill Devil Hills. A favorite hangout for the late-night crowd, Kwan's serves tasty Asian-inspired food, tropical drinks, and weekly live music with a laid-back vibe. Lunch $; dinner $$.

♪ ⅄ **MexiCali Brewz** (252-480-0069), 1200 Beach Road, MP 9, Kill Devil Hills. Another fun spot brought to you by the Mama Kwan folks, this one has a menu drawing on SoCal and Mexican influences, with lots of fish tacos, an outdoor patio with games and live entertainment, and late-night food. $–$$.

BEACH FAST FOOD American Pie Pizza and Homemade Ice Cream (252-441-3332; www.americanpieobx.com), 1600 Beach Road, MP 9.5, Kill Devil Hills. Award-winning ice cream and pizza converge at this spot, just across Beach Road from the Ramada. In addition to hand-tossed New York–style pies, the menu includes hot subs, corn dogs, salads, and fresh-fruit smoothies. $–$$.

♪ ↬ **Crabby Fries** (252-441-9607; www.crabbyfries.com), 1006 Beach Road, MP 9, Lifesaver Shops, Kill Devil Hills. Take-out-only spot serves a popular menu of pressed sandwiches, including some vegetarian choices, burgers, steamed blue crabs and shrimp, fried

---

HEALTHY TREATS

🌱 **Zen Pops** (252-573-0306; www.pintsandpops.com), with a new shop in KDH at 3105 Bypass, MP 5.5, in the Seagate North Shopping Center, makes organic and vegan popsicles and ice creams in a variety of flavors, many inspired by traditional Southern favorites, such as spiced pecan and blueberry cobbler. Products are made from all-natural ingredients, with the vegan pops made with organic coconut milk. Besides the shop in Kill Devil Hills, you can find Zen Pops at Tommy's Market, in Duck; Coastal Provisions, in Southern Shores; the Brewing Station, in Kill Devil Hills; and the Manteo Farmer's Market (May–September). Look also for vegan baked goodies created by **Kind Confections** (www.kindconfectionsobx.com), available at Zen Pops, Tommy's Market, and other OBX locations.

---

seafood, hand-squeezed lemonade, hush puppies, and fries from breakfast through dinner daily. Beer and wine available to go. $.

Kill Devil's Frozen Custard & Beach Fries (252-441-5900; www.killdevilsfrozencustard.com), 1002 Bypass, MP 8.5, Kill Devil Hills. Real frozen custard, made fresh hourly, and so much better than ordinary soft-serve ice cream, comes in a variety of flavors, such as Key lime, egg nog, and, of course, chocolate. Try the waffle sundae for a satisfying treat. The menu also includes never-frozen, hand-cut fries; Coney Island hot dogs; barbecue; and burgers, both meat and veggie. $.

BREAKFAST Ships Wheel Restaurant (252-441-2906), 2028 Beach Road, MP 9.5, Kill Devil Hills. Breakfast-only spot, located in front of the Ebb Tide Family Motel, wins rave reviews for huge portions at reasonable prices. Served 6 AM–noon. Home of the world's, or at least the beach's, largest pancakes. $.

COFFEE ❀ ♪ ☂ (ᵥᵢ) **Front Porch Café** (252-449-6616; www.frontporchcafeonline.com), 2200 Bypass, Milepost 6 Plaza, Kill Devil Hills; additional locations in Nags Head (252-480-6616; MP 10.5, Bypass) and Manteo (252-473-3160; 300 US 64). The original KDH location of the Kill Devil Coffee Roasters, voted the best beans on the beach, is the centerpiece of a complex, which also includes paint-your-own pottery and beading studios, making it a fun family stop. Besides a full-service espresso bar, Front Porch offers baked goods and a special children's menu. Wi-Fi is free, but there is no place to plug in to recharge at the KDH location. $.

DELI ❊ **KDH Deli** (252-255-1720; www.kdh -deli.com), 710 Bypass, MP 8.5, Kill Devil Hills. Features Boar's Head subs and sandwiches on freshly baked breads, plus homemade soups. $.

❊ **N.Y. Bagels** (252-480-0990; www.outer banksbagels.com), 1708 Bypass, MP 7.5, Dare Center, Kill Devil Hills; second location in Nags Head (252-480-0106; MP 14, Bypass, Outer Banks Mall). More than a dozen flavors of scratch-made bagels are baked fresh daily. The KDH location is open all year and serves lunch sandwiches made with Boar's Head meats and cheese, as well as breakfast sandwiches and treats. $.

❊ ✍ **Stop-N-Shop Beach Shop, Deli & Wine Shop** (252-441-6105; www.stopnshopobx.com), 100 Beach Road, MP 8.5, Kill Devil Hills. Everything you'll need for a picnic is available here, including deli sandwiches made of Boar's Head cold cuts, along with convenience and gourmet food items, beach supplies, and souvenirs. $.

SEAFOOD ↭ **Billy's Seafood** (252-441-5978), 1341 Colington Road, Colington Island. This little grocery sits in the heart of the Colington Island crabbing scene, making it a great place to pick up local blue crabs, "shedders," shrimp, or other seafood, plus groceries, beer, and wine. They'll even steam the shrimp or crabs for you. A gold member of Outer Banks Catch (www.outerbankscatch.com).

✍ ↭ **Carolina Seafood Buffet** (252-441-6851; www.carolinaseafoodbuffet.com), 2042 Beach Road, MP 6.5, Kill Devil Hills. All-you-can-eat seafood lovers will enjoy this locally owned buffet, operated by the same family as the Jolly Roger. Kids like the pirate theme and giveaways; parents like the price—kids pay their age, plus 99 cents. Most of the seafood is local catch, including all-you-can-eat blue crabs and

steamed clams, and there's always a prime rib roast. $$$.

VEGETARIAN ✍ **Thai Room Restaurant** (252-441-1180; www.thairoomobx.com), 710 Beach Road, MP 8.5, Oceanside Plaza, Kill Devil Hills. Longtime Asian spot on the Beach Road is a local favorite for its many vegetarian dishes and specials featuring local seafood, as well as its classic Thai and Chinese menu. Takeout and full bar available. Lunch $; dinner $–$$.

WINE AND BEER ((ೲ)) **Chip's Wine and Beer Market** (252-449-8229; www.chipswinemarket .com), 2200 Bypass, Milepost 6 Plaza, Kill Devil Hills. With 2,000 different wines and the Great Wall of Beer offering 450 brews, Chip's may well have the largest selection of adult beverages on the Outer Banks. The Tasting Lounge offers your choice of wines dispensed by an automated wine station, or try a flight of draft beers. Chip's also offers fun and informative wine classes conducted by a pro, and free beer and wine tastings each week.

BREW THRU: A BEACH TRADITION

Convenience is number one on vacation, and who wants to get out of the car to shop for beer, wine, coolers, or a soft drink? **Brew Thru** (www.brewthru.com), a local company founded in 1977, solved the problem, opening drive-through stores where you literally pull into the store to make your selection. Look for the locations in Corolla, Kitty Hawk, Kill Devil Hills, Nags Head, and at Jockey's Ridge. The company is also famous for its T-shirts, issued annually since 1977. The KDH location (MP 5.5) is also an outlet store, with lots of Brew Thru souvenirs, plus all the vintage tees from the '70s to today.

❊ Entertainment

CONCERT SERIES **Outer Banks Forum for the Lively Arts** (252-202-4289; www.outerbanks forum.org), First Flight High School Auditorium, 100 Veterans Drive, Kill Devil Hills. Nonprofit brings top international classical and popular music groups to town September to May. Tickets $12 (student) to $25.

NIGHTCLUBS ✍ ♈ **Boardriders Grill at the Pit Surf Shop** (252-480-3128; www.pitsurf.com), 1209 Bypass, MP 9, Kill Devil Hills. A hangout for surfers day and night, the Pit serves a surf-inspired menu all day, featuring wraps, quesadillas, pizzas, grinders, and tacos, with many vegetarian items. The tiny dining room, carved out of a log cabin, is a museum of cool surfer stuff. Alcohol-free teen dance nights with lots of giveaways are held several times a week during the summer. Add in frequent live bands and DJs spinning tracks, and this is one of the hottest nightlife scenes on OBX.

> **QUICK TIP:** Avoid the Tuesday crush at the Pit when the crowds arrive for $1 tacos. You can try the same tacos for the same price from 4 to 6 PM at the daily happy hour.

☿ **The Comedy Club** (252-441-2151; www.comedyclubobx.com), Ramada Plaza Resort, 1701 Beach Road, MP 9.5, Kill Devil Hills. Touring comedians keep the laughs coming at the longest-running comedy club on the beach.

⚓ ☿ ↶ **Just George's Sports Bar** (252-480-6677; www.captaingeorges.com), 705 Bypass, MP 8.5, Kill Devil Hills. Located next to Captain George's Seafood Buffet, this state-of-the-art sports bar has 28 flat-screen TVs carrying all the major sports packages. An à la carte menu featuring local seafood is served until close, or you can go next door and raid the buffet all through the game. Dishes $–$$$; buffet $$$$.

❋ ☿ ↶ **Port O' Call Restaurant & Saloon** (252-441-7484; www.outerbankspocrestaurant.com), 504 Beach Road, MP 8.5, Kill Devil Hills. Formerly a romantic piano bar stuffed with stained glass and Victorian antiques, Port O' Call now lives up to its potential as one of the best dance clubs in town, with frequent live music, DJ parties, a big dance floor, and two levels of bar seating. You can eat lunch or dinner at the adjacent restaurant or browse one of the beach's largest jewelry selections. This is also a popular spot for holiday buffets. Lunch $$; dinner $$$.

Other hot spots for nightlife in Kill Devil Hills include the Outer Banks Brewing Station, the Jolly Roger, Peppercorns in the Ramada Plaza, Goombay's Grille and Raw Bar, MexiCali Brewz, and Chilli Peppers Coastal Grill.

❋ Selective Shopping

ART GALLERIES **The Bird Store** (252-480-2951; www.thebirdstore.biz), 807 Bypass, MP 8.5, Kill Devil Hills. Antique decoys and fishing and hunting equipment on display, plus new carvings, paintings, and prints of wildfowl and other wildlife by local and regional artists.

✾ ☂ **KDH Cooperative Gallery & Studios** (252-441-9888; www.kdhcooperative.com), 502 Bypass, MP 8.5, Kill Devil Hills. Artist-operated gallery exhibits the works of over two dozen local artists. Frequent classes and openings are offered year-round.

BOOKS **Croatan Bookery Limited** (252-480-1890), 2006 Bypass, MP 10, Kill Devil Hills. Bookshop stocks over 100,000 volumes of mostly used and antiquarian books, including many books on North Carolina and Outer Banks topics.

SPECIAL SHOPS **A Penny Saved Thrift & Consignment Shop** (252-441-8024), Seagate North, MP 5.5, Bypass, Kill Devil Hills. Great spot to browse on a rainy day.

BrewThru Outlet (252-453-2878; www.brewthru.com), 3101 Bypass, MP 5.5, Kill Devil Hills. Licensed beer apparel and memorabilia, plus over 50 different Brew Thru T-shirts, including annual designs dating back to 1977.

The Cyber Dog USA Holistic Pet Shop (252-449-0331; www.thecyberdogusa.com), 3105 Bypass, Seagate North, MP 5.5, Kill Devil Hills. Healthy pet foods and remedies, plus doggie day care available by the hour.

Gold-N-Gifts (252-449-2900; www.obxgold.com), 3105 Bypass, Seagate North, MP 5.5, Kill Devil Hills. Locally owned store has the largest selection of charms on the beach, including the OBX bead and other locally inspired pieces.

Natural Creations Fine Jewelry (252-255-2015; www.obxjeweler.com), 2501 Bypass, MP 5.75, Kill Devil Hills. Custom jewelers let you design you own ring using virtual technology, and sell signature Outer Banks Destination bracelets and unique lighthouse and Outer Banks beads.

Shore-Fit Sunwear (252-441-4560; www.obxsunwear.com), 100 E. Helga Street, at MP 5.5, Bypass, Kill Devil Hills. Swimwear boutique offers fashionable solutions to fit every figure, including many plus-size selections, as well as beach cover-ups, bags, and sandals.

❋ Special Events

February: **Annual Chili Cookoff** (www.chilli-peppers.com); sponsored by Chilli Peppers Restaurant.

March: **Outer Banks Family YMCA Penguin Plunge** (252-449-8897; http://obxplunge.wordpress

.com/), Ramada Plaza Resort. **First Flight Cruisers Shamrock Car Show and Poker Run** (www.firstflightcruisers.com).

April: ✈ **Wilbur Wright's Birthday** (252-441-7430; www.nps.gov/wrbr), Wright Brothers National Memorial.

May: **Coastal Gardening Festival** (252-473-4290), Outer Banks Arboretum and Teaching Garden. Educational lectures, plus plant sale and vendors. Free. **Nags Head Woods 5K and 1-Mile Fun Run** (www.nagsheadwoods5krun.org). A beach party and buffet at the Ramada Plaza Resort follows the races. **Outer Banks Spring Festival of Arts and Crafts** (www.outerbankschamber.com), Baum Senior Center.

July: ✈ **Wright Kite Festival** (252-441-4127; www.kittyhawk.com), Wright Brothers National Memorial, MP 8. Giant animal and stunt kites fly over the national monument, and kids get to build a kite of their own. Free with NPS admission.

August: **Kitty Hawk Kites Ocean Games and Surf Kayak Competition** (252-441-4127; www.kittyhawk.com), Ramada Plaza Resort. Family beach day includes kayak and stand-up paddleboarding races, and free rentals all day. Free. ✈ **National Aviation Day** (252-441-7430; www.nps.gov/wrbr). Celebrate Orville Wright's birthday at the Wright Brothers National Memorial.

October: **Outer Banks Stunt Kite Competition** (www.kittyhawk.com), Wright Brothers National Memorial. Kite competition set to music. Free stunt and power kite lessons. ✈ **Artrageous Art Extravaganza Day** (252-473-5558; www.darearts.org), Dare County Family Recreation Park. ✈ **Wildfest** (252-475-4180; www.fws.gov/alligatorriver), Wright Brothers Pavilion. A day of conservation activities includes lots of activities for kids, including Wildlife Olympics, bird feeder making, beach-combing bingo, plus live animal exhibits. **OBX Horror Film Festival and Zombie Beach Walk** (www.obxhorrorfest.com), Ramada Plaza Resort.

December: **First Flight Anniversary** (252-473-2111; www.nps.gov/wrbr), Wright Brothers National Memorial. Free December 17th celebration includes flybys and guest speakers. **Man Will Never Fly Memorial Society Annual Banquet** (www.manwillneverfly.com). Held the night before the First Flight Anniversary—on December 16th—this evening event centers around disputing the "myth" of manned flight and traditionally lasts all night. The society's motto: "Birds fly, men drink." Open to the public. **Poulos Christmas Lights,** Ocean Acres Drive. The Poulos family was the 2005 national winner of NBC's *Today Show* lights contest, thanks to their unique, extensive, and ever-growing holiday lights display. Their house, also featured on HGTV, is decorated during the month of December.

NAGS HEAD AND WHALEBONE JUNCTION

THE UNUSUAL NAME OF NAGS HEAD appears on maps as early as 1738. Some say it was named for the wild horses that roamed the area, others that it reminded an early settler of a place on the coast of England that bears the same name. The most colorful tale attributes the name to the practice of placing a lantern around a horse's head and leading it along the shore to lure ships to their destruction. In those early days, much of the wood for building homes, as well as other supplies, came ashore from shipwrecks. The practice of luring ships, called "wrecking," has not actually been documented along this coast.

The region became the earliest summer resort on the Outer Banks in the 1830s, when a planter from nearby Perquimans County brought his family to Nags Head to avoid the fevers and insects of the interior. The area along the sound soon housed hotels and cottages with docks extending far out to accommodate the steamers that put in with vacationing families. By the 1860s, families began to build cottages along the oceanfront, some of which still survive in the historic Nags Head Beach Cottage Row, otherwise known as the Unpainted Aristocracy.

The largest surviving dune along the Banks is located in Nags Head. Named Jockey's Ridge, possibly for the horse races once held there, the dune is moving slowly southwest with the prevailing wind. The sand has buried many things over the years, including a church and a hotel. Along the Bypass opposite Jockey's Crossing shopping center, the top turrets of a castle, all that remains of a minigolf course, can be seen peeking above the sands.

THE REMAINS OF A MINIGOLF COURSE PEEK THROUGH THE SANDS OF THE LARGEST DUNE ON THE BANKS.

The origin of the name Whalebone Junction is another mystery, but the area where the Beach Road joins the Bypass, as well as the causeway coming from Manteo, does provide the backbone and nerve center of the area. Whalebone Junction is the oldest developed part of Nags Head, where you'll find long-lived establishments such as Sam and Omie's and Owens' Restaurant.

GUIDANCE Nags Head Town Hall (252-441-5508; www.townofnagshead.net), 5401 S. Croatan Highway, on the Bypass, MP 15, Nags Head.

POST OFFICE The **Nags Head Post Office** (252-441-0526) is located at 100 W. Deering Street. The zip code for Nags Head is 27959.

PUBLIC RESTROOMS Bathhouses with restrooms are located on the Beach Road at Bonnet Street, Hargrove Street, Epstein Street, and Jennette's Pier. On the Bypass, the Harvey Sound Access at MP 16 also has public facilities.

GETTING THERE Nags Head stretches from Eighth Street, about MP 10, south to MP 21 on Old Nags Head Road. The Nags Head–Manteo Causeway (US 64) comes from Roanoke Island and the mainland at Whalebone Junction.

GETTING AROUND The Beach Road (NC 12) and the Bypass (US 158) join together in Whalehead Junction. From the junction with the causeway to Roanoke Island, NC 12 continues south through the national park lands along an inland route, while the Beach Road, now named Old Oregon Inlet Road, continues south along the coast for a few miles before rejoining NC 12. This area, almost completely composed of residential and rental properties, is called South Nags Head.

MEDICAL EMERGENCY Outer Banks Hospital (252-449-4500 or 1-877-359-9179; www.theouter bankshospital.com), 4800 S. Croatan Highway/US 158, MP 14 on the Bypass. A full-service hospital offering inpatient, outpatient, and emergency services 24 hours a day all year.

Outer Banks Urgent Care Center (252-261-8040; www.outerbanksurgentcare.com), 4923 Bypass, MP 14.5. Extended hours are available for walk-ins.

Virginia Dare Women's Center (252-441-2144); 2518 Bypass, MP 10.5.

✳ To See

✳ ✑ ⚕ ✑ ⟿ **Jennette's Pier** (252-255-1501; www.jennettespier.net), 7223 Beach Road, MP 16.5. Originally erected in 1939, the pier is now part of the North Carolina Aquarium system and has been rebuilt with concrete pilings that hopefully will withstand hurricanes. Nature exhibits in the pier house include touch tanks and the state's largest collection of mounted trophy fish. The state facility's goal is to preserve the tradition of family pier fishing for future generations. Adult and children's fishing passes are available by the day, weekend, or week. Pier and surf fishing classes are offered for all

ARCHITECTURE

About 40 structures along a 1.5-mile stretch of the Beach Road make up the **Nags Head Beach Cottage Row Historic District.** Many of them are listed on the National Register of Historic Places. Nine cottages built before 1885 survive today. Most of the others date from 1900 to 1940.

A CLASSIC COTTAGE IN THE NAGS HEAD BEACH COTTAGE ROW HISTORIC DISTRICT.

The cottages share design elements that have come to define the Nags Head style: unpainted cedar-shake siding, wide hip-roofed porches with built-in benches, and windows covered by propped shutters.

Cottage Row runs between MP 12 and MP 13.5 on the Beach Road, from the C. H. White Cottage at 3905 S. Virginia Dare Trail on the north end to the Outlaw Cottage at 4327 S. Virginia Dare Trail and Dove Avenue in the south. Besides the private cottages, historic buildings include **St. Andrew's By-the-Sea Episcopal Church** (1915), the **First Colony Inn** (1932), and **Mattie Midgette's Store** (1914), now a museum. The oldest surviving cottage is the 1859 **Spider Villa,** at 4049 Virginia Dare Trail.

A paved multiuse path runs along the Beach Road past the historic cottages. To see the cottages from the beach side is more difficult, as there are no public beach accesses in the historic district. The closest are at Conch Street (3600 block, Beach Road) at the north end, and Small Street (4500 block, Beach Road) at the southern end.

This first cottage community was built close to the eastern flank of the Jockey's Ridge dune, and a fine overall view of the historic district can be gained from the observation tower at **Jockey's Crossing Shopping Center,** built on the site of the old dance pavilion.

In recent years, the Town of Nags Head has encouraged the use of local design elements, including cedar-shake siding, wraparound porches, wooden shutters, gable and hip roofs, cupolas, and lifesaving station watchtowers. These can now be seen in numerous new commercial and residential units along the Banks.

RECOMMENDED READING:

Bishir, Catherine. *Unpainted Aristocracy: The Beach Cottages of Old Nags Head.* Raleigh, NC: Division of Archives and History, North Carolina Department of Cultural Resources, 1978.

Roundtree, Susan Byrum. *Nags Headers.* Winston-Salem, NC: John F. Blair, 2001. Oral histories from Nags Head's oldest families.

Roundtree, Susan Byrum, and Meredith Vaccaro. *Nags Head: Then and Now.* Manteo, NC: One Boat Guides, 2004. Walking tour of the Unpainted Aristocracy district.

Siddons, Anne Rivers. *Outer Banks.* New York: HarperCollins Publishers, 1992. This best-seller introduced the Unpainted Aristocracy to the world.

ages. Other programs include beachcombing, crafts, and Parents' Night Out. Open all year and 24/7 during the summer season.

♂ ♿ **Jockey's Ridge State Park** (252-441-7132; www.jockeysridgestatepark.com), Carolista Drive, MP 12, Bypass. Sunset is the most popular time to visit Jockey's Ridge, when many make the pilgrimage up the 100-foot dune to enjoy a spectacular 360-degree view of the Outer Banks. The Visitor Center Museum provides exhibits and films explaining the unique ecosystems, and two nature trails explore the maritime thickets of stunted live oak slowly being buried by the sand. A handicapped-

SURFING COMPETITIONS AT JENNETTE'S

Ever since Jennette's Pier was completed, surfers have been eyeing the break. In 2011, the **ESA Eastern Surfing Championships** (www.surfesa.org), long a popular annual event at Cape Hatteras, moved its finals competition to Nags Head next to the pier. The event was a big success, and ESA, the largest amateur surfing organization in the world, now returns for its September competition every year. The **OBX Pro Surfing Competition** (www.facebook.com/OuterBanks Pro), an event in the Western Atlantic Surf Series (www.westernatlanticsurf.com) with a $30,000 purse, is held at Jennette's as well, usually a bit later in September. The **Bud Light Lime Surf Series** (www.budlightlimesurfseries.com) also stops at Jennette's for the OBX Labor Day Cup Pro Invitational.

accessible boardwalk leads out to the dune. Activities available include hang gliding and kite flying, as well as kayaking, windsurfing, and swimming at the Soundside Road access. Sandboarding is permitted during the off-season with a permit. Activity programs, including birding walks and kayak tours, are offered at the park all year. Admission and all programs are free.

Nags Head Gallery Row, located around MP 10 between the Beach Road and the Bypass. This area, encompassing both Gallery Row Road and Driftwood Road, was set aside by the town especially to encourage local arts and crafts. Most artists here live on the property. While several of the galleries have closed in recent years, you'll still find **Glenn Eure's Ghost Fleet Gallery** (252-441-6584; www .glenneureart.com), **Jewelry by Gail** (252-441-5387; www.jewelrybygail.com), and the **Morales Art Gallery** (1-800-581-0300; www .prints-r-us.com) here. See our listings for art galleries in the *Selective Shopping* section.

Nags Head Town Hall (252-441-5508; www .townofnagshead.net), 5401 Bypass, MP 15. The town's ever-growing collection of local art in all media is on display free Monday through Friday 8:30–5.

Outer Banks Beachcomber Museum in Mattie Midgette's Store (252-441-6259; www.oldnagshead.org), 4008 Beach Road, MP 13. Housed in a 1914 grocery store listed on the National Register of Historic Places, this museum exhibits treasures gathered by Nellie Myrtle Pridgen during a lifetime of beachcombing, including rare shells, sea glass, whalebone, messages in bottles, driftwood, and all sorts of curious artifacts. Check website for upcoming open house hours.

MANY BUILDINGS ON THE OUTER BANKS USE ARCHITECTURAL FEATURES DRAWN FROM HISTORY, INCLUDING THIS LANDMARK ON NAGS HEAD'S GALLERY ROW.

USS *Huron* Historic Shipwreck Preserve (910-458-9042; www.archaeology.ncdcr.gov), Bladen Street Beach Access, Beach Road, MP 11.5. North Carolina's first shipwreck preserve is the site of the wreck of the *Huron* just north of Nags Head Pier, about 250 yards off the beach. The *Huron*, one of the last iron steamships in the U.S. Navy, sank in heavy seas on November 27, 1877, with many lives lost. In summer, buoys mark the stern and bow of the wreck, now home to a great variety of sea life, and a popular destination for divers and snorkelers. A second wreck, a tugboat that went down in

KAYAKS ARE THE BEST WAY TO EXPLORE THE MARSH ON THE SOUND SIDE OF THE BANKS.
Betty Lou Wright

1919, is located halfway between the *Huron* and the pier. Collecting artifacts from the wrecks is prohibited. Look for an information kiosk at the Bladen Street Beach Access.

✳ To Do

BICYCLING In Nags Head, a multiuse path runs parallel to the Beach Road from MP 21 on Old Oregon Inlet Road north through Whalebone Junction to Eighth Street (MP 11.5), where it continues as a widened shoulder through Kill Devil Hills.

BOATING Fishing Unlimited (252-441-5028; www.fishingunlimited.net), 7665 Nags Head–Manteo Causeway. Rent an outboard skiff or pontoon boat for fishing, crabbing, or sight-seeing on Roanoke Sound by the full or half day.

Kitty Hawk Watersports (252-441-2756; www.kittyhawkwatersports.com), 6920 Bypass, MP 16. Rent a Hobie catamaran for a sail on the sound. Beginner sailing lessons available.

CANOEING AND KAYAKING The marshes that stretch between Nags Head and Roanoke Island, both north and south of the Causeway, although very shallow, are full of waterfowl and wading birds.

Kayaks and canoes can launch at the Nags Head Causeway Estuarine Access on the south side of the Causeway near its east end, where you'll also find a parking area, public dock, and fishing gazebo.

Another good place to put your kayak in is behind Jockey's Ridge State Park at the Soundside Access area, found by following the road that runs along the southern boundary of the park to its end. This is also a popular swimming beach for families.

See *Water Sports Centers* for kayak rentals and tours.

CRAFTS ✐ ☂ **Beach Memories** (252-441-7277; www.obxbeachmemories.com), 2236 Bypass, Plaza Del Sol, MP 10. Scrapbook supplies to preserve your vacation memories.

✐ ☂ **Cloud Nine** (252-441-2992; www.obeadx.com), 3022 Bypass, MP 11, Pirate's Quay Shopping Center. Long-established beading store offers classes for adults and children, with a huge selection of beads, beach glass, and jewelry-making supplies, plus gold and silver jewelry created by local artists.

✐ ☂ **Outer Banks Bear Factory** (252-255-5222; www.jockeysridgecrossing.com), 3941 Bypass, Jockey's Ridge Crossing, MP 12.5. A great spot for birthday parties.

DOLPHIN TOURS Causeway Watersports (252-441-8875; www.causewaywatersports.com), 7649 Causeway. Daily cruises aboard the *Miss Bodie Island* 40-foot pontoon boat offer sightings of dolphins and tours of Wanchese and Manteo harbors.

Jet Boat Dolphin Tours (252-441-WILD; www.obxwaterworks.com), 7612 Causeway. Wild Bill's Waterworks offers fast-paced tours in search of dolphins.

&. **Nags Head Dolphin Watch** (252-449-8999; www.dolphinwatch.com), 7517 Causeway. This group of independent researchers studies the Atlantic bottlenose dolphins that make their home in Roanoke Sound. Two-hour journeys aboard a canopied pontoon boat, offered May through September, are guided by naturalists with a wealth of information about the dolphins, many of whom have individual names.

FISHING AND CRABBING The so-called little bridge on the eastern end of the Nags Head–Manteo Causeway is a noted spot for fishing. Crabbing is good at the nearby Nags Head Causeway Estuarine Access at the eastern end of the Causeway. Rangers at **Jockey's Ridge State Park** (252-441-2588; www.jockeysridgestatepark.com) offer a free Crabby Clinic during the summer months.

❋ ✄ &. ♂ ✆ **Jennette's Pier** (252-255-1501; www.jennettespier.net), 7223 Beach Road, MP 16.5. A two-story pier house holds a tackle shop, gift shop, and exhibits. Adult and children's fishing passes are available by the day, weekend, or week. Pier and surf fishing classes are offered for all ages. Open all year and 24/7 during the summer season.

Joe Malat's Outer Banks Surf Fishing Schools (252-202-4189; www.joemalat.com). Joe Malat wrote the books, literally, on pier fishing, surf fishing, and crabbing. His three-night surf-fishing schools are held twice a year, with seminars and workshops scheduled year-round.

Nags Head Pier (252-441-5141; www.nagsheadpier.com), 3335 Beach Road, MP 11.5. The 750-foot Nags Head Pier has a full-featured tackle shop that rents rods and reels, rental cottages, and a restaurant serving breakfast, lunch, and dinner, where the motto is "You hook 'em, we cook 'em." Open 24 hours a day in season, with lights for night fishing.

Outer Banks Pier (252-441-5740; www.fishingunlimited.net), 8901 Old Oregon Inlet Road, MP 18.5. This 600-foot pier operated by Fishing Unlimited is open 24 hours a day and is lit for night fishing. Senior discount passes and rental rods and reels available. ♅ **Fish Heads Bar & Grill** on the pier serves inexpensive sandwiches, appetizers, and drinks, and hosts live music and dancing on the deck. $.

Roanoke Sound Pier (252-441-5028; www.fishingunlimited.net), 7665 Causeway. Fishing Unlimited also operates this 300-foot pier on the Causeway—a great place for crabbing or fishing for speckled trout or other inshore species. Tackle shop and boat rentals on-site.

Whalebone Tackle (252-441-7413; www.whalebonetackle.com), 7667 Causeway. Convenient shop in business since 1977 sells tackle, ice, and bait, as well as some of the finest custom rods on the Banks.

FOR FAMILIES ✄ **Friday Night Movies on the Sound** (www.childrenatplayobx.com), Windmill Point, 6800 Bypass. Free family movies outside on the sound. Fee for parking.

✄ **Kitty Hawk Kites** (252-449-2210; www.kittyhawk.com), 3933 Bypass, MP 13, Jockey's Ridge Crossing. Indoor 22-foot rock-climbing wall, lessons in kite flying, and kite-making workshops, plus a shop full of sportswear, colorful kites, and great gifts are on-site. Climb the tower for a view of Jockey's Ridge.

✄ **Kitty Hawk Watersports** (252-441-2756; www.kittyhawkwatersports.com), 6920 Bypass, MP 16. Bumper boats, a 26-foot-tall climbing wall, plus Jet Ski rentals, parasailing, windsurfing, and more are offered at this sound-side mecca. This stretch of the Bypass around MP 16 has a wealth of entertainment options, including several go-kart tracks and minigolf courses. **Jurassic Park Minigolf** (252-441-6841) is next door.

✄ &. **Mutiny Bay Adventure Golf** (252-480-6606), 6606 Bypass, MP 16. This 18-hole pirate-themed course has an arcade and snack bar, plus a pirate ship and a store with pirate souvenirs. **Full Throttle Speedway** (252-441-4499; 6504 Bypass), close by, is operated by the same family.

✄ **Nags Head Raceway** (252-480-4639), 7000 Bypass, MP 16. Indy-style track also has bumper cars, an arcade, and ice cream.

✄ **Outer Banks Family YMCA Water Park** (252-449-8897; www.ymcashr.org), 3000 Bypass, MP 11. Water park with two pools and a waterslide is open during the summer.

✄ ⊤ ⦿ **Outer Banks Gear Works Lasertag & Fun Center** (252-480-8512; www.obxgearworks.com), 2420 Bypass, MP 10.5, South Beach Plaza. Family amusement center with a wide variety of video games, as well as air hockey, laser tag, and a bounce house for the younger set, is a great place for a birthday party or rainy-day fun.

GOLF ∞ **Nags Head Golf Links** (252-441-8073; www.nagsheadgolflinks.com), 5615 S. Seachase Drive. Beautiful Scottish links–style course located in the Village of Nags Head development overlooks Roanoke Sound. The Ⓨ **Links Grille** serves lunch and after-golf libations, as well as Sunday brunch, and is open to the public.

HANG GLIDING AND PARAGLIDING
Jockey's Ridge State Park (252-441-7132; www.jockeysridgestatepark.com), Carolista Drive, MP 12, Bypass. People with USHGA Hang 1 or other agency-approved certification may hang glide free of charge on the dunes at Jockey's Ridge. Register with the park office.

∞ **Kitty Hawk Kites Hang Gliding School.** (252-441-2426; www.kittyhawk.com; MP 12, Bypass). The world's largest hang-gliding school has been teaching students from ages 4 to 84 how to catch the wind since 1974. Lessons are held on the soft sand dunes of Jockey's Ridge State Park. Other ways to get airborne include paragliding under a lightweight glider wing.

JOCKEY'S RIDGE, A FAVORITE LAUNCH POINT FOR HANG GLIDERS

Or—the ultimate thrill for early airplane buffs—fly a museum-quality replica of the 1902 Wright glider that paved the way for the first powered flight.

HEALTH AND FITNESS CLUBS **Ashtanga Yoga Center** (252-202-0345; www.ashtangayogaobx .com), Central Square Shopping Center, 2910 Bypass, MP 11. Introductory to advanced classes, special events, and retreats are offered in several disciplines of yoga.

Outer Banks Family YMCA (252-449-8897; www.ymcashr.org), 3000 Bypass, MP 11. Open daily, this 28,000-square-foot center offers a wide range of equipment, facilities, and classes. Indoor facilities include a lap pool, hot tub, sauna, racquetball courts, cycling studio, and fitness center with FitLinxx strength training. Outdoors is a water park with waterslides, plus a skate park. Massage therapy and free child care are available. Nonmembers can purchase day, week, or monthly passes for individuals or families. Many hotels and vacation cottages also offer free passes to the Y.

Outer Banks Sports Club (252-441-8361; www.obxsportsclub.com), 2423 Bypass, MP 10. Fully equipped sports club has the latest in equipment, plus an elevated running track, a variety of classes, and a smoothie bar.

KITEBOARDING AND WINDSURFING Windmill Point and the Nags Head Sound Access at MP 16 are considered excellent spots for beginners learning both kiteboarding and windsurfing. More advanced boarders can launch from the sound access at Jockey's Ridge, considered a prime "bump-and-jump" spot. On the ocean side, the Jennette's Pier access is a popular spot to launch.

SKATE PARK **Outer Banks Family YMCA Skatepark** (252-449-8897; www.ymcashr.org), 3000 Bypass, MP 11. Open to in-line skaters, bikers, and scooters, as well as skateboarders, the YMCA's skate park offers daily and weekly passes. Built by Grindline, the 15,000-square-foot park features a concrete bowl and large street course. Open all year. Helmets required, and pads for those under 18.

SNORKELING AND DIVING The wrecks of the USS *Huron* and the tugboat *Explorer*, both located just north of the Nags Head Pier, are two of the most popular shore diving sites on the Banks. See our description in the *To See* section.

Outer Banks Dive Center (252-449-8349; www.obxdive.com), 3917 Bypass, MP 12.5. Located across from Jockey's Ridge, this full-service dive shop offers sales, rentals, and repairs, plus instruction for all levels, and guided beach and charter boat dives to historic wrecks.

SPECTATOR SPORTS Many tournaments featuring some the top names in surfing, surf kayaking, and kiteboarding are held annually on the Banks. The sound behind Pamlico Jack's is a good place to check out the kiteboarding action.

Windmill Point, at MP 16.5 on the Bypass, was for many years a landmark in Nags Head, with a famous restaurant located here as well as a windmill, a replica of the many windmills that once ground grain along the Outer Banks. The restaurant was deemed unsafe and was burned to the ground as part of a training exercise for area firefighters in 2011. The artifacts of the SS *United States* that filled the restaurant were transferred to the Mariners Museum in Newport News, Virginia. The windmill was moved to the Island Farm on Manteo, where it will be restored. Windmill Point is currently the site a variety of outdoor events, including the new Outer Banks Seafood Festival.

SURFING Cavalier Surf Shop (252-441-7349; www.cavaliersurfshop.com), 4324 Beach Road, MP 13.5. Family-run shop, in operation since 1960, offers sales and rentals, as well as private and group surfing lessons.

Hukilau Surf Camp (252-441-7548; www.surfcampobx.com). Aimed at middle and high school students, these one-day introductions to surfing sponsored by the Nags Head Church are a real bargain, offering one-on-one instruction by experienced surfers, all equipment, and a safe environment.

Outer Banks Boarding Company (252-441-1939; www.obbconline.com), 103 E. Morning View Place, MP 10.5, Bypass. The shop of board-shaping legend Lynn Shell carries his signature Shell Shapes, plus high-tech boards from other top designers, and rents surfboards and wet suits. Surfing lessons from top pros available through the **Farm Dog Surf School** (252-339-4283; www.farmdog surfschool.com).

Scammell's Corner Surf Shop & Ice Cream Parlor (252-715-1727), 6406 Beach Road, MP 15.5. Tom Neilson custom-shaped boards are for sale, plus lots of surfer gear, from swimsuits to tie-dye, as well as Hawaiian tikis and artwork. Rental boards and surf lessons available, along with a full menu of ice cream treats.

Secret Spot Surf Shop (252-441-4030; www.secretspotsurfshop.com), 2815 Bypass, MP 11. One of the first surf shops on the Banks, this colorful spot showcases the shapes of founder Steve Hess and other custom and classic boards, plus an eclectic selection of surfer stuff from beater boards to tiki statues. New and used boards and stand-up paddleboards are for sale or rent, and lessons are available.

THE HUKILAU SURF CAMP TEACHES THE ESSENTIALS OF THE SPORT IN A SINGLE DAY.

Whalebone Surf Shop (252-441-6747 or 1-877-855-1975; www.whalebonesurfshop.com), 2214 Bypass, MP 10. Open for more than 30 years, Whalebone stocks boards by top shapers for sale and soft-tops for rent. Lessons for beginners never have more than three students per instructor. T-shirts with the shop's skull and crossed surfboards logo are popular even with nonsurfers.

TENNIS Public courts are located at MP 10 behind Kelly's Restaurant.

WATER SPORTS CENTERS Causeway Water Sports (252-441-8875; www.causewaywatersports .com), 7649 Causeway. Sweet spot on the Causeway is easy to find thanks to a 30-foot observation tower. Here you can rent kayaks, WaveRunners, and stand-up paddleboards (SUPs), take an ecotour, sign up for parasailing or a dolphin tour, or enjoy a free SUP lesson (with rental).

Kitty Hawk Kites–Whalebone Watersports (252-441-4112; www.kittyhawk.com), 7517 Causeway. Rent single or double kayaks, stand-up paddleboards, or Jet Skis to explore Roanoke Sound. Sign up for kayak ecotours of the Bodie Island marshes or a night bioluminescence tour, or take a Jet Ski tour down to the Bodie Island Lighthouse or north to Roanoke Island. Kiteboarding lessons are also available at this location.

Kitty Hawk Water Sports (252-441-2756; www.kittyhawkwatersports.com), 6920 Bypass, MP 16. Windsurfing and kiteboarding lessons are a specialty thanks to the location's shallow waters that are perfect for beginners. Sound-side spot also rents kayaks, windsurfers, sailboats, surfboards, stand-up paddleboards, and Jet Skis; offers Jet Ski and kayak tours; and books parasailing and dolphin tours.

Nags Head Waterworks (252-441-0477; www.obxwaterworks.com), 7612 Causeway, and sister store **Wild Bill's Waterworks** (252-441-WILD), 6900 Bypass. Second-generation Nags Head entrepreneur specializes in parasail trips and jet boat dolphin-watch tours. Kayak and WaveRunner rentals also available.

✳ Green Space

BEACHES More than three dozen public beach access points line NC 12 (the Beach Road) and Old Oregon Inlet Road in Nags Head, between the Eighth Street access on the border with KDH in the north, south to the national seashore.

Bathhouses with restrooms where you can shower and change are located at Bonnet Street, Hargrove Street, Epstein Street, and Jennette's Pier. Bathhouse locations have lifeguards during the summer months.

Handicapped access is available at many of the beach accesses. The Eighth Street access has a stability mat for easier access. Beach wheelchairs are available from the Nags Head Fire Department (252-441-5909), Jockey's Ridge State Park (252-441-7132), and the Bodie Island Lighthouse Visitor Center (252-441-5711). From Memorial Day to Labor Day, they are also available on a first-come, first-served basis at the Bonnett Street (MP 11) and Hargrove Street (MP 17) beach access areas. For assistance accessing the beach, call Nags Head Ocean Rescue at 252-305-6068. Permits to operate an ATV on the beach are also available for those with disabilities.

Fires on the Nags Head beaches are allowed with a Pit Fire Permit from the town's Fire and Rescue Department. Since permits are issued based on current wind and weather conditions, you must obtain the permit between 5 and 9 PM on the day you plan to use it at Station 16 (252-441-5909), MP 14.5 on the Bypass, or at the South Nags Head Station 21 (252-441-2910), 8806 S. Old Oregon Inlet Road. Permits are $10.

From October 1 through April 30 each year, you can drive on the Nags Head beach with a town permit, available at Town Hall, Jennette's Pier, and local tackle shops for $25.

Pets are allowed on Nags Head beaches at all times, as long as they are leashed and their owners clean up after them.

For current updates on regulations, visit the Town of Nags Head website (www.nagsheadnc.gov) or call 252-441-5508.

SOUND ACCESS ♿ ⚓ **Harvey Sound Access,** at MP 16 on the Bypass, is a favorite with windsurfers and kiteboarders. A picnic area, grill, and restrooms are available. This is also a demonstration site for sustainable coastal development, with cisterns, two rain gardens, and educational exhibits.

Jockey's Ridge Sound Access, located at the end of Soundside Road, which runs along the state park's southern boundary, is a popular place for families to swim.

♿ **Little Bridge,** on the Causeway, is a popular spot for fishing.

&. **Nags Head Causeway Estuarine Access,** on the south side of the Nags Head–Manteo Causeway near its east end, has a public dock, fishing gazebo, and kayak launch. Bring the chicken necks and string, because the crabbing is great here.

TRAILS ♪ &. Jockey's Ridge State Park (252-441-7132; www.jockeysridgestatepark.com), Carolista Drive, MP 12, Bypass. Two nature trails explore the maritime thickets of stunted live oak slowly being buried by the sand. One begins at the visitors center, the other at the sound-side access. A handicapped-accessible boardwalk leads out to the dune.

♪ **Nags Head Town Park and Town Trail** (252-441-5508; www.nagsheadnc.gov), 415 Health Center Drive, off MP 11 on the Bypass at Barnes Road. This shady park has a picnic shelter, grill, playground, and restrooms. The **Town Trail,** a 1.6-mile round-trip that runs over several forested dune ridges down to the shore of Roanoke Sound, begins at the end of the parking lot. A map of the trail is available on the Nags Head Woods website (www.nature.org).

☀ Lodging

BED & BREAKFAST INNS ❋ ♪ ♂ (ᵞᵖ) **First Colony Inn** (252-441-2343 or 1-800-368-9390; www.firstcolonyinn.com), 6720 Beach Road, MP 16. A "grand old lady" of the Outer Banks, this inn first welcomed guests in 1932 and is the sole survivor of the era of shingle-style beach hotels. In 1988, the revered inn was rescued from the ocean by moving it to the other side of the Beach Road, and an extensive renovation began. Placed on the National Register of Historic Places, the inn received an award from the Historic Preservation Society of North Carolina. Charmingly decorated throughout, the inn is a great favorite for wedding parties and other romantic occasions.

Today the two stories of rocking-chair-lined verandas that circle the building still look out on sunrise and sunset. Outside, a large swimming pool and hot tub sit amid award-winning landscaping next to a croquet court.

A hot breakfast buffet and afternoon tea are both included in the daily rate. The property is nonsmoking and kid friendly. Babysitting service and cribs are available. AAA, AARP, and military discounts offered. Open all year. $–$$$$.

(ᵞᵖ) **Nags Head Beach Inn Bed and Breakfast** (252-441-8466 or 1-800-421-8466; www.nagsheadbeachinn.com), 303 E. Admiral Street, off the Beach Road, MP 10.5. Eight guest rooms are available in this historic cottage, once used as a dance pavilion. A deluxe continental breakfast is served daily in the lobby, which is decorated with pictures of the building during its days as a dance hall. The Admiral Street beach access is a short walk away, and beach chairs, body boards, and bikes are available. Closed in winter. $–$$$.

CONDO RENTALS &. (ᵞᵖ) **Oasis Suites** (252-441-5211; www.oasissuites.com), 7721 Nags Head–Manteo Causeway. This boutique hotel offers luxurious suites on the north side of the Causeway. Leather furniture and Oriental rugs, beds topped with poofs, flat-screen plasma TVs,

full kitchens with stainless-steel appliances, balconies, and Jacuzzi tubs are standard in the family and executive suites, most of which sleep six. Pool and outdoor hot tub are fenced for privacy. Guests can dock their boats behind the hotel or fish from the dock. $$$–$$$$.

COTTAGE AND MOTOR COURTS To experience an "old Nags Head" vacation, make reservations for a week at one of the cottage courts that date from the 1950s to 1970s. A few still survive along the Beach Road, where you can enjoy the simple life filled with traditional beach activities. Cottages typically have kitchen facilities, private baths, and porches. Amenities usually begin and end with air-conditioning and a TV hooked to cable. Linens are usually provided; phones and pools are generally not. Fish-cleaning stations and grills are available for cooking up the daily catch. Some so-called cottages may actually be attached units. Cottage and motor courts usually close during the off-season.

Cahoon's Cottages (252-441-5358; www.cahoonscottages.com), 7213 Beach Road, MP 16.5. Oceanfront cottages located next to Cahoon's Variety Store, a longtime landmark on the beach, have between two and four bedrooms.

☀ **Nags Head Fishing Pier Cottages** (252-441-5141; www.nagsheadpier.com), 3335 Beach Road, MP 11.5. The pier rents several cottages of various sizes within walking distance. Docks available for small boats.

Ocean Side Court (252-441-6167; www.oceansidecourt.com), 6401 Beach Road, MP 15.5. No pets. Oceanfront.

☀ (ᵞᵖ) **Pelican Cottages** (252-441-2489; www.pelicancottages.com), 3513 Beach Road, MP 12. Two- and three-bedroom cottages on oceanfront. Outdoor hot showers. Complimentary bikes. Free YMCA passes. Linens are not furnished.

❋ **The Sandspur Motel & Cottage Court** (252-441-6993 or 1-800-522-8486; www.sandspur.net), 6607 Beach Road, MP 15.5. Two-night cottage rentals available off-season. Linens and towels are not provided. Outdoor pool, hot tub, playground, pay phone, coin laundry. Efficiencies and motel rooms also available.

MOTELS ❋ (ᵗᵖ) **Colonial Inn Motel** (252-441-7308; www.colonialinnmotel.com), 3329 Beach Road, MP 11.5. This low-rise classic enjoys an excellent location directly on the ocean and next door to the Nags Head Fishing Pier. The motel is now open all year, and it serves a continental breakfast included in the room rate. Thirty-one rooms and efficiencies, plus 12 one- and two-bedroom apartments, many paneled in knotty pine, are all first or second floor, with parking in front. The outdoor pool is open seasonally. Free YMCA passes are available to guests. Free Wi-Fi in the office. Fall and winter specials provide real bargains. $–$$.

🍴 **Sea Foam Motel** (252-441-7320; www.seafoam.com), 7111 Beach Road, MP 16.5. Now on the National Register of Historic Places, this 1948 landmark is hard to miss—it's painted the color of its name. Noted by the register as "one of the last and best preserved" motor courts of the post–World War II era, it's better noted by guests for its well-kept, clean rooms, friendly service, and oceanfront location. Poolside rooms are available at slightly lower rates. Cottages, one- and two-bedroom apartments, and efficiencies are available with fully equipped kitchens. During the summer season, these are only rented by the week and have a loyal repeat clientele. The motel wraps around a heated swimming pool, shuffleboard court, and children's playground. Children under 12 stay free. $–$$.

VACATION RENTALS ❋ **Cove Realty** (252-441-6391 or 1-800-635-7007; www.coverealty.com), 105 E. Dunn Street, MP 13.5. Weekly, yearly, and winter rentals, with many located in Nags Head, including Old Nags Head Cove. Some cottages have negotiable rates.

❋ 🐾 **Rentals on the Ocean** (252-441-5005; www.rentalsontheocean.com), 7128 Beach Road, MP 16.5. Group of pet-friendly cottages in South Nags Head are available all year.

❋ Where to Eat

DINING OUT
In Nags Head

🍴 🔆 **Blue Moon Beach Grill** (252-261-BLUE; www.bluemoonbeachgrill.com), 4104 Beach Road, MP 13, Surfside Plaza. Earning raves on the Beach Road, this chef-owned restaurant teams a menu of innovative dishes with a friendly family environment. Vegetarian entrées and daily chef specials available. Lunch and dinner $$–$$$.

🍴 🗡 🍸 ▼ **Kelly's Outer Banks Restaurant & Tavern** (252-441-4116; www.kellysrestaurant.com), 2316 Bypass, MP 10.5. An OBX institution, Kelly's is the flagship of restaurateur Mike Kelly's family of eateries, which also includes Mako Mike's and Pamlico Jack's. Kelly is a noted community booster, sponsor of the annual St. Patrick's Day celebration, and the walls of his restaurant are covered with Outer Banks memorabilia. This enormous restaurant has both a fine-dining and a more casual tavern menu, as well as a spacious nightclub and the largest dance floor on the beach. Kelly's has something for everyone: early-bird specials, late-night menu, and frequent live entertainment, everything from national touring bands to female impersonators. Tavern menu $–$$; dinner $$–$$$$.

🍴 ♿ **Old Nags Head Café** (252-441-1141; www.nagsheadcafe.com), 3948 Beach Road, MP 13. Formerly Jockey's Ribs, this historic property amid the Unpainted Aristocracy has been reinvented as an upscale dining experience, with a full bar, homemade desserts, and daily chef specials. Southern fried chicken and fried green tomatoes are specialties. Dinner only, $$–$$$.

🍴 ♿ 🍸 🔆 **Owens' Restaurant** (252-441-7309; www.owensrestaurant.com), 7114 Beach Road, MP 16.5. Bob and Clara Owens opened a 24-seat café on the beach back in 1946, among the first to gamble on the oceanfront property opened up by the causeways. Today, Owens' is one of the most storied restaurants on the coast, highly praised for its Southern coastal cuisine, fresh seafood, attentive service, and elegant decor. The entrées are classic preparations of soft-shell crab, shrimp, crabmeat, lobster, and beef, served with a crock of cheese and crackers as a before-meal treat, an old Southern tradition. Ordering fried seafood here is a waste; there are so many delicious and original dishes to choose from. Built to resemble a lifesaving station, Owens' exhibits a collection of logbooks, photographs, and historic memorabilia. The elegant upstairs lounge is a great place for a before-dinner drink. Dinner only, $$$$.

On the Causeway

🛥 ♿ 🍸 ✺ **Basnight's Lone Cedar Café** (252-441-5405; www.lonecedarcafe.com), 7623 Causeway. Longtime president pro tem of the North Carolina Senate Marc Basnight and his family operate this local favorite, located on the Causeway. Basnight is a native of Manteo and a strong supporter of the local fishing and farming industries. This is one place where you can be sure the fish is from local waters, the vegetables are locally grown, and the beef, pork, and chicken are all natural. The **Osprey Lounge** is a favorite at sunset and late night. Named for the ospreys that nest just outside, the lounge offers frequent live entertainment. Don't miss the mural depicting the history of the Outer Banks fishing fleet painted by the Tillett sisters. Sunday brunch $–$$; dinner $$–$$$$.

✺ **Brine and Bottle** (252-715-1818; www.thebrineandbottle.com), 7531 Causeway, Caribbean Professional Center. One of the new breed of chef-owned restaurants on the Outer Banks, this little spot with a deck on the sound delights diners with creative seasonal fare based on Southern classics—pimento cheese, deviled eggs, country ham, shrimp and grits—all with little gourmet twists that make them memorable. Fresh local seafood stars in the dinner entrées, juicy burgers and fried house-made pickles on the lunch menu, and bacon jam ranks top among the appetizers. Jars of pickles made by chef-owner Andrew Donovan and his staff are available to take home. Enjoy a glass of wine from the extensive wine list on the outside deck, with live music during the summer. Reservations available. Lunch $$; dinner $$–$$$$.

🛥 ♿ ✺ **Sugar Creek Soundfront Seafood Restaurant** (252-441-4963; www.sugarcreek seafood.com), Causeway, MP 16.5. Located on the north side of the Causeway, this soundfront restaurant is a favorite with families, thanks to all the wildlife visible from the dock and outdoor boardwalks. The menu is noted for its prize-winning shrimp and grits, and daily prime rib. The ✳ **Sugar Shack** (252-441-3888), a seafood market selling sandwiches, seafood baskets, steamer buckets, and seafood by the pound, is next door. Lunch $–$$; dinner $$–$$$$.

🛥 ✺ **Tale of the Whale** (252-441-7332; www.taleofthewhalenagshead.com), 7575 Causeway. A great choice for large groups; otherwise ask for a private booth with a water view. Prices are high, but portions are huge and

recipes are traditional at this longtime favorite. Many diners take advantage of the early-bird discount; seniors receive a price break all the time. Plan to spend any wait time at the outdoor bar and gazebo, where live music entertains at sunset in the summer months. (Or skip the meal and head straight for the water.) Dinner only, $$–$$$$.

EATING OUT
In Nags Head

✺ **Cafe Lachine** (252-715-2550; www.cafe lachine.com), 5000 Bypass, MP 14, Outer Banks Mall. Operated by a husband and wife team, Johanna and Justin Lachine, both chefs, this modest spot in the mall rose rapidly to one of the top-ranked eateries on the Banks. This is a great spot to pick up a fast, inexpensive breakfast or lunch that doesn't scrimp on flavor or healthy ingredients. The café opens at 6:30 AM every day and closes at 5 PM (3 PM on Sunday). Stop by for a box lunch for your day at the beach. Breakfast and lunch $.

Dirty Dick's Crab House (252-449-CRAB; www.dirtydickscrabs.com), 2407 Bypass, MP 10.5. Fun spot with a menu that is constantly being updated, this is one of Nags Head's most popular spots. See our description in the *Eating Out* section of "Avon (Kinnakeet)," where a sister location recently opened a new venue.

🛥 ♿ ✺ **The Dunes Restaurant and R-Bar** (252-441-1600; www.thedunesrestaurant.com), 7013 Bypass, MP 16. Big all-you-can-eat breakfast buffet with lots of fresh fruit is served every morning in summer, weekends in spring and fall. The R-Bar serves a full selection of cocktails and several North Carolina beers, plus a bar menu. Breakfast $; dinner $$–$$$.

🛥 **FireFly Restaurant** (252-480-0047; www.fireflyobx.com), 2706 Bypass, MP 11. The bright yellow exterior of FireFly belies its interior, where vine-twined trees blink with (artificial) fireflies. The ambience is Southern comfort, with drinks served in mason jars, country-fried steak, ribs, and crab potpie, followed by desserts such as deep-fried Moon Pie and cheese pie from a family recipe. Upstairs, a classy martini bar leads out to a balcony with a view. The children's menu is unusually extensive—even including a kids'-size version of the signature lobster mac and cheese. Dinner only, $$.

🛥 🍸 ✺ **Miller's Waterfront Restaurant** (252-441-6151; www.millerswaterfront.com), 6916 Bypass, MP 16. This family-owned spot was renovated after Hurricane Irene and now has a pier and gazebo to enhance its excellent soundside views, along with a bright new dining room.

SUNSET SPOTS

In Nags Head and along the Causeway, some of the best sunsets in the Outer Banks are on view every evening. Several restaurants have maximized this asset by building sound-side decks and gazebos for sunset viewing, and offer live music during the summer season to help ease day into night.

On the Causeway, live music at sunset can be found at **Basnight's Lone Cedar Café** (252-441-5405; www.lonecedarcafe.com), **Tale of the Whale** (252-441-7332; www.taleofthewhale nagshead.com), **Brine and Bottle** (252-715-1818; www.thebrineandbottle.com), and **Sugar Creek Soundfront Seafood Restaurant** (252-441-4963; www.sugarcreekseafood.com). All have great waterfront views on the sound.

On the Bypass, check out the sunset celebrations at **Pamlico Jack's Pirate Hideaway** (252-441-2637; www.pamlicojacks.com) and **Miller's Waterfront Restaurant** (252-441-6151; www.millerswaterfront.com). **South Beach Grille** (252-449-9313; www.southbeachgrillemp16 .com), though not on the water, still has great sunset views from its lofty patio.

Be sure to check schedules as days and times of live music performances vary.

Live music on the pier accompanies the sunset during the summer months. Lunch $–$$; dinner $–$$$.

♂ ゟ ♂ ♈ ↬ **Pamlico Jack's Pirate Hideaway** (252-441-2637; www.pamlicojacks.com), 6708 Bypass, MP 15.5. Enjoy a fabulous sunset view from the dining room, huge lounge, or outdoor deck at this sound-side landmark, formerly Penguin Isle. The restaurant's wine cellar, which survives from the previous incarnation, received the *Wine Spectator* Award of Excellence many times. Early-bird specials, daily happy hours, and drink specials help visitors stay within budget. Outdoors on the Sunset Deck, a bar designed to look like a pirate ship, and live entertainment nightly in season make this a destination for all ages. Reservations available. Dinner only, $–$$.

♂ ゟ ↬ **Pier House Restaurant** (252-441-4200; www.nagsheadpier.com/food.htm), Nags Head Pier, 3335 Beach Road, MP 11.5. A survivor from another time, this restaurant sits above the surf on the Nags Head fishing pier. The view can't be beat, even on a stormy day. This is a popular breakfast spot, where you'll find some unusual local dishes, such as salt herring. You can bring your own catch if you like, and the kitchen will prepare it for you. The Pier House has a full bar and daily happy hour. Dinner includes a free pass to the pier for an after-dinner stroll. Breakfast, lunch, and dinner $–$$.

♈ ↬ **Sam & Omie's** (252-441-7366; www.sam andomies.net), 7228 Beach Road, MP 16.5. Opened in 1937 by a couple of fishermen as a place to eat breakfast before the Oregon Inlet charter fleet set out for the day, Sam & Omie's is still serving breakfast more than 70 years later. Breakfast features "Omie-lettes" and Bloody Marys. Later in the day attention shifts to steamed seafood and cold ones, as fishermen gather to discuss the day's catch. Breakfast and lunch $; dinner $$.

♈ ♂ **South Beach Grille** (252-449-9313; www .southbeachgrillemp16.com), 6806 Beach Road, MP 16. Enjoy views of both ocean and sound from the lofty covered deck on this new Beach Road landmark. The wide-ranging menu is tinged with Caribbean flavors, from fish tacos to Costa Rica Baked Fish, and has plenty to offer vegetarian or gluten-free diners. Come early for happy hour or early-bird discounts backed by fabulous sunsets, or later for the nightly entertainment in season. Lunch $; dinner $$.

In South Nags Head

♈ **Fish Heads Bar & Grill** (see *Where to Eat* in "South Bodie Island and Oregon Inlet").

BARBECUE ♂ **Sooey's BBQ and Rib Shack** (252-449-4227; www.sooeysbbq.com), 3919 Beach Road, MP 12.5, Jockey's Ridge Crossing. Southern fried chicken and barbecued pork, beef brisket, and chicken, plus ribs by the rack and Southern-style sides, available for dine in or take out. Other locations in Corolla and Duck. $–$$$.

BEACH BARS ❄ ♂ ♈ ↬ **Lucky 12 Tavern** (252-255-LUCK; www.lucky12tavern.com), 3308 Beach Road, MP 12. A neighborhood favorite for its reasonably priced food, 20 beers on tap, HDTVs tuned to sports, pool table, laid-back attitude, and pizza served until 2 AM. Lunch and dinner $–$$.

❋ ⟡ **Mulligan's Raw Bar & Grille** (252-480-2000; www.mulligansobx.com), 4005 Bypass, MP 13. Fun spot across from Jockey's Ridge has a great second-floor deck and tiki bar with views of the beach and the historic Nags Head cottage district. An Orange Crush cocktail at sunset is rapidly becoming an OBX tradition. Steamed oysters, Greek salads, and buffalo burgers are specialties. Serving breakfast from 8 AM. Breakfast $; lunch $–$$$; dinner $$–$$$$.

⟡ **Red Drum Grille and Taphouse** (252-480-1095), 2412 Beach Road, MP 10.5. Over a dozen beers on tap, foosball, and pool, plus live entertainment and steamed seafood served late. The ribs in honey habanero barbecue sauce are legendary. Lunch and dinner $–$$.

❋ ⟡ **Slammin' Sammy's Offshore Grille and Stillery** (252-449-2255; www.slammin sammys.com), 2407 Bypass, MP 10.5. More than 40 TVs make this a favorite stop for sports fans. The lunch specials are real bargains. $–$$.

⟡ **Thumpers** (252-480-2228), 2519 Beach Road, MP 10.5. Formerly the Beach Road Grill, this oceanfront spot backed up to the beach offers a fun bar atmosphere, burgers, and unrivaled location. Frequent live local acoustic acts. $.

⬡ **Tortuga's Lie Shellfish Bar and Grille** (252-441-RAWW; www.tortugaslie.com), 3014 Beach Road, MP 11. Beachside spot features Caribbean-themed dishes made with local catch, late-night steamed seafood, sushi on Wednesday, beach volleyball, and cool vibes year-round. Lunch $; dinner $$.

BEACH FAST FOOD Dune Burger (252-441-2441), 7304 Beach Road, MP 16.5. Get your burgers, hot dogs, fries, and other fast-food favorites from the window at this throwback to another age, strategically placed in Whalebone Junction. Open seasonally. $.

Fat Boyz Ice Cream & Grill (252-441-6514; 7208 Beach Road, MP 16.5. Full line of ice cream delights, plus hand-patted burgers, veggie burgers, fresh grilled tuna, crabcakes, onion rings, and other take-out favorites are served at this pink landmark on the Beach Road. Shady side deck has tables where you can eat. Homemade ice cream cakes for special occasions are a specialty. $.

❋ ⟐ ⬡ **King Tut's Wiener Hut** (252-715-3200; www.kingtutswienerhut.com), 3022 Bypass, MP 11, Pirates Quay. Everything comes in a bun at this spot, featuring locally made Weeping Radish preservative and hormone-free hot dogs, bratwurst, and sausages. The game room is great for both kids and adults, with everything from old-school Ping-Pong, darts, billiards, and pinball to the latest Wii and cornhole. Daily specials. Beer available. $.

⟡ **The Snowbird** (252-441-0000), 3522 Beach Road, MP 12. Try your choice of 24 different flavors of soft-serve ice cream, plus burgers and seafood "boats," at this sweet little takeout spot on the Beach Road. Don't miss the cool penguin T-shirts. Stays open very late in summer. $.

BREAKFAST ❋ **Grits Grill** (252-449-2888; www.gritsgrill.com), 5000 Bypass, MP 14, Outer Banks Mall. Retro diner serves breakfast and burgers from 6 AM to 2 PM. Huge biscuits, fresh Krispy Kreme doughnuts, and reasonable prices on everything from corned-beef hash to shrimp and grits make it a real find. $.

COFFEE SHOPS ❋ ⟡ ⬥ ⟐ ((•)) **Front Porch Café** (252-480-6616; www.frontporchcafeon line.com), 2515 Bypass, MP 10.5. Beyond the freshly roasted artisanal coffees, pastries baked on-site, and free Wi-Fi, each Front Porch location is a little distinctive. The Nags Head store has a stage for live music performances and kids' story hours, plus a special Wi-Fi bar with comfy couches and plenty of plug-in space.

⟡ ✿ ((•)) **Morning View Coffee House** (252-441-4474; www.themorningview.com), 2707 Bypass, MP 11, Forbes Building. Fair-trade and organic beans from around the world are roasted on-site by owner Ashley Barnes.

DELI Country Deli (252-441-5684; www.countrydeliobx.com), 4107 Beach Road, MP 13, Surfside Plaza. Overstuffed subs, deli meats, cheeses, and salads, plus a selection of beverages available to take out or delivered free along the Central Beaches. $

⟡ ((•)) ⬡ **Waveriders Coffee and Deli** (252-715-1880; www.waveriderscoffeeanddeli.com), 6705 Bypass, MP 15.5. Bagel breakfast sandwiches, muffins, smoothies, and Boar's Head sandwiches, and a full coffee bar, served in a friendly family environment. $.

ICE CREAM AND SWEETS The Fudgery (252-480-0163; www.fudgeryfudge.com), 3933 Bypass, MP 12.5, Jockey's Ridge Crossing. Handcrafted fudge, cooked in copper kettles the old-fashioned way.

Scoops Ice Cream Parlor (252-441-4485), 3941 Bypass, MP 12.5, Jockey's Ridge Crossing. Old-fashioned ice cream shop conveniently located across from the often burning sands of Jockey's Ridge.

(ɴ) **Surfin' Spoon** (252-441-7873; www.surfin spoon.com), 2408 Beach Road, MP 10.5. Frozen yogurt with a difference at this spot, operated by a former professional surfer. There's a game room, walls covered with local surfing memorabilia, and creative frozen yogurt and sorbet creations by Jesse Hines and his wife, Whitney.

MARKETS Cahoon's Market and Deli (252-441-5358; www.cahoonscottages.com), 7213 Beach Road, MP 16.5. Cahoon's, for four decades a one-stop shopping destination along the Beach Road, has gone gourmet, adding cheese, pâté, and locally grown vegetables to its offerings of wine, beer, meats cut in-house, and other groceries, plus beach, fishing, and camping supplies.

Nags Head Produce (252-564-7344; www .outerbanksproduce.com), 3711 Bypass, MP 12.5. Seasonal stand next to the Austin Fish Market provides locally sourced fruits, vegetables, baked goods, and jams, most from farms in the surrounding counties.

PIZZA Maxximmuss Pizza (252-441-2377; www.nagsheadpizza.com), 5205 Bypass, MP 14.5. Authentic New York–style thin-crust pizza, stromboli, and calzone, plus hot subs, jumbo wings, salads, and Middle Eastern specialties such as gyros, falafel, and hummus, available to eat in or take out. Gluten-free pizzas and desserts are a specialty, along with lots of vegetarian items. Beer available. Delivery as far as Manteo and MP 8. Second location in Rodanthe (252-987-0050). $$.

SEAFOOD TO GO (ɴ) ✧ **Austin Fish Company** (252-441-7412; www.austinfishcompany .com), 3711 Bypass, MP 12.5. Family owned and operated, Austin's has been selling fresh fish and seafood from the same location next to Jockey's Ridge for over 50 years. Freshness is guaranteed, and most of the seafood here comes from local waters. Fried seafood dinners and sandwiches, as well as a variety of steamed seafood and locally famous mac and cheese, are available to go, or to eat at the picnic tables outside.

The Sugar Shack (252-441-3888; www.sugar creekseafood.com), 7340 Nags Head–Manteo Causeway, MP 16.5. Get a bucket of seafood to "go-go" or a seafood pizza from the shack, located at the edge of the sound next to sister restaurant **Sugar Creek.** Delivery of raw or steamed seafood available. A seating area overlooks the sound.

✳ Selective Shopping

ANTIQUES Antique Mall of Nag's Head (252-449-6363); **Mystic Antiques & Collectibles** (252-441-1710); **Southern Soldier Antiques** (252-715-0144; www.southernsoldierantiques.com), 2910 Bypass, MP 11, Central Square. Three antiques stores located in Central Square present the Central Beaches' largest concentration of vintage collectibles and antiques.

ART GALLERIES
On the Beach Road

Seagreen Gallery (252-715-2426; www.seagreengallery.com), 2404 Beach Road, MP 10.5. Gallery specializing in art made from found or cast-off items has a huge collection of jewelry made from sea glass and natural seeds, plus gourds, vintage quilts, and more.

Seaside Art Gallery (252-441-5418 or 1-800-828-2444; www.seasideart.com), 2716 Beach Road, MP 10. Established in 1961, this gallery carries over 2,000 originals by local and contemporary artists. Special collection of original animation art from Disney, Hanna-Barbera, and others.

Yellowhouse Galleries (252-441-6928; www.yellowhousegallery.com), 2902 Beach Road, MP 11. Housed in a 1935 beach cottage along the Beach Road, this gallery invites you to browse through its huge collection of antique maps, charts, and prints, most over 100 years old, as well as many modern reproductions and works by local artists.

On Gallery Row—MP 10

Ann's Beach Crafts (252-441-7459), 206 E. Driftwood Street. Consignment shop displays crafts handmade by local residents, at very reasonable prices.

Glenn Eure's Ghost Fleet Gallery (252-441-6584; www.glenneureart.com), 210 E. Driftwood Street. Unique gallery displays the sculptural watercolors and oils, woodcuts, and etchings of the talented Eure, a fixture for over 30 years on the local art scene.

Morales Art Gallery (1-800-581-0300; www.prints-r-us.com), 207 E. Gallery Row. Exhibits a wide variety of art forms, from X-ray botanical photography to Disney prints.

JEWELRY **Dare Jewelers** (252-441-1112), 5000 Bypass, MP 14, Outer Banks Mall. Handcrafted 14-carat gold sea-life jewelry, OBX watches, and locally created stained-glass designs.

Halloran & Company (252-480-3132; www.halloranandco.com), 4711 Bypass, MP 14, Croatan Centre. Established in 1996, this is the only jeweler on the Outer Banks licensed to sell official Wright Brothers First Flight Centennial jewelry and ornaments.

Jewelry by Gail (252-441-5387; www.jewelrybygail.com), 207 E. Driftwood Street, Gallery Row. Award-winning jeweler Gail Kowalski creates original pieces using diamonds, colored pearls, amethysts, and corals. Her designs include a popular line of Outer Banks lighthouse charms. The shop features a magnificent amethyst chandelier.

Lone Wolff Trading Co. (252-449-5111; www.facebook.com/Lonewolfftrading), Surfside Plaza, MP 13. Specializing in affordable jewelry made of sterling silver and semiprecious stones.

SHOPPING CENTERS Fun shopping destinations in Nags Head, arranged north to south:

Gallery Row, MP 10. Set between the highways, this is the largest concentration of galleries on the beach.

Central Square, MP 11, Bypass. Noted for its group of antiques stores.

Pirate's Quay Shoppes, MP 11.5, Bypass. Sophisticated and fun shops and boutiques next to the YMCA skate park. Look for the huge boat propeller out front.

🦐 ✐ **Jockey's Ridge Crossing** (www.jockeysridgecrossing.com), MP 12.5, Bypass. Located at the site of the original Nags Head Pavilion across from the Jockey's Ridge dunes, this two-story center offers refreshments, shopping, and an indoor climbing wall, plus planned activities and daily sunset celebrations throughout the summer.

Outer Banks Mall (www.nagsheadshopping.com), MP 14, 5000 Bypass. Over two dozen specialty shops, restaurants, department stores (including Sears), and a Food Lion grocery are located next to the Outer Banks Hospital. Restaurants here include **New China** (252-449-8000), **Taiko Japanese Sushi Bar** (252-449-8095; www.taikosushiobx.com), Cafe Lachine (see *Eating Out*), a N.Y. Bagels, and Grits Grill (see *Breakfast*). Check website for coupons.

Tanger Outlet Mall (252-441-5634; www.tangeroutlet.com/nagshead), MP 16.5, Bypass. Discount shopping for name brands. Check for coupons on the website.

SPECIAL SHOPS **Chameleon Clogs** (252-441-2550; www.facebook.com/Chameleon.Clogs), 2515 Bypass, MP 10.5, Shoppes at 10.5. Design your own Swedish-style wooden clog with your choice of leather, velvet animal print, or customized handwoven textile upper.

🎄 **Christmas Mouse** (252-441-8111; www.christmasmouse.com), 2401 Bypass, MP 10.5. It's Christmas all year at this store, full of holiday cheer and gift ideas. Second location in Duck.

The Cotton Gin (252-449-2387; www.cottongin.com), 5151 Bypass, MP 14.5. Southern tradition meets coastal charm in room after room of gifts, home and garden decor, decoys, dolls, collectibles, and holiday decorations. The original store in Jarvisburg (252-491-2387; US 158) has an even bigger selection, plus a wine-tasting room.

✐ 🎄 **Life on a Sandbar** (252-449-9066; www.lifeonasandbar.com), Jockey's Ridge Crossing, MP 12.5, Bypass. Popular logo'd souvenirs are available all over the Banks, but the shop at Jockey's Ridge offers the full range, plus local art and jewelry, Del Sol products that change color in the sun, make-your-own sand art, and hair wraps and braiding.

Lil' Grass Shack (252-441-1922; www.lilgrassshack.net), 2707 Bypass, MP 11. Try on a fun dress for beach or evening in a grass shack changing room or browse silver jewelry made by a local silversmith.

✐ 🎄 **Pirates and Pixies Toystore** (252-441-8697; www.toysobx.com), 7332 Beach Road, MP 17. Cool toy store has a playroom with a dollhouse, train set, and plenty of games.

Rock-A-Bye Baby (252-480-2297; www.rockabyebabyobx.com), 4711 Bypass, MP 14, Croatan Centre. New and used baby clothes, furniture, toys, and maternity and baby shower supplies, plus baby equipment rentals for vacationing families.

Salty Paws Biscuits (252-480-2284; www.saltypawsbiscuits.com), Jockey's Ridge Crossing, MP 12.5, Bypass. Healthy all-natural dog treats are made fresh daily.

Shipwreck (252-441-5739), 7746 Causeway. Stop on the Causeway for driftwood and shells, plus local crafts and scenic views.

✳ Special Events

January: **Frank Stick Memorial Art Show** (252-473-5558; www.darearts.org), Glenn Eure's Ghost Fleet Gallery. Local artwork on display through mid-February.

February: **The Elizabethan Rendezvous Pirate's Jamboree** (252-473-1061; www.elizabethr.org), Pamlico Jack's. Fun-filled gala produced by Elizabeth R and Company includes an Elizabethan seven-course feast and cabaret entertainment.

March: **Kelly's Restaurant and Tavern's St. Patrick's Day Parade** (252-441-4116; www.kellys restaurant.com), Beach Road, MP 12–10.5. **Annual George Barnes Oyster Roast** (252-441-7132; www.jockeysridgestatepark.com), Jockey's Ridge State Park. Help create new oyster beds, then enjoy the party afterward for free.

April: **Kitty Hawk Kites Easter Egg-stravaganza** (252-449-2210; www.kittyhawk.com), Kitty Hawk Kites, MP 12.5. The largest egg hunt on the Outer Banks is held at the Kitty Hawk Kites store. Free. **Kitty Hawk Kites Fly Into Spring** (252-449-2210; www.kittyhawk.com), Jockey's Ridge State Park. Kite flyers from around the country demo stunt kites and teach lessons in honor of National Kite Month. Free. **Earth Day OBX** (252-255-1501; www.jennettespier.net), Jennette's Pier.

May: **International Miniature Art Show** (252-441-5418; www.seasideart.com), Seaside Art Gallery, Beach Road, MP 11. **Kitty Hawk Kites Hang Gliding Spectacular and Air Games** (252-441-2426; www.kittyhawk.com), Jockey's Ridge State Park. The world's longest running hang gliding competition.

Early June: **Rogallo Kite Festival** (252-449-2210; www.kittyhawk.com), Jockey's Ridge State Park, MP 12.5. Weekend festival honors the inventor of the flexible wing. Night flight on the beach at the Ramada Plaza Resort. **Family Fishing Tournament** (252-255-1501; www.jennettespier.net), Jennette's Pier.

Late June: **Kitty Hawk Kites Sand Sculpture Festival** (252-449-2210; www.kittyhawk.com). Professional sand-sculpting company creates a sand masterpiece and gives sand clinics during a week that culminates with a full day of entertainment at Jockey's Ridge Crossing. Free.

August: **Outer Banks Watermelon Festival** (252-441-4124; www.kittyhawk.com), Kitty Hawk Kites, MP 12.5. A day of hometown fun and contests. Free.

September: **Outer Banks Pirate Festival** (252-441-4127; www.outerbankspiratefestival.com). Weekend festival sponsors swashbuckling events at various venues, with a pirate encampment and a Scallywag School for Young Scoundrels at the Kitty Hawk Kites store. Free. **ESA Eastern Surfing Championships** (757-233-1790 or 1-800-937-4733; www.surfesa.org), Jennette's Pier. The grand finale of the amateur surfing competition season on the East Coast.

Early October: **Nags Head Surf Fishing Club Invitational Tournament** (www.nagsheadsurf fishingclub.org).

October: **Outer Banks Seafood Festival** (www.outerbanksseafoodfestival.org), Windmill Point, MP 16, Bypass. Free festival with live music, cooking demonstrations, and kids' activities showcases Outer Banks seafood.

Late November: **Kites with Lights** (252-441-4127; www.kittyhawk.com), Jockey's Ridge State Park, MP 12.5. Giant illuminated kites fly over Jockey's Ridge at sunset. Refreshments and Santa at the Kitty Hawk Kites store. Free. **Kitty Hawk Kites Hanging with Santa** (252-441-4127; www.kitty hawk.com), Kitty Hawk Kites, MP 12.5. Free pictures with Santa in a demonstration hang glider. **Outer Banks Gobbler 5K and Little Giblet Fun Run** (www.outerbanksrunningclub.org). Course follows Roanoke Sound.

December: **New Year's Eve 5K** (252-441-7299; www.tortugaslie.com), Tortuga's Lie Restaurant, Beach Road, MP 11.5. Go for a run, then head back to the restaurant for a champagne toast.

SOUTH BODIE ISLAND
AND OREGON INLET

PRONOUNCED BAH-DEE ISLAND by natives, and named supposedly for the many bodies that washed up here during the worst years of the Graveyard of the Atlantic, this end of the peninsula forms the northernmost segment of Cape Hatteras National Seashore. The Bodie Island Lighthouse, Coquina Beach, and a campground are maintained by the park rangers.

Bodie Island comes to an end at Oregon Inlet and the Bonner Bridge, stretching to Pea Island, Hatteras Island, and beyond. The Bonner is scheduled to be rebuilt and perhaps replaced with a bridge taking a different route across the inlet, a matter of great debate among local residents and national wildlife advocates.

Just before the Bonner Bridge, Oregon Inlet Fishing Center is home to one of the world's most storied fishing fleets. Crowds gather here in the afternoons to see what the boats bring in.

GUIDANCE At the entrance to the Cape Hatteras National Seashore on NC 12, the **Whalebone Welcome Center** (252-441-6644 or 1-877-629-4386; www.outerbanks.org) dispenses friendly advice on activities in the national park and on the route south. Open daily except Thanksgiving and Christmas Day.

The **Bodie Island Visitor Center** (252-473-2111; www.nps.gov/caha) at the Bodie Island Lighthouse is open daily except for Christmas Day.

PUBLIC RESTROOMS Public facilities can be found at the Whalebone Welcome Center; the Bodie Island Visitor Center, at the base of the lighthouse; at the Coquina Beach Bath House; and at the Oregon Inlet Fishing Center.

GETTING THERE NC 12 is the only through road on this stretch of the Outer Banks. It runs from Whalebone Junction to the Bonner Bridge and beyond. Old Nags Head Road, a continuation of the Beach Road, runs through South Nags Head before joining NC 12.

GETTING AROUND **Outer Banks Chrysler Dodge Jeep** (252-441-1146 or 1-855-459-6555; www .outerbanksjeep.com), on the Bypass MP 5.5, in Kill Devil Hills, rents four-wheel-drive Jeeps if you want to drive on the beach. You must also obtain a permit from the National Park Service.

✷ To See

✐ **Bodie Island Lighthouse and Keepers Quarters** (252-473-2111; www.nps.gov/caha), NC 12, South Nags Head. The 156-foot, black-and-white-striped tower, built in 1872, and its first order Fresnel lens have been under renovation for the past several years. As of press time, the lighthouse is expected to open for climbing in 2013. Check the NPS website for current updates. The Double Keepers Quarters building at its base contains exhibits on the history of the lighthouse, a National Park Service visitors center, and a bookstore. Several other historic buildings—the 1878 Bodie Island Lifesaving Station, its boathouse, and the 1925 Bodie Island Coast Guard Station—have been moved from the oceanfront and are now located along the lighthouse entrance road. Follow the path behind

---

The **Outer Banks National Scenic Byway** (1-877-629-4386; www.outerbanksscenicbyway .org) begins at Whalebone Junction and follows NC 12 south over the Bonner Bridge and down Hatteras Island, across the ferry to Ocracoke Island, then takes the ferry to Cedar Island to meander through the small Down East communities where decoy carving and boat building still rule. The 138-mile route (plus two ferry rides) passes through 21 maritime villages with strong traditions tied to the sea, as well as some of the most spectacular coastal scenery accessible by automobile. The byway runs past four lighthouses, plus several wildlife refuges and museums, and is a great trip any time of year. The route is also a North Carolina Scenic Byway, and an interactive map can be found on the North Carolina Department of Transportation website (www.ncdot.gov/travel/scenic). The **NCDOT Scenic Byways Book,** containing a detailed description of the Outer Banks Scenic Byway as well as other scenic drives in the region, can be downloaded from the same website.

the quarters to a ♿ boardwalk where you can spot wading birds and waterfowl in a freshwater pond. Daily ranger programs, including bird walks, turtle talks, sound-side seining, and evening campfires, are offered June through Labor Day.

Oregon Inlet Fishing Fleet. The history of the famous Oregon Inlet Fishing Fleet began about 1951, when the state paved the sand road from Whalebone Junction to Oregon Inlet. Sambo Tillett, a local fisherman and owner of a little restaurant named Sambo's, decided to dock his boat in a canal at the southern end of the road where he would be closer to the inlet, and the open ocean waters beyond. Others followed, and soon a marina was built, the first at Oregon Inlet.

Today, the little restaurant in Whalebone Junction, renamed Sam and Omie's after Sambo's son Omie joined the business, is still serving breakfast and beer to fishing captains, and the Tillett family remains a force on the Oregon Inlet fishing scene. Omie, and his brother Tony, went on to become two of the most famous captains the Inlet has ever known.

BODIE ISLAND LIGHTHOUSE IS ONE OF THREE LIGHTHOUSES LOCATED IN THE CAPE HATTERAS NATIONAL SEASHORE.

Omie is retired after a lifetime of building and captaining boats, and Tony is semi-retired, having sold his famous *Carolinian*, built by Omie, and considered the epitome of the Carolina-style boat. However, Tony wasn't quite ready to quit fishing yet and teamed up with Jordan Croswait to refurbish a Buddy Cannady–built boat, renaming it the *Legacy.*

Look for the ***Legacy*** (252-305-7960; www.legacyfishingobx.com) at the Oregon Inlet docks, along with a number of other Cannady-built boats, many with captains bearing famous names in the Outer Banks fishing world, including the *Rebait,* skippered by Capt. Harry Baum; the *Skirt Chaser,* skippered by Capt. Barry Daniels; and Cannady's latest, *Trophy Hunter.* Several boats built by Omie Tillett at his famous Sportsman Boat Works are also still on the water. Look for the *Fight-N-Lady, Fintastic,* and *Rigged Up.*

Carolina boats, constructed by hand in the traditional manner with juniper planks, last just about forever. Many of these boats, built by the big names in Roanoke Island boatbuilding, are still taking out charters from Oregon Inlet. There's even a boat in the Oregon Inlet marina built by the legendary Warren O'Neal, considered the father of Roanoke Island boatbuilding and the Carolina style, the ***Sinbad*** (252-473-2398; www.sinbadsportfishing.com).

All of these boats are available for a day of fishing through the Oregon Inlet Fishing Center website. Many of the captains also offer sunset cruises, ecotours, bird-watching, and other trips. See the "Manteo" chapter for more information on Warren O'Neal, and the "Wanchese" chapter for more on Dare County boatbuilders.

Shipwrecks (www.nps.gov/caha), Hatteras National Seashore beaches. Several victims of the Graveyard of the Atlantic can be seen along the South Bodie Island beaches. The remains of the *Laura Barnes,* a four-masted wooden schooner that came ashore in 1921, can be seen at Coquina Beach. Farther south, the wreck of the *Lois Joyce,* a fishing trawler lost in 1981, can be seen on the ocean side of the hook on the north side of Oregon Inlet at low tide.

✳ To Do

BOATING The National Park Service operates a free boat ramp at Oregon Inlet behind the fishing center. About 75 vehicles and trailers can park here. You cannot launch personal watercraft (Jet Skis) at this facility.

FISHING ✐ ***Miss Oregon Inlet*** (252-441-6301 or 1-800-272-5199; www.oregon-inlet.com), Oregon Inlet Fishing Center. Does not sail on Sunday. Spend a morning or afternoon on the water, fishing with an experienced crew aboard this 65-foot headboat. Family-friendly rates include all the equipment needed to fish. In summer, a twilight sight-seeing cruise is offered.

CAROLINA FISHING BOATS

The unique Carolina-style fishing boats developed from necessity, as the boatbuilders, most of them fishing captains during the summer, adapted the boats they built during the winter months to cope with the unique conditions they faced in Oregon Inlet, bucking the choppy surf at the mouth of the inlet, then venturing far out to sea to fish the Gulf Stream.

The most distinctive feature of a Carolina-style fishing boat is the so-called Carolina flare—an exaggerated upward and outward curvature of the hull that pushes waves away. Another practical feature is the sharply pointed bow, designed to help the boat cut through the waves and chop. Other features, such as the broken shear line and extra-wide spray rails, are designed to deflect the spray thrown up during a high-speed trip to the Gulf Stream—and keep the paying customers dry.

To find out more about Carolina-style boats and their builders, pick up a copy of *Carolina Flare: Outer Banks Building and Sportfishing Heritage,* by Neal, John, and Jim Conoley.

Oregon Inlet Fishing Center & Marina (252-441-6301 or 1-800-272-5199; www.oregon-inlet.com), 98 NC 12. Nearly 50 fishing boats are docked at Oregon Inlet Fishing Center, one of the most famous fishing destinations in the world, thanks to the many big fish brought to its docks. At the fishing center's website, you can browse pictures and specs for each boat and visit their individual websites, check availability, and book online, or sign up for a makeup charter that will match you with other anglers with similar interests. Prices are standardized and run about $1,500 a day for offshore charters, $900 for nearshore, $600 for inshore and sound fishing in an open boat. Half-day morning or afternoon trips, and shorter evening trips, also available. The ship's store carries groceries, tackle, sandwiches, and Oregon Inlet souvenirs.

Outer Banks Fly Fishing and Light Tackle Charters (252-449-0562; www.outerbanksflyfishing .com). If you prefer fly and light tackle fishing, captains Brian Horsley and Sarah Gardner will take you out after bluefish, speckled trout, redfish, little tunny, stripers, and just about anything else that will hit a fly.

Outer Banks Pier (252-441-5740; www.fishingunlimited.net), 8901 Old Oregon Inlet Road, MP 18.5. This 600-foot pier in South Nags Head is the closest to Oregon Inlet and the campground. Senior discount passes and rental rods and reels available. Y **Fish Heads Bar & Grill** on the pier serves inexpensive sandwiches, appetizers, and drinks. $.

RECOMMENDED READING Brown, William K. *Mullet Roar and Other Stories by an Outerbanker.* Manteo, NC: Maritime Kids' Quest Press, 2007. Written by the founder of the Oregon Inlet Fishing Center and the son of legendary photographer and early PR genius Aycock Brown, these fascinating stories of fishing and hunting in the "old days" are illustrated by the author's original artwork.

THE *MISS OREGON INLET* HEADBOAT TAKES ANGLERS AND THEIR FAMILIES OUT DAILY.

FOR FAMILIES ✍ Head down to the south end of Bodie Island in the late afternoon when the charter boats come in at the **Oregon Inlet Fishing Center** (252-441-6301; www.oregon-inlet.com) to see the different fish that have been caught and watch the crews weigh the really big ones. The store here can provide an impromptu picnic. Be sure to see the world record blue marlin and the 805-pound bluefin tuna mounted in cases outside the store.

HUNTING The National Park Service allows waterfowl hunting on Bodie Island by registration request only and limits hunting through a lottery to 20 requests a day. The NPS website (www.nps.gov/caha) has details.

Lottery winners must be present at the

Whalebone Junction Information Station for the hunting blind drawing at 4:30 AM on the day of the reservation. Any blinds remaining after the day's drawing are assigned on a first-come, first-served basis to walk-in hunters.

✳ Green Space

BEACHES The Cape Hatteras National Seashore maintains a large beach facility at the ♿ **Coquina Beach Bath House,** opposite the Bodie Island Lighthouse. Amenities include changing rooms, showers, walkway to the beach, large paved parking lot, and lifeguards (in season).

Beach wheelchairs are available at the Bodie Island Lighthouse Visitor Center (252-441-5711).

Street-legal four-wheel-drive vehicles can be driven on the beach with an ORV permit, available from the NPS office at the north end of the Coquina Beach parking lot or at other Cape Hatteras welcome centers. Permits are currently available for one week ($50) or one year ($120). You must show your driver's license and car insurance, and watch a seven-minute informational video, to get a permit. Be sure to pick up a map that shows where you may drive. ATVs and motorcycles are not allowed on the beach.

Fires are allowed on the beaches of the national seashore with a free permit, available online. Fireworks, metal detectors, and personal watercraft are forbidden. Pets must be crated or on a 6-foot leash, and cannot go on designated swimming beaches.

KIDS LOVE WATCHING THE FLEET COME IN AT THE OREGON INLET FISHING CENTER.

COQUINA BEACH IS JUST OPPOSITE THE BODIE ISLAND LIGHTHOUSE.

TRAILS ♿ **Bodie Island Dike Trail** (252-473-2111; www.nps.gov/caha), a short signed nature trail, leads through the marsh to a freshwater pond near the Bodie Island Lighthouse. A longer (and unsigned) trail off the entrance road leads down to the sound, with views of ramshackle fish camps across the water.

✳ Lodging

CAMPGROUND Oregon Inlet Campground (252-441-0882; www.nps.gov/caha), NC 12. The 120 sites at the NPS campground opposite the Oregon Inlet Marina have no utility hookups but are located on level ground. Campground amenities include modern restrooms, potable water, unheated showers, grills, and tables. The ocean is just across the dune line. Open from April to October; 14-day maximum. Reservations not accepted, except for the group campsite for 7–30 campers, which must be made at least two weeks in advance. Tent, trailers, and motor homes $20; group site $4 per person.

VACATION COTTAGES See our suggestions for South Nags Head rentals in the "Nags Head and Whalebone Junction" chapter.

✳ Where to Eat

EATING OUT ♈ **Fish Heads Bar & Grill,** on Fishing Unlimited's Outer Banks Pier (252-441-5740; www.fishingunlimited.net), off Old Oregon Inlet Road at MP 18.5, is the closest spot to the Oregon Inlet Campground to get food and drink. This fun spot serves inexpensive sandwiches, appetizers, and drinks, plus hosts live music, karaoke, and dancing on the oceanfront deck. Stop by for a late breakfast, a fish taco, or the steamed shrimp happy hour. $.

Roanoke Island and the Albemarle Peninsula

ROANOKE ISLAND AND THE ALBEMARLE PENINSULA

Mystery and the Mother Vine

ONLY 12 MILES LONG and about 3 miles wide, Roanoke Island packs a lot of history into a small, conveniently toured area. Visitors staying elsewhere on the Outer Banks often make a day trip to Roanoke. However, if you are especially interested in history, you'll find a stay on the island rewarding. This is the location of the famous Lost Colony, the earliest attempt by England to settle men, women, and children in the New World. No one is sure what became of the colony, although speculation and archaeological investigations continue. Visitors have plenty of opportunity to form their own opinions. *The Lost Colony* outdoor drama, Fort Raleigh National Historical Park, and the state-run Roanoke Island Festival Park all present pieces of the puzzle.

The island of Roanoke rose to importance even before Sir Walter Raleigh attempted to place his ill-fated colony here. Its Native American name, unchanged from then till now, indicates that it was a major manufacturing point for roanoke, elsewhere called wampum, the shell beads used as currency by the natives. The word *roanoke* literally meant "money."

Early settlers thought they were coming to a paradise. Besides the ample fish and shellfish in the surrounding waters, the area was renowned for its grape vines. The colonists all disappeared, but one of the grape vines growing then lives on. The so-called Mother Vine, estimated to be more than 400 years old, continues to thrive in Manteo.

Many landmarks refer to the island's history. The two major towns, Manteo and Wanchese, are named for two Native American chiefs. The youths were taken to England by an early voyage of exploration and returned with Raleigh's expeditions. Their roles in the history of the settlement are part of the mystery, but Manteo is generally believed to have been friendly with the newcomers, while Wanchese proved to be hostile. The story is told in fictionalized form in a film shown daily at Roanoke Island Festival Park. Oddly, the feelings of the two chiefs are reflected today in the attitudes of the two villages on the island. Manteo, at the northern end of Roanoke, welcomes guests with a wide variety of attractions and accommodations. Wanchese, on the island's southern tip, works hard to maintain its traditions as a fishing village. You'll find few restaurants here, and fewer hotels. But the natives these days are friendly.

GUIDANCE **The Outer Banks Welcome Center on Roanoke Island** (252-473-2138 or 1-877-OBX-4FUN; www.outerbanks.org), located on the US 64/264 Bypass just over the Virginia Dare Memorial Bridge, is the logical first stop as you reach the Banks. Besides an abundance of information on Outer Banks attractions in Dare County, the expansive complex also offers an accommodation reservation service, a picnic area, and restrooms that are open 24/7. Staffed by friendly natives, the center is open 9–5 every day except Thanksgiving and Christmas. Pick up an **Outer Banks Getaway Card** for local discounts.

Dare County (252-475-5000; www.co.dare.nc.us), 962 Marshall C. Collins Drive, Manteo.

TOP 10 DON'T MISS: ROANOKE ISLAND

1. Walk the Manteo boardwalk and circle Roanoke Island Festival Park's island.
2. Bike to the Umstead Bridge and learn the history of the Freedmen's Colony.
3. Discover the history of flight in Manteo at the Dare County Regional Airport Museum, then take a flight-seeing tour to see the Banks from above.
4. Go backstage at *The Lost Colony.*
5. See a film at the Pioneer Theatre.
6. Enjoy a glass of wine at the copper bar in the Tranquil House's 1587 Restaurant.
7. See the purple martins fly in to roost under the Umstead Bridge.
8. Hear the red wolves howl and see the black bears stroll at Alligator River Wildlife Refuge.
9. Visit Roanoke Island Festival Park to learn the story of chiefs Manteo and Wanchese.
10. Watch the fishing fleet come in at Fisherman's Wharf Restaurant in Wanchese.

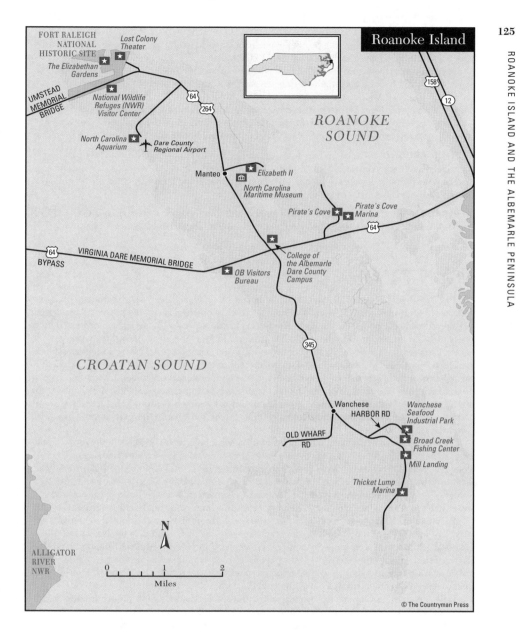

Roanoke Island

FORT RALEIGH NATIONAL HISTORIC SITE
Lost Colony Theater
The Elizabethan Gardens
UMSTEAD MEMORIAL BRIDGE
National Wildlife Refuges (NWR) Visitor Center
North Carolina Aquarium
Dare County Regional Airport
Manteo
Elizabeth II
North Carolina Maritime Museum
Pirate's Cove
Pirate's Cove Marina
ROANOKE SOUND
64
264
158
12
64
VIRGINIA DARE MEMORIAL BRIDGE
64 BYPASS
OB Visitors Bureau
College of the Albemarle Dare County Campus
CROATAN SOUND
345
Wanchese
HARBOR RD
Wanchese Seafood Industrial Park
Broad Creek Fishing Center
Mill Landing
OLD WHARF RD
Thicket Lump Marina
ALLIGATOR RIVER NWR
N
0   1   2
Miles
© The Countryman Press

GETTING THERE *By Air:* **Dare County Regional Airport (MQI)** (252-475-5570; www.darenc .com/airport), Manteo. General aviation airport offers car rentals, air tours, an aviation museum, 24-hour fuel service, two lighted runways of 3,300 and 4,300 feet, and amenities for visiting pilots.

By Car: To reach Roanoke Island and the Central Banks from the west, you have your choice of two major roads, US 64 and US 264, both of them now four-lane, limited-access highways for most of the distance. The roads start out together from Raleigh, then separate to sweep along either shore of the great Albemarle Peninsula, joining again in Manns Harbor, on the mainland opposite Roanoke Island.

US 64 is the most direct and fastest route, being four-lane as far as Columbia. The trip from Raleigh to Roanoke Island takes about four hours via this route, with a rest stop in Columbia, or about three hours from I-95.

US 264 is currently four-lane as far as Washington. Beyond, it makes its winding way past Lake Mattamuskeet and tiny fishing villages on the peninsula's southern and eastern shores. You can turn off US 264 at Swan Quarter to catch a toll ferry to Ocracoke.

Once they join, the highways split again in Manns Harbor, this time into the older US 64 and the newer US 64/264 Bypass. Each route has its own causeway bridge to Roanoke Island: the older William B. Umstead Memorial Bridge at the northern tip of the island, and the newer Bypass bridge, dubbed the Virginia Dare Memorial, the longest bridge in the state at 5.25 miles.

From Nags Head, the Nags Head–Manteo Causeway (US 64/264), an extension of the Bypass, crosses marshy Roanoke Sound, connecting Manteo and Wanchese with NC 12.

GETTING AROUND The island is easy to navigate. The Bypass bisects the island and continues on to Nags Head and the main beaches of the Outer Banks via the Nags Head–Manteo Causeway. A second road runs north/south down the length of the island from the Umstead Bridge to the docks in Wanchese. The two roads meet at a traffic light.

MEDICAL EMERGENCY Island Medical Center (252-473-2500; www.albemarlehealth.org), 715 N. US 64, Manteo. A family practice associated with Albemarle Hospital in Elizabeth City.

MANTEO

TO OUTWARD APPEARANCES, Manteo might be any other small fishing village turned to tourism. Narrow streets lead down to the bay. Waterside shops offer practical goods and souvenirs. Boats from far and wide line the docks. But in most fishing villages, you won't find ladies and gents dressed in the finery of 400 years ago strolling the streets and gardens. In Manteo it's not unusual to encounter Queen Elizabeth I, dressed in her brocades, lace ruffs, and strings of pearls, several times a day.

The northern end of Roanoke Island is virtually a historical park, where the year 1587, when Raleigh's colony is believed to have occupied the site, is celebrated. Here, under live oak trees hundreds of years old, the outdoor drama *The Lost Colony* has been presented nightly every summer for over 70 years. Its **Waterside Theatre** sits adjacent to **Fort Raleigh National Historic Site,** where a visitors center displays the latest archaeological findings, and the **Elizabethan Gardens,** a living tribute to the 16th century.

The main town of Manteo lies a few miles south down a broad avenue. Many of the town's restaurants, motels, and a new complex of government buildings lie along this avenue, US 64, which runs along the back of the town's historic downtown. Stretching from the highway to the waterfront, this historic district, about 10 blocks square, is small, charming, and easily walked. A boardwalk rims the water's edge, with great views any time of day that turn superb at dawn and dusk. Locally owned shops and bed & breakfast inns have colonized the historic homes and renovated storefronts.

An ambitious 20-year plan revitalized the historic waterfront of Manteo. Adopted to prepare the town for the 400th anniversary of Raleigh's original colony, the plan resulted in the building of the *Elizabeth II* replica ship, christened at a ceremony attended by Princess Anne of Britain in 1984. In the years since, many other elements of the plan have come to fulfillment, including a boardwalk and public marina, as well as shops and condominiums along the waterfront. The **Tranquil House Inn,** built to resemble a hotel that welcomed guests in the early 1900s, opened its doors in 1988.

The state of North Carolina has taken an active interest in Manteo and its history, resulting in a cluster of government-subsidized attractions. **Roanoke Island Festival Park,** which completely transformed the environmentally challenged Ice Island, is located directly across Dough Creek from the historic waterfront. It provides the community with a history museum, indoor and outdoor performance venues, plus much else, including a large, free parking lot close to downtown. Other state-funded attractions in Manteo include branches of the **North Carolina Aquarium** and the **Roanoke Island Maritime Museum.**

Manteo's most precious resource, however, is the people who make this their home. A mix of old boat-building families and newer residents who fell in love with the small town's story, the citizens of Manteo extend a warm welcome to visitors from near and far.

GUIDANCE Manteo Town Hall (252-473-2133; www.townofmanteo.com), 407 Budleigh Street.

Dare County Offices (252-475-5000; www.co.dare.nc.us), 962 Marshall C. Collins Drive.

POST OFFICE The **Manteo Post Office** (252-473-2534) is located at 212 US 64. The zip code for Manteo is 27954.

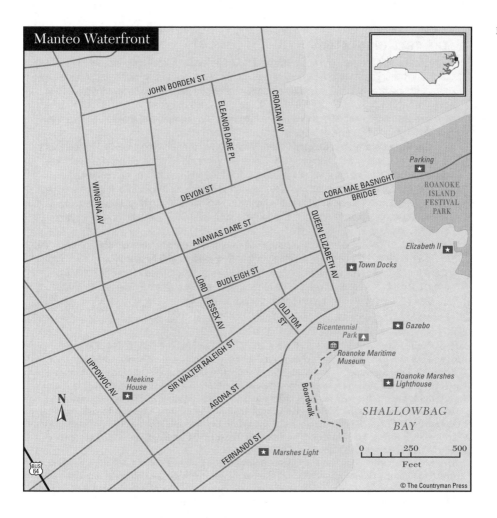

Manteo Waterfront

JOHN BORDEN ST
ELEANOR DARE PL
CROATAN AV
WINGINA AV
DEVON ST
CORA MAE BASNIGHT BRIDGE
Parking
ROANOKE ISLAND FESTIVAL PARK
ANANIAS DARE ST
QUEEN ELIZABETH AV
Elizabeth II
Town Docks
LORD ESSEX AV
BUDLEIGH ST
OLD TOM ST
Bicentennial Park
Gazebo
Roanoke Maritime Museum
UPPOWOC AV
Meekins House
SIR WALTER RALEIGH ST
AGONA ST
Roanoke Marshes Lighthouse
Boardwalk
SHALLOWBAG BAY
N
FERNANDO ST
Marshes Light
0   250   500
Feet
BUS 64
© The Countryman Press

PUBLIC LIBRARY ♂ (ᵧ) **Dare County Library in Manteo** (252-473-2372; www.earlibrary.org /manteo), 700 US 64.

GETTING THERE See *Getting There* in "Roanoke Island and the Albemarle Peninsula."

GETTING AROUND *By Bicycle:* Bicycling is an excellent option for getting around the island, thanks to the paved multiuse path that runs from the Business/Bypass junction all the way to the Umstead Bridge. Several bike rental companies are located along US 64 and down by the boardwalk.

By Car: US 64 is the main drag through Manteo, running from the William B. Umstead Memorial Bridge in the north to the traffic light where it meets Bypass US 64/264. Locals usually just refer to it as US 64 or "the highway." Although many businesses are found along this stretch of road, the main business district lies just off it, a compact and walkable 10 square blocks along the waterfront of Shallowbag Bay.

✳ To See

ARCHITECTURE Residents of Manteo have taken a remarkable interest in the community's architectural character through the years, and the town recently enacted measures to preserve the village's traditional character.

Much of the downtown waterfront was destroyed by a catastrophic fire in 1939. Local historians used the rebuilding process as an opportunity to rename the streets with more evocative titles. Water Street became Queen Elizabeth Avenue, with other streets named for Sir Walter Raleigh, Ananias

THE ARTS IN MANTEO

Rarely has history played such an important part in the development of a cultural scene as it has here. The history of the arts in Manteo began in 1937 when local history buffs first presented the outdoor symphonic drama *The Lost Colony* to commemorate the 350th birthday of Virginia Dare, the first English child born in the New World. Although it was supposed to run just one summer, the outdoor drama, the first of its kind, gave birth both to a new genre of theater and an active arts community in the town of Manteo.

The Dare County Arts Council (252-473-5558; www.darearts.org), organized by volunteers in 1975, carries this artistic energy into the community through an active program of exhibitions, performances, and classes in visual arts, dance, film, and music. It sponsors an annual series of exhibits at several venues, including its own gallery in Manteo's historic district, at the Roanoke Island Festival Park gallery, at artist Glenn Eure's Ghost Ship Gallery in Nags Head, and elsewhere. During the council's annual studio tour in March, over 30 artists from Duck to Hatteras open their doors to art lovers.

Don't miss any of the frequent gallery openings at both the **Dare County Arts Gallery** in the old courthouse and the gallery across the creek at **Roanoke Island Festival Park,** if you find yourself in the area. The arts community turns out in force, the art itself is always worth a look, and the local ladies put out a memorable refreshment table of traditional Southern party food.

Check *Special Events* for specific galas, annual events, and exhibitions.

Dare, and other characters in *The Lost Colony*. Tudor-style architectural details became popular in the 1940s and can still be found in some commercial structures, such as the Pioneer Theatre.

Several buildings escaped both fire and development. Today, Manteo's historic downtown is a mix of architectural styles ranging from late Victorian to the Western Plains style popularized by Frank Lloyd Wright. There's even a Sears mail-order arts-and-crafts cottage at 505 Croatan Street.

Two properties are on the National Register of Historic Places: the Queen Anne–style Meekins House at 319 Sir Walter Raleigh Street, today the White Doe Inn; and the George W. Creef Jr. House, at 308 Budleigh Street. The **Manteo Preservation Trust** (MPT) places bronze MPT plaques on buildings that predate the 1939 fire.

To protect its historic look and small-town atmosphere, Manteo adopted guidelines that all new construction and renovations must follow. At the town's website, www.townofmanteo.com, you can download both a sketchbook of historic properties and a manual of the *Manteo Way of Building*, illustrated with numerous photos. Picket fences are encouraged. Cul-de-sacs are not.

You can see the Manteo Way in action at the new Marshes Light development (www.marshes light.com)at the southern end of the Manteo waterfront, designed to blend seamlessly with the historic village.

ART EXHIBITS Manteo's historic waterfront district makes an attractive location for a variety of art studios and galleries. Most are located within a few blocks of each other. The town's monthly First Friday celebrations include a gallery crawl. See the *Selective Shopping* section for a listing of commercial galleries.

🤿 ♿ ♟ ♂ **The Art Village** (252-473-1500; www.outerbanksartvillage.com), 525 US 64. This nonprofit art cooperative occupies part of an enormous complex next door to the Christmas Shop. More than a dozen local artists are in residence, creating one-of-a-kind works and handcrafted gifts. The gingerbread house holds a bead shop offering a huge selection of beads, plus free lessons for all. The broad grounds are a great place to relax and let the kids run. An open-air stage hosts music, improv comedy, and more.

College of the Albemarle Professional Arts Gallery (252-475-9248; www.albemarle.edu), 205 S. US 64. The new Professional Arts Building overlooking Roanoke Sound on the COA Roanoke Island campus houses a gallery that presents changing shows, many associated with the Professional Crafts programs in jewelry and pottery offered at the college.

Dare County Arts Council Gallery (252-473-5558; www.darearts.org), 300 Queen Elizabeth Avenue. The arts council sponsors several competitions every year, as well as art classes and changing exhibitions at its gallery on the first floor of the historic 1904 Dare County Courthouse in the heart of historic Manteo. Highlights on the gallery calendar include monthly First Friday exhibit openings.

Roanoke Heritage Art Gallery and Military Museum (252-473-2632), 543 Ananias Dare Street. Artist and collector Herbert Bliven displays his original photographs and artwork of local wildlife, lighthouses, and other local scenes, plus driftwood carvings and handcrafted wooden frames, at a rustic shop behind his home. The outside is surrounded by buoys, driftwood, and fig trees, all for sale. Inside, glass cases display finds Bliven has made in a lifetime of relic hunting on the Outer Banks, including artifacts from the Civil War, antique hunting decoys, old bottles, and Native American artifacts, plus his collection of uniforms and equipment from World War I through the Korean conflict. Call for hours. More of Bliven's work can be seen at his son's **Roanoke Heritage Extended** gallery downtown (see *Selected Shopping*).

Roanoke Island Festival Park Art Gallery (252-475-1500; www.roanokeisland.com), 1 Festival Park Boulevard. Part of the state-operated Festival Park complex, this gallery presents important shows of local and regional art in many media. Annual events include the Quilt Extravaganza in March and the Mollie Fearing Memorial Art Show in May.

QUICK TIPS:

• On the Manteo Weather Tower, check out the sign showing the high-water mark (7 feet, 11 inches) reached in downtown Manteo during Hurricane Irene on August 11, 2011.

• The story of the Pea Island Life-Saving Station and Richard Etheridge's struggle for civil rights in the 1880s is told in the book *Fire on the Beach*, written by David Wright and David Zoby, recently made into the documentary film *Rescue Men*. For younger readers, Carole Weatherford's *Sink or Swim: African-American Lifesavers of the Outer Banks* tells the story of the heroes of the Pea Island Life-Saving Station.

ATTRACTIONS IN DOWNTOWN MANTEO ✍ **Manteo Weather Tower** (www.townofmanteo .com), Manteo waterfront. One of the few remaining Coastal Warning Display towers left in the country, and possibly the only one with all its original signal lights intact, this tower was restored and moved back to the Manteo waterfront. An information board at the base of the tower explains the meaning of the various flag combinations.

✻ ♿ **Outer Banks History Center** (252-473-2655; www.obhistorycenter.net), 1 Festival Park Boulevard, Roanoke Island Festival Park. Open weekdays. This branch of the North Carolina State Archives collects and preserves documentary evidence relevant to Outer Banks history, including books, magazines, newspapers, photographs, maps, and a collection of oral histories. The center is open to all, and most services are free. Permanent and temporary exhibits are on display in the **History Center Gallery.**

✍ **Pea Island Cookhouse Museum and African American Heritage Center at Collins Park** (252-473-2133; www.townofmanteo.com), 1013 Sir Walter Raleigh Street at Bideford Street. Free tours are offered Monday, Wednesday, and Friday 11–3. This new museum preserves the history of the Pea Island Lifesaving Station, the only one to have an all African American crew. Exhibits detail the many daring rescues performed by these brave men, awarded the Gold Lifesaving Medal in 1996, one hundred years after they rescued the crew of the *E. S. Newman* in hurricane-force seas. The museum is housed in the station's original cookhouse, moved to this site and restored by descendants of the lifesavers. A bronze statue honors Richard Etheridge, the first African American United States Life-Saving Service Keeper at Pea Island Station. Free.

♟ ✍ ♿ ⬆ ✍ **Roanoke Island Festival Park and** *Elizabeth II* (252-475-1500; www.roanokeisland .com). Open March through December, daily 9–5. Closed January and February. Located across from the Manteo docks, this state-run facility offers a full roster of activities and amenities to visitors and the Manteo community. Its most visible attraction, the *Elizabeth II*, a replica of a 16th-century sailing vessel like the ones that carried Sir Walter Raleigh's colonists, is docked opposite the Manteo waterfront. Her bright colors advertise the fact that the history interpreted here, the Elizabethan Age, has little in common with the grim groups of Puritans who later settled farther north. The ship is staffed by costumed characters speaking Elizabethan dialect.

The **Settlement Site** explores the daily life of the settlers both at work and play. Nearby at the **American Indian Town,** visitors experience a different way of life, building a log canoe, working a fish trap, and participating in tribal dances.

THE *ELIZABETH II,* AN AUTHENTIC RE-CREATION OF THE SHIPS THAT BROUGHT SIR WALTER RALEIGH'S COLONISTS TO THE NEW WORLD.

There's plenty of inside fun at the Festival Park as well, making it a popular rainy-day destination. In the **Roanoke Adventure Museum,** kids can dress in Elizabethan ruffs and bum rolls or American Indian skin tunics, become sailors, pirates, lifesavers, and duck hunters. The excellent docudrama *The Legend of Two Path,* exploring Native American attitudes toward the settlers in their midst, screens several times a day in the film theater.

Admission is charged to visit the interpretive areas, the film, and the museum, but other areas of the park, which covers a small island, are free to the public. These include an excellent museum store with many pirate-, Elizabethan-, and American Indian–themed gift items; an art gallery with changing exhibits; the Outer Banks History Center; an interpretive boardwalk; picnic tables; and a Fossil Pit.

FREE SAILS ON AN AUTHENTIC SHAD BOAT ARE OFFERED EVERY SUMMER BY THE MARITIME MUSEUM IN MANTEO.

Not least of the free attractions is the spacious parking lot, located across a short bridge from the busy Manteo waterfront, where parking is often hard to find during the summer season. Art gallery and grounds are free; admission to the *Elizabeth II,* the museum, film, and historical interpretation areas: adults $10, students (6–17) $7, children 5 and under free; tickets are good for two consecutive days.

✇ ⅃ ↑ **Roanoke Island Maritime Museum** (252-475-1750; www.townofmanteo.com or www.roanokeisland.com), 104 Fernando Street. The historic Creef Boathouse on the Manteo waterfront is named for George Washington Creef, creator of the shad boat, the official state boat of North Carolina. On exhibit are several traditional small watercraft, including an 1883 Creef shad boat, dubbed the "pickup truck of the Banks"; spritsail skiffs; and a 1948 Buddy Davis runabout. The *Elizabeth II* replica at Roanoke Island Festival Park was built on-site. Volunteers and staff repair historic boats and build new ones, take visitors on sailing excursions in a shad boat, give classes in boatbuilding and maritime skills, and every summer teach hundreds of children how to sail in the Outer Banks Sailing Program (www.townofmanteo.com).

⅃ ✇ **Roanoke Marshes Lighthouse** (252-475-1750; www.townofmanteo.com), end of the pier on the Manteo waterfront. A reproduction of the cottage-style screw-pile lighthouses that once aided navigation in nearby sounds now helps mariners

THE ROANOKE MARSHES LIGHTHOUSE, AT THE ENTRANCE TO SHALLOWBAG BAY, IS A REPLICA OF THE SCREWPILE LIGHTS THAT ONCE LINED THE NORTH CAROLINA SOUNDS.

enter Shallowbag Bay. Inside are exhibits on the history of the lighthouse, a wooden hydroplane used in local speedboat races in the 1960s, and an exhibit on local pioneering boatbuilder Warren O'Neal. Outside, you may find *Island Time,* considered one of O'Neal's masterpieces, berthed at the dock. Visiting boaters can tie up to this pier for complimentary overnight mooring. Free.

ATTRACTIONS AT THE NORTH END OF ROANOKE ISLAND ❄ ⬥ **Dare County Regional Airport Museum** (252-475-5575; www.darenc.com/airport/museum.asp), 410 Airport Road. Open daily 8–7. The aviation history of Dare County may have begun with the Wright brothers, but it didn't end there. Find out the rest of the story at these exhibits, housed in the regional airport at the north end of Roanoke Island. The airport, commissioned as a Naval Auxiliary Air Station during World War II, served as a base for Civil Air Patrol antisubmarine searches and as a training facility for many famous Navy air squadrons, including the VF-17 "Jolly Rogers." The Ready Room of aviator Dave Driscoll details the history of aviation in the region from the barnstorming days of the 1920s to the dawn of the jet era. Free.

❄ ✿ ✎ ✦ **The Elizabethan Gardens** (252-473-3234; www.elizabethangardens.org), 1411 National Park Drive. Open daily; hours vary seasonally. Begun as a project of the Garden Club of North Carolina during the 1950s, the site, on the shores of Roanoke Sound, has developed into a rich complex of gardens that delights history lovers, art lovers, and nature lovers alike. The gardens are embellished with many works of sculpture and include a Shakespearean herb garden, a sunken garden, and superb collections of camellias and rhododendrons, with something in bloom year-round. The Queen's Rose Garden features the Queen Elizabeth rose, a gift from Queen Elizabeth II. Many special programs are included with admission, including weekday programs for children during the summer season. Adults $8; youths $5; children under 5 free; reduced admission on Virginia Dare's birthday, August 18.

❄ ✎ ⬥ **Fort Raleigh National Historic Site** (252-473-5772; www.nps.gov/fora), 1401 National Park Drive. The NPS Visitor Center is open 9–5 daily year-round (except Christmas Day), and grounds are open dawn to dusk. June–Labor Day, the visitors center stays open until 6 PM, and the grounds remain open until the completion of *The Lost Colony* outdoor drama. Located between the Elizabethan Gardens and *The Lost Colony*'s Waterside Theatre, the Lindsay Warren Visitor Center exhibits artifacts

WARREN O'NEAL AND ROANOKE ISLAND BOATBUILDING

Credited as the father of boatbuilding on Roanoke Island and the originator of the Carolina style of sportfishing boat, Warren O'Neal was born on Manteo in 1910 and worked as a commercial fisherman and charter boat captain. In 1959, he designed and built a boat with a deep V hull to help him cut through the chop at Oregon Inlet and the rough seas beyond. Up until then, most boats on the Banks had flatter bottoms to help them keep afloat in the shallow inshore waters, but blue marlin had recently been striking in the Gulf Stream, and charter captains and their customers were eager to go out after this legendary game fish. Many of the boatbuilders who would become famous for their Carolina-style sportsfishing boats worked with O'Neal in the early years, including Omie Tillett, Sheldon Midgett, and Buddy Davis. To delve deeper into the O'Neal legacy, visit the Outer Banks History Center at Roanoke Island Festival Park, where the papers from his boat works are archived. (See the "South Bodie Island and Oregon Inlet" chapter for more on the Carolina-style boat, and the "Wanchese" chapter for boats being built on Roanoke Island today.)

found on Roanoke Island and tells the story of early explorations and the first English attempts at colonization in the New World. A documentary, *Roanoke: The Lost Colony,* is shown daily. The site contains an earthen fort built in the style used by the adventurers and a nature trail with signs that identify the native plants found in the area in 1585 by naturalist Thomas Hariot. A longer trail leads to an interpretive display on the Freedmen's Colony on the shores of Roanoke Sound. Archaeological investigations are ongoing. In summer a range of free activities are offered, including nature hikes and visits to the park's museum collection building, as well as special programs on the Freedmen's Colony. Free.

The Freedmen's Colony of Roanoke Island

(www.roanokefreedmenscolony.com) existed from 1862 to 1867 and was home to an estimated 3,500 people, nearly all of them enslaved people who had fled Confederate-controlled areas and sought protection by the Union army. The actual site of the timber town remains lost. It's yet another of Roanoke Island's archaeological mysteries.

THIS STATUE, REPRESENTING VIRGINIA DARE AS AN INDIAN MAIDEN, GRACES THE ELIZABETHAN GARDENS.

An interpretive display is located at the northern end of the Manteo Bike Path at the foot of the William Umstead Bridge in a small park, which also has a sandy beach and parking lot on the sound. Another site connected with the Freedmen's Colony is **Cartwright Park,** at 303 Bideford Street. The park sits on the grounds of the first church, dated to 1865, of Andrew Cartwright, founder of AME Zion churches in the Albemarle area. Cartwright Park has a picnic shelter, restrooms, grills, and a playground. Free.

✍ **Island Farm** (252-473-5440; www.theislandfarm.com), 1140 US 64 at Buzzy Lane. Open April–November. The last remaining pre–Civil War farmhouse on Roanoke Island is now living-history museum. A dozen farm buildings have been restored, including a windmill relocated from Nags Head. Farm animals of the types raised in the 1850s, including sheep, oxen, chickens, and Banker horses, now live in the barns and pastures. A new welcome center houses exhibits on island culture, boatbuilding, windmills, and the Freedmen's Colony. Adults $6; children 5 and under free.

✍ ↑ **National Wildlife Refuges Gateway Visitor Center** (252-473-1131; www.fws.gov/ncgate wayvc), 100 Conservation Way. Open 9–4 daily, except Thanksgiving and Christmas. Manteo's newest attraction, located across US 64 from Fort Raleigh, offers exhibits and information on 11 different wildlife refuges along the Carolina and Virginia coasts. Interactive exhibits include a Cessna "fly-over" of the refuges; dioramas of many indigenous species, including red wolves, black bear, and eagles; and a theater showing three different productions. Free.

❄ ✍ ♿ ↑ ✍ **North Carolina Aquarium at Roanoke Island** (252-473-3494 or 1-800-832-3474; www.ncaquariums.com), 374 Airport Road. Open daily 9–5 year-round. Closed Thanksgiving Day, Christmas Day, and New Year's Day. One of three state aquariums located along the coast, this one presents exhibits exploring the waters of the Outer Banks, from the rivers pouring into the sounds to the marine communities offshore in the deep ocean. Highlights include a one-third scale model of the USS *Monitor* in the Graveyard of the Atlantic gallery and the new Operation: Sea Turtle Rescue exhibit. A nature trail leads to exhibits along the sound. A changing menu of activities is offered daily, including films, feedings, and dive shows. Adults $8; seniors (62+) $7; children (3–17) $6; 2 and under free.

QUICK TIP: For more information about the Freedmen's Colony, read *Time Full of Trial: The Roanoke Island Freedmen's Colony, 1862–1867,* written by Patricia C. Click (University of North Carolina Press, 2000).

EXPLORING THE MYSTERY OF THE LOST COLONY

A couple of different organizations, in addition to the National Park Service and various university archaeology departments, are investigating the Lost Colony.

The **First Colony Foundation** (www.firstcolonyfoundation.org), a group of historians, archaeologists, and concerned citizens, are concentrating their efforts on finding the area occupied by the 1587 colonists at the north end of Roanoke Island. They have conducted underwater surveys in the nearby sound, as well as archaeological digs within the national historic park.

The **Lost Colony Center for Science and Research** (252-792-3440; www.lost-colony.com), 9192 NC 171, Williamston, is dedicated to exploring the mystery of the Roanoke colony. The center takes a multidisciplinary approach, using geography, geology, history, biology, anthropology, and oceanography to investigate clues. Most recently, the center has embarked on DNA studies aimed at identifying present-day descendants of the colonists. The center runs research field trips to sites under investigation that are thought to be connected with the colonists and other early residents of the coastal region. Call for schedule.

✳ To Do

AIR TOURS Aviation companies based at the **Dare County Airport** (252-475-5570; www.darenc .com/Airport), at the northern end of Roanoke Island, take you high above dunes and surf, providing a unique view of the fragile environment we call the Outer Banks. Lighthouses, marine wildlife, shipwrecks on the bottom of the ocean—all can be seen best from above.

Barrier Island Aviation (252-473-4247; www.barrierislandaviation.com), 407 Airport Road. Air tours in a vintage Waco biplane or a high-winged Cessna. Sunrise and sunset flights available.

Coastal Helicopters (252-475-4354; www.obxhelicopters.com), 410 Airport Road. Get pictures from high above the Banks in a thee-seat, air-conditioned 'copter.

OBX Biplanes (252-216-7777; www.obxbiplanes.com), 407 Airport Road. Tour the Banks in an open-cockpit 1990 reproduction Waco biplane.

Outer Banks Air Charters and Tours (252-256-2322; www.outerbanksaircharters.com), 410 Airport Road. Five people can tour aboard this Piper craft. Charter flights are available to any OBX airport from your home airport, as well.

BICYCLING Manteo is blessed with a wide, paved multiuse path, suitable for walking, jogging, cycling, and rollerblading, that runs along US 64 from the Umstead Memorial Bridge to the junction with NC 345 and the US 64/264 Bypass. From the light at that intersection, it continues as a wide paved shoulder over the Washington Baum Causeway Bridge to Whalebone Junction in Nags Head. More than 8 miles long, the multiuse path joins downtown Manteo with the Lost Colony district at the north end of the island, ending at the Freedman's Colony Memorial. The ride is both cool and colorful, running beneath live oak trees and crape myrtles that bloom all summer. A nice side trip takes bikers around a loop composed of Scuppernong and Mother Vineyard roads. Along the way you'll pass the oldest-known grape vine in the country, the so-called Mother Vine, estimated to be more than 400 years old. The vine is now on private property, so take a look from the road.

If you are coming to Manteo to ride the bike path, good paved parking areas are located at Roanoke Island Festival Park, at the Fort Raleigh National Historic Site, and at the end of the path at the Umstead Bridge. The paved paths within the national park are also open for biking.

Manteo Kitty Hawk Kites (252-473-2357; www.kittyhawk.com), 307 Queen Elizabeth Street. Single, tandem, and children's bikes, plus infant seats and trailers, are available by the hour, day, or week, at this shop on the Manteo waterfront.

Olde Towne Creamery (252-305-8060; www.oldetownecreamery.com), 500 US 64. Adult and children's bikes, plus adult trikes, have baskets for your convenience. And the rates are great.

Roanoke Island Outfitters and Dive Center (252-473-1356; www.roanokeislandoutfittersanddive

THE MOTHER VINE

Now located on private property along Mother Vineyard Road in Manteo, this scuppernong vine still produces fat, white grapes. Experts estimate its age to be at least 400 years old and speculate that it may have been first cultivated by the American Indians in the area before Raleigh's English colonists arrived. The Mother Vine has a central trunk about 2 feet around, and its vines cover about half an acre.

In 2010, the ancient vine had a brush with destruction when a contractor killing weeds under power lines inadvertently sprayed an outlying runner with a powerful herbicide that follows vines to their roots. The Mother Vine began to wither and die. Agriculture specialists rushed to Manteo to treat the injured plant, and the vine seems to have survived the attack.

Early explorers reported that the shores of North Carolina, when first discovered, were thick with grape vines. These grapes, native to the Southeast, were muscadines, a particularly hearty species with an extra chromosome that defends them from the diseases and insects that plague European varietals planted here. Scuppernongs are one of the 250 varieties of muscadine.

The discovery of the many health benefits of the muscadine grape has sparked increased interest in both the grape and the wine made from it. Two extremely powerful antioxidents—resveratrol and quercetin—are found in concentrated form of muscadine juice. The **Mothervine Nutraceutical Company** (www.themothervine.com) uses grapes grown from Mother Vine cuttings to create supplements, juices, and other healthful products. You can even order your own Mother Vine cutting, ready for planting.

Other companies have used cuttings from the Mother Vine to create new vineyards. **Duplin Winery** (www.duplinwinery.com), in Rose Hill, North Carolina, just off I-40, is the world's largest muscadine wine producer and has mature vines grown from Mother Vine cuttings. Its **Mother Vine Scuppernong Wine** (www.mothervinewine.com), first released in 2008, was the first wine made from Mother Vine grapes in 100 years.

No wines are currently produced on Roanoke Island, but if you'd like to sample muscadine wines, the closest winery is the **Vineyard on the Scuppernong** (www.vineyardsonthescuppernong.com), located just off US 64 in Columbia, about 40 miles west of Manteo.

Quick tip: Scuppernong and other muscadine grapes are often available at local farmer's markets during the late summer. The skins are quite tough and are not eaten. The proper way to eat these grapes is to pop the inside into your mouth while keeping hold of the skin.

center.com), 312 US 64. Explore Manteo's bike paths with some of the lowest-priced rentals on the island. Family-friendly bike tours also available.

BIRD-WATCHING Roanoke Island and the adjacent Albemarle Peninsula contain exceptional opportunities for birding year-round. The **North Carolina Birding Trail** (919-604-5183; www.ncbirding trail.org) identifies 11 places to look for birds in the area. Trail guides, including detailed maps and directions, can be downloaded from the North Carolina Birding Trail website.

Manns Harbor Purple Martin Roost (252-394-6205; www.purplemartinroost.com). The Umstead Memorial Bridge at the north end of Roanoke Island has gained fame as a roosting location for huge flocks of purple martins every summer. Over 100,000 birds can be observed returning to roost under the bridge at dusk. The **Coastal Carolina Purple Martin Society** coordinates educational programs at the Betty Dean "BeBop" Fearing fishing pier and observation platform on the Manns Harbor side of the bridge on selected evenings from July 15 to August 25, when the martins reach their greatest numbers. The *Crystal Dawn* headboat out of Pirate's Cove offers guided sunset ecocruises during the last two weeks of July and the first two weeks of August to the watch the martins come in to roost. Funds raised benefit the Coastal Carolina Purple Martin Society. Call 252-473-5577 for reservations.

BOATING AND BOAT CRUISES North Carolina Fish and Wildlife (www.ncwildlife.org) maintains free public boat ramps into Croatan Sound at the west end of &. Bowsertown Road in Manteo and in Manns Harbor on US 64.

Manteo has a public boat ramp downtown at **Edward's Landing,** on Queen Elizabeth Avenue at the foot of the Basnight Bridge.

THE SCHOONER *DOWNEAST ROVER* OFFERS DAILY CRUISES FROM SHALLOWBAG BAY.

Public docks are available for daytime use on the Manteo waterfront along the boardwalks leading to the Roanoke Marshes Lighthouse and the town gazebo.

Charter Private Sailing (252-473-2719; www.sailouterbanks.com), Manteo waterfront. Charter the *Sea'Scape*, a 41-foot Gulfstar ketch, for a private sight-seeing or sunset sail with up to six people.

♂ ***Downeast Rover* Sailing Cruises** (252-473-4866; www.downeastrover.com), Manteo waterfront. If you are visiting Manteo late spring through early fall, you're sure to notice the lovely ship with red sails entering Shallowbag Bay. This is the *Downeast Rover,* a 55-foot topsail schooner, offering three cruises a day, including one at sunset, from the Manteo boardwalk.

Outer Banks Cruises (252-473-1475 or 1-866-473-1475; www.outerbankscruises.com). Dolphin watches (sightings guaranteed), sunset cruises, bird-watching tours, and fishing trips for shrimp and crab on a covered, pontoon-style boat (complete with restroom) depart from the Manteo waterfront.

🐚 **Shallowbag Bay Sail About** (252-475-1750; www.townofmanteo.com), Roanoke Island Maritime Museum, 104 Fernando Street. Every Tuesday during the summer months, volunteers from the maritime museum take visitors out for a free sunset sail on an authentic shad boat, the official state boat of North Carolina. Suggested donation $5.

CANOEING AND KAYAKING Kitty Hawk Kayaks (252-261-0145 or 1-866-702-5061; www.khkss .com). Experienced guides offer paddling tours of the Alligator River National Wildlife Refuge, as well as Roanoke Island ecotours and full-moon paddles.

Manteo Kitty Hawk Kites (252-473-2357; www.kittyhawk.com), 307 Queen Elizabeth Street. Rent single or tandem kayaks or stand-up paddleboards right on the waterfront to explore Shallowbag Bay and surrounding waters. You can launch from a floating dock behind the shop. This location also offers guided kayak trips along the Manteo waterfront as well as paddles into the Alligator River National Wildlife Refuge to explore the cypress swamp that concealed one of Prohibition's most famous moonshine capitals. For reservations, call 1-877-359-8447.

🛶 **Roanoke Island Outfitters** (252-473-1356; www.roanokeislandoutfittersanddivecenter.com). Pam Malec Landrum, the author of *Guide to Sea Kayaking in North Carolina,* leads kayak ecotours and special children's activity tours. Her company also offers kayaking lessons and rents kayaks, including fishing kayaks, with free delivery to put-ins on Roanoke Island.

DOLPHIN WATCHING Captain Johnny's Dolphin Tours (252-480-9151 or 252-473-1475; www .outerbankscruises.com), Manteo waterfront. Guaranteed sightings on Dolphin watch cruises June to October. Dolphin mating and births are often observed.

DRIVING TOUR Civil War Trail Sites (www.civilwartraveler.com). Although fortified by Confederate troops, Roanoke Island fell to the Union army in February 1862. Former slaves came to the island to be under the protection of the Federal authorities and built the Freedmen's Colony on a site now lost.

Several brown markers recounting Civil War events are scattered around the island. A sign about the **Battle of Roanoke Island** is located on the east side of NC 345 just south of the US 64/264 traffic light. One on the **Burnside Expedition of 1862,** describing the Union capture of the island, is at the Manteo Outer Banks Welcome Center on US 64/264 Bypass. The **Gateway to the Albemarle** marker, explaining the strategic importance of Roanoke Island, is located on the mainland side of the Umstead Bridge on US 64.

FISHING A North Carolina Coastal Recreational Fishing License is required at these free public piers.

BeBop's Multi Purpose Pier (www.darenc.com/grntswtrways), west end of the Umstead Bridge in Manns Harbor. Noted for purple martin viewing (see *Bird-Watching*), crabbing, fishing, and photography.

Roanoke Sound Boat Access and Fishing Pier (www.ncwildlife.org), western end of the Nags Head–Manteo Causeway.

FOR FAMILIES Public playgrounds are located in Manteo next to the Old Fishing Hole on Airport Road; at Manteo Elementary School, 701 N. US 64; at Cartwright Park, Sir Walter Raleigh Street; and on the Manteo waterfront.

Ghost Tours of the Outer Banks (252-573-1450; www.ghosttoursoftheobx.com). Walking tours begin at the Manteo Town Center Kiosk. Reservations required.

Lost Colony **Children's Show** (252-473-2127; www.thelostcolony.org), Waterside Theatre. Tuesday and Wednesday afternoons, June–August. Every year, the cast of *The Lost Colony* presents a special play just for kids. Performances are held in the air-conditioned Gazebo Theatre. Tickets $7.50. The company also offers five-day Theatre Arts Camps with sessions for kids from rising first graders to age 16.

Pirate Adventures of the Outer Banks (252-473-2007; www.piratesobx.com), 408 Queen Elizabeth Avenue, Manteo waterfront. The pirate ship *Sea Gypsy* sets sail from the Manteo docks several times a day during the summer for a pirate adventure complete with messages in a bottle, sunken treasure, and battles with water cannon. Arrive early for dress-up and face painting to transform the young ones into pirates or mermaids.

Roanoke Island Festival Park Children's Shows (252-475-1500; www.roanokeisland.com). University theater departments from around the state offer special plays for children, often with audience participation, on selected mornings. Tickets $5 for six and up; five and under free. The park also sponsors one-day summer activities for kids, ranging from crabbing to watercolor painting. Fees vary.

HEALTH AND FITNESS **Dare County Center** (252-475-9270; www.darenc.com/DCCenter), Dare County Government Complex, 950 Marshall C. Collins Drive off US 64. This facility for all ages has a state-of-the-art fitness room, a variety of exercise classes offered at low rates, health and wellness programs, plus arts and crafts classes, trips, and a media room with free computers to use as well as free Wi-Fi. Most programs are free for seniors. Stop by for an orientation tour.

Nautics Hall Health & Fitness Complex (252-473-2101; www.elizabethaninn.com), 814 US 64. The Elizabethan Inn's fitness center offers exercise equipment, a free-weight room, and the largest heated indoor pool on the Outer Banks, plus a whirlpool and sauna. Passes available for those not staying at the inn.

OBX Zumba (704-998-1323), Westcott Park Lions Club Building, 1000 Westcott Park Road. Certified instructor Maria Williamson (also an owner of the Avenue Grille) offers Zumba, Pilates, and yoga classes for all ages and abilities. Drop-in rates available.

SAILING LESSONS The **Outer Banks Sailing Program** at the Roanoke Island Maritime Museum (252-475-1750; www.townofmanteo.com) gives school-age sailors five days of sailing experience, with special classes in racing. Applications can be submitted as early as January 1 and can be found online.

SKATE PARK **Manteo Skateboard Park** (252-473-2133; www.townofmanteo.com), Uppowac Street, between Marshes Light and College of the Albemarle's Roanoke Island campus. Free and open to the public.

SKYDIVING Skydive OBX (252-678-5867; www.skydiveobx.com), Dare County Regional Airport, 410 Airport Road. Discounts available for students and military.

TENNIS Tennis courts at **Manteo Middle School** (252-473-5549; http://mms.darecounty schoolsonline.com), 1000 US 64, and at **Manteo High School** (252-473-5841; http://mhs .darecountyschoolsonline.com), 829 Wingina Avenue, are open for public use after school hours.

WATER SPORTS Manteo Kitty Hawk Kites (252-473-2357 or 1-877-359-8447; www.kittyhawk .com), 307 Queen Elizabeth Street, Manteo waterfront. In addition to kayak and bike rentals, this location offers stand-up paddleboard (SUP) rentals and lessons, and parasailing for singles, doubles, or triples over Shallowbag Bay. Prices rise with the altitude, up to 1,200 feet.

Roanoke Island Outfitters and Dive Center (252-473-1356; www.roanokeislandoutfittersanddive center.com), 312 US 64. Formerly Nags Head Diving, this outfitter, operated by Matt and Pam Landrum, has expanded to offer even more outdoor adventures. On the diving side, a wide variety of scuba courses, plus shore dives and kayak dives to historic wrecks, are available, along with rental scuba and snorkel gear. Spearfishing lessons and charters are a new activity, as are stand-up paddleboarding lessons, rentals, and ecotours. Kayak rentals and tours and bike rentals and tours are specialties. The Landrums also rent tents and other camping equipment, and have a camping supply store and bike repair shop.

✳ Green Space

SWIMMING HOLES While you won't find much surf on the shores of Roanoke Island, you can join the locals at their favorite swimming holes. It's a long-standing community tradition to swim just off the Manteo waterfront, and you'll often see local kids keeping cool next to the Basnight Bridge, which arches over Dough Creek to Festival Park.

For a more structured experience, take a dip at the **Old Swimming Hole** (252-475-5910; www .darenc.com/ParksRec), on Croatan Sound at 410 Airport Road next to the North Carolina Aquarium. Maintained by Dare County, the park has a sandy beach, playground, volleyball court, picnic tables, grills, and restrooms. A lifeguard is on duty daily 10–6 from Memorial Day to Labor Day.

WALKS Manteo High School Wetland Boardwalk (252-473-5841; http://csi.northcarolina.edu/ mhswetland.htm), Manteo High School, 829 Wingina Avenue. This project, still in development, is being completed by the students of Manteo High with assistance from the new UNC–Coastal Studies Institute. Elements of the project include a cistern, rain garden, and a public education boardwalk, located behind the high school.

((•)) ✧ **Manteo Waterfront Boardwalk & Roanoke Island Festival Park** (www.townofmanteo .com or www.roanokeisland.com). Take a stroll along the Manteo waterfront for relaxing views of marsh and sound. The boardwalk stretches all the way to the **Marshes Light Marina,** curving around a bit of marsh, and passes in front of the maritime museum. Continuing along the town docks, you pass a pirate-themed playground, the **Roanoke Marshes Light,** and the town gazebo. Next walk over the Cora Mae Daniels Basnight Bridge. The sidewalk will take you to another boardwalk, this one along the shores of the island that houses Festival Park, with a view of the high white dunes of Jockey's Ridge across the sound. Interpretive signs tell of the environmental restoration of this once badly damaged shoreline. Public restrooms and parking are located at Roanoke Island Festival Park and next to the maritime museum on Fernando Street.

Roanoke Island Marsh Game Land (252-482-7701; www.ncwildlife.org), NC 345, south of Manteo. Short walking trail leads to views of a 40-acre waterfowl impoundment and a black needlerush marsh.

ㅎ **Trails at Fort Raleigh National Historic Site** (252-473-5772; www.nps.gov/fora), 1401 National Park Drive. The 1.25-mile **Freedom Trail** leads from the parking lot in front of the Elizabethan Gardens to the Freedman's Colony exhibit at the foot of the Umstead Bridge. Along the way, signs identify plants used in the native Algonquian culture. The shorter **Thomas Heriot Nature Trail** winds on sandy paths under old live oaks down to the shore. Signs here hold quotes from Heriot's journals on the local flora he found in the New World, and the ways colonists used them. Both trails are paved and open to both pedestrians and bicycles.

✳ Lodging

Roanoke Island is a rarity among major vacation destinations. Not even one chain hotel or motel has taken root here. Nearly all accommodations are locally owned and operated, often by families who have lived on the Outer Banks for generations.

Seasonal demand can drive up prices to extravagant heights. A room that rents for $59 a night in January may go for $199 in July. Valentine's Day weekend is also a time of high tariffs in Manteo, with its many romantic bed & breakfasts, as are May and June, when wedding parties come to town.

Many accommodations require two-night minimum stays on the weekends and three-night minimums on holiday weekends. Some also require notice of cancellations many days in advance in order to retrieve your deposit, up 50 percent of the total price.

Many accommodations on Roanoke Island are now pet friendly, often with an additional pet fee required.

BED & BREAKFAST INNS ((ɕ)) **Burrus House Inn Waterfront Suites** (252-475-1636; www .burrushouseinn.com), 509 S. US 64. Away from the bustle but within walking distance of the Manteo waterfront, this classic Carolina beach house offers views of Shallowbag Bay from all eight elegantly appointed guest suites, all with both bedrooms and sitting rooms, fireplaces, ceiling fans, refrigerators, microwaves, and coffeemakers. Baths feature Jacuzzi tubs and showers big enough for two. Kitchens are stocked with continental breakfast items, coffee, tea, wine, cheese, and crackers. The tower suites with cathedral ceilings are popular with honeymooners. Private and quiet with few distractions, the Burrus is best suited to couples seeking a romantic getaway. $$$$.

✿ ✿ ♂ ((ɕ)) **Cameron House Inn** (252-473-6596 or 1-800-279-8178; www.cameronhouse inn.com), 300 Budleigh Street. Just a block from the Manteo waterfront, this restored 1919 Arts and Crafts bungalow features comfortable rooms with period decorations, plus lots of common areas where you can relax and mix with other guests. Favorite gathering places are the front porch, furnished with wicker furniture and an antique swing, and a large jasmine-vine-covered back porch, where rocking chairs surround a fireplace. Breakfasts of muffins, juice, coffee, or tea are served in the dining room, and fresh-baked cookies and other goodies are available around the clock. The innkeepers are guidebook writers and very helpful in suggesting local activities. The inn is home to several cats.

Children are welcome. Bicycles are included in the room rate. No smoking is allowed inside. $$–$$$.

((ɕ)) **The Outdoors Inn** (252-473-1356; www.the outdoorsinn.com), 406 Uppowoc Avenue. Operated by scuba and kayaking instructor Pam Landrum and her boat-building husband Matt, this inn occupies a historic house close to the Manteo waterfront with a swimming pool and hot tub. Two ground-floor rooms have refrigerators and private baths, and come with complimentary bicycles and a full breakfast. A no-smoking policy is enforced both inside and on the grounds. $–$$.

✿ ♂ ((ɕ)) **Roanoke Island Inn** (252-473-5511 or 1-877-473-5511; www.roanokeislandinn.com), 305 Fernando Street. With an unsurpassed Manteo location and a long tradition of hospitality, the Roanoke Island Inn garners rave reviews from guests. Built in the 1860s for the current innkeeper's great-great-grandmother, the white building is surrounded by distinctive gardens and has grown into a sprawling hostelry looking out over the marsh at Shallowbag Bay. The inn's eight guest rooms each have private entrances, as well as access to a big porch overlooking the water. Two of the rooms are family suites that have small adjoining rooms with twin beds for children. Through the arched carriageway, you'll find a lush garden and koi pond, as well as a two-bedroom bungalow. Bicycles, crab dipping nets, and continental breakfast are included, and the innkeeper's pantry offers refreshments 24 hours a day. The Roanoke also has a private boat dock and a wedding chapel on the grounds. Open seasonally. $$–$$$$.

The same innkeeper rents other unique properties in the area. The **Island Camp** is on a private island accessible only by boat and comes complete with crab traps. You must have your own boat and cell phone. The **Croatan Cottage** is a restored Sears Kit home with three bedrooms and three baths. The backyard faces the water.

((ɕ)) **Scarborough House Bed & Breakfast** (252-473-3849; www.scarboroughhouseinn .com), 323 Fernando Street. Innkeepers Sally and Phil Scarborough, both natives of the Outer Banks, frequently chat with guests in their comfortable living room or while rocking on their porch overlooking the garden. All the guest rooms are furnished with genuine antiques and mementos of Roanoke Island history. The house enjoys a terrific location facing the harbor, just a block from the activity on Queen Elizabeth Avenue.

The Scarborough rents five rooms in the main house, plus two suites in a separate guesthouse and a cottage loft on the grounds. A light continental breakfast is offered in your room. The guesthouse suites have Jacuzzi tubs for two complete kitchen facilities. $–$$.

 ⚟ **Scarborough Inn** (252-473-3979; www .scarborough-inn.com), 524 US 64. The younger generation of the Scarborough family operates this inn, on the main highway, with the same island hospitality, outstanding cleanliness, and reasonable rates found at the Scarborough homestead not far away. The cedar-shake main inn has two-story covered porches to catch the island breezes. Twelve rooms, each with private bath, cable TV, refrigerator, microwave, and coffeemaker, are distributed among three buildings. A light continental breakfast is served. $–$$.

 ⚟ **Tranquil House Inn** (252-473-1404 or 1-800-458-7069; www.tranquilhouseinn.com), 405 Queen Elizabeth Avenue. Located directly on the Manteo boardwalk across from the *Elizabeth II*, this elegant inn is top-of-the-line among local hostelries. Richard Gere and Diane Lane stayed here while filming *Nights in Rodanthe,* and other notables seem to find their way here as well. Maybe it's the room service. The hotel's restaurant, **1587,** is one of the finest in the area.

Built of cypress, cedar, and stained glass to resemble historic inns of the past, the Tranquil House is in the heart of downtown Manteo, but its focus is outward toward Shallowbag Bay. The spacious second-floor patio overlooking the harbor is a favorite gathering spot at sunset. Each of the inn's 25 rooms is unique. The three-story hotel does not have an elevator, but a ramp makes the first floor accessible to wheelchairs, with one guest room equipped for the handicapped. Up to two children under 18 may stay free with their parents. Continental breakfast, daily newspaper, bicycle rental, and an afternoon wine and cheese reception are included in the room rate. $$–$$$$.

 ⚟ **The White Doe Inn** (252-473-9851 or 1-800-476-6091; www.whitedoeinn.com), 319 Sir Walter Raleigh Street. Its turret, wraparound porches, elaborate woodwork, balconies, and extensive gardens make the Queen Anne–style Theodore Meekins house, built in 1910 and on the National Register of Historic Places, stand out. Today it is the White Doe Inn, Manteo's most romantic bed & breakfast. Decorated in the Victorian style, its eight uniquely designed bedrooms offer a range of amenities, including private gardens, balconies, canopied beds, stained-glass windows, soaking tubs, and Jacuzzis for two. Both masculine and feminine color schemes are available. All rooms have guest bathrobes, and a fireplace. Room rates include a four-course seated breakfast served in the dining room or on the veranda, as well as coffee, dessert, and sherry every evening. In-room spa services are available, as are special picnic, wedding, honeymoon, champagne, and chocolate packages; a 24-hour butler's wine pantry; and cappuccino and espresso service. $$$–$$$$.

CONDO RENTALS Shallowbag Bay Club (252-475-1617; www.shallowbagbaymarina .com), 90 N. Bay Club Drive. Several of the fully equipped luxury one- to four-bedroom condos in this sound-front community are available as rentals. Community amenities include a swimming pool and hot tub, fitness center, and game room, as well as the popular **Stripers Bar & Grille.** Slips at the marina are available for transient boaters.

GUESTHOUSES AND COTTAGES ⚐ **Booth Guest House** (252-305-1205 or 252-473-3515; www.theboothhouse.com), 135 Morrison Grove Road. Located on the sound at the north end of Roanoke Island, this home, filled with family antiques, is within walking distance of *The Lost Colony.* The soundfront gazebo is a popular spot for weddings. $–$$.

 ❀ **Clemons Cottage** (252-256-2662; www .clemonscottage.com), 406 Budleigh Street. Quiet cottage in the middle of the historic district offers two bedrooms and a full kitchen, plus a private garden with barbecue grill. Weekly rates are available. $$–$$$.

 ❀ ⚐ ⚟ **Island Guesthouse and Cottages** (252-473-2434; www.theislandmotel.com), 706 US 64. The guesthouse, a cottage located on the main highway through town, offers friendly service and bright, clean accommodations at surprisingly reasonable rates both on and off-season. The 14 rooms each have two double beds with fold-out cots available, plus cable TV and air-conditioning. The property is popular for weddings, and an on-site wedding planner is available. A block away, at 708 Wingina Avenue, three themed cottages that offer more privacy as well as more upscale amenities are operated by the same proprietors. Each cottage has a full kitchen, Dolby surround sound home theater with a flat-screen TV, bath with two-person whirlpool tub, fireplace, Wi-Fi. The owners are avid surfers and offer guests discounted surfing lessons. $–$$$$.

 ⚟ **Magnolia Cottage** (252-256-2662; www .magnoliacottage.us), 310 Ananias Dare Street.

Vacation in one of Manteo's most distinguished residences. This three-bedroom, two-bath cottage has wraparound porches and an arbor, plus an Elizabethan-style garden and every modern convenience. Two bikes included in rental. $$$$.

🐾 (ᵗ) **Neva Midgett House** (252-256-2662; www.midgetthouse.com), 406 Budleigh Street. This Arts and Crafts bungalow in the historic district has two bedrooms; a big covered porch; living, dining, and bath; plus a completely equipped kitchen; two HDTVs; washer/dryer; DVD player; and dishwasher. Or select the **Island Loft** (www.islandloft.com) upstairs, with two bedrooms, a tree-top deck, and private entry. Both rentals come with complimentary bikes. $$$–$$$$; three-night minimum.

(ᵗ) **The Roanoke Bungalow** (252-305-4473; www.roanokebungalow.com), 511 Ananias Dare Street. Luxuriously appointed inside and out, this two-bedroom cottage with shared bath is great for a family or friends traveling together. Outside, a fireplace on a covered deck and outdoor garden shower expand the living space into the lovely garden. Breakfast is served on the deck, where drinks and snacks are available all day. $$$.

MARINAS Several marinas on Roanoke Island welcome transients who want to cruise in and stay aboard their boats, or just stop by for dinner on the docks. Most host excursion boats or charter fishing vessels, so a marina can be an exciting place to hang out, even if you don't have a boat.

(ᵗ) **Manteo Waterfront Marina** (252-473-3320; www.townofmanteo.com), 207 Queen Elizabeth Avenue. Numerous transient berths with full hookups are available on the waterfront in downtown Manteo. Showers, Laundromat, ship's store, and many onshore amenities are nearby. The town hosts free Wi-Fi along the entire waterfront.

Marshes Light Marina (252-475-9863; www.marsheslight.com/marina), 201 Fernando Street. New marina with full-service transient slips is connected to downtown Manteo by a boardwalk. Shower and laundry available, plus a ship's store.

Shallowbag Bay Marina (252-305-8726; www.shallowbagbaymarina.com), 100 Bay Club Drive. Boat slips come with all club amenities, including a pool and hot tub, fitness center, bicycles, cable and phone hookups, laundry and shower facilities, and a courtesy car. A ship's store and restaurant are located on-site, with slip space available for customers.

MOTOR LODGES 🐾 (ᵗ) **Dare Haven Motel** (252-473-2322; www.darehaven.com), US 64. The 26 courtyard units in this family-run motel have been recently renovated. Each has a color TV, phone, and minifridge. Pleasant porches have swings and rockers. Room service and boat trailer parking available. $–$$.

🐾 ♿ **Duke of Dare Motor Lodge** (252-473-2175), 100 S. US 64. This very basic motel, owned and operated by the local Creef family, offers some of the lowest nightly rates around and is within walking distance of the Manteo waterfront. Built in 1964, the lodge's 57 rooms clearly have a few miles on them, but anglers and bargain hunters will appreciate the inexpensive price. An outdoor pool (open in summer), cable TV, heat and air-conditioning, and in-room phones complete the amenities. Most rooms have two double beds, and some are handicapped accessible. $.

🐾 ♿ (ᵗ) **The Elizabethan Inn** (252-473-2101 or 1-800-346-2466; www.elizabethaninn.com), 814 US 64. Roanoke Island's largest accommodation, with 78 units, has an attractive Tudor-style, timbered exterior that fits in well with the island's historic theme. Opened in 1954 and renovated in 2003, the motor lodge now has a professionally staffed spa with heated indoor pool, whirlpool, sauna, aerobic and yoga classes, and the latest fitness equipment, as well as a seasonal outdoor pool. Guests can borrow bicycles to explore the bike path that runs in front of the inn. A variety of room types are available, including deluxe rooms with whirlpool bath and king bed, handicapped-accessible rooms, smoking and nonsmoking rooms, pet-friendly rooms, and efficiencies. All rooms have cable TV, and most have refrigerators. ♪ **La Dolce Vita Italian Cuisine & Pizzeria** (252-473-9919; www.ladolcevitamanteo.com) is on-site. $–$$$.

☀ Where to Eat

With the exceptions of McDonald's, Subway, and Pizza Hut, Roanoke Island remains free of chain restaurants. Most eateries are family-owned and operated. Often the fresh seafood on the menu comes directly from the family's fishing boat to the table. Keep an eye out for blackboard specials. These change frequently and usually represent what is literally "the catch of the day."

DINING OUT ♂ ♀ **Avenue Grille and Events** (252-473-4800; avenueeventsobx.com), 207 Queen Elizabeth Street, Waterfront Shops. Closed Sunday and Monday. This chef-owned spot is a favorite location for weddings and other events, thanks to its lofty views over Shallowbag Bay and clean contemporary decor, but it is also a favorite with diners looking for something a little upscale. Chef Thomas Williamson creates a seasonally changing menu. There's a nice lounge area as well, with and occasional live entertainment. Reservations suggested. Lunch $$; dinner $$$–$$$$.

♂ & ❧ **1587 Restaurant** (252-473-1587; www.1587.com), Tranquil House Inn, 405 Queen Elizabeth Avenue. Relax over a glass of wine and watch the moon rise over Shallowbag Bay, then order up a selection of the creative cuisine the Tranquil House Inn's signature restaurant. The chefs here exhibit a fine touch with the fresh local ingredients at hand and are constantly designing new, but always delicious, combinations. The menu changes seasonally and features fresh local seafood, char-grilled chops, and, often, local game. A full vegetarian menu is available upon request. If you're just in the mood for something light, stop by the restaurant's copper-top bar, a work of art in itself, for an appetizer or a glass of wine. The cellar selection at 1587 received favorable mention in *Wine Spectator*. You'll be favorably surprised by the prices, both for bottles and wines by the glass. One of the Outer Banks' unique fine-dining experiences, this is a don't-miss. Reservations recommended. Dinner only, $$$.

♨ ♂ ♥ & ❧ **Full Moon Café & Brewery** (252-473-6666; www.thefullmooncafe.com), 208 Queen Elizabeth Avenue, Creef's Corner. Catch the laid-back pulse of Manteo at this restaurant, located in the heart of it all, under the town clock. The eclectic menu brings together cuisines from several continents, ranging from hummus to shrimp-and-crab enchiladas, and includes many creative vegetarian suggestions. Owner Paul Charron recently opened his own microbrewery. His unique small-batch British- and Irish-style beers, as well as a selection of outstanding North Carolina drafts, are available at the beer pub on-site. Sign up for the Brew & Chew tour to get Paul's beer-geek take on the operation. Pets are welcome on the patio. Lunch $–$$; dinner $$–$$$.

♂ ❧ **Ortega'z Southwestern Grill** (252-473-5911; www.ortegaz.com), 201 Sir Walter Raleigh Street. Closed Sunday and Monday. Occupying a location with a history of fun—former site of the Green Dolphin Pub and before that Fernando's Ale House—in downtown Manteo, this classy spot offers indoor and outdoor dining, and fresh takes on Southwestern cuisine, featuring slow-cooked beef and pork, local seafood, gluten-free dishes, house-made desserts, paella, and build-your-own kebabs. The bar in the cen-

DID YOU KNOW? Liquor by the drink became available in Manteo for the first time after a referendum in 2011. However, many restaurants have been slow to make the change, still offering just beer and wine.

ter of the restaurant offers fun appetizers and a full cocktail menu. Check out the restored mural of the Albatross Fleet on the back wall. Lunch $–$$; dinner $–$$$.

♂ & ♀ **Stripers Bar & Grille** (252-473-3222; www.stripersbarandgrille.com), 1100 S. Bay Club Drive, Shallowbag Bay Club. This restaurant is a little hard to find, tucked away from the road inside the Shallowbag Bay Club. The secret to finding it: Turn east between McDonald's and Darrell's on US 64. Or come by boat. You can tie up at the dock outside. The three-story building sits right on the waterfront, guaranteeing great views from every seat. Downstairs, the steamed and raw bar is a fun-loving hangout where locals gather for happy hour, with an outdoor patio and screened porch overlooking the docks. Upstairs, you'll find sophisticated dining with quiet background jazz, a lounge and roof-top deck. Signature dishes include the Rockfish Rueben, a tasty take on the classic, featuring the restaurant's namesake fish, the rockfish or striped bass, known locally as a striper. The Sunday brunch, voted a favorite by locals, features a variety of eggs Benedict creations, as well as blueberry French toast, breakfast quesadillas, and omelets. Live music and karaoke some evenings. Sunday brunch $; lunch and dinner $–$$$.

EATING OUT ♨ ♂ & **Big Al's Soda Fountain & Grill** (252-473-5570; www.bigalsobx.com), 716 S. US 64. Local fishing boat captain Al Foreman, known as Big Al to his friends, grew up around ice cream and always wanted his own old-fashioned soda fountain. Big Al's ended up as a complete 1950s-themed restaurant with multiple dining rooms, a big dance floor next to a jukebox full of rock 'n' roll classics, and a soda fountain counter long enough for a dozen people to spin around on those shiny red stools.

Kids can get all their favorites here, for about what you'd pay for a Happy Meal. Meanwhile, adults and teens enjoy a wide selection of burgers, melts, finger food, blue-plate specials, and fresh local seafood, straight off Big Al's *Country Girl* and other local fishing boats. The dessert menu features all the classics, from a banana split to peanut butter pie. You'll have fun here just reading the menu, but there's plenty more to do: Play the jukebox, admire the incredible collection of Coke memorabilia, visit the game arcade, or browse the gift shop full of 1950s-themed souvenirs. Lunch and dinner $–$$.

✒ ♿ ⌖ **Darrell's Seafood Restaurant** (252-473-5366; www.darrellsseafood.com), 523 S. US 64. Closed Sunday. The motto on the menu says it all: "Eat More Fish." This family-owned favorite, operated by the Daniels family, has been serving local fish and other seafood straight from the boat for over 50 years. The fried oysters are what people rave about, but Darrell's does things like marinated grilled tuna well, too. The surf and turf is a local favorite, as is the super-budget take-out lunch. Dessert features a legendary hot fudge ice cream cake. If you'd rather eat at home, Darrell's has a great family-style take-out menu featuring hickory-smoked barbecue and Southern fried chicken. Breakfast and lunch $; dinner $$.

Garden Deli & Pizzeria (252-473-6888; www.gardenpizzeria.com), 512 S. US 64. Known for its New York–style thin-crust pizzas, including a delicious white Greek pie, this spot has chefs who like to press the envelope. The menu also has vegan pizzas and salads. Free delivery to Roanoke Island and Pirate's Cove, or eat on the shady deck. $–$$.

✒ **Hungry Pelican Deli and Bakery** (252-473-9441; www.thehungrypelican.com), 207 Queen Elizabeth Avenue, Waterfront Shops. Sandwiches at this shop overlooking the harbor are made with Dietz and Watson "Healthier Lifestyle" deli meats on breads baked on-site. Salads, dressings, soups, and sides are all made in-house, as are the desserts. $.

✒ **La Cabana Restaurant** (252-473-9364; www.lacabanaobx.com), 112 US 64. Authentic homestyle Latin American dishes, plus reasonable prices, make this spot next to the Piggly Wiggly grocery a favorite with locals. Owned by a family from Belize, La Cabana features dishes ranging from mild to spicy, including Honduran fried fish with plantains, Guatemalan chicken, and Salvadoran *pupusas*, plus the more familiar tamales, tacos, and enchiladas, including many local seafood selections. The Sunday brunch menu offers many interesting takes on Latin American breakfast cuisine. Sunday brunch $; lunch and dinner $–$$.

▾ (((•))) **Poor Richard's Sandwich Shop** (252-473-3333; www.poorrichardsmanteo.com), 303 Queen Elizabeth Avenue. A presence on the Manteo waterfront since 1984, Poor Richard's is easy to find, with a door opening onto Queen Elizabeth Avenue and another leading directly onto the docks. A full breakfast menu is served until 10:30 AM. Hot and cold sandwiches are made with Boar's Head meats and cheese or house-made deli salads. You can check your e-mail, thanks to the complimentary Wi-Fi access along the waterfront. Live music is offered several nights a week, and the newly enlarged pub opens at noon on Sunday. $.

T.L.'s Country Kitchen (252-473-3489), 812 S. US 64. Breakfast is served anytime at this family-owned local favorite, where Southern home cooking is the specialty. Lunch and dinner features homestyle dishes, sandwiches, and a salad bar. Don't miss the homemade pies. $.

BAKERY Carolina Cupcakery (252-305-8501; www.carolinacupcakery.com), 205 Budleigh Street. Over 200 different flavors of cupcakes, with at least 15 available daily, are offered by this bakery, started by a North Carolina mother and her daughters. Call ahead to order vegan, gluten-free, sugar-free, or kosher cupcakes, or one of the bakery's famous cupcake towers.

COFFEE SHOPS ❋ **The Coffeehouse on Roanoke Island** (252-475-1295), 106-A Sir Walter Raleigh Street. Located in the heart of historic Manteo, the coffeehouse uses fresh-ground beans from around the world to make an array of coffee drinks both hot and iced, plus teas, fresh-baked breads, pastries and desserts, handmade chocolates, ice cream, and milk shakes.

❋ (((•))) **Front Porch Café** (252-473-3160; www.frontporchcafeonline.com), 300 US 64. Front Porch's newest location, on the road into town, has both Wi-Fi and secure Ethernet options at its "wireless bar," plus a wine bar with a selection of vintages available by the glass or to go in bottles, and hosts wine tastings on First Fridays.

FARMER'S MARKETS ⌖ **Four Seasons Fresh Market** (252-370-6360), 110 Sir Walter Raleigh Street. This store, operated by the Coastal Farmers Co-op, sells locally grown vegetables and grains, plus eggs, meats, honey, and more produced at local farms, including several organic and natural operations. Call for hours.

Island Produce (252-473-1303), S. US 64, corner of Patty Lane. Open seasonally, this roadside stand sells fresh vegetables, herbs, and fruits all summer, then shifts to pumpkins, Christmas trees, and other holiday decor in fall.

Manteo Farmer's Market (252-473-2133; www.townofmanteo.com), George Washington

Creef Park. Held in the park next to the maritime museum on the Manteo waterfront every Saturday morning from mid-May to early September, this market, sponsored by the Town of Manteo, features local produce, jellies and pickles, home-baked goodies, and crafts.

ICE CREAM *♪* **((ϱ))** **Mabel's Scoop Shop** (252-473-1636), 107-F Budleigh Street, Phoenix Shops. Locally owned sweet shop near the Pioneer Theatre offers Breyer's ice cream, a variety of candies, and natural sodas. Kids will love the arcade upstairs.

♨ ♪ Olde Towne Creamery (252-305-8060; www.oldetownecreamery.com), 500 US 64.

✳ Entertainment

CINEMA ♨ ♪ Pioneer Theatre (252-473-2216), 113 Budleigh Street. The first, and still the only, movie theater in Manteo, Pioneer opened in 1918. Today, the Creef family continues to operate the local landmark and keeps prices low to make it affordable for families. One first-run movie plays each week (Friday to Thursday) at 8 PM nightly. The theater, the largest in both seating and screen size in the county, recently updated with an extra-powerful digital projector and new surround-sound speakers. Tickets are $5; add fresh made popcorn, candy, and a drink, and you'll still be spending under $10 for the evening.

Southern Circuit Film Series (252-473-5558; www.darearts.org), Roanoke Island Festival Park Indoor Theatre. Screenings of independent films feature postfilm discussions with filmmakers. September–April. $5–10.

NIGHTLIFE You'll usually find a crowd of locals lifting a glass at **Poor Richard's After Hours** (252-473-3333), 303 Queen Elizabeth Avenue, the pub located in Poor Richard's Sandwich Shop on the Manteo waterfront. Live music is offered nearly every night of the week.

THEATER, MUSIC, AND DANCE ♨ Elizabeth R & Company (252-475-1500; www .elizabethr.org), Roanoke Island Festival Park Indoor Theatre. Of all the actresses who played Queen Elizabeth in *The Lost Colony* through the years, none took to the role more naturally than Barbara Hird. After her stint in the Water-

Located on the main road into town, this full-service ice cream shop stocks a wide range of both ice cream and frozen yogurt flavors, plus Italian ice, fudge, gourmet chocolates, an espresso bar, and a huge menu of desserts. The creamery serves "real food" as well; choose between North Carolina barbecue, beef franks, grilled chicken sandwiches, or an authentic Italian meatball sub. The creamery offers bike rentals, too.

WINE AND SPIRITS Dare County ABC Store (252-473-3557; www.ncabc.com), US 64. Most state ABC stores are open Monday to Saturday 10–9 and are closed Sunday.

> **DID YOU KNOW?** The Pioneer Theatre is recognized by Hollywood as the oldest movie theater in the country continuously owned and operated by the same family.

MISS BARBARA HIRD BRINGS *ELIZABETH R* TO LIFE EVERY SUMMER IN SEVERAL THEATRICAL PRODUCTIONS.

side Theatre ended, Miss Hird went on the road portraying the queen in a one-woman show, *Elizabeth R*, written and directed by Elizabethan scholar lebame houston. The combination of script and actress accurately captures the wit and charisma of the Virgin Queen and has played to critical and audience acclaim. Every summer Hird and houston return to Manteo with *Elizabeth R*, along with *Bloody Mary and the Virgin Queen*, a fun romp through the messy family relations of the Tudors, and *Shepherd of the Ocean*, exploring the relationship between Sir Walter Raleigh and his queen. The company also produces a number of other theatrical performances at the Festival Park during the off-season. Check park schedules for dates and times. Afternoon performances are free with park admission.

♪ *The Lost Colony* **Outdoor Drama** (252-473-2127; www.thelostcolony.org), Waterside Theatre, 1409 National Park Drive. Nightly except Sunday, June–August. Over 4 million visitors have seen the outdoor drama *The Lost Colony* since it debuted in 1937. Commissioned by the residents of Manteo, the symphonic drama scripted by Pulitzer Prize winner Paul Green was the first of its kind, telling the story of the original English colony and of Virginia Dare, the first English child born in the New World, through song, dance, and dramatic narrative. The show has always been lucky in its talent. Andy Griffith started his career playing Sir Walter Raleigh here. The magnificent costumes are created by William Ivey Long, winner of multiple Tony awards for production design and himself a local boy who began his theatrical career at the Waterside Theatre. $9.50–35. In the event of rain, tickets are honored at a future performance.

QUEEN ELIZABETH I MAKES NIGHTLY APPEARANCES IN *THE LOST COLONY* DURING THE SUMMER MONTHS.

Roanoke Island Festival Park Performance Series (252-475-1500; www.roanokeisland .com). Music and theater departments from the many campuses of the University of North Carolina system come to Manteo to perform plays, concerts, and revues on the stages at the Festival Park during the spring and summer. $10 adults, $5 students (6–12); under six free.

Theatre of Dare (252-261-4064; www.theatreofdare.org). An all-volunteer cast and crew present several musicals and comedies every fall and spring in the company's new home, the auditorium of the College of the Albemarle Roanoke Island campus in Manteo. $5–10.

♪ **Waterside Theatre Backstage Tours** (252-473-2127; www.thelostcolony.org). Evening tours conducted before each show give a behind-the-scenes look at *The Lost Colony* theater, prop rooms, and costume shop as the actors warm up to go onstage. Summer only. $7 or $25 for four. VIP tickets include the backstage tour, *The Lost Colony* performance, souvenirs, and more.

✳ Selective Shopping

Manteo has no malls and only one strip shopping center. Most of the shopping options are located in downtown Manteo close to the historic waterfront. There you'll find numerous shops offering a variety of practical and gift items.

ART GALLERIES Manteo's historic waterfront district makes an attractive location for a variety of art studios and galleries. Most are located within a few blocks of each other. The town's monthly First Friday celebrations include a gallery crawl. See also **The Art Village,** listed under *To See—Art Exhibits.*

Andrus Gallery & Studio (252-305-5411; www.andrusgallery.com), Waterfront Shops, Queen Elizabeth Street. Longtime Banks resident and founder of the local high school arts program, Steve Andrus, displays his light-drenched watercolors of boats, harbors, and other marine subjects.

Gallery 101 (252-473-6656; www.gallery101manteo.com), 101 Budleigh Street. Fine arts and crafts from some of the area's top artists, including pottery, metal and wood art, photography, paintings in many media, and art glass.

Island Art Gallery (252-473-2838; www.outerbankschristmas.com), 621 S. US 64. Gallery established in 1967 exhibits arts and crafts created by over 100 local and regional artists, plus originals by P. Buckley Moss and Albert Swayhoover. The original Outer Banks Christmas Shop is located next door.

John Silver Gallery (252-475-9764; www.johnsilvergallery.com), 105 Fernando Street. Oils by John Silver, including many of local scenes, as well as artwork by other professional artists. Silver also conducts en plein air painting workshops.

Mellow Dog Gallery (252-473-4777; www.mellowdoggallery.com), 104 Sir Walter Raleigh Street. Stop by to meet Jake, the original mellow dog, and browse the works of some 30 local artists at this waterfront shop with a view.

Nancyware Pottery (252-473-9400; www.nancywareobx.com), 402 Queen Elizabeth Avenue, Magnolia Market. Nancy Huse creates high-fired functional pottery in her studio. In the gallery next door, her collectible ornaments and God jar are customer favorites.

✍ ↑ **Roanoke Heritage Extended** (252-475-1442; www.manteogifts.com), 100 Sir Walter Raleigh Street, Suite 109. The home of Stumpy the Pirate Cat, hero of several popular children's books written by Jeremy Bliven, exhibits artwork by its illustrator Herbert Bliven, Jeremy's father. The building is full of fascinating treasure, including seashells, driftwood, duck decoys, handcrafted ceramic jewelry, and nautically themed gifts for children and adults. You can even create your own driftwood sculpture.

Silver Bonsai (252-475-1413; www.silverbonsai.com), 905 S. US 64. The home gallery of jewelry artists Ben and Kathryn Stewart also exhibits the fine arts and crafts of other select artists, as well as a large collection of bonsai. Among the art and miniature trees, you'll find Ben Stewart's secret passion: Etch A Sketch art.

Wanchese Pottery (252-473-2099), 107 Fernando Street. Potters Bonnie and Bob Morrill create handcrafted pottery in this attractive building, facing Washington Creef Park on the Manteo waterfront.

BOOKS Burnside Books (252-473-3311), 610 US 64. Stocks new and used books, many of them titles on local history and lore issued by Penny Books, a local imprint, published by Burnside's parent company, Times Printing, which also puts out the *Coastland Sentinel* three times a week.

🦆 ✍ **Duck's Cottage Downtown Books** (252-473-1056; www.duckscottage.com), 101 Sir Walter Raleigh Street. The much-loved Manteo Booksellers closed after suffering extensive flood damage after Hurricane Irene, but Duck's Cottage, a stalwart on the North Banks scene, stepped in to continue the location's reputation as a refuge for book lovers. The hand-picked selection includes regional titles and local authors, cookbooks, graphic novels, best-sellers, and more, with a special area devoted to young readers. The shop also carries a large selection of toys and games that encourage creativity, including the popular Melissa & Doug series, and has a comfy refreshment corner offering fresh brewed coffee, tea, and treats.

SHOPPING CENTERS Chesley Mall, 210 S. US 64. All the stores you simply have to find—grocery, post office, video store, drugstore—are conveniently centralized in this strip mall, anchored by a Food-A-Rama IGA grocery, on the main highway. Look for **La Playa** (252-475-9846), a Latin bakery and minimarket, and **Top China** (252-473-6660), a favorite for Chinese take-out or delivery, here.

SPECIAL SHOPS 🦆 ↑ **Christmas Shop and Island Gallery** (252-473-2838; www.outerbanks christmas.com), 621 S. US 64. One of Manteo's most popular shops, famous for its Christmas displays, has reopened, now augmented by a Halloween room, plus fudge, candy, antiques, jewelry, craft, and books shops. Wander around the grounds for a great shopping experience.

🦆 ↑ **Endless Possibilities** (252-475-1575; www.ragweavers.com), 105 Budleigh Street. Unique hand-woven and handcrafted items made from recycled clothing are produced and sold here to benefit the Outer Banks Hotline Women's Shelter. Pick up a diva boa, a purse made of men's cast-off ties, or a one-of-a-kind wall hanging. You can watch the weavers at work on the looms or get behind the shuttle yourself. Lessons are available.

Inspired by the Sea (252-473-9955; www.furnitureinspiredbythesea.com), 107 Budleigh Street, Phoenix Shops. Hand-painted scenes of lighthouses, shells, and seascapes grace functional furniture items.

Mike Keller Ltd. (252-473-5007 or 1-800-683-8464; www.mikekellerltd.com), 416 Russell Twiford Road. Sports outfitter carries foul-weather gear, crabbing supplies, cast nets, fishing accessories, and Grundens' "Eat Fish" line of clothing.

Modern Heirloom (252-475-1413; www.modernheirloom.com), 905 US 64. Husband-and-wife team Ben and Kathryn Stewart create timeless masterpieces from precious metals and gemstones.

Muzzie's Antiques (252-473-4505; www.muzziesantiquesobx.com), 101-A Fernando Street. Vintage, estate, and antique jewelry is Muzzie's specialty, along with vintage clothing, garden statuary, and unique engagement rings.

My Secret Garden (252-473-6880), 101 Sir Walter Raleigh Street. A favorite stop for residents and visitors alike displays a wealth of ornaments for your garden, plus gift items, stuffed animals, mermaids, and fairies.

Outer Banks Quilts and Antiques (252-473-4183; www.obxquilts.com), 108 Sir Walter Raleigh Street. An antiques mall with a dozen different dealers shares space with quilting fabrics and supplies. Antique quilts are on display.

✳ Special Events

February: **Freedman's Colony Blues Jam** (252-305-5789; www.roanokefreedmenscolony.com), College of the Albemarle, Roanoke Island Campus.

March: **Albemarle Green Building Seminar and Expo** (www.albemarle.edu), College of the Albemarle–Roanoke Island campus. Vendor expo showcases green technologies and products. **Priceless Pieces Quilt Extravaganza** (252-475-1500; www.roanokeisland.com), Roanoke Island Festival Park Gallery. Annual quilt show includes a vendor day. **Roanoke Island 1862—A Civil War Living History Weekend** (252-473-2655; www.obhistorycenter.ncdcr.gov).

April–December: **First Friday on Roanoke Island** (252-473-2133; www.firstfriday-roanokeisland .com), downtown Manteo waterfront. Manteo's galleries, boutiques, and restaurants host open house events, plus there's live music, family activities, a climbing wall, historical interpreters in period costumes, and more, 6–8 PM April–December.

April: **Easter Egg-stravaganza** (252-473-3234; www.elizabethangardens.org), Elizabethan Gardens. Celebrate spring with Easter egg hunts, live bunnies, egg rolls, Easter bonnet contest, and a day of fun at the gardens. **Spring for the Arts Home and Garden Tour** (252-473-3234; www.elizabethan gardens.org).

May: **Mollie Fearing Memorial Art Show** (252-473-5558; www.darearts.org), Roanoke Island Festival Park Gallery. Juried show honors the founder of the Dare County Arts Council.

Summer: **Tuesdays in Manteo** (www.facebook.com/imaginemanteo), Magnolia Marketplace. Events may include wine and beer tastings, art shows, craft demonstrations, children's story hours, Mad Hatter tea parties, pirate ship tours, chalk art contests, an evening tapas crawl, a free sail in a shad boat, and a summer concert.

June: **Dare Day** (252-475-5629; www.townofmanteo.com), downtown Manteo. Annual free festival takes place on the waterfront. **Gardens-a-Glow** (252-473-1554; www.elizabethangardens.org). Visit the Elizabethan Gardens by night for a hot dog cookout and campfire sing.

July: **Fourth of July Celebration and Fireworks** (252-475-5629; www.townofmanteo.com), downtown Manteo. Old-fashioned event with apple pie eating contest, patriotic ceremony, live music, and fireworks. **Red Nose Wine Festival** (www.rednosewinefestival.com), Marshes Light. Event benefits the Outer Banks Relief Foundation.

August: **New World Festival of The Arts** (252-473-2133; www.townofmanteo.com), Manteo waterfront. Two-day outdoor event is a juried exhibition of 80 select artists. **Roanoke Island American Indian Cultural Festival & Powwow** (757-477-3589; www.ncalgonquians.com), Airport Pavilion Lawn, Airport Road. **Virginia Dare Faire** (252-473-3414; www.thelostcolony.org), Fort Raleigh National Historic Site. Free family festival celebrates the birthday of the first English child born in America.

September: **"Get Pumped for Pink" All Out Road Race Dance** (252-473-3234; www.elizabethan gardens.org), Elizabethan Gardens. **Oregon Inlet Billfish Roundup** (www.oregoninletbillfishround up.com), Marshes Light Marina. Contest to catch the famous Oregon Inlet white marlin is wrapped in concerts, great meals, and a barbecue cookoff.

October: **Beach Book Cover Art Competition** (252-473-5558; www.darearts.org), Historic Courthouse Gallery. **Harvest Hay Day and Diamonds and Denim Harvest Dance** (252-473-3234; www.elizabethangardens.org). **Outer Banks Bluegrass Festival** (www.bluegrassisland.com), Roanoke Island Festival Park.

Late October: **Wooden Boat Show** (252-473-2133; www.townofmanteo.com), Creef Boathouse and Park. **Trick or Treat Under the Sea** (252-473-3494 or 1-866-332-3475; www.ncaquariums.com), North Carolina Aquarium at Roanoke Island.

November: **Manteo Rotary Rockfish Rodeo** (252-473-6644; www.rockfishrodeo.com), Roanoke Island Festival Park. Family-oriented tournament celebrates the return of the rockfish.

Late November: **Island Foodways** (www.theislandfarm.com), Island Farm.

December: **Christmas by the Sea** (252-473-2133; www.townofmanteo.com), downtown Manteo. Friday night lighting of the town tree; Saturday Christmas parade featuring Queen Elizabeth I and Santa. **Holiday Small Works Show** (252-473-5558; www.darearts.org), Historic Courthouse Gallery. **WinterLights** (252-473-3234; www.elizabethangardens.org), Elizabethan Gardens. The gardens transform into an illuminated winter wonderland full of holiday decor, accompanied by gift shop and plant sales. **Holiday Tour of Homes** (252-473-7336; www.facebook.com/manteopreservationtrust). Fund-raiser for the Manteo Preservation Trust tours local homes decorated for the holidays. **Christmas Past at Island Farm** (www.theislandfarm.com). Candlelight tour explores Christmas traditions of the 1850s.

RECOMMENDED READING: Harrison, Molly, and Meredith Vaccaro. *Roanoke Island: Then and Now.* Manteo, NC: One Boat Guides, 2004. Walking tour with map and many old photos of Manteo.

houston, lebame, and Barbara Hird, eds. *Roanoke Revisited: The Story of the First English Settlements in the New World and the Fabled Lost Colony of Roanoke Island.* Manteo, NC: Penny Books, 1997. houston and Hird, the team behind the successful Elizabeth R theatrical troupe, translate the documents relating to the Lost Colony into modern English.

Hudson, Marjorie. *A Journey Into History, Memory, and the Fate of America's First English Child.* www.searchingforvirginiadare.com, 2007

Tate, Suzanne. *Memories of Manteo and Roanoke Island, N.C.* (as told by the late Cora Mae Basnight). Nags Head, NC: Nags Head Art, 1988. Oral history recalls details of Basnight's 25 years performing in *The Lost Colony.*

THE ALBEMARLE PENINSULA

JUST OVER THE BRIDGES from Roanoke Island lies the Dare County mainland, a network of wildlife refuges, state parks, conservation and game lands, preserves, a wilderness of brackish marsh, freshwater lakes, and wooded wetlands. US 64 and US 264, which run together through Roanoke Island, divide as they reach the mainland and sweep out north and south to embrace this immense area of undeveloped land called the Albemarle Peninsula.

Man has made few inroads into this wilderness, although not for lack of trying. Numerous land development companies over the years have sought to drain Lake Mattamuskeet and convert the rich bottomland into farms, and a great pumping station still stands as a monument to the endeavor. But the water always comes creeping back. Today, a few farms grow cotton, sweet potatoes, and onions as sweet as Vidalias. Along the marshy coast, US 264 passes the little fishing villages of Stumpy Point and Engelhard and Swan Quarter, largely untouched by tourism. The towns along US 64, Columbia and Plymouth, once important seaports along Albemarle Sound, quietly dream of their historic pasts. Most of the vast interior is managed by a patchwork of federal and state agencies. Wildlife, including black bear, deer, and American alligator, is found here in abundance. The U.S. Fish and Wildlife Service is reintroducing the endangered red wolf into the area.

MANY DIFFERENT SPECIES MAKE THEIR HOMES ON THE ALBEMARLE PENINSULA.

Every winter, the lakes in the region host huge flocks of migrating tundra swans, ducks, and snow geese, making this one of the best bird-watching areas on the East Coast. Bald eagles, ospreys, and wading birds live here all year. Spring and fall, migrating songbirds stop here on their journeys, filling the forests and swamps with their music.

GUIDANCE The ✸ ↑ **National Wildlife Refuges Gateway Visitor Center** (252-473-1131; www.fws .gov/ncgatewayvc), just over the Umstead Bridge in Manteo, provides an overview of the natural preserves on the Albemarle Peninsula and beyond. Open 9–4 daily, except Thanksgiving and Christmas. Free.

PUBLIC RESTROOMS The **Tyrell County Visitor Center** (www.visittyrrellcounty.com), US 64, Columbia, and the **Mattamuskeet National Wildlife Refuge** ranger station, near Swan Quarter, have public facilities.

GETTING THERE *By Car:* US 64 and US 264, which run together through Roanoke Island, divide as they reach the mainland in Manns Harbor. US 64 runs along the northern side of the peninsula through the Alligator River Wildlife Refuge, Columbia, past Pettigrew State Park and Somerset Place, and Plymouth on the Roanoke River. US 264 runs along the eastern and southern side on the peninsula, passing Stumpy Point, Engelhard, Lake Mattamuskeet, Swan Quarter, Belhaven, and Bath.

By Ferry: The **North Carolina State Ferry** (1-800-BY FERRY; www.ncferry.org) operates a route between Ocracoke Island and Swan Harbor.

✸ To See

Columbia (US 64; www.visittyrrellcounty.com). The **Tyrell County Visitor Center** provides a welcome stop at the foot of the bridge on US 64, offering restrooms and travel information. Next door is the **Walter B. Jones Center for the Sounds** (252-796-3008; www.partnershipforthe sounds.org), with exhibits on red wolves and other native species, as well as the **Scuppernong River Interpretive Boardwalk,** along the waterfront. A few blocks away on Main Street, the **Pocosin Arts & Crafts Gallery** (252-796-2787; www.pocosinarts.org) and the **Columbia Theater Cultural Resources Center** (252-766-0200), located in a renovated movie palace, provide insight into life along the Scuppernong.

Engelhard (US 264; www.hydecounty.org). The unique eight-sided **Octagon House** (252-945-2781; www.octagonhousenc.com), on US 264, is currently open on Saturday 10–3, but call for hours.

Mattamuskeet Lodge (www.mattamuskeetlodge.com). The grand pumping station on the shores of Lake Mattamuskeet is currently being renovated by the state of North Carolina for use as a lodge, event space, and museum. Meanwhile, it presides over one of the country's largest gatherings of swans and other waterfowl every winter.

Plymouth (US 64; www.visitplymouthnc.com). The **Port O' Plymouth Museum** (252-793-1377; www.livinghistoryweekend.com) follows the history of the area from the Native Americans to the Civil War. There's a working 63-foot replica of a Confederate ironclad tied to the dock outside, and in season it cruises the river, firing its guns. Stroll down Water Street to discover the **Roanoke River Lighthouse and Maritime Center** (252-217-2204; www.roanokeriverlighthouse.org) and the **Rail Switch Nature Trail,** plus unique eateries and shops.

Somerset Place State Historic Site (252-797-4560; www.nchistoricsites.org), 2572 Lake Shore Road, Creswell. Open Tuesday through Saturday; closed Sunday and Monday. One of the largest plantations in the upper South before the Civil War, Somerset Place, on the shores of Lake Phelps, is today preserved as a state historic site offering a realistic view of the life of all its inhabitants, from the plantation owners to the workers of African descent, both enslaved and free. In 1986, Somerset was the location of the first reunion of slave descendants to be held at the original planta- tion where their ancestors were enslaved, an event credited with starting the national homecoming movement. The plantation is located south of US 64 about an hour's drive west of Manteo. Free.

Swan Quarter (US 264; www.swanquarter.net). Attractions in this charming fishing village include the historic **1854 Hyde County Courthouse** (252-926-1171; www.hyde1854courthouse.org) and **Providence United Methodist Church,** known as "the church moved by the Hand of God," both on Main Street. You can catch the North Carolina Ferry here to go to Ocracoke Island.

Vineyards on the Scuppernong (252-796-4727; www.vineyardsonthescuppernong.com), located just off US 64, about 40 miles west of Manteo, makes a variety of muscadine wines and offers tours and tastings. Free boat tours up the scenic Scuppernong River are offered from the Tyrrell County Visitor Center on US 64 in Columbia during the summer months.

✸ To Do

BOATING North Carolina Fish and Wildlife (www.ncwildlife.org) maintains free public boat ramps in the Alligator River Wildlife Refuge on ♿ Mashoes Road and at East Lake Ferry into the Alligator River.

River Roaming on the Scuppernong (252-796-1000; www.partnershipforthesounds.org). Free boat tours on the scenic Scuppernong are offered April to October, departing from the Tyrell County Visitor Center on US 64 in Columbia. Shorter cruises go to Vineyards on the Scuppernong. Reservations required.

CANOEING AND KAYAKING PADDLE TRAILS Alligator River Wildlife Refuge Paddle Trails (252-216-9464; www.fws.gov/alligatorriver), Buffalo City Road off US 64. The 15 miles of canoe and kayak trails on Milltail Creek provide one of the best ways to see this wilderness. The trailhead is about a 20-minute drive from Roanoke Island. Guided canoe tours offered May through September. Reservations required; call 252-475-4180. More paddling trails are located at the **Palmetto-Peartree Preserve, Mattamuskeet National Wildlife Reserve,** and **Pettigrew State Park** (see *Green Space*).

DRIVING TOURS Historic Albemarle Tour (1-800-734-1117; www.historicalbemarletour.org). Brown signs lead visitors to over 25 sites, most of historical significance, along with natural history and ecotourism highlights, on the Albemarle Peninsula and beyond. The entire guide can be printed from the website for easy reference.

Hyde County Talking Houses and Historic Places Driving Tour (252-926-9171; www.hyde county.org). Sites on both the mainland and Ocracoke Island include historic churches, the Mattamuskeet Lodge, and the Octagon House. Watch for signboards giving the frequency of radio transmitters at each site, so you can tune in and listen to the history of the area.

Murphy Peterson Wildlife Drive (www.fws.gov/alligatorriver), Alligator River National Wildlife Refuge. Follow this gravel drive out to Bear Road, where, like many visitors before you, you will very likely see a black bear.

GOLF The Sound Golf Links (252-426-5555 or 1-800-535-0704; www.albemarleplantation.com), 101 Clubhouse Drive, Hertford. On the shores of Albemarle Sound, this Dan Maples course is worth a drive.

HUNTING AND SHOOTING Hunting is permitted at several national wildlife refuges on the Albemarle Peninsula under strict national and state regulation. Seasons vary greatly even year to year, and each refuge and species has its own set of regulations. White-tailed deer are the most numerous, and most frequently hunted, species. Waterfowl hunting is allowed on a very limited basis, with permits awarded by lottery. A special Youth Waterfowl Hunt is held annually. Visit the North Carolina Wildlife Resources Commission website (www.ncwildlife.org) for seasons, regulations, license locations, and lottery details.

AJ's Sea Duck and Trophy Swan Hunts (252-925-9903 or 1-866-UNC-SWAN; www.ajseaducks andswans.com), P.O. Box 578, Engelhard 27824. Adam Jones guides hunts for sea duck, swan, and bear.

& **Dare County Shooting Complex** (252-473-6655; www.obxgc.org), 1541 Link Road, US 264, Manns Harbor. Public shooting facility has archery, pistol and rifle ranges, plus trap house sporting clays.

DPlace (252-542-0342; www.dplacellc.com), P.O. Box 194, Engelhard 27824. Jim Stevens leads bow and gun hunts for trophy bucks and black bear, featuring state-of-the-art game retrieval and processing facilities.

Jennette's Guide Service (252-925-1521; www.ncduckhunts.com), 11281 N. Lake Road, Engelhard. Teddy "Tadpole" Gibbs will take you out for sea ducks, divers, and swans on Pamlico Sound and Lake Mattamuskeet.

✳ Green Space

♂ & **Alligator River National Wildlife Refuge** (252-473-1131; www.fws.gov/alligatorriver), US 64. Alligator River is one of the most accessible of the area's refuges, thanks to its location just west of Roanoke Island and the Outer Banks. Several public-use areas and programs are located on US 64, including the ♂ **Red Wolf Howlings,** held weekly in the summer months and less frequently the rest of the year. & Guided tram tours are also offered during the summer months. Summer howlings and tram tours cost $7 per person (12 and under free); howlings and tram tours are free in the off-season. Reservations are required for tram tours.

THE RED WOLVES OF NORTH CAROLINA

Alligator River and a few other refuges in eastern North Carolina are home to over 100 free roaming wild red wolves. The species was declared officially extinct in the wild in 1980. The wolves in eastern North Carolina are descended from a captive breeding program using 14 wolves from southern Louisiana. In 1987, some of these wolves were released at the Alligator River refuge, where they continue to multiply and expand their territory. For more about the Red Wolf Recovery Program, visit the Fish and Wildlife Service website (www.fws.gov/redwolf) or contact the Red Wolf Coalition (252-796-5600; www.redwolves.com).

The Howlings begin at the ♿ **Creef Cut Wildlife Trail,** US 64, a paved, half-mile, universally accessible, interpreted trail that leads to a freshwater marsh. A universally accessible fishing platform is located at the trailhead. A North Carolina fishing license is required.

Peterson Wildlife Drive, where sightings of black bears are very frequent, also begins here. The 5-mile unpaved drive is appropriate for cars or mountain bikes. During the summer, a free program, **Bear Necessities at Alligator River,** is offered before the Howlings some nights. Creef Cut is about a 20-minute drive from Manteo.

Another cluster of public-use areas is located at the end of unpaved Buffalo City Road, which turns off to the south a few miles farther west on US 64. Here you'll find the ♿ **Sandy Ridge Wildlife Trail,** a half-mile earth path and boardwalk through a cypress swamp, and a boat ramp for the refuge's 15 miles of paddling trails on Milltail Creek.

Mattamuskeet National Wildlife Refuge (252-926-4021; www.fws.gov/mattamuskeet or www.mattamuskeet.org), 38 Mattamuskeet Road off US 264, Swan Quarter. Lake Mattamuskeet, North Carolina's largest natural lake, is the winter home of huge flocks of tundra swans, snow geese, Canada geese, and ducks. A paved road (NC 94) runs on a causeway across the center of the refuge. A 5-mile unpaved wildlife drive leads to park headquarters, next to the historic **Lake Mattamuskeet Pumping Station**. A short nature trail begins in this area. Other refuge amenities include three boat ramps and several observation decks and towers. The lake is very shallow and appropriate only for small boats, including canoes and kayaks. A paddle trail leads along the lake's southern shore. Fishing is permitted March through October. Sign up in advance for the open-air wildlife tram tours offered during the annual open house every December. Free.

THE MATTAMUSKEET NATIONAL WILDLIFE REFUGE IS HOME TO HUGE FLOCKS OF SWANS EVERY WINTER.

THE LAKE MATTAMUSKEET PUMPING STATION IS BEING RESTORED BY THE STATE OF NORTH CAROLINA.

Palmetto-Peartree Preserve (252-796-0723 or 919-967-2223; www.palmettopeartree.org), northeast of Columbia, about 38 miles from Manteo. The Conservation Fund manages this 10,000-acre preserve, known locally as P3. It's a top birding site and contains one of the last large populations of the endangered red-cockaded woodpecker. Several trails and boardwalks lead through the preserve, as well as a paddling trail with a camping platform on Hidden Lake for overnight stays. A network of old logging trails welcome biking and horseback riding. A visitors center with restrooms is in the works. Free.

Pettigrew State Park (252-797-4475; www.ncparks.gov), 2252 Lake Shore Road, Creswell. Centered on 5-mile-wide Lake Phelps, one of the cleanest lakes in North Carolina, Pettigrew State Park is a paradise for paddling, bass fishing, and hiking through sweet gum and cypress forests. A family campground (no hookups), a boat ramp, a fishing pier, and numerous hiking trails are available. Native American dugout canoes dated to nearly 5,000 years ago are on display in the park's information center. Admission is free; fees for camping.

🦆 **Pocosin Lakes National Wildlife Refuge** (252-796-3004; www.fws.gov/pocosinlakes), 205 S. Ludington Drive, Columbia. This 110,000-acre refuge is home to black bear and a variety of birds. Tundra swans, snow geese, and ducks winter here in great numbers. Fishing for black crappie, sunfish, and catfish is popular in the refuge's canals. The park's welcome center in Columbia offers interpretive exhibits and a scenic boardwalk along the Scuppernong River, as well as restrooms, making it a great pit stop on the way to the Outer Banks. Free.

✳ Where to Eat

White's Shopping Center, Manns Harbor (252-473-2256), 7395 US 64/264, Manns Harbor. General store and grill on the mainland offers fishing supplies, souvenirs, burgers, and beach equipment at prices usually less than you'll find on the beach.

✳ Special Events

February: **Stumpy Point Oyster Feast** (252-473-5869; www.bayviewchapel.com), Stumpy Point Civic Center. All-you-can-eat down-home seafood feast on the Dare County mainland.

April: **Battle of Plymouth Living History Weekend** (www.livinghistoryweekend.com), Plymouth. Civil War reenactments include torchlight tours led by costumed docents and land and naval battles featuring a replica ironclad.

October: **Scuppernong River Festival** (www.visittyrrellcounty.com), Columbia.

November: **Soul Food Celebration** (www.partnershipforthesounds.org), Columbia.

WANCHESE

NO ONE IS SURE what the word wanchese meant in the native Algonquian language, but there's no doubt what the word stands for today. The village of Wanchese is all about fishing, and all about preserving this traditional way of life. A leisurely drive or bicycle ride along the village's winding roads takes you past houses with boats, crab pots, and horses in the backyard. Family homes often have their own docks and piers, with fishing boats tied up alongside. There may be a boat-building shed around back. A recently adopted zoning plan preserves the traditional right of families to both live and work on their land. It also puts some major roadblocks in the way of development, which local residents feared would drive up their property values, a process already witnessed in Manteo.

Many of the roads bear the names of local families, some of whom have been here for centuries, including Etheridge, Daniels, Baum, and Tillett. The Etheridge and Daniels families founded the now international **Wanchese Fish Company** (www.wanchese.com), which remains under family control. If you find yourself in a long line of slowly moving traffic, be patient. A new boat is likely making its way from boat shed to water. These frequent events turn into impromptu parades as utility teams take down and replace wires to let the big boats pass.

So Wanchese residents continue, as they have for centuries, to harvest the sea. There are only a few restaurants and a couple of bed & breakfast inns. The tourists who do find their way here come to board a charter fishing boat, to shop for a boat of their own, or to enjoy a meal snatched fresh from the ocean at the **Fisherman's Wharf Restaurant.**

The state has been busy in Wanchese, as in Manteo—but with a different aim. The state-sponsored **Wanchese Seafood Industrial Park,** devoted exclusively to marine-focused industries, opened in 1988. Locals were slow to warm to it, but in recent years the park on Harbor Road has become a beehive of boatbuilding and boat repair, specializing in custom sportfishing boats and commercial trawlers.

HUGE BOATS SOMETIMES TAKE TO THE ROADS IN WANCHESE.

GUIDANCE Wanchese is an unincorporated community in Dare County. Information is available at the **Outer Banks Welcome Center on Roanoke Island** (252-473-2138 or 1-877-OBX-4FUN; www.outerbanks.org), located on the US 64/264 Bypass, and at the offices of **Dare County** (252-475-5000; www.co.dare.nc.us), 962 Marshall C. Collins Drive, Manteo.

POST OFFICE The **Wanchese Post Office** (252-473-3551) is at 3525 Mill Landing Road. The zip code for Wanchese is 27981.

PUBLIC RESTROOMS Public facilities are located at **"Pigum" Walker Park** (252-473-6638; www.darenc.com/parksrec) on Pond Road.

GETTING THERE To find Wanchese, head south down the main highway from Manteo to the other end of Roanoke Island. The road, now NC 345/Mill Landing Road, meanders through marsh before reaching the more populated area at the southern tip of the island. You'll look in vain for a downtown commercial district. All the business of Wanchese takes place on the docks.

GETTING AROUND The quiet streets at the southern end of Roanoke Island are excellent for getting around by bicycle. Be prepared to turn around a lot. Most roads end at the water's edge.

✳ To See

Decoys by Nick Sapone (252-473-3136), 292 The Lane. Call ahead to visit the studio of Sapone, a carver of traditional Outer Banks–style canvas-covered hunting decoys.

✦ **University of North Carolina—Coastal Studies Institute** (252-475-3663; http://csi.north carolina.edu), 850 NC 345. This new campus, located in the Skyco neighborhood, about halfway between Manteo and Wanchese, opened in late 2012. Dedicated to the study of estuarine ecology, ocean energy, sustainability, and North Carolina's maritime heritage, the campus hosts a variety of educational and outreach community programs. The LEED-certified campus, located amid marshland, is landscaped with native plants.

Wanchese Seafood Industrial Park (252-473-5867; www.nccommerce.com/wanchese), 615 Harbor Road, off NC 345. North Carolina's ocean industries are on display in this bustling compound. Fishing boats dock to unload their catch at seafood processing plants, and shipbuilders create and repair everything from custom yachts to seagoing commercial trawlers. A large charter fishing fleet makes its home here at **Broad Creek Fishing Center,** and **O'Neal's Sea Harvest** offers fresh seafood at a dockside market.

BOATBUILDERS If you're in the market for a sportsfishing boat or cruising yacht of your own, you've come to the right place. Boats custom built in Carolina are considered the best available by many anglers and mariners around the world. Contact local professional boatbuilders to see their prebuilt models, or design your own customized boat. Many also offer repair and upgrade services, haul-out, and storage.

In Manns Harbor

Mann Custom Boats Inc. (252-473-1716; www.paulmanncustomboats.com), 6300 US 64. Mann-built boats are proven winners in fishing tournaments.

In Manteo

BB Boats (252-473-1097; www.bbboatsinc.com), 135 Berry Drive. Legendary boatbuilder Buddy Cannady teams up with charter captain Billy Maxwell to create custom Carolina-style boats.

Bayliss Boatworks (252-473-9797; www.bayliss boatworks.com), Wanchese Seafood Industrial Park, 600 Harbor Road. Custom boats are built the old-fashioned way—from the keel up. A marine supply store is located on-site.

> **QUICK TIP:** Sunday is not the best day to visit Wanchese, since most restaurants and other businesses are closed in this traditional religious community.

Blackwell Boatworks (252-473-1803; www.black wellboatworks.com), Wanchese Seafood Industrial Park, 932 Harbor Road. In business for over 20 years, Blackwell's owner formerly worked for the famed Buddy Davis.

Bluewater Outer Banks Yacht Service (252-475-1420; www.bluewateryachtsales.com), Wanchese Seafood Industrial Park, 920 Harbor Road.

Briggs Boatworks (252-473-2393; www.briggsboatworks.com), Wanchese Seafood Industrial Park, 370 Harbor Road. Boats from Briggs are noted for speed.

Briglia Boatworks (252-473-1981; www.brigliacustomyachts.com), Wanchese Seafood Industrial Park, 625 Harbor Road. Briglia specializes in boats designed by Wanchese native and veteran boatbuilder Billy Baum.

Scarborough Boatworks (252-473-3646; www.scarboroughboatworks.com), 273 Thicket Lump Road. Ricky Scarborough, a major proponent of the Carolina style and 30-year boat-building veteran, hand builds his boats from juniper planks.

Spencer Yachts Inc. (252-473-6567; www.spenceryachtsinc.com), 31 Beverly Drive. Producers of high-performance sportfishing yachts also have a full-service marine facility.

✳ To Do

BIRD-WATCHING Pelican Island Cruises (252-473-1475 or 1-866-473-1475; www.outerbanks cruises.com), departing from Wanchese, take birdwatchers to Pelican Island, where over 4,000 of the big birds roost. Along the way, you'll see osprey, dolphins, old hunting lodges, and commercial trawlers at work.

BOATING The free **Dare County boat ramp** (www.darenc.com/grntswtrways) is on Mill Landing Road between the Fisherman's Wharf Restaurant and Moon Tillett's Fish Company. **Thicket Lump Marina** also offers a public boat ramp.

DOLPHIN WATCHING ♿ **Paradise Dolphin Cruises** (252-573-0547; www.outerbanksdolphin cruises.com), Wanchese Marina, 4457 Mill Landing Road. Dolphin sightings are guaranteed aboard the *Kokomo*, a 40-foot catamaran with restroom, cushioned seats, and sun shade.

FISHING Wanchese is home to a large charter fishing fleet, as well as a commercial fishing fleet that ships its catch around the world. Check these marina websites for charter fishing options departing from their docks:

Broad Creek Fishing Center and Marina (252-473-9991; www.broadcreekfishingcenter.com), Wanchese Seafood Industrial Park, 708 Harbor Drive. This fully equipped marina offers new floating dock slips for boats from 28 to 70 feet, and smaller transient slips with all the amenities, plus a 70-ton travel lift; engine, electronic, and welding services; canvas repair; and a dry stack facility. The headboat *Miss Broad Creek* calls the marina home, as does a big charter fishing fleet, offering light-tackle sound fishing, shrimping, and shark trips, as well as inshore, offshore, and fishing at deepwater ocean wrecks. A two-for-one special includes both Gulf Stream fishing and wreck fishing on the same trip. The marina has a full-service ship's store and a professional fish-cleaning station.

✦ **Grandpa Shrimp and Crab Charters** (252-305-8862; www.grandpascharters.com), Broad Creek Marina, 705 Harbor Road. Experience the life of a professional fisherman with Capt. Russell Firth, as he drags a commercial-style shrimp net behind the boat, then takes you to check a line of crab pots. You sort the catch and keep everything of legal size—a favorite with families. Light tackle, inshore fishing, and half and half crabbing/shrimping and fishing also available.

✦ *Miss Broad Creek* (252-473-5344; www.broadcreekmarinaobx.com), 708 Harbor Road. Sailing out of Broad Creek Fishing Center in Wanchese Seafood Industrial Park, this 61-foot headboat takes up to 46 people on morning and afternoon half-day fishing trips, dolphin watches, and sunset cruises.

Thicket Lump Marina (252-473-4500), 219 Thicket Lump Road. Located just 5 miles from Oregon Inlet at the end of Thicket Lump Road, this is a full-service marina with fuel, a ship's store, and private slips. Dolphin tours, charter fishing, and headboat trips are available from the docks. The shaded patio of the **Great Gut Deli** is a favorite lunch stop.

FOR FAMILIES ✔ **"Pigum" Walker Park** (252-473-6638; www.darenc.com/parksrec) on Pond Road has a playground, picnic shelter, tennis courts, and restrooms.

SCUBA DIVING Ghost Fleet Dive Charters (252-202-1784; www.ghostfleetdivecharters.com), 212 Thicket Lump Road. Enjoy voyages of discovery to some of the most famous wrecks in the Graveyard of the Atlantic, including the steamer *Oriental* and several German U-boats. Top-notch rental equipment, air and nitrox fills, instruction, and lodging packages available.

✳ Lodging

BED & BREAKFAST INNS 🥾 📶 **Island House of Wanchese Bed & Breakfast** (252-473-5619; www.islandhouse-bb.com), 104 Old Wharf Road. Located in a rambling historic home, this inn serves a full country-style breakfast buffet every morning. Guests are welcome to use the freezer to store their catch, or borrow beach chairs, umbrellas, and towels for trips to the beach. They also have access to a 24-hour pantry with refrigerator, microwave, and ice machine. A screened gazebo is available for smokers or just to relax. $$–$$$.

✳ 📶 **Wanchese Inn Bed and Breakfast** (252-475-1166 or 252-473-0602; www.wancheseinn .com), 85 Jovers Lane. Especially popular with anglers, this historic house in Wanchese offers four rooms, including a master suite with king bed and Jacuzzi. A full breakfast is served every morning. After that, you can lounge on the porch, take the complimentary beach towels and chairs to the shore, or go fishing. There's a freezer to stash your catch and a 35-foot boat slip where you can dock your boat. Boat and

WANCHESE INN

trailer parking is available on-site. Pets are not allowed, but the inn will help you arrange boarding nearby. Smoking is not permitted inside the building. Winter $–$$; otherwise $$.

RV RESORTS While overnight parking or camping is not permitted there, the Outer Banks Roanoke Island Welcome Center (252-473-2138) on the US 64/264 Bypass provides visiting RVers with a free waste dump station. 🦽 📶 **The Refuge RV Park on Roanoke Island** (252-473-1096; www.therefuge-roanoke island.com), 2881 NC 345. Campground offers full hookups, including some waterfront sites. Amenities include a bathhouse, pavilion with picnic tables and grills, fishing pond, outdoor pool, Wi-Fi, cable TV, and a dock and boardwalk over the marsh.

✳ Where to Eat

DINING OUT ✔ 🦽 ✿ **Fisherman's Wharf Restaurant** (252-473-6004; www.fishermans wharfobx.com), 3683 Mill Landing Road. Closed Sunday. The Daniels family, owners of the mighty Wanchese Fish Company, recently reopened this dining destination, closed for several years after a 30-year run. Along with spectacular views of Wanchese harbor and the commercial fishing fleet unloading its catch, Fisherman's Wharf serves up the freshest seafood, accompanied by locally famous hush puppies and chocolate fudge pie. Try the shrimp dip or bacon-wrapped scallops served with Southern pepper jelly, before a platter of local seafood right off the boat or a scallop cake, a Daniels family invention. No alcohol is served. Kids love the live touch tank out front. Lunch $; dinner $$–$$$.

EATING OUT ✔ **Great Gut Deli** (252-473-2479), 219 Thicket Lump Road, Thicket Lump Marina. Closed Sunday. The deli upstairs in Thicket Lump Marina serves sandwiches made of Boar's Head meats and cheeses, plus delicious house-made shrimp, chicken, and tuna salads. Eat indoors or out on the shaded deck. $.

Mann's Luncheonette (252-473-3787), NC 345. Friendly staff will fill your orders at the counter located next to **Mann's Grocery and Hardware.** Spencer sausage, a local favorite, is the featured meat in breakfast sandwiches, or you can have eggs with your choice of sausage, bacon, "city ham" or country ham. The luncheonette serves rib eyes, barbecue, daily specials, and buckets of fried chicken (but no seafood) until 5 PM. $.

🍴 ✦ **O'Neal's Sea Harvest Restaurant and Retail Store** (252-473-4535; www.onealssea harvest.com), Wanchese Seafood Industrial Park, 622 Harbor Road. Closed Sunday. This casual café serves fried fish or shrimp baskets and soft-shell crabs. Add a crabcake or oysters to your order for a small additional fee. In the retail store, fresh seafood is available according to the season, but most varieties are also available flash frozen year-round. The store will pack your cooler full of seafood to take home or will ship it direct to you. Lunch only, $.

QUICK TIP: To see the shrimp trawlers unloading their catch, visit Fisherman's Wharf from mid-July through September on a Friday or Saturday during lunch hours (11–3).

SEAFOOD TO GO ✦ **Captain Malc's Market** (252-473-5525; www.captmalcs.com), NC 345. Cut out the middleman and get your seafood straight off the Wanchese Fish Company boats at this retail store, belonging to the Daniels family, which sits right next to the docks and the Fisherman's Wharf Restaurant. The market carries shrimp, scallops, lump blue crabmeat, soft shells, and a variety of fin fish, depending on the current catch, and will steam your selection for you. You can also order some Daniels family specialties here, including bacon-wrapped scallops and scallop cakes.

✳ Selective Shopping

Mann's Sentry Hardware and Mann's Red and White (252-473-5664), 2991 NC 345/Mill Landing Road. Owned and operated by the Mann family, Wanchese's version of a shopping center includes a grocery store, old-fashioned hardware, and a luncheonette, all connected by interior doors. You can fill up on gas out front.

PIRATE'S COVE

LOCATED BETWEEN ROANOKE ISLAND and the main beaches to the east, Pirate's Cove is clearly visible—some would say all too visible—from the Manteo waterfront.

Today the site of a gated community, a resort, and a marina boasting a large and successful charter fishing fleet, Pirate's Cove was once called Midgett's Hammock, and before that, Ballast Point. Various bars and restaurants were established on the Hammock, and in the late 1980s development began on one of the region's first gated communities. Developer Glenn Futrell remains committed to keeping Pirate's Cove compatible with its unique location in the midst of a salt marsh. Nearly 500 acres here are protected as a bird sanctuary and wildlife preserve.

GUIDANCE Pirate's Cove is officially part of the town of Manteo (and shares its zip code, 27954). See *Guidance* in "Manteo" for visitor information.

GETTING THERE Pirate's Cove is located at the western end of the Washington Baum Bridge on the Nags Head–Manteo Causeway (US 64/264).

GETTING AROUND Many visitors arrive by boat and either stay onboard at the marina or rent a vacation home with its own dock.

✳ To Do

BIRD-WATCHING *Country Girl* (252-473-5577; www.countrygirlcharters.com), Pirate's Cove Marina. Charter this boat that can carry up to 27 people for pelagic birding on the Gulf Stream led by experts.

FISHING Pirate's Cove Yacht Club (252-473-3906 or 1-800-367-4728; www.fishpiratescove.com), 2000 Sailfish Drive. The 20 or so charter fishing boats based here head out to the Gulf Stream for tuna, dolphin, wahoo, and marlin; stay nearshore for cobia or Spanish mackerel; or fish the inlet for trout, flounder, bluefish, and striped bass. Makeup charters available.

&. **Washington Baum Bridge Roanoke Sound Boating Access Area** (www.ncwildlife.org). The public dock and pier under the Washington Baum Bridge on the south side of the Nags Head–Manteo Causeway, just opposite Pirate's Cove, is a popular spot for crabbing and fishing. Large parking lot, restrooms, and public boat ramp available.

HEADBOATS *Country Girl* (252-473-5577; www.countrygirlcharters.com), Pirate's Cove Marina. The 57-foot *Country Girl,* owned by the family who runs Big Al's Grill, takes larger groups out for private Gulf Stream charters and winter rockfish trips, headboat-style bottom fishing, Ashes at Sea memorial services, and pelagic birding expeditions.

Crystal Dawn (252-473-5577; www.crystaldawnheadboat.com), Pirate's Cove Marina, 2000 Sailfish Point. A 65-foot party boat, sister boat to the *Country Girl,* takes up to 150 anglers out for half-day fishing trips in inlet and sound. All bait, tackle, and licenses furnished. Families with children welcome. Sunset sight-seeing cruises are also available at very reasonable rates.

✳ Lodging

MARINA ♂ **Pirate's Cove Marina** (252-473-3906 or 1-800-367-4728; www.fishpiratescove .com), 2000 Sailfish Drive. Transient slips include electric, water, and cable TV in the dockage rate, with access to the gated community's pool and hot tub, fitness center, sauna, and tennis courts, plus laundry facilities, showers, private fish-cleaning house, and a courtesy van. Internet access is available in the ship's store.

VACATION RENTALS ♂ 🐾 &. **Pirate's Cove Realty** (1-800-537-7245; www.pirates-cove .com), 1 Sailfish Dive. A wide variety of vacation rentals are available in the gated Pirate's Cove community, from seven-bedroom homes to smaller villas and condominiums, including some with private boat slips. Many rental units come complete with bicycles, beach and fishing equipment, and some are equipped for infants. Rentals include linen service and housekeeping.

Guests can use the community amenities, including a clubhouse, game room, pool and hot tub, fitness center, playground, volleyball courts, fossil search area, horseshoe pits, putting green, and lighted tennis courts, and receive reduced greens fees at the nearby Nags Head Golf Links.

✳ Where to Eat

EATING OUT ♂ ♂ **Harbor Point Bar and Grill and Mimi's Tiki Hut** (252-473-4011; www.manteorestaurants.com), Pirate's Cove Marina, 2000 Sailfish Drive. Dine upstairs on the porch, with great views of the Pirate's Cove Marina, or downstairs in the casual bar, where steamed and raw seafood rule. Outside, the tiki hut brightens up the night with live music in season and a fun happy hour. Lunch $–$$; dinner $$–$$$.

✳ Special Events

The Tournament Pavilion at Pirate's Cove serves as the headquarters of many fishing tournaments each year. Most include a variety of events, including meals, that are open to the public for a fee. For information on any of the following events, contact **Pirate's Cove Big Game Tournaments** (252-473-1015; www.pcbgt.com).

Early June: Tuna Roundup.

Late June: Small Fry Tournament.

July: Carolina Boat Builders Challenge (www. dcbbf.org). Fishing tournament open only to those with custom boats built in North or South Carolina.

August: Alice Kelly Ladies Only Tournament. Billfish tournament benefits the Outer Banks Cancer Support Group. Pirate's Cove Billfish Tournament.

September: East Coast White Marlin Championship.

October: Fishing Tackle Flea Market.

November: Rockfish Rodeo (www.rockfishrodeo.com). Contest for anglers of all ages benefits the college scholarship fund of the Manteo Rotary Club.

FAST FACT: Don't miss the huge blue marlin displayed outside near the tiki hut. It's a replica of the North Carolina state record holder, a giant weighing in at 1,228.5 pounds, caught in the 25th Annual Pirate's Cove Billfish Tournament in 2008.

Hatteras Island 4

PEA ISLAND

THE TRI-VILLAGES:
RODANTHE, WAVES, SALVO

AVON (KINNAKEET)

BUXTON

FRISCO

HATTERAS VILLAGE

HATTERAS ISLAND
One Road On, One Road Off

HATTERAS ISLAND is the most fragile section of the Outer Banks, and the heart of the Cape Hatteras National Seashore. Here you can see nature at work, as wind and water compete to build land, and to wash it away. In the past, one continuous strip of sand stretched from the Virginia border to the tip of Ocracoke. A great unnamed storm opened both the Oregon and Hatteras inlets in 1846, creating the Hatteras Island we know today. Experts say that within not too many years, Hatteras will break into separate islands, as new inlets open across the sandy barrier, which at some points is less than a quarter mile wide. In fact, this process is already in motion. In 2011, Hurricane Irene moved these speculations out of the realm of possibility into the world of fact. Overwash coming from the sound side created several breaches, both in the Pea Island Refuge and in the Mirlo Beach neighborhood of Rodanthe near the famous S curves.

GUIDANCE The islands south of the Bonner Bridge are long and narrow. For the first 13 miles, the **Pea Island Visitor Center** (252-987-2394) is the only place to stop. The villages on the rest of Hatteras are broken into two groups. Rodanthe, Waves, and Salvo, sometimes called the Tri-Villages, and Avon, a few miles farther south, form the Kinnakeet Township, still unincorporated but pulling together for mutual benefit. After Hatteras Island takes a sharp bend to the west at Cape Point, where the famed Hatteras Lighthouse is located, come the towns that make up Hatteras Township, also unincorporated: Buxton, Frisco, and Hatteras Village.

> **QUICK TIP:** To get a handle on the changes confronting the region, pick up a copy of *The Battle for North Carolina's Coast: Evolutionary History, Present Crisis, and Vision for the Future* (Univeristy of North Carolina Press, 2011), written by four experts on coastal dynamics.

A note on addresses: The somewhat charming method of giving addresses on Hatteras Island combines the number address along NC 12 with the name of the (short) cross street.

For information on attractions and traveling conditions on Hatteras Island, consult the **Whalebone Welcome Center** (252-441-6644 or 1-877-629-4386; www.outerbanks.org), on NC 12 in South Nags Head, or the **Outer Banks Visitors Bureau Hatteras Welcome Center** (252-986-2203; www.outerbanks.org), 57190 Kohler Road, in Hatteras Village.

GETTING THERE *By Boat:* At the southern end of the Hatteras Island, free ferries run from Hatteras Village to Ocracoke Island, where NC 12 continues south. The ferries run every day on a regular schedule that changes with season and demand. Ferry service will, however, occasionally be canceled in times of storm or high seas. Check the ferry website at www.ncferry.org for the schedule. You can call 252-986-2353 or toll-free 1-800-368-8949 for current conditions. The crossing takes about 40 minutes.

THE HERBERT C. BONNER BRIDGE CONNECTS HATTERAS ISLAND WITH THE REST OF THE WORLD.

By Car: Without taking a boat or airplane, there is only one way on and off Hatteras Island: the Herbert C. Bonner Bridge. Built in 1962, it replaced the state ferry service that began in 1935.

Now showing its age, the Bonner Bridge is being replaced but should remain open during construction of a new, four-lane bridge parallel with the current bridge. If all goes well, it is scheduled to open in 2016. A part of the old bridge will be retained for use as a fishing pier. (For details on the fight to replace the bridge, visit www.replacethebridgenow.com.)

If storm or other accident should render the Bonner impassable, the state plans to immediately begin ferry service across Oregon Inlet. You can check on the progress of roadwork

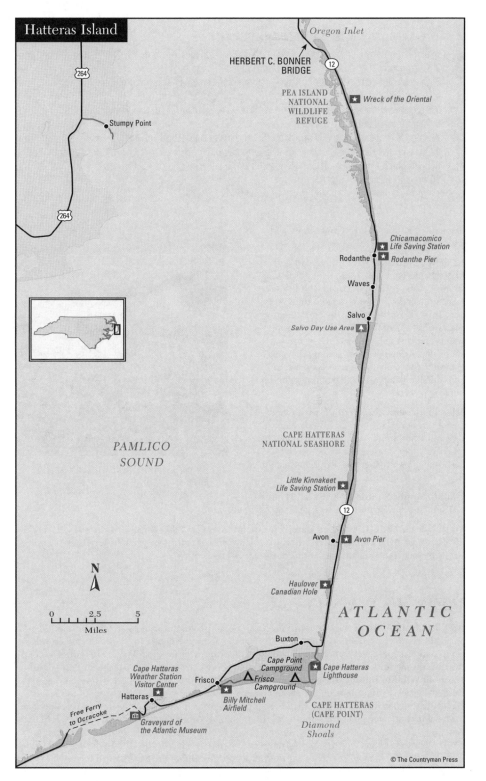

Hatteras Island

Oregon Inlet

HERBERT C. BONNER BRIDGE

12

PEA ISLAND NATIONAL WILDLIFE REFUGE

⭐ *Wreck of the Oriental*

Stumpy Point

264

264

Chicamacomico Life Saving Station ⭐

Rodanthe ⭐ *Rodanthe Pier*

Waves

Salvo

Salvo Day Use Area 🅿

PAMLICO SOUND

CAPE HATTERAS NATIONAL SEASHORE

Little Kinnakeet Life Saving Station ⭐

12

Avon ⭐ *Avon Pier*

Haulover Canadian Hole ⭐

N

0   2.5   5
Miles

ATLANTIC OCEAN

Buxton

Cape Hatteras Weather Station Visitor Center

Frisco

Cape Point Campground

△ *Frisco Campground* △

⭐ *Cape Hatteras Lighthouse*

Hatteras ⭐

Billy Mitchell Airfield

Free Ferry to Ocracoke

🏛 *Graveyard of the Atlantic Museum*

CAPE HATTERAS (CAPE POINT)

Diamond Shoals

© The Countryman Press

along this coast by visiting www.obtf.org and www.ncdot.gov.

GETTING AROUND NC 12, here part of the Outer Banks National Scenic Byway, is the only through road on Hatteras Island. It is just two lanes wide and subject to frequent traffic back-ups. Tucked just behind the dunes, the narrow roadway is frequently overwashed by storm waters and covered with sand. However, the state's department of transportation remains committed to keeping the road open and invests considerable manpower and equipment in this ongoing project.

Island Cruisers (252-987-2097; www.island cruisersinc.com), 26248 NC 12, Rodanthe, will rent you a fun, street-legal VW buggy, a four-wheel drive for heading out to the beach for surf fishing, or a vintage classic for cruising the island roads. Golf carts are also available.

ROADS ON HATTERAS ISLAND ARE OFTEN COVERED IN SAND.

Island Hopper Shuttle (252-995-6771) offers taxi and limo service on Hatteras Island and beyond.

MEDICAL EMERGENCY Vidant Family Medicine Avon (252-995-3073; www.vidanthealth.com), 40894 NC 12, Avon. Center associated with the University Health Systems of Eastern Carolina offers family medicine by appointment, with a doctor on call 24 hours.

PEA ISLAND

AS YOU COME ACROSS the Bonner Bridge from Bodie Island, the abandoned Oregon Inlet Life-Saving Station sits awash in sand, its tower just peeking above the dunes. Just beyond, sand crowds close to the narrow pavement of NC 12, frequently blowing over the road. Waves often wash across this area during storms. The first 13 miles south of the bridge are part of the 6,000-acre **Pea Island National Wildlife Refuge,** the wintering grounds of more than a dozen waterfowl species. Large fresh and brackish water impoundments and natural ponds take up most of the width of the island. Biologists studying the ecosystem have determined that periodic overwash is a natural process and an essential part of maintaining the habitat. NC 12, running between the ponds and the dunes, is in the way.

The North Carolina Department of Transportation has decided to build a 2.5-mile elevated road-way around the area most frequently overwashed by storms. But in the meantime, this stretch of

THE ABANDONED OREGON INLET LIFE-SAVING STATION IS NEARLY BURIED IN DUNES.

NC 12 is a fascinating showcase of nature in motion and brings the rich wealth of waterfowl close to the road for convenient viewing.

Continuing south from the Pea Island Visitor Center, you will cross a temporary bridge over the newly opened inlet caused by Hurricane Irene. The area around this inlet is closed to the public due to erosion danger. Farther south, you'll enter the famed "S curves," a section of beach noted for its exceptional surfing and its tendency to wash over.

GUIDANCE The **Pea Island Visitor Center** (252-987-2394) is the best place to stop. Here you can pick up a map of the very easy walking trails in the refuge and get help identifying the species you will see. If you cross the dunes here to walk along the ocean, you may see the boiler of a steamer that wrecked in 1862, the *Oriental,* above the waves. Public restrooms are available here as well.

Also see *Guidance* in "Hatteras Island."

✳ To See

&. **Pea Island National Wildlife Refuge** (252-473-1131 or 252-987-2394; www.fws.gov/pea island), NC 12. The refuge offers superb bird-watching and handicapped-accessible hiking trails, as well as a pristine stretch of beach where endangered shorebirds and loggerhead sea turtles nest. Paved parking areas are located at the base of the Bonner Bridge next to Oregon Inlet, and at the visitors center, about 4 miles south of the bridge. The &. visitors center, with a bookstore and spotting scope trained on the North Pond, is open 9–4 daily; hours are shorter December–March.

✳ To Do

BIRD-WATCHING The **Pea Island National Wildlife Refuge** is considered one of the finest birding destinations in North Carolina, with habitats ranging from salt marsh to freshwater impoundments to beach and dune. The bird list for the refuge includes 365 different species. During the winter months, large numbers of

THE BROAD PONDS OF PEA ISLAND NATIONAL WILDLIFE REFUGE ARE A FAVORITE STOP FOR WATERFOWL AND PHOTOGRAPHERS.

ducks, geese, and swans are in residence. Several observation decks overlook the refuge, as well as a more remote blind for photography or serious birding. Ask about access.

❋ **Pea Island Bird Walks** (252-473-1131; www.fws.gov/peaisland). Free bird walks are offered year-round from the visitors center. Special ecotours focus on shorebirds and sea turtles during the summer months.

BOATING Kayaks are a very popular way to tour the wildlife refuge, both to spot birds and to see the aquatic life through the usually extremely clear, shallow water. The **New Inlet Boat Ramp,** a free public ramp, accommodates small boats only. The parking lot is on the west side of NC 12, about a half mile south of the bridge over the new Pea Island Inlet caused by Hurricane Irene, and about 6 miles south of Oregon Inlet.

✇ **Pea Island Canoe Tours** (www.fws.gov/peaisland). Canoe tours in Pamlico Sound led by a naturalist are offered for a fee, with a special tour for families. Call 252-475-4180 to register.

Several commercial outfitters offer kayak tours of the Pea Island National Wildlife Refuge. Among them, **Kitty Hawk Kites Sunset Tour** (252-987-2528; www.kittyhawk.com), **Kitty Hawk Kayaks** (252-261-0145; www.khkss.com), and **Coastal Kayak** (252-441-3393; www.outerbankskayaktours.com), are recommended for birders.

Pea Island is also extremely popular with for kayak fishing. **Roanoke Island Outfitters** (252-473-1356; www.theoutdoorsoutfitters.com) will rent you an equipped kayak or take you on a guided outing.

FISHING Bonner Bridge, NC 12. A catwalk from the southern end of the Bonner lets you fish around the pilings out in Oregon Inlet. There's a large paved parking lot at the base of the bridge. When the Bonner is replaced in the next few years, the old bridge will be adapted as fishing piers. It is free to fish here, but you do need a North Carolina Coastal Recreational Fishing License.

SHORE SNORKELING AND DIVING Strong swimmers can reach a few of the wrecks along the Hatteras Island coast. The *LST 471,* which sank in 1949, is about 100 yards offshore, a mile north of the Rodanthe Fishing Pier, in 15 feet of water. The *Oriental,* also called the *Boiler Wreck,* a Federal transport that sank in 1862, lies off the beach opposite the Pea Island National Wildlife Refuge visitors center in 20 feet of water. The boiler is usually visible above the waves.

❋ Green Space

♿ **Pea Island National Wildlife Refuge Trails.** The refuge has two handicapped-accessible trails around North Pond, where bird-watching is good all year, and spectacular in the winter months when the migratory waterfowl are in residence. The **North Pond Trail** leads along the south side of the pond to a dual-level observation tower. The shorter **Salt Flats Wildlife Trail** leads along the north side of the pond to an observation deck. A service road connects these two trails along the west side of the pond, and many people walk the entire loop. The final leg of the loop, however, runs along the shoulder of NC 12, a sometimes dangerous proposition. Instead, cross over the dunes and return along the beach, where you'll see the boiler of the *Oriental,* about 100 yards offshore. No vehicles are allowed on the beach in the refuge, and fires and camping are prohibited. The refuge trails and beach are open during daylight hours all year.

THE CHARLES KURALT TRAIL

Television journalist Charles Kuralt's love of America, and especially his native state of North Carolina, is well documented in his books *Charles Kuralt's America* and *North Carolina Is My Home.* One of the memorials to him that he might have liked best is the Charles Kuralt Trail, linking 11 national wildlife refuges and a national fish hatchery. Located on barrier islands, blackwater swamps, and inland waterways in eastern North Carolina and along the Virginia border, these refuges provide homes for a host of species, many endangered by habitat loss. Each also offers special opportunities for nature lovers to enjoy the splendor and solitude that left Kuralt, in his own words, "a dazzled Odysseus, dizzy with the wonders of the world."

For information on the Charles Kuralt Trail, look for red-roofed signboards detailing hiking and paddling routes, boardwalks, observation towers, and scenic drives. Or contact the **Coastal Wildlife Refuge Society** (252-473-1131; www.northeast-nc.com). An audio tour of the refuges, narrated by Kuralt's brother, Wallace, is available and highly recommended.

June: **Pea Island Crabbing and Fishing Rodeo** (www.fws.gov/peaisland), Pea Island National Wildlife Refuge.

THE TRI-VILLAGES: RODANTHE, WAVES, SALVO

TOWERING ABOVE THE WILD DUNES, the tall cottages of Mirlo Beach are the first signs of human habitation on Hatteras. Named for a torpedoed ship that sank close by, and a famous rescue, Mirlo is the most quickly eroding stretch of beach on Hatteras.

In the late 1800s, villages formed around lifesaving stations established by the federal government, when numerous shipwrecks gave this coast the well-deserved name, Graveyard of the Atlantic. With no reliable means of summoning help, lifesavers patrolled every foot of coast, 24 hours a day, on the watch for ships in distress. In the shadow of the Mirlo Beach cottages, the **Chicamacomico Life-Saving Station** sits facing the ocean, as it has since 1874. The restored buildings are filled with memories of heroic rescues, violent storms, daily drills, and the harsh life along these shores in years past.

> **FAST FACT:** The northern half of Hatteras was originally called the Chicamacomico (chik-a-ma-CO-mee-ko) Banks, taking its name from an Algonquian word meaning sinking or subsiding sands.

The village of Chicamacomico was renamed Rodanthe (roe-DAN-thee) when the U.S. Postal Service arrived in 1874. Over time, South Rodanthe and Clark received new postal service names as well, becoming Waves and Salvo. Today you have to look closely to see boundaries between these villages. In fact, there is a growing trend to refer to this section of Hatteras as the Tri-Villages. It's noted for its many campgrounds and great king mackerel fishing from the pier.

One name you're sure to encounter is Midgett. Descended from a man who purchased land in this area as early as 1717, members of the family today run stores and restaurants, operate one of the area's largest real estate firms, and continue the family's long tradition of serving in the Coast Guard. At the time of the *Mirlo* rescue, five of the six lifesavers on duty were named Midgett. The sixth was married to a Midgett girl.

Most recently, the Tri-Villages have become a nationally recognized hot spot for the growing sport of kiteboarding, due to become an official Olympic sport in the 2016 games in Rio. Two large resorts dedicated to kiteboarding have opened along the shores of Pamlico Sound, with numerous other water sports venues offering rentals and lessons.

GUIDANCE See *Guidance* in "Hatteras Island."

POST OFFICE The **Rodanthe Post Office** (252-987-2273) is located at 25969 NC 12. The zip code for Rodanthe is 27968; for Salvo and Waves, 27982.

PUBLIC RESTROOMS Restrooms are located inside the **Rodanthe Community Center** (252-475-5650), at 23186 Myrna Peters Road, and at the **Salvo Day Use Area** (see *To See*), south of the villages.

GETTING THERE Hatteras Island is narrow along this stretch. NC 12 runs north–south, with just a few short roads leading off to either side.

GETTING AROUND As you drive into the Tri-Villages from the north, you will pass first through Rodanthe, then Waves, then Salvo, before reentering the national seashore. Avon is about 10 miles to the south.

Across the street from the lifesaving station, a short road leads down to Rodanthe Harbor, site of a Civil War battle.

To See

Chicamacomico Life-Saving Station Historic Site (252-987-1552; www.chicamacomico.net), 23645 NC 12, Rodanthe. Open Mid-April to November, Monday through Friday 10–5. This historic site is dedicated to the amazing history and valiant heritage of the U.S. Life-Saving Service, which

EARLY LIFE-SAVING STATION ARCHITECTURE

In 1874 the U.S. Life-Saving Service began building stations along the East Coast. The earliest stations were designed by architect Frances W. Chandler in an eclectic style with medieval and Renaissance influences. The stations' architecture, called Carpenter Gothic, used a board-and-batten style put together with wooden pegs that reminds many people of Scandinavian ski lodges. Most of these stations have been lost to fire or flood, or altered over the years, but Hatteras Island has two of the best preserved of all the 1874 stations, plus one very authentic replica of this unique architectural style.

The best, most completely restored station is the very first one built along this coast, now part of the **Chicamacomico Historic Site** (252-987-1552; www.chicamacomico.net). The National Park Service is restoring the **Little Kinnakeet Station,** also built in the 1870s, located just north of Avon. The **Pea Island Art Gallery** (252-987-2879), the last building on the sound side as you leave Salvo heading south, authentically reproduces much of the intricate woodwork that is the hallmark of Carpenter Gothic style.

THE 1874 CHICAMACOMICO LIFE-SAVING STATION IS AN EXAMPLE OF THE UNIQUE CARPENTER GOTHIC ARCHITECTURE.

gave birth to the U.S. Coast Guard in 1915. The service achieved many daring rescues along this coast in the days when the area was earning its title as Graveyard of the Atlantic. The complex of buildings in Rodanthe is the most complete lifesaving station complex remaining on the East Coast. It includes the 1874 station, the first to be built on the Outer Banks, and the 1911 Life-Saving Station, now restored as a gift store and museum. Exhibits detail the daily drills of the lifesavers, as well as the many rescues and wrecks that took place along this coast. Other buildings on the site include the 1907 Midgett House, with original furnishings. Volunteer crews from nearby Coast Guard stations reenact the breeches buoy drill every week during the summer season. Adults $6; seniors (65 and up) and students $4.

Civil War Trails (www.civilwartraveler.com). A marker across NC 12 from the Chicamacomico Life-Saving Station in Rodanthe tells the tale of the infamous Chicamacomico Races, during which Confederates and Federals chased each other up and down the island in October 1861. A marker in a picnic area on the sound nearby describes the capture of the *Fanny,* a Union supply ship, on October 1, 1861.

Rodanthe Fishing Pier (252-987-0030; www.rodanthepierllc.com), 24251 Atlantic Avenue, Rodanthe. Repaired after extensive damage in the stormy 2012 season, Rodanthe Pier is one of the island's longest; played a cameo role in the 2008 movie *Nights in Rodanthe.* The large pier house has an air-conditioned game room with pool table, air hockey, arcade games, snack bar, and a jukebox. The tackle shop sells bait, tackle, gifts, and snacks, and rent rods, reels, and other equipment. Sight-seers can walk out on the pier for a dollar. Closed most of the winter. Call for hours.

Kiteboarding. One of the most watchable sports around, kiteboarding is booming in the Tri-Villages and is scheduled to replace windsurfing as an Olympic sport in 2016. To check out the action (without getting wet), visit **Kitty Hawk Kiteboarding Resort at Waves Village** (252-987-2297; www.kitty hawk.com), or **REAL Kiteboarding Center** (252-987-6000 or 1-866-REAL-548; www.realwater sports.com), located along the west side of NC 12. Both have restaurants and decks overlooking Pamlico Sound where you can kick back with a microbrew and enjoy the show.

Pea Island Art Gallery (252-987-2879; http://artonhatteras.blogspot.com), 27766 NC 12, Salvo. Housed in a replica of one of the lifesaving stations, a work of art in itself, Kim Robertson's gallery exhibits her own artwork as well as the work of some 100 other talented artists. A portion of sales benefits the Pea Island National Wildlife Refuge and the Chicamacomico Life-Saving Station.

Salvo Day Use Area (www.nps.gov/caha), NC 12. As you leave the Tri-Villages and enter the national seashore, this former campground along Pamlico Sound is a great rest stop where you can check out the shallow waters, sunbathe, or windsurf. There's an old cemetery here as well, with many local names on the headstones.

Salvo Post Office, NC 12, Salvo. Famous as the country's smallest post office until it was decommissioned in 1992, the tiny white building with blue and white trim is now listed on the National Register of Historic Places. It sits on private land along the west side of NC 12 just south of the Park Road junction.

Serendipity Cottage, 23289 Beacon Road, Rodanthe. Mirlo Beach's most northern oceanside house, Serendipity, served as a major location in the movie *Nights in Rodanthe*, starring Richard Gere and Diane Lane. Waves frequently washed over this section of NC 12, gradually eroding the beach away and leaving the towering cottage standing with its pilings in the surf. New owners moved the house about a mile south to its new oceanfront location. It's not open to the public, but it is available for rental through Sun Realty (252-441-7035; www.sunrealtync.com). Look for it under its new name (and name in the movie), the Inn at Rodanthe. Both interior and exterior—cue the bright blue shutters—have been restored to appear as they did in the film.

Wreck of the *G.A. Kohler*, NPS Ramp #27, 4 miles south of Salvo. The charred remains of this four-masted schooner that was driven ashore in a hurricane in 1933 are sometimes visible through the shifting sands.

RECOMMENDED READING Nicolas Sparks's novel *Nights in Rodanthe* is set in this seaside town, and the 2008 Warner Brothers film, starring Richard Gere and Diane Lane, shot all its location scenes locally.

✳ To Do

BIKING A paved off-road multiuse path parallels the west side of NC 12 through the Tri-Villages, from the Rodanthe/Waves/Salvo Community Building, at 23186 Myrna Peters Road, to the Salvo Day Use Area.

Duck Village Outfitters (252-987-1222; www.duckvillageoutfitters.net), 26689 NC 12, Salvo. DVO rents beach cruisers for the whole family, plus geared bikes, surfboards, kayaks, and a variety of other useful beach equipment.

BOATING AND KAYAKING It is easy to launch kayaks and other shallow-bottom craft at any soundside access point. Jet Skis and power boats are allowed only in the waters off the island's villages, as the National Park Service does not allow you to launch or operate power craft within park boundaries.

The Dare County boat ramp (www.darenc.com/grntswtrways) in Rodanthe is on Myrna Peters Road. If you are staying at **Camp Hatteras Campground** (252-987-2777; www.camphatteras.com), you can launch your boat there.

The **Salvo Day Use Area** (see *To See*), south of the Tri-Villages, is a great alternative to the crowds at Canadian Hole, and an excellent spot to launch a kayak, windsurfer, or kiteboard. A bathhouse provides showers and restrooms.

Charlie's Boat Rentals (757-477-6475; www.charliesboatrentals.com), 25628 NC 12, Waves. Rent flat-bottomed skiffs or pontoon boats that seat 5–16 people, or a three-seater Yamaha WaveRunner, by the hour, day, or week. You can launch at Charlie's sound-side location.

Kitty Hawk Kites (252-995-6060; www.kittyhawk.com), Island Shops, Corbina Drive West, Rodanthe. Rental kayaks and other sport equipment available.

CRAFTS ✎ ↑ **The Glass Bead and Beach Mugs** (252-987-2005), 24267 NC 12, Rodanthe. Create your own jewelry from the thousands of beads in stock while you stoke your creativity with the wide selection of coffees, teas, and mugs available.

FISHING Hatteras Jack (252-987-2428; www.hatterasjack.com), 23902 NC 12, Rodanthe. Master caster Ryan White's shop will build you a custom rod and reel, repair the equipment you've got, or provide guide services for whatever kind of fishing you have in mind. Casting instruction available.

Mac's Tackle & Island Convenience (252-987-2239), 23532 NC 12, Rodanthe. This tackle shop also has a wrecker service if you get stuck in the sand and a popular deli where you can get lunch to go, plus gas, beer, and all the usual convenience store items.

Also see **Rodanthe Fishing Pier** under *To See.*

FOR FAMILIES ☙ **Rodanthe Community Center Playground** (252-475-5650; www.darenc.com /parksrec), 23186 Myrna Peters Road, Rodanthe. Playground and picnic area. Restrooms inside community center.

In Rodanthe, the enormous ☙ **Waterfall Action Park** (252-987-2213; www.waterfallactionpark.com) has waterslides and seven racetracks, including speedboats, dune buggies, and sprint cars, plus kiddie rides, miniature golf, bumper boats, and bungee jumping. No admission; ticket package specials available. Summers only. Closed Sunday.

SURF SHOPS Hatteras Island Surf Shop (252-987-2296; www.hatterasislandsurfshop.com), 25410 NC 12, Waves. HISS stocks new and used surf, skim, and body boards, and offers rentals and lessons.

Rodanthe Surf Shop (252-987-2412), 23580 NC 12, Rodanthe. Run by hard-core surfers, this shop sells Hatteras Glass Surfboards, shaped on-site and a longtime local favorite. Call 252-987-2435 for the daily Hatteras surf report.

TENNIS The **Down Under Restaurant** (252-987-2277; www.downunderrestaurant.com), 25920 NC 12, Waves, has some tennis courts out back, available to the public for a small fee. Call for a court time.

WATER SPORTS Among the numerous water sports shops on Hatteras Island, several offer good destinations for a daylong excursion, with rentals of watercraft, plus showers, restrooms, and picnic facilities. All are located on the shores of Pamlico Sound.

Kitty Hawk Kiteboarding Resort at Waves Village (252-987-2297; www.wavesvillage.com), 24502 NC 12, MP 40, Rodanthe. Located on the sound side, Kitty Hawk's new kiteboarding resort also offers WaveRunner, stand-up paddleboard, and kayak rentals and surfing lessons, in addition to signature Fast Track kiteboarding camps, private lessons, supervised riding, and the popular Fly & Ride one-day introductory course. The free launch site here, with restrooms and hot showers, is open to the public. Waves Village also has a coffee shop, restaurant, and several retail stores, as well as on-site accommodations.

Hatteras Island Sail Shop (252-987-2292; www.hatterasislandsurfshop.com), Vela Court, behind the Dairy Queen in Waves. This HISS location offers kayak, paddleboard, windsurfing, kiteboarding, and sailboat rentals and lessons, with an on-site launch.

Hatteras Watersports (252-987-2306; www.hatteraswatersports.com), 27130 NC 12, Salvo. Rent WaveRunners, kayaks, and Hobie Cat sailboats at this friendly, family-operated water sports mecca located in the former Pea Island Life-Saving Station. A large lawn with picnic tables, observation deck, and volleyball court; restrooms with hot showers; plus a beach on the sound make this a great place to spend a relaxing afternoon for all ages.

☙ **REAL Kiteboarding Center** (252-987-6000 or 1-866-REAL-548; www.realwatersports.com), 25706 NC 12, Waves. Founded by Trip Forman and Matt Nuzzo, both legends in kiteboarding, REAL offers a wide variety of kiteboarding lessons for all ability levels from beginner to advanced, including the award-winning three-day Zero to Hero camp and special lessons for young riders, as well as stand-up paddleboarding and surfing instruction. The rental shop offers top kiting, surfing, and stand-up gear. A huge deck overlooks the action on "the Slick," and music plays throughout the property. The launch site is reserved for customers. **MoJo's Sunset Café** is part of the complex, as well as the Waterman's Retreat condos. Check the REAL Watersports webpage (www.realwatersports.com) for a map of the best kiting and surfing "session" spots on Hatteras Island, rated by ability level.

Rodanthe Watersports and Campground (252-987-1431; www.watersportsandcampground.com), 24170 NC 12, Rodanthe. Rent Jet Skis, kayaks, stand-up paddleboards, and sailboats here, and enjoy the sound-side beach and hot showers. Wet suits, beach equipment, and surf, boogie, and skim boards also for rent.

✴ Green Space

BEACHES Hatteras Island faces the Atlantic with a long, unspoiled beach for some 50 miles, from the Bonner Bridge to the spit south of Hatteras Village. The island bends to the west after Cape Hatteras, and the water and waves along the southern shore are often warmer and less wild than the eastern-

THE BEACH IN THE TRI-VILLAGES GETS CROWDED DURING THE SUMMER MONTHS.

facing Kinnakeet beaches farther north. Most of the beach is under the management of the National Park Service as part of the **Cape Hatteras National Seashore** (www.nps.gov/caha), which maintains several spots along NC 12 where you can park and cross the dunes. It's not advisable to pull off on the shoulders of NC 12, as the sand there can be deceptively deep. There are no lifeguards along this stretch of beach. If your car has four-wheel drive, you can drive onto the beach at off-road vehicle ramps located along the island after obtaining a permit from the NPS (see the "South Bodie Island and Oregon Inlet or "Buxton" chapter for details). The beaches in front of the island's villages are generally closed to vehicle traffic from March 15 to September 15.

On the sound side of the park, the **Salvo Day Use Area,** formerly a national park campground, is just south of the village of Salvo and has a nice, shallow beach for children.

✳ Lodging

MOTELS Salvo Inn (252-987-2240; www.salvo innmotel.com), 27219 Sand Street, Salvo. Rates are low both on and off-season for the standard rooms, efficiencies, and cottages, at this basic accommodation just a short walk to the beach. Weekly rates available. $.

☀ **Sea Sound Motel** (252-987-2224; www.sea soundmotelobx.com), 24224 Sea Sound Road, Rodanthe. Just a short walk from the beach, this family favorite is noted for its hospitality and economical rates, with many guests returning every year. Guests can enjoy an outdoor pool, fish-cleaning table, and picnic area with grills. $.

RESORTS ♂ ((ṗ)) **Watermen's Retreat** (252-987-6060; www.watermensretreat.com), 25682 NC 12, Waves. Luxuriously appointed two- and three-bedroom condo units next to the REAL Watersports flagship store have teak floors, leather furniture, flat-screen TVs with cable, down duvets, granite cocktail bars, and full kitchens. Each unit has a private balcony with

water views. **MoJo's Sunset Café** on-site serves meals and hosts frequent live music. Off-season $$; high season $$$$.

☀ ♿ ((ṗ)) **Waves Village Soundfront Resort** (1-866-595-1893; www.wavesvillage.com), 24502 NC 12, MP 40, Rodanthe. Part of the Kitty Hawk Kiteboarding Resort, these condominiums each have three bedrooms and three baths, electric fireplace, full kitchen with granite counters, multiple LCD TVs with cable, washer/dryer, plus a private balcony with a hot tub, gas grill, and view of the sound. Each unit sleeps up to eight people. Guests have access to an outdoor pool, an on-site restaurant, and kayak, stand-up paddleboarding, surfing, and kiteboarding rentals and lessons just outside the door. Minimum stay may be required. $$$$.

RV CAMPGROUNDS The Tri-Villages are the last stronghold of oceanfront camping, once prevalent from one end of the Banks to the other. Frequent devastating storms have made this stretch of coast less attractive to developers, keeping oceanfront property prices low and allowing campgrounds to continue this longtime tradition.

❄ 🦞 ✂ (((•))) **Camp Hatteras RV Resort & Campground** (252-987-2777; www.camp hatteras.com), 24798 NC 12, Rodanthe. Located on both sides of NC 12, this camping resort offers paved full-hookup sites with cable TV; plus three swimming pools, including one indoors; a hot tub; clubhouse; lighted tennis courts; miniature golf; a sound-side marina and boat ramp; stocked fishing ponds; and free Wi-Fi access. Jet Ski and kayak rentals are located on-site. Off-season $; summer $$.

❄ ✂ 🐾 (((•))) **Cape Hatteras KOA** (252-987-2307 or 1-800-562-5268; www.capehatteraskoa.com), 25099 NC 12, Waves. Large campground on the ocean side of NC 12 has over 300 campsites for RVs and tents, plus upgraded one- and two-bedroom Kamping Kabins. Bathhouses are all new. Amenities include a pool, a hot tub, snack bar, game room, playground, and planned activities, including campfires and outdoor movies. A kids' train, jumping pillow, minigolf, bike rentals, Wi-Fi access, cable TV hookups, and pancake breakfasts require additional fees. Canine campers enjoy a fenced dog park where they can run free. Off-season $; summer $$.

(((•))) **Midgetts Campground** (252-986-2284 or 252-216-7033), 23532 NC 12, Rodanthe. Sites available for tents and RVs behind Island Convenience, with full bathhouse, and playground for the kids; plus propane, diesel, and gas sales; and on-site store and deli. $.

❄ (((•))) **Ocean Waves Campground** (252-987-2556; www.oceanwavescampground.com), 25313 NC 12, Waves. Quiet oceanfront campground has over 60 sites with full hookups, cable TV, game room, camp store, swimming pool, hot showers, laundry, and free Wi-Fi, plus direct access to the ocean. Tent sites available. $.

Rodanthe Watersports and Campground (252-987-1431; www.watersportsandcamp ground.com), 24170 NC 12, Rodanthe. This small campground on Pamlico Sound is a favorite with windsurfers, kiteboarders, and kayakers, who can launch on-site. Water and electric hookups for 15 RVs under 25 feet, and 20 tents; full bathhouse. Campers get discounts on water sport rentals on-site. $.

(((•))) **Saint Clair Landing Campground** (252-987-2850; www.stclairlandingcampground.com), 25028 NC 12, Rodanthe. Small, quiet campground on the sound for RVs and tents was

completely rebuilt after Hurricane Irene, so all facilities are new. Boat rentals, Mom's Produce Stand, and Wi-Fi on-site. $.

✳ Where to Eat

DINING OUT ✂ ♿ ↝ **Boardwok South** (252-987-1080; www.boardwoksouth.com), 26006 NC 12, MP 41.5, St. Waves Plaza, Waves. Closed Sunday. Specialties at the Boardwok are Asian stir-fried dishes made with rice, lo mein, or rice noodles. There are surf and turf entrées as well, including an excellent crabcake; and a tasty crab bisque, plus chocolate egg rolls for dessert. Dinner only. $$.

✂ ♿ 🍸 ↝ **Good Winds Seafood & Wine Bar** (252-987-1100; www.goodwindsrestaurant.com), 24502 NC 12, Rodanthe. This restaurant, above the Kitty Hawk Kites store in Waves Village, has a casual vibe, but the chef-designed cuisine goes beyond the usual beach menu. The views of the sound, the sunset, and the kiteboarders are terrific. Ditto the fresh local catch and other chef creations. Or drop by the bar to try the 12 craft beers on draft. Live music some nights. Lunch and dinner $$–$$$.

EATING OUT ✂ (((•))) ↝ **Atlantic Coast Café** (252-987-1200; www.atlanticcoastcafe.com), 25150 NC 12, Waves. This Internet hotspot is a favorite with campers from the KOA located just across NC 12. A big breakfast menu is served from 7 AM, with breakfast wraps and sandwiches available all day. For lunch or dinner, try a crabcake or shrimp Reuben "Hatteras style" with slaw, a dish of mac and cheese laced with crab, or a platter of local seafood. Beer and wine are served. Take-out and party trays available. $–$$.

✂ **Lisa's Pizzeria** (252-987-2525; www.lisas pizzeria.net), 24158 NC 12, Rodanthe. Hand-tossed pizza heads the menu, along with lasagna, spaghetti, burgers, subs, and more. Eat in, take out, or get free delivery (after 4 PM). $–$$.

(((•))) **Marilyn's Deli** (252-987-2239), Island Convenience, 23532 NC 12, Rodanthe. Popular stop with surfers and locals for the home-cooked specials at breakfast and lunch. $.

✂ 🍸 **MoJo's Sunset Café** (252-987-1600; www.mojossunsetcafe.com), 25706 NC 12, Waves. Open April to November. Closed Sunday. Located on the sound behind REAL Watersports's flagship store, this new hot spot has it all—awesome sunsets, cold draughts of the local microbrew variety, fish tacos and ribs that have folks raving, plus live music several nights a week right through the fall. Opens at

8 AM for breakfast. Breakfast and lunch $; dinner $$.

🐾 **Top Dog Café** (252-987-1272; www.topdog cafeobx.com), 27982 NC 12, Waves. Enjoy huge burgers, fish tacos, seafood, hot dogs, and beer and wine on the deck or screened porch of this casual, family-friendly spot with a pirate theme. Lunch $; dinner $–$$.

BEACH BARS 🍸 **Down Under Restaurant and Lounge** (252-987-2277; www.downunder restaurant.com), 25920 NC 12, Waves. Indulge your hunger with a kangaroo burger or pot of steamed seafood, then linger on the deck for sunset over a cocktail as live music plays. Full bar. $–$$$.

🐾 🐾 **Sting Wray's Bar & Grill** (252-987-1500), 24394 NC 12, MP 40, Rodanthe. Fun spot in the former Uncle Pauly's location has good fish sandwiches, cold beer, and live entertainment during the summer months. The dog-friendly outdoor deck yields great sunset views. $–$$.

COFFEE SHOPS 🐾 ☂ **Beach Mugs/The Glass Bead** (252-987-2005), 24267 NC 12, Rodanthe. A wide selection of coffees and teas are served at this interesting bead store.

(📶) **Forbes Candies, Coffee and Tea** (252-987-2320; www.forbescandies.com), Waves Village, 24502 NC 12, Rodanthe. In addition to the candies, taffy, brittles, and fudge this candymaker is known for, this location also has a full-service espresso and coffee bar, teas, smoothies, and a variety of baked goods for a fast breakfast.

ICE CREAM Village Conery (www.facebook .com/VillageConery), 26204 Monitor Lane, MP 42, Salvo. Soft-serve and hand-dipped ice cream and frozen yogurt come in your choice of shakes, sundaes, splits, or cones.

TAKE-OUT ⤷ **Austin's South Island Seafood and Produce** (252-987-1352), 24202 NC 12, Rodanthe. Fresh local seafood is available raw or cooked to order, including steamer pots, fried seafood baskets, sandwiches and po'boys, plus fruits and produce. Open April–October. $$.

Leonardo's Pizza (252-987-6522; www .leonardospizzaobx.com), St. Waves Plaza, 26006 NC 12, MP 41.5, Waves. In a new location since Hurricane Irene, this little spot operated by locals is the go-to choice for thin-crust New York–style pizza. Delivery available after 5 PM. $–$$.

Waves Market and Deli (252-987-2352), St. Waves Plaza, 26006 NC 12, Waves. Small grocery has a good selection of craft beer, wine, and seafood, plus barbecue smoked in-house, burritos, Boar's Head sandwiches, thick-cut Belgian-style fries, homemade tuna salad and pimento cheese, and daily specials. Open late all summer. $.

✳ Entertainment

During the summer season, check the schedules at Sting Wray's, Down Under Lounge, MoJo's Sunset Café, and Good Winds in Waves Village for live music.

Skye Blue Summer Concert Series (252-987-6000 or 1-866-REAL-548; www.realwater sports.com), REAL Watersports, 25706 NC 12, Waves. Live concert series on the waterfront is family friendly and free.

✳ Selective Shopping

Blue Whale (252-987-2335), 27307 NC 12, Salvo. Fun stop sells groceries, including steaks and chops, and gas, beer, and wine, plus a popular logo tee and a huge selection of hot sauces.

Island Dyes (252-987-2121; www.islanddyes .net), 26651 NC 12, Salvo. Colorful tie-dye clothing and hand-blown glass for sale in this friendly shop. Classes in glassblowing available.

SHOPPING FOR A CAUSE
Hotline Thrift Shops (252-473-5121; www.obhotline.org), with five locations on the Outer Banks, offer outstanding browsing and great deals, all for a good cause. Proceeds from sales benefit the local women's shelter and crisis intervention center. Look for Hotline stores in Manteo (US 64), Nags Head (MP 9.5 Bypass), Kitty Hawk (MP 3.5 Bypass), Rodanthe (NC 12), and Buxton (NC 12).

Endless Possibilities (252-475-1575; www.ragweavers.com), a unique weaving shop in downtown Manteo, also benefits the Outer Banks Hotline.

Ocean Gourmet and Sea Treasures (252-987-1166), 24753 NC 12, Rodanthe. Shop offers homemade fudge, ice cream, and candy, plus a wealth of souvenirs, all within walking distance of Camp Hatteras.

⚓ ⚓ **Pirates of Chicamacomico** (252-489-9022; www.piratesofchicamacomicomarket.com), 23904 NC 12, Rodanthe. Ahoy, mateys: This is the spot to score your pirate garb.

✳ Special Events

January: **Old Christmas** (252-987-1303; www.rwscivic.org), Rodanthe/Waves/Salvo Community Building. Celebrated on the Saturday closest to January 6, this 100-year-old custom includes an appearance by "Old Buck," plus oyster roasts, music, and bonfires.

May: **Hatteras Demo Days** (252-987-2297; www.kittyhawk.com), Waves Village. Kiteboarding demos and clinics, giveaways, and a stand-up paddleboarding race.

Late May: **Endless Summer Weekend** (252-987-6000; www.realwatersports.com), REAL Watersports. Surf sessions, live music, screening of original *Endless Summer* movie. Free.

Early June: **Triple-S Invitational and Annual Sunset Charity Swim** (252-987-6000; www.realwatersports.com), REAL Watersports. Weeklong Surf, Slick and Slider competition brings top kiteboarding pros and fans together for riding, live music, dancing, and autograph sessions, topped with an awards ceremony by the sound.

July: **Fourth of July Celebration** (252-987-1303; www.rwscivic.org), Rodanthe/Waves/Salvo Community Building. A reading of the Declaration of Independence precedes a patriotic musical performance.

August: **American Heroes Day** (252-987-1552; www.chicamacomico.net), Chicamacomico Life-Saving Station Historic Site, Rodanthe. Flyovers and demonstrations of lifesaving techniques, both historic and modern, by military organizations, honor our armed forces.

Late August: **Hatteras Kite Week** (252-987-2297; www.kittyhawk.com), Waves Village. Free clinics and demos on all the latest gear.

October: **Halloween Parade and Party** (252-987-1303; www.rwscivic.org), Rodanthe/Waves/Salvo Community Building. Pumpkin signs indicate homes and businesses welcoming trick-or-treaters after the parade.

November: **End of Season Festivities** (252-987-1552; www.chicamacomico.net), Chicamacomico Life-Saving Station Historic Site, Rodanthe.

December: **Community Holiday Dinner** (252-987-1303; www.rwscivic.org), Rodanthe/Waves/Salvo Community Building.

AVON (KINNAKEET)

TEN MILES FARTHER DOWN NC 12, Avon is another village that received a name change from the U.S. Postal Service. Many residents still refer to it by its earlier name, Kinnakeet, a village that grew up between the Little Kinnakeet and Big Kinnakeet lifesaving stations.

The **Avon Fishing Pier** is the town's most notable landmark, famed as a spot to catch red drum. The main part of the town lies west of NC 12 along the sound.

Just south of Avon, back in the national seashore, you'll pass Canadian Hole, famous among windsurfers worldwide. The National Park Service calls it the **Haulover Day Use Area** and provides restrooms and showers here. The name refers to a pre-windsurfing use of the area, when locals would haul their boats across this narrow stretch of island to avoid the long sail around.

Avon remains a worldwide center for windsurfing and wavesailing, and is the only East Coast stop on the international **American Windsurfing Tour** (www.americanwindsurfingtour.com). Many shops specializing in windsurfing rentals and lessons are found near the Avon Pier.

GUIDANCE See *Guidance* in "Hatteras Island."

POST OFFICE The **Avon Post Office** (252-995-5991) is at 41196 NC 12. The zip code in Avon is 27915.

GETTING THERE NC 12 runs through Avon. The Avon Pier is on the east or ocean side of the road. Turn west at the Harbor Road traffic light to find the village of Avon, on the shores of Pamlico Sound.

ONE OF HATTERAS ISLAND'S MOST FAMILIAR
LANDMARKS: THE AVON PIER

GETTING AROUND Bikes are a great way to explore old Avon Village, with its many scenic lanes and older cottages. Rent a bicycle or motor scooter at **Island Cycles** (see To Do—*Bicycling*).

✻ To See

Avon Fishing Pier (252-995-5480), 41001 NC 12. This 600-foot pier is a hot spot for red drum and stays open all night during the fall run. The pier house store stocks a full range of fishing gear and tackle for sale or rent; bait, snacks, and beverages; plus some cool souvenirs. An 18-hole short-game golf course and the Atlantic Coast Café are located next to the pier. You can walk down the pier and have a look without fishing for $1, or fish all day for about $12.

❧ ⊤ **Hatteras Histories and Mysteries Museum** (252-995-4241; www.hatterashistoriesand mysteries.com), Kinnakeet Shoppes, 40534 NC 12. This museum explores Hatteras Island history, with an emphasis on the Croatoan Native American people and the survivors of the Lost Colony believed to have taken refuge with them. Among the artifacts on display are many found during archaeological digs at the site of the Native American village on Hatteras, as well as heirlooms from islander families. Free.

Little Kinnakeet Life-Saving Station (252-995-4474; www.nps.gov/caha), Cape Hatteras National Seashore, NC 12. Located down a short road on the sound side of NC 12, just north of the town of Avon, the Little Kinnakeet Station is being restored by the National Park Service. The station complex includes an 1870s building and a 1904 building, both similar to the already restored buildings at Chicamacomico, and offers an interesting perspective on the challenges faced by preservationists. The National Park Service is also restoring stations at Bodie Island and Creeds Hill, near Frisco.

✻ To Do

BICYCLING A 4-foot-wide paved shoulder for bikes and pedestrians runs along NC 12 through Avon. Plans will extend this as far as national seashore ramps to the north and south of town. Avon Village west of NC 12 makes a pleasant place to bike, with little traffic and some shade.

Island Cycles (252-995-4336; www.islandcycles.com), Hatteras Island Plaza, 41934 NC 12. Shop next to the Food Lion rents bikes, including tandems, recumbent, and adult trikes; baby joggers; and bikes with training wheels, as well as motor scooters, kayaks, and surf, body, and skim boards. Professional mechanics here also repair bikes and scooters.

Ocean Atlantic (252-995-5868 or 1-800-635-9559; www.oceanatlanticrentals.com), 40809 NC 12. Beach cruisers for adults and kids, plus surfboards, kayaks, and a variety of beach equipment for rent. Delivery available.

BOATING AND KAYAKING Avon has a boat ramp, but it can be tricky to find. Ask for directions at one of the local bait and tackle stores.

Kayaks and other nonpowered craft can be launched at ocean- and sound-side access points in the national seashore. You can rent kayaks to use in the ocean or sound at the shops listed under *Bicycling*.

Koru Adventure Tours (252-995-3125; www.koruvillage.com). Koru Village offers a variety of fitness adventures. Kayak tours range from easy paddles in the salt marsh to challenging three-day trips from Avon to Ocracoke. You can try a yoga workout on top of a floating stand-up paddleboard. Other activities include hikes, photography tours, and four-wheel-drive beach expeditions suitable for families.

CRAFTS *❧ ⊤* **The Glass Bead** (252-995-7020; www.facebook.com/GlassBeadJavaJunction), 39774 NC 12. Make your own jewelry at this spot, with a huge selection of beads and jewelry supplies.

❧ ⊤ **Studio 12** (252-995-7899; www.studio12hatteras.com), Kinnakeet Shoppes, 40534 NC 12, MP 55. Create your own pottery, mosaic, and glass projects or browse local art at this popular spot for rainy days and parties.

✦ 🌱 **Uglie Mugs** (252-995-5590), 40534 NC 12. Another spot to get your bead on, this one next to Studio 12 in the Kinnakeet Shoppes.

FISHING Frank and Fran's Fisherman's Friend (252-995-4171; www.hatteras-island.com), 40210 NC 12. This friendly, family-run gathering spot for anglers carries everything you'll need for fishing from surf or pier, including North Carolina fishing licenses, the best bait for the season, and cigars for when the fish aren't biting. The 94.2-pound world-record red drum, caught from the beach just south of the Avon Pier in 1984, and the rod that brought it in, are on display. Fishing advice, weather reports, and coffee are all complimentary.

See also **Avon Fishing Pier,** under *To See.*

FOR FAMILIES ✦ **Avon "Kinnakeet Village" Playground** (252-475-5650; www.darenc.com/parks rec), 40184 Harbor Road. Fenced-in grassy area has a nice playground and picnic pavilion. Turn off NC 12 at the light toward Kinnekeet Village.

✦ **Club Hatteras** (252-489-4333; www.hatterasrealty.com), 41156 NC 12, operated by Hatteras Realty, offers kids' programs, including the Kinnakeet Sound Safari day camp and Kids' Night Out.

✦ 🌱 **Hatteras Island Toy Store** (252-995-7171; www.hatterastoystore.com) offers daily children's activities during the summer, including Paint with Thomas Play Day, and hermit crab races.

✦ **Ketch 55 Seafood Grill** (252-995-5060) has a large game arcade with pool tables and video games.

✦ **Koru Village Beach Klub** (252-995-0285 or 252-995-3125; www.koruvillage.com), located next to the Avon Pier, has a large oceanfront pool, a concession stand with drinks and snacks, a large stage, and private beach access, plus plenty of beachfront parking. Day passes are available for $10. Children five and under enter free.

✦ **R/C Theatres Hatteras Movies 4** (252-995-9060), in the Hatteras Island (Food Lion) Plaza on NC 12, is the only movie theater on Hatteras Island.

GOLF Avon Golf (252-995-5480), Avon Fishing Pier, 41001 NC. 12. This 18-hole putting range with well-kept natural-grass greens makes a good spot to practice your short game. Play all day right up to midnight for one price. Get your clubs and balls in the pier house.

SPAS AND FITNESS Pam Bailey Massage & Body Work (252-305-8822; www.pambailey.biz), 40246 NC 12. Pam, a gifted healer and licensed massage therapist, offers treatments in cranio-sacral, polarity, cranial rolfing, and other therapies. She also teaches yoga classes at several locations around the Banks and is an avid windsurfer.

Spa Koru (252-995-3125; www.spakoru.com), 40920 NC 12. Salon and spa offers a full menu of beauty and body treatments, including Hungarian facial massage; coffee, sugar, or lava scrubs; and herbal wraps; acupuncture; waxing; hair care; and special services for men and teens. A complete fitness center with daily classes is located on-site, with daily and weekly passes available.

JET SKIS ARE POPULAR ON HATTERAS ISLAND.

WATER SPORTS The combination of steady winds and shallow water makes Hatteras Island the best destination in the East for windsurfing and kiteboarding. Pamlico Sound, with its 35-mile-wide expanse of waist-deep water, provides some of the best flat-water riding in the world. Located just south of Avon, **Canadian Hole,** officially named the Haulover Day Use Area, is a favorite with windsurfers (no kiteboarding). Just across NC 12 and over the dunes lies **Ego Beach,** a hot spot for wave sailing.

Kiteboarders congregate just south of Canadian Hole at **Kite Point.** Ramp 34, about a mile north of Avon, is a popular spot to launch for oceanside downwinders.

Avon itself is the region's top hot spot for windsurfing shops, with kiteboarding and surf shops running close behind.

NOW A WATER SPORTS CAPITAL, THE OUTER BANKS ATTRACTS WINDSURFERS FROM AROUND THE WORLD.

Avon Sail House (252-995-7954 or 541-806-4117; www.avonsailhouse.com), 39235 N. Kinnakeet Drive. Locally owned shop sells top windsurfing equipment and will arrange to have your gear repaired.

❋ **Avon Surf Shop** (252-995-4783; www.facebook .com/AvonSurfShop), 40136 NC 12. Run by Jennifer and Eric Harmon, a couple who are passionate about surfing and skateboarding, this shop offers surfboard rentals and lessons, plus a full-service skate shop and some rad fashions. Formula Surfboards, shaped by local Eric Holmes, are available here, as are boards shaped by top competitor Mark Newton.

Hatteras Island Boardsports (252-995-6160 or 1-866-442-9283; www.hiboardsports.com), 41056 NC 12. Surfing specialists offer some of the best intro to surfing lessons around and rent kayaks, surf and body boards, wet suits, and fins. A two-bedroom, two-bath apartment over the shop is available for rent by the night or week.

Kite Club Hatteras (202-549-7693; www.kiteclub hatteras.com). Kiteboarding school offers kite camps and lessons for beginners, including a three-day course leading to certification by the International Kiteboarding Organization (www.ikointl.com).

((ɯ)) **OceanAir Sports** (252-995-5000; www.oceanairsports.com), 39450 NC 12. At this great water sports hangout right on the sound, you can enjoy windsurfing, kiteboarding, kayaking, and stand-up paddleboarding; rent a Hobie Cat or WaveRunner; or just watch all the action from the shore. The OceanAir Academy offers a progressive series of lessons in windsurfing or kiteboarding including special windsurfing lessons for children, plus free windsurfing and kiteboarding clinics. You can test out a variety of equipment with the try-before-you-buy program including the Aquaglide Multisport, a unique craft that converts to a sailboat, kayak, windsurfer, or towable.

Outer Banks Kiting (252-305-6839; www.outerbankskiting.com). Kiteboarding specialists offer private lessons for all abilities using the latest Naish and Jimmy Lewis gear, plus kite charters, kite camp, sailboat lessons, wakeboarding instruction, and sunset cruises.

Ride Hatteras (252-995-6755; www.ridehatteras.com), 40168 NC 12. Shop specializing in windsurfing lessons and rentals also offers personalized kiteboarding and surfing lessons, plus kayak and stand-up paddleboard rentals.

Wind-NC (252-995-4400; www.wind-nc.com), 41056 NC 12. Shop across from the Avon Pier specializes in windsurfing, with lessons from beginner to high-wind freestyle moves. Stand-up paddleboarding and windsurfing rentals available, as well as a huge selection of skateboards and gear.

❋ Green Space

There are many places to access the typically quiet waters of Pamlico Sound along the west side of Hatteras Island. Most are reached via sand roads suitable for four-wheel-drive vehicles. The national seashore's **Haulover Day Use Area** (www.nps.gov/caha), just south of Avon on NC 12, has a bathhouse with showers and restrooms, as well as paved parking. The water here is shallow, making this a good spot for youngsters to get into the water if the windsurfers aren't too numerous.

❋ Lodging

Accommodations in Avon are mostly of the weeklong, vacation cottage rental variety. The exceptions are a new spa and fitness resort and a set of weather-worn motel units.

CAMPGROUND Sands of Time Campground (252-995-5596; www.sandsoftime campground.com), 125 North End Road. Quiet

park set in a fishing village has full hookups with cable TV for 57 RVs, plus a two-bedroom rental cottage and 15 shady tent sites with water and electric, plus bathhouse, laundry, lighted fish-cleaning table, and a fish freezer.

MOTEL ☀ ((ɯ)) **Avon Motel** (252-995-5774; www.avonmotel.com), 40230 Younce Drive at

NC 12. Located on the same block as an ocean beach access, this clean but slightly dated family-owned property at the north end of Avon offers 45 first-floor motel rooms, as well as two- and three-room efficiency apartments, a fish-cleaning station, and coin laundry. The same family operates the Avon Cottages (see *Vacation Rentals*). Off-season $; high season $$.

RESORT ♂ (ᵞ) **Koru Village** (252-995-3125; www.koruvillage.com), 40920 NC 12. Six fully equipped two- and three-bedroom villas located in the resort's Meditation Garden are themed to the nature: Air, Earth, Water, Fire, Sun, and Stars. Guests enjoy free access to the Koru Fitness Center, with yoga classes, Zumba, and more; backyard volleyball and horseshoe area; and the Beach Klub, with ocean access, parking, and pool; plus free beach bikes and discounted prices on activities such as kayak tours and stand-up paddleboarding. A boutique offering salon and fitness products, local art, and a gourmet tea bar is located on the property. Minimum stay may be required. Off-season $$; summer season $$–$$$.

VACATION RENTALS ☃ (ᵞ) **Avon Cottages** (252-995-4123; www.avoncottages.com), 40279 Younce Road. Cottages with two to four bedrooms rent mostly by the week, but a few efficiencies are available by the night. $$–$$$.

Colony Realty (252-995-5891 or 1-800-962-5256; www.hatterasvacations.com), 40197 Bonito Road at NC 12. Specializing in smaller, affordable homes suitable for one or two families, Colony also has longer rentals available on Hatteras Island.

♣ ♂ **Hatteras Realty** (252-995-5466 or 1-800-HATTERAS; www.hatterasrealty.com), 41156 NC 12. The more than 500 vacation homes of every description represented by Hatteras come with member privileges at Club Hatteras, the company's private clubhouse in Avon, with a large heated pool, tennis courts, putting green, playground, snack bar, and changing rooms with showers. Many homes are also part of the Klub Koru program, offering access to the Koru Fitness Center and daily schedule of classes. Last-minute three-night stays available.

☃ ♿ **Outer Beaches Realty** (252-995-4477 or 1-800-627-3150; www.outerbeaches.com), 40227 Tigrone Boulevard. Additional offices in Hatteras Village (252-986-2900) and Waves (252-987-2771). Operating exclusively on Hatteras Island, Outer Beaches lists over 550 properties, including cottages especially suited to windsurfers, and handicapped-accessible properties.

QUICK TIP: Koru Village offers several special facilities for couples ready to tie the knot. The Love Boat, an enormous, three-level sound-side mansion with seven bedrooms, a private pool and hot tub, honeymoon suite, and the Love Shack for parties on the sound, can accommodate large weddings or other special events. Koru Village has a bridal registry and a full-time wedding concierge on call.

✳ **Where to Eat**

DINING OUT ♂ **Cafe 12** (252-995-3602; www.facebook.com/avoncafe12), 41934 NC 12, Hatteras Island Plaza. A creative, Mediterranean-tinged menu of wildly popular Hatteras Flats (open-faced quesadillas), by-the-glass wine list, shrimp happy hour, vegetarian options, and great bread pudding, make this unpretentious spot next to the Food Lion a favorite gathering spot among locals. Lunch $–$$; dinner $$–$$$.

♂ ♿ ↭ **Dolphin Den** (252-995-7717; www.dolphindenrestaurant.com), 40126 NC 12. Owned by an island family who took root here in the 1700s, this family favorite serves seafood; house-smoked pork; Italian pasta dishes; prime rib; and steaks. Desserts are homemade, and the Key lime pie is award winning. Early-bird specials before 5 PM. Full bar. Take-out available, and large groups welcome. Dinner only, $$–$$$.

♂ ♿ ♈ **Ketch 55 Seafood Grill** (252-995-5060; www.mackdaddysobx.com), 40396 NC 12. The former Mack Daddy's now has a chef-designed seasonal menu full of creative options, such as shrimp hot pot in a spicy lime stock, tuna bacon poke, and free-range chicken, all with suggested wine pairings. There's also a large selection of microbrews on tap, plus live music some nights. Dinner only, $$–$$$.

✳ ♂ ♿ ♈ **Oceana's Bistro** (252-995-4991; www.oceanasbistro.com), 40774 NC 12. Restaurant across from Outer Beaches Realty is the only restaurant in Avon serving breakfast, lunch, and dinner all year. Sit at the bar and enjoy a rare sesame seared tuna appetizer, the house specialty. Occasional live entertainment, creative cocktails, and a large TV make this a local favorite for hanging out. Breakfast and lunch $; dinner $–$$.

♣ ↭ **Open Water Grill** (252-995-0003; www.openwatergrill.com), 39450 NC 12. Lovely sunsets on the waterfront deck are one good reason to visit this new entry on the Avon dining scene; excellent food is another. You may actually smell this restaurant before you see it—much of the food is cooked over charcoal on an outdoor grill, sending up a mouthwatering aroma to guide diners to the table. Inside, it's a bit elegant, especially for Hatteras Island, with actual table-cloths, or you can sit on the patio overlooking the water. Chocoholic alert: Don't miss the World's Ugliest Chocolate Cake. The restaurant also offers free limo service and will pick you up for an evening at the restaurant, or just ferry you home if you've had a few too many. Full bar. Lunch $$; dinner $$–$$$.

EATING OUT ♫ ((•)) ⇝ **Woodies OBX** (252-995-7000; www.woodiesobx.com), 41934 NC 12. New family spot in Hatteras Island Plaza hails from the Jersey Shore, with a menu of hand-patted burgers and foot-long hot dogs, available with a wide range of toppings, plus Philly-style cheesesteaks, paninis and sandwiches, prepared to order. The Maryland-style blue crab cake is a stand-out. Breakfast sandwiches are served all day. Breakfast and lunch $.

♫ ♿ ((•)) **Dirty Dick's Crab House** (252-995-3425; www.dirtydickscrabs.com), Hatteras Island Plaza, 41934 NC 12. In honor of Hat-teras Island's new liquor-by-the-drink rules, Dirty Dick's has built a large new restaurant in Hatteras Island Plaza. (No more tent!) Crabs every which way, from a crab martini to crab lasagna, are the name of the game at this fun spot, with lots of different kinds of crustacean on the menu, from local blue crabs and soft-shells to king, snow, and Dungeness brought in from the Pacific. Barbecue, steaks, and Louisiana specialties, such as crawfish and frog's legs, fill out the menu. Stop by the on-site store for the world-famous "I Got My Crabs at Dirty Dick's" logo'd attire. A second Dirty Dick's (252-449-2722) is in Nags Head at MP 10 on the Bypass. Lunch $$; dinner $$–$$$.

♫ ♿ ♉ **Froggy Dog Restaurant & Groggy Pirate Pub** (252-995-5550; www.froggydog .com), 40050 NC 12. A landmark in Avon, the Froggy Dog provides food early to late, plus entertainment and some great souvenirs. The all-new Groggy Pirate Pub serves crab legs and boiled shrimp at special prices in the afternoon, as well as an inexpensive lounge menu of sand-wiches and burgers, and stays open late with karaoke and sports on the surfboard TV. Kids enjoy the Tadpole Corner play area and meals served in a Frisbee. Ribbit's Gifts, upstairs, offers a variety of froggy mementoes. Live music on the outside deck in season. Lunch $; dinner $$–$$$.

♫ ♿ ♉ **Mad Crabber** (252-995-5959; www.face book.com/themadcrabber), 40369 NC 12. New location of this longtime favorite has a cool log-cabin vibe accented with homespun quilts. The food that made it popular remains the same—huge piles of fresh seafood. To get a taste of everything, order the Mad Crabber Platter, a pizza pan heaped high with steamed crab legs, mussels, clams, oysters, crawdads, shrimp, and scallops. Pool and poker tournaments, plus live music and sushi, make this a nightlife destina-tion. Dinner only, $$–$$$.

BEACH FAST FOOD Avon is unique among the villages on Hatteras Island for having several chain fast-food restaurants, including a **Dairy Queen** (252-995-5624) and **Subway** (252-995-7827). For a more local experience, try **Burger Burger** (252-995-0311), next to the Village Market. It's a chain, too, but a local one. The original store is in Buxton. Locals are crazy for the Smile Burger, which comes with a crispy layer of cheese bigger than the bun. The burg-ers here are all hand-patted and cooked to order.

Kinnakeet Corner (252-995-7011), NC 12 and Harbor Road. Located at the road that will take you down to Avon's fishing harbor, this little store and gas station stocks groceries and serves hot breakfast and lunch.

COFFEE SHOPS ☕ ♫ ♿ **Island Time Cups and Cones** (252-995-0202), 40146 NC 12. Cof-fee is just one of the offerings at this bright pink spot along the main highway. Get a Hawaiian shave ice cone, hand-dipped scoops of Her-shey's ice cream, or an Italian ice. There are games and puzzles to play, and on summer evenings Island Time is open late, with family films playing on an outdoor screen.

KINNAKEET FISH FRY

For a real taste of local fare, head down to the **Avon Volunteer Fire Department** (252-995-5021) at 40159 Harbor Road, 5–7 PM on Saturdays between Memorial Day and Labor Day, for the weekly Kinnakeet Fish Fry. The fish are caught by local water-men and cooked by the local ladies, along with hush puppies, baked beans, and coleslaw. Funds raised benefit the nonprofit Kinnakeet Civic Association and its many community projects. Adults $9; seniors and children $6. Don't miss the homemade desserts, just $1 extra.

Java Junction (252-995-7020; www.facebook.com/GlassBeadJavaJunction), 39774 NC 12. On Hatteras Island, it seems like coffee and beading go together. This coffee shop is located in the Glass Bead, next to the Dairy Queen.

✄ ☂ ((ɣ)) **Uglie Mugs Coffee House** (252-995-5590), 40534 NC 12, Kinnakeet Shoppes. Internet hotspot next to the Subway has a computer you can use, plus a creative selection of high-octane espresso and tea drinks, cinnamon buns, and breakfast goodies. You can create your own bead jewelry here as well, or browse works by local artists.

MARKETS Breeze Thru Avon (252-995-3347; www.breezethruavon.com), 40374 NC 12, MP 55. No need to get out of your car to score beer and soft drinks at this drive-through convenience store. **Mill Creek Gifts** (252-995-3188), in the same building, has a nice selection of beachy gifts and local art, so maybe you'll want to get out of the car after all.

Island Spice & Wine (252-995-7750), 40246 NC 12. Fun store stocks hundreds of wines and champagnes, microbrews, and imports, plus locally made jellies and tons of supplies for gourmet cottage meals, including sushi-making sets. Check the schedule for wine tastings.

The Village Grocery (252-995-4402), 40618 NC 12. Upscale grocery in the heart of Avon has a great craft beer selection, many organic and gluten-free items, local products, Boar's Head deli, fresh baked breads and desserts, hand-cut steaks and seafood, and a little bit of most everything.

PIZZA ❄ ✄ ((ɣ)) **Gidget's Pizza and Pasta** (252-995-3109; www.pizzagidget.com), 41934 NC 12, Hatteras Island Plaza. Family-run local favorite, formerly Toppers, serves specialty pizzas, pastas, calzones, and oven-baked subs, plus daily specials made from family recipes. Beer and wine available. Delivery in Avon. $–$$.

Nino's Pizza (252-995-5358), 41188 Palazzolo Road. Hand-tossed pizzas by the pie or by the

> **QUICK TIPS:**
> • Lines can be outrageously long at the Food Lion in Avon (Hatteras Island's only large chain grocery) on the weekends, as everyone checks into their vacation cottages and shops for the week ahead. Avoid the crowds by shopping at one of the small local groceries that have served the islanders for generations, at a local seafood market, or at one of the many gourmet food shops that flourish on Hatteras. You can always visit the Food Lion later; it's open 24/7 during the summer season.
>
> • A few pounds of steamed shrimp make an inexpensive and delicious meal. Most seafood markets will steam shrimp or crabs for you at no additional charge.

slice, seafood pastas, and Italian specialties such as stuffed peppers and baked ziti, plus burgers, subs, and salads. Beer available. Free delivery in Avon. $–$$.

SEAFOOD TO GO Risky Business Seafood Market (252-995-7003; www.riskybseafood.com), 40658 NC 12 at Kinnakeet Corner. Second location in Hatteras Village (252-986-2117) at Oden's Dock. Run by a former commercial fisherman, these markets, where the quality of the seafood is anything but risky, offer a variety of fresh seafood, plus steamed blue crabs and shrimp, smoked tuna and tuna spread, famous secret-recipe crabcakes, clam chowder, and cocktail sauce.

Surf's Up Seafood Market (252-995-3432), 41838 NC 12, Hatteras Island Plaza. Local and imported seafood includes live lobsters, king and snow crab legs, salmon, and red snapper. Get some shrimp steamed and ready to eat, or pick up a clambake with all the fixings to cook at home.

❋ Entertainment

Entertainment is sparse in Avon during the winter, when many spots close or cut back their hours. The nightlife scene gathers steam during the summer months, when you'll find live entertainment at the Froggy Dog, the Mad Crabber, Oceana's Bistro, Ketch 55, and the Open Water Grill.

Papawack Theatre (252-995-3125; www.koruvillage.com). Located in the newly opened Koru Village Beach Klub, next to the Avon Pier, this 4,000-square-foot theater's large stage brings a major entertainment venue to Avon.

❋ Selective Shopping

ART GALLERIES Gaskins Gallery (252-995-6617), 40462 North End Road. This gallery, in a traditional cedar-shake cottage in Old Avon Village, displays paintings and pottery by local artists, as well as photography and prints, and offers a framing service. Collectors of Fenton art glass and Annalee dolls will enjoy shopping here.

Kinnakeet Clay Studio and Showroom (252-995-0101; www.kinnakeetclay.com), 39774 NC 12, Dairy Queen Shops. Stop by the studio of Antoinette Gaskins Mattingly, the fourth generation of her family creating art on Hatteras Island, to see her distinctive tiles, stoneware pottery, and other hand-made items, as well as art by other local artists.

Sandcastles (252-995-0147; www.sandcastlesavon.com), 39774 NC 12, Dairy Queen Shops. Eclectic gallery carries locally produced arts and crafts, from paintings, handblown glass, and metal work to mosaics, stained glass, and jewelry, including a big selection of sea glass and shells.

SHOPPING CENTERS Dairy Queen Shops (252-995-5624), 39774 NC 12. Besides the frozen treats that make Dairy Queen famous, you'll find several art shops and an Internet café.

Hatteras Island Plaza, 41934 NC 12. Universally known as the Food Lion shopping center, this is the island's largest strip mall. In addition to the 24/7 **Food Lion** (252-995-4488; www.foodlion.com), it is home to more than a dozen shops, restaurants, and the island's only cinema, the **RC Hatteras Movies 4** (252-995-9060). Look for the **Beach Pharmacy** (252-995-3811), which carries craft supplies, and **Sweet & Simple Pleasures** (252-995-0012), where you can sample some excellent fudge. Restaurants located here include **Woodies OBX** (252-995-7000), serving breakfast and lunch; **China-town** (252-995-0118), with daily specials; and **La Fogata** (252-986-1118; www.lafogatamexican restaurant.com), a Mexican favorite with another location in Kitty Hawk.

Kinnakeet Shoppes, 40534 NC 12. This cedar-shingled row of shops is a great stop for families, with toys, pottery, beading, coffee, and Wi-Fi.

SPECIAL SHOPS Askins Creek Store (252-995-6283; www.askinscreek.com), 42676 NC 12. This convenience store at the far southern end of Avon carries a wide variety of souvenirs, including authorized OBX merchandise, beach stuff, groceries, and grab-and-go meals, but its real claim to fame is its car wash, where you can rinse the sand and salt off your car.

☂ **Fisherman's Daughter** (252-995-6148), 39455 NC 12. Two stories of fashion, accessories, home decor, books, and just cute stuff make for a great day of browsing.

The Slough (252-995-9000; www.facebook.com/TheSlough), 48103 NC 12. This little ladies' boutique carries a carefully selected collection of fashion, locally made jewelry, and fresh cut flowers.

✳ Special Events

Monthly: **Really, Really Free Markets,** held the first Saturday of every month at the Avon Fire Station (252-995-5021), 40159 Harbor Road, are swap meets where you can bring your extra clothing, furniture, and other stuff to share with others. Anything left over is donated to local thrift stores and the library.

March: **St. Baldrick's Day.** Avon Surf Shop sponsors this St. Patrick's Day head-shaving event to raise money for childhood cancer research.

Late May: **Shore Break 5K and Tide Pool Fun Run** (www.hatterasyouth.com), Koru Village Beach Klub. Benefit held annually on Memorial Day weekend.

July: **Fourth of July Fireworks,** Avon Pier.

August: **Junior Fishing Tournament,** Avon Pier.

September: **Hatteras Wave Jam** (www.americanwindsurfingtour.com). The only East Coast stop on the American Windsurfing Tour features five days of parties and competitions at local venues. Wind-NC is the local organizer. **North Carolina Beach Buggy Association Red Drum Tournament** (www.ncbbaonline.com).

October: **Frank and Fran's Red Drum Tournament** (252-995-4171; www.hatteras-island.com). **Hatteras Island Cancer Foundation Fun Run** (www.hicf.org). Begins at Sun Realty in Avon.

November: **Veterans Day History Potluck Dinner,** Avon Fire Station. Honors local veterans. **Hatteras Island Oyster Roast** (252-305-1722), Avon Volunteer Fire Department. Buy tickets in advance for this benefit for wounded warriors. Contact Kinnakeet Civic Association (P.O. Box 291, Avon, NC 27195) for details.

BUXTON

TRAVELING SOUTH FROM AVON, you often see kiteboarders' foils above the sound, and up ahead the Banks' most famous landmark, the spiral-striped Cape Hatteras Light, comes into view. A climb up the lighthouse offers a staggering view of the cape. To the west and south stretch Buxton Woods, one of the largest remaining maritime forests on the East Coast. To the east, the treacherous Diamond Shoals stretch 8 miles out to sea, a constant menace to navigation.

Before the post office renamed it for a Fayetteville judge, this area was called simply the Cape. Buxton has a reputation as a casual family-oriented resort, popular for surf fishing, surfing, and—on the sound side—windsurfing and kiteboarding.

GUIDANCE The Double Keepers House at the base of the **Cape Hatteras Lighthouse** (252-995-4474; www.nps.gov/caha), Lighthouse Road, houses a visitors center for the area. You can also sign up for beach driving permits here.

Also see *Guidance* in "Hatteras Island."

POST OFFICE The **Buxton Post Office** (252-995-5755) is located at 48042 NC 12. The zip code in Buxton is 27920.

PUBLIC RESTROOMS Facilities are located at the **Cape Hatteras Lighthouse Welcome Center** (252-995-4474; www.nps.gov/caha), on Lighthouse Road, and at the **Dare County Fessenden Center** (252-475-5650; www.darenc.com/ParksRec), 46830 NC 12.

GETTING THERE NC12 takes a sharp turn to the west as it reaches Buxton, doglegging past Cape Point.

GETTING AROUND *By Bicycle:* Bicycles are a great way to explore the many roads and trails running through Buxton Woods, and the small residential roads leading off NC 12. The loop formed by NC 12 and the Buxton Back Road is a popular biking excursion.

By Car: Most commercial development in Buxton lies along NC 12 and the Buxton Back Road. Old Lighthouse Road runs along the Atlantic coast, with many motels along its length. The newer Lighthouse Road leads to the Cape Hatteras Light itself, as well as camping and hiking in the Cape Point area.

✷ To See

⚓ **Cape Hatteras Lighthouse** (252-995-4474; www.nps.gov/caha), Lighthouse Road. Visitors center and museum open all year: daily 9–6, Memorial Day weekend to Labor Day; daily 9–5 the rest of the year, except Christmas Day. The lighthouse is open for climbing from mid-April to Columbus Day. Tours begin at 9 AM and run every 10 minutes until 5:30 PM in summer, 4:30 in spring and fall. The iconic landmark of Hatteras Island continues to flash its warning out to sea, as it has since 1870. The

FAST FACT: In 1999, the 210-foot Cape Hatteras Lighthouse was moved inland from its precarious perch just 100 feet from the ocean. The 2,900-foot trip took 23 days to complete along a set of tracks laid especially for the purpose. It is the tallest brick building ever moved and the tallest lighthouse in the United States.

210-foot tower, the tallest lighthouse in the nation, is painted with a distinctive black-and-white spiral pattern and flashes every 7.5 seconds. Visitors at least 42 inches tall can climb the 268 steps to the walkway at the top of the light for great views over Hatteras Island and Diamond Shoals. Next to the lighthouse, the two-story Double Keepers Quarters has been restored and houses a visitors center, bookstore, and the **Museum of the Sea,** with exhibits on the history and ecology of the Outer Banks and information on the lighthouse and its dramatic move inland in 1999. A video, *The Move of the Century,* is shown daily at the museum. During the summer months, park rangers offer a variety of free programs on shipwrecks, lifesavers, and pirates. Climbing tour tickets are $7 for adults; $3.50 for seniors 62 or older and children 12 and under. Admission to the park and museum is free.

Special night climbs of the **Cape Hatteras Light** are offered weekly during the summer months, as well monthly full moon climbs. Buy tickets in advance, and bring a flashlight as there are no lights inside the tower.

The Old Gray House (252-995-6098; www.outerbanksshells.com), Light Plant Road. Open daily; closed in winter. Take a step back in time with a visit to this traditional homestead, owned by a family who has been on the island since the 1600s. Built largely from salvaged ship timbers, the house today is filled with local crafts. A path leading through the woods to the **Cape Pines Motel** is posted with signs about island lore. Free.

✳ To Do

BIRD-WATCHING Buxton Woods and the Cape Point area of the Cape Hatteras National Seashore are noted birding destinations and important stops for birds on the East Coast Flyway. The trails in Buxton Woods are good for sighting songbirds during the spring and fall migrations; ponds within the woods harbor wading birds in summer and diving ducks in winter. Salt Pond, near the tip of Cape Point, and best reached by four-wheel-drive vehicle, yields views of a variety of fowl, both summer and winter. After severe winter weather, the Point is a refuge for many varieties of gulls, and in late May, pelagic species, such as storm petrels, shearwaters, and jaegers, migrate north along this route. A Birds of the Outer Banks checklist is available on the NPS site and at the visitors center. Maps and site descriptions can be found online at the website of the **North Carolina Birding Trail** (www.ncbirdingtrail.org).

FISHING One of the most storied beaches for surf fishing in the United States is located at Cape Point south of the lighthouse, accessed by four-wheel-drive vehicle from Ramps 43 and 44. A beach driving permit from the NPS and a fishing license from the state of North Carolina are required. Talk to the folks at local tackle shops about what's biting where, and how to catch them.

Dillon's Corner (252-995-5083; www.dillonscorner.com), 47692 NC 12. Downstairs you'll find a complete selection of fishing gear and tackle, upstairs a gallery of gifts, apparel, and art. Fishing cottage rentals available.

The Red Drum (252-995-5414; www.reddrumtackle.com), 46813 NC 12. Serving the fishing public since 1954, the tackle shop anchors a gas station and market complex.

FOR FAMILIES Minigolf and ice cream just go together in Buxton. See our listings under *Where to Eat* for info on **Uncle Eddy's Frozen Custard and 18-Hole Minigolf,** next to the Falcon Hotel in Buxton, and **Cool Wave Ice Cream Shoppe and Minigolf,** another spot in Buxton offering the popular ice cream/minigolf combination.

The game room in the back of ✍ **Angelo's Pizza/Burger Burger Arcade** (252-995-6364), with pool tables, air hockey, and lots of video games, is a hit with kids. Small children have their own section.

The entire lower floor of the **Sandbar and Grille** (252-995-3413; www.sandbarandgrille.com) is given over to a game room equipped with a jukebox, pool table, pinball, and classic video games. It's a popular hangout for teens while the parental units enjoy a sunset cocktail on the deck upstairs. At ✍ 🐦 **Double L Bird Ranch and Petting Zoo** (252-996-0412), at 47051 Buxton Back Road, kids can meet and feed more than 200 birds of many different species. Call for hours.

✍ **Junior Ranger and Seashore Ranger programs** at the Cape Hatteras National Seashore (252-995-4474; www.nps.gov/caha) include a variety of free, family-friendly activities during the summer months at the Cape Hatteras Lighthouse Visitor Center.

HEALTH AND WELLNESS Hatteras Island Chiropractic (252-489-1688; www.hatterasisland chiropractic.com), 47761 NC 12. Dr. Howard Ruderfer offers adjustments, therapeutic massage, reflexology, aromatherapy, cranial-sacral work, and chakra balancing. House calls available as far away as Ocracoke.

SKATE PARK ✍ **Dare County Fessenden Center** (252-475-5650; www.darenc.com/ParksRec), 46830 NC 12, Buxton, boasts a state-of-the-art skateboard park with street course and a reportedly gnarly bowl. Helmets are required. The Fessenden is a Dare County community activity center with a full roster of classes and activities for all ages.

TENNIS On Hatteras Island, tennis courts are located in Buxton at the **Fessenden Center** (252-475-5650; 46830 NC 12) and at the **Cape Hatteras High School** (252-995-5730; 48576 NC 12). Courts at the school are available for public use after school hours.

WATER SPORTS Blow Kite (252-995-0260; www.blowkite.com), 47661 NC 12, MP 62. Learn kiteboarding from these kite enthusiasts at their private Pamlico Sound beach. They can get you on a board even on days when the wind isn't blowing.

Fatty's Treats N Tours (252-995-3288; www.capehatterasmotel.com/fattys-treats-n-tours), 46618 NC 12. Take a guided kayak tour along the sound-side waterfront to discover the history of Hatteras, once the home of the Croatan people.

Fox Watersports (252-995-4102; www.foxwatersports.com), 47108 NC 12. Founded by the late surfboard shaper and windsurfing pioneer Ted James, Fox is still run by his family and carries custom boards based on his best designs, as well other top brands, plus quality equipment for windsurfing and stand-up paddleboarding (SUP). You can rent windsurfers, kayaks, SUPs, and surfboards; get lessons to bump you to the next level; or just stop by and talk surf. Repairs available.

Kite Hatteras (252-305-5290; www.kitehatteras.net), Inn on Pamlico Sound docks. Ty Luckett's custom kite boats and tower apparatus let you develop boarding skills in a controlled environment. Kite camps, charters, and wakeboarding also available.

Natural Art Surf Shop (252-995-5682; www.surfintheeye.com), 47331 NC 12. Owner Scott Busbey shapes his custom In the Eye boards at this shop in Buxton, a haven for surfers since 1977. Board rentals and repairs, plus rad surf gear for sale. Locally made **Shortbus Skimboards** (www.shortbus skims.com) are also sold here.

✳ Green Space

BEACHES ♿ **Cape Hatteras National Seashore** (252-995-4474; www.nps.gov/caha), Lighthouse Road. The beach next to the old lighthouse site is the only one on Hatteras with a lifeguard, on duty Memorial Day to Labor Day. The park service offers a busy schedule of free activities on Hatteras every summer, ranging from bird walks to snorkeling trips on the sound. Beach wheelchairs can be borrowed from the park service by calling 252-995-4474 or 252-473-2111.

Driving on the beaches of the national seashore is a hot topic these days, with bird lovers battling it out with fishermen. The NPS has worked out a court-ordered compromise that puts in place closures of various parts of the beach to protect nesting shorebirds and sea turtles. Those who want to drive their four-wheel vehicles on the sand must now purchase a permit and watch a short film before proceeding. Permits are available at the Cape Hatteras Lighthouse Visitor Center, with expanded hours during the summer season, as well as the Coquina Beach and Ocracoke visitors centers. Check the NPS website (www.nps.gov/ca) for current regulations and requirements, and a map of current ORV routes. Some stretches of beach are also reserved for pedestrians.

TRAILS **Buxton Woods Coastal Reserve** (252-261-8891; www.nccoastalreserve.net), NC 12. Over 1,000 acres of maritime forest, the largest remaining on the Banks, occupies the southeast coast of Hatteras Island from Cape Point to Hatteras Village. Rare plants and animals make their homes here, and the woods are noted for bird-watching, and rare butterflies, including the giant swallowtail and gossamer-winged northern hairstreak. A number of trails and multiuse paths run through this maritime forest. The **NPS Buxton Woods Nature Trail** (252-995-4474; www.nps.gov/caha) begins at a picnic area just beyond the Cape Hatteras Lighthouse. This shady three-quarter-mile loop runs along pine-needle-covered paths where interpretive signs explain the ecosystem of the area. Many creatures are seen along this trail, including cottonmouth snakes, so be wary. The **Open Ponds Trail** begins farther down the road near the old British cemetery and connects with other trails that enter the woods from roads off NC 12, eventually reaching the NPS campground in Frisco. An information kiosk and parking are found at the end of Old Doctor's Road off NC 12. Four-wheel-drive vehicles can drive down this road to another parking area near the **Lookout Loop Trail.** Two-wheel-drive vehicles can follow Water Association Road off NC 12 to a parking area and information kiosk. The reserve is open year-round. ATVs are not allowed on trails, and horses can only use the Piney Ridge Trail. Camping and campfires are not permitted. Pets must stay on a leash. Be cautious during hunting season, as some hunting is allowed.

✳ Lodging

BED & BREAKFAST INNS 🌊 ♂ ((•)) **Cape Hatteras Bed and Breakfast** (252-995-6004; www.capehatterasbandb.com), 46223 Old Lighthouse Road. Enjoy a stay in one of this inn's nine guest rooms, each named for a famous hurricane. Located a short walk from the beach, the inn is smoke-free and received three diamonds from AAA. You can watch the Cape Hatteras Lighthouse from the great room, or the large sundeck furnished with comfortable tables and chairs and a gas grill. Guests have the use of bicycles, beach chairs, and coolers, as well as lockable surfboard and sailboard storage. Gourmet breakfasts are a highlight of a stay here, with menus that change daily. $$–$$$.

🦪 ♿ ⚓ (ᵂⁱᶠⁱ) **The Inn on Pamlico Sound** (252-995-7030 or 1-866-PAMLICO; www.innon pamlicosound.com), 49684 NC 12. A favorite for honeymoons and romantic getaways, this quiet inn enjoys a lovely setting along the sound where stunning sunsets are nightly events. Innkeeper Steve Nelson has created a retreat that manages to be both casual and elegant. The inn's 12 rooms range from modest queens to new king rooms with whirlpool tubs and private porches. The rate includes a gourmet three-course breakfast with menus that change daily; afternoon cookie breaks; complimentary beverages and snacks; use of the inn's kayaks, stand-up paddleboards, bicycles, beach chairs, towels, and field glasses; and all the chocolate you can eat. Other amenities include a pool, a 14-seat HD theater with 1,800 DVD titles, computers, and a lending library of books to enjoy on the many porches and decks where hammocks and lounge chairs overlook the sound. The property was ranked as the top hotel on the North Carolina coast in 2012 by TripAdvisor readers. The inn's restaurant, **Café Pamlico** (see *Where to Eat*), is locally renowned for its cuisine. Reservations are highly recommended. Chef Forrest Paddock and his staff prepare everything from elegant picnics to breakfast in bed for guests. They'll also cook the fish or ducks you catch. The inn excels at special events, hosting weddings, private film festivals, and corporate retreats with equal ease. $$–$$$$.

CAMPGROUNDS AND CABINS 🐾 **Cape Woods Campground** (252-995-5850; www.capewoods.com), 47649 Buxton Back Road. Occupying a shady pond-side location in Buxton Woods, this family-run campground has sites for RVs and tents, plus cabin rentals, pool, heated bathhouse, laundry, playground, and fish-cleaning stations. Fifty-amp service available.

(ᵂⁱᶠⁱ) **Island Hide-A-Way Campground** (252-995-6628; www.alphaadv.net/hideaway), 1254 Buxton Back Road. Small, quiet campground accommodates 30 RVs and 15 tents, with hookups, cable TV, and a bathhouse.

National Park Service Cape Point Campground (252-473-2111; www.nps.gov/caha), 46700 Lighthouse Road. Located within walking distance of the lighthouse and the beach, 202 sites for RVs and tents are paved, with picnic tables and grills, but no hookups. No reservations; stays limited to 14 days. Restrooms, cold-water showers, drinking water, dump station, and pay phone provided. Open summer only.

COTTAGE COURTS ❄ 🐾 (ᵂⁱᶠⁱ) **Dillon's Corner Cottages and Village Homes at the Outer**

Banks Motel (252-995-5601 or 1-800-995-1233; www.outerbanksmotel.com), 46577 NC 12. Located in Buxton just north of the lighthouse, this complex offers a wide range of accommodations, from motel rooms and ocean-front cottages to homes in the village, at great prices. All guests can use the pools, hot tub, rowboats with crab nets, and Wi-Fi at the motel. Off-season $; in season $$.

MOTELS ❄ 🐾 (ᵂⁱᶠⁱ) **Buxton Beach Motel** (252-995-5972; www.buxtonbeachmotel.com), Old Lighthouse Road. Small, pet-friendly property on the oceanfront has a variety of accommodations, many with screened porches, and all on the ground floor. Off-season $; in season $$.

❄ 🦪 (ᵂⁱᶠⁱ) **Cape Hatteras Motel** (252-995-5611 or 1-800-995-0711; www.capehatterasmotel.com), 46556 NC 12, MP 61. With units on both the ocean and the sound, this low-key inn has nonsmoking rooms, efficiencies, and apartments for rent close to the lighthouse. A lighted swimming pool, hot tub, two fish-cleaning stations, and a fish freezer make this a popular spot both for anglers and families. The inn also anchors a complex of retail, restaurants, and recreation at the entrance to Buxton Village. **Fatty's Treats N Tours** (see *Where to Eat*), located next to the motel office, offers light meals, ice cream, and kayak tours on the sound. The ⚓ **Shipwreck Grill** (252-995-5548; www.capehatterasmotel.com/shipwreck-grill), in the same complex, serves inexpensive meals at breakfast, lunch, and dinner. The **Daydreams Boutique** is next door. Off-season $; in season $$$.

❄ ⚓ 🐾 (ᵂⁱᶠⁱ) **Cape Pines Motel** (252-995-5666 or 1-866-456-9983; www.capepinesmotel.com), 47497 NC 12. Located just a half mile from the Cape Hatteras Lighthouse, the Cape Pines is an older property but is immaculately maintained and professionally run. It offers clean, comfortable, freshly renovated rooms in a two-story main building and cottages set amid lush landscaping. Guests enjoy a large pool, gas and charcoal grills in the picnic area, a fish-cleaning station, and a playground with swings, horseshoe pit, and croquet. The property is very pet friendly. Off-season $; in season $$.

❄ ⚓ (ᵂⁱᶠⁱ) **Lighthouse View Motel** (252-995-5680 or 1-800-225-7651; www.lighthouseview.com), 46677 NC 12. Located directly on the oceanfront, with no road to cross to get to the beach, the Lighthouse View has been operated by the Hooper family since the 1950s. Over the years, the property has grown to include 85 diverse units, ranging from standard rooms and efficiencies to one- and two-bedroom villas and cottages. A heated pool and hot tub are located on the oceanfront. Other amenities include a playground, barbecue grills, and lighted fish-cleaning tables. Most units require guests to climb at least one flight of stairs. No pets, although a number of cats make their homes here. Off-season $; in season $$$.

✳ Where to Eat

DINING OUT ♪ ⅃ ♀ ♡ **Café Pamlico** (252-995-7030 or 1-800-PAMLICO; www.innon pamlicosound.com), 49684 NC 12. Definitely the class act when it comes to dining on Hatteras Island, the restaurant of the elegant Inn on Pamlico Sound accepts a limited number of outside reservations for dinner. Menus change nightly as the talented chefs create gourmet dishes based on the freshest local produce and seafood available, as well as organic grain-fed beef and vegetable-fed chicken. Vegetarian and vegan choices are also available. The café is also open to the public for breakfast, named "Best on the Outer Banks" by *National Geographic Traveler*. You can dine on the deck overlooking Pamlico Sound or in the white-tablecloth dining room. Reservations are highly recommended. Extensive wine and cocktail lists, and occasional live music. Breakfast $$; dinner $$$–$$$$.

♪ ⅃ ♀ **Rusty's Surf and Turf** (252-995-4184; www.rustyssurfnturf.com), 47355 NC 12, Osprey Shopping Center. This popular seafood restaurant, operated by Rusty Midgett, a local boy who went to the big city to learn to cook and traveled the islands of the world in pursuit of big surf, brings his experience of both back home, preparing local seafood with tropical touches—a nice change from the fried-or-broiled selection at most Hatteras restaurants. Rusty's also serves a killer Sunday brunch during the summer. The full bar carries several local microbrews and is a popular hangout for locals. Brunch $–$$; dinner $$–$$$.

EATING OUT 〔𝕞〕 ♡ **Buxton Munch Company** (252-995-5502; www.buxtonmunch.com), 47355 NC 12, Osprey Shopping Center. Closed Saturday and Sunday. Small sandwich shop serves fish tacos, crabcakes, wraps, quesadillas, fried chicken, and vegetarian dishes for lunch on weekdays, all at low prices, amid '70s music and groovy memorabilia. Lunch only, $.

♪ ⅃ ♡ **The Captain's Table** (252-995-3117), 47048 NC 12. Locally owned restaurant receives high marks for both its fresh, wild-caught seafood and its friendly service. Donna Scarborough, the owner, is married to a commercial fisherman, so the Captain's Catch of the Day is always a good bet here. Sides and desserts are made in-house. Beer and wine available. Lunch $; dinner $$; senior menu $.

♨ ♪ ⅃ ♀ ♡ **Diamond Shoals Restaurant, Sushi Bar, and Lounge** (252-995-5217; www.diamondshoals.net), 46843 NC 12. Reliable local spot serves satisfying meals at reasonable prices. The creamy clam chowder, made with local Ocracoke clams, is award winning. Sushi is served nightly in the lounge, one of the first on Hatteras to offer cocktails, where you'll also enjoy live music. Diamond Shoals has numerous aquariums filled with tropical fish—the largest collection on the island—making it a favorite with kids. An on-site seafood market (252-995-5521), is open daily 10–7. Breakfast and lunch $; dinner $$.

♪ ♀ **Hurricane Heather's Oyster Bar** (252-995-3060), 46948 NC 12. Located at the turnoff to the lighthouse and a popular stop for surf fishers just off the beach, this newly renovated spot in the former Finnegan's location is a great find for late-night action, live entertainment during the summer season, and sports on TV the rest of the year. Lunch and dinner feature burgers, barbecue with homemade slaw, fresh fish, and a raw bar. $–$$.

✳ ⅃ ♀ **Pop's Raw Bar** (252-995-7734), 48967 NC 12. Closed Sunday. Pop's is open all year, and most evenings it's crowded with locals playing darts, watching sports on TV, and enjoying fresh steamed seafood, bowls of Hatteras chowder, burgers and barbecue. Locally made crab-cakes and fish cakes, spicy steamed shrimp, really cold beer, occasional live music, and lots of local gossip make this place an experience. Not good for large groups, as most seating is at the bar or small tables. $–$$.

✳ ♪ ⅃ ⬆ ♀ **Sandbar and Grille** (252-995-3413; www.sandbarandgrille.com), 49252 NC 12. Great location on the sound along NC 12 makes a super destination for sunset cocktails with a view and live acoustic music on the back deck. The bar crowd loves the place, too, thanks to a late-night menu, poker tournaments, and schedule of live entertainment and karaoke. Downstairs, the game room is a draw for all ages. Dinner only, $–$$.

BEACH FAST FOOD ✳ ♪ **Angelo's Pizza** (252-995-6364), 46903 NC 12. Nice eat-in or take-out spot has good deep-dish pizza, plus other Italian favorites, and a mean Philly cheesesteak sub. Kids like the arcade room. $.

♪ **Burger Burger** (252-995-0065), 46903 NC 12. Sharing the same building (and arcade room) as Angelo's, this popular spot has hand-patted burgers cooked to order, sweet potato fries, veggie wraps, wings, and fresh squeezed lemonades. Several specialty burgers are on the menu, but the Smile Burger, surrounded by a crispy ring of cheddar cheese bigger than the bun, is the favorite. $.

Fatty's Treats N Tours (252-995-3288; www .capehatterasmotel.com/fattys-treats-n-tours), 46618 NC 12. Located next to the office at the Cape Hatteras Motel, Fatty's is a good spot for Hershey's ice cream, root beer floats, and fudge, or made-from-scratch beignets, cinnamon rolls, brownies, and other goodies. A brief menu of wings, chicken fingers, and hot dogs fills the bill for a quick lunch. Sign up for a kayak tour of the sound here as well. $.

BREAKFAST Orange Blossom Bakery & Café (252-995-4109; www.orangeblossom bakery.com), 47206 NC 12. Open mornings only, 6:30–11. Closed off-season. Famous for its huge Apple Uglies, this café, located near the entrance to Cape Hatteras Lighthouse, also serves breakfast sandwiches and burritos, fair-trade organic coffees, yummy Meyer's rum raisin cinnamon rolls, hand-glazed doughnuts, and the soon-to-be-famous Chocolate Ugly. The bakery sells freshly baked bread and special-order cakes, as well. $.

ICE CREAM AND MINIGOLF ♫ **Cool Wave Ice Cream Shoppe and Minigolf** (252-995-

6366), 47237 NC 12. Both soft-serve and hand-scooped ice cream are served in homemade waffle cones at this shop, next to the minigolf course at the fork where the Back Road cuts off from NC 12. Play cornhole or have a turn on the swings for free.

♫ **Uncle Eddy's Frozen Custard and 18-Hole Minigolf** (252-995-4059), 46860 NC 12. Enjoy homemade frozen custard in an ever-expanding list of custom flavors including fig (a local favorite), sorbet smoothies, or coffee drinks while the kids play unlimited minigolf for a single fee next door or talk with the resident parrots.

MARKETS Buxton Seafood (252-995-5085), 49799 NC 12. Fresh local seafood, plus steaks, wine, produce, and other groceries.

Conner's Supermarket (252-995-5711; www .connerssupermarket.com), 47468 NC 12. Three generations of the Conner family have operated this grocery, serving locals and visitors for half a century.

Diamond Shoals Seafood Market (252-995-5521; www.diamondshoals.net), 46843 NC 12. Stocks a variety of locally caught seafood, crabcakes, soups, seafood salads, pick-your-own herbs, and kids' meals to-go.

✳ Entertainment

Hatteras Island is something of a hot spot for live music, especially of the acoustic variety, perhaps because of its proximity to Ocracoke Island, where many musicians make their homes. During the summer season, look for live music in Buxton at Café Pamlico, Diamond Shoals, Hurricane Heather's, the Sandbar and Grille, and Pop's.

✳ Selective Shopping

Buxton Village Books (252-995-4240; www.buxtonvillagebooks.com), 47918 NC 12. Located in a Civil War–era cottage, this charming store carries an amazing range of new and used books for all ages. Specialties include sea stories, fishing guidebooks, Southern fiction, and books on Hatteras history. Owner Gee Gee Rosell hosts frequent book signings and stocks note cards by local artists.

Osprey Shopping Center, 47355 NC 12. This strip of shops houses the island's **ABC Liquor Store** (252-995-5532); **Buxton Munch** (252-995-5502), a retro-themed sandwich shop; and **Papa Nino's** (252-995-0060), with New York–style pizza and a lunch buffet. Out front there's a picnic area and **Rusty's Surf and Turf** (see *Where to Eat*), a popular seafood restaurant.

✳ Special Events

Early August: **Hatteras Island Arts and Craft Guild Arts and Crafts Show** (252-441-1850), Cape Hatteras Secondary School, 48576 NC 12. Money raised sponsors scholarships for local students. Free.

October: **Bike the Light** (252-995-3125; www.hatteras-kiwanis.org), 48576 NC 12. Annual costume contest and bike ride from the Cape Hatteras Secondary School to the Cape Hatteras Lighthouse raises money for the Kiwanis Club of Hatteras's children's charities. **Capital City Four Wheelers Annual Surf Fishing Tournament** (www.capitalcityfourwheelersva.com).

Early November: **Annual Invitational Surf Fishing Tournament and Bob Bernard Open Individual Tournament** (252-995-4253; www.capehatterasanglersclub.org), 47231 Light Plant Road.

Events include an open house, tackle show, Brag Night, cocktail hour, and awards dinner. It's in the *Guinness World Records* as the largest surf fishing tournament in the world. Registration for the individual tournament is free for youth and juniors, $10 for adults.

Late November: **Hatteras Island Arts and Craft Guild Holiday Show** (252-441-1850), Cape Hatteras Secondary School, 48576 NC 12. Local food and artworks; held annually on the Friday and Saturday after Thanksgiving. Free admission.

FRISCO

FORMERLY THE TOWN OF TRENT, Frisco is a quiet family resort town once famous for its fishing pier on the ocean. Known for the numerous king mackerel caught from its deck, the landmark was destroyed by a series of storms culminating in the 2010 blow from Hurricane Earl, which left the pier in ruins. Attempts to rebuild it have been delayed by the economic downturn, but fishermen who fished here still hope for a reprieve.

Back in the 1920s, locals had front-row seats as Gen. Billy Mitchell, a World War I flying ace and early supporter of airpower, struggled to build an airfield in the sand. A squad of airplanes soon arrived, then bombed and sank two former battleships just offshore. This early demonstration of airpower is credited with sparking the development of the U.S. Air Force as well as naval aviation. Mitchell was later court-martialed for his outspoken statements, but his views were vindicated by events. Frisco's airport, not far from the fishing pier, is named for Mitchell, as was the famous B-25 Mitchell bomber, a key to victory in World War II.

The area was also the location of an immense Indian town, perhaps Croatoan, the home of Manteo, friend of the Lost Colony. The site is being excavated in sections by East Carolina University and other archaeological teams.

GUIDANCE See *Guidance* in "Hatteras Island."

POST OFFICE The **Frisco U.S. Post Office** (252-995-5017) is located at 53590 NC 12. The zip code for Frisco is 27936.

PUBLIC RESTROOMS & **Frisco Beach Bath House,** on the south side of NC 12 just beyond the cutoff to the old pier, has public restrooms.

GETTING THERE *By Air:* **Billy Mitchell Airfield (HSE/HNC)** (252-995-3646; www.nps.gov/caha) in Frisco is an unattended airfield with 3,000 feet of runway, but no facilities. Air tours available.

By Car: Frisco occupies a narrow section of Hatteras Island, with NC 12 the only through road.

GETTING AROUND Frisco is a good spot for biking, particularly down Billy Mitchell Road, to the NPS campground at the end, set on the highest natural point on Hatteras Island. You can ride out the boardwalk here and along the beach.

✳ To See

Cape Hatteras Fishing Pier (Frisco Pier), 54221 Cape Hatteras Pier Drive. Better known as the Frisco Pier, this was a noted spot for catching king mackerel. The pier was destroyed by Hurricane Earl in 2010 and needs a complete rebuild. The owner hopes to find the funding, to interest the National Park Service, or may attempt to form a nonprofit to raise money for repairs. Meanwhile, the pier remains a scenic ruin, with just portions standing in the surf. Fishermen often cast into the surf around the pilings from the beach.

Frisco Native American Museum & Natural History Center (252-995-4440; www.native americanmuseum.org), 53536 NC 12. Open Tuesday–Sunday 11–5. Built close to the site of an early Indian village, this museum displays an amazing collection of Native American artifacts from precolonial to modern times. Of special interest are the dugout canoe found on museum property and items from the archaeological dig nearby. The museum also contains galleries of art and antiques, a natural history room, a bookstore, and a gift shop offering the work of over 30 Native American artists. Outside, enjoy the bird garden, or follow the nature trail that begins in the back of the parking lot and winds through 3 acres of maritime forest. $5 per person; $15 per family; $3 seniors.

AIR TOURS Burrus Flightseeing Tours (252-986-2679; www.outerbanksairtours.com), Billy Mitchell Airport, 53252 Billy Mitchell Road. Local pilot Dwight Burrus offers air tours that provide fabulous views of the Cape Hatteras Lighthouse, shipwrecks, Ocracoke ponies, and more.

FISHING Frisco Rod and Gun (252-995-5366; www.friscorodgun.com), 53610 NC 12. Bryan Perry, chief of the Frisco Volunteer Fire Department, owns and operates this tackle and gun shop, along with the Frisco Market next door, at the junction of NC 12 and Billy Mitchell Road. This is an official weigh station and sells North Carolina fishing licenses.

FOR FAMILIES ✐ Frisco Mini-Golf and Go-Karts (252-995-6325; www.friscominigolfandgokarts .vpweb.com), 50212 Trent Lake Lane, MP 65, NC 12. Kids under six play free on the 18-hole minigolf course. Other fun things to do include a game room with pool table and video games, a snack bar, go-karts, and bumper cars. The nicely landscaped property has a deck and goldfish pond, and stays open until late in the evening.

HORSEBACK RIDING Horses are allowed on the beaches of the national seashore but must follow the same rules and use the same access ramps as off-road vehicles.

Driftwood Ranch (252-489-8488; www.drift woodranchobx.com). If you'd like to bring your horses with you on vacation, to ride on the beaches or in Buxton Woods, you can board at this Frisco stable with easy access to trails. Dry camping also available.

Equine Adventures (252-995-4897; www .equineadventures.com), Piney Ridge Road. Horseback rides take groups through the maritime forest and onto the beach, where you can trot or canter, depending upon your riding ability. Rides are offered all year.

MARINA Scotch Bonnet Candies and Marina (252-995-4242), 51684 NC 12. Twenty slips with water and electric are available for transients up to 30 feet long, with showers, ice, and marina store, as well as a boat ramp open to the public for a fee. Scotch Bonnet is worth hunting out for the awesome fudge sold in the marina store, even if you never set foot on a boat.

HORSEBACK RIDING ALONG THE HATTERAS ISLAND BEACH

SPAS In Touch Massage & Wellness Center (252-995-4067; www.intouchmassageandwellness .com), 50840 NC 12. Spa treatments here use only natural and organic products. Acupuncture, massage, and a boutique of organic beauty products available.

WATER SPORTS Cape Hatteras Kiteboarding (252-216-7228; www.capehatteraskiteboarding .com), Frisco Woods Campground. Learn the basics or improve your skill with a kiting camp or private lesson that launches from Frisco Woods, well away from the busy waters off Avon and Rodanthe. These friendly folks will also take your family out clamming, for a sunset cruise, or for a session of wakeboarding.

✳ Green Space

BEACHES The **Cape Hatteras National Seashore** (www.nps.gov/caha) has two facilities close to each other along NC 12 in Frisco. The ♿ **Frisco Beach Bath House,** on the south side of NC 12 just beyond the cutoff to the old pier, has restrooms, changing rooms, showers, and a fully wheelchair-accessible beach-access boardwalk. The **Sandy Bay Sound Access** offers a large parking area on the north side of NC 12 with paths over to Pamlico Sound and, across the street, a stairway to the ocean beach. Kiteboarders have recently renamed this sound-side beach Isabelle's Inlet, after the hurricane that opened a new inlet here (now filled in) back in 2003.

✳ Lodging

CAMPGROUNDS 🐾 🐕 🛜 **Frisco Woods Campground** (252-995-5208; www.thefrisco woodscampground.com), 53124 NC 12. Large, shady campground with 150 RV sites, 100 tent sites, and air-conditioned cabins is popular with windsurfers and kayakers, thanks to its easy launch on Pamlico Sound. Full hookups with cable, pool, laundry, LP gas sales, fish-cleaning station, and a camp store are available, plus kayak, stand-up paddleboard, and windsurfing rentals and lessons.

National Park Service Frisco Campground (252-473-2111; www.nps.gov/caha), 53415 Billy Mitchell Road. Located amid sand dunes on the oceanfront, the 127 sites here have no hookups. Restrooms, cold-water showers, and drinking water are available. No reservations; 14-day maximum stays. Open April to October.

✳ Where to Eat

DINING OUT 🍴 ⤷ **Quarterdeck Restaurant** (252-986-2425; www.quarterdeckfamily restaurant.com), 54214 NC 12. There's a bit of a time warp as you enter this spot that's been serving since 1978. The seafood is mostly fried, steaks are hand-cut and char-grilled, and the salad bar is no-frills. But the Hatteras chowder and homemade pies are worth a visit. There's a lunch menu of inexpensive sandwiches and a full bar. Large groups welcome. Lunch $; dinner $$–$$$.

EATING OUT 🍸 **Capt'n Rolo's Raw Bar & Grill** (252-995-3663; www.facebook.com/captn rolo), 53060 NC 12. Fun eatery serves up local seafood, along with live music on weekends and happy hour specials. Best bets are the fresh fish

special, fish tacos, and raw oysters. With a full bar and cheap PBR on draft, things can get rowdy at this local hangout as the evening wears on. $–$$.

🍴 **Frisco Sandwich Company** (252-995-3354; www.friscosandwich.com), 53674 NC 12. Operated by two chefs who also own the **Catering Company of Hatteras Island** (www.catering companyhatteras.com), this cool shop, with a great location across from the Ramp 49 beach access and the NPS campground, serves gourmet soups, sandwiches, and house-smoked barbecue that are very much worth seeking out. The fried pickles are great, when available, or get a jar of house-made pickles to take home. Get a Beach Box to go. Lunch only, $.

🍴 ♿ **Gingerbread House Bakery** (252-995-5204; www.gbhbakery.com), 52715 NC 12. Hansel and Gretel–style cottage offers delicious baked goods, fresh-squeezed orange juice, breakfast sandwiches, French toast, and omelets, served until 11:30 AM. In the evening, it reopens to serve some of the best pizza on Hatteras Island, a salad bar, and root beer floats. A favorite with kids. Breakfast $; pizza $$.

COFFEE Captain Beaners Coffee House (252-986-0008), 53688 NC 12. Coffee shop next to the Frisco Sandwich Company is also a bakery selling fresh-baked pastries, doughnuts, and cheesecake, as well as ice cream treats blended on a cold slab of marble.

ICE CREAM Hatteras Sno-Balls (252-995-5331), NC 12, MP 67. Hatteras-style snowballs, combining ice cream and shave ice, are a specialty. Mix and match your way through 39 snow cone flavors and 12 ice creams.

✳ Entertainment

Banjo Island (252-256-0148; www.banjoisland.org), 50062 Timber Trail. During the summer months, the **Red Drum Pottery** (see *Selective Shopping*) hosts bluegrass performances by the band Banjo Island, followed by a bluegrass jam. The small theater next to the pottery usually sells out its weekly shows, so get there early. Refreshments available. Banjo Island (the theater) also hosts acoustic music workshops, yoga classes, and other events. Call for schedule.

> **SOUNDTRACK FOR HATTERAS ISLAND:** John Golden's *Hatteras Memories,* Soundside Records (www.soundsiderecords.com), 2005.

Frisco Jubilee (252-995-3540; www.friscojubilee.com). This group of local musicians performs bluegrass, blues, pop, and some gospel at various locations around the island. *Nights in Rodanthe* fiddler Herb "Speedy" Price is often the featured performer. Call for current schedule.

✳ Selective Shopping

ART AND CRAFTS Catfish Pottery and Gallery (252-986-2220; www.facebook.com/CatfishPottery), 53688 NC 12. This gallery is full of original "ugly mugs," plus amusing clay sculptures of animals and decorative items, all with a sense of humor.

Frisco Art Center (252-995-3400; www.friscoartcenter.smugmug.com), 53460 NC 12. Three galleries under one roof—the Art Cottage, Sea Glass Gallery, and the Christmas Shop—display original art created by dozens of artists from the Outer Banks, and other coastal locales. The artists are often on hand doing live demos.

Indian Town Gallery (252-995-5181; www.indiantowngallery.com), 50840 NC 12. One-of-a-kind artworks by Outer Banks and regional artists are displayed at this gallery, where you may catch Wayne Fulcher, grandson of a Cape Hatteras lightkeeper, or other local artists at work. Classes are available as well, including photography classes with Pulitzer-nominated photographer Don Bowers. Arts and craft shows are held every Memorial Day and Columbus Day, with music and barbecue dinners.

Red Drum Pottery (252-995-3686; www.reddrumpottery.com), 50062 Timber Trail. The studio of potters Rhonda Bates and Wes Lassiter displays their original pieces, including a collection of hand-painted beach and nautical-theme Christmas ornaments. Wes, familiar to Molasses Creek fans as "Banjo Wes," is often at work in the studio. During the summer the gallery hosts **Banjo Island** (252-256-0148; www.banjoisland.org), evenings of original bluegrass tunes, at a theater next door.

(⌘) **The Space Between** (252-995-5729; www.facebook.com/TheSpaceBetweenBoutique), 50840 NC 12, MP 65. This fun boutique goes a step beyond the ordinary. It's a full-service espresso bar and also the working studio of artist Jen Ray, filled with her whimsical sterling silver jewelry, crocheted items, painted hats, and much more.

🦐 🐚 🌴 **Sunsational Designs Gallery and Beads of Paradise** (252-995-5960), 53255 NC 12. Owned by a family of artists native to Hatteras Island, this little gallery carries jewelry and unique island works painted on rocks, shells, and driftwood. They will help you make your own jewelry from the huge selection of beads, charms, and sea glass they have in stock. A great rainy-day stop for kids.

SPECIAL SHOPS **Scotch Bonnet Candies and Gifts** (252-995-4242 or 1-888-354-4242; www.scotchbonnetfudges.com), 51684 NC 12. This shop, with 30 flavors of homemade fudge made on the premises, saltwater taffy, jelly beans, and doggie treats, has been featured on the Food Network. Stop by on Friday afternoons in summer for the hermit crab races.

✳ Special Events

April: **Frisco Woods WindFest** (252-995-5208; www.thefriscowoodscampground.com), Frisco Woods Campground. Weekend of windsurfing and kiteboarding, with demos, clinics, and parties. **Journey Home** (252-995-4440; www.nativeamericanmuseum.org), Frisco Native American Museum. Sharing of cultures includes dancing, drumming, crafts, and foods from many tribal traditions.

June: **OBX Paddle Palooza** (www.obxpaddlepalooza.com), Frisco Woods Campground. Stand-up paddleboard races, plus clinics, free demos, live bands, sunset paddles, pig pickin', and family events.

Early December: **Annual Christmas Bonfire** (www.hatteras-kiwanis.org), Frisco Woods Campground. The Kiwanis Club of Hatteras Island hosts this free Christmas party for children, with Santa in attendance.

HATTERAS VILLAGE

SOON AFTER HATTERAS INLET opened in 1846, watermen began moving to the area to enjoy easy access to the rich fishing grounds offshore. In 1935 the Hatteras Development Co. installed an electric generator and ice plant where Oden's Dock now stands, bringing Hatteras into the modern age. Two years later, Capt. Ernal Foster began taking anglers out after blue marlin aboard his boat the *Albatross*, founding the charter fishing industry in North Carolina. Despite booming tourism and lots of new construction, the village of Hatteras is actively seeking to preserve its traditional commercial and sportfishing culture. Life here still revolves around the town's marinas and docks, and many of the inhabitants are members of old island families. The Hatteras watermen share their heritage every September at the annual Day at the Docks and Blessing of the Fleet.

In September 2003, Hurricane Isabel cut the village off from the rest of the island, throwing a new inlet across NC 12 north of town and causing widespread devastation. The Army Corps of Engineers filled the new inlet in record time, but this section of the island is still considered unstable.

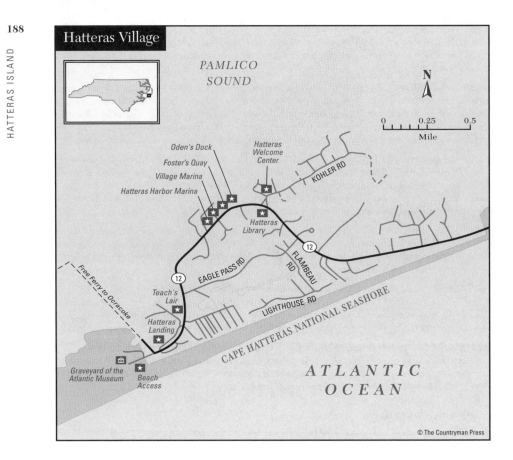

Hatteras Village

PAMLICO SOUND

N

0   0.25   0.5
Mile

ATLANTIC OCEAN

KOHLER RD

Oden's Dock
Foster's Quay
Village Marina
Hatteras Harbor Marina
Hatteras Welcome Center
Hatteras Library
Free Ferry to Ocracoke
12
EAGLE PASS RD
FLAMBEAU RD
12
Teach's Lair
Hatteras Landing
LIGHTHOUSE RD
CAPE HATTERAS NATIONAL SEASHORE
Graveyard of the Atlantic Museum
Beach Access

© The Countryman Press

At the southern end of NC 12 sit the ferry docks where the free state ferry leaves for Ocracoke Island every day, year-round. On the far side of the ferry landing, the **Graveyard of the Atlantic Museum** presents the dramatic tales of many ships and sailors brought to grief.

GUIDANCE Hatteras Welcome Center (252-986-2203 or 1-877-629-4386; www.outerbanks.org) in the restored 1901 U.S. Weather Bureau Station is located next to the Burrus Red & White grocery in the heart of Hatteras Village, at 57190 Kohler Road, and is open daily 9–5 all year.

POST OFFICE The **Hatteras U.S. Post Office** (252-986-2318) is at 57689 NC 12. The zip code for the town of Hatteras is 27943.

PUBLIC RESTROOMS Public facilities are found at the **Hatteras Welcome Center** (252-986-2203), 57190 Kohler Road; at **Hatteras Landing,** 58848 Marina Way; and at the state ferry docks at the end of the road.

PUBLIC LIBRARY ((ᵧ)) **Dare County Library in Hatteras** (252-986-2385; www.earlibrary.org /hatteras), 57709 NC 12, has a section on local history and exhibits of Croatoan Indian artifacts (www.cashatteras.com).

GETTING THERE *By Boat:* If you are arriving on Hatteras from Ocracoke, the **North Carolina State Ferry** (252-986-2353 or 1-800-

THE NORTH CAROLINA STATE FERRY SYSTEM RUNS EVERY DAY ALL YEAR.

THE 1901 U.S. WEATHER BUREAU STATION, NOW A WELCOME CENTER FOR HATTERAS ISLAND

368-8949; www.ncferry.org) runs 5 AM–midnight every day, unless conditions are too rough, departing about every half hour from May to October, every hour the rest of the year. Free.

By Car: Hatteras Village is hard to miss as you come down NC 12 on Hatteras Island. Just keep going south. NC 12 runs directly to the state ferry docks.

GETTING AROUND *By Bicycle:* Hatteras Village has a quiet residential side, with streets lined with historic houses and old family cemeteries—perfect for getting around by bike. Take a right on Kohler Road at the Burrus Red & White, or turn off on Eagle Pass Road, to discover this side of island life.

Waterboy Equipment Rentals (252-995-2295 or 252-986-2222), along NC 12, rents bikes and golf carts to help you get around.

By Car: Most of the action—lodging, food, activities—in Hatteras Village centers on the six marinas located here. However, since they are oriented toward the water, these can be a bit hard to find. All are located on the west side of NC 12. Four are next to each other just past the traffic triangle marked by the Burrus Red & White grocery. North to south, these are: Oden's Dock, Foster's Quay (home of the Albatross Fleet), Village Marina, and Hatteras Harbor Marina. Teach's Lair is a large marina a bit farther down NC 12, followed closely by Hatteras Landing, next to the state ferry docks, where the (paved) road ends.

MEDICAL EMERGENCY Hatteras Village Medical Center (252-986-2756), 57635 NC 12, Hatteras. Community nonprofit rural health center offers care for children and adults.

✳ To See

Albatross Fleet at Foster's Quay (252-986-2515; www.albatrossfleet.com), 57976 NC 12. The Outer Banks' very first charter fishing fleet originated here in 1937 and still takes anglers to the Gulf Stream after the big ones. Stop by to see the unique Hatteras-style boats with sharp, flared prows and rounded sterns, designed to help boats safely run the breaking waves of the inlet. A history of the Albatross Fleet and the early days of sportfishing can be found on its website.

Barnett Graveyard, Hatteras Landing, NC 12. An evocative graveyard dating to 1859 can be reached by a boardwalk over the marsh north of Hatteras Landing. Buried amid the twisted cedars are Stephen and Rebecca Barnett, lost when their schooner broke up on the Ocracoke shoals.

THE BARNETT GRAVEYARD PROVIDES A STARK CONTRAST TO THE LARGE VACATION HOMES AND UPSCALE SHOPPING OF HATTERAS LANDING.

Civil War Trails (www.civilwartraveler.com). Markers in the parking lot of the Graveyard of the Atlantic Museum describe the capture of Fort Hatteras and Fort Clark in 1861, the sinking of the USS *Monitor* in 1862, and other wartime shipwrecks. A marker in the parking lot of the Hatteras Village Civic Center on NC 12 describes the amphibious assault on Forts Hatteras and Clark. Nearby, a marker located on the grounds of Eastern Carolina Bank (57197 Kohler Road, a block west of NC 12) describes the Hatteras islanders' attempt to reconstitute a Union-oriented government.

Graveyard of the Atlantic Museum (252-986-2995; www.graveyardoftheatlantic.com), 59200 Museum Drive. Open Monday–Saturday 10–4. This fascinating museum, now a part of the North Carolina state history museum system, is dedicated to conserving the maritime heritage of the area and memories of the hundreds of shipwrecks that line the coast. On display are shipwreck artifacts from the age of pirates through World War II, including some recovered from the wreck of the iron-clad *Monitor,* an Enigma machine from a German submarine, and relics from the *Titanic.* The star of the collection is the 1854 Fresnel lens from the first Cape Hatteras Lighthouse; the lens disappeared during the Civil War and was only recently recovered and restored. Maritime movies, history lectures, children's programs, and other special events take place daily. The dramatic building, with a sweeping design resembling the bones of a shipwreck, sits at the end of NC 12, beside the state ferry docks. Free.

RECOMMENDED READING For more on the Fresnel lens in the Graveyard of the Atlantic Museum, read *The Lost Light: The Mystery of the Missing Cape Hatteras Fresnel Lens* (Raleigh, NC: Looking Glass Productions, 2003), by Kevin Duffus, a factual and dramatic account of how the author found the lens, missing since the Civil War.

For more on the Graveyard of the Atlantic, read Bland Simpson's *Ghost Ship of Diamond Shoals: The Mystery of the Carroll A. Deering* (Chapel Hill: University of North Carolina Press, 2005).

❋ **U.S. Weather Bureau** (252-986-2203 or 1-877-629-4386; www.outerbanks.org), 57190 Kohler Road. Open daily 9–5, all year. Built in 1901, this first U.S. Weather Bureau Station played a key role in the nation's developing meteorological network and in the lives of local residents, giving warning of oncoming storms. The building, in Hatteras Village, now on the National Register of Historic Places, has been restored to its original appearance, with a cedar-shingled widow's walk. Today, it houses an Outer Banks Visitor Center. Free.

✎ ♿ ✦ ❧ **Hatteras Island Ocean Center** (www.hioceancenter.org), 57204 NC 12, Beacon Shops. The first phase of a project that will eventually include an ocean fishing pier has exhibits on sea turtles, local history, the fishing fleet, and local ecology. Wetland trails lead to scenic overlooks and launches for kayaks and paddleboards. Free.

BICYCLING Hatteras Village is a pleasant spot to bike, with lots of roads besides NC 12 to tour. You can also take your bike on the ferry to Ocracoke to explore there.

Bike rentals are available at **Nedo Shopping Center** (252-986-2545), **Waterboy Rentals** (252-995-2295), and **A. S. Austin Company** (252-986-1500).

BIRD-WATCHING Charter trips out of Hatteras Village offer unique opportunities to see species of sea birds that rarely come to shore, but migrate along the Gulf Stream, feeding off schools of fish found in its warm waters. The best times for birding trips at sea are May–September and January–March.

Stormy Petrel II (252-986-1363; www.seabirding.com), Hatteras Landing Marina. Pelagic trips operated by Capt. Brian Patterson and an experienced band of volunteer bird experts have made some impressive sightings, including a rare black-browed albatross in 2012. Participants may also sight sea turtles, dolphins, and whales. Private trips and makeup charters available.

BOATING In Hatteras Village you can launch your boat at the Dare County boat ramp at **Village Marina** (www.villagemarinahatteras.com), or for a fee at **Teach's Lair Marina** (www.teachslair.com). Rent a Carolina skiff or kayak from **Hatteras Parasail & Kayak** (252-986-2627 or 252-986-2243; www.hatterasparasail.com), at Oden's Dock. See the *Water Sports* section for more options.

The free trip aboard the **Hatteras-Ocracoke Ferry** (252-986-2353; www.ncferry.org) is not to be missed. Ferries run 5 AM–midnight every day, unless conditions are too rough.

The original *Albatross*, grand old man of the famous **Albatross Fleet** (see *To See*), offers inexpensive Salt Marsh Tours that combine history and ecology.

RECOMMENDED READING Carlson, Tom. *Hatteras Blues: A Story from the Edge of America*. Chapel Hill: University of North Carolina Press, 2005. Memoirs of deepwater fishing and the families of Hatteras.

DRIVING TOUR Follow the route of the virtual tour of Hatteras Village on the website of the **Hatteras Village Civic Association** (www.hatterasonmymind.com) to see the local side of life here. Links show pictures of some of the storms that have hit the island, as well as historic sites, some still standing, some washed away.

FISHING Just 12 miles from the docks in Hatteras Village is the Gulf Stream, the highway used by the big-game fish, here closer to shore than at any point north of Stuart, Florida. Because this is the southernmost range of some species and the northernmost of others, the waters off Cape Hatteras where the cool Labrador Current, headed south, meets the warm Gulf waters flowing north earned the name Gamefish Junction, with more types of fish caught here than any other destination on the East Coast. Billfish anglers from around the world come to attempt the rare Grand Slam by catching a blue marlin, a white marlin, and a sailfish. Tarpon and wahoo, renowned for their fighting spirit, swim these waters as well.

The fishing is equally good for "meat fish" in the area, with numerous bass, bluefish, king mackerel, tuna, and dolphin (mahimahi) brought to boat. In winter, giant bluefin tuna, often weighing 200 to 500 pounds, are the most sought-after fish.

Follow the links in our listings under *Marinas* to find an offshore or nearshore sportfishing charter.

🐟 **Custom Sound Charters** (252-216-6765; www.customsoundcharters.com), Oden's Dock. Capt. Rick Caton offers educational Waterman trips especially suitable for families and children, which include dragging a shrimp net and

THE GRAVEYARD OF THE ATLANTIC MUSEUM HOUSES A RESTORED FRESNEL LENS.

identifying the species caught, followed by rod and reel fishing, in the calm back waters of the sounds. Inlet adventures involve several different types of fishing, with anglers trying sight casting, trolling, and light tackle wreck fishing.

North Carolina State Sport Fishing School (919-515-2277; https://onece.ncsu.edu). North Carolina State University sponsors an annual sportfishing school in Hatteras every June, with two days of classroom instruction, two offshore excursions hunting big-game fish, and a half day of inshore fishing. Open to the public.

The Roost Bait & Tackle (252-986-2460; www.teachslair.com), Teach's Lair Marina. The Hissey brothers, well-known locally for their expertise, offer advice and top-notch equipment at this store.

FOR FAMILIES ✔ **Kitty Hawk Kites** (252-986-1446) supervises a 32-foot outdoor climbing wall at Hatteras Landing. There's also a playground at this location.

The ✔ ⌕ **Graveyard of the Atlantic Museum** (see *To See*) offers a First Mates Program every summer, where students ages 8–12 can earn a Certificate of Rank and a First Mate's Wristband after completing a series of activities at the museum. Free.

The evening ✔ **Little Pirate Adventure Cruise** aboard the *Cap'n Clam* out of Oden's Dock (see *Marinas*) in Hatteras Village is a must for Jack Sparrow fans. The fee includes free swords, eye patches, root beer grog, and plenty of swashbuckling. Birthday parties are a specialty.

HEADBOATS ✔ **Cap'n Clam** (252-986-2365; www.hatterasfishingcaptain.com), Oden's Dock. The 68-foot *Cap'n Clam* makes daily trips in season around Hatteras Inlet fishing for flounder, sea bass, trout, and other inshore and sound fish. In the evening the headboat offers the inexpensive **Little Pirate Adventure Cruise,** a great way for kids to go to sea.

✔ **Miss Hatters** (252-986-2365; www.hatterasfishingcaptain.com), Oden's Dock. To experience fishing on the Gulf Stream, sign up for this headboat's 10-hour trip and bottom fish for snapper, triggerfish, grouper, and sea bass. A shorter four-hour trip is offered to nearshore waters, or try the **Dolphin and Wildlife Sunset Cruise.**

Stormy Petrel II (252-986-1363 or 252-473-9163; www.thestormypetrel.com), Hatteras Landing Marina. This 61-foot boat is able to handle larger groups, up to 24 people, for bottom or inshore fishing or trolling in the Gulf Stream. It also offers party boat cruises for sight-seeing or pelagic bird-watching.

HORSEBACK RIDING ✔ ♿ **Hatteras Island Horseback Riding** (252-216-9191; www.hatteras islandhorsebackriding.com), Ramp 55, NC 12. Ultra-safe rides on the beach can accommodate any age, kids to seniors, even those in a wheelchair, or with other disabilities. The family package is a great bargain, with the whole family riding for a single price. Rides happen on the NPS beach at the end of NC 12.

HUNTING Ken Dempsey's Guide Service (252 986-2102; www.kendempseyguide.com), Hatteras Landing Marina. Dempsey takes hunters to blinds located in Pamlico Sound. Charters include use of Ken's handcrafted decoys. He also offers light tackle inshore charters.

MARINAS Each of the marinas in Hatteras Village hosts its own charter fleet. Each has something a little different to offer. Check the websites listed for current details.

Charter boats typically accommodate groups of up to six. If your group is smaller, ask about a makeup charter.

Trips on the calm waters of Pamlico Sound are usually the favorite for family fishing trips, offered by many inshore captains.

Albatross Fleet at Foster's Quay (252-986-2515; www.albatrossfleet.com), 57976 NC 12. The experienced captains of the Outer Banks' very first charter fishing fleet can take you out to the Gulf Stream after the big game fish or on a hunt for good-eating Spanish mackerel and other nearshore fish. See the Albatross website for good pictures and descriptions of the fish caught in these waters.

Hatteras Harbor Marina (252-986-2166 or 1-800-676-4939; www.hatterasharbor.com), 58058 NC 12. Protected, full-service marina is home to the area's largest charter fishing fleet and offers

THE CHARTER FLEET HEADS BACK TO THE MARINAS OF HATTERAS VILLAGE AT THE CLOSE OF ANOTHER DAY OF OFFSHORE FISHING.

deepwater slips with water and electric for transients up to 60 feet. Showers and a coin laundry are available for visiting boaters, or you can rent an efficiency apartment over the marina. Makeup charters available. The **Harbor Deli** (252-986-2500) specializes in bag lunches for charters.

Hatteras Landing Marina (252-986-2077; www.hatteraslanding.com/marina), 58848 Marina Way. Located in the Hatteras Landing Resort, immediately adjacent to the ferry docks, this marina has a 9-foot-deep basin and more than three dozen slips that can accommodate boats up to 75 feet. Hookups include cable TV and telephone. Showers, laundry, and a huge ship's store and deli are on-site. Inshore and offshore charters, sight-seeing cruises, clamming, bird-watching, and makeup charters available.

Oden's Dock (252-986-2555 or 1-888-544-8115; www.odensdock.com), 57878 NC 12. Oden's is a center of activity in Hatteras Village, as the home of charter fishing and duck hunting outfitters, kayak tours, WaveRunner rentals, and parasailing; the **Breakwater Inn and Restaurant** and **Risky Business Seafood Market;** and two headboats offering fishing and sight-seeing cruises. Transient boat slips with utility hookups are available by the night or month.

Teach's Lair Marina (252-986-2460 or 1-888-868-2460; www.teachslair.com), 58646 NC 12. Transient boaters can dock at this 87-slip marina, one of the farthest south in Hatteras Village, by the day, week, or month. Dry storage, boat ramp, ship's store, bait and tackle shop, and restaurant are on-site. More than a dozen offshore and inshore charter boats dock here. Makeup charters available.

♿ (•) **Village Marina** (252-986-2522; www.villagemarinahatteras.com), 57980 NC 12. This full-service marina caters to anglers bringing their own boats to Hatteras, offering slip rentals, a boat ramp, dry storage, a ship's store, and a 12-suite motel, plus **Dinky's Waterfront Restaurant.**

SCUBA DIVING Some of the following dive outfitters offer trips to the *Monitor* site (www.monitor .noaa.gov), open only by permit.

♿ **Capt. J.T.'s Wreck Diving** (757-537-6524; www.capt-jt.com), Hatteras Landing Marina. The dive boat *Under Pressure* is available for dive charters or open boat recreational dives. The boat is equipped with a diver lift to make it easier for those with mobility issues to get back on the boat.

Dive Hatteras (703-818-1850 or 703-517-3724; www.divehatteras.com), Saxon Cut Drive. Specializing in the shipwrecks of Diamond Shoals, dive masters Ann and Dave Sommers take small groups some of the deeper, more challenging sites. They also offer blue water spearfishing charters for SCUBA or free divers.

Outer Banks Diving (252-986-1056; www.outerbanksdiving.com), 57540 NC 12. Experienced NAUI dive master John Pieno offers recreational and deeper technical dives, as well as trips to shallow-water wrecks suitable for snorkeling, plus underwater photography, treasure hunting, and spearfishing trips. The dive shop, offers gear sales, repairs, and rentals, including underwater cameras and computers.

WATER SPORTS Crisscrossed by creeks, inlets, and canals, and surrounded by salt marsh, Hatteras Village is a super spot to kayak or stand-up paddleboard, and especially good for beginners to practice without going out into the open water.

A.S. Austin Company (252-986-1500; www.facebook.com/AsAustinCo), 57698 NC 12. The Austin family store opened in Hatteras Village back 1915 and is still operated by the latest generation, Capt. Eddie Skakle and his wife, Gail, who help visitors discover the islalnd's secrets by kayak or stand-up paddleboard. They offer guided ecotours, including highly recommended full moon and sunset kayak trips, or will map out a self-guided tour for you. A put-in is next to the shop. Surfboard lessons and rentals, bike rentals, and fishing charters on the *Sea Bear* are other options, or you can rent clamming equipment or snorkel gear. The shop also sells local artwork, plus beach attire, hats, and more.

Hatteras Parasail & Kayak (252-986-2627 or 252-986-2243; www.hatterasparasail.com), Oden's Dock. Morning and evening kayak ecotours explore the waterways and marshes on the sound side of Hatteras Village. Single and double kayaks available, along with child booster seats. Single, double, and triple parasail rides depart from Oden's Dock. WaveRunner, kayak, and Carolina skiff rentals also available.

Kitty Hawk Kites (252-986-1446; www.kittyhawk.com), 5848 Hatteras Landing. Kayaks and stand-up paddleboards available for rent. Launch into the sound from Hatteras Landing.

Waterboy Equipment Rentals (252-995-2295 or 252-986-2222), NC 12. This stand along the main drag through town rents bikes, kayaks, surfboards, and stand-up paddleboards, along with fun stuff like cornhole games, and golf carts to help you get around.

✳ Green Space

BEACHES In Hatteras Village, the **Ramp 55 Public Beach Access** boardwalk is located across from the Graveyard of the Atlantic Museum parking lot, where there's plenty of free parking. A second beach access is located at the end of Flambeau Lane.

Beyond the ferry docks, sand roads run on through the National Seashore to the tip of Hatteras Island. A popular surfing break called the Water Tower is located along the ocean side. Check with the NPS for current ORV routes.

The Sea Breeze Trail in the new Hatteras Village Park on Eagle Pass Road has a boardwalk leading to a scenic overlook of the salt marsh. Other nature trails can be found behind the new Hatteras Island Ocean Center on NC 12.

✳ Lodging

BED & BREAKFAST INN ✽ ⚇ ♂ (ᵞ) **SeaSide Inn** (252-986-2700 or 1-800-635-7007; www.coverealty.com), 57321 NC 12. Originally named the Atlantic View Hotel, this was the first hostelry to receive guests in Hatteras Village. The historic 1928 inn was completely renovated with modern amenities after Hurricane Isabel, but it retains its cedar-shingle charm. Six suites and four standard rooms are furnished in antiques and wicker. Several, including a honeymoon suite, have Jacuzzi tubs. Spacious decks with grills and common rooms with fireplaces make this a popular place for special events, including weddings. Room rate includes a continental breakfast. The inn is a block from the ocean. No smoking permitted. $–$$.

CAMPGROUNDS AND CABINS ♂ ✽ (ᵞ) **Hatteras Sands RV Resort** (252-986-2422; www.hatterassandscampground.com), 57316 Eagle Pass Road. Highly rated Good Sam campground has over 100 full-hookup and tent sites, as well as six two-story air-conditioned cabins that look like dollhouses. Resort-style amenities include a large pool area with kids' pool and spa, fitness room, a bathhouse that is both heated and air-conditioned, laundry, adult lounge, free cable TV, and a game room with pool tables and Ping-Pong. Paddleboats and pedal cars are available for rent. $.

CONDO RENTALS ✽ (ᵞ) **Hatteras Cabanas** (252-986-2562 or 1-800-338-4775; www.dolphin-realty.com), 57980 NC 12. Each efficiency condo in this oceanfront complex has a kitchen, two sundecks, covered parking, and is topped by a "crow's nest." Originally built in 1968, every unit was extensively remodeled (or rebuilt entirely) in 2005. Weekly and shorter stays available. $–$$.

&. ((p)) **Hatteras Landing Rooftop Residences**
(252-986-2841 or 1-800-527-2903; www.hatteras
landing.com), 58848 Marina Way, Hatteras
Landing. Upscale lodgings atop the Hatteras
Landing shopping complex have two or three
bedrooms, 2.5 baths, a kitchen equipped with
GE appliances and granite countertops, several
cable TVs with DVD players, stereos with CD
players, washer/dryers, and private balconies.
Elevator access to on-site shopping and dining.
No smoking. $$$–$$$$.

SeaWorthy Condos (252-986-6510; www
.seaworthygallery.com), 58401 NC 12. Fully
equipped luxury condos above the SeaWorthy
Art Gallery rent by the week. $–$$$.

((p)) **The Villas at Hatteras Landing** (252-986-
1110; www.villasofhatteras.com), 58822 Marina
Way. This complex, next to the Hatteras ferry
dock, once a Holiday Inn Express, has 53 one-
bedroom units available for nightly or weekly
rental. Each condominium has a king bed and
sleeper sofa, fully equipped kitchen, and a private balcony or patio. Free guest laundry, swimming pool, sundeck, and boardwalk to the
beach. No smoking. $$–$$$.

MARINA LODGING ✳ ☕ ((p)) **Breakwater Inn**
(252-986-2565; www.breakwaterhatteras.com),
57896 NC 12, Oden's Dock. The former Hatteras Harbor Motel continues its tradition of
welcoming anglers and hunters. A newer sound-
front building houses 21 nonsmoking rooms,
each with two queen beds, a kitchenette, cable
TV, and private deck with fabulous sunset views.
The older Fisherman's Quarters building offers
standard rooms that can accommodate pets, and
some are smoker friendly. Guests enjoy a continental breakfast and a pool. The **Breakwater
Restaurant** and Oden's Dock and Marina Store
are next door. Off-season $; in season $$.

♪ ((p)) **Hatteras Harbor Marina Efficiencies**
(252-986-2166 or 1-800-676-4939; www.hatteras
harbor.com), 58058 NC 12. Five efficiency units
on the second floor of the marina building each
have private balconies overlooking the harbor,
full kitchens, cable TV, and sleep six. $$.

✳ &. ((p)) **Village Marina Motel** (252-986-2522;
www.villagemarinahatteras.com), 57980 NC 12.
A dozen suites, new in 2004, overlook the
sound, each with a living area equipped with
day bed, flat-screen TV, kitchenette, and bed-
room sleeping three. Boat slips, restaurant,
marina store, and laundry are on the property.
Off-season $; in season $$.

MOTOR LODGES ✳ &. ((p)) **Hatteras Marlin
Motel** (252-986-2141 or 1-866-986-2141; www
.hatterasmarlin.com), 57783 NC 12. Enjoying a

central location in Hatteras Village, this well-
kept property has 39 rooms, including suites
and efficiencies, spread among four buildings.
A seasonal swimming pool, outside showers,
fish-cleaning table, picnic area, and parking for
boats are available for guests. Off-season $; in
season $$$.

✳ ☕ ((p)) **Sea Gull Motel** (252-986-2550; www
.seagullhatteras.com), 56883 NC 12. Completely
refurbished after Hurricane Isabel in 2003, the
Sea Gull sits on the oceanfront with its own
beach. Amenities include morning coffee, an
oceanfront swimming pool, a picnic area with
grills, and a fish-cleaning table. Off-season $;
in season $$$.

✳ **Where to Eat**

DINING OUT ♪ ☕ ↪ **Breakwater Restaurant
& Bar** (252-986-2733; www.breakwaterhatteras
.com), 57878 NC 12, Oden's Dock. Enjoy the
fabulous sunset views from this restaurant, on the
second floor at Oden's Marina. The menu is creative, offering unusual appetizers and specials,
including a highly praised dish of mussels sim-
mered in a blue cheese sauce. You can eat in the
white-tablecloth dining room or in more casual
surroundings at the bar or on the large covered
deck, where you'll often encounter a band playing music to end the day in style. Dinner only,
$$$.

✳ ♪ &. **Dinky's Waterfront Restaurant** (252-
986-2020; www.dinkysrestaurant.com), 57980
NC 12, Village Marina. Open all year, this is
a hot spot for locals who gather around the
mahogany bar after the fishing fleet comes in.
Regulars recommend the crabcakes, soups, and
Friday night's prime rib. The restaurant is small,
with just 48 seats, but offers great sunset views
over the water. An elevator is available. If you
were lucky on your fishing trip, ask Dinky's to

cook up your catch. Full bar. Dinner only, $$–$$$$.

EATING OUT ✐ ♈ ↭ **Channel Bass Seafood Restaurant** (252-986-1250; www.facebook.com/ ChannelBassRestaurant), 57571 NC 12. Spot in the center of Hatteras Village backs up to "the Slash," a creek running through town, and has a nice waterside dining area with tables on the lawn. Take your soft-shell crab sandwich out there and kick back. You can play a game of putt-putt or drop a crab pot in the water. An old fishing boat has been converted to a stage where live music rocks several nights a week in the summer. Breakfast and lunch $; dinner $$.

↭ **Hatteras Harbor Deli** (252-986-2500; www.hatterasdeli.com), 58058 NC 12, Hatteras Harbor Marina. Enjoy breakfast and lunch sandwiches at dockside tables or on the enclosed, air-conditioned porch. If you like seafood, don't miss the unique grilled shrimp burger or the family-recipe Islander fishcake sandwich. For bag lunches or fried chicken (an island favorite, especially among boat captains) to take aboard your fishing charter, order by 3 PM the day before. The deli case has grab-and-go items. Opens at 5 AM most days; closed Sunday. Breakfast and lunch $.

✐ ❊ **Rocco's Pizza and Italian Restaurant** (252-986-2150), 57331 NC 12, MP 70. Thin- and thick-crust hand-tossed pizzas are the draw, plus subs, calzones, Italian pastas, and burgers. $–$$.

✐ ⚲ **Sonny's Waterfront Restaurant** (252-986-2922), 57947 NC 12. Opens at 6 AM for breakfast. After more than three decades serving Hatteras diners, Sonny's has breakfast figured out: homemade biscuits and home fries, big servings, friendly service. Full bar. Breakfast and lunch $; dinner $$.

✐ ♈ **Billfish Bar & Grill** (252-986-0080; www.teachslair.com), 58646 NC 12, Teach's Lair Marina. Awesome views of Pamlico Sound and the docks team with a menu of freshly caught seafood and fun appetizers. Lunch features sandwiches; dinner expands into steaks, pastas and Mexican dishes. Sunset celebrations on the outdoor deck are a Hatteras tradition. Lunch and dinner $$–$$$.

✐ ❀ ♈ **The Wreck Tiki Bar** (252-996-0162; www.thewreckobx.com), 58848 Marina Way, Hatteras Landing Marina. Rockin' spot right next to the ferry docks, with seating indoors and out, live music at sunset, a menu of paninis and Tex-Mex fare, plus beer chilled down in ice. Late-night hours during the summer. Take-out available. $.

BEACH FAST FOOD Hatteras Sol Deli & Café (252-986-1414; www.hatterassol.com), 56910 NC 12. New cafe in Stowe on Twelve Shops serves a variety of deli items, including house-made mozzarella and pasta salads, as well as gourmet take-out and delivery. Evenings feature open mic nights and sushi specials. $.

Gringo's Tacos (252-986-1088), 58848 Marina Way, Hatteras Landing. Great spot to grab a burrito or taco to go, right next to the ferry docks. $.

✐ (•) **The Hatterasman** (252-986-1005), 57449 NC 12. Small family spot serves inexpensive breakfast, lunch, and dinner. Better-than-fast-food burgers and fries are joined by pork barbecue, fried veggies, crabcakes, and fresh fish sandwiches. Eat in or take out. Cash only. $.

COFFEE ❀ (•) **The Dancing Turtle Coffee Shop** (252-986-4004; www.thedancingturtle.com), 58079 NC 12. Dog-friendly Internet hotspot serves a full menu of coffee drinks, plus iced tea, and tasty muffins, cookies, and other treats.

ICE CREAM (•) **Happy Belly Ice Cream, Smoothies and Candies** (252-995-2037), 57204 NC 12, MP 71, Beacon Shops. Score a big waffle cone full of Maola Ice Cream (www.maolamilk.com), a local brand made by a farmer in New Bern, North Carolina, to enjoy on the screened porch.

MARKET ❊ **Burrus Red & White Supermarket** (252-986-2333; www.burrusmarket.com), 57196 Kohler Road. Located in the heart of Hatteras Village, this family-run grocery has been serving locals since 1866. Excellent deli items, fresh meat, seafood, and produce, plus all the necessities and a friendly staff.

SEAFOOD TO GO ↭ **Harbor House Seafood Market** (252-986-2039), 58129 NC 12. Family-owned market sells raw seafood off its own trawler, plus lots of prepared items, including oven-ready seafood dishes, shrimp and crab enchiladas, chowder, shrimp dip, seafood salads, smoked fish, crabby patties, steamed shrimp, and clams.

✐ ↭ **Risky Business Seafood Markets** (252-986-2117; www.riskybseafood.com), 57878 NC 12, Oden's Dock. Spiced steamed crabs and shrimp, smoked tuna, and the famous secret-recipe crabcakes are specialties, along with a wide variety of fresh local seafood. They will also clean, vacuum pack, and freeze your catch, then pack it for travel when you leave, or ship it to you. Kids enjoy watching the fish being cleaned at this spot, under the Breakwater Restaurant.

✳ Entertainment

Look for live music at Billfish Bar, the Wreck Tiki Bar, Channel Bass, and Breakwater, most often around sunset during the summer.

✳ Selective Shopping

ART GALLERIES The beauties of storm and sun have attracted a large colony of artists to Hatteras, including many fine photographers specializing in wildlife, sunsets, and surfscapes.

Blue Pelican Gallery (252-986-2244; www.bluepelicangallery.com or www.photosfromtheporch .com), 57762 NC 12. Hatteras Island native Jenn Johnson displays her photography and unique jewelry, along with the work of other local artists, at this gallery, next to the Burrus Red & White.

Light Keeper Gallery (252-986-4034; www.lightkeepergallery.com), 58848 Marina Way, Hatteras Landing. Coastal art and home decor, including the colorful works of Hatteras Island artist Stephanie Kiker (www.stephaniekiker.com).

((ψ)) **Roads End Gallery & Wine Shop** (252-995-2037), 57204 NC 12, MP 71, Beacon Shops. Enjoy a glass of wine or a beer on the porch after browsing this selection of works by exclusively North Carolina artists and artisans.

Sandy Bay Gallery (252-986-1338), 57544 NC 12, At The Slash. Lovely selection of art, blown glass, sculpture, and jewelry includes many local works.

SeaWorthy Gallery (252-986-6510; www.seaworthygallery.com), 58401 NC 12, MP 72. Stop by to browse the wide selection of art, including a huge collection of North Carolina pottery, in the bright blue building. Artist Carole Nunnally has arranged everything by subject—boats, birds, lighthouses, marine life—for a uniquely compelling display. Classes are offered in jewelry making, painting, and other media.

SHOPPING CENTERS At The Slash, 57544 NC 12. Look for the new home of the **Sandy Bay Gallery** (252-986-1338) and **Sailor Jo's Stand Up Paddleboard Excursions** (252-216-6123; www.sailorjo.com) at this new set of shops.

((ψ)) **Beacon Shops,** 57204 NC 12, MP 71. Now part of the Hatteras Island Ocean Center, the complex houses an ecology center, plus a boutique, gallery, and sweet shop.

♂ ((ψ)) **Hatteras Landing** (252-986-2205; www.hatteraslanding.com), 58848 Marina Way. Located next to the ferry docks, this large, modern center contains a number of shopping, dining, and activity options. Turnover is rather high, with new shops moving in every year, but there's always something fun to see and tasty to eat while you wait for the ferry. The **Hatteras Landing Marina Ship Store** (252-986-2077) is the one perennial, with snacks, souvenirs, beach necessities, and free Wi-Fi. You can get married or celebrate other special occasions here as well, at a new events venue, the **Affairs at Austin Creek** (www.hatterasevents.com), a lovely, light-filled space with superb views looking out over the harbor.

Shops at Stowe on Twelve (252-986-2024), 56910 NC 12. Fun shops are run by some of the island's coolest ladies. A gourmet deli and surf shop add to the mix.

SPECIAL SHOPS A.S. Austin Company. See *To Do—Water Sports.*

Family Jewels (252-986-2323; www.hatterasjewels.com), 56882 NC 12, Stowe on Twelve. Wendy Stowe Sisler designs jewelry of Murano glass beads she makes herself, freshwater pearls, and semiprecious stones.

Lee Robinson's General Store (252-986-2381; www.leerobinsongeneralstore.com), 58372 NC 12. This island classic, opened in 1948 and the survivor of many hurricanes, stocks lots of necessary items, fun souvenirs, and beer and wine. Don't miss the upstairs gallery of gifts. In season, Robinson's operates a produce stand just across the street.

Nedo Shopping Center (252-986-2545), 57866 NC 12. They aren't kidding when they say Nedo's has a little of everything. If you like to browse in hardware stores, this is your spot. You'll find shoes, hats, fishing tackle, and toys among the tools and nails. You can also rent a bike here.

✳ Special Events

May: **Hatteras Village Offshore Open** (252-986-2579; www.hatterasoffshoreopen.com), Hatteras Village Civic Association. Cash and trophies for largest billfish and blue marlin, followed by evening events, including a Taste of the Village. **Hatteras Storytelling Festival** (www.hatterasyarns.org). A weekend of top storytellers and local music.

June: **Hatteras Marlin Club Invitational Tournament** (252-986-2454; www.hatterasmarlinclub .com), Hatteras Marlin Club. The state's oldest billfish tournament.

September: **Day at the Docks—A Celebration of Hatteras Island Watermen** (252-986-2515; www.dayatthedocks.org), Hatteras Village. Chowder cook-off, kids' fishing contest, crab races, traditional wooden boat exhibits, and a working boat parade followed by the Blessing of the Fleet. **Hatteras Village Invitational Surf Fishing Tournament** (252-986-2579; www.hatterasonmy mind.com), Hatteras Village Civic Association.

Late October: **Ocracoke/Hatteras Blackbeard's Pirate Jamboree** (www.piratejamboree.com). Cross-island festival celebrates the region's maritime and pirate history.

November: **United Methodist Women's Holiday Craft Bazaar** (252-986-2149), Hatteras Village Civic Association. Community lunch made by the local ladies is served.

Late November: **Thanksgiving Day Surfin Turkey 5K and Drumstick Dash Fun Run** (www .hatterasyouth.com), Hatteras Village Civic Center. Benefits the Hatteras Island Youth Education Fund and OBX Go Far.

Early December: **Christmas Parade** (252-986-2579; www.hatterasonmymind.com), Hatteras Village. Parade is followed by open houses at area businesses.

Ocracoke Island 5

OCRACOKE ISLAND
Off the Grid

If once you have slept on an island
You'll never be quite the same . . .
—RACHEL FIELD

OCRACOKE IS A TRUE ISLAND. No bridge links it to the mainland, so to get here you must take a boat or plane. The state of North Carolina obligingly provides three different ferries to Ocracoke. The one from Hatteras is free, while the other two cost money; but however you arrive, the trip lends a sense of isolation to the island. You cannot easily leave this place. Someone must ferry you away. Although, locals say, once the sand gets between your toes, you may not ever want to leave.

For eons, the island belonged to the birds and the waves. Later, the ponies arrived and flourished, survivors perhaps of Spanish attempts to establish colonies along the Carolina coast. The local natives, the Woccon tribe, used to come to the island for oyster roasts. Their name for the island, "Wococon," appears on John White's 1585 map. The island's name had morphed into Occocok by Blackbeard's day. No one is sure how the "r" sneaked into the present-day name of Ocracoke. Locals today will tell you: "Pronounce it like the vegetable and the soft drink."

The island's location, next to an inlet that gives access to the great Pamlico and Albemarle sounds, gave Ocracoke a unique prominence during the age of sail. In colonial days, two-thirds of all North Carolina shipping passed through Ocracoke Inlet, the only gap in the northern Outer Banks that has remained open continuously since the 1500s. The first to take advantage of this position were the pirates. Blackbeard and his cohorts would lurk here, waiting for rich ships to pass. Between raids they came ashore to drink rum and roast pigs. The island became a known gathering spot for pirates, and it was here that Lieutenant Maynard of the British Navy hunted Blackbeard down. The fateful battle, which ended with the pirate's head hanging from the bowsprit of Maynard's ship, took place just offshore at a place known today as Teach's Hole.

The constantly shifting sands of the inlet made passage dangerous for ships, and in 1715 the North Carolina colonial government sought to establish a community of pilots on Ocracoke to guide ships through. By the 1730s, Pilot Town was well established at what is today Springer's Point. Many of the families who live on the island are descendants of those early pilots. The names of Howard, Williams, Garrish, Balance, O'Neal, Gaskill, Stryon, and Wahab all appear on census records from the 1700s, and you'll meet people with the same names running the shops, charter boats, and restaurants of Ocracoke today. Perhaps most notable among these are the Howards, descended from a William Howard, who bought the island in 1759. Legend connects him with Blackbeard's quartermaster, also a William Howard, the only member of the pirate crew to escape hanging. Look for the **Village Craftsmen** shop on Howard Street, established by the eighth generation of the family to live on Ocracoke.

The first lighthouse built in the area, a wooden structure on Shell Castle Island in 1798, was replaced in 1823 by the current white tower of the Ocracoke Light. It's the oldest operating lighthouse in North Carolina and the second-oldest continuously operating lighthouse in the United States. In 1846, a great storm opened Hatteras and Oregon inlets, and from that date the importance of Ocracoke Inlet began to decline. Shipwrecks along this coast did not, however, and many local families joined the Life-Saving Service or turned to commercial fishing and hunting.

During World War II, the U.S. Navy established a base on Ocracoke to chase the German subs that were decimating shipping along the coast. The 500 men stationed there complained it was "the Siberia of the East Coast" due to the lack of amusements navy men typically enjoyed, but more than one ended up marrying a local girl and staying on after the war. The navy base has disappeared except for a large cistern, but the military left a lasting legacy on the island's footprint. Cockle Creek, until then just a swampy inlet in the marsh, was dredged for the navy boats, becoming **Silver Lake Harbor,** today the centerpiece of Ocracoke Village. This, the island's lone town, occupies less than a third of the island on the southwest Pamlico Sound side. The 16 or so miles of oceanfront beach remain completely undeveloped, part of the **Cape Hatteras National Seashore** established in 1953. This is one of the last places on the East Coast of the United States where you can look both ways, up and down the shore, and not see a single structure built by man.

Until the 1950s, when North Carolina began regular ferry service, Ocracoke remained largely isolated from the rest of the world. Through the centuries, the local residents developed their own

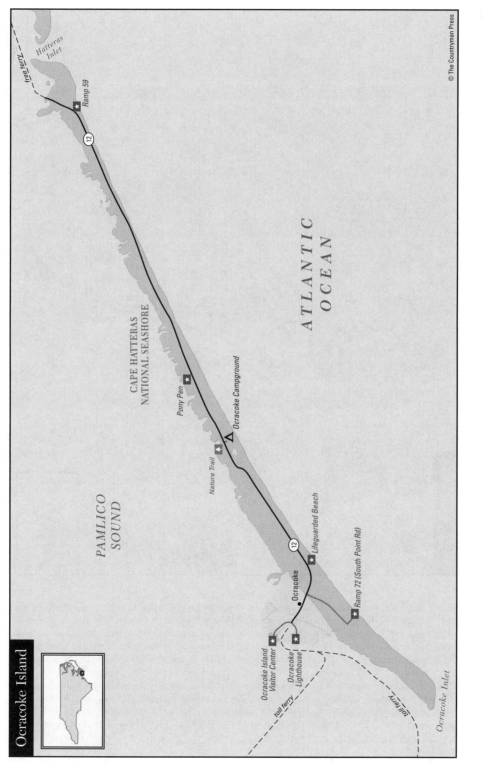

© The Countryman Press

Ocracoke Island

Hatteras Inlet

free ferry

Ramp 59

12

PAMLICO SOUND

CAPE HATTERAS
NATIONAL SEASHORE

Pony Pen

Ocracoke Campground

Nature Trail

ATLANTIC OCEAN

Lifeguarded Beach

Ramp 72 (South Point Rd)

12

Ocracoke

Ocracoke Island
Visitor Center

Ocracoke
Lighthouse

toll ferry

toll ferry

Ocracoke Inlet

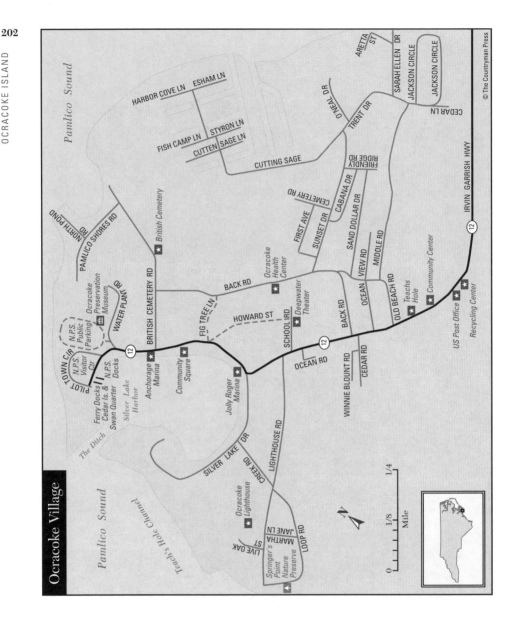

unique style of speech, known to linguists as the Ocracoke brogue. Visit the docks around Silver Lake, and you may hear the boat captains and mates still using terms you won't hear elsewhere and commenting on the "hoi toide." The ferries brought a steadily increasing tide of visitors to Ocracoke, and tourism is now the major industry. The village of 800 year-round residents swells to over 7,000 during the summer season. Tourism reached storm force after Dr. Beach named Ocracoke the best beach in America in 2007. Ferry operators reported an immediate jump in number of visitors to the island.

Locals, feeling the glare of the spotlight, hope that all the publicity doesn't attract a new breed of pirates to their island. It's hard to imagine waterslides or minigolf courses on Ocracoke. But the year-round residents also welcome the increase in tourism—and the income it brings. Villagers, both the descendants of the old residents, who call themselves the O'Cockers, and newer settlers, are determined to preserve the family traditions, laid-back lifestyle, and close-knit community that make Ocracoke special.

Many visitors catch just the briefest glimpse of Ocracoke and its unique qualities as they drive

TOP 10 DON'T MISS: OCRACOKE ISLAND

1. Sail or paddle out to Teach's Hole.
2. Cross the inlet to the ghost village of Portsmouth.
3. Adopt an Ocracoke pony.
4. Bike the Back Road, stopping at all the galleries.
5. Pay your respects at the British Cemetery.
6. Swim at Dr. Beach's Top Beach in the United States, Ocracoke's Lifeguarded Beach.
7. Visit the Village Craftsmen gallery of American crafts.
8. Stroll Springer's Point.
9. Learn to weave for a good cause at Tapestry.
10. Enjoy the sunset on a dock at Silver Lake, picking up lessons in the Ocracoke brogue.

from one ferry landing to the other. To them, the island is just a traffic jam around the harbor and another two-lane stretch of road through the dunes. However, for those who park their vehicles in the large lot behind the **National Park Service Ocracoke Island Visitor's Center** next to the docks and wander out into the village on foot, Ocracoke often becomes a favorite vacation memory.

Visit the dockside watering holes. Wander the old lanes paved with oyster shells. Look for galleries hidden amid the gnarled live oaks. Listen to some local music. Stroll the beach, looking for shells or shipwrecks. Take time to watch the sun set. Relax. You're on island time.

GUIDANCE A good place to begin a tour of the island is the **National Park Service Ocracoke Island Visitor's Center** (252-928-4531; www.nps.gov/caha), 38 Irvin Garrish Highway, NC 12. Located next to the ferry docks in Ocracoke Village, the visitors center offers information on both the national seashore and the town, and a bookshop full of local-interest books. Rangers lead programs during the summer at various locations around the park, including history and ecology talks, bird walks, and excursions that teach crabbing and seining techniques.

The **Village of Ocracoke's** official website (www.ocracokevillage.com) offers guidance on dining, lodging, fishing, places of worship, events, and entertainment, plus a guide for those who would like to get married on Ocracoke. The **Ocracoke Community Center** (252-928-3162; www.ocracoke communitycenter.com), at 999 NC 12, is the setting for many local events. Check the billboard here, and others at the Variety Store and Community Square for notices of interest.

Ocracoke is an unincorporated town in Hyde County, which is otherwise located on the mainland Albermarle Peninsula. Additional tourism information is available from:

Hyde County (252-926-9171 or 1-888-493-3826; www.hydecountync.gov), 30 Oyster Creek Road, Swan Quarter.

Hyde County Chamber of Commerce (252-926-9171 or 1-888-493-3826; www.hydecounty.org), P.O. Box 178, Swan Quarter, NC 27885.

POST OFFICE The **Ocracoke U.S. Post Office** (252-928-4771) is located at 1122 Irvin Garrish Highway/NC 12. The zip code for the entire island is 27960.

> **FAST FACT:** Beaches named as number one in the nation by **Dr. Beach** (www.drbeach.org) on his annual list, as Ocracoke's Lifeguarded Beach was in 2007, are retired from consideration on future lists.

PUBLIC RESTROOMS Public facilities can be found at both of the ferry docks, at the national park visitors center in Ocracoke Village; at the Community Square docks; at the Lifeguarded Beach, about 1.5 miles north of the village; and at the NPS campground.

PUBLIC LIBRARY The ♪ ♈ (ᵠ) **Ocracoke Community Library** (252-928-4436; www.bhmlib.org) shares its location at 225 Back Road with the Ocracoke School. Hours vary due to school activities but are generally late afternoons and evenings on weekdays, mornings on Saturdays during the school year, with expanded hours in summer. The library's collection includes works on the Civil War, World

War II, and pirate and Ocracoke family history. Free Wi-Fi is available at the library, and several computers are available for public use. The Friends of the Library host an annual book sale during the month of July on the library's porch.

GETTING THERE *By Air:* You can reach Ocracoke Island by air—if you have a private plane. The
↝ **Ocracoke Island Airport (W95)** (252-928-5111 or 919-840-0112; www.ocracokeairport.com), a 3,000-foot asphalt strip operated by the National Park Service, is unattended and unlighted. Tiedowns are available, but no fuel. The beach is just 100 yards away.

By Boat: A typical Outer Banks island, about 16 miles long and just 5 miles across at its widest point, Ocracoke lies about 20 miles off the mainland. State-operated ferries arrive at both the north and south ends. NC 12 runs between the ferry docks.

The free ferry at the north end of the island connects with Hatteras Village, a trip that takes about 40 minutes.

Two ferries come to the docks in the south, at the far side of Ocracoke Village. From here you can go to Cedar Island, where a short drive brings you to Beaufort and the Crystal Coast; or to Swan Quarter, the Hyde County seat, on the Albemarle Peninsula. Both trips take about one and a half hours. Reservations are recommended for these ferries, especially in the summer, and a fee is charged. Contact the **North Carolina Ferry Division** (1-800-BYFERRY; www.ncferry.org) for prices and schedules. For immediate information on local conditions, contact the Ocracoke ferry docks at 252-928-1665.

A note on hours: As the tourist trade increases into the spring, fall, and winter seasons, hotels, restaurants, and other establishments are expanding their hours to meet demand. Although a listing may say that the place you'd like to go is closed seasonally, a telephone call will often reveal that the welcome mat is out.

Ocracoke Village is the only town on Ocracoke Island, and all establishments listed here, except the National Park Service campground and beach, the pony pens, and the ferry docks to Hatteras Island, are located within its boundaries.

GETTING AROUND *By Bicycle or Golf Cart:* Bikes and golf carts (locally referred to as "Ocracoke turtles") are two of the best ways to get around Ocracoke Village. Numerous bike and cart rental stands are located throughout the village. Golf carts are only permitted on public streets within the limits of the village, and not on NPS land. Children under 18 cannot drive golf carts on public streets.

Beach Ride 4x4 Rentals (252-916-0133; www.ocracoke4x4rentals.com), 1070 NC 12. Four-wheel-drive vehicles rent by the day or half day and include ORV beach driving permits. Shuttles from your hotel or cottage to the beach or the ferry are also available.

Round Creek Rickshaws (252-588-2149). Rent a pedicab to take you to your evening destination or on a tour of the village. Call for pickup.

T & J Outfitters (256-541-7891; www.tjout fitters.com), 285 NC 12. Rent bikes or golf carts at this stand, across from Community Square.

Wheelie Fun Scooter and Golf Cart Rentals (252-928-6661), 180 NC 12, Anchorage Marina.

On Foot: There's a large parking lot behind the visitors center. Leave your vehicle there and set off on foot to explore the town, or rent a bike or golf cart at one of the nearby stands. Walking

BICYCLES ARE THE BEST WAY TO GET AROUND IN OCRACOKE VILLAGE.

MANY LOCAL BUILDINGS ARE CONSTRUCTED FROM WOOD SALVAGED FROM THE OCEAN.

tour maps are available at the visitors center and at the **Ocracoke Preservation Society Museum,** next door, on the other side of the parking lot.

A note on addresses: Who was Irvin Garrish anyway? Many of the addresses listed here are officially located on Irvin Garrish Highway, named for the first Hyde County commissioner from Ocracoke and one of the first captains of the Cedar Island Ferry. This road is identical with NC 12, the scenic byway that runs from the Hatteras ferry dock down the length of the island until it reaches the waterfront. There, it makes a sharp right turn to the west, running along the water to the ferry docks that will take you to Cedar Island or Swan Quarter. At this T intersection (sometimes referred to as Kayak Corner) where NC 12 meets the water, Silver Lake Drive is to your left, running around the eastern edge of the harbor.

MEDICAL EMERGENCY Ocracoke Health Center (252-928-1511; after hours: 252-928-7425), a certified rural health clinic at 305 Back Road, offers nonemergency health care. Call for an appointment.

✳ To See

Thanks to their centuries of isolation, Ocracoke islanders developed a unique culture, creating their own forms of entertainment and creativity. Sea chanteys blended with folk music around winter fires, decoy carving developed into fine art, and always there was—and is—the inspiration of sea, wind, and sand.

Thanks to a remarkable commitment to community, Ocracoke Village retains its unique spirit and, equally remarkable, has found ways to share it with visitors, without losing its island identity.

ARCHITECTURE Some 200 acres of the village (about half the total area) is officially identified as the **Ocracoke Historic District.** Concentrated around Silver Lake, the district includes 232 historic buildings, 15 cemeteries, plus the lighthouse, cisterns, picket fences, and docks dating from 1823 to 1959, when Ocracoke is considered to have entered the modern era. Many of the older houses are traditional "story-and-a-jump" cottages with steep gable roofs, front porches, chimneys on the end, tongue-and-groove interior walls, and rooms in the attic. The outside is usually covered with cedar shakes, and there may still be a cistern to catch the rain, the island's only source of fresh water in the early days. Many of the homes in the historic district display wooden plaques giving the construction date and name of the original occupant.

Sam Jones, a native son turned Norfolk industrialist, was another major influence on Ocracoke architecture. During the 1950s Jones engaged local craftsmen in a variety of construction projects, most of his own fanciful design. Two significant examples survive along the waterfront: the many-gabled Castle, now a bed & breakfast inn, and Berkley Manor, recently renovated as an event and adventure destination.

> QUICK TIP: **The Ocracoke Preservation Society** (252-928-7375; www .ocracokepreservation.org) has developed a booklet documenting the Ocracoke Village historic district and its special architectural features. It's available at the society's museum bookstore or through its website, for those wishing to know more about the Ocracoke style.

Beach Jumper Historical Marker on Loop Shack Hill (www.beachjumpers.com). This granite marker on the west side of NC 12 just before Ocracoke Village commemorates an almost forgotten episode in World War II history. During the war, German submarine activity was monitored from a facility on Loop Shack Hill via a top-secret magnetic cable that ran between Ocracoke and Buxton. In 1943, Loop Shack became a training base for an undercover Navy program, dubbed the Beach Jumpers, amphibious commando units deployed on tactical missions, a precursor of the famed Navy Seals of today. The original idea for the Beach Jumper commando units came from Lt. Douglas Fairbanks Jr., a famous movie star both before and after the war.

British Cemetery (www.nps.gov/caha), British Cemetery Road. The bodies of four British sailors who lost their lives when a German submarine torpedoed the HMS *Bedfordshire* on May 12, 1942, are buried here under a British flag. The U.S. Coast Guard performs an honor guard ceremony every year on the anniversary of the ship's sinking.

Community Square, NC 12 and Silver Lake. Centered on the beloved Community Store, the shops and docks at this location have been the center of Ocracoke life since the days when mailboats, once the island's only contact with the outside world, tied up here. Since 1918, local folks have gathered on the porch, or around the potbellied stove, of the Community Store to share news and talk story. Today, the complex includes several historic buildings, including those housing the **Working Watermen's Exhibit** and the Black Schooner Nautical Store. The Community Store itself is being transferred to the ownership of the Ocracoke Preservation Society, and will house an Ocracoke Village visitors center, educational exhibits on the Ocracoke Clean Water Initiative, and increased shoreline access for pedestrians.

THE BRITISH CEMETERY HONORS SAILORS WHO DIED IN THESE WATERS.

Fort Ocracoke Historical Marker. Located at the back of the parking lot behind the National Park Service visitors center, this marker gives information about Fort Ocracoke, once located just offshore. The site of the Civil War fort is now underwater but has been excavated by divers, and some of the artifacts are on display in the Ocracoke Preservation Museum.

Howard Street (www.ocracokevillage .com). Shaded with live oak, yaupon, and myrtle trees, this lane, paved with oyster shells, was once one of the village's main streets. The houses still belong to the island's oldest families, and the live oaks here are the most ancient on the island.

THE OCRACOKE PRESERVATION SOCIETY MUSEUM

North Carolina Center for the Advancement of Teaching Campus at Ocracoke Island (www.nccat.org). The historic 1940 U.S. Coast Guard station, located beyond the ferry docks at the mouth of Silver Lake Harbor, has been restored for use as a campus offering enrichment programs for North Carolina teachers. A historic bell, on loan from the Coast Guard, sits on the harbor side of the facility. Around back, a boardwalk leads to a dock on the sound.

Ocracoke Lighthouse (252-928-4531; www.nps.gov/caha), Lighthouse Road. Most visitors to the island make their way to its most prominent landmark, the 70-foot lighthouse that continues to help guide ships today as it has since 1823. A short boardwalk leads to the base of the lighthouse, past the old keeper's cottage surrounded by twisted trees. The lighthouse is not open for climbing, but during the summer you can have a look inside the base if a docent is on duty. Free.

Ocracoke Pony Pens (252-928-4531; www.nps.gov/caha), NC 12. Ocracoke, like other Banks islands both north and south, has its own herd of wild horses. No one has ever been sure where they came from, but they played an important role in island life for several centuries, serving as mounts for local residents and pulling lifesaving equipment to wreck sites. In the late 1950s, when the road, now NC 12, was paved down the length of the island, collisions between cars and ponies, which then numbered in the hundreds, became a problem. The National Park Service initially wanted to remove all the ponies from Ocracoke, but at the request of island residents agreed to keep a small herd in a 180-acre pasture. A boardwalk leads from a parking area along NC 12 to a viewing deck where the ponies, now numbering under two dozen, can be observed. National Park Service rangers present a program on the ponies during the summer months. Genetic testing reveals that they are likely the descendants of Spanish horses who were stranded or shipwrecked on these shores. The pony pens are located on the sound side of NC 12, about 6 miles south of the Hatteras Ferry docks and 7 miles north of Ocracoke Village. Free.

Ocracoke Preservation Society Museum (252-928-7375; www.ocracokepreservation.org), 49 Water Plant Road. Located in a historic 1900 house next to the National Park Service visitors center, this museum is a community-based effort with strong support from local families. The rooms are furnished with donated antiques, decoys, model boats, and quilts. Special exhibits explore the island's hunting and fishing traditions, Civil War and World War II history, and the distinctive Ocracoke Island brogue. Outside, the yard, enclosed in a rose-twined picket fence, contains

DID YOU KNOW? Ocracoke Island once had the only mounted Boy Scout troop in the country, with each boy taming and training his own horse.

an original cistern, a life car used by the U.S. Life-Saving Service, and a 1934 fishing boat. During the summer, local residents, many of them cultural treasures themselves, give talks on the porch. The museum's gift shop is an excellent source of books on local history and culture. Free.

Ocracoke Seafood Company Fish House (252-928-5601; www.ocracokeseafood.com), 416 NC 12. The last surviving fish house on Ocracoke remains in its historic spot on the waterfront due to an intense community effort led by the nonprofit Ocracoke Working Watermen's Association (www.ocracokewatermen.org). Visitors are welcome. Come by to watch seafood being unloaded on the dock or to pick up some fresh catch for dinner.

Ocracoke Working Watermen's Exhibit (www.ocracokewatermen.org). The historic Will Willis Store & Fish House on the Community Square docks houses exhibits explaining the crucial connection between fishing and the local economy, past, present, and future, through historic photos and artifacts, plus video clips on many related topics. It also serves as a clearinghouse for classes, birding tours, and community events. Free.

Ocrafolk Performances. Ocracoke is home to an impressive number of musicians and story-tellers who have developed a unique "Ocrafolk" style based on island traditions. Annual festivals

THE GHOST VILLAGE OF PORTSMOUTH LIES JUST ACROSS THE INLET FROM OCRACOKE.

and folk schools, plus an island-based recording studio, help spread the traditions, and during the summer, performances are held several nights a week at the Deepwater Theater, featuring Molasses Creek, the Ocrafolk Opry, and local storytellers. See our *Entertainment* section for more info.

Portsmouth Island (252-728-2250; www.friendsofportsmouthisland.org or www.nps.gov/calo). Once larger and more prosperous than Ocracoke, on the other side of the inlet, today Portsmouth is a ghost town, maintained in pristine yet lonely splendor by the National Park Service as part of Cape Lookout National Seashore. The NPS offers guided tours of the village, or you can take a self-guided tour. Maps, restrooms, and historical exhibits can be found at the visitors center, close to the dock where boat shuttles drop off day-trippers. Several buildings are open to the public and contain exhibits on village history, including the general store and post office, the Methodist church, and the lifesaving station.

Teach's Hole Blackbeard Exhibit (252-928-1718; www.teachshole.com), 935 NC 12. This pirate store, with over 1,000 pirate-related items, offers educational exhibits, including weapon and pirate flag displays, old bottles, and a film on Ocracoke's most famous resident and his pirate associates.

Village Craftsmen (252-928-5541; www.villagecraftsmen.com), 170 Howard Street. Gallery in an old island cottage stocks a wide variety of crafts by over 300 American crafters, including many from the Outer Banks. Gallery founder Philip Howard, an eighth-generation Ocracoker, is a wealth of information on the island, past, present, and future, and admits he just may be descended from one of Blackbeard's pirate crew. Drop by to chat, or check out his wonderful blog on Ocracoke life at www.villagecraftsmen.blogspot.com. The store also offers history and ghost tours of Ocracoke Village.

✳ To Do

If you want to play golf on vacation or have young ones who need to ride roller coasters, Ocracoke is not the destination for you. The attractions here are walking and swimming at one of the best beaches

SOUNDTRACK: OCRAFOLK

Lots of local music is made—and recorded—on Ocracoke. Check the offerings of **Soundside Records** (www.soundsiderecords.com), including the *CoastalFolk* and the *Ocrafolk Sampler* compilations, for great tunes and fascinating stories. Also from Soundside Records:

Molasses Creek. *Ocracoke Island,* 2008 (remastered). New version of the original 1993 recording by the group that is the guiding force behind the folk music revival on Ocracoke, with eight other CDs to date.

Parsons, Roy. *Songs and Tales from Ocracoke Island,* 1999. An Ocracoke original, much missed by the community.

Temple, Rob. *The Rumgagger,* 2006. Sea stories, pirate poetry, and nautical tunes from the captain of the schooner *Windfall.*

in the country, exploring the historic village, slowing down, reading a book, or just relaxing. You can find more action out on the water, but even there you'll encounter the island's laid-back vibe, locally referred to as the Ocracoma.

BICYCLING The best way to see Ocracoke Village is by bike. Ride the Loop Road to the lighthouse, visit Springer's Point and the British Cemetery, and gallery-hop along the Back Road. Especially seek out the old lanes paved with crushed oyster shell, such as Howard Street and Fig Tree Lane.

A paved, multiuse path connects the village with the National Park Service campground and the Lifeguarded Beach.

Most hotels and inns rent bicycles, if they aren't included for free in the room rate. Shacks and stands along NC 12 also offer convenient daily rentals.

Beach Outfitters (252-928-6261; www.ocracokeislandrealty.com), 1053 NC 12. Large bike stand sits outside the Ocracoke Island Realty office at the north end of the village.

The Slushy Stand (252-928-1878), 473 NC 12. Popular ice cream stand near the Silver Lake T rents adult, kid, and tandem bikes; adult tricycles; and baby seats, by the hour, day, or week. Locks are included.

THE CHURCH AT PORTSMOUTH VILLAGE

T & J Outfitters (256-541-7891; www.tjoutfitters.com), 285 NC 12. Rent bikes or golf carts at this stand, across from Community Square.

Wheelie Fun Scooter and Golf Cart Rentals (252-928-6661; www.theanchorageinn.com), Anchorage Marina, 180 NC 12. Shop at the marina rents both bikes and scooters, by the hour or day. Helmets provided.

BIRD-WATCHING The sections of the Cape Hatteras National Seashore located on Ocracoke are some of the most isolated and undisturbed on the East Coast and are popular nesting sites for a variety of shorebirds, including the endangered piping plover. Sections of the national seashore are frequently closed during the summer to protect nesting shorebirds and sea turtles. On offshore islands, brown pelicans, black skimmers, and terns can be seen during nesting season.

Wading and marsh birds, as well as migrating songbirds, are often seen along the Hammock Hills Nature Trail, across NC 12 from the National Park Service campground, and at Springer's Point.

In spring and fall, **Portsmouth Island ATV Excursions** (252-928-4484; www.portsmouthisland atvs.com) offers bird-watching trips from the Jolly Roger Marina over to Portsmouth Island's tidal flats to see shorebirds such as rare curlew sandpipers and bar-tailed godwits.

Captains Rudy and Donald Austin at **Austin Boat Tours** (252-928-4361 or 252-928-5431; www .portsmouthnc.com) take visitors to Beacon Island to see an amazing brown pelican rookery in season.

BOATING Most of the recreation on the island, beyond the beach, is found at the docks along Silver Lake. Several fun establishments have sprung up on the waterfront, where you can kick back with a cold beverage and watch the nautical action.

Those who arrive by boat will find consistent depths of 8 feet in Silver Lake Harbor and in the well-maintained channels leading to it.

Several boat ramps are available in the village. The National Park Service maintains a free boat ramp at the back of the large parking lot next to the visitors center, but you cannot launch personal watercraft such as Jet Skis from here—they are not allowed in the waters of the national seashore. Boat ramps charging a fee are located at the Anchorage Marina and at the Harborside Motel.

Anchorage Marina (252-928-6661; www.theanchorageinn.com), 180 NC 12. Full hookups including cable, fuel, and pump-out service are available for transient boaters, with access to showers and a swimming pool. Vessels up to 100 feet can dock. **SMacNalley's Raw Bar** serves local seafood and cold ones on the dock in season. Bikes and scooters are rented by the hour, day, or week. **Restless Native Small Boat Rentals** (252-921-0011) operates out of this marina.

Community Square Docks, 324 NC 12. Sign up here for boat tours and ferry service to historic Portsmouth or sunset sails aboard the *Windfall II* or *Wilma Lee.* Fuel for boats is available, as are occasional slips for transients, a dinghy dock, and kayak launch area.

Gun Barrel Point Marina, located at the T intersection where NC 12 meets the water, sometimes referred to as Kayak Corner.

Jolly Roger Pub & Marina (252-928-3703; www.silverlakemotelandinn.com), 396 NC 12, across the street from the Silver Lake Motel. Parasail Ocracoke, Ocracoke Wave Runners, Native Son Boat Tours, and several charter-fishing boats dock here, convenient to the refreshments and fun served up daily by the pub. **Ocracoke Parasail** (252-928-2606; www.ocracokeparasail.com) operates from the dock.

National Park Service Docks (252-473-2111; www.nps.gov/caha). Located next to the ferry docks at the far end of Silver Lake, these government-run docks host boats up to 80 feet at low rates. Dockage is first come, first served, and there is a 14-day limit on stays during the summer. Services include electric hookup, available in summer only; low-pressure water connections; and bathrooms across the street.

BOAT RENTALS AND BOAT TOURS ✐ **Beach Ride Rentals** (252-928-0007; www.ocracoke4x4 rentals.com), 294 NC 12, Community Square Docks. Rent a pedal boat for a family-friendly cruise on Silver Lake.

✐ ♿ ✐ **Native Son Boat Tours** (252-928-4484; www.ocracokecruises.com), Jolly Roger Marina, 410 NC 12. Board a 40-foot motorized catamaran equipped with canopy and restroom for a day of swimming and sunning on an isolated sandbar or for a sunset cruise with the Austin family.

Portsmouth Island Boat Tours (252-928-4361; www.portsmouthnc.com), Community Square

Docks. Captains Rudy and Donald Austin run a shuttle service from the Ocracoke waterfront to the ghost village of Portsmouth. $20 round-trip.

The Austins also offer a narrated sight-seeing tour of Pamlico Sound, visiting the sites of Fort Ocracoke, Shell Castle Island, Pelican Island, and other local landmarks. During the tour the Austins tell local tales in the fast-disappearing Ocracoke brogue.

Restless Native Small Boat Rentals (252-921-0011 or 252-928-1421; www.ocracokeboatrentals .com), Anchorage Marina, 180 NC 12. Be your own captain in a flat-bottom skiff with outboard motor. After a brief orientation, explore the harbor and sound on your own, go fishing or clamming, or head over to Portsmouth Village for the day. Daily and package rates available.

The Wilma Lee (www.ocracokealive.org), Community Square Docks. This restored 1940 shipjack is used for educational programs and offers cruises for up to 44 passengers under Capt. Ron Temple. Stop by the Black Schooner Nautical Store (see *Selective Shopping*) to see the current schedule and sign up for sails on both the *Wilma Lee* and *Windfall II*.

The Windfall II (252-928-7245; www.schoonerwindfall.com), Community Square Docks. Capt. Rob Temple takes small groups on sails aboard his Lazy Jack schooner, April through October. She's hard to miss, with the Jolly Roger flying from her mast. During the hour-long sails, Temple tells tales about Ocracoke's most infamous resident, Blackbeard, including many little-known facts. Temple also offers sunset sails, a Pirate Cruise, and sailing lessons. No credit cards are accepted.

CRAFTS **Glass Bead of Ocracoke** (252-928-2838), Spencer's Market, 587 NC 12. Beading shop offers lessons in jewelry making and wire wrapping, and stocks a huge selection of beads and fittings.

Tapestry, a Studio on Ocracoke (252-928-0113), Spencer's Market, 587B NC 12. Drop by to weave on the studio's loom or browse the local crafts, sold to benefit the Hyde County Crisis Hotline.

DOLPHIN AND WHALE WATCHING The waters of Pamlico Sound and offshore on the ocean side are rich in sea life year-round. Boats making their way through Ocracoke Inlet often encounter groups of bottlenose dolphin. More rare are whale sightings. Whale hunting was once a lucrative pursuit in these parts. Today, more different species of whales migrate along the coast of North Carolina than any other stretch of the East Coast. While no organized whale-watching tours are taking place at this time, the experienced captains of Ocracoke know where to look, if asked. Sperm whales and the extremely rare northern right whales migrate past the coast in springtime; humpback and fin whales pass in fall. Pilot whales can be seen all year. Some whales, such as the orcas, stay far from shore in deep water, but juvenile humpbacks can sometimes be seen from the Ocracoke beaches, breaching and forming bubble nets in the rich waters.

Austin Boat Tours (252-928-4361 or 252-928-5431; www.portsmouthnc.com). Captains Rudy and Donald Austin take visitors out to see the dolphins in Pamlico Sound.

Devereux II (252-921-0120; www.devereuxfishing.com), Anchorage Marina. Locals recommend contacting Capt. Reid Robinson, one of the area's top charter fishing captains, about whale-watching trips.

FISHING CHARTERS Docked less than 20 miles from the Gulf Stream, Ocracoke's charter-fishing fleet conducts some of the most successful, and reasonably priced, offshore trips on the coast, and the rich waters of Pamlico Sound are just outside the harbor.

Many of Ocracoke's charter fleet captains are descendants of families who have fished this region for generations, and they will take you to productive spots that the out-of-town fisherman will never find.

Although Ocracoke has no fishing piers, surf fishing is tremendously popular along the unspoiled beaches of the island. A four-wheel-drive vehicle is a must. A permit is required to drive on the beach. Consult the National Seashore website (www.nps.gov/caha) for current regulations and closures.

Drum Stick (252-921-0011 or 252-928-1421; www.drumstickocracoke.com), Anchorage Marina. Capt. Farris O'Neal's charter boat has the distinction of catching the state-record king mackerel, an 82-pound, 66-inch monster, and more recently a world-record snowy grouper. A wide variety of excursions are possible, including makeup trips, night drum fishing, shark fishing, Gulf Stream trolling, and winter fishing for giant bluefin tuna.

SURF FISHING ON THE BEACHES AROUND OCRACOKE

Fish Tale (252-921-0224 or 252-928-3403; www.ocracokeisland.com/fish_tale.htm), Jolly Roger Marina. Educational family trips using light tackle on Pamlico Sound include lessons in fish identification, perfect for first-time anglers. The Catch Your Dinner special offers a quick two-hour trip after good "eating" fish. Tackle, bait, ice, and fish filleting are included in per-person rates.

Ocracoke Sportfishing (252-928-4841; www.ocracokesportfishing.com), Community Square Docks. The O'Neals, father and son, belong to a native Ocracoker family with a fishing heritage that dates back to the 1600s. Join Capt. Ronnie O'Neal (252-928-8064) for a full or half day aboard the *Miss Kathleen*. Or set out with Ronnie's son, Capt. Ryan O'Neal (252-928-9966), in the 24-foot *Tarheel*, for a day of inshore light-tackle fishing, clamming, or a night trip to gig flounder. Makeup charters available.

FISHING TACKLE SHOPS ✳ Ocracoke Variety Store (252-928-4911; www.ocracokevarietystore .com), 950 NC 12. This one-stop shop offers groceries and microbrews, as well as bait and tackle, beach supplies, and much more. Open all year.

O'Neal's Dockside II Tackleshop (252-928-1111), 800 NC 12. A huge variety of fishing gear is available for sale or rent, plus free fishing advice from members of one of the oldest families on the island. Hunting, camping, and marine supplies also in stock.

Tradewinds Bait & Tackle (252-928-5491; www.fishtradewinds.com), 1094 NC 12. The place to find the right gear for surf, inshore, and offshore fishing, plus clam rake rentals, crab nets, camping and beach supplies. Surf fishing is a passion of the owners, and they have an official weigh station where you can register your citation fish.

FITNESS CLASSES ✳ (ᵞᵖ) Angie's Gym (252-928-2496; www.angies-gym.com), 141 Sand Dollar Road. Full-service gym offers cardio and strength machines, plus exercise classes and a sauna. Daily, weekly, and single-class passes available.

✳ Free Fitness Classes at Ocracoke Community Center (252-928-3162; www.ocracoke communitycenter.com), 999 NC 12. Free exercise classes for all ages and abilities are offered on weekday mornings.

✳ Yoga with Amy (252-921-0182; www.yogawithamy.net), Deepwater Theater, 82 School Road. Local health professional Amy Hilton teaches Anusara yoga classes at the Deepwater Theater. Drop-ins welcome.

FOR FAMILIES If you have a young pirate in the family, Ocracoke is a great place to explore the real episodes of Blackbeard's life, with lots of pirate-themed attractions to visit. You can stay at Blackbeard's Lodge, tour a Blackbeard exhibit, take a pirate cruise to the site of Blackbeard's final battle, eat at the Jolly Roger pub, and stroll through Springer's Point, where Blackbeard once made his camp.

The village also offers a growing list of water sports that appeal to the younger set, including surf camps, boat cruises, Jet Ski rentals, and parasailing. The **Windfall Sailing School** (252-928-7245) offers basic sailing, cruising, and navigation lessons for the novice sailor.

HORSEBACK RIDING ❋ **Morning Star Stables** (252-921-0383). Horseback rides on the beach are available all year.

HUNTING Shooting waterfowl is a treasured winter tradition for many Ocracoke families. Some native Ocracokers now offer guide services, taking visiting hunters after the redheads, bluebills, black ducks, pintails, brants, widgeons, and geese that winter in Pamlico Sound. You'll find a unique kind of blind in use here: the curtain blind, a kind of sink box developed in the area that is legal only in Hyde and Dare counties.

Curtain Box Hunting (252-588-0185). Native guide Russell Williams specializes in curtain blind trips. Packages including accommodations can be arranged through the Pony Island Motel (see *Lodging*).

Island Guide Services (252-928-2504 or 252-928-2509; www.islandguideservice.com). Ken Tillett and Earl Gaskins continue the hunting traditions of their forefathers, who were guides at the legendary Green Island Hunting Club. Trips include stake and pit blinds, decoys, and transport.

Mason's Guide Service (252-928-2887 or 252-921-0351). Native Rodney Mason offers waterfowl hunting in stake blinds and curtain boxes, plus inshore and offshore fishing.

Ocracoke Sportfishing (252-928-4841 or 252-928-8064; www.ocracokesportfishing.com). Ronald O'Neal Jr., descended from eight generations of Ocracokers, takes hunters out to the family duck blinds in Pamlico Sound during the winter season.

Ocracoke Waterfowl Hunting (252-928-5751). Native Monroe Gaskill provides bush blinds, transport, and a resting area for dogs, and deploys more than 100 decoys at each blind.

Open Water Duck Hunting (252-928-7170; www.ocracokeduckhunting.com). Wade Austin is the fourth generation of his family to guide hunters. Curtain boxes and bush blinds available.

Named for two adjacent counties, **Dare to Hyde** (252-926-9453; www.daretohyde.com) seeks to make the outstanding outdoor opportunities of the region more available to visitors through a surprisingly wide range of all-inclusive packages. Options range from traditional tours of lighthouses and historic properties on both the Banks and the mainland, to trophy hunts for 500-pound black bear, to turkey and deer hunting. Other adventures take you aboard the charter fishing boat *Salvation*, horseback riding along wildlife trails, or on a hunt for waterfowl in a traditional curtain blind. Birding and photography trips are another popular option. You can spend a day with a commercial fisherman, or with a professional trapper learning to set snares. The "Dude" farming and construction packages let you participate in planting and harvesting on a working farm or learn to operate heavy machinery. The big bonus: Multiple-day packages include overnight accommodations at ⚥ (ᵞ) **Berkeley Manor**, Sam Jones's first home in Ocracoke Village, now a marvelously lavish inn.

KAYAKING AND STAND-UP PADDLEBOARDING Ocracoke Village is an ideal location for kayaking and stand-up paddleboarding (SUP). The calm waters of Silver Lake, with the lighthouse visible in the background, make a safe and scenic spot for a family paddle. Just stay clear of the ferry docks.

Outside the harbor, the sound side of the island is covered in salt marsh where many wading birds can be seen, especially at dawn and dusk. A favorite paddle is southeast along the coast toward Springer's Point.

More-experienced paddlers may want to cross Ocracoke Inlet to Portsmouth but should get local advice on winds, tides, and weather before setting out.

Kayak fishing is quite rewarding in the area. Contact **Ken DeBarth** (252-475-0869) for information on guided kayak fishing trips.

Kayaks and other nonmotorized craft can launch at the Community Square Docks and at a sandy, sound-side launch at the back of the parking lot next to the national seashore visitors center.

Rental kayaks and SUPs are available at several stands along the harborfront; at **Kitty Hawk Kites** (252-928-4563; www.kittyhawk.com), in Community Square; and at **Ride the Wind Surf & Kayak** (252-928-6311; www.surfocracoke.com), which also offers a variety of tours, including a paddle out to a secluded beach for a session of tai chi and yoga. See *Water Sports* for more information.

SHELLING Some of the best shelling in the state is found along the Atlantic side of Ocracoke. Lucky beachcombers may collect a variety of different whelks, sand dollars, and possibly a rare Scotch bonnet, the North Carolina state shell. The best time to search for shells is right after high tide or after a storm. The northern end of the island has a gentle slope, good for finding unbroken shells.

SPAS AND WELLNESS Ann Ehringhaus Massage Therapy (252-928-1311; www.annehringhaus .com), 660 NC 12. Licensed massage therapist offers treatments and classes in a variety of bodywork techniques, including Reiki, Chinese acupressure, and the Rosen Method of Emotional Healing. Ann is the innkeeper at Oscar's House B&B (see *Lodging*).

Deep Blue Day Spa (252-921-0182; www.deepbluedayspa.com), 260 O'Neal Drive. Amy Hilton offers massage therapy, Moor Mud facials, and a variety of body treatments.

Float with Grace (252-996-0198; www.floatwithgrace.com). Licensed massage therapist offers Watsu treatments, a gentle form of therapeutic massage conducted while the client floats in a warm-water indoor pool, as well as tai chi classes and swimming classes for all ages.

Island Path Massage and Retreats (252-928-1821 or 1-877-708-7284; www.islandpath.com). Ruth Fordon and Ken DeBarth offer therapeutic massage, life coaching, personal path retreats, and creativity camps. Ken (252-475-0869) trained at the Cayce/Reilly School of Massotherapy and offers treatments at his studio in the Thurston House Inn (see *Lodging*).

Stillwater Spa and Wellness (252-588-0267; www.stillwaterspaandwellness.com), 72 Back Road. Licensed therapist Laura Hardy offers bodywork and spa treatments, and sells her handmade aromatherapy and herbal products, including a pest potion designed to repel the local insects.

WALKING TOURS Ocracoke Ghost and History Walks (252-928-6300; www.villagecraftsmen .com), Village Craftsmen, 170 Howard Street. Eighth-generation Ocracoker Philip Howard and his trained staff lead two different walking tours of Ocracoke Village, and both include plenty of ghost stories. Tours last about 90 minutes and cover 1.5 miles. Adults $12; ages 12 and under $6. Self-guided MP3 tours also available.

WATER SPORTS Although the water-sports industry here is not yet as organized as you'll find farther north on the Banks, the area has a plenty of opportunities for extreme water fun.

Surfing experts say Ocracoke has some of the best, and least crowded, waves on the East Coast. Locals here consider surfing an important part of island life. Ocracoke's high school was the first east of the Mississippi to offer a surfing class.

Ocracoke Parasail (252-928-2606; www.ocracokeparasail.com), Jolly Roger Marina, 395 NC 12. Get the big picture as you fly high with this locally owned outfitter. A kiosk outside the Jolly Roger takes reservations.

Ocracoke Wave Runners (252-928-2600; www.ocracokejetski.com), Jolly Roger Marina, 395 NC 12. Half-hour and hour-long rentals let you explore Silver Lake and the waters of Ocracoke Inlet on your own. Tours also available.

Ride the Wind Surf & Kayak (252-928-6311; www.surfocracoke.com), 486 NC 12. Kayak and surf specialists offer kayak tours, including full-moon tours, a history tour to Teach's Hole, and a morning yoga/tai chi paddle. Kayaks, including boats equipped for fishing, surfboards, stand-up paddleboards, skim boards, and boogie boards with fins rent by the hour, day, or week. From May to August, students ages 9–17 can attend a three-day Surf Camp to learn both technique and safety procedures. Members of the staff surf every morning of the year and invite island visitors to join them.

✳ Green Space

BEACHES Ocracoke Island's more than 16 miles of undeveloped beach, managed by the National Park Service as part of the Cape Hatteras National Seashore, are its greatest assets, and in recent years they brought Ocracoke to international prominence. After ranking Ocracoke for four years among his top three, in 2007 Dr. Beach named **Ocracoke's Lifeguarded Beach** the best in the country. The shoreline's wide, uncrowded, and unpolluted sands, plus the warm Gulf Stream waters

NAMED THE BEST BEACH IN THE UNITED STATES IN 2007, THE SANDS OF OCRACOKE ISLAND ARE THE PERFECT PLACE TO RELAX.

that allow swimming into the late fall, attracted Dr. Beach's attention. Surfing, shelling, surf fishing, bird-watching, and just plain old loafing are the favorite activities on this beach, where no high-rises block the sun. Parts of the 16.5 miles of beach on Ocracoke Island are open to both off-road vehicles (ORVs in park parlance) and pedestrians. There are six places where you can park and walk over the dunes to the beach, and several beach access ramps for four-wheel-drive vehicles.

Driving on the beach requires an ORV permit from the National Park Service. You can get one at the ORV Permit Office at the Cape Hatteras National Seashore Visitor Center in Ocracoke Village. See the seashore's website (www.nps.gov/caha) for current updates on prices, regulations, and maps of ORV routes. The northern end of the island, accessed via ramp 59, and the southern end, accessed by ramp 72, also known as South Point Road, are popular spots for surf fishing, although they are subject to closures to protect nesting birds and sea turtles.

The boardwalk opposite the pony pens is a popular spot to cross to the beach. Ramp 70, also called the Airport Road, is the beach access most used by locals.

The parking lot for the award-winning Lifeguarded Beach can be found about a half mile north of ramp 70, about 1.5 miles north of the village, on NC 12. This beach also has changing rooms and showers. Look for the brown swimmer sign. Lifeguards are on duty Memorial Day to Labor Day.

Fires are allowed on the beach only with a free permit, available on the park website or at the Ocracoke Visitor Center next to the village ferry dock. From May 1 to November 15, beach fires can only be lit in the Ocracoke Day Use area. Pets are allowed if kept on a 6-foot leash or in a crate, but they cannot be brought onto the lifeguarded swimming beach.

Current information on beach closures, activities, and regulations can be found on the Cape Hatteras National Seashore website (www.nps.gov/caha) or by calling 252-473-2111.

For an even more remote beach adventure, cross the inlet to the unspoiled beaches of Portsmouth Island, part of the **Cape Lookout National Seashore** (www.nps.gov/calo). Primitive beach camping is allowed on the beach just beyond Portsmouth Village for a maximum of 14 days without a permit. Beach fires are allowed on the ocean side of the dunes below the high tide line, but you should plan on bringing your own wood. A compost comfort station is located at the gate into the historic district on the beach side, with flush toilets available at the visitors center near the ferry dock (open April–November). Pets must remain leashed at all times.

Personal watercraft (Jet Skis, etc.) and other boats and kayaks may land at the Wallace Channel dock located east of the ferry dock in Portsmouth Village and on the beach to the east of this dock. The water here is very shallow.

For a do-it-yourself tour to the Portsmouth beaches, **Portsmouth Island Boat Tours** (252-928-4361; www.portsmouthnc.com) runs a shuttle service from the Community Square Docks on the Ocracoke waterfront to the ghost village of Portsmouth. You have time for quick self-guided tour of the town, a swim, and some beachcombing on the unspoiled beach before your pickup four hours later. Bring insect repellent, drinking water, sunscreen, a hat, and good walking shoes. The beach is 1.5 miles from the village. The shuttle may transport pets on request. It can also drop you off and pick you up nearer the beach, depending on current conditions. Be sure to set this up in advance. The shuttle costs $20 round-trip.

✍ **Portsmouth Island ATV Excursions** (252-928-4484; www.portsmouthislandatvs.com), Jolly Roger Marina. Wade and Gwen Austin take groups to Portsmouth Island for a four-hour tour of the deserted village and nearby beach April through November. The ATVs can accommodate a family of four.

TRAILS Hammock Hills Nature Trail (252-473-2111; www.nps.gov/caha), Cape Hatteras National Seashore, NC 12, 3 miles north of

NUMEROUS BOARDWALKS LEAD OVER THE DUNES TO THE FAMOUS OCRACOKE BEACH.

Ocracoke Village, across NC 12 from the National Park Service campground. This 30-minute hike over remnant dunes covered with maritime forest and through salt marsh leads to an overlook on Pamlico Sound. There is ample parking and good birding here.

Springer's Point Nature Preserve (252-449-8289; www.coastallandtrust.org), Loop Road. The North Carolina Coastal Land Trust protects 121 acres of maritime forest overlooking Ocracoke Inlet and Teach's Hole. Once known as Teach's Plantation, legend says the infamous Blackbeard, aka Edward Teach, had an island outpost here where he roasted pigs and drank rum with his fellow pirates. The property today is heavily wooded with significant stands of ancient live oaks. A nature trail leads down to the sound where a sand path runs along the beach. Teach's Hole, where Blackbeard met his fate, lies just offshore. Plaques along the trail identify local plants. The preserve is an excellent birding spot, with a rookery containing white ibis, heron, and egret nests. Keep an eye out for ruins from the original pilots village and the graves of entrepreneur Sam Jones buried next to Ikey D, his favorite horse, marked by a rearing horse statue. Locals claim the cemetery, in fact the entire point, is haunted. No parking is available, so walk or bike to the gate off the Loop Road.

Windmill Point (252-928-7375; www.ocracokepreservation.org), end of Silver Lake Road. A conservation easement protects the area on the far side of Silver Lake from future development. Once the site of a windmill used to grind grain, the area is now heavily wooded. Locals recommend taking Robbie's Lane, a sandy path found at the end of Silver Lake Road, out to an uninhabited beach along Pamlico Sound to catch a spectacular sunset. This is also a great spot to dig for clams.

✳ Lodging

Like the village itself, Ocracoke inns generally have a little more character than those elsewhere on the Banks. You may find yourself passing a family of cats in the hall or renting a room from a published author. What you won't find is cookie-cutter resorts or chain hostelries.

Lodgings in Ocracoke Village are eclectic, no two the same. Mostly the inns are owned by local families, some of whom have returned to their roots to open hostelries after successful careers off-island.

While more innkeepers are staying open all

year, Ocracoke Island is still a very seasonal place, quiet in the winter months, but welcoming to visitors. In fact, for many regular guests, this is their favorite time of year, when the traffic dies down and the beach is deserted.

In season and out, rental fees tend to be a bit less than in other areas of the Banks—another advantage of an island that can't be reached by bridge.

BED & BREAKFAST INNS ((ŋ)) **Cove Bed & Breakfast** (252-928-4192; www.thecovebb .com), 21 Loop Road. Closed January. The Cove's location at the far end of Lighthouse Road guarantees a peaceful experience but is only a short walk from village attractions. Suites designed for romantic getaways, with queen beds, two-person Jacuzzis, and private decks, occupy the top floors of each wing, and a suite with private entrance and screened porch is located on the first floor. Several rooms can accommodate three guests, but all must be at least age 15. Innkeepers John and Kati Wharton serve a full plated breakfast and afternoon wine and "goodie" hours. Bicycles, beach chairs, and towels are complimentary. You can launch a kayak from the inn's dock. The inn is smoke-free, but smoking is allowed on balconies. A shuttle will pick guests up from the airport or docks. Off-season $$; in season $$$.

Crews Inn Bed & Breakfast (252-928-7011; www.ocracokers.com), 503 Back Road. Step into the lives of old-time Ocracokers at this historic 1908 inn, once the home of the O'Neal and Garrish families. It sits in the midst of live oaks at the end of an oyster shell driveway, not far from Silver Lake. Rooms are furnished with iron bedsteads, quilts, and the simple antiques typical of island homes. They do not have TVs or phones, but do have individual air conditioners. Two rooms on the first floor have private baths, while the two on the second share a bath. Up top is the Captain's Quarters, with private deck and clawfoot tub. A continental breakfast is served every morning. The wraparound porch, partially screened and furnished with rockers and swings, is a great place to read *Ocracokers*, a book on local history written by the inn's owner, Alton Ballance. Proceeds from the sale of the book benefit the Ocracoke School, where Ballance once taught English and journalism. $.

Oscar's House Bed & Breakfast (252-928-1311; www.oscarsbb.com), 660 NC 12. Closed winters. Built in 1940 by one of the island's last lighthouse keepers, Oscar's has four charming guest rooms with original bead-board walls, private half-baths, and a laid-back, creative vibe

nourished by innkeeper Ann Ehringhaus, a photographer, massage therapist, and interfaith minister. Guests share a private outdoor shower under a cedar tree. Ann serves a healthy breakfast daily and can accommodate special diets. A deck with barbecue grill and bicycles are free for guests to use. $.

☀ ((ŋ)) **Pam's Pelican Bed & Breakfast** (252-928-1661 or 1-888-7PELICAN; www.pams pelican.com), 1021 NC 12. This inn, located close to the airport, the beach, and Howard's Pub, rents four rooms, each with private bath, minifridge, microwave, and cable TV. Rates include a home-cooked breakfast. Guests can relax on the deck on top of the building or in a shady gazebo. Complimentary shuttle to airport or marina. Free bikes, grills, and coolers are available for guest use. $–$$.

♿ ((ŋ)) **Thurston House Inn** (252-928-6037; www.thurstonhouseinn.com), 685 NC 12. Operated by members of an old island family, this charming historic cottage rents 10 rooms, surrounded by several lovely outdoor porches and a courtyard with outdoor shower. The generous Southern-style breakfast, served on the porch when weather allows, features homemade Ocracoke Fig Cake, a local specialty. $$.

CAMPGROUNDS Because it takes a boat trip to reach the island, it's a good idea to always make advance reservations to camp, especially during the busy summer season. Even the National Park Service takes reservations for its campground here, unlike its other facilities on the Banks.

❋ ✿ ☀ **Beachcomber Campground** (252-928-4031; www.ocracokecamping.com), 990 NC 12. This big-rig-friendly campground, situated behind Ocracoke Station, a busy gas station and convenience store at the north end of the village, has water and electric sites for 29 RVs, plus a few tent sites, a bathhouse with hot showers, dump station, picnic tables, and grills. Cable TV at some sites. Bike, golf cart, and four-wheel-drive rentals available. Free Sunset Music series during the summer months.

☀ ♿ **Ocracoke Campground** (252-928-5111; reservations: 1-877-444-6777; www.nps.gov /caha), 4352 NC 12. Closed November to April. The National Park Service operates this 136-site campground, on the oceanfront about 4 miles from the village ferry docks. Paved sites can be used by either tents or RVs. An unspoiled beach is just over the dunes. Amenities are basic: cold showers, running water, flush toilets, dump station, picnic tables, and grills. Rangers lead evening programs and campfires during the summer months. Maximum stay is 14 days. Reservations and mosquito repellent recommended.

🐾 **Teeter's Campground** (252-588-2030 or 1-800-705-5341; www.teeterscampground.com), 200 British Cemetery Road. Open March through November. Located in the historic district, Teeter's has the island's only full hookups (two sites), plus a dozen more shady sites with water and electric, and 10 for tents. Hot showers, picnic tables, grills, and cable TV are available.

COTTAGE AND CONDO RENTALS The vast majority of rentals on Ocracoke are cottages handled by local real estate companies. While a few of the newer ones are large multiroom constructions, the majority are small, neat houses crouched among gnarled live oaks that protect them from the weather. Some have waterfront locations on canals leading to Pamlico Sound, but none is on the beach. The Atlantic side of the island remains totally undeveloped, under the care of the National Park Service.

🐾 ♿ **Blue Heron Vacation Rentals** (252-928-7117 or 1-866-576-7117; www.blueheron vacations.com), 585 NC 12, Spencer's Market. This company, started by an island native, Jennifer Esham, offers friendly, personal service and a variety of houses all over the village, including several historic cottages. You can browse and book online. Bicycle, golf cart, and linen rentals available.

🐾 ((ψ)) **Ocracoke Island Realty** (252-928-6261 or 1-877-646-2822; www.ocracokeislandrealty .com), 1075 NC 12. The island's premiere real estate company handles the rental of over 300 privately owned properties that run the gamut from small but historic cottages to luxurious sound-front properties with private docks and swimming pools. Most rent by the week, but some shorter getaway packages are available, especially off-season. Most properties come without linens, but you can rent them and other vacation essentials from Beach Outfitters on Ocracoke Island Realty's website, where you'll also find extensive pictures of all rental properties.

GUESTHOUSES AND APARTMENTS A number of smaller cottages, apartments, and guest rooms are for rent in Ocracoke Village, often at rates less than the more luxurious hotels and rental houses.

🐾 **Corinne's Studio Apartments** (252-928-5851), 59 Silver Lake Drive. Three studios on the waterfront have cable TV, decks, and hot tubs. $–$$.

((ψ)) **Lightkeeper's Guest House** (252-928-1821; www.lightkeepersguesthouse.com), 61 Creek Road. Air-conditioned rooms, including one double-decker with a futon in the cupola, rent by the day or week. Most rooms share baths. Guests have kitchen privileges and access to the big deck out back. $–$$.

Wagon Wheel Cottages (252-928-5321), Silver Lake Drive. Small cottages with a great location are popular with hunters and anglers, as well as families on a budget. $.

HISTORIC INNS AND RESORTS ❄ 🖉 🐾 ♿ ((ψ)) **Blackbeard's Lodge** (252-928-3421 or 1-800-892-5314; www.blackbeardslodge.com), 111 Back Road. The hotel that started Ocracoke's tourism industry in 1936 has been completely refurbished and is now back in the family of the original owner. Stanley "Chip" Stevens, who bought the hotel in 2007, is the great-grand-nephew of the man who built the hotel, Robert Stanley Wahab. Today, a statue of Blackbeard the pirate greets guests as they enter the spacious lobby. Comfortable couches and a wood-burning stove invite both hotel guests and day-trippers to sit and relax awhile. The yellow frame lodge has 38 air-conditioned units with a wide variety of sleeping arrangements, from regular doubles to full-kitchen efficiency apartments that sleep eight, all nonsmoking. The lodge has a heated pool, wide porches furnished with rocking chairs and swings, and a game room with pool table, foosball, and video and board games. Bicycles and golf carts are available for rent, and a free shuttle takes guests to the harbor or airport. Rates are higher if you stay only one night during the peak season or on weekends. Free Wi-Fi in common areas. Off-season $; in season $$.

((ψ)) **The Castle on Silver Lake and Castle Courtyard Villas** (252-928-3505 or 1-800-471-8848; www.thecastlebb.com), 155 Silver Lake Drive. Once the domain of the legendary Sam Jones, this house, built by local craftsmen in the mid-1900s, soon earned the nickname of "The Castle" thanks to its many-gabled roof and lofty cupola. After many years of neglect, the landmark building has been completely refurbished as a bed & breakfast inn with 11 elegant rooms, all paneled with beautiful wood. Each has a private bath with shower. A hot breakfast buffet is served daily. The common rooms are spectacular, including a den with big-screen TV and custom pool table, a parlor, formal dining room, and a screened porch with swings. High atop the inn, occupying the entire third floor, the Lighthouse Suite is the inn's most requested accommodation. The bed & breakfast does not allow children under 12. Behind the Castle, the ♫ ((ᵠ)) **Castle Courtyard Villas,** 11 units ranging from studios to three-bedroom suites, are available for larger parties or families with children. All guests can enjoy the Castle's amenities, which include an, outdoor heated pool, pool house with sauna and steam shower, bicycles, and complimentary dockage at the inn's dock. Be sure to climb the outside stairs up to the widow's walk around the inn's cupola for a spectacular view. B&B $$–$$$; villas $$$–$$$$.

❋ ((ᵠ)) **Island Inn and Villas** (252-928-4351; www.ocracokeislandinn.com), 25 Lighthouse Road. Built of shipwrecked wood in 1901, the part of the inn fronting on Silver Lake is the island's oldest commercial building, originally built as an Oddfellows Lodge, and reputedly haunted. Today the building houses 16 rooms furnished with antiques, including the unique Crow's Nest rooms, with soaring ceilings and lofty balconies under the eaves. Some of the inn rooms have TV, and all include a full breakfast, but do not accommodate children. The 12 villas are new one- and two-bedroom condo units with balconies overlooking the inn's heated pool. The villas have Jacuzzi tubs, washers and dryers, and full kitchens. $–$$$$.

MOTELS ❋ ((ᵠ)) **Bluff Shoal Motel** (252-928-4301; www.bluffshoal.com), 306 NC 12. Small, '60s era motel has seven well-maintained rooms, each with a small refrigerator, a great location in the center of the village action, and a nice waterfront deck out back. Parking is right outside your room. Off-season $; in season $$.

((ᵠ)) **Edwards of Ocracoke** (252-928-4801 or 1-800-254-1359; www.edwardsofocracoke.com), 226 Old Beach Road. Laid-back motel rooms, efficiencies, and private cottages, all with screened porches or covered decks, are located on a quiet street and have plenty of simple island charm. The courtyard is a favorite location for cookouts. The **Duck Cottages** (www.ocracokeduckcottages.com), two larger properties located near the lighthouse, rent by the week. $–$$.

((ᵠ)) **Harborside Motel** (252-928-3111 or 252-928-4141; www.ocracokeharborside.com), 244 NC 12. Closes mid-November to Easter. Located just across the street from the waterfront, Harborside has been a popular destination since 1965. Family owned and operated, the motel offers 14 rooms with two double beds, refrigerator, television, and private bath and four efficiencies. Room rates include continental breakfast, making this a good bargain. A sundeck with seats overlooking the harbor, boat dock, and boat ramp are across the street.

Guests share the motel with a colony of cats. AAA and senior discounts are available. Nonsmoking. Off-season (April and November) $; in season $$.

❋ ((ᵠ)) **Pony Island Motel & Cottages** (252-928-4411 or 1-866-928-4411; www.ponyislandmotel.com), 785 NC 12. One of the largest inns on the island, Pony Island rents 50 guest rooms and efficiencies, plus four classic island cottages. All rooms are air-conditioned and nonsmoking, and all have TVs and refrigerators. Several suites have Jacuzzi tubs. A swimming pool, picnic area with grills, and a popular family restaurant are on-site. Bike rentals and boat docks available. Off-season $; in season $$.

❋ ((ᵠ)) **Sand Dollar Motel** (252-928-5571 or 1-866-928-5571; www.sanddollarmotelocracoke.com), 70 Sand Dollar Road. Motel built in the 1960s has 12 motel-style rooms paneled in knotty pine renting by the night, plus a suite and several cottages that rent by the week. Guests can enjoy a pool and picnic area with grills. Off-season $; in season $–$$.

PET ACCOMMODATIONS ❦ **Sandy Paws Bed & Biscuit Inn** (252-928-3093), 136 West End Road. Hotels and rental cottages that don't allow pets recommend you board your family friend at Sandy Paws. Doggie day care is also available.

WATERFRONT INNS ❦ ♿ **Anchorage Inn & Marina** (252-928-1101; www.theanchorageinn.com), 180 NC 12. Located on Ocracoke's harbor, the Anchorage Inn has its own marina, a private pool, a sundeck, a cafe, plus terrific views of the harbor at sunset. The four-story brick inn contains 35 modern rooms and 2 suites, served by an elevator. Small boats, bikes, golf carts, and scooters are available for rent. Open from March to November, the inn accepts reservations only by phone. $$–$$$$.

♿ ((ᵠ)) **Captain's Landing** (252-928-1999; www.thecaptainslanding.com), 324 NC 12. Located directly on the waterfront of Silver Lake, Captain's Landing lets guests put the traffic literally behind them. Owner Betty Chamberlin, a descendant of some to the island's oldest families, designed this inn on the old Howard property to maximize views of the harbor and the island's renowned sunsets. Eight spacious suites each sleep four and have a full kitchen and one and a half baths, as well as a private deck. A penthouse with all the comforts of home sleeps eight. The Captain's Cottage, formerly a 1950s post office building, sits next to the inn, offering modern amenities, including a big-screen LCD television and gourmet kitchen, in a private setting. All guests enjoy access to a DVD library, bicycles for exploring the island, and complimentary boat dockage with hookups just outside their doors. $$$–$$$$.

&. (φ) **Ocracoke Harbor Inn and Cottages** (252-928-5731 or 1-888-456-1998; www .ocracokeharborinn.com), 144 Silver Lake Road. Modern lodging on the quiet end of the harborfront offers 16 standard rooms and 7 suites on three floors, plus apartments and cottages for longer stays. Guests can access a picnic area with grills and outdoor showers. Boat docking is complimentary with advance reservation. Bikes and golf carts can be rented. A continental breakfast is included. $$–$$$.

❄ ❦ (φ) **Silver Lake Motel & Inn** (252-928-5721 or 1-855-758-7525; www.theinnonsilver lake.com), 395 NC 12. Located across the street from the Jolly Roger Pub and Marina, this property has two segments, an older two-story motel-style unit and a newer three-story inn with both motel rooms and suites with full kitchens. Many of the inn units have private balconies with hammocks, while the motel units share a balcony furnished with rocking chairs. The property, now being managed by Ocracoke Island Realty, is being updated and renovated. A continental breakfast is included. Off-season $; in season $$.

❋ Where to Eat

To see what's biting in local waters, visit the historic Ocracoke Seafood Company on the waterfront. Here local fishing trawlers land their catches. Some seafood is available for retail sale; some makes its way to local restaurants. The friendly staff here will help you identify what you see. You may want to check out some of the more unusual local fish, such as sheepshead or spadefish, said to taste much like grouper and red snapper. Shrimp, clams, oysters, and blue crab are plentiful in these waters.

If you plan on doing a lot of cooking in your vacation rental, consider shopping on your way to the island to pick up your favorite foods and essential items. Groceries are limited on Ocracoke, although improving, and a specialty store now offers many gourmet-cooking items. The one thing you won't need to bring is fish; the Ocracoke Seafood Company should be able to meet your needs with its fresh catch.

A major change came to the Ocracoke dining scene in 2007 when liquor by the drink came to Hyde County. While a few restaurants immediately added a full cocktail menu, many took a go-slow approach to the change. However, mixed drinks are becoming more common and today are widely available.

OCRACATS

Island visitors often comment on the large number of feral cats on Ocracoke. Many locals believe they arrived along with the island ponies, survivors of shipwrecks along this coast, since the cats seem to have been here even before the village. Perhaps some are even descendants of cats that lived aboard Blackbeard's pirate ship, since every captain kept cats aboard to battle rats. **Ocracats** (252-921-0281; www .ocracats.org) is a nonprofit organization dedicated to caring for these community cats, through catch-and-release vaccination and spay-neuter services. Donations to this cause are tax-deductible and greatly appreciated. Ocracats also often has kittens available for adoption.

DINING OUT &. ↝ **Back Porch Restaurant and Wine Bar** (252-928-6401; www.backporch ocracoke.com), 110 Back Road. A favorite with local Ocracokers, the Back Porch has a warm, inviting atmosphere, with low lights and white tablecloths. Twisted trees and a fence of cacti shield the outside of the old building, increasing the intimacy. The menu changes seasonally but always features fresh fish caught locally. Many of the preparations, such as the Vietnamese lime sauce available on the fresh catch, have an Asian fusion slant. Big appetites will enjoy the seafood platter, a local favorite loaded with broiled fish, sautéed shrimp, scallops, and signature crab beignets. Half portions of some dishes are available for smaller appetites. Cocktails and a casual bar menu are available, along with an extensive wine list. Dinner only, $$–$$$.

♪ &. **Café Atlantic** (252-928-4861), 1129 NC 12. Closed Tuesday. Seafood comes in interesting combinations at this tall beach house on the northern edge of town. Try the Pesto Scallops or the Tomatillo Shrimp for something a little different, or go with the baked Parmesan fish of the day. The crabcakes and clams casino are popular, and, for a local treat, sample the rosemary chèvre and fig preserve appetizer. Desserts here are fabulous and homemade, including bread pudding in a wide variety of flavors, Ocracoke fig cake, plus numerous other tasty treats. Take time over a glass of wine to enjoy the views out over marsh and dunes, and the artwork by local artists on the walls. Vegetarian entrées and senior menu available. Dinner only $$.

✐ ✹ ♿ ⛾ **Dajio Restaurant and Patio Bar**
(252-928-7119; www.dajiorestaurant.com), 305
NC 12. Located in the historic house across
from the waterfront once occupied by the popular Pelican Bar, this new addition to the Ocracoke scene retains the relaxed atmosphere and
shady, dog-friendly patio of its predecessor
while updating the menu with touches like
ceviche, crab mac and cheese, free-range
chicken, and a vegan quinoa salad. The Ciop-
pino, chock-full of local seafood in a saffron
broth, deserves a shout-out. The Pelican's
"Shrimp Hour," 3–5 PM, and the live music that
follows, remain in place, making Dajio a favorite
party place after a day on the water. This laid-
back spot also serves breakfast daily, featuring
apple pancakes, shrimp and grits, omelets, and a
variety of à la carte items. Breakfast $–$$; lunch
and dinner $$–$$$.

✐ ♿ ↝ **The Flying Melon** (252-928-2533),
181 Back Road. Calling the menu eclectic does-
n't really do it justice, but whatever you order,
you will likely come away singing the praises of
the Flying Melon. The bright, even funky dining room is the scene of daily brunch, served
9–2,where the specialties are *pain perdu* (New
Orleans–style French toast) and sweet potato
pancakes. Creole- and Cajun-style dishes, Ocracoke broth-based chowder, and fresh local fish
prepared with creative flair star at dinner, and
the homemade desserts are to die for. The
restaurant moved to larger quarters on the Back
Road in 2013. Brunch $; dinner $$.

✐ ♿ ⛾ **Topless Oyster** (252-928-2800; www
.toplessoyster.com), 875 NC 12. Located in the
former Captain Ben's, a longtime local favorite,
this new restaurant specializes in oysters, served
raw, steamed, or in a variety of special dishes,
but always "topless," as well as local clams,
shrimp, fish, and Low Country boils, plus a
number of New Orleans–style dishes, such as
barbecue shrimp, authentic po'boys, and bread
pudding, perfected at the owners' previous
restaurant on the Gulf Coast. Gourmet burgers
and wood-smoked North Carolina barbecue
round out the menu. A few Captain Ben
favorites remain, including the famous Angus
prime rib. You can watch sports or live music,
play cornhole, or enjoy happy hour on the
screened porch. $–$$$.

EATING OUT ✐ ⛾ **Creekside Café** (252-928-
3606; www.ocracokecreekside.com), 621 NC 12.
Eat on the screened porch or on the patio at the
casual Creekside, now offering a variety of trop-
ical cocktails, as well as beer and champagne
drinks. The menu includes popular blackened
shrimp, burgers, seafood baskets, and locally
famous Key lime pie, all at reasonable prices.

QUICK TIP: If you'd like to re-create some
authentic Ocracoke recipes at home, check
out the website of the **Island Cookbook**
(www.islandcookbook.com). Be sure to try
Frances O'Neal's Fig Cake, for an authentic
taste of the island. Several local restau-
rants publish their best recipes as well,
including the Back Porch and Café Atlantic.

Live music on the patio in season. Breakfast
served 8–10 AM. $–$$.

✳ ⛾ (ᵖ) **Gaffer's Sport Pub** (252-928-3456;
www.gafferssportspub.com), 1050 NC 12. Enjoy
live music and sports on numerous TVs at this
fun pub, with a bar-oriented menu featuring a
dozen flavors of wings, burgers, nachos, and
daily drink specials. $–$$.

✐ ♿ ⛾ **Howard's Pub & Raw Bar** (252-928-
4441; www.howardspub.com), 1175 NC 12.
Open seasonally. For lots of Outer Banks visitors, a trip to Howard's is an annual pilgrimage. Some of them ride over on the free ferry and
never make it any further than this restaurant
and bar, which sits at the northern limit of Ocracoke Village. An on-site store sells Howard's
famous T-shirts, license plates, and other collectibles. Barbecued ribs, char-grilled rib eyes,
steamed shrimp, and the Ocracoke oyster
shooter (served with hot sauce and beer in a
souvenir glass) are the specialties, but everyone
will find something to like on the extensive
menu. After a day of fishing or beachcombing,
relax with a cold one from Howard's list of 200
beers on the big screened porch or up on the
rooftop deck with a view over the dunes to the
ocean. This is entertainment central, with live
bands, bar games, and sports on the numerous
TVs. Kids' meals come served on a take-home
Frisbee. $–$$.

✐ ♿ ↝ **Jason's Restaurant** (252-928-3434;
www.jasonsocracoke.com), 1110 NC 12. Closed
Sunday. Casual low-key spot is a favorite hangout for locals and visitors alike. The big bar here
offers several beers on tap, by the glass or
pitcher, plus a complete selection of all the most
popular bar food. Take a seat on the screened
porch and choose among pasta; vegetarian
lasagna; pizzas; steaks; jerk chicken; and fresh
local seafood. Tuesday is sushi night. Full bar.
$–$$.

✐ ♿ ⛾ **Jolly Roger Pub & Marina** (252-928-
3703; www.silverlakemotelandinn.com), 396 NC
12. A casual, open-air spot that sits right on the
docks in front of the Silver Lake Motel serves

sandwiches and baskets of fried or grilled fish, shrimp, and crab cakes, ribs, and wraps, plus burgers and some Mexican offerings. The best bet is the catch of the day. All tables are outside, on a deck or under umbrellas and awnings. Food comes in plastic baskets with throw-away utensils. The main attraction here, however, is the location, directly on the waterfront. In fair weather, a crowd gathers at cocktail hour to see what the charter fleet brings in. Live music adds to the sunset vibe. A great place to develop that Ocracoma. $$.

❋ ✐ **Pony Island Restaurant** (252-928-5701; www.ponyislandmotel.com), 51 Ocean View Road. Big breakfasts at reasonable prices make this place a favorite with families. Try the famous Pony Potatoes, topped with cheese, sour cream, and salsa, and the awesome biscuits. Open for breakfast and Sunday brunch all year, and for dinner during the summer season. Breakfast $; dinner $–$$.

✐ ⚒ ♈ ↝ **SMacNally's Raw Bar and Grill** (252-928-9999; www.smacnallys.com), 180 NC 12, Anchorage Inn Marina. Located on the docks at the Anchorage Inn Marina, this is a great place to kick back with a cold one while you check out the catch of the charter fishing boats. SMacNally's keeps its beer on ice and claims it's the coldest in town. Local seafood comes grilled or fried, but this place is known for its juicy half-pound Angus burgers dressed in a variety of toppings. Live music on the weekends features local songsmiths. $–$$.

BAG LUNCHES AND TAKE-OUT Many, if not most, of the restaurants in town offer take-out or have self-serve windows. This reflects the big need for bag lunches and picnics experienced by both locals and visitors. People stock up on provisions before heading to the beach, boarding a charter fishing boat, or taking the shuttle to Portsmouth Island. Getting a bag lunch to take on the state-run ferries is also a good idea, as they offer very limited food options—vending machines and coffee. If you have a ferry to catch or other time constraint, call ahead to order.

✐ ⚒ **Back Porch Lunchbox** (252-928-3651; www.backporchocracoke.com), 747 NC 12. Pick up a gourmet bag lunch for the ferry at this to-go window, located next to the Pony Island Motel. Unique sandwiches, drinks, ice cream, smoothies, and home-baked cookies are available. $.

✐ **Corner Crêpe** (252-588-2100), 110 Back Road. Dine alfresco at a café table under the trees at this food stand, at the corner of the

Back Road and Old Beach Road. Yet another spin-off from the creative Back Porch kitchen, this classic French crêperie serves sweet and savory crêpes beginning at 8 AM. You can get a glass of wine or bottle of sparkling water to complete the mood. $.

❋ **Eduardo's Taco Stand** (252-588-0202), 950 NC 12. Eduardo Chavez Perez, a top chef at the Back Porch, serves authentic Mexican cuisine, made with love, at this food truck, in the Variety Store parking lot. $–$$.

✐ **Fig Tree Bakery and Deli and the Sweet Tooth** (252-928-3481), 1015 NC 12. The Fig Tree/Sweet Tooth combo has what it takes to assemble a great picnic or bag lunch for ferry or beach. Try a deli sub or the pimento cheese sandwich, a Southern favorite. Baked goods and breakfast sandwiches also available, along with delish cinnamon rolls, homemade fudge, and chocolates. Outdoor shaded seating. $.

❋ (ᵞ) **Ocracoke Station Deli** (252-928-4031; www.facebook.com/OcracokeBeachcomber Campground), 990 NC 12. Locals drop by this gas station and deli in front of the Beachcomber Campground for breakfast biscuits and the latest news. A popular spot to pick up a box lunch of fried chicken, sub sandwiches, or local fried fish for the ferry, or a day of fishing or beach-combing, this is also the island's only gas station. Free Wi-Fi and charging station. $.

Thai Moon Carry-Out and Sushi (252-928-5100; www.thaimooncarryout.com), Spencer's Market, 589 NC 12. Take-out-only spot that earned a write-up in *Gourmet Magazine* serves traditional Thai dishes such as Tom Yum soup, curries, and pad thai, plus Asian takes on local seafood, sushi, and vegetarian choices. Cash only. $–$$.

COFFEE (ᵞ) **Live Oak Coffee** (252-928-0115; www.liveoakcoffeeocracoke.com), 271 NC 12. Located in a vintage house across the street from Community Square, this new coffee shop features espresso drinks, drip coffee, and pour-overs by the cup using sustainable single-origin beans from Counter Culture Coffee, plus Italian sodas, shaken iced teas, and lemonade. Free Wi-Fi, a 6 AM opening time, and a variety of baked goods sweeten the pot. $.

🍴 ((ᵖ)) **Ocracoke Coffee Co. & Island Smoothie** (252-928-7473; www.ocracoke coffee.com), 226 Back Road. With a wide porch, a shady yard, coffee drinks created with specially selected roasted beans, fruit smoothies, fresh baked goods, and free Wi-Fi, this coffee shop is a community gathering spot for island residents as well as visitors. The **Village Thrift Store** (252-928-4743), offering lots of clothing and used books, is located in the back of the coffee shop. Proceeds from the thrift shop benefit the Ocracoke Youth Center. $.

ICE CREAM ((ᵖ)) **The Slushy Stand** (252-928-1878), 473 NC 12. Located at the three-way junction where NC 12 meets the water, this landmark serves ice cream, frozen yogurt, homemade Italian gelato, breakfast items, and coffee. You can read the paper or check your e-mail on the porch. The stand rents bikes as well.

MARKETS **ABC Store** (252-928-3281; www.ncabc.com), 950 NC 12, Variety Store Shops. The state-run liquor store here has some unusual hours, especially off-season. Check for the latest.

Island Natural Health Store (252-928-6211), 170 Back Road. This shop within the Sunflower Center stocks supplements, teas, gluten-free breads, soy products, and organic foods, including fresh organic produce in season.

La Isla Mexican Grocery (252-928-2626), 588 NC 12, Spencer's Market. Small market carries Latin American groceries and treats.

The Vegetable Man, 782 NC 12. Look for fresh produce, local honey, and homemade jams and preserves being sold on the lawn of the East Carolina Bank, several days a week.

((ᵖ)) **Zillie's Island Pantry** (252-928-9036; www.zilliespantry.com), 538 Back Road. A godsend to gourmet cooks on the island, Zillie's stocks items from around the world, including pâtés, smoked salmon, cheeses, and much, much more. The shop also has a huge selection of wine and the island's best stock of imported beers and microbrews. Enjoy a beer or glass of wine on the Wine and Wi-Fi Deck or make reservations for the weekly wine tasting.

SEAFOOD ⋈ **Captain Puddle Duck's Steamer Pots** (252-588-0107; www.facebook .com/puddleducks.seafoodsteamerpots). Commercial fisherman Fletcher O'Neal and his family will assemble a pot of seafood for you to steam at your cottage, or will do it for you for an extra $10. He gathers the blue crabs, clams, and oysters (in season) himself.

⋈ **Fat Boys Fish Company** (252-921-0134), 300 Lighthouse Road. Seasonal market next to the historic Albert Styron Store sells local clams, crabs, and shrimp, plus whatever the charter fishing fleet brings in.

⋈ **Local Shellfish.** A couple of outfits on Ocracoke will deliver shellfish in quantity for clambakes or crab boils. Contact Jackson Seafood (252-588-0036; www.ocracokeclams .com) for wild harvested quahog clams and blue crabs, or Corky's Clams (252-928-2887 or 252-921-0351) for aquacultured clams in bulk.

🍴 ⋈ **Ocracoke Seafood** (252-928-5601; www .ocracokeseafood.com), 416 NC 12. Seafood arrives fresh off the boats that dock just behind this community market. Offerings vary by day and season, but you'll often find shrimp, crabs, clams, flounder, and mahimahi (dolphin) harvested in local waters, as well as two island favorites, spadefish and sheepshead, not often seen on menus.

✳ Entertainment

For a small island, Ocracoke makes a lot of music. The island traditions of impromptu back-porch jam sessions, potluck dinners, and community square dances have morphed into something the locals call Ocrafolk, a unique form of American music melded from old and new musical styles.

The original members of **Molasses Creek** (www.molassescreek.com), Gary and Kitty Mitchell and Fiddler Dave, are at the heart of the movement. The trio plays a fusion of folk, bluegrass, and humorous ballads, writing songs inspired by their location on Pamlico Sound. They began performing weekly at the Deepwater Theater and inviting local talents, such as native legend Martin Garrish, leader of the Ocracoke Rockers, and Roy Parsons, a local boy who toured with the Barnum & Bailey

Circus band way back when, to sit in. Band membership has changed and grown in the years since the band formed. Along the way Molasses Creek won an award on Garrison Keillor's *Prairie Home Companion*, and in recent years has toured extensively off-island.

In 1996 Gary Mitchell recorded a compilation album of songs by local musicians, called *Ocrafolk*. Its popularity led to recurring performances by the Ocrafolk Opry and to the ever-growing **Ocrafolk Festival of Music and Storytelling** (www.ocrafolkfestival.org), held every year in June.

Soundside Records (www.soundsiderecords.com), a label run by Molasses Creek members, offers an impressive list of discs by local and regional artists, including the popular series of Ocrafolk samplers.

During the summer you'll have several choices for live music most nights of the week. In addition to the Deepwater Theater shows, you can regularly find music at Howard's Pub, the Jolly Roger, Creekside Cafe, SMacNally's, the Topless Oyster, Gaffer's, Beachcomber Campground, and Dajio. Local bands to watch for include the Ocracoke Rockers, playing island-style rock 'n' roll, and Lou Castro and his Mighty Jazzcasters.

Deepwater Theater and Music Hall (252-921-0260 or 252-928-3411; www.deepwater theater.com), 25 School Road. From June to September, you can catch some of the brightest stars of the local music scene at the Deepwater Theater, an intimate space that regulars compare to an overgrown screen porch. While schedules vary every year, performers usually include **Captain Ron Temple** and his Rumgagger Pirate Show (www.schoonerwindfall .com), Noah Paley and songwriting duo **Coyote** (www.coyotemusic.net), *Prairie Home Companion* award winners **Molasses Creek** (www .molassescreek.com), and the ever-evolving **Ocrafolk Opry.** Classes in yoga and tai chi are also held at the theater.

Ocrafolk School (252-928-4280; www.ocrafolk school.org). Weeklong seminars by island experts offer classes ranging from basketry, cooking, and sea chanteys to Ocracoke history, ecology, and sailing. Students participate in community events including evening sings, square dances, and storytelling.

> **LOCAL UPDATES**
>
> Two great options for keeping up with local events and musical gigs on the island are the online newsletter **Ocracoke Current** (www.ocracokecurrent.com) and the non-profit **Ocracoke Community Radio WOVV FM 90.1** (252-928-WOVV; www .wovv.org). Broadcasting 24 hours a day, the radio's studio is on the harborfront, across from the Anchorage Motel, and welcomes visitors daily 10–1. Programming features an eclectic mix of local and regional music, plus interviews with local celebs and coverage of island events. You can listen live online.

✳ Selective Shopping

Most shops on Ocracoke Island are small and eclectic, mixing practical items with souvenirs for visiting tourists. The "necessities" can be found in general-store-type shops, which carry a large variety of different and useful groceries and goods, but perhaps not the selection of brands that people are used to at home. Locals make regular runs "up the beach" across the Hatteras Ferry to get items unavailable on Ocracoke, returning as quickly as possible with full trunks and sighs of relief.

ANTIQUES Annabelle's Florist and Antiques (252-928-4541; www.annabellesofocracoke.com), 324 Back Road. Local floral designer and folklorist Chester Lynn sells treasures and artifacts related to Ocracoke's past, as well as seedlings of the island's some dozen varieties of figs.

Ocracoke Restoration (252-928-2669 or 252-291-0060; www.ocracokerestoration.com), 341 NC 12. Fascinating shop in an old cottage stocks a huge selection of English antique stained glass, plus vintage jewelry, wrought-iron yard art, and locally made spa products.

ARTS AND CRAFTS The funky personality, natural beauty, and relative isolation of the island have led many creative folk to settle here. Information on Ocracoke's galleries and artists, plus gallery openings, the annual Artwalk, and other events, can be found at www.ocracokecurrent.com.

Bella Fiore Pottery (252-928-2826), 80 Back Road. The vivid hues of Sarah Fiore's microwave- and oven-safe stoneware pottery reflect the beauty of the island environment. Watercolors, silk mobiles, handblown glass, and other locally created artwork also on display.

Deepwater Pottery (252-928-3936; www.bookstobered.com), 34 School Road. Dedicated to artful living, Deepwater is a focus of Ocracoke culture. The pottery shares the historic 1898 Dezzie Bragg house with **Books to Be Red,** and the **Deepwater Theater** is next door.

Down Creek Gallery (252-928-4400; www.downcreekgallery.com), 260 NC 12. This waterfront gallery, winner of a 2009 award from *Niche Magazine* as one of the Top 25 Retailers for American Craft in North America, represents over 125 local and regional artists and craftspeople. Art openings during the summer season showcase local artists.

Downpoint Decoys (252-928-3269), 340 NC 12. David O'Neal, a noted carver and collector of decoys, carries on the historic traditions of his forefathers. The shop is full of decoys, old fishing lures, scrimshaw, and other nautical memorabilia.

The Gathering Place (252-928-7180; www.ocracokegatheringplace.com), 290 Sunset Drive. Unique wooden pens and darts handmade on Ocracoke mix with handcrafted folding knives from around the world, at this small shop.

Island Artworks (252-928-3892; www.islandartworks.com), 89 British Cemetery Road. Artist Kathleen O'Neal's original jewelry, made of precious metals, gemstones, and beachcombed treasures, forms the heart of a collection of works by local and regional artists.

Over the Moon (252-928-3555; www.overthemoongiftshop.com), 64 British Cemetery Road. Handmade arts and crafts of every kind, selected by Cathy Scarborough, a sixth-generation islander, crowd this old island house.

Pamlico Gifts (252-928-6561), 486 Lighthouse Road. In her cute shop, at the end of a path next to the lighthouse, Elizabeth Parsons sells shell art, folk-art paintings, hand-crocheted bags, decoys, and hand-etched glass created by herself and her late husband, Roy, plus much more, including CDs of Roy's music. Roy, a much-loved local treasure known for his model boats and yodeling singing style, passed in September 2007.

Secret Garden Gallery (252-928-2598), 72 Back Road. Jewelry designer Barbara Hardy and her husband, Ray, a painter and collage artist, exhibit their own art, plus works by many other artists, including 20 jewelry designers. An upstairs gallery hosts rotating exhibits.

Sunflower Center for the Arts (252-921-0188), 170 Back Road. Carol and Jim O'Brien present their original handcrafted jewelry as well as a large collection of estate pieces. The upstairs gallery is devoted to art and glass by local artists. Classes in arts and crafts are also offered, and there's a herbal pharmacy on-site.

🐾 ⸙ **Tapestry, a Studio on Ocracoke** (252-928-0113; www.hydecountyhotline.org), 587 NC 12, Spencer's Market. Unique woven rugs, hangings, handbags, and other crafts made of worn-out clothing and other recycled fabrics, as well as local crafts sold on consignment, crowd this studio, where all proceeds benefit the Hyde County Hotline for crisis intervention and services to victims of domestic abuse and sexual violence.

Tree Top Studio (252-928-9997), 402 Back Road. Featuring paintings and photography by local artists, this little studio also does professional framing and sells organic produce.

Village Craftsmen. See *To See.*

Woccocon Nursery and Gifts (252-928-3811), 439 Lighthouse Road. Della Williams, the sister of Elizabeth Parsons, whose shop, Pamlico Gifts, is just across the road, preserves many old Ocracoke crafts and sells the results at this shop, next to the Assembly of God Church. Fruit butters, fig jams and preserves, peach rum jam, plus needlepoint, beaded jewelry, and hand-loomed bags, are a few of the treasures found here.

BOOKS AND MUSIC Books to Be Red (252-928-3936; www.bookstobered.com), 34 School Road. Sharing a historic building with the Deepwater Pottery, this small bookstore has an excellent selection of local and regional book titles and music CDs. Redheaded owner Leslie Ann Lanier stocks her shelves with titles ranging from light beach reading to historical research, with a special section of books and puzzles for children. If you prefer to write your own story, you'll find a nice selection of journals here, as well.

Ocracoke Preservation Society Museum Gift Shop (252-928-7375; www.ocracokepreservation .org), 49 Water Plant Road. The museum's gift shop stocks a range of books relating to Ocracoke for

BOOKS BY OCRACOKERS

The people who live on Ocracoke year-round are a creative bunch and find plenty of time to write during the long off-season. Some books to look for:

Digging Up Uncle Evans: History, Ghost Tales & Stories from Ocracoke Island (www.blacksquall books.com), the latest from Philip Howard;

Hoi Toide on the Outer Banks: The Story of the Ocracoke Brogue, by Walt Wolfram and Natalie Schilling-Estes, the definitive 1997 work published by Chapel Hill's University of North Carolina Press;

The Lady and the Moon, a novel written by Mary Chandler Newell, a co-owner of the Island Inn;

Ocracoke Odyssey: A Naturalist's Reflections on her Home by the Sea, by Pat Gerber;

Ocracokers, written by Alton Ballance, historian and owner of the Crew Inn, is considered the definitive book about the islanders and their culture; and

The Sheltering Cedar, a children's book written by Anne Marshall Runyon, about a Christmas Eve storm that threatens the wildlife on Ocracoke. For ages four to eight.

all ages, plus cookbooks published by local churches and restaurants, DVDs of local storytellers, and music CDs by local musicians. Sales benefit the society.

Village Thrift Store (252-928-4743), 226 Back Road. Proceeds from the sale of used books (and other items) at this shop, in the back of Ocracoke Coffee, benefit the Ocracoke Youth Center.

FASHION Harborside Gift Shop and Art Gallery (252-928-3111; www.ocracokeharborside.com), 229 NC 12. Shop at the Harborside Motel carries top-label resort wear, batik dresses, popular Sea Dog T-shirts, and the original island art of Douglas Hoover.

↬ **Natural Selections Hemp Shop** (252-928-4367; www.ocracokeislandhemp.com), 35 School Road. Environmentally conscious shop carries a wide range of clothing, handbags, hats, and even snacks made of hemp, bamboo, and other natural fibers, plus an all-natural line of soaps made on Ocracoke.

((ツ)) **Negozio** (252-928-4351; www.ocracokeislandinn.com), 25 Lighthouse Road. Shop inside the Island Inn carries jewelry handmade by owner Mary Chandler Storrs, plus fun fashion and accessories, lighthouse souvenirs, and a large selection of beer, wine, and cold drinks, to take out or try on-site. Several wines come from the vineyard owned by inn operator Thomas Storrs.

SHOPPING DESTINATIONS Back Road Loop, British Cemetery and Back roads. Over a dozen interesting shops and galleries line these shady lanes, and traffic is generally light, making it ideal for a stroll or a bike ride. Here you'll find a gourmet restaurant, a neat coffeehouse and bookstore, and the Ocracoke Library, with Internet access and a porch full of rocking chairs.

Captain's Landing Shops, NC 12 and Silver Lake. Clustered around Captain's Landing Hotel are several shops, most in historic buildings that once housed the post office, which has since moved to the north end of town.

Community Square Shops and Dock, NC 12 and Silver Lake. Centered on the beloved Community Store, the shops and dock at this location have been the center of Ocracoke life since the days when mail boats, once the island's only contact with the outside world, tied up here. Today, the complex houses the **Working Watermen's Exhibit,** as well as several shops, including the Ice Cream and Fudge Store, Island Quest Gifts, Mark's Dogs, and the Black Schooner Nautical Store. The **Pagoda** (252-902-5058), a tobacco store carrying fine cigars, homemade candles, blown glass, biodegradable flip-flops, and more, has a small shady smoking deck out back where you can light up that cigar.

❋ **Ocracoke Variety Store and True Value Hardware** (252-928-4911; www.ocracokevarietystore .com), 950 NC 12. A one-stop store where you'll find groceries, fresh meats, beer, wine, and ice, plus souvenirs and beach, boating, and camping gear. The ABC store is located here, as well as a gourmet Mexican food truck. Check the bulletin board for local events.

The Shops at Spencer's Market, NC 12 and School Road. This complex, set a bit back from the harbor, contains an international selection of shops and a unique nonprofit weaving shop.

SPECIAL SHOPS **Albert Styron Store** (252-928-2609), 300 Lighthouse Road. This 1920 landmark on the National Register of Historic Places lives on, run by Albert's granddaughter, thanks to its initials, offering T-shirts with the popular ASS and Fat Boys Fish Company logos, plus a wide variety of wine, gourmet food items, gifts, and ice cream. The leather-bound ledgers dating to 1925, antique cash register, and original adding machine, feed scales, and roll-top desk, raise Styron's to near-museum status.

Black Schooner Nautical Store (252-928-SAIL; www.schoonerwindfall.com), Community Square, 284 NC 12. The new shore-side office of the schooner *Windfall II* and shipjack *Wilma Lee* offers a wealth of nautical art from scrimshaw to ropework, plus locally crafted items made from salvaged parts of the original *Windfall,* including tote bags made from the old sails and ship models mounted on mahogany hatches.

Captain's Cargo (252-928-9991; www.thecaptainslanding.com), 326 NC 12. Former post office on the Captain's Landing property displays an eclectic collection of nautical gifts, shells, bath products, and island arts and crafts, tucked into the old postal boxes.

Home Grown Hettie's (252-333-2597), 107 Aretta Street. Plant lovers will enjoy a visit to this off-the-beaten-track nursery that specializes in plants that grow well on the island, including herbs, vegetables, succulents, and flowering plants.

Island Quest Gifts (252-573-1126; www.islandquest.us), 276 NC 12. Little shop in Community Square sells surfer jewelry you can wear into the ocean, one-of-a-kind metal art, and a variety of gifts. You can score lunch outside at **Mark's Dogs,** a New York City–style pushcart offering Sabrett natural casing hotdogs, smoked sausages, and jumbo pretzels.

Island Ragpicker (252-928-7571), 515 NC 12. Seemingly assembled from driftwood, the 10 rooms of this shop, near the Slushy Stand, contain original hand-loomed Ragpicker rugs, created here since 1973, plus crafts, apparel, wind chimes, and the Title Wave Room, filled with cards and books of local interest.

Mermaid's Folly (252-928-RAGS; www.mermaidsfolly.com), 259 NC 12. The former owners of the Island Ragpicker present a selection of their best-selling "sea-spirited" clothing.

Ocracoke Island Woodworks (252-928-7001; www.ocracokeislandwoodworks.com), 158 Ocean View Road. Comfortable Adirondack chairs, swings, and other outdoor furniture are handcrafted by local Ocracokers from white cedar, the same wood used to build boats. It doesn't splinter and looks better the longer is sits out in the weather. You can see examples of this furniture at the Ocracoke Variety Store.

Pirates Chest Gift Shop (252-928-4992), 11 Back Road at NC 12. Fun shop has a huge selection of shells and driftwood, plus an upstairs full of discounted T-shirts.

T & J Outfitters (256-541-7891; www.tjoutfitters.com), 285 NC 12. You can rent bikes, golf carts, kayaks, and surfboards at this stand, across from Community Square, but there's also great flea-market-style browsing amid beach wear, pirate gear, and a variety of bamboo items, such as tiki torches and gigs for flounder fishing, plus great homemade ice cream.

Teach's Hole Pirate Specialty Shop (252-928-1718; www.teachshole.com), 935 NC 12 at West End Road. All things pirate are on sale at this shop, stocking over 1,000 items of "piratical piratephernalia."

✸ Special Events

April: **Portsmouth Village Homecoming** (www.friendsofportsmouthisland.org), Portsmouth Village, Cape Lookout National Seashore. Held on even-numbered years, this old-fashioned homecoming brings together descendants of Portsmouth residents and visitors for music, fellowship, and a picnic-style dinner. Open to all.

Early May: **Ocracoke Invitational Surf Fishing Tournament** (252-928-5491; www.hydecountync.gov), Ocracoke Community Center. Some 400 anglers hit the beach for this competition, which concludes with a big community dinner open to all.

May: **British Cemetery Military Honors Ceremony** (www.hydecounty.org). Graveside ceremony at the British Cemetery is followed by a reception and pig pickin' at the Ocracoke Community Center.

Late May: **Ocracoke Volunteer Firemen's Ball** (www.ocracokevfd.org). A pig pickin' is followed by live and silent actions, and a dance at the Ocracoke Community Center.

Early June: **Ocrafolk Music and Storytelling Festival** (252-928-4280 www.ocrafolkfestival .org), Deepwater Theater and other venues. A free weekend of acoustic music, storytelling, art exhibits, live auction, potluck dinner, and a community square dance.

Early July: **Ocracoke Island Independence Day Celebration** (www.ocracokevillage.com). A sand sculpture contest, patriotic parade, and classic car contest mark the Fourth of July.

October: **Ocrafolk School** (252-928-1541; www.ocrafolkschool.org), Deepwater Theater. Weeklong school offers classes in traditional music, arts, crafts, cooking, and history, plus an immersion in local culture.

DID YOU KNOW? Ocracoke Island for many years was noted for its fireworks display on the Fourth of July. Tragically, this tradition ended in July 2009 when a truck full of fireworks exploded near the ferry docks while being unloaded. Three people were killed. The investigation that followed resulted in new safety regulations that canceled fireworks shows up and down the Banks for several years. In 2012, July Fourth fireworks returned to Hatteras Island, and many locals and return visitors hope that Ocracoke may yet reboot this treasured tradition.

Late October: **Annual Halloween Carnival and Spook Walk,** Ocracoke School. **Ocracoke/ Hatteras Blackbeard's Pirate Jamboree** (www.piratejamboree.com). Cross-island festival celebrates the region's maritime and pirate history.

November: **Ocrafolk Festival Fall Fundraiser Concert** (252-928-7375; www.ocrafolkfestival.org), Ocracoke Community Center. Thanksgiving weekend tradition.

December: **Island Caroling** (252-928-5541; www.villagecraftsmen.blogspot.com). Meet at the United Methodist Church. **Ocracoke Seafood Company Oyster Roast and Shrimp Steam** (252-928-5601; www.ocracokewatermen.org), Ocracoke Fish House. **Wassail and Tree Lighting** (252-928-7375; www.ocracokepreservation.org), Ocracoke Preservation Museum.

The Crystal Coast and South Banks

6

THE CRYSTAL COAST
AND SOUTH BANKS

THE CRYSTAL COAST, sometimes known as the Southern Outer Banks is a place of contrasts. Recorded history here stretches back over 300 years and has always had a close relationship with the sea. Beaufort, North Carolina's third oldest town, was an early seaport of vital importance to the state during the Age of Sail. Pirates and privateers made cameo appearances throughout the region's history, including the infamous Blackbeard, who wrecked his flagship, *Queen Anne's Revenge,* on the shoals off Bogue Banks. Commercial fishing and boatbuilding have been the backbone of the economy here for centuries.

In 1858, the railroad arrived when former North Carolina governor John Motley Morehead extended the rails to the deepwater port he built across the inlet from Beaufort. The community that grew up around the port took its name from the visionary governor, becoming Morehead City. The area's first beach resort, Atlantic Beach, was established on Bogue Banks across from Morehead City to serve travelers arriving by rail.

Atlantic Beach and Emerald Isle, communities at either end of Bogue Banks, evolved into popular vacation destinations for families and servicemen from the Marine Corps at nearby Camp Lejeune and Cherry Point air station. Today, Bogue Banks is home to a string of increasingly upscale resort communities catering to vacationers attracted by the area's largely undiscovered white-sand beaches and family-friendly activities. However, the South Banks have another face. The area north of Beaufort, called Down East by locals, has been among the last along the coast to be caught up in development. Here families still carve decoys, build boats, and sew quilts as their ancestors have done for generations. Just offshore lie the islands of Core and Shackleford banks, areas once home to thriving communities that were swept away by storms in the 1890s. Today, National Park Service caretakers and herds of wild ponies are the only year-round inhabitants of these lonely isles.

GUIDANCE The **Visitor's Center for Carteret County and the Crystal Coast** (252-726-8148 or 1-877-206-0929; www.crystalcoastnc.org), 3409 Arendell Street, Morehead City, has helpful counselors and lots of local information, as well as restrooms, a boat ramp, and a pleasant picnic area overlooking Bogue Sound.

A second visitors center is located in Cedar Point (252-393-3100), 262 NC 58, just before the bridge to Emerald Isle.

GETTING THERE *By Air:* Commercial air service is available at:

Albert J. Ellis Airport (OAJ) (910-324-1100; www.onslowcountync.gov/OAJ), Richlands. This airport, operated by Onslow County, is about 60 miles from Beaufort.

TOP 10 DON'T MISS: CRYSTAL COAST

1. Take a boat ride to Shackleford Banks to pick up shells and see wild horses.
2. Plan a progressive dinner by visiting some of Beaufort's numerous fine eateries.
3. Paddle—or take a boat taxi—over to the Rachel Carson nature trail on Carrot Island.
4. Stroll the downtown waterfront in Morehead City, checking out the artwork, the seafood restaurants, and the otters.
5. Take a day trip to Jacksonville, North Carolina, to visit the moving Beirut Memorial and other monuments at the Marine Corps' Camp Lejeune (www.lejeune.marines.mil) or to follow the African American Heritage Trail (www.onslowcountytourism.com).
6. Hunt down a Bogue Sound watermelon, chill, and enjoy.
7. Climb the Cape Lookout Lighthouse.
8. Visit the iconic Circle at Atlantic Beach and take in a concert at historic Fort Macon.
9. Look for endangered red-cockaded woodpeckers among the longleaf pines at Patsy Pond Nature Trail.
10. Make the journey out to Bear Island in Hammocks Beach State Park to see a truly unspoiled dune system—and swim on an uninhabited beach.

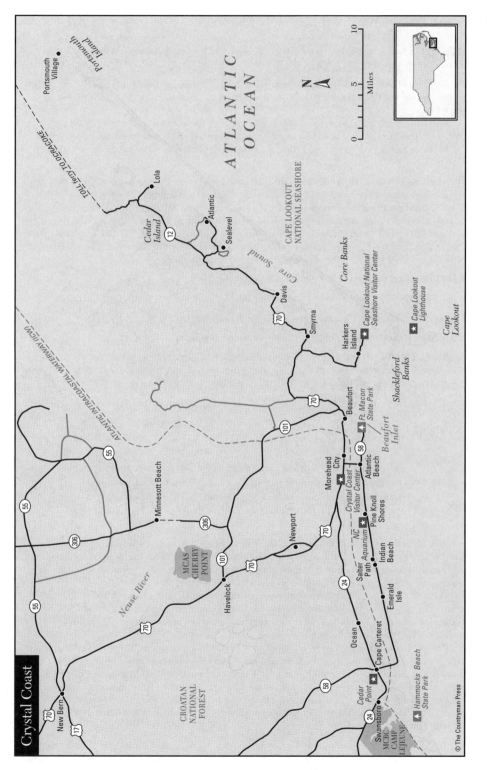

Crystal Coast

© The Countryman Press

Craven Regional Airport (EWN) (252-638-8591; www.newbernairport.com), New Bern. About 45 miles from Beaufort.

Wilmington International Airport (ILM) (910-341-4125; www.flyilm.com), Wilmington. About 85 miles from Beaufort.

By Car: From the west, US 70E, a good four-lane, is the most direct route from Raleigh and points west to the Crystal Coast, crossing both I-40 and I-95 along the way. Drive time to Beaufort is about three hours.

From the south, US 17 runs from Wilmington north to the Virginia border, passing through many old Inner Banks towns. To reach the Crystal Coast, turn east on NC 24 in Jacksonville.

From the north, NC 12 arrives via the Ocracoke–Cedar Island ferry, then heads south to meet US 70.

By Train and Bus: In 2012, **Amtrak** (1-800-USA-RAIL; www.amtrak.com) began a new Thruway bus service to Morehead City, connecting with the daily Amtrak Palmetto train running between New York City and Savannah. The bus makes stops in Havelock, New Bern, and Greenville before arriving in Wilson, North Carolina, to meet both the north- and southbound Palmetto. Buses depart from the restored 1905 train station (252-808-0440) at 1001 Arendell Street, used as a community center by the Downtown Morehead City Revitalization Association (www.downtownmoreheadcity.com). The return of passenger train service to the area is one of the organization's longterm goals.

GETTING AROUND Area rental car companies include:

Avis (252-247-5577; www.avis.com), Morehead City.

Enterprise (252-240-0218; www.enterprise.com), Morehead City.

Stars Auto Rentals (252-728-2323), 150 Airport Road, Beaufort.

MEDICAL EMERGENCY Carteret General Hospital (252-808-6000; www.carteretgeneral.com), 3500 Arendell Street, Morehead City. A full-service hospital offering inpatient, outpatient, and emergency services 24 hours a day all year.

DOWN EAST

> *A Downeaster is best defined as one who prefers salt fish (notably spots)*
> *for breakfast. But mostly it is a state of mind, where the people like wood-*
> *en boats and build them in back yards beneath big live oak trees . . .*
> —FROM WHEN THE WATER SMOKES BY BOB SIMPSON

AS YOU LEAVE THE CEDAR ISLAND FERRY from Ocracoke, you enter a region of marshes and forests dotted with small communities where generations of Down East families continue their traditions of boatbuilding, decoy carving, hunting, fishing, and farming. The people here retain an exceptional sense of place and are actively involved in preserving their way of life.

The Down East region includes many small unincorporated towns, spread on the shores and streams that lace this area. Most are dedicated to fishing, and during much of their history could be reached only by boat. Some, such as Portsmouth on North Core and Diamond City on Shackleford, no longer exist, swept away by storms or passed over by history.

Harkers Island is the largest community Down East, and there is no better place to discover the region's maritime traditions than the **Core Sound Waterfowl Museum and Heritage Center** located here. Next door, the recently expanded **Cape Lookout National Seashore Visitor Center** offers exhibits on the ecology, history, and culture of the region. Island Road, the main drag on Harkers, is lined with marinas offering ferry trips to the South Core Banks and Cape Lookout, and to Shackleford Banks where the wild horses live, uninhabited islands that draw tourists, beachcombers, and surf fishers year-round.

GUIDANCE To become acquainted with the history and lore of these fascinating small villages just north of Beaufort, take the virtual **Down East Tour** (www.downeasttour.com), developed by members of the Core Sound Waterfowl and Heritage Museum. Another online tour of the Core Sound region is maintained by the **North Carolina Folklife Institute** at www.ncfolk.org.

POST OFFICES Many of the little towns Down East have a U.S. Post Office and a unique zip code:

Atlantic (252-225-5081), 755 Seashore Drive. Zip code: 28511.

Cedar Island (252-225-2131), 3553 Cedar Island Road. Zip code: 28520.

Harkers Island (252-728-2924), 823 Island Road. Zip code: 28531.

Sea Level (252-225-4791), 751 US 70. Zip code: 28577.

Smyrna (252-729-4951), 467 US 70. Zip code: 28579.

PUBLIC RESTROOMS Public facilities are available at the ferry docks on Cedar Island, and at the National Seashore Welcome Center on Harkers Island.

PUBLIC LIBRARY Down East Public Library (252-728-1333; carteret.cpclib.org), 702 US 70, Otway. Computers available for public use, plus many classes, and a used-book sale on Friday and Saturday.

GETTING THERE *By Car:* From the south, the Down East communities are reached by following US 70 from Beaufort. NC 12, leading out to the ferry docks, branches off from US 70, passing through many miles of marsh and forest before reaching the dock, with no services along the way— not a fun trip in the dark. At the end of the road, on Cedar Island, there's a convenience store, the Driftwood Motel and Restaurant, a campground and boat ramp, plus many miles of unspoiled beach.

By Ferry: The **North Carolina State Ferry** (1-800-BYFERRY; www.ncferry.org) makes between three and six trips a day between Ocracoke and Cedar Island, depending on the season. Scenic Byway NC 12 crosses over with the ferry. The trip takes about two and a quarter hours. One-way fares at the time of publication are $1 for pedestrians; $3 for a bike and rider; $10 for motorcycles, scooters, golf carts, and ATVs; and $15 for passenger cars, with higher fees for longer vehicles and trailers. Reservations are strongly recommended but not required. You can reserve online at the state ferry website, or by calling 1-800-293-3779.

The ferries are sometimes canceled due to rough weather or other emergencies. If you need to check on whether the ferry is running, call the Cedar Island terminal at 252-225-7411, or the Ocracoke terminal at 252-928-1665.

GETTING AROUND NC 12, part of the Outer Banks National Scenic Byway, comes over the ferry from Ocracoke, then runs south across Cedar Island and through the forests and marshes of the Cedar Island Wildlife Refuge, before intersecting with US 70.

US 70, one of the major east–west highways in the nation before the interstate system was built, begins in Arizona and runs 2,385 miles before ending in the little Down East community of Atlantic.

MEDICAL EMERGENCY Eastern Carteret Medical Center (252-225-1134), US 70, Sea Level. Down East clinic associated with Carteret General.

❊ To See

❊ ⅃ **Cape Lookout National Seashore Harkers Island Visitor Center** (252-728-2250; www.nps .gov/calo), 1800 Island Road, Harkers Island. Open daily 9–5, except Christmas and New Year's days. Located at the very end of Harkers Island, this visitors center provides an introduction to the Cape Lookout islands. An award-winning documentary, *Ribbon of Sand,* is shown daily. Nearby on the waterfront, several ferry services will take you across to South Core Banks, where you can climb the lighthouse from mid-May to late September. Admission to the visitors center is free; the ferry across the inlet costs $10 and up depending on the season; tickets to climb the lighthouse cost $4–8. For more things to do in the national seashore, see "Cape Lookout and the Core Banks."

❧ **Core Sound Decoy Carvers Guild Hall** (252-838-8818; www.decoyguild.com), 1574 Harkers Island Road, Harkers Island. Local carvers and waterfowling enthusiasts gather at the historic H. Curt Salter Building, located at the foot of the Harkers Island bridge. Classes for adults and children are available, as well as decoy merchandise. Thursdays are Guild Carving Day; stop by to meet the carvers and talk decoys. Kids Carving Days are held on the third Saturday of the month; preregistration required. Free.

✳ ♿ **Core Sound Waterfowl Museum and Heritage Center** (252-728-1500; www.core sound.com), 1785 Island Road, Harkers Island. Open Monday–Saturday 10–5, Sunday 2–5; closed Easter Sunday, Thanksgiving Day, Christmas Day, and New Year's Day. Near the end of the road on Harkers Island, this important new museum is filled with hand-carved decoys, boat models, quilts, and other artifacts donated by local families. Each of the Down East communities has its own exhibit, and traditional decoy carvers and quilters demonstrate their crafts on-site. Outside, a nature trail leads to a pond frequented by migrating waterfowl. Several full-size boats built locally have been restored, including the *Jean Dale*, a 40-foot Harkers Island sink netter with a classic flared bow, handbuilt by the legendary Brady Lewis. The center sponsors a full schedule of activities featuring Down East cooking, music, and crafts, including the Waterfowl Weekend every December. Climb the lookout tower for a great view of the lighthouse. $5.

CARVING DECOYS IS A WAY OF LIFE FOR MANY DOWN EASTERS.

James A. Rose Model Boat Shop (252-728-1742), Harkers Island. Rose, a former boatbuilder and North Carolina Heritage Award winner, devotes his retirement to creating incredibly detailed and accurate models, based on the traditional boats of Harkers Island. To arrange a visit to his shop, contact the Core Sound Waterfowl Museum, where several of his models are on display.

Snug Harbor on Nelson Bay (252-225-4411; www.snugharboronnelsonbay.com), 272 US 70, Sea Level. Now an upscale retirement community, this originally was Sailor's Snug Harbor, a home for retired sailors founded on Staten Island in 1833. The sailors were moved to this location in 1976, while the original location in New York became an outstanding cultural center. The Sea Level facility has lovely grounds with several statues.

THE CORE SOUND WATERFOWL MUSEUM PRESERVES THE HERITAGE OF THE DOWN EAST COMMUNITIES.

BOATING The North Carolina Wildlife Resources Commission (www.ncwildlife.org) has boat ramps at ♿ **Straits Landing** (1648 Harkers Island Road), at the northern end of the bridge to Harkers Island; and at ♿ **Oyster Creek** (1300 US 70, Davis), into Core Sound; at **Salters Creek** (200 Wildlife Ramp Road, Sea Level), under the US 70 highrise bridge; and at **Cedar Island** (115 Driftwood Drive), into Pamlico Sound. No public facilities at any of these ramps.

The **Cedar Island National Wildlife Refuge** (252-225-2511 or 252-926-4021; www.fws.gov/cedarisland) maintains two free boat ramps. One, at the end of Lola Road past the refuge office at the east end of Cedar Island, gives access to the sounds; the other, at the Thorofare Bridge on NC 12, puts you into the heart of the marsh. These are available for both powerboats and kayaks or other unmotorized craft.

On Harkers Island, you can use boat ramps at several marinas for a fee, including the **Harkers Island Fishing Center** (252-728-3907; www.harkersmarina.com), **Rose's Marina** (252-728-2868; www.rosesvacationrentals.com), and **Cape Pointe Marina** (252-728-6181; www.capepointemarina.com).

A harbor of refuge is located near the mouth of the North River at the southern end of Harkers Island.

DRIVING TOUR Follow the **Outer Banks National Scenic Byway** (www.outerbanksscenicbyway.org) through the small towns and fishing villages of Down East, where you'll see working fish houses, docks full of fishing boats, yards full of crab pots and skiffs, plus many historic structures. The **Down East Green Map** (www.greenmap.org) identifies numerous points of interest and maritime history along the route.

FISHING A public fishing pier is located on the small island that sits in the middle of the bridge to Harkers Island. A North Carolina fishing license is required. On Harkers Island, you can buy a fishing license at **Billy's Grocery** (252-728-4393; 1016 Island Road) or Harkers Island Tackle and Trading Post (see listing that follows). The inshore waters near Harkers Island are considered some of the finest on the East Coast for light tackle and fly-fishing, especially in the late fall when the giant false albacore (little tunny or "fat Alberts") run, and in the late summer when tarpon enter the sounds.

A number of Down East charter captains will take you out for light tackle or saltwater fly-fishing. False albacore, king and Spanish mackerel, cobia, red drum, trout, lady fish, and shark are the most popular catches. The shallow waters are also great for flounder gigging. You can even fish for them with bow and arrow.

Harkers Island Tackle and Trading Post (252-269-6967 or 252-838-1126; www.harkersislandtackle.net), 989 Island Road, Harkers Island. Full-service bait and tackle shop books a variety of fishing charters, including night flounder gigging, day or night bow fishing after rays, old drum fishing, and inshore and offshore charters.

Last Cast Charters at Harkers Island Fishing Center (252-728-3907; www.harkersmarina.com), 1002 Harkers Island Road, Harkers Island.

Noah's Ark Fishing and Tour Charters (252-342-6911 or 252-504-3139; www.noahsarkfishingcharters.com), at Cape Pointe Marina, 1390 Harkers Island Road, Harkers Island.

HORSEBACK RIDING Outer Banks Riding Stables (252-225-1185; www.horsebackridingonthebeach.com), 120 Driftwood Drive, Cedar Island. Rides aboard well-trained horses offer opportunities to trot and canter, and ride through the water on the open beach. Located next to the Cedar Island ferry docks.

HUNTING Hunting waterfowl during the winter months is a treasured tradition among Down East families. Loons were a favorite target, both for eating and for their leg bones, used to make fishing lures, until loon shooting was outlawed. Today, huge numbers of ducks, geese, and swans arrive each year to winter in the marshes and protected waters. The **Cedar Island National Wildlife Refuge** (www.fws.gov/cedarisland) has 400 acres open to waterfowl hunters with the proper permits. Consult its website for more info. Hunting is also allowed on the Core Banks of the Cape Lookout National Seashore.

Lucky Duck's Guide Service (252-723-8711; www.capelookout.com), 476 US 70, Bettie. Capt. Bernie Corwin will accompany you on a hunt for ducks or geese. Dogs are welcome. Corwin also offers light tackle and saltwater fly-fishing, including fall trips after fat Alberts.

KAYAKING Sea kayaking is a popular activity in the region. You can launch on the sandy beach at the picnic area in front of the NPS visitors center on Harkers Island, or at nearby Shell Point at the end of Island Road, and park your car in the large picnic area lot. It's a 2- to 3-mile paddle over to the Core Banks from this spot, and conditions can sometimes be hazardous. The National Park Service asks that you file a float plan before setting off. Paddle maps are available inside the center. The many streams and canals that lace the Down East region are ideal for kayaking and stand-up paddleboarding. The canals through the black needlerush marsh of the Cedar Island National Wildlife Refuge are good spots for birding or fishing from a kayak. Other popular spots to launch kayaks include the beach at Cedar Island and the boat ramp areas in Cedar Island National Wildlife Refuge.

SHELL POINT ON HARKERS ISLAND

♿ **Cape Lookout Cabins & Camps Ferry Service** (252-729-9751; www.calocabins-camps inc.net), 125 Grady Lane, Davis. You can rent a kayak here, or put your craft aboard the ferry for a day of paddling over on Core Banks.

Down East Kayaks (252-838-1336; www.down eastkayaks.com), 1604 Harkers Island Road, Straits. You can rent kayaks at this shop, on the north side of the Harkers Island bridge, with an easy launch into the North River, or sign up for a guided ecotour.

WATER SPORTS Shell Point, at the end of Island Road on Harkers Island, is a popular spot for windsurfers to launch. You can park in the lot at the NPS visitors center. The beach at Cedar Island is another option.

✳ Green Space

BEACHES Public beaches are located at the southeast end of the Harkers Island drawbridge and next to the ferry docks on Cedar Island, but neither offers any facilities besides parking. Most beach fans head to Core or Shackleford banks for their day on the sand.

TRAILS Cedar Island National Wildlife Refuge (252-225-2511 or 252-926-4021; www.fws.gov /cedarisland), 829 Lola Road, Cedar Island. This refuge, about 40 miles north of Beaufort, contains nearly 15,000 acres, about 10,000 of it brackish marsh, the rest pocosin and woodland. Kayaks or canoes are the best way to explore the black needlerush marshes, and the best time to visit is in winter when huge numbers of redhead ducks are in residence and the local mosquitoes are least fierce. A number of gated, unimproved roads can be used for hiking, biking, or horseback riding. The refuge is open during daylight hours. No camping or motorized vehicles are allowed.

FAST FACT: Archaeologists believe that Shell Point, at the east end of Harkers Island, is the remnant of a causeway across the sound to Core Banks built entirely from seashells by the Tuscarora Indians.

Harkers Island Trails. Two connecting trails are located in the maritime forest behind the NPS visitors center and the Core Sound Waterfowl Museum. The **Willow Pond Trail,** a short trail with interpretive signs, begins at the Core Sound Waterfowl Museum (see *To See*) and circles a freshwater pond where waterbirds can be observed. The longer **Soundside Loop Trail** leads from the Cape Lookout National Seashore Visitor Center out to the marsh.

☀ Lodging

BED & BREAKFAST INNS Cape Lookout Bed and Breakfast (252-728-3662; www.cape lookoutbedandbreakfast.com), 349 Bayview Drive, Harkers Island. Two pleasant rooms offer great views over the marsh and of the wild horses on Browns Island, across Core Sound Straits. A hot breakfast is served on your schedule. $$.

🐾 ♿ Otway House Bed & Breakfast (252-728-5636; www.otwayhouse.com), 68 US 70, Otway. Located on 6 acres in the quiet little town of Otway, this dog-friendly inn rents four elegantly furnished rooms with private baths, ceiling fans, and cable TV. The canine members of the party enjoy quality dog food, indoor and outdoor kennels, and a doggy play area. Human guests can indulge in a full breakfast, often including the inn's signature whole-wheat pancakes with bananas and pecans, before an active morning of rocking on the porch. Several free boat ramps are located close by, and the property has plenty of room for boat trailers. $$.

CAMPGROUNDS Cape Pointe Marina & Campground (252-728-6181; www.cape pointemarina.com), 1390 Harkers Island Road, Harkers Island. Boat slip rentals, boat ramp, ship's store, and RV site rentals.

(ᵠ) Cedar Creek Campground & Marina (252-225-9571; www.cedarcreekcampground andmarina.com), 111 Canal Drive, Sea Level. Family-run Good Sam park has swimming pool, boat ramp, saltwater fishing dock, and game room. Tent area available. Cash or checks only.

COTTAGE RENTALS Cape Lookout Realty (252-728-2375; www.capelookoutrealty.com), 834 Island Road, Harkers Island.

Vacation Rentals by Owners (www.vrbo .com) lists several houses for rent in Down East communities.

MOTELS 🐾 Driftwood Motel, Restaurant, and Campground (252-225-4861; www.clis .com/deg), 3575 Cedar Island Road, Cedar Island. Located next to the Cedar Island Ferry, this motel, built in the 1950s and showing its age, has 37 standard units and a great location on a beach with no other development for miles. Rates include continental breakfast. The campground across the street has full hookups, a dock, and boat ramp. The **Drift-wood Restaurant** serves lunch during the summer and dinner year-round. $

(ᵠ) Harkers Island Fishing Center (252-728-3907; www.harkersmarina.com), 1002 Harkers Island Road, Harkers Island. Basic budget motel rooms and efficiencies, transient boat slips, boat ramp, fly and light tackle fishing charters (252-504-3823). $.

(ᵠ) Rose's Vacation Rentals (252-728-2868; www.rosesvacationrentals.com), 287 Bayview Drive, Harkers Island. An old island family rents several well-maintained units next to Rose's Marina. A few RV sites and boat slips are also available. The boat-building sheds of the L. R. Rose Boat Works are still intact on the property. $.

☀ Where to Eat

DINING OUT ✐ ♿ Driftwood Motel's Pirate's Chest Restaurant (252-225-4861; www.clis.com/deg), 3575 Cedar Island Road, Cedar Island. Located next to the ferry docks, the Driftwood is a convenient stop before or after a trip to Ocracoke. Seafood combination platters, pasta dishes, baby back ribs, and vegetarian entrées are featured. A cup of cream of crab soup or Core Sound chowder is a good way to warm up on a blustery day. Locals come here for the prime rib special on the weekends. The homemade lemon meringue pie is much praised. Beer and wine are available, or you can bring your own brown bag. $–$$.

EATING OUT ✐ ↬ Fish Hook Grill (252-728-1790; www.fishhookgrill.com), 980 Island Road, Harkers Island. Southern-style diner food is served by friendly locals at this unpretentious spot near the Cape Lookout Visitor Center. Order a platter of local seafood, North Carolina pork barbecue sandwich, or a Southern veggie plate with squash casserole, pickled beets, and fried okra, washed down with fresh brewed tea. Don't miss the local broth-based clam chowder, crabcakes, and delicious pies, all specialties of Ms. Faye, the 80-year-young owner. $–$$.

Morris Marina Grill (252-225-4261; www .portsmouthislandfishing.com), 1000 Morris Marina Road, Atlantic. A favorite stop for breakfast before catching the ferry to North Core Banks for a day of surf fishing. Try the Core Sound shrimp burger for lunch. $.

Outer Island General Store (252-504-2672), 499 US 70, Otway. This family-owned convenience store and grill serves home cooking, Down East style. $.

✳ Selective Shopping

Captain Henry's Gift Store (252-728-7316; www.capthenrysgiftstore.com), 1341 Island Road, Harkers Island. Browse a wide variety of gifts and collectibles, including locally carved decoys.

Core Sound Waterfowl Museum Store (252-728-1500; www.coresound.com), 1785 Island Road, Harkers Island. Features art and crafts by local people, including decoys, Core Sound crab pot trees, and locally produced books and music.

Harvey & Sons Net & Twine (252-729-1731; www.harveyandsons.com), 804 US 70, Davis. Visit the shop where Nicky Harvey makes his ingenious crab pot Christmas trees—the must-have souvenir of a trip to the Crystal Coast.

✳ Special Events

February: **Taste of Core Sound–Winter Edition** (252-728-1500; www.coresound.com), Core Sound Waterfowl Museum and Heritage Center, Harkers Island. Enjoy a dinner of Down East specialties.

August: **Taste of Core Sound–Summer Edition** (252-728-1500; www.coresound.com), Core Sound Waterfowl Museum and Heritage Center, Harkers Island.

September: **Kids Showcase Day** (252-838-8818; www.decoyguild.com), Core Sound Decoy Carvers Guild, Harkers Island. Hunting and fishing safety, wildlife preservation, decoy painting, loon calling, archery, a BB gun shoot, hot dog lunch, and other fun activities. **NC Challenge** (www.watertribe.org/nc-challenge), Driftwood Motel, Cedar Island. One-hundred-mile race for sea kayaks, canoes, and small sailboats circumnavigates the entire Down East.

October: **Born to Raise Sail** (718-548-1188; www.baloghsaildesigns.com), Driftwood Motel, Cedar Island. Annual gathering of sailing kayaks and canoes.

Early December: **Core Sound Decoy Festival** (252-838-8818; www.decoyguild.com), Core Sound Decoy Guild, Harkers Island. Weekend of decoy competition includes a decoy auction, retriever demonstrations, loon calling, and children's decoy painting. **Core Sound Waterfowl Weekend** (252-728-1500; www.coresound.com), Core Sound Waterfowl Museum and Heritage Center, Harkers Island. Held the same weekend as the decoy festival, this event celebrates Down East traditions of boatbuilding, fishing, music, arts and crafts, cooking, and fellowship.

Mid-December: **Core Sound Christmas Crèche Celebration** (252-728-1500; www.coresound.com), Core Sound Waterfowl Museum and Heritage Center, Harkers Island.

CAPE LOOKOUT AND THE CORE BANKS

THE FIVE UNINHABITED ISLANDS stretching from Ocracoke Inlet to Beaufort Inlet, making up the Cape Lookout National Seashore, have more than 55 miles of pristine ocean beach wiped nearly clean of all traces of human occupation. Originally used as hunting and fishing grounds by the Coree Indians, from whom they take their name, the Core Banks remain today, as then, a rich ecological treasure, one of the most significant undeveloped barrier island systems in the world.

At the north end of Core Banks, once-prosperous **Portsmouth Village,** now a ghost town administered by the National Park Service, is most easily reached from Ocracoke Island. See our coverage in that chapter. The national seashore is generally divided into the North Core and South Core Banks islands, plus Shackleford Banks nearer Beaufort, although the park service has decided to let the shape of these islands be determined entirely by natural causes. Inlets open and close, depending on storms and tides. **Cape Lookout Lighthouse** is located near the southern hook of South Core. Nearby lie the remnants of **Cape Lookout Village,** including an old lifesaving station. This area is reached via passenger ferries from Harkers Island, where the **Cape Lookout National Seashore Visitor Center** is located, and from Beaufort's waterfront. Private watercraft can also land on the Banks at designated spots.

From Cape Lookout, the **Shackleford Banks** stretch west to a point opposite Fort Macon on Bogue Banks. Once the location of the whaling village of **Diamond City,** Shackleford was abandoned by its inhabitants after a hurricane in 1899 sent a storm surge over the island. Today, the island's sole residents are about 150 ponies of Spanish descent who have adapted to the harsh conditions.

GUIDANCE For a complete rundown on things to do on Cape Lookout, how to get there, and reservations at the NPS cabin camps, visit the website of the **Cape Lookout National Seashore** (252-728-2250; www.nps.gov/calo) or go by the visitors center on Harkers Island.

GETTING THERE During the summer months, many passenger ferries ply the shallow waters of Core Sound and Beaufort Inlet, taking visitors to the offshore, uninhabited islands of the region. Ferries licensed by the National Park Service make their way to the national seashore's islands from several ports on the mainland and on Harkers Island. Ferries from Atlantic go to North Core. Ferries from Davis go to the middle of South Core. The ferries from these ports carry vehicles, including passenger vehicles, ATVs, golf carts, and utility vehicles, as well as passengers, and dock near cabin camps maintained by the National Park Service. Ferries from Harkers Island carry only passengers and go to the Cape Lookout Lighthouse area and Shackleford Banks. Ferries from Beaufort and Morehead City also carry passengers to the lighthouse and Shackleford, plus a variety of other small islands in Beaufort Inlet where you can enjoy a private beach experience.

Harkers Island is the closest point to the Cape Lookout Lighthouse, and the National Park Service licenses a number of concessionaires to make the 3-mile run. Ferries usually operate from mid-March to November, but a few may operate during the winter, weather permitting, with increased rates (see listings marked ❋ and call for details). Leashed pets are accepted on most ferries, but you may be charged a child's fare for them. Call to make arrangements in advance.

Expect to pay $10–16 per person for your ferry ride. Children are sometimes offered lower rates. Rates go up if you are taking camping gear aboard. Note: Ferry service from Harkers Island and Beaufort will be changing dramatically during the next few years, as the National Park Service consolidates and standardizes services. Ferries will depart from NPS terminals on Harkers and the Beaufort waterfront beginning as early as 2014. Check the NPS website for current information.

From Atlantic: **Morris Marina Ferry Service** (252-225-4261; www.portsmouthislandfishing.com), 1000 Morris Marina Road, Atlantic. Ferries carrying pedestrians, vehicles, trailers, and ATVs depart for Long Point on the North Core Banks daily from March to mid-December.

From Davis: よ **Cape Lookout Cabins & Camps Ferry Service** (252-729-9751; www.calocabins-campsinc.net), 125 Grady Lane, Davis. Passenger and vehicle ferry departs from Davis to Great Island on South Core. Kubota utility vehicles, four-wheel-drive trucks, and kayaks available for rent. Guided waterfowl hunting and fishing charters to Drum Inlet and other hot spots.

Davis Shore Ferry Service (252-729-3474; www.davisferry.com), 148 Willis Road, Davis.

From Harkers Island: ❋ **Calico Jack's Ferry** (252-728-3575; www.capelookoutferry.com), 1698 Island Road, Harkers Island. Ferries go to the east end of Shackleford Banks and to Cape Lookout Lighthouse area. For an additional fee, you can also be dropped off at Les and Sally Moore's former fishing camp, near the historic Cape Lookout Village; at the 1915 Coast Guard Station across the Bight; at the rock jetty; or at Power Squadron Spit. Food and supplies are available at the marina. Most ferries use small open skiffs, but Calico Jack's also has a larger 49-passenger motor catamaran with sun shade for use during peak periods.

❋ **Cape Pointe Marina** (252-728-6181; www.capepointemarina.com), 1390 Island Road, Harkers Island. The former Barbour's Marina.

Harkers Island Fishing Center (252-728-3907; www.harkersmarina.com), 1002 Island Road, Harkers Island. Passenger shuttles to Cape Lookout and Shackleford. Food and supplies available at the marina.

❋ **Local Yokel Ferry and Tours** (252-728-2759; www.tourcapelookout.com), 516 Island Road, Harkers Island. Shuttle service from Harkers Island to Cape Lookout. Free parking.

From Beaufort: **Island Ferry Adventures** (252-728-7555; www.islandferryadventures.com), 610 Front Street, Beaufort. Daily passenger service in season from the Beaufort waterfront to Sand Dollar Island, Carrot Island, Bird Shoals, and the west end of Shackleford Banks.

❋ **Outer Banks Ferry Service** (252-728-4129; www.outerbanksferry.com), 326 Front Street, Beaufort. Passenger ferry to Cape Lookout from Beaufort.

From Morehead City: ❋ **Waterfront Ferry Service** (252-726-7678; www.portsidemarina.com), 209 Arendell Street, Morehead City. Ferries depart from Portside Marina on the Morehead City waterfront to Sugarloaf Island just offshore and to Shackleford Banks.

GETTING AROUND *By Four-Wheel Drive:* Much of the ocean beach and the unpaved sand roads on North and South Core banks within the Cape Lookout National Seashore are open to ORV use. Vehicles can reach the seashore aboard ferries located at Atlantic (for North Core) and Davis (for South Core). No permit is required for driving on the beach.

Most driving is done on the harder surface along the tide line, although a sandy road, referred to as the Back Road, runs behind the dunes. Vehicles must remain on the beach or the sand roads, and are not allowed on dunes or in areas restricted due to bird or sea turtle nesting activities. Four-wheel-drive vehicles are strongly recommended; there are no tow trucks or emergency vehicles on the Core Banks. You are on your own, so come prepared.

By Shuttle: **Cape Lookout Conch Tours** (252-732-4578) offers shuttle service from the ferry dock near the lighthouse to the Cape Point beaches, as well as tours of historic Cape Lookout Village. You can pay by credit card at the ferry offices on Harkers Island, or by cash on the island. $15.

On Foot: The sand on Core Banks is soft and difficult to walk through. A boardwalk leads across to the beach from the ferry dock near the lighthouse.

❋ To See

Cape Lookout Lighthouse & Keepers' Quarters Museum (252-728-2250; www.nps .gov/calo), South Core Banks. The lighthouse is open for climbing 10–3:45 Wednesday–Saturday, May–September, although these hours may expand; the Keepers' Quarters Museum, at the base of the tower, and the Light Station Visitor Center, near the ferry dock, are open 9–5 daily, April–November. The 169-foot-tall Cape Lookout Lighthouse was first lit in 1859 but didn't receive its distinctive black and white diamond paint job until after the Civil War. Its 207 steps are roughly the equivalent of a 12-story building. The adjacent **Keepers' Quarters** holds a museum detailing the history of the lighthouse and the Core Banks. Ferries make the run from Harkers Island, the nearest land access, docking near the **Light Station Pavilion,** which houses a ranger station, bookstore, and restrooms. During the summer months, park rangers conduct free programs on the history of the lighthouse and the surrounding area. A ferry ride ($10–16) is required to reach South Core Banks from Harkers Island, and the fare does not include lighthouse climbing tickets. The museum is free. Tickets to climb the lighthouse cost $8 adults; $4 children 12 and under and seniors 62 and up. You can buy tickets at the Light Station Pavilion the day of your visit, or make reservations at least one day in advance by calling 252-728-0708. The view is well worth both the price and the climb.

Cape Lookout Village (252-728-1500; www.friendsofcapelookout.com), Cape Point, South Core Banks. Located about a mile south of the lighthouse, this cluster of buildings on

THE DIAMOND PATTERN ON THE CAPE LOOKOUT LIGHT TAKES ITS INSPIRATION FROM DIAMOND SHOALS.

the National Register of Historic Places is all that remains of the village that once thrived here. There are currently 16 buildings, built from 1887 to 1960, including the 1887 Life-Saving Station and its boathouse, and various private residences and fishing cottages, all unoccupied. The 1915 Coast Guard Station is just across the bight. Interpretive signs are located throughout the village. The village can be reached by foot, by private vehicle or boat, or by shuttle service from the Light Station Visitor Center.

Portsmouth Village (252-728-2250; www.friendsofportsmouthisland.org or www.nps.gov/calo). This eerie ghost village is located at the northern tip of North Core Banks and is most easily reached by private ferry from Ocracoke. (See our recommendations in that chapter.) The National Park Service maintains a visitors center in the restored Theodore and Annie Salter House, open Tuesday–Saturday April–November, with restrooms, maps of the village, and exhibits on Portsmouth history. Free tours of the village are offered by rangers during the summer months. You can also reach Portsmouth Village by bringing your vehicle across to North Core on the ferry from Atlantic, then driving about 16 miles up the beach.

Shackleford Banks Horses (252-728-6308; www.shacklefordhorses.org). A herd of about 100 horses descended from Spanish stock lives the wild life on Shackleford Banks. The island can be reached only by boat. A tour guided by a naturalist is recommended for the best and safest views of the wild horses.

RECOMMENDED READING Prioli, Carmine. *The Wild Horses of Shackleford Banks.* Winston-Salem, NC: John F. Blair, 2007.

✴ To Do

BOATING You can get to the various deserted islands aboard your private boat, although caution is advised since the average depth in the sound is just 5 feet, and there are numerous shifting sandbars. Docks where you can off-load passengers are located just north of the lighthouse on South Core and at the western end of Shackleford near Beaufort. Two docks are located near Portsmouth Village at the tip of North Core. You cannot tie up at any of these docks, but must anchor offshore. Many shallow draft boats simply pull up on the sandy beach.

Sailboats and deeper draft vessels can best moor in Cape Lookout Bight behind the Cape Point spit, a truly beautiful anchorage with awesome views of both the lighthouse and the Shackleford horses. You can anchor for a maximum of 14 days in national seashore waters.

Personal watercraft (PWC) such as Jet Skis and WaveRunners can currently land on the islands of Cape Lookout National Seashore at 10 designated locations. However, these regulations change frequently, so check with the National Park Service before launching your watercraft.

FISHING Next to the lighthouse, surf fishing is Cape Lookout's biggest draw, with numerous fishing enthusiasts bringing their four-wheel-drive vehicles over on the ferries from Atlantic and Davis, and spending weeks at a time roaming the tide line, camping out, and fishing the break, then cooking their catch for dinner. Fall and spring are the busiest seasons for fishing, highlighted by the Cape's famous run of red drum during the autumn months.

HUNTING Waterfowl hunting is allowed on the Core Banks islands, with the correct permits, during certain times of the year. Contact the park service for more details.

SHELLING The Core and Shackleford banks, and other islands of Cape Lookout National Seashore, are great places to find shells, including Scotch bonnets, olives, petrified clams, whelks, conchs, and Queen's helmets. The beach on the west side of Cape Point south of the lighthouse is noted for the large whelk shells, some a foot long, found there.

Sand dollars are also abundant, especially on the small sandbar called Sand Dollar Island that lies between Carrot Island and Shackleford Banks. This little sandbar is barely above water and is only accessible at low tide.

A limit of 2 gallons of shells a day may be taken from national seashore beaches. Shelling is best in the early spring, about two hours before or after high tide, and especially after big storms.

SNORKELING AND SCUBA The rock jetty near the west end of the Cape Lookout spit (officially Power Squadron Jetty) is a great spot for seeing the local aquatic life. The area is best reached by boat.

SWIMMING The Cape Lookout National Seashore does not have a lifeguarded beach. All swimming is at your own risk.

WATER SPORTS The uninhabited beaches of Cape Lookout offer surfers, kiteboarders, and windsurfers a unique opportunity to practice their sports in a truly natural environment.

✳ Green Space

Core Banks, Cape Lookout National Seashore (www.nps.gov/calo) has more than 55 miles of pristine, undeveloped beaches stretching from Portsmouth Island in the north to Cape Point, south of the lighthouse. Accessible only by boat, the seashore's beaches have few amenities and can be hard to travel by foot. A boardwalk stretches from the Light Station Pavilion near the ferry dock, over to the ocean beach and to the Keepers' Quarters museum. Drinkable water, restrooms, and picnic areas are located at Cape Point, the Light Station area, and Great Island on South Core; at Long Point and Portsmouth Village on North Core. North Core and South Core are separated by the fairly deep New Drum Inlet. Check the park service website for current amenities and recommended supplies. (Such as insect repellent, a must for a trip to Cape Lookout. The insects here have well-deserved reputations for ferocity.) During the summer, rangers and volunteers from the North Carolina Coastal Federation (252-808-3301) lead free programs exploring barrier island ecology.

Endangered sea turtles and shorebirds nest along the shore, especially in the Cape Point area. Wading birds frequent the marsh. Visitors can hike along the shores of the ocean or sound to observe birds, or along the sandy roads and trails.

Wheelchairs are available on a limited basis at the Light Station Pavilion. Fires are permitted only on the beach below the high tide line. Plan to bring your own wood. Pets are allowed within the national seashore but must be leashed at all times.

Shackleford Banks (252-728-2250; www.nps.gov/calo). Home to a herd of wild horses (proved through DNA studies to be descended from colonial-era Spanish stock) and little else, this island is a popular spot for shelling and sunning. Access is by ferry or private boat. Park rangers offer Horse Sense and Survival Tours during the summer season. Reservations required. Restrooms are located near the passenger ferry landing at the western tip of the island, and at Wade's Shore, a short distance east. See "Beaufort" section for details on tours and ferries to Shackleford.

NUMEROUS FERRIES MAKE THE TRIP TO THE CORE AND SHACKLEFORD BANKS.

✷ Lodging

CAMPING There are no established campgrounds within the national seashore; however, primitive camping with both tents and vehicles is allowed. Tents are permitted anywhere except on dunes or within 100 feet of any structure. Vehicles, allowed on Core only, must park on the ocean side of the dune line. Because of the softness of the sand, and the likelihood of becoming stuck, large RVs are not recommended. There are no stores on the Banks, and campers should bring along all supplies they'll need, including drinking water, and plan to carry out all trash. Dump stations and restrooms are available at the picnic area near Cape Point, and at the two cabin areas. Showers for public use and fuel for vehicles are available at the cabin camps. Camping is limited to 14 consecutive days. Free.

CAPE LOOKOUT CABINS Two groups of cabins on Core Banks are available for rent, and they are popular with fishers and kayakers, and for family getaways. Rentals are available from mid-March through the end of November. Rates are higher during the spring and fall fishing seasons, and less during the summer. Renters must provide their own linens, bedding, cookware, food, and other supplies. Gas and ice are sold at the camp offices. Pets are allowed in cabins, but they must be kept in crates or tied up on the cabin porch and not left unattended. Each cabin camp also has a hot shower and restroom facility open to campers.

Reservations for these cabins can be made online at the **Recreation.gov** website, or by calling 1-877-444-6777. Reservations are accepted beginning in early January. Plan ahead, as these cabins book up quickly.

&. **Great Island Cabin Camp** (1-877-444-6777; www.nps.gov/calo), South Core Banks. The 26 rustic cabins sleep 4–12 people; one is fully accessible. Accommodations are basic, with screened porches, bunk beds, hot water, full baths with showers, and propane stoves, but no electricity. Most are wired for generators, which must be provided by individual renters. Great Island is reached by ferry from Davis or by private boat. $–$$.

&. **Long Point Cabin Camp** (1-877-444-6777; www.nps.gov/calo). Ten duplex cabins each sleep up to six people on each side. Units 1–8 are in hexagonal buildings; four of these units have air-conditioning. The other units are in rectangular buildings with propane heaters. All cabins have electricity, private baths, ceiling fans, bunk beds, and kitchen stoves. Cabins at Long Point are reached by ferry from Atlantic or by private boat. One cabin is accessible. $$.

✷ Special Events

April: **Junior Ranger Day** (www.nps.gov/calo).

October: **Davis Island Fishing Foundation Surf Fishing Tournament** (www.diffclub.com), Great Island Camp and South Core Banks.

BEAUFORT

THE CHARMING VILLAGE that is today the seat of Carteret County began life as Beaufort-by-the-Sea back in 1709, making it the state's third oldest town. Pronounced in the French manner with a long *o* (in contrast to the South Carolina Beaufort, pronounced BYOO-furt), the town is a favorite stop for yachts cruising the Atlantic Intracoastal Waterway (ICW) as well as visitors seeking history, water-based recreation, and fine cuisine. The pedestrian-friendly historic district centers on Front Street, facing the town docks. Here you'll find a variety of restaurants, bed & breakfasts, historic houses, and boat tours and water taxis to nearby islands. The wild ponies on Carrot Island can often be seen just across the water.

Shops along the waterfront offer an eclectic blend of nautical items, antiques, and local artwork. **The Beaufort Historic Site** and the **North Carolina Maritime Museum** provide context on the area's rich background of pirates, merchants, and commercial fisheries. Beaufort is also the home port of North Carolina's last privateer, Capt. Horatio Sinbad. His ship, the brigantine *Meka II*, can often be found at the Gallant's Channel docks, and the captain himself frequents the establishments along Front Street.

GUIDANCE The historical center at the **Beaufort Historic Site** (252-728-5225; www.beaufort historicsite.org), on the first block of Turner Street, serves as a welcome center for the town of Beaufort.

Additional information can be found at:

Beaufort Town Hall (252-728-2141; www.beaufortnc.org), 701 Front Street, Beaufort.

Carteret County Offices (252-728-8450; www.carteretcountygov.org), Courthouse Square, at Cedar and Turner streets, Beaufort.

POST OFFICE The **Beaufort U.S. Post Office** (252-728-1812) is at 1903 Live Oak Street. The zip code in Beaufort is 28516.

PUBLIC RESTROOMS Public facilities are found at the Beaufort Historic Site's historical center; at the Town Docks, on Front Street; at Perry Park, at the east end of Front Street; and at the W. Beaufort Road Water Access. On the US 70 causeway to Morehead City, look for restrooms and bathhouses at the Newport River Park on the north side of the road, and across the street at the Radio Island Water Access.

PUBLIC LIBRARY The main branch of the ((ᵠ)) **Carteret County Public Library** (252-728-2050; http://carteret.cpclib.org) is at 1702 Live Oak Street in Beaufort. Services include children's story time, faxing, public-use computers, and a paperback exchange.

THE *MEKA II*, BASED IN BEAUFORT, IS AN AUTHENTIC REPRODUCTION OF A PIRATE SHIP, CAPTAINED BY HORATIO SINBAD.

GETTING THERE *By Air:* **Michael J. Smith Field Airport (MRH)** (252-728-1928; www.flysouthern air.com), 150 Airport Road, Beaufort. Car rentals, fuel, and tie-downs, as well as air tours and aircraft rentals, are offered at this field, named for the astronaut, a local man, who commanded the space shuttle *Challenger* on its final, fatal flight.

By Boat: Beaufort is a popular stop for boats traveling the Atlantic Intracoastal Waterway. Boat slips for transients are located at the **Beaufort Docks** (252-728-2503), 500 Front Street, in the heart of town.

By Car: US 70 comes over the bridge from Morehead City, then runs along the north side of Beaufort's historic district before making a sharp turn to the north and heading toward the Down East communities.

GETTING AROUND *By Trolley:* For those staying elsewhere and arriving for a day visit to the historic village, parking is sometimes a challenge, especially during the busy summer season. In recent years, the **Mullet Line Trolley** (252-838-1524; www.facebook.com/BeaufortOpenAirTrolleyboat), officially the Beaufort Open Air Trolley, or B.O.A.T., provides a solution to this problem, offering rides aboard a motorized trolley from a large free parking lot at the eastern edge of town at 2400 Lennoxville Road during the busiest season, Memorial Day to Labor Day. The 2.5-mile route runs down Front Street, with stops at the North Carolina Wildlife boat ramps (Curtis Perry Park), Beaufort Town Hall, the North Carolina Maritime Museum, and the Waterfront Boardwalk at the Dock House. The trip costs $1 each way, takes about 30 minutes, and runs 9–7. A narrated tour of local history and attractions is given during the ride. The trolley is sponsored by **Front Street Village** (252-838-1524; www.front streetvillage.com), a new mixed-use development under way at the east end of Front Street where it meets Lennoxville Road.

On Foot: Beaufort is a great walking destination. Everything you need for a great vacation is within a block or two of Front Street. Many visitors arrive, park their car at their hotel, and walk to museums, restaurants, and nightlife. Even boat tours are easy to reach, with the docks right on Front Street.

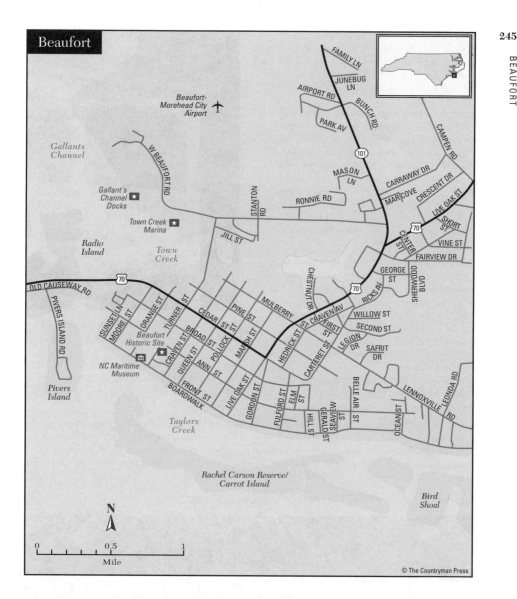

Beaufort

Gallants
Channel

Gallant's
Channel
Docks

Town Creek
Marina

Radio
Island

Town
Creek

Pivers
Island

Taylors
Creek

Beaufort-
Morehead City
Airport

FAMILY LN

JUNEBUG
LN

AIRPORT RD

BUNCH RD

PARK AV

CAMPEN RD

101

MASON
LN

CARRAWAY DR

CRESCENT DR

MARLCOVE

LIVE OAK ST

RONNIE RD

SHORT
ST

70

VINE ST

FAIRVIEW DR

W BEAUFORT RD

STANTON
RD

JILL ST

CHESTNUT DR

70

RICKS AV

GEORGE
ST

SHERWOOD BLVD

OLD CAUSEWAY RD

70

SUNSET LN

MOORE ST

ORANGE ST

TURNER ST

CEDAR ST

PINE ST

MULBERRY

CRAVEN AV

FIRST
ST

WILLOW ST

SECOND ST

BROAD ST

POLLOCK ST

MARSH ST

HEDRICK ST

CARTERET ST

LEGION
DR

SAFRIT
DR

PIVERS ISLAND RD

Beaufort
Historic Site

CRAVEN ST

QUEEN ST

ANN ST

LIVE OAK ST

GORDON ST

FULFORD ST

ELM
ST

SEAVIEW
GERALD ST

BELLE AIR
ST

LENNOXVILLE RD

LEONDA RD

NC Maritime
Museum

FRONT ST

BOARDWALK

HILL ST

OCEAN ST

Rachel Carson Reserve/
Carrot Island

Bird
Shoal

N

0   0.5   1
Mile

© The Countryman Press

MEDICAL EMERGENCY The nearest emergency room is located at **Carteret General Hospital** (252-808-6000; www.ccgh.org), 3500 Arendell Street, Morehead City.

✳ To See

Architecture. The Beaufort Historic District contains over 100 buildings bearing plaques with the original owner and date of construction listed. Victorian and Queen Anne influences are reflected in the elaborate millwork found on many of the houses. Beaufort also has a distinctive style of picket fence, characterized by an undulating, up-and-down top line and square pickets. **The Beaufort Historical Association** (252-728-5225 or 1-800-575-7483; www.beauforthistoricsite.org) sponsors an Old Homes and Gardens Tour every June.

✳ ♂ **Beaufort Historic Site** (252-728-5225 or 1-800-575-7483; www.beauforthistoricsite.org), 100 block, Turner Street. Open daily June–August; Monday–Saturday September–May. The Beaufort Historical Association, a private, membership-based organization formed in 1960, has gathered, restored, and furnished six historic buildings—including the 1732 Rustell House, now an art gallery, and Federal and Victorian residences—in the 100 block of Turner Street. Other buildings around the wide green lawn include the 1786 Carteret County Courthouse; the Old Jail, reputed to be haunted; and the 1859 Apothecary Shop and Doctors Office, filled with fascinating medical artifacts. Gardens on the grounds include a colonial-era kitchen garden and herb gardens. The **Safrit Historical Center** houses exhibits, the museum gift shop, and restrooms, in addition to serving as an information center. Free admission to grounds, gardens, and art gallery; tours of the historic buildings, Old Burying Ground, and double-decker bus tours $8 adults, $4 children.

Beaufort Town Hall (252-728-2141; www .beaufortnc.org), 701 Front Street. Step into the lobby of Beaufort's town hall, formerly the post office, to see four large murals depicting scenes related to the town's history and culture, including the 1886 wreck of the schooner *Crissie Wright*, a mailboat, a hunting scene, and the "sand ponies" still found on several islands. The

MANY HOMES IN BEAUFORT VILLAGE HAVE ELABORATE WOODWORK.

murals are the work of immigrant artist Simka Simkhovitch, who began work soon after the post office opened in 1937, as part of a federally funded project that put artists to work during the Great Depression. The lobby also houses exhibits from the NPS, which operates its ferry concession from this location (beginning in 2014); the Rachel Carson Reserve; and other organizations. Free.

❄ ✎ & ↑ **North Carolina Maritime Museum in Beaufort** (252-728-7317; www.ncmaritime.org or www.ncmm-friends.org), 315 Front Street. Open daily except Thanksgiving, Christmas holidays, and New Year's Day. The state's maritime museum in Beaufort includes three separate facilities: the main galleries on Front Street; the **Watercraft Center,** across the street on the waterfront; and

DISTINCTIVE WHITE PICKET FENCES LINE YARDS IN BEAUFORT.

SIGN UP TO BUILD A BOAT IN A SINGLE DAY AT THE NORTH CAROLINA MARITIME MUSEUM'S WATERCRAFT CENTER.

INSIDE THE RESTORED 1859 APOTHECARY SHOP AT THE BEAUFORT HISTORIC SITE

the **Gallant's Channel Docks,** about 1 mile west of downtown. The main galleries contain an extensive shell collection, examples of traditional boats, an excellent collection of hand-carved decoys, and the skeleton of a 35-foot sperm whale, as well as a new **Blackbeard's Queen Anne's Revenge** exhibit, featuring artifacts from the pirate ship and interactive activities. The Watercraft Center specializes in the building and restoration of wooden boats, and houses a ship model-making shop. The maritime museum sponsors a wide variety of boat-building, boating, and environmental education programs, including many kayak tours, throughout the year. Free.

Old Burying Ground (252-728-5225; www .beauforthistoricsite.org), bounded by Ann, Craven, and Broad streets. Open dawn to dusk. A leisurely walk beneath the 100-year-old live oaks that shade the Old Burying Ground is a fascinating trip through local history. The nearly 300-year-old cemetery contains some 400 graves dating back to 1731. Two notable occupants are Otway Burns, the famous privateer whose grave is marked with a cannon from his ship, and a young girl buried in a barrel of rum, whose grave is decorated with toys and gifts left by visitors over the years. A self-guided tour booklet is available at the **Beaufort Historic Site,** and costumed interpreters offer guided tours ($8) with many additional stories several times a week. Free.

Rachel Carson National Estuarine Research Reserve (252-728-2170; www .nccoastalreserve.net), 135 Duke Marine Lab Road. The complex of islands, accessible by boat ferry, includes Carrot Island, Town Marsh, Bird Shoal, and Horse Island, all less than a mile wide. Feral horses, not related to the Spanish descendants on Shackleford Banks, roam the islands. A local farmer released them here in the 1940s. The horses on Carrot Island, located directly across Taylor's Creek from the Beaufort waterfront, are frequently sighted from dockside restaurants.

THIS CANNON MARKS THE GRAVE OF OTWAY BURNS, A FAMOUS PRIVATEER.

✳ To Do

AIR TOURS Southern Air (252-728-2323; www.flysouthernair.com), 150 Airport Road. For a unique perspective, see Cape Lookout, the wild ponies, and Fort Macon from the air. You can also take an introductory flight lesson or rent an aircraft.

BICYCLING The **Beaufort Bicycle Route** makes a 6-mile loop around the historic village. The quiet side streets generally make for good riding.

Beaufort Bicycles (252-728-1203), 127 Briar Patch Lane, rents bikes.

BOATING The **Friends of the Maritime Museum** (252-728-1638; www.ncmm-friends.org) sponsors many different boating programs, including two-week long Junior Sailing Programs, the Beaufort Oars Rowing Club, and family sailing on traditional skiffs or a 30-foot keelboat available by reservation.

Several free boat ramps are available to the public. ⑤ **Curtis A. Perry Park,** at the east end of Front Street, has four boat ramps maintained by the North Carolina Wildlife Service (www.ncwildlife .org), plus a dock, picnic area with grills, tennis courts, and restrooms. ⑤ **Town Creek Water Access** (Turner Street and W. Beaufort Road) has two ramps, easiest to use at high tide, plus a boardwalk, fishing pier, floating docks, and restrooms, with access to Gallant's Channel.

Rent a Carolina skiff or pontoon boat from **Ahoy Boat Rentals** (252-726-1900; www.ahoyboat rentals.com), 232 W. Beaufort Road at the Town Creek Marina.

Beaufort is a popular destination for boaters traveling the Intracoastal Waterway. A couple of marinas cater to live-aboards:

Beaufort Docks (252-728-2503), 500 Front Street. Transient slips are located in the heart of historic Beaufort.

Town Creek Marina (252-728-6111; www.towncreekmarina.com), 232 W. Beaufort Road. Transient slips, restaurant, tiki bar with live entertainment, and terrific sunset views.

BOAT TOURS The Beaufort waterfront is very active, with many tours leaving from docks all along Front Street. The trip over to Shackleford Banks for shelling and viewing the wild horses, offered by several different companies, is not to be missed. Naturalist-led tours are recommended and well worth the small additional cost.

Beginning in 2014, the National Park Service will operate a ferry concession out of the Beaufort Town Hall, recently moved to the old post office building at the corner of Front and Pollock streets. The ferries will depart for Shackleford Banks and the Cape Lookout Lighthouse from a dock in the current Grayden Paul Park, directly across Front Street.

Barrier Island Adventures (252-728-4129; www.outerbanksferry.com), 326 Front Street. Water taxis and tours to Carrot Island, Bird Shoal, Sand Dollar Island, Shackleford Banks, and the Cape Lookout Lighthouse.

❧ *Crystal Coast Lady* **Cruises** (252-728-8687 or 252-728-7827; www.crystalcoastlady.com), 617 Front Street. The largest and newest cruiser on the Beaufort waterfront hosts narrated harbor tours, lunch cruises, dolphin watches, and a special pirate treasure hunt for kids.

❦ **Island Ferry Adventure** (252-728-7555; www.islandferryadventures.com), 610 Front Street. Award-winning boat tours include a horse and waterfront sight-seeing cruise that circles the islands in front of Beaufort. Water taxi service will drop you off for a day of relaxation on Shackleford Banks, Bird Shoal, Sand Dollar Island, or Carrot Island. Small dogs can ride along.

Lookout Cruises (252-504-7245; www.lookoutcruises.com), 600 Front Street. A 45-foot sailing catamaran offers dolphin watching, day trips to Cape Lookout with lunch and snorkeling, plus sunset and moonlight cruises.

✆ **Port City Tours Company** (252-772-9925; www.pctourco.com), 610 Front Street. Tours offered by this outfitter include dolphin hunts, sunset cruises, and romantic, adult-only moonlight cruises. The Kid's E.C.O. Adventure promises a day of education and discovery on an offshore island.

❋ **Shackleford Wild Horse and Shelling Safari** (252-772-9925; www.tourbeaufort.com). Join a naturalist guide to look for the herds of wild ponies that inhabit the island, then search for shells along the oceanfront.

Water Bug Harbor Tours (252-728-4129; www.waterbugtours.com), 324 Front Street. Cruise the historic Beaufort waterfront on a one-hour tour.

FISHING Public-access fishing piers are located at the ♿ **Town Creek (West Beaufort) Water Access** (298 W. Beaufort Road) and at ♿ **Newport River Park,** on the causeway between Beaufort and Morehead City. A North Carolina Coastal Recreational Fishing License is required.

Crystal Coast Lady **Cruises** (252-728-8687 or 252-728-7827; www.crystalcoastlady.com), 617 Front Street. Headboat operating from the Beaufort waterfront offers reasonably priced half-day bay fishing trips, with lower rates for children, seniors, and spectators. All equipment, bait, and licenses are included. Night fishing also available.

THE BEAUFORT WATERFRONT IS THE CENTER OF MARITIME ACTIVITIES ON THE CRYSTAL COAST.

FOR FAMILIES The ✍ **North Carolina Maritime Museum** (252-728-1638; www.ncmaritime museums.com) offers a weeklong Summer Science School for students entering grades 1–10, introducing the natural environments and maritime history of coastal North Carolina.

✍ **Pirate Island Treasure Hunt** (252-772-9925; www.pctourco.com). Take a ferry to a deserted island where you'll help solve the mystery of Blackbeard's lost treasure.

GHOST TOURS Beaufort Ghost Walk (252-772-9925; www.tourbeaufort.com). On Beaufort's most popular tour, a pirate guide leads you to the Hammock House, once the residence of Blackbeard, then on to a 300-year-old cemetery for more tales of horror.

Port City Pirates & Ghosts Tour (252-772-9925; www.pctourco.com). Tour a haunted house, learn to fight with a sword, and fire a cannon on this fun tour.

GOLF North River Club (252-728-5525; www.northrivergolfclub.com), 300 Links Drive. Semiprivate course designed by award-winning architect Bob Moore.

HUNTING Waterdog Guide Service (252-728-7907 or 919-423-6310; www.waterdogguideservice .com). Join captains Tom Roller and Scott Crocker on a hunt for sea ducks, operated with the highest ethical standards. As a bonus, your guide remains with you in the blind and cooks up a filet mignon and oyster brunch.

KAYAKING Thanks to the many close-by islands, Beaufort is a great kayaking destination. One favorite paddle crosses Taylor's Creek from the town waterfront to Carrot Island. Several small beaches along Front Street are good for launching a kayak, including **Topsail Marine Park,** at the end of Orange Street; **Grayden Paul Park,** at the end of Pollock Street; and **Fisherman's Park,** at the end of Gordon Street.

A handicapped-accessible kayak and canoe put-in is located at the ♿ **Town Creek Water Access** (298 W. Beaufort Road).

PARASAILING Beaufort Inlet Watersports & Parasail (252-728-7607), 500 Front Street.

SCUBA AND SNORKELING Discovery Diving Company (252-728-2265; www.discoverydiving .com), 414 Orange Street. Full-service dive shop offers headboat trips on three dive boats to more than 30 offshore wrecks, plus lobster hunting and spearfishing trips, classes and equipment sales, repairs, and rentals. A diver's lodge is available for groups and divers who opt for the discounted weekday package.

✳ Green Space

BEACHES The uninhabited islands that make up the **Rachel Carson Reserve,** especially Carrot Island, are popular beaches and are uncrowded since they are accessible only by boat. **Island Ferry Adventures** (252-728-7555; www.islandferryadventures.com) and ✳ **Outer Banks Ferry Service** (252-728-4129; www.outerbanksferry.com) offer ferry service to Sand Dollar Island, Carrot Island, Bird Shoals, and the west end of Shackleford Banks. No concessions are available on any of these islands, so take a cooler, sunscreen, hats, and plenty of water along. Shackleford has public restrooms.

On the causeway between Beaufort and Morehead City, ♿ **Newport River Park** has a bathhouse, pier, sandy beach, and shallow-water boat ramp. Across US 70 is the entrance to **Radio Island,** where a popular regional beach access has a picnic area with grills, sandy beach, bathhouse, and a great view of downtown Beaufort and Carrot Island across the channel.

TRAILS ✳ Rachel Carson National Estuarine Research Reserve Nature Trails (252-728-2170; www.nccoastalreserve.net), Carrot Island, across from the Beaufort waterfront. Two loop nature trails introducing this unique island habitat are each about 1 mile long. Access is by boat from the northwest beach on Carrot Island. Low tide is the best time to hike. You can also hike about 1.5 miles down sandy Bird Shoal, with perhaps some wading. The Carrot Island Boardwalk is located farther east, directly across from the boat ramp at Front Street and Lennoxville Road. It leads across the island to a viewing platform that is a good spot for birding. Carrot Island is home to a small herd of feral horses.

Sea Gate Woods Preserve (252-634-1927; www.coastallandtrust.org). Located about 8 miles west of Beaufort off NC 101, this unique habitat preserves one of the rarest community types, a nonriverine wet hardwood forest, and provides a critical feeding and nesting area for more than 25 species of migrant songbirds. Contact the Coastal Land Trust to join one of their guided walks.

✳ Lodging

CAMPGROUNDS Coastal Riverside Campground (252-728-5155; www.coastalriverside.com), 216 Clark Lane. Shady campground just north of the village has a 320-foot pier and a boat ramp.

HISTORIC BED & BREAKFASTS Ann Street Inn (1-877-266-7814; www.annstreetinn.com), 707 Ann Street. Beautifully restored 1832 house has porches lined with wicker and rocking chairs, a full hot breakfast, afternoon cocktails, and an award-winning water garden. $$$.

☀ ♂ (ૐ) The Cedars Inn and Restaurant (252-838-1463; www.cedarsinn.com), 305 Front Street. Located directly on Front Street facing the water, the Cedars occupies the 1768 William Borden House. Set amid cedars and lush landscaping, the inn rents six guest rooms and suites, furnished with claw-foot tubs and antiques. Continental breakfast is included. Children over 10 are welcome. Recently reopened under new management, the Cedars is now also home to a much-acclaimed new restaurant, serving a gourmet dinner nightly. Reservations highly recommended. Rooms $$-$$$. Dinner $$$-$$$$.

♂ ☀ ♂ (ૐ) County Home Bed & Breakfast and Poor House Pavilion (252-728-4611; www.countyhomeb-b.com), 299 NC 101. A bed & breakfast like no other, this inn was once the county home for the local poor, beginning in 1914. Abandoned for many years, the sturdy tin-roofed structure, now listed on the National Register of Historic Places, survived to be completely renovated into 10 spacious two-room suites, each with two private entrances: one opening onto a veranda with rocking chairs, and a second giving access to a back deck with barbecue grills, overlooking the landscaped grounds dotted with hammocks and swings. Each suite has a refrigerator stocked with juices, fruit, yogurt, and bottled water. A basket of warm muffins and bagels is delivered to your room every morning. The County Home is located on the edge of town, with parking for boats. $$.

♨ (ૐ) Cousins Bed and Breakfast (252-728-3917 or 1-877-464-7487; www.satansbreath.com), 305 Turner Street. Three brightly decorated rooms loaded with amenities are available for guests in this casual, friendly B&B in the 1820s Jarvis Brown House. Downstairs, Chef Elmo whips up goodies in the kitchen, making for memorable breakfasts. There's a spice shop on-site. $$.

♨ (ૐ) Pecan Tree Inn (252-728-6733 or 1-800-728-7871; www.pecantree.com), 116 Queen Street. Innkeepers Dave and Allison DuBuisson make relaxation and charm the norm at the Pecan Tree, housed in a Victorian building that started life as the town's Masonic lodge back in 1866. Rock the morning away on the upstairs balcony, have a cup of tea on the wraparound front porch or just chill out next to the lily pond with the neighborhood cats. The seven guest rooms are elegantly appointed with antiques. Two suites have king beds and double Jacuzzis. A downstairs parlor is stocked with books of local interest, and an ample breakfast buffet with fresh fruit and baked goods is served in the dining room. A refrigerator with ice maker is available for all guests. Beyond the parking lot a large flower and herb garden includes many unusual species. The garden is open to the public. Complimentary bikes are available for guests, and the location is just a few steps from Front Street. Children under 10 cannot be accommodated. $$.

HOTELS ♨ (ૐ) Inlet Inn (252-728-3600 or 1-800-554-5466; www.inlet-inn.com), 601 Front Street. Located at the corner of Front and Queen streets, the 36-room Inlet Inn enjoys the best location in town. Several fine restaurants are just across Queen Street, the boat-tour docks lie directly across Front Street, and all the town's dining and shopping action is just steps away. The three-story building has an elevator, and a top-floor lounge where a widow's walk balcony overlooks the waterfront. All rooms are spacious and have private, but no-frills, baths. All rooms have refrigerators, cable TV, hair dryers, telephones, and coffeemakers, and many of the first-floor rooms have gas fireplaces. A call in the morning brings a complimentary tray of fresh baked muffins, bagels, and juice, plus a newspaper, to your door. Boat slips are available. $-$$.

HOUSEBOAT RENTALS ☀ Outer Banks Houseboats (252-728-4129; www.outerbankshouseboats.com), 324 Front Street. Houseboats for weekend, weekday, or full-week rentals come with a Carolina skiff for getting around. An experienced captain pilots your houseboat to your preferred mooring place.

VACATION RENTALS Beaufort Realty (1-800-548-2961; www.beaufortrlty.com), 325 Front Street. Lists cottages and condos in Beaufort, including many on the waterfront and in the historic district.

✳ Where to Eat

DINING OUT ⅋ ↶ **Aqua** (252-728-7777; www.aquaexperience.com), 114 Middle Lane. Seasonal menus at Aqua showcase fresh local seafood and produce in creative combinations, and fine wines from around the world. The menu is divided into small plate and large plate dishes. Small plates may range from a Japanese bento box with seared yellowfin tuna and seaweed salad to a Mozzarella Napoleon layered with local eggplant. Large plates are sturdier fare, but still creative: a fillet of choice beef rubbed with coffee, or fresh triggerfish crusted with wild mushrooms. The wine menu is extensive, and a nightly "wine discovery" is available by the glass at a special price. You can dine in the stylishly decorated contemporary dining room or outside on the roofed patio. The whole place is quite a contrast to the company's other restaurant, **Clawson's,** around the corner. Dinner only, $$–$$$$.

⅋ **Beaufort Grocery Co.** (252-728-3899; www.beaufortgrocery.com), 117 Queen Street. A casual spot for lunch, this local favorite becomes a sophisticated fine-dining experience every evening. Executive chef/owner Charles Park gives many creative twists to seasonally changing menus. All desserts, including a variety of cheesecakes and a great pecan pie, are homemade. The take-out deli counter is a great spot to assemble a quick lunch. Lunch and Sunday brunch $$; dinner $$$$; extra charge for sharing.

✳ ⚘ ✐ ⅋ ↶ **Clawson's 1905 Restaurant & Pub** (252-728-2133; www.clawsonsrestaurant .com), 425 Front Street. This landmark on the Beaufort waterfront occupies a series of historic buildings over 100 years old. Decorated with memorabilia from the town's history and other period items, the restaurant is often crowded with tourists during the summer months. The menu ranges from burgers to some excellent seafood bisque and the famous stuffed potato "dirigibles." The mud pie, made with Oreos and rocky road ice cream, is another local favorite and well worth the calories. The cozy bar is a favorite retreat among locals who know they can find the best beer selection in town here, including many North Carolina microbrews. Order a beer sampler and settle in to watch the game on the big-screen TVs. Lunch $; dinner $$.

✐ ♈ ↶ **FishTales Waterfront Restaurant and Tiki Bar at Town Creek Marina** (252-504-7263; www.fishtaleswaterfront.com), 232 W. Beaufort Road. This restaurant, located above the Town Creek Marina, is a great place to eat

or meet for a cocktail as the sun sets. Local seafood is featured in the daily specials, and the sunset view is great from the veranda. Diners arriving by boat can tie up at the dock. Live entertainment at the tiki bar n summer. Lunch and Sunday brunch $–$$; dinner $$–$$$.

♈ **Front Street Grill & Rhum Bar at Stillwater Café** (252-728-4956; www.frontstreet grillatstillwater.com), 300 Front Street. Casual waterfront setting meets creative cuisine in the best possible combination. The unpretentious street front belies an elegant interior dining room, where you dine on white linen. Or have your meal beneath an umbrella on the casual Afterdeck, with unexcelled views of the harbor. Sunsets here are spectacular, and after dark the deck is romantically lit by hurricane lamps. The outdoor Rhum Bar stocks a great selection of imported rums, and serves a fun casual menu. Dock space is available for diners arriving by boat. Lunch and Sunday brunch $–$$; dinner $$–$$$.

✐ ⅋ ↶ **Old Salt Restaurant and Oyster Bar** (252-728-2002; www.oldsaltbeaufort.com), 113 Turner Street. Conveniently located across the street from the Beaufort Historic Site, this casual family restaurant, formerly the Net House, has upped its game with a chef-designed menu and now serves both lunch and dinner, plus Sunday brunch, and has a full bar. Soups, dressings, and desserts are house made, including excellent seafood bisques. The kitchen uses only locally sourced fish and seafood. The adjacent lounge serves a casual menu, and oysters and clams steamed or raw on the half shell. Lunch $; Sunday brunch $$; dinner $$–$$$.

✐ ⅋ ↶ **Spouter Inn** (252-728-5190; www.the spouterinn.com), 218 Front Street. Superb waterfront views and friendly service make this a winner for lunch or dinner. You can dine inside or out on the partially covered deck, where you may spot porpoises or the Carrot Island horses. On Sunday, a special brunch menu offers Eggs Orleans, sitting atop crabcakes; seafood omelets; and crab-stuffed portobellos. Desserts prepared in the on-site bakery are fabulous, as is the Banana Crème Crepe, a

SHOPS AND RESTAURANTS ALONG BEAUFORT'S FRONT STREET FACE DIRECTLY ON THE HARBOR.

house specialty for over 30 years. Freshly baked breads and luscious desserts, including éclairs and napoleons, fill the bakery's display case. Dock available. Full bar. Lunch and Sunday brunch $; dinner $$–$$$.

EATING OUT ⦚ **Boardwalk Café** (252-728-0933), 510 Front Street. One of Beaufort's most popular spots for breakfast has tables on the dockside boardwalk, or you can eat inside in the comfortable dining room decorated with historic photos from Beaufort's past. Live music on summer weekends. Breakfast and lunch $; dinner $$.

⦚ (( )) **Cru Wine Bar and Beaufort Coffee Shop** (252-728-3066; www.thecruwinebar.com), 120 Turner Street. Comfortable, sophisticated shop sells wine by the bottle or glass, along with a light menu. A coffee shop with handcrafted chocolates made with Escazu one-source beans and homemade ice cream is just through the archway, serving breakfast sandwiches and baked goods. Locals love this place for the live music several nights a week. $.

No Name Pizza & Subs (252-728-4978), 408 Live Oak Street. The No Name serves much more than pizza and subs, including pasta and Greek dishes, in its dining room and at the drive-through window. Beer and wine available. $.

Roland's Barbecue (252-728-1953), 1507 Live Oak Street. Stop by this top caterer's for some eastern North Carolina pulled pork and ribs accompanied by Roland's famous vinegar-based sauce, or "pig out" on classic fried chicken, catfish, shrimp burgers, and other Southern favorites. $.

⦚ & ⦚ **Royal James Café** (252-728-4573), 117 Turner Street. Beaufort's oldest business in continuous operation is this casual spot, named after a pirate ship. Take a seat at the counter for a Southern breakfast, or one of the café's signature cheeseburgers, topped with secret chili

QUICK TIP: Foodies should plan their visit to the Crystal Coast to coincide with the **Toast to the Coast Restaurant Weeks** (www.toasttothecoast.org) offering special menus at some of the area's best restaurants, culinary tours, and more.

sauce. The menu features Beaufort's version of fast food: shrimp burgers, local steamed shrimp, and Down East clam chowder, all washed down by your choice from a lengthy list of beers. The bar is a local hangout and a favorite spot to "rack up" on the antique Brunswick pool tables, so expect to meet some characters if you visit late in the evening. $.

Taylor's Creek Grocery (252-838-1495; www.taylorscreekgrocery.com), 525 Front Street. Convenience-style store in a great location has a deli counter in the back serving salads and sandwiches made with Boar's Head products, Bright Leaf North Carolina hot dogs, breakfast items, and a terrific sherry-laced crab bisque. $.

CANDY AND ICE CREAM The Fudge Factory (252-728-6202; www.thefudgefactory .com), 400 Front Street, Somerset Square. Old-fashioned handmade fudge, ice cream, and frozen yogurt available overlooking the docks.

The General Store (252-728-7707), 515 Front Street. Carries 32 flavors of ice cream, plus souvenirs and gifts. Out back you'll find a coin laundry, great for campers or boaters.

MARKETS ⚓ **Chandlery at Front Street Village** (252-838-1524; www.frontstreetvillage .com), 2400 Lennoxville Road. This ship's store, located next to the boathouse at Front Street Village, has a huge selection of boutique wines and ice-cold beers, along with gourmet groceries, fishing supplies, outdoor gear, and souvenirs. Wine tastings are held on Saturday.

⚓ **Coastal Community Market** (252-728-2844; www.coastalcommunitymarket.com), 606 Broad Street. Earth-friendly store carries locally grown and organic produce, dried fruits, wines, and soy products; locally baked bread; and free-range eggs. Cooking classes using natural foods and local products, and yoga classes are offered.

⚓ **Fishtowne Seafood Center** (252-728-6644; www.fishtowneseafood.com), 100 Wellons Drive. Certified Carteret Catch retailer sells locally sourced fish, and shellfish including conch meat, raw oysters, blue crabs, and clams.

Martha's Spices and Gifts (1-877-464-7487; www.satansbreath.com), 305 Turner Street. Stock up on Chef Elmo's award-winning hot sauces, spice blends, and handmade sausages.

✳ Entertainment

CONCERT SERIES American Music Festival (252-728-4488; www.americanmusicfestival.org). Chamber music series sponsors performances by top regional and national artists in Beaufort and Morehead City from September to May.

Down East FolkArts Society Concert Series (252-504-2787; www.downeastfolkarts.org). Folk and roots music concerts are held September to May at Clawson's Restaurant.

LIVE MUSIC CLUBS ❄ ☕ **Backstreet Pub** (252-728-7108; www.facebook.com/TheBackstreetPub), 124 Middle Lane. Cool little spot behind Clawson's features a big wine list, cold beer, and live music year-round. No food here—unless it's free. Check out the upstairs lending library.

Dock House Restaurant & Bar (252-728-4506; www.dockhousenc.com), 500 Front Street. This landmark on the docks serves up daily live music on the boardwalk during the summer season. The inside is quite small, but you can get some pub grub or a big mug of coffee and breakfast with a view in the upstairs lounge.

Hannah's Haus (252-728-3757; www.facebook.com/hannahshaus), 900 Live Oak Street. Fun pub inside Gaskill's Hardware has 16 beers on tap and live music until midnight.

Queen Anne's Revenge (252-504-7272; www.facebook.com/QARBeaufort or www.qarbeaufort .com), 510 Front Street. Choose a beverage from the huge selection of craft beers and wines, then enjoy it on the covered deck along with some sunset music and views of the docks.

Additional spots to hear live music in Beaufort include the Cru Wine Bar, Boardwalk Café, and Fish-Tales Tiki Bar. (See *Where to Eat.*)

✳ Selective Shopping

On Beaufort's historic Front Street, a multitude of nautically themed shops carry everything you might need for a life at sea, from books and charts, to Bloody Mary mix, to shipboard cat and dog accessories.

THE BEAUFORT FOOD AND WINE WEEKEND IS A FAVORITE LOCAL EVENT.

ANTIQUES The Marketplace and Marketplace II Antiques and Collectibles (252-728-2325 or 252-728-2507), 131 and 126 Turner Street. Dozens of dealers display estate pieces from local and New Orleans's families, plus a selection of folk art.

Taylor's Creek Antiques & Collectibles (252-728-2275), 513 Front Street. Get a peek inside an old Beaufort mansion while shopping for vintage furniture, china, and bottles.

ART GALLERIES Handscapes Gallery (252-728-6805; www.handscapesgallery.com), 410 Front Street. Exquisite selection of pottery, jewelry, art glass, and works in other media created by more than 200 artists across the nation. Special section of Banker pony–themed art.

Mattie King Davis Art Gallery (252-728-5225; www.beauforthistoricsite.org), 130 Turner Street. Occupying the 1732 Rustell House on the grounds of the Beaufort Historic Site, this gallery displays juried works by over 100 local and regional artists.

BOOKS Rocking Chair Bookstore (252-728-2671; www.rockingchairbookstore.com), 400 Front Street, Somerset Square. Independent bookstore on the Beaufort waterfront is owned by writers and specializes in books by North Carolina authors, collectible books, and local interest titles for children and adults.

SPECIAL SHOPS The Bag Lady (252-728-4200), 413 Front Street. Browse Suzie the Bag Lady's huge collection of collectible handbags, ranging from clever to outrageous, or pick up one of Suzie's handmade Sun Totes.

Jarrett Bay Boathouse (252-728-6363; www
.jarrettbay.com/boathouse), 507 Front Street.
Retail store of a local boatbuilder carries classic
yachting garb, plus gifts and Jarrett Bay commissioned art and prints.

Old Beaufort Shop (252-728-5225; www
.beauforthistoricsite.org), 130 Turner Street.
Shop at the Beaufort Historic Site stocks histori-
cally related gifts and toys, as well as books on
local and regional history.

❀ 🐾 **Seagrass Whimsical Gift Shop** (252-
728-2775), 519 Front Street. Fun shop that
welcomes dogs offers a wide variety of fun
clothing and accessories, plus local art and handmade decor. Upstairs, a Christmas shop carries unique
holiday decorations.

Tierra Fina (252-504-2789; www.tierrafinanc.com), 415 Front Street. Bright and bold ceramics from
around the world, including popular Spanish ceramic house-number tiles.

The **Crystal Coast Countdown**
(www.crystalcoastcountdown.com), a multiday event at the end of December with
bonfires, live music, tours, hikes, sand
sculpture contest, and more, plus shopping
and dining deals, from Beaufort to Emerald
Isle, leads up to the Pirate Plunge and
Crabpot Drop with fireworks on New Year's
Eve.

✳ Special Events

April: **Beaufort Wine and Food Weekend** (www.beaufortwineandfood.com). Five-day event
includes wine and food tastings, seminars, dinners, art shows, and more. 🐚 **Easter Egg Hunt**
(www.beauforthistoricsite.org), Beaufort Historic Site. Free event for children seven and under.
Publick Day (www.beauforthistoricsite.org), Beaufort Historic Site. Colonial-style flea market and
period children's games. Free.

May: **Beaufort Music Festival** (www.beaufortmusicfestival.com). A weekend of free music and family fun featuring national and local performers. **Wooden Boat Show** (www.ncmaritimemuseum.org),
North Carolina Maritime Museum.

June: **Beaufort Old Homes & Gardens Tour** (www.beauforthistoricsite.org), Beaufort Historic Site.

July: **Barta Boys & Girls Club Billfish Tournament and Art Show** (252-808-2286; www.barta
billfish.com), Beaufort Docks.

August: **Beaufort Pirate Invasion** (252-728-3917; www.beaufortpirateinvasion.com). Captain Sinbad
fires on the town docks, then invades with his buccaneer crew for a weekend of feasting, dancing, and
other pirate merriment.

October: **Beaufort Historical Association Fall Gala and Art Show** (www.beauforthistoricsite.org).
Fall In-The-Water Meet (www.ncmaritimemuseums.com), Gallant's Channel docks.

November: **Community Thanksgiving Feast** (www.beauforthistoricsite.org).

December: **Beaufort ArtWalk and Historic Beaufort Candlelight Homes Tour** (www.beaufort
historicsite.org).

MOREHEAD CITY AND NEWPORT

JUST ACROSS THE BRIDGE FROM BEAUFORT lies the commercial center of Morehead City, one
of North Carolina's two deepwater state ports. The adjacent waterfront area is home to an active
charter fishing fleet, as well as seafood restaurants and markets featuring fish fresh from the sea.
Several of these, including the **Sanitary Fish Market** and **Captain Bill's,** have been in operation
since before World War II and are landmarks along the coast. The town is a center for marine
research, as well, with several government and university facilities.

The tracks of **Governor Morehead's railroad** run right down the center of the town's main
drag, Arendell Street, US 70. Many of Morehead City's attractions, restaurants, and shops lie along
either side.

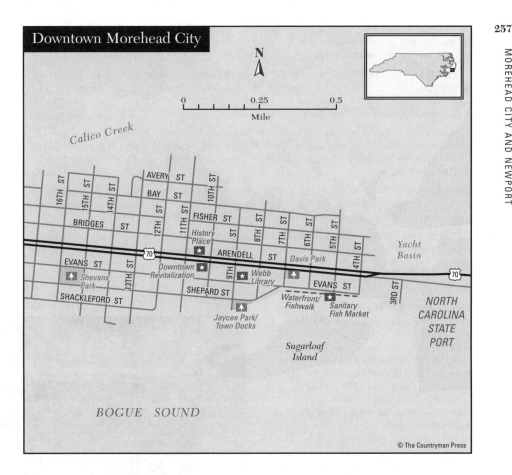

Downtown Morehead City

N

0   0.25   0.5
Mile

Calico Creek

© The Countryman Press

BOGUE SOUND

GUIDANCE The ✤ 🌊 **Visitor's Center for Carteret County and the Crystal Coast** (252-726-8148 or 1-877-206-0929; www.crystalcoastnc.org) at 3409 Arendell Street in Morehead City has helpful counselors and lots of local information, as well as restrooms, a boat ramp, and a pleasant picnic area overlooking Bogue Sound. The **Downtown Morehead City Revitalization Association** (252-808-0440; www.downtownmoreheadcity.com), 1001 Arendell Street, Morehead City. Visitors center housed in a historic 1904 train depot has information on Morehead City's history, maps of the historic downtown, and other info.

Morehead City Town Hall (252-726-6848; www.moreheadcity.nc.gov), 706 Arendell Street, Morehead City.

Carteret County Chamber of Commerce (252-726-6350 or 1-800-622-6278; www.nccoastchamber .com), 801 Arendell Street, Morehead City.

POST OFFICE The **Morehead City U.S. Post Office** (252-726-0920) is at 3500 Bridges Street. The zip code in Morehead City is 28557.

The **Newport U.S. Post Office** (252-223-4638) is at 460 Howard Boulevard. The zip code in Newport is 28570.

PUBLIC RESTOOMS Public facilities in Morehead City are found at the Crystal Coast visitors center, 3409 Arendell Street; the community center, 1600 Fisher Street; and at the Downtown Morehead City visitors center, 1001 Arendell.

PUBLIC LIBRARY ♂ 🕈 (ᵱ) **Webb Public Library** (252-726-3012; www.thewebblibrary.com), 812 Evans Street. Morehead City's historic library makes a good rainy-day destination. The Kids' Room has many books for young children, plus games and computers filtered for appropriate content. The Sports, Exploration and Adventure (S.E.A.) Room displays artifacts from local shipwrecks and contains documents of interest to historians, boaters, and divers.

GETTING THERE US 70 enters Morehead City from the north, becoming Arendell Street and running straight down the center of town, and over the causeway to Beaufort. NC 24 follows the shore of Bogue Sound west from Swansboro and Cape Carteret, joining US 70 just at the point where it heads north toward Havelock and New Bern.

The downtown section of Newport lies along US 70 north of Morehead City, while another, unconnected, section of Newport, often called Ocean, lies along NC 24 and the shores of Bogue Sound. The Croatan National Forest lies just beyond the development on the north side of NC 24 from Morehead City to Cape Carteret.

GETTING AROUND The waterfront area in Morehead City's downtown is fun to walk around in, strolling along the waterfront to see the fishing fleet, poking around in the area's shops, then checking out the bars and restaurants that line Arendell Street, just a block or two away.

MEDICAL EMERGENCY Carteret General Hospital (252-808-6000; www.ccgh.org), 3500 Arendell Street, Morehead City. Full-service hospital offers inpatient, outpatient, and emergency services 24 hours a day all year.

✳ To See

Architecture. The Morehead City Historic District, running along Fisher Street and Bridges Street, is a mix of Victorian mansions and Craftsman bungalows. Between 10th and 12th streets, the area known as the **Promise Land** has cottages in the Banker style, some of them ferried across Bogue Sound after hurricanes in the 1890s. The **Downtown Morehead City Revitalization Association** (see *Guidance*) sponsors an annual Homes and Heritage Tour every May.

Art. The Fish Walk, a series of bas-relief sculptures created by local artists Keith Lambert and Willie Baucom of **Shipyard Earthworks Studio** (252-241-2613; www.shipyard earthworks.com) celebrating the region's fishing heritage, runs along the city's boardwalk beginning at S. 4th Street. At S. 7th and Shepard, the new **Jib Plaza** features a triangular fountain topped by a 17-foot statue of a leaping marlin, the first phase of the Big Rock Blue Marlin Tournament's new home.

The **Arts Council of Carteret County** (252-726-9156; www.artscouncilcarteret.org), 812 Evans Street, Morehead City, sponsors the Adopt an Artist program, which places changing exhibits of artwork in local businesses. Consult the website for current shows.

More local art can be found at the **Morehead City Markets** (252-723-0311; www .mhcsaturdaymarket.com), held on the second Saturday of the month in City Park, 1001 Arendell Street, in Morehead City's waterfront district, from April to December.

SCULPTURES ALONG THE FISH WALK REPRESENT THE LOCAL CATCH.

DAY TRIP

Tryon Palace State Historic Site & Gardens (252-514-4900 or 1-800-767-1560; www.tryon palace.org), 610 Pollock Street, New Bern. Open daily except Thanksgiving, December 24–26, and New Year's Day. About 40 miles north of Morehead City up US 70 lies one of North Carolina's historical gems, the colonial capital of New Bern. Tryon Palace, a magnificent Georgian structure designed by architect John Hawks, has been reconstructed based on the original 1767 plans and archaeological evidence, and its 14 acres of gardens replanted in the Colonial Revival style. The one-day pass includes admission to the palace, plus three nearby historic houses, the surrounding gardens, and the New Bern Academy, now a museum detailing the city's history through the Civil War. The objects on display in the palace and other buildings are considered one of the top 10 collections of American and European decorative arts in the United States. One-day pass: adults $20, students grades 1–12 $10; other passes covering just the galleries and gardens are available.

TRYON PALACE IN NEW BERN IS AN ACCURATE RE-CREATION OF THE ROYAL GOVERNOR'S RESIDENCE IN COLONIAL TIMES.

The History Place (252-247-7533; www.thehistoryplace.org), 1008 Arendell Street, Morehead City. Open Tuesday–Friday 10–4. Operated by the Carteret County Historical Society, this is a museum of both history and art. Exhibits explore the history and traditions of the region, including menhaden fishing, duck hunting, the first yacht club, the railroad, the porcelain dolls of Sally Beatty, and artifacts relating to local Confederate spy Miss Emeline Pigott. The historical society sponsors many special events, including the popular Lunch with a Dash of History series, featuring storyteller Rodney Kemp. Free.

North Carolina Coastal Federation (252-393-8185; www.nccoast.org), 3609 NC 24, Newport. Nonprofit sponsors many conservation and coastal restoration projects. The headquarters building is open to the public and houses exhibits explaining the organization's works, plus an exhibit of some 15,000 shells, a library dedicated to works and videos on nature and conservation, and a shop with ecofriendly books and gifts for all ages. The **Patsy Pond Nature Trail** is located directly across the street.

North Carolina State Port (252-726-3158; www.ncports.com), 113 Arendell Street, Morehead City. Groups can schedule tours in advance by contacting communications@ncports.com. Free tours are also offered during the annual North Carolina Seafood Festival. Adults must show photo ID upon entry.

Outer Banks Wildlife Shelter (OWLS) (252-240-1200; www.owlsonline.org), 100 Wildlife Way, off NC 24, Newport. Tours of this hospital that cares for injured, sick, and orphaned wild animals are offered for a small fee. A nature trail leads to outdoor exhibits on the grounds.

Sugarloaf Island, off the downtown Morehead City waterfront. Easily visible across the water from the downtown boardwalk, this uninhabited island belongs to the Town of Morehead City. There are boat docks, a bathhouse with restrooms, and a nature trail on the island. You can reach Sugarloaf by ferry, private boat, or kayak.

University of North Carolina Institute of Marine Sciences (252-726-6841; http://ims.unc.edu), 3431 Arendell Street, Morehead City. Free seminars on marine topics offered weekly during the school year.

✳ To Do

AIR TOURS Crystal Coast Helicopters (252-514-2242; www.cchelitours.com), 5962 US 70, Newport Flea Mall, Newport. Get a real bird's-eye view of the many islands and beaches of the Crystal Coast.

BICYCLING The **MATS Morehead Alternative Transportation System,** a multiuse trail for bikes and pedestrians, runs along Bridges Road between Country Club Road and North 35th Street in Morehead City, connecting with the Calico Creek Boardwalk and the Rotary Park Fitness Trail.

Bike rentals are available from **EJW Outdoors** (252-247-4725; www.ejwoutdoors.com), 4667 Arendell Street, Morehead City.

BOATING ♿ **North Carolina Wildlife Intracoastal Waterway Boat Ramp** (www.ncwildlife.org), 3407 Arendell Street, Morehead City. Facility behind the Crystal Coast visitors center has restrooms and a shady picnic area.

South 10th Street Water Access & Boat Ramp (252-726-5083; www.moreheadcity.nc.gov), 1001 Shepard Street, Morehead City. City-operated facility has parking, a pier, and a boat ramp for boats up to 16 feet.

Morehead City Docks (252-726-7678; www.downtownmoreheadcity.com). Transient slips at S. Ninth Street, adjacent to Jaycee Park, in the heart of the downtown action.

(ᵗᵖ) **Morehead City Yacht Basin** (252-726-6862 or 1-888-726-6292; www.moreheadcityyachtbasin .com), 208 Arendell Street, Morehead City. Transient slips at the foot of the causeway to Beaufort.

Portside Marina (252-726-7678; www.portsidemarina.com), 209 Arendell Street, Morehead City. Harbor tours, Carolina skiff rentals, transient slips, and ship's store, plus ferries to Shackleford Banks and Sugarloaf Island.

THE BOAT RAMP BEHIND THE CRYSTAL COAST VISITORS CENTER IS A POPULAR SPOT TO LAUNCH.

BOAT TOURS AND RENTALS Crystal Coast Ferry Service (252-503-1955; www.crystal coastferry.com), 201 S. Sixth Street, downtown Morehead City. Ferry service to Shackleford Banks, Bird Shoals, Sand Dollar Island, and Sugarloaf Island for a day of shelling, sunning, surfing, fishing, bird-watching, or watching wild horses.

🐚 *Good Fortune* **Coastal Ecology Charters** (252-241-6866; www.goodfortunesails.com), Peltier Creek Marina, Morehead City. During the summer season, this 41-foot yacht sails on coastal ecology charters conducted by biologist Ron White. Cruises may include snorkeling, shelling, bird- and dolphin watching, and kayaking.

FISHING PIERS Public fishing piers are located all along the downtown Morehead City waterfront, at the north ends of 7th and 11th streets and the south ends of 9th and 10th streets. You'll need a North Carolina Coastal Recreational Fishing License if you are 16 years old or over.

FITNESS CENTER Morehead City Community Center (252-726-5083; www.morehead city.nc.gov), 1600 Fisher Street, Morehead City. Nonresident passes are available at this city facility, offering a wide range of exercise classes and a fully equipped fitness room.

FOR FAMILIES 🐚 **The Morehead City Parks and Recreation Department** (252-726-5083; www.moreheadcity.nc.gov) sponsors a summer camp program for children ages 3–15.

SEAGULLS GREET VISITORS ALONG THE MOREHEAD CITY WATERFRONT.

🐚 **Sea of Dreams** public playground, designed by kids for kids, is located at **Shevans Park** (252-726-5083; www.moreheadcity.nc.gov), at 16th and Evans streets in Morehead City.

GOLF Brandywine Bay Golf Club (252-247-2541; www.brandywinegolf.com), 224 Brandywine Boulevard, Morehead City. Award-winning semiprivate course.

The Golf Farm (252-223-3276; www.thegolffarminc.com), 612 Tom Mann Road, Newport. Driving range set amid old-growth pines offers lessons and clinics with LPGA pro Nina Foust. Special days for ladies, seniors, and military.

HEADBOAT FISHING *Carolina Princess* (252-726-5479 or 1-800-682-3456; www.carolinaprincess .com), Sixth Street Waterfront, Morehead City. Full- and half-day trips to the edge of the Gulf Stream. For hard-core fishers, the *Princess* also offers an 18-hour bottom-fishing marathon, and stand-up big game sportfishing.

Continental Shelf (252-726-7454 or 1-800-775-7450; www.continentalshelf.com), Eighth Street Waterfront. Day-long, 24-hour, and 48-hour fishing trips aboard a comfortable boat with a grill on board, and fully heated and air-conditioned indoor lounge.

KAYAKING The most popular paddle in Morehead City is out to uninhabited Sugarloaf Island, just off the downtown waterfront, where visitors can enjoy a nature trail, floating dock, and restrooms. A great spot for a picnic.

Numerous launch sites are located all along the southern waterfront of Morehead City (252-726-5083; www.moreheadcity.nc.gov). Popular spots to put in include Conchs Point (608 Bay Street), South 6th Street Day Docks (S. Sixth and Evans), the small sandy beach at the S. 11th Street canoe launch (S. 11th and Shepard), and South 13th Street Boardwalk and Dock (S. 13th and Shackleford).

SNORKELING AND SCUBA DIVING Olympus Dive Center (252-726-9432; www.olympus diving.com), 713 Shepard Street, Morehead City. Three dive boats docked at the Morehead City waterfront next to a full-service dive shop offer day and night dives to the area's many wrecks, lobster and spearfishing charters, and popular shark dives. A diver's lodge nearby provides inexpensive bunkrooms.

SURFING Action Surf Shop (252-240-1818; www.actionsurf.com), 4130 Arendell Street, Morehead City. Surfboards hand-shaped on-site by owner Bob Webb, plus skateboards, motocross, and accessories.

TENNIS Lighted tennis courts are found in Morehead City at **Swinson Park** (252-808-3301; www.ccparksrec.com), 4319 Country Club Road, and **Shevans Park** (252-726-5083; www.more headcity.nc.gov), 16th and Evans streets. In Newport, **Fort Benjamin** (252-808-3301; www.cc parksrec.com), 100 McQueen Avenue, has lighted courts, plus a walking trail, shuffleboard, a playground, a band shell, and restroom.

✳ Green Space

Croatan National Forest (252-638-5628; www.fs.usda.gov/nfsnc), 141 E. Fisher Avenue, New Bern. The 160,000-acre forest is the natural habitat of carnivorous plants such as the Venus flytrap and pitcher plant. Numerous recreational opportunities include camping, hiking, mountain biking, fishing, paddling, and swimming. Two of the forest's campgrounds have hookups for RVs. Primitive camping is also available at numerous sites. The 21-mile Neusiok Trail for hikers runs across the forest; other trails include the **Pine Cliff Equestrian Trail** and the Black Swamp OHV Trail. Flanners Beach on the Neuse River is a popular spot for freshwater swimming. Other areas of interest within the forest include **Fisher's Landing**, off US 70, site of the 1862 Battle of New Bern and a historic CCC camp; and **Long Point Recreation Area** on the White Oak River, once the site of a large Native American village. The Croatan ranger station, with maps and further information, is on US 70, about 10 miles south of New Bern and 30 miles north of Morehead City.

TRAILS Neusiok Trail (252-638-5628; www.neusioktrail.org), Croatan National Forest. The 20.4-mile Neusiok Trail, running between the Neuse and Newport rivers, features carnivorous plants and cypress wetlands. Primitive camping is allowed at three camping shelters along the trail, and at other undeveloped sites.

OWLS Nature Trail (252-240-1200; www.owlsonline.org), 100 Wildlife Way, Newport. Half-mile loop passes 40 labeled plant species, duck pond, raptor enclosures, and interactive exhibits. In-depth guided tours of the Wildlife Shelter are offered Tuesday, Thursday, and Saturday. Small fee.

Patsy Pond Nature Trail (252-393-8185; www.nccoast.org), 3609 NC 24, Newport. The trailhead for this easy 3.7-mile hike through longleaf pines is on NC 24 between Morehead City and Cape Carteret, across from the North Carolina Coastal Federation. Maps and restrooms available at the federation office.

Sugarloaf Island Nature Trail (252-726-5083; www.moreheadcity.nc.gov). Located across from the Morehead City waterfront and accessible only by boat.

WALKS Calico Creek Boardwalk (252-726-5083; www.moreheadcity.nc.gov), N. 19th and Bay streets to N. 22th Street, Morehead City. Easy mile-long walk with good bird-watching opportunities. Restrooms at community center, 1600 Fisher Street.

Fish Walk (252-808-0440; www.downtownmoreheadcity.com). Stroll along the Morehead City Waterfront Boardwalk, beginning at Fourth Street and Evans, to see 12 glazed plaques depicting sea life species common to the area.

Promise Land Waterfront Walk (252-808-0440; www.downtownmoreheadcity.com). Easy 2.3-mile fitness heritage trail leads from Morehead City Park along Bogue Sound. Maps and restrooms are available at the office of the Morehead City Downtown Revitalization Association at 811 Arendell Street.

Rotary Park Exercise Trail (252-726-5083; www.moreheadcity.nc.gov), 2200 Mayberry Loop Road, Morehead City. This 0.89-mile loop with fitness stations circles Rotary Park and Big Rock Stadium.

* Lodging

Morehead City is the home of numerous national chain hostelries, including EconoLodge, Budget Inn, Hampton Inn, Comfort Inn, Quality Inn, and Holiday Inn Express and Suites.

CAMPGROUNDS & **Neuse River Campground in the Croatan National Forest** (252-638-5628; www.fs.usda.gov/nfsnc), located off US 70, has 40 sites, 24 with electric hookups, flush toilets, warm showers, drinking water, and a dump station. Sites are first come, first served. A stairway leads down to sandy **Flanners Beach,** a popular spot for swimming and picnicking. A handicapped-accessible paved path circles the campground, and the longer **Beede Loop Trail,** for hiking or mountain biking, runs on a boardwalk through a tupelo swamp. $12–17.

* & **Oyster Point Campground in the Croatan National Forest** (252-638-5628; www.fs.usda.gov/nfsnc), FR 181 off SR 1154, Newport. Tent and dry RV campground along the Newport River has 16 campsites, handicapped-accessible restrooms, drinking water, and a shallow-water launch for kayaks and canoes. This is the southern trailhead for the 21-mile-long Neusiok Trail, and also a popular spot to rake for oysters. $8.

* **Water's Edge RV Park** (252-247-0494 or 252-247-0709; www.watersedge-rvpark.com), 1463 NC 24, Newport. Campers enjoy full hookups, a pier on Bogue Sound, paddleboats, kayaks, and planned activities.

* **Whispering Pines RV Park and Campground** (252-726-4902; www.wprvpark.com), 25 Whispering Pines Road, Newport. Situated amid tall pines, full-hookup RV and tent sites include access to a large pool and a freshwater fishing pond.

* Where to Eat

DINING OUT *&* (( )) **Beaufort Grocery Too** (252-727-0815; www.beaufortgrocery.com), 913 Arendell Street, Morehead City. Closed Tuesday. Formerly Shepard's Point, the sister restaurant of **Beaufort Grocery** provides a sophisticated dining option in downtown Morehead City. A favorite with locals who come for the weekday specials, Friday wine pairings, and Burger and a Brew deal, the restaurant serves a great prime rib, Southern fried chicken and waffles, barbecue cooked in its own smoker, and local seafood in well thought out preparations. On Sunday, a buffet loaded with breakfast

specialties, shrimp and grits, carved prime rib, cold salads, and a variety of breads and pastries begins at 11 AM. Full bar. Sunday brunch $$; dinner $–$$$.

& **Captain Bill's Waterfront Restaurant** (252-726-2166; www.captbills.com), 701 Evans Street, Morehead City. Fresh local seafood, available fried, broiled, panned in butter, or topped with an au gratin cheese sauce, has been the specialty here for over 75 years. Many of the dishes are from old family recipes. Arrive on a Wednesday or Saturday to sample the famous conch stew. This is a family favorite, with large tables in the dining room, and a deck overlooking the harbor where kids can visit the seagulls and the family of otters that makes its home here. You can get ice cream and candy at the counter up front, if you're walking the waterfront. $–$$.

& **Sanitary Fish Market Restaurant** (252-247-3111; www.sanitaryfishmarket.com), 501 Evans Street, Morehead City. A landmark

THE SANITARY FISH MARKET HAS BEEN SERVING CUSTOMERS SINCE 1938.

on the Morehead City waterfront since 1938, when the first 12-seat counter opened in the fish market here, Sanitary now seats 600, plus new expanded outdoor seating, but waits can be long when the tour buses roll in. Lunch features fish sandwiches, shrimp and oyster burgers, plus salads made of shrimp and fresh tuna. This is a good place to sample some of the more unfamiliar fish favored by locals, such as bluefish, jumping mullet, spots, wahoo, king mackerel, or mahimahi, all available in season. The hush puppies here are famous: You can buy a bag of mix to take home. The new Tall Tales Bar hosts live music on weekends. Overnight moorage available at the dock. Seniors' menu. Lunch $; dinner $$.

EATING OUT ♪ **Beach Bumz Pub & Pizzeria** (252-726-7800; www.beachbumzpub.com), 515 Arendell Street, Morehead City. Located at the corner of Sixth Street in the downtown district, this casual spot is a great place for a quick bite and a beer before or after a fishing trip or a visit to Sugarloaf Island. $.

El's Drive-In (252-726-3002), 3706 Arendell Street, Morehead City. Family-owned fast food joint has been serving burgers since 1959. Waitresses deliver burgers and more right to your car. Open late. $.

Garden Gate Cafe & Deli (252-247-4061), 278-L NC 24, Morehead Crossing, Morehead City. Sandwich shop in the Walmart plaza serves breakfast and lunch, including some great sweet potato pancakes and house-made pimento cheese amid lovely garden murals. $.

♪ (ʸ) **Raps Grill and Bar** (252-240-1213; www.rapsgrillandbar.com), 715 Arendell Street, Morehead City. Historic building makes a stunning sports bar, with nightly appetizer and drink specials, seafood combos, and plenty of TVs. Full bar and late-night menu. Lunch $; dinner $–$$.

❋ ↦ **Ruddy Duck Tavern** (252-726-7500; www.ruddyducktavern.com), 509 Evans Street, Morehead City. Casual waterfront spot in the original Sanitary Fish Market building serves a wide variety of creative cuisine, much of it with a spicy twist, from seafood-laden jambalaya to crispy duck to the ever-popular fish taco. You can eat outside on a deck overlooking Bogue Sound. Local produce is featured, and much of the seafood comes off the owner's boat. Full bar. $–$$.

COFFEE AND TEA Alex & Brett Coffee, Tea and Wine Bar (252-622-4688; www.alexand bretts.com), 513 Arendell Street, Morehead

City. Sweet spot in downtown Morehead City features delicious pastries baked on the premises.

(ʸ) **Coffee Affair** (252-247-6020; www.coffee affair.com), 2302 Arendell Street, Morehead City. Internet hotspot has a full menu of coffee and tea drinks, baked goods, box lunches, and terrific chicken salad croissants.

Infusion Cafe (252-240-2800; www.facebook .com/TheInfusionCafe), 1012 Arendell Street, Morehead City. Elegant tearoom next door to the **History Place** stocks more than 120 whole-leaf and herbal teas, single-origin coffees, and other infusions from around the world, and serves light lunches, desserts, and afternoon tea with scones and savories. Make reservations in advance for a formal high tea, served 2–4 PM. Live acoustic music is scheduled most weekend evenings. $.

PRODUCE Carteret County Curb Market (252-222-6359; http://carteret.ces.ncsu.edu), 1213 Evans Street, Morehead City. Shop for local produce, fresh seafood, flowers, and baked goods at the oldest continuously operating curb market in North Carolina from 7:30 to noon Saturday from May to Labor Day. A demonstration garden is located next door.

SEAFOOD ↦ **Captain Jim's Seafood** (252-726-3454; www.captjimsseafood.com), 4665 Arendell Street, Morehead City. The motto here is, "If it swims, we've got it." A certified Carteret Catch retailer.

WINES Somerset Cellars Winery (252-725-0029 or 252-727-4800; www.somersetcellars .com), 3906 Arendell Street, Morehead City. The Crystal Coast's first federally bonded winery offers tours and tastings.

☀ Entertainment

FILMS CCCF International Film Series (www.carteret.edu/foundation), Joslyn Hall, on the Carteret Community College Campus, 3505 Arendell Street, Morehead City. Series of four foreign films are preceded by live music and refreshments. The Dinner and a Movie option includes a dinner themed on the nationality of the film served in the Historic Camp Glenn Building on campus. Reservations required (252-222-6056).

MUSIC AND THEATER Carteret Arts Forum (252-247-6409; www.carteretartsforum.com). Annual subscription series brings professional music and theatrical performances to the Crystal Coast. Individual tickets $35.

Carteret Community Theatre (252-726-6340; www.carteretcommunitytheatre.org). Amateur theatrical group with an impressive 50-year history mounts an average of three productions each year, including musicals and children's plays.

Crystal Coast Choral Society (910-324-6864; www.crystalcoastchoralsociety.org). This chorus of 70 voices, recently guest artists at New York's Carnegie Hall, performs several concerts annually, including a Christmas performance of Handel's *Messiah*.

♂ Crystal Coast Civic Center (252-247-3883 or 1-888-899-6088; www.crystalcoastcivicctr.com), 3505 Arendell Street, Morehead City. Hosts concerts by regional and national touring groups, plus many annual events, at its location on the waterfront.

Morehead Center for the Performing Arts (252-726-1501; www.themoreheadcenter.com), 1311 Arendell Street, Morehead City. Spacious theater offers a variety of shows, including comedy, magic, popular music, gospel, and country, plus special holiday shows for the whole family. Special Crystal Coast Jamboree Christmas at the Beach show in December combines country, oldies, lots of laughs, and plenty of patriotism.

Also see *Entertainment* in the "Beaufort" chapter.

NIGHTCLUBS ☐ Arendell Room (252-240-2753; www.arendellroom.com), 715 Arendell Street, Morehead City. Hole-in-the-wall downtown bar is surprisingly plush and has the most creative mixologists—and best selection of liquors—in town.

❊ ☐ ✎ Bistro-By-The-Sea (252-247-2777; www.bistro-by-the-sea.com), 4031 Arendell Street, Morehead City. This popular eatery hosts a piano bar on Friday and Saturday nights all year.

☐ Jack's Waterfront Bar (252-247-2043; http://site.jackswaterfrontbar.com), 513 Evans Street, Morehead City. Locally owned spot offers live bands every weekend, plus daily drink specials and a great waterfront deck to enjoy them on. In accordance with North Carolina law, this is a private club. Bring your ID.

OUTDOOR CONCERTS Alive at 5 (252-808-0440; www.downtownmoreheadcity.com), Katherine Davis Park, Arendell Street between Sixth and Seventh. Free twilight concerts take place on First Fridays spring to fall.

Saturday in the Park Concert Series (252-726-5083; www.moreheadcity.nc.gov), Jaycee Park, Ninth and Shepard streets, Morehead City. Free concerts every Saturday evening from Memorial Day to Labor Day at 7 PM.

☀ Selective Shopping

On Evans Street in Morehead City, a stroll takes you past a variety of fascinating shops located in historic surroundings. Along the docks, you'll find a cluster of seafood restaurants and galleries.

ANTIQUES Downtown Morehead City has quite a nice selection of antiques shops, all within a few blocks of the waterfront along Evans and Arendell streets, most in the 500 to 700 blocks. Shops to look for include Evans Street Company Antiques, Light Tender's Cottage, Jib Street Museum, Seaport Antique Market, and Tir Na N Og. A bit farther down Arendell, **Olde Towne Theatre Antiques** (252-247-7478), 1308 Arendell, specializes in old coins and silver. Several art galleries are found in the same area. The Downtown Morehead City website (www.downtownmoreheadcity.com) has current listings.

ART GALLERIES Arts & Things Gallery (252-240-1979; www.arts-things.com), 704 Evans Street, downtown Morehead City. Gallery carries the area's largest selection of art supplies and sponsors a calendar of classes in many media.

♪ **BluSail Gallery** (252-723-9516; www.blu-sail.com), 903 Arendell Street, Morehead City. Intriguing gallery in downtown Morehead City offers lovely local art, a wide range of classes in various art forms—including cooking—and a fully equipped pottery studio (252-723-3271).

Carolina Artists Studio Gallery (252-726-7550; www.facebook.com/CASGMorehead), 800 Evans Street, downtown Morehead City. The area's largest gallery displaying original local art also offers classes and workshops.

Carteret Contemporary Art (252-726-4071; www.twogalleries.net), 1106 Arendell Street, Morehead City. Changing exhibits of original, cutting-edge artwork.

BOOKS The Book Shop (252-240-1163; www.moreheadcitybookshop.com), Parkway Shopping Center, 4915 Arendell Street, Morehead City. New and used books, DVDs, and audiobooks; trade-ins accepted.

Dee Gee's Gifts and Books (252-726-3314 or 1-800-DEE-GEES; www.deegees.com), 508 Evans Street, Morehead City. Established in 1934, this is one of the oldest continuously operating bookstores in the state. Selections and events showcase the many writers living in the region.

SHOPPING CENTERS AND MALLS In recent years, Morehead City has seen many big box stores, such as Walmart and Lowe's, move in, making it the shopping destination for the region. These are concentrated in **Cypress Bay Shopping Center,** at the junction of US 70 and NC 24, with Sears, Belk, and a number of specialty stores. Another center, **Pelletier Harbor Shops,** 4426 Arendell Street/US 70, has a concentration of upscale shops.

Newport Flea Mall (252-223-2085; www.newportfleamall.com), 196 Carl Garner Road, hosts dozens of vendors in covered stalls every weekend. A restaurant is on-site.

SPECIAL SHOPS Concepts Jewelry Factory Outlet Store (252-247-5244 or 1-800-926-3277; www.conceptsjewelry.com), 508-C Evans Street, downtown Morehead City. Earrings guaranteed not to irritate sensitive ears at discount prices.

Golden Gull (252-726-2333), Pelletier Harbor Shops, 4426 Arendell Street, Morehead City. A local favorite for stylish women's apparel since 1976.

Waterfront Junction (252-726-6283; www.facebook.com/waterfrontjunction), 412 Evans Street, Morehead City. Supplies for all kinds of needlework and other crafts, plus nautically themed gifts.

✳ Special Events

January: **Bridal Fair** (252-247-3883; www.crystalcoastcivicctr.com), Crystal Coast Civic Center, Morehead City.

February: **Art From The Heart** (252-726-9156; www.artscouncilcarteret.org). **Carolina Chocolate Festival** (252-354-9500; www.carolinachocolatefestival.com). Chocolate dinners, cooking demonstrations, and other events surround the main tasting festival at the Crystal Coast Civic Center. **Empty Bowls Fundraiser** (252-354-5278; www.emptybowls.net), Crystal Coast Civic Center.

March: **Coastal Home and Garden Show** (252-247-3883; www.crystalcoastcivicctr.com), Crystal Coast Civic Center. **Crystal Coast Half Marathon and 5K Race** (252-247-3883; www.ncraces .com), Crystal Coast Civic Center.

April: **Newport Pig Cookin'** (252-223-3112; www.newportpigcooking.com), Newport Community Park. Newport goes whole hog with more than 80 pigs on the grill. **Women's Fair** (252-247-3883; www.crystalcoastcivicctr.com), Crystal Coast Civic Center.

May: **Coastal Stars Quilt Show** (252-247-2316; www.crystalcoastcivicctr.com), Crystal Coast Civic Center.

June: **Big Rock Blue Marlin Fishing Tournament** (252-247-3575; www.thebigrock.com). Week-long event includes men's and ladies' divisions, social mixers, and a fireworks display. **Spanish Mackerel–Dolphin Fishing Tournament** (www.carteretsmt.com), Carteret Community College Boat Yard. **MCAS Cherry Point Air Show** (1-866-WINGS-NC; www.cherrypointairshow.com),

Marine Air Corps Station Cherry Point, Havelock. The state's largest air show features two days of military and civilian aerobatic demonstrations, aircraft on display, live music, and the famous "Night Show" featuring skydivers and aerial pyrotechnics topped off by the region's largest fireworks display.

July: **Morehead City Fireworks** on Sugarloaf Island, July 4th. View from the downtown waterfront. **N.C. Ducks Unlimited Band The Billfish Tournament** (252-237-3717; www.ncdubillfish.com), Crystal Coast Civic Center.

September: **Crystal Coast Grand Prix Speedboat Races and Car Show** (www.ccgrandprix.com), downtown Morehead City waterfront and North Carolina State Port. Free.

October: **North Carolina Seafood Festival** (252-726-6273; www.ncseafoodfestival.org), Morehead City waterfront. Weekend celebrating the commercial fishing industry includes seafood tastings, live music, fishing and sailing competitions, a free boat show, and Blessing of the Fleet.

November: **Veterans Day Parade** (www.downtownmoreheadcity.com), Arendell Street, Morehead City.

December: **Christmas Flotilla** (www.downtownmoreheadcity.com), downtown Morehead City waterfront, early December. **Festival of Trees** (252-247-3883; www.crystalcoastcivicctr.com), Crystal Coast Civic Center. **Morehead City Christmas Parade** (www.downtownmoreheadcity.com), Arendell Street.

ATLANTIC BEACH AND PINE KNOLL SHORES

UNIQUELY SITUATED along the Carolina coast, Bogue Banks, comprised of the beach towns of Atlantic Beach, Pine Knoll Shores, Indian Beach, Salter Path, and Emerald Isle, runs east to west, so both sunrise and sunset can be enjoyed from your oceanfront balcony. The long white-sand beaches that gave the area its Crystal Coast nickname face south, bringing warmer water and different surf than ocean beaches farther north. On the north side of Bogue, quiet sound waters make this a great destination for paddling and boating, and provide a breeding ground for many birds, as well as the seafood that has made this coast famous.

THE BEACHES OF BOGUE BANKS ARE PROTECTED BY FORESTED DUNES.

While the original resort on Bogue Banks, located opposite Morehead City, had its first beach pavilion back in the 1880s, military forts have occupied the eastern tip of the island since before the Revolutionary War. Today's Fort Macon, an impressive pentagon-shaped masonry structure, is also North Carolina's most popular state park, thanks to its fine public beach.

The heart of Atlantic Beach lies at the end of the causeway from Morehead City. On the ocean-front lies the area once famous as **The Circle,** a collection of rides, dance halls, taverns, and hotels. Most of the establishments were demolished to make way for a mixed-use project dubbed The Grove, to include several condominium towers and commercial buildings. Some of the local color, including an ice cream shop, a few taverns, and the area's best diner, remain, however, as does the public board-walk and the wide, white-sand beach adjacent to public parking. Plans for The Grove proceed, but very slowly, thanks to a number of environmental concerns.

Just west of Atlantic Beach, dense growths of twisted live oaks shield most of Pine Knoll Shores (often referred to as PKS) from passing eyes. This was once the private estate of heiress Alice Hoff-man, who willed the land to her cousins, the children of President Theodore Roosevelt. The kids of the national parks founder followed in their father's footsteps, setting aside much of the maritime forest as the Theodore Roosevelt Natural Area, now the home of the North Carolina Aquarium, and developing the rest with an eye on ecology. The island's only golf course is located on stunning terrain here.

GUIDANCE Atlantic Beach Town Hall (252-726-2121; www.atlanticbeach-nc.com), 125 W. Fort Macon Road, Atlantic Beach.

Pine Knoll Shores Town Hall (252-247-4353; www.townofpks.com), 100 Municipal Circle, Pine Knoll Shores.

The **Visitor's Center for Carteret County and the Crystal Coast** (252-726-8148 or 1-877-206-0929; www.crystalcoastnc.org), 3409 Arendell Street, Morehead City. The Cedar Point branch of the visitors center (252-393-3100) is located at 262 NC 58, on the mainland side of the bridge to Emerald Isle.

POST OFFICE The **Atlantic Beach U.S. Post Office** (252-726-5630) is at 1516 W. Fort Macon Road. The zip code for both Atlantic Beach and Pine Knoll Shores is 28512.

PUBLIC LIBRARY ((•)) **Bogue Banks Public Library** (252-247-4660; http://carteret.cpclib.org), 320 Salter Path Road, Pine Knoll Shores. Services include children's story time, faxing, public-use computers, free Wi-Fi, a changing exhibit of local art, and a free paperback exchange.

GETTING THERE Two high-rise bridges join Bogue Banks with the mainland. The Atlantic Beach Causeway begins in downtown Morehead City. The Cameron Langston Bridge, at the western end of Bogue Banks, joins Emerald Isle with Cape Carteret. NC 58 runs about 25 miles between the bridges, crossing to the mainland on the Emerald Isle bridge. Numerous beach access points are located along the south side of US 58 as it runs down Bogue Banks. Look for the signs with a pelican flying in an orange circle. (In our beach sections, we list accesses with bathhouses and restrooms.)

GETTING AROUND A series of mile markers (MM) help judge distances along NC 58. MM 0 is at Fort Macon at the eastern end of the island. The road has several different names along its length—it is called Fort Macon Road in Atlantic Beach, changing from East to West at the Atlantic Beach Causeway, and it is Salter Path Road in PKS. We'll call it NC 58 to avoid confusion.

MEDICAL EMERGENCY Atlantic Beach Urgent Care Center (252-247-2464; www.ouchcenter .com), 600 Atlantic Beach Causeway. Open during the summer season.

✳ To See

✳ ☙ ✍ ⚲ **Fort Macon State Park** (252-726-3775 or 252-726-2295; www.ncparks.gov), 2300 E. Fort Macon Road, Atlantic Beach. Open all year, daily 9–5; closed Christmas Day. Hours for the surrounding grounds, bathhouse, and swimming area vary by season. The eastern tip of Bogue Banks was fortified as early as 1715. The present pentagon-shaped fort was begun in 1826, fell to Union forces in the Civil War, and was garrisoned for the final time during World War II. Today it is the second oldest state park in the North Carolina system and also the most visited. The 27 vaulted casements in the restored fort house a comprehensive museum detailing the history of the facility and the men who saw service here. Guided tours, musket and cannon firing demonstration, and nature walks are offered, and Civil War reenactments take place in July and September. The **Friends of Fort**

THE CANNON AT FORT MACON STILL FACE THE OCEAN.

Macon (friendsoffortmacon.org) hosts a very popular free Friday night summer concert series on the fort's parade ground. The **Coastal Education and Visitor Center** houses ecology exhibits. Free.

North Carolina Aquarium at Pine Knoll Shores (252-247-4003 or 1-866-294-3477; www.ncaquariums.com), 1 Roosevelt Boulevard, Pine Knoll Shores. Open daily 9–5, until 9 on Thursdays in July; closed Thanksgiving, Christmas, and New Year's days. This branch of the state aquariums takes visitors on a journey from a waterfall in the North Carolina mountains, down through many streams and bays, to the deep offshore realm of the big saltwater game fish. Along the way, visitors meet live native brown trout, giant catfish, playful river otters, sea turtles, sharks, and red drum. Several huge tanks holds replicas of famous wrecks located on the floor of the ocean nearby, including a German U-boat; the *Caribsea,* torpedoed in 1942; and Blackbeard's flagship, *Queen Anne's Revenge,* discovered on the bottom just off Fort Macon, all now home to tiger sharks and other large fish. Outdoors, a boardwalk leads over the marsh to a snake exhibit and Bogue Sound overlook. Free programs are offered daily; kayak trips, marsh explorations, and fishing lessons require a small additional fee. Adults $8; seniors 62 and over $7; children 3–12 $6; children 2 and under free. Free admission on Martin Luther King Jr. Day and Veterans Day.

JELLYFISH AT THE NORTH CAROLINA AQUARIUM AT PINE KNOLL SHORES

BEACH READING Duncan, Pamela. *The Big Beautiful.* New York: Dial Press, 2007. A romantic comedy set in Salter Path.

Morris, Bill. *Saltwater Cowboys.* Winston-Salem, NC: John F. Blair, 2004. A fun fish tale set on the Crystal Coast.

✳ To Do

BICYCLING Beach Wheels Bike Rentals (252-240-2453 or 1-800-504-2450; www.beachwheels bikerentals.com), 607 Atlantic Beach Causeway, Suite 103, Atlantic Beach. Free baskets, helmets, locks, and delivery.

BOATING Anchorage Marina (252-726-4423; www.anchoragemarina.net), 517 E. Fort Macon Road, Atlantic Beach. Boat ramp, transient slips, ship's store.

Shackleford Charters (252-725-5941; www.fishthenccoast.com), 2300 E. Fort Macon Road, Atlantic Beach. Fishing and beachcomber outings, ecology and history tours.

FISHING Capt. Joe's Bait and Tackle (252-222-0670; www.saltwaterbaitandtackle.com), 601 Atlantic Beach Causeway, Atlantic Beach. Fishing writer Capt. Joe Shute specializes in saltwater fly-fishing after redfish and speckled trout. Shop stocks gear for both inshore and offshore fishing.

Captain Stacy Fishing Center and Headboat (252-247-7501; www.captstacy.com), Atlantic Beach Causeway. *Captain Stacy IV* headboat specializes in full-day and 24-hour excursions and night shark-hunting trips. Charter fishing also available.

((ᵧ)) **Fisherman's Inn Charters** (252-726-2273; www.fishermansinn.net), 200 Atlantic Beach Causeway. Fishing charters, boat slips, inexpensive motel rooms, and a bunkhouse are available.

((ᵧ)) **Oceanana Fishing Pier** (252-726-4111; www.oceanana-resort.com), 700 E. Fort Macon Road, Atlantic Beach. The centerpiece of the family-friendly **Oceanana Resort** is open to the public. The pier grill serves breakfast.

FOR FAMILIES Playgrounds and picnic areas are located in Atlantic Beach at the **Circle Beach Access,** and at the town's new **Coral Bay Park,** 915 W. Fort Macon Road, across Atlantic Station.
✎ **Kites Unlimited & Bird Stuff** (252-247-7011; www.kitesandbirds.com), 1010 W. Fort Macon Road, Atlantic Station, Atlantic Beach. Full-service kite store sponsors kite-flying events every Sunday morning at Fort Macon State Park.

✎ **The North Carolina Aquarium at Pine Knoll Shores** (252-247-4003) sponsors annual Holiday Adventure Camps at Thanksgiving and Christmas.

✎ **The Trinity Center** (252-247-5600; www.trinityctr.com), located in Pine Knoll Shores, offers a Sound to Sea Summer Day Camp focused on environmental education.

GOLF The Country Club of the Crystal Coast (252-726-1034; www.crystalcoastcc.com), 152 Oakleaf Drive, Pine Knoll Shores. Semiprivate course set amid maritime forest with views of Bogue Sound. Rental clubs available.

PARASAILING Dragonfly Parasail (252-422-5500; www.dragonflyparasail.com), 517 Fort Macon Road, Atlantic Beach. Located at the Anchorage Marina.

SCUBA DIVING Atlantic Beach Diving Services (443-255-3775; www.atlanticbeachdiving.com). The comfortable dive boat *Mutiny II* docks next to the Fisherman's Inn on the Atlantic Beach Causeway, Atlantic Beach.

♿ **Atlantis Charters** (252-728-6244; www.atlantischarters.net), Atlantic Beach Causeway, Atlantic Beach. The spacious *Atlantic IV* dive boat carries up to six passengers out to dive World War II wrecks or to snorkel at the Cape Lookout jetties. The boat also goes out on fishing charters, including bluefin tuna trips every winter.

Diver Down Diving Charters (252-240-2043; www.diverdownscubadiving.com), 212 Atlantic Beach Causeway, Atlantic Beach. Trips include shark dives, live bottom hunting, and World War II and artificial reef wrecks. Walk-ons available.

SURFING AB Surf Shop (252-726-9382; www.absurfshop.com), 515 W. Fort Macon Road, Atlantic Beach. The Crystal Coast's oldest surf shop stocks over 300 boards, including the house brand, Outer Banks Custom Shapes.

Bert's Surf Shop (252-726-1730; www.bertsurfshop.com), 304 W. Fort Macon Road, Atlantic Beach; two additional locations in Emerald Isle at 8202 Emerald Drive (252-354-2441) and 300 Islander Drive (252-354-6282). The places to find Bert's logo wear.

TENNIS **Country Club of the Crystal Coast** (252-726-1034 or 252-736-1134; www.crystalcoastcc .com), 152 Oakleaf Drive, Pine Knoll Shores. Semiprivate club offers court time and lessons to non-members on a fee basis.

✳ Green Space

BEACHES In Atlantic Beach, bathhouses are located at ♿ Fort Macon State Park, the Les and Sally Moore Public Beach Access (177 New Bern Street), and the new ♿ Tom Doe Memorial Beach Access on Ocean Boulevard. The West Atlantic Boulevard/Circle Regional Access at the Circle (201 W. Atlantic Boulevard) is the town's main beach access, with a boardwalk, sand volleyball, on-the-sand swings, and three lifeguard stands. There is a fee to park in the lots here during the summer.

Pine Knoll Shores has a bathhouse and 50 parking spaces at **Iron Steamer Regional Beach Access** (345 US 58, MM 7.5).

Driving is allowed on Atlantic Beach sands from October 1 to March 15 with a permit, $75 for nonresidents.

TRAILS **Alice Hoffman Nature Trail** (252-247-4003; www.ncaquariums.com), 1 Roosevelt Boulevard, Pine Knoll Shores. Half-mile trail leads along marsh to a brackish pond frequented by white ibis and other wading birds. Access is through the North Carolina Aquarium with an entrance fee.

Hoop Pole Creek Clean Water Preserve Nature Trail (252-393-8185; www.nccoast.org), NC 58, Atlantic Beach. Easy half-mile walk to the shore of Bogue Sound begins in the parking lot of Atlantic Station Shopping Center. Interpretive signs explain the maritime forest.

Theodore Roosevelt Nature Trail (252-726-3775), Theodore Roosevelt State Recreation Area, Pine Knoll Shores. The 1.5-mile trail leads through maritime forest and marsh frequented by painted buntings and songbirds. Trailhead is located in the North Carolina Aquarium's parking lot, and access is free.

QUIET TIMES ON THE BEACH

✳ Lodging

OCEANFRONT INN ✳ 🐾 ✐ 🐾 ((·)) **Atlantis Lodge** (252-726-5168 or 1-800-682-7057; www.atlantislodge.com), 123 Salter Path Road, Pine Knoll Shores. A. C. and Dot Hall operate this retro retreat with a friendly vibe set amid the live oaks along the oceanfront. Pets of all kinds are welcome here as long as they are well behaved, and many guests return every year, so reservations should be made in advance. Standard rooms with two doubles or a king bed, and completely equipped efficiencies, open onto balconies or a peaceful, grassy courtyard where feeders attract many birds. A wooden boardwalk leads to a wide beach with complimentary lounges, chairs, and umbrellas during the summer months. Lovely landscaping surrounds a quiet pool, where a little waterfall leads to a baby pool. High atop the three-floor building, a sundeck and lounge with pool table, Ping-Pong, library, and big-screen TV provides a gathering spot where guests can socialize. Nonpet rooms are also available, and all rooms have coffeemakers and cable TV. Off-season $; in season $$$.

MOTOR INN ✐ 🐾 ((·)) **Caribbe Inn** (252-726-0051; www.caribbe-inn.com), 309 E. Fort Macon Road, Atlantic Beach. Brightly painted and immaculately clean, the Caribbe Inn is a favorite among bargain hunters, with prices half of what you'd pay in a chain hotel. The inn is located across the street and a short walk from the beach, but it backs up to Bogue Sound with its own boat dock and slips. If you fish, you can use the fish-cleaning station, then store your catch in the deep freezer or cook it up on the grill in the waterfront barbecue area. Rooms here are cheerfully decorated with murals of sea life, a hit with kids. Two children under 12 stay free. $.

RETREAT Pelican House at the Trinity Center (252-247-5600; www.trinityctr.com /pelican), 618 Salter Path Road, Pine Knoll Shores. Part of the lovely property stretching from the sound to the ocean given to the Episcopal Diocese of East Carolina by Alice Hoffman and the heirs of Theodore Roosevelt, Pelican House offers guided spiritual retreats, silent retreats, and individual "personal time" for people of all faiths. Guests have access to the paths that thread the property's maritime forest, a prayer garden, ocean beach, sound-side docks, and other facilities. Rates include meals in the Trinity Center dining room. $.

VACATION RENTALS Atlantic Beach Realty (252-240-7368 or 1-800-786-7368; www.atlantic beachrealty.net), 513 Atlantic Beach Causeway, Atlantic Beach. Voted Best Beach Cottage & Condo Company on the Crystal Coast, Atlantic handles over 200 properties.

Atlantic Sun Properties (252-808-2786; www .atlanticsunproperties.com), 205 Atlantic Beach Causeway, Atlantic Beach.

✳ Where to Eat

DINING OUT ✐ 🕭 ♈ **Amos Mosquito's Restaurant & Bar** (252-247-6222; www.amos mosquitos.com), 703 E. Fort Macon Road, Atlantic Beach. Cleverly decorated, fun restaurant has great views over the sound. The menu ranges from sushi to brown sugar glazed meat loaf. Kids have a great time at "Skeeters," ordering Slimewiches (grilled cheese) and Snake Skins (buttered noodles) off the children's menu. For dessert, s'mores, cooked over a brazier at the table, are another kid favorite. Adults without children in tow may want to dine in the bar or on the patio, as the dining room is often packed with family groups. Gluten-free options available. Dinner only, $$–$$$.

✳ ♈ **Channel Marker Restaurant & Lounge** (252-247-2344; www.thechannelmarker.com), 718 Atlantic Beach Causeway, Atlantic Beach. Waterfront spot with a big deck and great view at the foot of the Causeway is a favorite gathering spot for locals, with live jazz several nights a week. Try the she-crab soup or clam chowder, and the seafood lasagna, if it's on special. A limited menu is served at lunch, but it includes the Baltimore Burger, a winner with both an Angus beef patty and crabcake, plus asparagus, on a house-baked bun. Lunch $–$$; dinner $$–$$$$.

✐ ♈ ✎ **Crab's Claw Restaurant** (252-726-8222; www.crabsclaw.com), 201 W. Atlantic Boulevard, Atlantic Beach. Closed Wednesday, sometimes Tuesday. Awesome beachfront location next to the Circle public access teams with fresh seafood at this longtime favorite, with decks overlooking the waves. Appetizers range from local littleneck clams from Harkers Island to a spicy crab dip praised by *Southern Living*. Steamer pots with seafood and vegetables are a specialty. Lunch and dinner $$–$$$.

EATING OUT ✐ 🕭 ♈ **Clam Digger Inn Restaurant** (252-247-4155 or 1-800-338-1533; www.clamdiggerinn.com), 511 Salter Path Road, Atlantic Beach. Popular with locals for its daily specials, the restaurant serves all the breakfast favorites from 6:30 AM. Full bar with DJ dance parties in the Cutty Sark Lounge on weekends. Breakfast $; lunch $–$$; dinner $–$$$.

DINING ON A DECK OVERLOOKING THE OCEAN IN ATLANTIC BEACH

4 Corners Diner (252-240-8855), 100 E. Fort Macon Road, Atlantic Beach. Breakfast is served all day at this classic diner located at the Circle. Breakfast and lunch $; dinner $–$$.

Roma Pizza & Subs (252-247-2040), 100 Charlotte Avenue, Atlantic Beach. Locally owned spot serves great pizza, hot subs, and Italian specialties, all made from scratch. Try the house-made chips. Delivery available. $–$$.

The Shark Shack (252-726-3313; www.face book.com/SharkShackAtlanticBeach), 100 S. Durham Avenue, Atlantic Beach. Serving burgers and baskets, this is fast food with a difference: live music on the grassy lawn; a beach-y menu of oyster, shrimp, and scallop burgers; plus beer and wine. $.

White Swan Bar-B-Q & Fried Chicken (252-726-9607; www.whiteswanatlanticbeach.com), 2500A W. Fort Macon Road, Atlantic Beach. Slow cooked Eastern North Carolina–style barbecue, ribs and barbecue chicken star on the menu, along with fried shrimp, flounder, and chicken, plus a wide range of Southern sides. Most folks get take-out since seating is limited. $.

ICE CREAM AND CANDY AB Ice Cream and Candy Shoppe (252-648-8623; www.ab icecream.com), 1010 W. Fort Macon Road, Atlantic Station, Atlantic Beach. Cool off with a banana split, sundae, smoothie, or Hershey's cone, or satisfy your sweet tooth with saltwater taffy or homemade fudge.

✳ Entertainment

CONCERT SERIES Fort Macon Summer Concert Series (252-726-3775; www.friendsoffort macon.org). Free concerts sponsored by the Friends of Fort Macon are held inside the fort Friday 7–8 PM, June to August.

FILM SERIES During the summer, the town of Atlantic Beach (252-726-2121; www.atlanticbeach-nc.com) sponsors free family movies on an outdoor screen at the Circle Beach Access. Free.

NIGHTCLUBS ✳ Beach Tavern Bar and Grill (252-247-4466; www.beachtavernonline.com), 413 W. Fort Macon Road, Atlantic Beach. Known to locals at BT's, this casual spot has been serving burgers and beers around its horseshoe bar since 1972. Poker, pinball, pool, darts, and sports on TV supplement the live bands and karaoke, and daily specials on food and drink. Lunch and dinner $–$$.

✳ ℽ **Memories Beach Club** (252-240-7424; www.memoriesbeachclub.net), 128 E. Fort Macon Road, Atlantic Beach. DJs spin beach rhythm and blues, otherwise known as shag music. The big hardwood dance floor hosts free dance lessons and meetings of the **Atlantic Beach Shag Club** (www.atlanticbeachshagclub.com).

✳ Selective Shopping

Shopping options abound in **Atlantic Station Shopping Center,** 1010 W. Fort Macon Road/NC 58 at MM 3, where you'll also find several restaurants. The **Atlantic Station Cinema** (252-247-7016; www.atlanticstationcinema.com) screens first-run films.

Both sides of the causeway to Morehead City are lined with docks, water sports, and fishing tackle stores, plus several restaurants with waterfront decks.

ART GALLERY Vision Gallery (252-247-5550; www.twogalleries.net), 407 Atlantic Beach Causeway, Atlantic Beach. Changing exhibits of original paintings and sculpture by state and regional artists.

BOOKS ✐ Beach Book Mart (252-240-5655), 1010 Atlantic Station, Atlantic Beach. Adults enjoy the best-sellers and local-interest books, while kids are crazy for the action figures and other toys at this independent bookstore.

SPECIAL SHOPS Coastal Crafts Plus (252-247-7210), 16 Atlantic Station, Atlantic Beach. A wide selection of gifts, including lots of nautical and collegiate items, shares space with the area's largest selection of knitting supplies in this family-owned shop.

Island Furniture & Accessories (252-727-4778; www.shopislandfurniture.com), 407 Causeway Shopping Center, Atlantic Beach. Big selection of wicker and lawn furniture, plus nautically themed decor and locally made shell art.

✳ Special Events

February: **Atlantic Beach Shaggers Hall of Fame Induction Weekend** (www.memoriesbeachclub.net). **Summertime Blues Art Auction** (www.buddy.pelletier.com)

Early July: **Atlantic Beach Fourth of July Fireworks** (www.atlanticbeach -nc.com), the Circle. Family event includes amusement rides and waterslides.

September: **Atlantic Beach King Mackerel Tournament** (www.blue waterpromo.com).

October: ✐ **Carolina Kite Fest** (www.kitesandbirds.com), Atlantic Beach Public Beach Access at the Circle. Includes a Night Fly with illuminated kites, daytime events with huge character kites, and a Candy Drop.

Late October: ✐ **Trick Or Treat Under the Sea** (www.ncaquariums .com), North Carolina Aquarium at Pine Knoll Shores.

Early December: **Atlantic Beach Christmas by the Sea** (www.atlantic beach-nc.com), Atlantic Beach Town Park. Visits from Santa and the illumination of the town tree.

KITES FLY HIGH AT THE ANNUAL CAROLINA KITE FEST, HELD IN ATLANTIC BEACH.

INDIAN BEACH
AND SALTER PATH

*If there was ever a heaven on earth, it was here. There was wild country on
each side of us. We had a church. We had a school. If anybody got sick, they
helped out. They had a feeling for each other, a love for one another . . .*
—LILLIAN SMITH GOLDEN, 1901–1985, NATIVE OF SALTER PATH

IN THESE TWO TOWNS, located in the middle of the island, the past and future of Bogue Banks
meet. Salter Path, one of the oldest villages on the island, is home to descendants of the original
settlers, some of whom floated their houses over from Diamond City, the lost town of Shackleford
Banks. Officially part of the Hoffman estate, the land was awarded to the established families
through a series of court cases. Today, the residents continue their traditional lifestyle as commercial
fishermen, selling their catch at local markets. To take advantage of the increasing tourist trade,
they've also branched out into Jet Ski and kayak rentals, and offer a variety of water sports
adventures.

The modern world crept up on the fishing port, however, with several large condominium projects
built on either side. In 1973, these areas incorporated as the town of Indian Beach, wrapping unincorporated Salter Path in a doughnut of upscale development. Together, the two towns offer a range of
accommodation and dining options from down-home to world-class.

GUIDANCE **Indian Beach Town Hall** (252-247-3344; www.indianbeach.org), 1400 Salter Path
Road, Indian Beach.

The **Visitor's Center for Carteret County and the Crystal Coast** (252-726-8148 or 1-877-206-
0929; www.crystalcoastnc.org), 3409 Arendell Street, Morehead City. The Cedar Point branch of
the visitors center (252-393-3100) is located at 262 NC 58, on the mainland side of the bridge to
Emerald Isle.

POST OFFICE The closest post office is the
Atlantic Beach U.S. Post Office (252-726-5630),
1516 W. Fort Macon Road, Atlantic Beach. The zip
code for both Salter Path and Indian Beach is 28575.

GETTING THERE See *Getting There* in "Atlantic
Beach and Pine Knoll Shores."

GETTING AROUND See *Getting Around* in
"Atlantic Beach and Pine Knoll Shores."

✳ To Do

FOR FAMILIES ✐ **Professor Hacker's Lost
Treasure Golf & Raceway** (252-247-3024;
www.losttreasuregolf.com), 976 NC 58, Salter Path.
A full day of fun with 36 holes of minigolf, a mining
train ride, go-karts, bumper boats, arcade games, ice
cream parlor, and picnic area.

SPA AND WELLNESS **The OC Spa and Wellness Center** (252-247-2035 or 1-888-237-2035;
www.theoceanclubnc.com), 1701 NC 58, Indian
Beach. This world-class spa facility at the Ocean
Club offers a wide variety of health and beauty
treatments, including full-day beauty retreats, in an
elegant and tranquil setting. Weeklong Health and
Wellness Weeks include luxury accommodations,
gourmet meals, a Vichy experience, yoga classes,
and much more.

THE GRACIOUS SPA AT THE OCEAN CLUB

For a beach soundtrack, listen to Mark Fielding Darden's 2004 CD, *Will This Town Survive? Songs and Stories from Salter Path,* released by Salter Path Records (www.salterpathnc.com). The disc comes with a 60-page book recounting the fast-disappearing life of one of the Banks' original fishing villages.

WATER SPORTS **Water Sports Rentals** (252-247-7303; www.h20sportsrentals.com), 1960 NC 58, Indian Beach, near the Emerald Isle border. Shoot into the sky on a FlyBoard, the newest water sports thrill; rent a Jet Ski or kayak; or sign up for a Banana Boat ride. You can launch into Bogue Sound from the 200-foot pier, then return for a sunset cocktail at the two-story Dolphin Deck and Tiki Bar, a cool way to end the day.

* Green Space

In Indian Beach/Salter Path, outside showers, restrooms, and 75 parking places are located at **Salter Path Regional Public Beach Access** (1050 NC 58). The **Indian Beach Regional Public Access** (1425 NC 58) has a four-wheel-drive access ramp.

* Lodging

HOTEL **William and Garland Motel** (252-247-3733; www.williamandgarlandmotel.com), 1185 NC 58, Salter Path. This small family-owned and family-operated hotel offers simple, clean lodgings, personal service, and great rates and location. Direct access to the beach is via a lovely nature trail. The property is pet friendly. $.

RESORT **The Ocean Club** (252-247-2035 or 1-888-237-2035; www.theoceanclubnc.com), 1700 NC 58, Indian Beach. Stretching across Bogue Banks with both ocean-front and sound-front units, the Ocean Club rents villas with one to three bedrooms in mostly three-story buildings with elevators and covered parking. This unique resort employs ecologically advanced technology to cause the least impact on the local environment. Each unit is cleverly decorated and fully equipped, with two baths, full kitchens, washer/dryers, large-screen TVs, and covered decks with water views. Linens are provided. Many units also have video game players, and Wi-Fi. Outdoor amenities include pool complexes on both the beach and sound, with a heated pool and

PARASAILING OVER BOGUE SOUND

whirlpool, a children's pool and cabana, an activity pavilion and boccie ball area, a golf putting course, lighted clay tennis courts, and a fishing pier great for sunset views. Beach attendants are on duty during the summer season with chairs and umbrellas. Guests can use the state-of-the-art fitness center, with its full menu of classes, and receive discounts at the Ocean Club's luxurious spa. Most rentals are weekly, but some nightly rates are available in the off-season. $$$–$$$$.

* Where to Eat

DINING OUT (OR IN) **Carlton's To Go** (252-808-3404; www.carltonsathome.com), 1701 NC 58, MP 11.5, Indian Beach. Chef Patrick Hogan offers a menu of popular dishes, including a lump crabcake that is Carlton's most famous dish. Located in the Ocean Club, the restaurant is now open only on holidays and for special events. However, you can order a Beach Bake of steamed seafood or a crabcake dinner delivered to your vacation rental. Or host your own dinner party either at home or around the patio fireplace at the Ocean Club Spa. $$–$$$$.

EATING OUT **Big Oak Drive In & Bar-B-Q** (252-247-2588; www.bigoakdrivein.com), 1167 NC 58, Salter Path. The specialty at this old-time take-out stand is the shrimp burger, reputed to be the best on the coast.

SALTER PATH'S BIG OAK DRIVE IN HAS THE BEST SHRIMP BURGER AROUND.

✴ Entertainment

☿ **Frank and Clara's Restaurant & Lounge** (252-247-2788; www.frankandclaras.com), 1440 NC 58, Salter Path. Tucked behind an old live oak, this classic surf-and-turf place has an upstairs lounge with balcony offering cocktails, a DJ spinning oldies, and occasional live music.

EMERALD ISLE

DEVELOPED AS A RESORT IN THE 1950S, Emerald Isle was named for the dense maritime forest that dominated the area. Today this is a family-oriented destination with many kid-friendly activities, and a large selection of beach cottages in every size and price range. The town has several public parks along both the ocean and sound, all the way down to the western tip of island, and a new system of multiuse paths. NC 58 crosses back to the mainland on the scenic Cameron Langston Bridge, intersecting with NC 24 at a busy shopping corner of big box stores.

GUIDANCE Emerald Isle Town Hall (252-354-3424; www.emeraldisle-nc.org), 7500 Emerald Drive/NC 58, Emerald Isle.

A branch of the **Crystal Coast visitors center** (252-393-3100; www.crystalcoastnc.org) is located in Cedar Point, 262 NC 58, just before the bridge to Emerald Isle.

POST OFFICE The **Emerald Isle U.S. Post Office** (252-354-6677) is located at 142 Eastview Drive. The zip code for Emerald Isle is 28594.

PUBLIC RESTROOMS Both the ♿ **Eastern and Western Regional Beach Accesses** have public restrooms, as do **Blue Heron Park,** behind the Town Hall; ♿ **Emerald Isle Woods Park** (9404 Coast Guard Road); **Merchant's Park** (8401 NC 58); and the ♿ **Emerald Isle Boating Access** (6800 NC 58).

GETTING THERE See *Getting There* in "Atlantic Beach and Pine Knoll Shores."

GETTING AROUND Emerald Drive is the main road through this beach community. It is the same road as NC 58 until the state road turns off to cross the Cameron Langston Bridge to the mainland. From that intersection, Coast Guard Road continues to the Point.

Beach Butler Rentals (252-241-0590; www.beachbutlerrentals.com). Rent beach bikes or a golf cart for your week at the beach. Free delivery within Emerald Isle.

MEDICAL EMERGENCY Med First Urgent Care (252-354-6500; www.thinkmedfirst.com), 7901 Emerald Drive/NC 58.

✳ To See

Bogue Inlet Fishing Pier (252-354-2919; www.bogueinletpier.com), 100 Bogue Inlet Drive. Emerald Isle's last pier, at 932 feet, is the state's longest. After a brush with the developer's wrecking ball, the pier's future seems secure, at least for the time being. It was completely rebuilt in 2011 after the visit of Hurricane Irene, with an improved king and Spanish mackerel area and an upper observation deck. The funky old Bushwackers Lounge is being replaced with SurfBurger, an open-air grill with a tropical twist. Spectators can stroll down the pier to watch the action for free.

✳ To Do

BICYCLING In keeping with its family-friendly identity, the town of Emerald Isle has wide multi-use paths stretching alongside many of its roads, including Emerald Drive (NC 58) and Coast Guard Road. The town's goal is to have every destination connected by 10-foot-wide paved paths that all interconnect with each other and a similar path in Indian Beach. Restrooms, bike racks, and parking can be found at ♿ **Emerald Isle Woods Park** (9404 Coast Guard Road), at the west end of the path; **Merchant's Park** (8401 NC 58); and the ♿ **East Ocean Regional Access** (2701 NC 58). The paths can be used by pedestrians, bikers, in-line skaters, and handicapped-accessible motorized vehicles. Maps of the paths can be found on the Emerald Isle website (www.emerald isle-nc.org).

Ocean Drive, one block back from the beach, is another good biking option in Emerald Isle, with paths connecting the occasional dead-ends.

Emerald Isle Beach Gear & Linens (252-354-4404 or 1-866-593-4327; www.emeraldislebeach gear.com), 9106-C Coast Guard Road, Bell Cove Village. Rents bikes by the week for the whole family at one low price, plus beach equipment and baby gear packages, with free delivery and pickup. Kayaks and stand-up paddleboard rentals also available.

Hwy 58 Bicycles @ E.I. (252-354-9006 or 252-393-7762; www.hwy58bicycles.com), 8802 US 58 (entrance on Reed Road). Dedicated bike shop goes beyond basic beach cruisers, offering a variety of bikes to meet your needs, from geared and mountain bikes to tandems and adult trikes—all nicely maintained.

BOATING The ♿ **Emerald Isle Boating Access** (www.ncwildlife.org), located on Bogue Sound/ICW at 6800 NC 58, MM 18, about 3 miles east of the Causeway, is the largest on the North Carolina coast, with four ramps; 112 boat trailer spaces, plus additional spaces for passenger vehicles; a kayak/canoe launch; and restrooms. Future plans call for a fishing pier, playground, and picnic area as part of this complex.

✳ ♦ **Bogue Sound Adventures** (252-422-7873; www.boguesoundadventures.com), Island Harbor Marina, 510 W. Marina Drive. Family fishing trips and boat tours to Bear Island.

Emerald Isle Adventures (910-538-2749; www.emeraldisleadventures.com), Island Harbor Marina. 510 W. Marina Drive. Pontoon boat rentals and light tackle fishing charters.

FISHING Once the home of several popular oceanfront piers, Emerald Isle is down to just one, the **Bogue Inlet Fishing Pier** (see *To See*). However, there is a movement afoot to save the family tradition of pier fishing, and the state recently announced plans to build a new concrete fishing pier at the former site of the Emerald Isle Pier, currently the Eastern Regional Ocean Access. Called the **Aquarium Pier,** the new facility will be operated as an outreach of the North Carolina Aquarium in Pine Knoll Shores, following the general blueprint of Jennette's Pier in Nags Head. The first part of the project, which will stretch across the island, has already been built—a fishing pier in **Cedar Street Soundside Park,** directly north of the beach access.

Emerald Isle also has a number of other public piers on the Bogue Sound side where you can cast a line or dip for crabs, including those at **Bluewater Drive** and **Emerald Woods.** Fishing license required.

FITNESS CENTER Emerald Isle Parks & Recreation Community Center (252-354-6350; www.emeraldisle-nc.org), 7506 NC 58. Town-operated recreation center has a fully equipped exercise room and indoor gym. Nonresident passes available.

FOR FAMILIES ❋ ✎ **Emerald Isle Parks and Recreation** (252-354-6350; www.emeraldisle-nc.org), 7500 NC 58, sponsors a year-round program of family-oriented Friday Free Flicks, on the second Friday of the month at 7 PM. Admission is free; popcorn and a drink are just $1.

✎ **Emerald Isle Speedway** (252-354-2313), 9102 Coast Guard Road, next to the Holiday Trav-L-Park Resort.

✎ **Playland and Lighthouse Golf** (252-354-6616), 204 Islander Drive. Go-karts, bumper cars and boats, located next to 18 holes of minigolf and a snack bar.

✎ **Water Boggan of Emerald Isle** (252-354-2609), 8915 Reed Drive. Cool fun for all ages, with waterslides, wading pools, and tubing.

KAYAKING Several of Emerald Isle's sound-side water access points are suitable for kayaks and windsurfers to launch, including the north ends of Cedar Street, Park Street, and 15th Street, each with a small sandy area. There are also undeveloped boat ramps at the ends of 13th Street and Kelly Lane.

Flatwaters Paddling (910-703-7878; www.flatwaterspaddling.com), 3102 Emerald Drive/NC 58. Specializes in rentals of kayaks and the new BOTE stand-up paddleboards (SUPs) equipped for fishing, complete with coolers, rod holders, and, on the SUP, a seat.

See *Water Sports* for more options.

TENNIS Lighted tennis courts are found at **Blue Heron Park,** behind the Emerald Isle Town Hall (252-354-6350), 7500 NC 58. Other facilities here include a grill and picnic area, playground, basketball court, and fossil pit.

WATER SPORTS See *Kayaking* for spots to launch your windsurfer. The Point, at the end of Inlet Drive, is a favorite spot for kiteboarders.

Carolina Kitesurfing and SUP (252-659-2534; www.carolinakitesurfing.com), 142 Fairview Drive. Take a kiteboarding lesson out on Emerald Isle Point, paddle out on a stand-up paddleboard (SUP) ecotour, or try stand-up paddlesurfing. SUP rentals available.

Hot Wax Surf Shop and Surf Camp (252-354-6466; www.hotwaxsurf.com), 200 Mallard Drive. Surfboard, stand-up paddleboard, and kayak rentals; kayak fishing tours; and surfing and paddlesurfing instruction, including day- and weeklong camps, taught by experienced locals who are on the water daily.

❋ Green Space

BEACHES Emerald Isle has a public ocean access at the southern end of nearly every cross street, a total of nearly 90. Two larger areas have bathhouses, picnic pavilions, grills, large parking lots, and other amenities: the ⚐ **Eastern Regional Access** (2701 NC 58) and the ⚐ **Western Regional Access** (299 Islander Drive). Both have lifeguards on duty Memorial Day to Labor Day and charge $10 for parking on weekends and holidays, April through September. Beach wheelchairs can be checked out from the Emerald Isle Fire Station. No. 1 (7508 NC 58). You can find detailed information on Emerald Isle's numerous public beach accesses at the town's website, www.emeraldisle-nc.org.

Driving on the beach is permitted from September 15 to April 30, with the exception of the 10-day period around the Easter holidays. Permits are required and cost $80 for nonresidents. Handicapped individuals are eligible to receive a free permit, with appropriate documentation. To get a permit, go in person to the Town Administration Building (252-354-3424) at 7509 NC 58.

Dogs are permitted on the beach but must be leashed at all times. Fires and fireworks are not allowed.

WALKS Emerald Isle Woods Park (252-354-6350; www.emeraldisle-nc.org), 9404 Coast Guard Road. Nature trail leads from Coast Guard Road to Bogue Sound. The area is a stop on the North Carolina Birding Trail (www.ncbirdingtrail.org).

✳ Lodging

CAMPGROUNDS Camp Ocean Forest Campground (252-354-3454; www.campocean forest.com), 100 Fairview Drive. RV park just west of the Bogue Island Pier has private ocean access and is within walking distance of several restaurants. A few tent sites are available. Minimum stays required. $–$$.

𝄞 ((ᵢ)) **Holiday Trav-L Park Resort** (252-354-2250; www.htpresort.com), 9102 Coast Guard Road. Oceanfront resort, rated five-star by Woodall, offers 325 sites with full hookups, Wi-Fi, and cable TV. Planned activities, a pool, raceway, beach concessions, and modern bathhouse are among the amenities. Rentals of on-site travel trailers available. $–$$.

VACATION COTTAGE RENTALS 𝄞 🐾 **Emerald Isle Realty** (252-354-3315 or 1-800-849-3315; www.emeraldislerealty.com), 7501 NC 58. Representing 750 cottages and luxury "sand castles," this company has a "no worries" policy that minimizes extra fees, and adds free perks such as continental breakfast, free ice cream, and concierge services.

Shorewood Real Estate (252-354-7873 or 1-888-557-0172; www.shorewoodrealestate.net), 7703 NC 58.

✳ Where to Eat

DINING OUT ♿ **Kathryn's Bistro & Martini Bar** (252-354-6200; www.kathrynsbistro.com), 8002 NC 58. A favored destination for date nights or special occasions, Kathryn's keeps its wood-fired grill busy searing fork-tender steaks, fresh local seafood, and free-range chicken. The Maryland-style crabcakes are considered the best on Bogue Banks. If you're just looking for something light, sit at the elegant mahogany and granite bar and enjoy your choice of 30 martinis, plus a lengthy list of excellent appetizers ranging from baked stuffed oysters to Firecracker Shrimp. Dinner only, $$$–$$$$.

EATING OUT ✳ ☥ **Ballyhoo's Island Sport Grill** (252-354-9397; www.facebook.com/BallyhoosIslandSportsGrill), 140 Fairview Drive, MM 19.5. A dedicated sports bar with TVs tuned to all the big games, Ballyhoo's is also a reliable spot for live music year-round and serves a solid menu of burgers and seafood from early morning right through late night. Breakfast $; lunch and dinner $–$$.

𝄞 **Mike's Place** (252-354-5277; www.eatat mikesplace.com), 8302 NC 58. Popular spot near the Bogue Inlet Pier serves a full breakfast menu and a long list of inexpensive sandwiches

KATHRYN'S BISTRO OFFERS FINE DINING IN EMERALD ISLE.

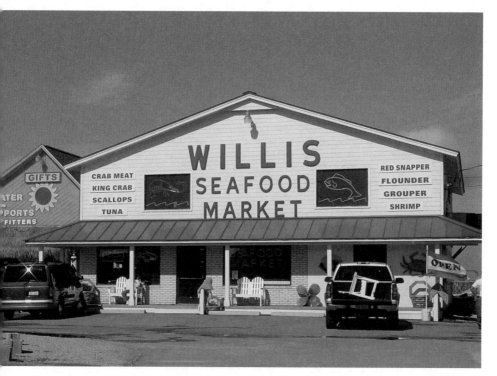

THE WILLIS FAMILY OF FISHERMEN OPERATES SEVERAL SEAFOOD MARKETS ON BOGUES BANKS.

daily until the 2 PM close, plus a breakfast buffet on summer weekends. $.

♪ ♿ ♉ **RuckerJohn's** (252-354-2413; www .ruckerjohns.com), 8700 NC 58, Emerald Plantation. Overlooking the lake behind Emerald Plantation Shopping Center, RuckerJohn's has a huge menu of popular favorites, including many dishes prepared on a charcoal grill. Music plays on the lakeside patio on summer evenings. Lunch and dinner $–$$.

COFFEE ☂ (ᵖ) **Beans-N-Screens Internet Café** (252-354-4336), 8700 NC 58, Emerald Plantation. Cool spot with free Wi-Fi access serves coffees and teas hot and iced, frappes, and lattes, plus homemade muffins. Table games and comfy seating make this a nice place to hang out. $.

ICE CREAM AND CANDY ♪ ☂ **Sweet Spot Ice Cream Parlor and Candy Shoppe** (252-354-6201; www.sweetspotei.com), 8201 NC 58, MM 19.5. Ice cream parlor features 48 flavors of Hershey's premium ice creams, frozen yogurt, Italian ice, and 46 flavors of saltwater taffy, plus lots of specialty coffees, teas, and candies, as well as a wide range of gifts, artworks,

and jewelry to browse. Kids have their own corner full of toys.

PIZZA ♪ **Michaelangelo's Pizza** (252-354-7424; www.michaelangelosinc.com), 8700 NC 58, Emerald Plantation. Local favorite serves New York–style pizza, whole or by the slice; pasta dishes; salads; gyros; and subs every day until late at night—a real lifesaver when you arrive in town hungry after all the other family restaurants are closed. Gluten-free pies and delivery available.

SEAFOOD **Cap'n Willis Seafood Market** (252-354-2500), 7803 NC 58. Operated by the Willis family, providing seafood to Bogue Banks for four generations, this shop stocks local fish and shellfish depending on what's in season, plus tartar sauce, slaw, crabcakes, and Key lime pie made with secret family recipes.

WINES AND BEER **Emerald Isle Wine Market** (252-354-8466; www.eiwinemarket .com), 9102 Coast Guard Road. Located inside the **Holiday Trav-L-Park** RV resort, this wine store stocks microbrews and wines from around the world, as well as gourmet chocolates and ready-to-eat items from the famed Beaufort Grocery.

✷ Entertainment

CONCERTS **Emerald Fest** (www.seasideartscouncil.com), Western Ocean Regional Beach Access. Free music concerts, ranging from reggae to country, most Thursdays, June through August, 6:30 to 8 PM. Bring your lawn chairs and picnics, but no alcohol is allowed.

NIGHTCLUB 🍸 **Emerald Club** (252-354-2929; www.facebook.com/eclub.isle), 8102 NC 58. Live beach and classic rock music in a smoke-free atmosphere.

✷ Selective Shopping

The **Emerald Plantation Shopping Center,** a huge collection of shops and services at 8700 Emerald Drive, MM 20 on NC 58, is an inevitable stop in Emerald Isle. There you'll find the **Emerald Plantation Cinema** (252-354-5012; www.emeraldplantationcinema.com), as well as a Food Lion supermarket, restaurants, and numerous gift, book, toy, and clothing stores that make for great browsing.

BOOKS **Emerald Isle Books & Toys** (252-354-5323; www.emeraldislebooks.com), Emerald Plantation. Family-run independent bookshop sponsors book clubs for children and adults, besides stocking a wide variety of toys, pirate loot, and bath items.

SPECIAL SHOPS **Flip Flops Gift Shop** (252-354-3446), 7702 NC 58. Cute shop carries all things flip-flop, from sandals you can wear to flip-flop wall hangings.

Lollipups Doggie Bakery & Boutique (252-354-7877; www.lollipupsonline.com), 9104D Coast Guard Road. Treats, fashion, and healthy food for your furry friends.

✷ Special Events

March: **St. Patrick's Day Celebration** (www.emeraldisle-nc.org), Emerald Plantation Shopping Center.

April: **Spring Home Tour and Art Show** (252-393-6500; http://carteret.cpclib.org). Tour of local homes and gardens, plus art show at the Lands End Clubhouse, benefits the Western Carteret Public Library.

July: **"The Buddy" Longboard Classic** (www.buddy.pelletier.com), Bogue Inlet Pier. Surfing competition honors the memory of a local East Coast Surfing Hall of Fame member, Buddy Pelletier.

October: **Bogue Inlet Pier King Mackerel Tournament** (www.bogueinletpier.com). **Emerald Isle Triathlon** (www.emeraldisle-nc.org). **Gordie McAdams Speckled Trout Surf Fishing Tournament** (www.emeraldisle-nc.org).

Late November: **Emerald Isle Holiday Parade and Christmas Tree Lighting** (www.emerald isle-nc.org), Merchant's Park. Weekend events include caroling, visits with Santa, merchant open houses, and a Holiday Arts and Crafts Fair in the parks and rec gymnasium.

SWANSBORO, CEDAR POINT, AND CAPE CARTERET

BACK ON THE MAINLAND, NC 58 continues north through the Croatan National Forest after crossing NC 24 coming from Morehead City. From the junction, home to a variety of national chain stores and an entertainment complex, NC 24 continues west over the White Oak River to Swansboro, another historic fishing village with an eclectic downtown. Just to the west of town, **Hammocks Beach State Park** offers daily boat trips to Bear Island, site of some of the most impressive and unspoiled natural dunes on the East Coast.

Swansboro sits at the eastern edge of Onslow County, home of the Marine training base **Camp Lejeune.** The camp itself has many historic sites; however, NC 172 across the base is generally closed due to security concerns. The impressive and moving **Beirut, Vietnam, and World Trade Center monuments** in Jacksonville, however, are open to all.

THE BEIRUT MEMORIAL AT CAMP LEJEUNE IN JACKSONVILLE

GUIDANCE For information on Swansboro, contact the **Swansboro Area Chamber of Commerce** (910-326-1174; www.swansboro chamber.org), 502 Church Street, Swansboro, or **Onslow County Tourism** (1-800-932-2144; www.onslowcountytourism.com), 1099 Gum Branch Road, Jacksonville.

A branch of the **Crystal Coast Visitor's Center** (252-393-3100; www.crystalcoastnc.org) is located in Cedar Point, 262 NC 58, just before the bridge to Emerald Isle.

More sources of local information:

Cape Carteret Town Hall (252-393-8483; www.townofcapecarteret.com), 102 Dolphin Street, Cape Carteret.

Cedar Point Town Hall (252-393-7898; www .cedarpointnc.org), 427 Sherwood Avenue, Cedar Point.

Swansboro Town Hall (910-326-4428; www.swansboro-nc.org), 502 Church Street, Swansboro.

POST OFFICE The **Swansboro U.S. Post Office** (910-326-5959) is at 664 W. Corbett Avenue. The zip code in Swansboro, Cedar Point, and Cape Carteret is 28584. The area code in Swansboro changes to 910.

PUBLIC LIBRARY (ᵂ) **Western Carteret Public Library** (252-728-2050; http://carteret .cpclib.org), 230 Taylor Notion Road, Cape Carteret. Services include children's story time, faxing, public-use computers, free Wi-Fi, changing exhibits of local art, and a free paperback exchange.

(ᵂ) **Onslow County Library–Swansboro Branch** (910-326-4888; www.onslowcountync.gov), 1460 W. Corbett Avenue, Swansboro.

GETTING THERE NC 58, coming over the bridge from Emerald Isle, and NC 24 meet in the town of Cape Carteret. The communities known as Bogue and Ocean are to the east of this junction; the town of Cedar Point lies to the west on the banks of the White Oak River. Swansboro is just across the river.

GETTING AROUND *By Boat:* **Marsh Cruises and Water Taxi** (910-330-8750; www.marshcruises .com). Traveling by water is the best way to get around the Crystal Coast. This company will take you out to Bear Island, to dinner along the docks in Swansboro, or on a sunset cruise.

On Foot: Swansboro's historic downtown, located along the south bank of the White Oak River, is ideal for a walking tour.

✳ To See

Carteret County Speedway & Entertainment Complex (252-393-1245; www.carteretcounty speedway.com), 501 Whitehouse Forks Road, Swansboro. Historic racetrack, currently under renovation, will host the NASCAR Racing Series, plus concerts, car shows, and other fun events.

Hammocks Beach State Park (910-326-4881; www.ncparks.gov), 1572 Hammocks Beach Road, Swansboro. Located just outside Swansboro, this state park includes several uninhabited islands. Bear Island, the most popular, is a barrier island about 3 miles long and less than a mile wide with a pristine beach, extensive dune system, and pockets of maritime forest. Accessible only by boat, the island is a popular spot for ocean swimming, primitive camping, kayaking, and birding. On the mainland, the park visitors center, with ecological exhibits, is free and open daily all year (except for Christmas Day);

THE BOARDWALK AT HAMMOCKS BEACH STATE PARK

however, the ferry to Bear Island runs only April to October on a variable schedule. Fares are $5 round-trip for adults; $3 for seniors ages 62 and up and for children ages 6–12.

Swansboro Historic District & Bicentennial Park (910-326-1174; www.swansborohistory.blog spot.com), bounded by NC 24 and the White Oak River. Listed on the National Register of Historic Places, Swansboro's waterfront is home to an eclectic selection of architectural styles. **Bicentennial Park,** located on the waterfront at the base of the NC 24 bridge, features a statue of native son Otway Burns, captain of the *Snap Dragon* privateer during the War of 1812 and the first person to build a steamboat in North Carolina. The 1901 **William Edward Mattocks House,** 107 Front Street, now houses the Tidewater Gallery.

✳ To Do

BICYCLING The 25-mile **Swansboro Bicentennial Bicycle Trail** makes a loop into the Croatan National Forest before returning to the historic fishing village. The 19-mile signed **City to the Sea Bike Trail** (www.onslowcountytourism.com) runs from Jacksonville to Hammocks Beach State Park. Maps of these trails can also be ordered from the North Carolina Department of Transportation website (www.ncdot.org).

Bikes-R-In (252-393-7161 or 1-888-393-7161; www.bikes-r-in.com), 1020 NC 24, Cedar Point. Rents adult and kids bikes, plus strollers and bike racks.

BOATING The North Carolina Wildlife Service (www.ncwildlife.org) maintains free boat ramps at ♿ **Cedar Point** (144 Cedar Point Boulevard/NC 24), a large facility that also has a canoe/kayak launch, a fishing pier, and restrooms. A smaller boat ramp is located at **Shell Rock Landing** (250 Shell Rock Landing Road, Hubert), south of Hammock Beach State Park. Free boat ramps are located throughout the **Croatan National Forest** (252-638-5628; www.fs.usda.gov/nfsnc). Those at Catfish Lake, Great Lake, and Oyster Point are best suited to shallow-bottom boats.

Dudley's Marina (252-393-2204; www.dudleysmarina.net), 106 NC 24, Cedar Point. Family-owned marina offers dockage for transients, courtesy car, charter fishing fleet, and ship's store. Several charter fishing boats dock here. Check www.nccharterfishing.com for options.

Marsh Cruises and Water Taxi. See *Getting Around.*

ECOTOURS ✍ **Sandbar Safari Eco-Tours** (252-725-4614; www.sandbarsafari.com), 328 Live Oak Drive, Cape Carteret. Custom-designed boat tours can include shelling, shrimping, crabbing, digging for clams, dolphin and bird-watching, or some light tackle fishing.

Second Wind Eco-tours (910-325-3600; www.secondwindecotours.com), 208 W. Main Street, Swansboro. Tours combine yoga, biking, and kayaking. Bicycle, kayak, and stand-up paddleboard rentals, plus yoga classes, also available.

FITNESS CENTER Cape Carteret Aquatic and Wellness Center (252-393-1000; www.ccaw.net), 300 Taylor Notion Road, Cape Carteret. Temporary memberships and day passes are offered at this full-service fitness facility, with an indoor pool, hot tub, steam room, and fitness equipment.

FOR FAMILIES The many military families based at Camp Lejeune ensure that there's lots of fun for families in the area. A day at the farm, learning about what rural life was like, is a popular family activity. Visit ✍ **Mike's Farm** (910-324-3422; www.mikesfarm.com), 1600 Haw Branch Road, Beulaville, to meet a variety of farm animals, see a bakery in action, then have a fried chicken family-style meal at the on-site restaurant.

✍ **Golfin' Dolphin Family Recreation Center** (252-393-8131; www.thegolfindolphin.com), 134 Golfin Dolphin Drive, at the corner of NC 58 and NC 24, Cape Carteret. Minigolf, driving range, go-karts, bumper boats, batting cages, and a summertime water wars area.

✍ ⍍ **Mac Daddy's Bowling Center** (252-393-6565; www.mymacdaddys.com), 130 Golfin Dolphin Drive, Cape Carteret. Bowling center with a huge video game arcade, plus a sports bar and grill with beer for the grown-ups.

GOLF Paradise Point Golf Course (910-451-5445; www.mccslejeune.com), Brewster Boulevard, Camp Lejeune. The general public is invited to play the two 18-hole courses on the Marine Corps base just west of Swansboro, including the Gold Course, designed by George Cobb, renowned architect of Augusta National and a former marine.

Silver Creek Golf Club (252-393-8058; www.golfemeraldisle.com), 601 Pelletier Loop Road, Swansboro. Club rentals and driving range available.

SWANSBORO HARBOR AT SUNSET

Star Hill Golf Club (252-393-8111; www.starhillgolf.com), 202 Clubhouse Drive, Cape Carteret. Semiprivate club offers 27 holes of golf with bent grass greens.

HEADBOAT FISHING Nancy Lee Fishing Center (252-354-3474 or 910-326-4304; www.nancylee fishingcharters.com), 128 W. Corbett Avenue, Swansboro. Two headboats, both named *Nancy Lee,* offer five-hour fishing trips from a dock between the bridges in Swansboro.

HORSEBACK RIDING ♂ **Equine Country USA** (910-347-4511; www.equinecountryusa.com), 1259 McAllister Road, Jacksonville. Horse resort offers trail and carriage rides, plus lessons with English or Western tack. Inexpensive cabin rentals available.

KAYAKING The area around Swansboro is one of the best for kayaking and canoeing on the East Coast, with opportunities for paddling both open saltwater inlets and slow-flowing blackwater rivers. On the saltwater side, two marked paddle trails in the protected waters of **Hammocks Beach State Park** (910-326-4881; www.ncparks.gov) thread their ways from the dock at the visitors center to Bear Island, with its unspoiled dunes, and to Huggins Island, with a large maritime forest of many live oaks. Both are great spots for birding and shelling.

The **White Oak River Paddle Trail** (1-800-932-2144; www.onslowcountytourism.com) travels down the upper regions of this blackwater stream, through cypress swamps draped in Spanish moss, ending at Stella, about 10 miles north of Swansboro. The 20-mile trail begins at the **White Oak River Campground** (910-743-3051; www.whiteoakrivercampground.com), US 17, Maysville, where White Oak River Outfitters (910-743-2744) rents kayaks and canoes, as well as offers guided tours and a shuttle service. Below Stella the White Oak widens to over a mile, becoming first a freshwater, then a saltwater tidal estuary. Paddlers can continue to the Cedar Island campground or beyond, to the Swansboro waterfront.

The **New River Paddle Trail** (1-800-932-2144; www.onslowcountytourism.com), with unusual limestone formations along its upper course, begins in Richlands and ends in downtown Jacksonville, about 20 miles from Swansboro.

Ambitious paddlers will enjoy the **Croatan Saltwater Adventure Trail,** a 100-mile route that can take up to seven days. Beginning at the Brice's Creek Paddle Trail near New Bern, it almost circumnavigates the Croatan National Forest, traversing the Trent River, Neuse River, historic Harlowe Canal, Bogue Sound, and White Oak River in turn, visiting historic sites and camping along the way. A search of the national forest website (www.fs.fed.us) should turn up a map.

Barrier Island Kayaks (252-393-6457; www.barrierislandkayaks.com), 160 NC 24, Swansboro. This Nigel Dennis Kayaks Expedition Center rents kayaks and stand-up paddleboards, and offers lessons and tours, including a marsh ecotour and a paddle to Bear Island. Excursions around the tip of Cape Lookout, into the Atlantic to listen to dolphins, and longer island-to-island trips are also available.

MUD BOGGING AND RACING Dirt trail bikes and mud racing are popular in the Camp Lejeune area north of Swansboro. Two facilities in the area are **Half Moon MX Park** (910-382-4394; www .halfmoonmxpark.com), 1037 Ramsey Road, Jacksonville, and ♂ **Jumping Run Creek Mudbog** (910-326-1511 or 910-326-6999; www.promud.com), Riggs Road, Hubert.

In the **Croatan National Forest** (252-638-5628; www.fs.usda.gov/nfsnc), the 8-mile **Black Swamp Trail** is designed for off-road vehicles. A $5 permit, available at the district office in New Bern (141 E. Fisher Avenue), is required.

PRIMITIVE CAMPING Fourteen primitive campsites, are located on **Bear Island in Hammock Beach State Park** (910-326-4881; www.ncparks.gov). Water and restroom facilities are available on the island, except mid-November to mid-March. Fires are not permitted. Reservations are highly recommended.

Numerous primitive campsites are available in the **Croatan National Forest** (252-638-5628; www.fs.usda.gov/nfsnc). Those accessible by US 58 from Cape Carteret include Long Point Landing, along the White Oak River, as well as Catfish Lake and Great Lake, blackwater pocosin ponds in the forest's interior.

TENNIS Lighted tennis courts are found at **Western Park** (252-808-3301; www.ccparksrec.com), on Old Highway 58 in Cedar Point, along with a picnic area, playground, and restrooms.

✳ Green Space

BEACHES The beach at Bear Island, part of **Hammocks Beach State Park** (910-326-4881; www .ncparks.gov), south of Swansboro, is one of the wildest and least touched of any barrier island. It can only be reached by boat, and no vehicles are allowed. On the ocean side of the island, a boardwalk connects shaded picnic pavilions and a bathhouse with restrooms, drinking water, and cold water showers. A concession stand is open Memorial Day to Labor Day, when lifeguards are also on duty. Primitive camping sites are available ($13) year-round. Reservations recommended.

TRAILS Tideland Trail (252-638-5628; www.trailsofnc.com/croatan), Croatan National Forest. This designated National Recreation Trail winds through the marsh on boardwalks from the Cedar Point Campground.

✴ Lodging

BED & BREAKFAST INN ♿ ☎ **Harborlight Guest House** (252-393-6969 or 1-800-624-8439; www.harborlightnc.com), 332 Live Oak Drive, Cape Carteret. Selected as one of the best undiscovered bed & breakfasts in the country by BedandBreakfast.com, the Harborlight sits slightly off the beaten track on a peninsula jutting into Bogue Sound. The isolation and gracious amenities make this a favorite for romantic getaways. Seven elegantly appointed suites offer two-person whirlpool tubs, fireplaces, waterfront decks, and awesome views. Gourmet breakfasts, served in your suite or on the deck, include creative dishes such as baked grapefruit, peach glazed French toast, and sausage stuffed mushrooms. One ground floor suite is handicapped accessible. Guests may use the inn's beach chairs and umbrellas, and fishing rods. Romance packages with in-room massage available. $$–$$$$.

MOTEL ♿ ☎ **Waterway Inn** (252-393-8027 or 1-877-216-4206; www.waterwayinn.net), 160 Cedar Point Boulevard/NC 24, Cape Carteret. Motel with 16 recently remodeled rooms sits directly on the Intracoastal Waterway (Marker 46), making it a favorite with boaters and kayakers. A boat pier and 90-foot fishing pier are on the property. $.

MOTOR INN ♿ ☎ **Best Western Plus Silver Creek Inn** (252-393-9015 or 1-877-459-1448; www.bestwestern.com), 801 NC 24, Swansboro. Conveniently located to both Swansboro and Emerald Isle, this hotel has all the amenities, plus a friendly staff of locals. The AAA three-diamond hotel has an elevator, an outdoor pool and whirlpool, and serves free continental breakfast daily. Children ages 17 and under stay free. $$.

RV CAMPGROUNDS ✳ ♿ **Cedar Point Campground in Croatan National Forest** (252-638-5628; www.fs.usda.gov/nfsnc). Campground near Swansboro has 42 sites, all with electric hookups, a bathhouse with warm showers and flush toilets, drinking water, and a boat ramp for kayaks or other shallow-bottomed boats.

✳ ☂ **Goose Creek Resort** (252-393-2628 or 1-866-839-2628; www.goosecreekcamping.com), 350 Red Barn Road, Ocean. A favorite with families and anglers thanks to its large swimming pool, 135-foot waterslide, beach area, Jet Skis, boat ramp, and a 250-foot fishing pier. Open all year.

✴ Where to Eat

DINING OUT ☂ ♿ ☜ **Riverside Steak & Seafood** (910-326-8847; www.the-riverside-swansboro.com), 506 W. Corbett Avenue, NC 24, Swansboro. Daily specials supplement a menu of fresh local seafood and hand-cut aged beef at this longtime favorite. Try the Carpetbagger, a rib eye stuffed with jumbo shrimp. All meals come with famous homemade sweet potato muffins. Reservations recommended. Dinner only, $$–$$$$.

EATING OUT ☂ **Carteret Café** (252-764-0304; www.facebook.com/TheCarteretCafe), 1000 NC 24, Cape Carteret. Hard-to-miss bright yellow building on NC 24 serves satisfying breakfast and lunch at easy-on-the-wallet prices. Southern-style breakfasts, and peach fritters like the ones at sister restaurant Yanamama's in Swansboro, keep locals coming back. $.

🍴 ☂ **Church Street Irish Pub & Deli** (910-326-7572; www.churchstreet-deli-pub-inn.com), 105 Church Street, Swansboro. This local favorite, with a nice patio, is a deli and an Irish pub where you can lift a pint of Guinness. You can even spend the night. The adjacent **Church Street Inn** (910-326-7573) offers five uniquely decorated suites overlooking the historic downtown. Sandwiches $. Rooms $$$.

Yanamama's Restaurant & 50's Memorabilia Shoppe (910-326-5501; www.yanamamas.com), 117 Front Street, Swansboro. Locals rave about the fruit fritters at this cool soda shop, complete with milk shakes and a jukebox loaded with rock 'n' roll hits. The adjacent shop has the perfect collectibles for fans of Elvis, Marilyn, Betty Boop, the Lone Ranger, and many more '50s icons. Breakfast and lunch $.

PRODUCE STANDS Guthrie Farm Stand (252-393-2254 or 252-241-4918), 5417 NC 24, Bogue. Farmer Guthrie is the founder of the Bogue Sound Watermelon Growers Association.

Winberry Farm (252-393-2281; www.ncagr .gov/ncproducts), 1006 NC 24, Cedar Point. An old tobacco barn houses one of the area's best farm stands, a great place to find local tomatoes and Bogue Sound watermelons.

✳ Entertainment

SwanFest (www.seasideartscouncil.com). Free concerts are held every Sunday evening in Swansboro's Olde Town Square, May to September.

✳ Selective Shopping

Historic Front Street in Swansboro is home to an eclectic group of gift shops specializing in one-of-a-kind items.

ANTIQUES Swansboro Antiques & Uniques (252-326-0043; www.swansboroantiques.com), 675 W. Corbett Avenue, NC 24, Swansboro. Art glass and pottery, sterling, jewelry, and much more, selected by top "pickers."

ART GALLERY Tidewater Gallery (910-325-0660; www.tidewatergallery.com), 107 Front Street, Swansboro. Historic house is stuffed with art, from local works to international offerings.

AUCTIONS Sterling Auction House (910-545-9831; www.auctionhousesterling.com), 675 W. Corbett Avenue, Swansboro. Estate auctions offer unique opportunities to buy local antiques and collectibles.

SPECIAL SHOPS Russell's Olde Tyme Shoppe (910-326-3790; www.russellsofswansboro.com), 116 Front Street, Swansboro. Marvelous hand-painted objects for every room in the house.

Yanamama's 50's Memorabilia Shoppe. See *Where to Eat.*

✳ Special Events

March: **Oyster Roast** (910-326-6175; www.swansbororotary.com), Swansboro Rotary Civic Center.

April: **Swansboro Rotary Beach Bash** (910-326-6175; www.swansbororotary.com), Swansboro Rotary Civic Center.

May: **King Mackerel Blue Water Fishing Tournament** (910-326-3474; www.kingbluewater.com), Hammocks Beach State Park. Memorial Day weekend competition is one of the country's largest.

June: **Arts by the Sea and Storytelling Festival** (910-326-7370; www.swansborofestivals.com), downtown Swansboro.

July: **Fourth of July Fireworks** (910-326-7370; www.swansborofestivals.com), downtown Swansboro.

October: **Swansboro Mullet Festival** (910-326-7370; www.swansborofestivals.com), downtown Swansboro.

November: **Holiday Flotilla** (910-326-7370; www.swansborofestivals.com), downtown Swansboro. Decorated boat parade along the Swansboro waterfront on Thanksgiving weekend.

THE INNER BANKS: NORTH CAROLINA'S SECRET SHORE

ONCE YOU'VE MADE YOUR JOURNEY down the Outer Banks, jumping by bridge and ferry from Nags Head to Hatteras to Ocracoke to the Crystal Coast, loop back via an inland route, traveling US 17, once the major route down the East Coast in preinterstate days. In North Carolina, it passes through many of the early ports, located on the great rivers and sounds of the Inner Banks, North Carolina's secret shore. Here history blends seamlessly with ecotourism, offering paddling trails, historic and walkable downtowns, public docks, and interesting inns. We present these towns south

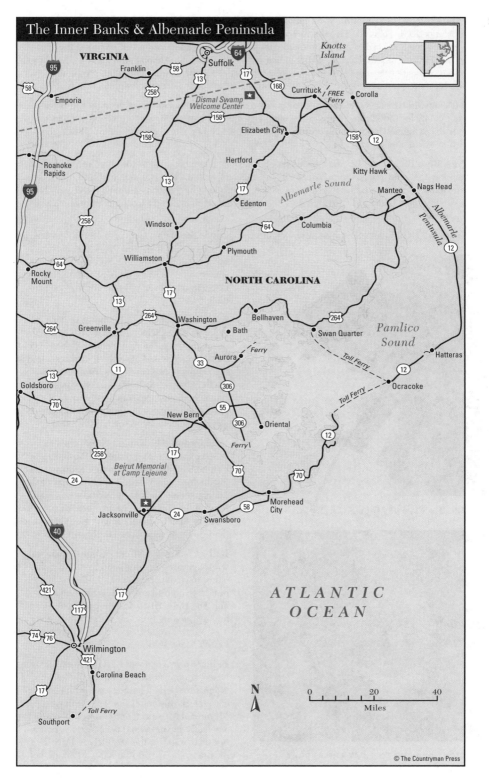

The Inner Banks & Albemarle Peninsula

VIRGINIA

Franklin

Suffolk

Knotts Island

Emporia

Currituck

FREE Ferry

Corolla

Dismal Swamp Welcome Center

Roanoke Rapids

Elizabeth City

Hertford

Kitty Hawk

Edenton

Albemarle Sound

Manteo

Nags Head

Windsor

Columbia

Albemarle Peninsula

Rocky Mount

Plymouth

Williamston

NORTH CAROLINA

Greenville

Washington

Bellhaven

Swan Quarter

Pamlico Sound

Bath

Aurora

Ferry

Toll Ferry

Hatteras

Goldsboro

New Bern

306

55

Oriental

Ocracoke

Toll Ferry

258

Beirut Memorial at Camp Lejeune

Ferry

Jacksonville

Swansboro

Morehead City

ATLANTIC OCEAN

Wilmington

Carolina Beach

N

0   20   40
Miles

Southport

Toll Ferry

© The Countryman Press

to north along US 17, starting from Jacksonville, just a few miles inland from Swansboro, and ending at Elizabeth City, close to the Virginia border. Most of US 17 is now four lanes, and limited access highways, such as US 264 and US 64, provide quick "escape routes" out to I-95, if time runs short. Where destinations are located off US 17, we give brief directions. Although the list is arranged south to north, the itinerary could as easily be followed north to south, starting in Virginia. Numerous shorter routes, or day trips from the Outer Banks, can be devised with the help of a map.

Jacksonville (US 17; www.onslowcountytourism.com or www.jacksonvilleonline.org). The support community for the Marine Corps Base Camp Lejeune and Marine Air Station New River, Jacksonville is home to the moving **Beirut Memorial** (www.beirut-memorial.org) and the oldest USO in the nation still in operation.

New Bern (US 17 and US 70; www.visitnewbern.com). The second oldest town in North Carolina and the home of royal governor William Tryon, this historic town has several house museums in addition to the reconstructed 1770 governor's palace, surrounded by gorgeous gardens. Walking and trolley tours visit colonial and Civil War sites, the soda fountain where Pepsi-Cola was invented, and the numerous bear mascots that dot the town.

Oriental (NC 55 east of New Bern; www.visitoriental.com). The Sailing Capital of North Carolina, located on the tip of the Pamlico Peninsula, hosts regattas nearly every weekend. Popular with visiting yachters, this dog-friendly town sits in the heart of over 300 miles of marked paddling trails.

THE BEAR IS THE MASCOT OF NEW BERN.

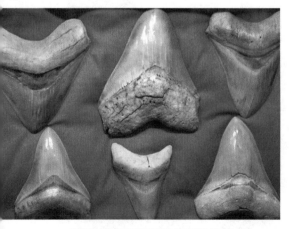

GIANT SHARK'S TEETH AT THE AURORA
FOSSIL MUSEUM

Aurora (NC 33 east of Washington; www.co.beaufort.nc.us). The **Aurora Fossil Museum** (www.aurorafossilmuseum.com) exhibits huge shark skeletons and other ancient relics found in the nearby phosphate mines. **Bennett Vineyards** (www.bennettvineyard.com) makes muscadine wines using colonial techniques. From here, catch a free state ferry north to Bath, or south to Havelock and the Crystal Coast.

Washington (US 17 and US 264; www.littlewashingtonnc.com). Located in Washington's historic downtown, the **North Carolina Estuarium** explains the unique ecology of the estuary system and offers free boat tours on the Pamlico-Tar River. Nearby, the **Beaufort County Arts Council** displays local artwork in the former Atlantic Coastline Train Depot.

Bath (US 264 and NC 92 east of Washington; www.nchistoricsites.org/bath). North Carolina's oldest town, incorporated in 1705, was home, briefly, to both Blackbeard and the royal governor. The **Bath Historic Site** preserves several buildings dating from the 18th century. Just west of town, you can swim or hike at **Goose Creek State Park.**

Belhaven (US 264 east of Bath; www.belhavennc.us). A popular stop on the ICW, Belhaven is a picture-perfect harbor town with commercial and sportfishing fleets. The **Belhaven Memorial Museum,** on the second floor of city hall, contains a unique collection of oddities. Plan a stop at the 1899 **River Forest Manor,** today a world-famous restaurant, hotel, and marina.

Williamston (US 17 and US 64; www.visitmartincounty.com). The Martin County seat, located on the Roanoke River, is a nexus of hiking and paddling trails. Nearby attractions range from the Old West town of **Deadwood** to the **East Carolina Speedway.** A self-guided walking tour begins at the 1831 **Asa Biggs House,** now a visitors center. Along the way, enjoy a heritage meal at the **Cypress Grill** or the **Sunny Side Oyster Bar.**

Windsor (US 17 and US 13; www.windsorbertiechamber.com). The **Roanoke/Cashie River Center** interprets both the ecology and history of these river bottomlands, with special emphasis on the native wild turkey. The adjacent **Cashie Wetlands Walk** leads through a cypress swamp. **Hope Plantation,** just west of town, re-creates 19th-century Bertie County life.

Edenton (US 17; www.visitedenton.com). Often called "the prettiest town in the South," Edenton overlooks an idyllic harbor off Albemarle Sound. The site of the 1774 Edenton Tea Party, one of the earliest political actions organized by women, the colonial town preserves a collection of bed & breakfast inns, historic sites, and house museums, including the distinctive **Cupola House.** Guided walking and trolley tours begin at the state historic site.

Hertford (US 17; www.visitperquimans.com). Another of North Carolina's lovely harbor towns, Hertford is home to the 1730 **Newbold-White House,** the oldest dwelling in the state open to the public, and a replica periauger, a form of boat used by early colonists. A stroll of the historic downtown takes you past antiques stores, Queen Anne mansions, and a unique S-shaped swing bridge—the only one of its type remaining in the United States— that inspired the classic song "Carolina Moon."

Elizabeth City (US 17 and US 158; www.discoverelizabethcity.com). Known as the Harbor of Hospitality, Elizabeth City is a favorite stop for boaters traveling the ICW and a popular weekend getaway for visitors from Virginia. The quiet streets of the town, perfect for a walking tour, are lined with historic houses and inns, revitalized shops, even a restored movie palace. On the waterfront, exhibits at the free **Museum of the Albemarle,** one of the state museums of history, explore 10,000 years of ecology and culture in the region. Elizabeth City is also the home of one of the country's largest U.S. Coast Guard bases and TCOM, a company that builds lighter-than-air craft, otherwise known as blimps. Tours of both are available on a limited basis.

THIS PERIAUGER IS A REPLICA OF A BOAT USED BY EARLY SETTLERS.

See "Roanoke Island and the Albemarle Peninsula" for information on towns near Manteo on the Albemarle Peninsula.

These websites provide more information on the attractions and events of the Inner Banks: www.partnershipforthesounds.org, www.visitncne.com, www.historicalbemarletour.org, www.homegrown handmade.com, and www.ibxarts.com.

INDEX